BRITISH ARMY UNIFORMS

FROM 1751 TO 1783

Including the Seven Years' War and the American War of Independence

INCLUDING BOTH CAVALRY AND INFANTRY
AN ILLUSTRATED GUIDE TO
UNIFORMS, FACINGS AND LACE

A fully illustrated account of the uniforms and distinctions of each numbered regiment of cavalry and infantry in the British Army with a full and complete list of regimental facings, lace and distinctions including the tartans of the highland regiments

C.E. FRANKLIN

Pen & Sword

MILITARY

To Barbara and Lindsey
and all those without whose help this book
could not have been written

First published in Great Britain in 2012 and
reprinted in this format in 2016 by
Pen & Sword Books Ltd
47 Church Street
Barnsley
South Yorkshire
S70 2AS

Page design by C.E. Franklin

ISBN 978 1 47388 666 7

A CIP catalogue record for this book is available from the British Library.

Pen & Sword Books Ltd incorporates the Imprints of Pen & Sword Aviation, Pen & Sword Family History, Pen & Sword Maritime, Pen & Sword Military, Pen & Sword Discovery, Wharncliffe Local History, Wharncliffe True Crime, Wharncliffe Transport, Pen & Sword Select, Pen & Sword Military Classics, Leo Cooper, The Praetorian Press, Remember When, Seaforth Publishing and Frontline Publishing

Printed in India by Replika Press Pvt. Ltd.

For a complete list of Pen & Sword titles please contact
PEN & SWORD BOOKS LIMITED
47 Church Street, Barnsley, South Yorkshire, S70 2AS, England
E-mail: enquiries@pen-and-sword.co.uk

List of Contents

Preface

To enable the reader to grasp fully the changes that occurred during the eighteenth century, George I ruled from 1714 to 1727, George II from 1727 to 1760 and George III, from1760 until 1820. When the Seven Years War ended in 1763 the British standing army was subject to severe reductions. The Foot Guards had three regiments but the infantry of the line was reduced to seventy, and the cavalry fared little better with the number of regiments reduced to eighteen. This book illustrates and identifies the different uniforms of the numbered regiments of cavalry and infantry within the British Army during 1751, 1768 and the end of the War of Independence in 1783. Named but un-numbered regiments or foreign regiments in British pay and the regiments especially recruited for service in the colonies, loyalist regiments or the veteran or Garrison battalions, have not been included. In each case the uniform is shown for a man of a nominal stature and five feet nine inches tall.

The uniforms of the Army uniforms of 1751 are taken from the Morier Paintings, to these have been added the uniforms after 1768 up to 1783. The 1751 paintings by Morier are used by the courtesy of 'The Royal Collection © 2009, Her Majesty Queen Elizabeth II', show in detail the regimental uniforms of the Army. These purport to show those regiments in the Army at this time; there is some discussion regarding this and many feel that they are not truly representative and may have been drawn over a longer time-scale.

The American War of Independence
Earlier incidents had begun to ferment dissatisfaction but it is considered by many that armed conflict began at Lexington and Concord on 19 April 1775. On 4 July 1776 the Second Continental Congress adopted a Declaration of Independence formally declaring the American War of Independence. Congress formally declared an end to hostilities in April 1783, with the final Peace Treaty being signed on 3 September 1783. During this period the British Army increased in size to thirty-three regiments of cavalry and one hundred and five regiments of infantry. The numbers of British Army regiments during the period varied considerably. It peaked about 1783 when there were, apart from Household troops, nineteen numbered regiments of heavy cavalry and twelve of light cavalry. The infantry similarly rose to include the three regiments of Foot Guards and one hundred and five regiments of Foot, but many of these higher numbered regiments only existed for a very short time and most had been disbanded by 1783. Most of the infantry regiments were allocated a county or area title in 1782, this ostensibly being the area from which the regiment drew recruits, although this was often not the case.

The exact nature of the dress of a unit at any one time is difficult to resolve as there were no official dress regulations published before 1833, just a random series of orders and individual regulations published by Horse Guards, most of which are recorded in the papers of the National Archives. There are the contemporary illustrations of the period and these, with those known extant examples, have been consulted during the preparation of this study. It may be that other regulations and items exist in private hands, but those in the public domain have been consulted. In some of the regimental illustrations, hat plates, breast plates and buttons have been included; these are selected examples to give a feel for the type and style and do not attempt to record the changes in pattern for any particular regiment throughout the period.

Provision of the uniforms for the other ranks was the responsibility of the Colonel of the regiment. Colonels arranged for manufacture and supply according to the laid down pattern, or their whim, on repayment from the Treasury and regimental variations were common. Officers purchased their own uniforms, usually following the practice and tradition of the regiment rather than regulations and it must also be remembered that it was the practice of officers, to adopt whatever variations of dress they considered the colonel would allow. It is quite clear that, whatever the regulations prescribed, the personnel serving in North America and abroad were often dressed in a manner contrary to the current regulations and, in most cases, the significant factors were regimental practice, the size of the purse, being dressed à la mode and, in many cases, what was available.

The history of dress for any regiment invariably relies upon many influences; not least among these were the decisions of the Colonel. In many cases, the apparent absence of any surviving clothing or records has meant that many of the previous studies have been limited. This book draws together contemporary information to provide a new insight into the uniforms and regimental identification of the different regiments of the period. While some of the material has been considered before, much is placed in the public domain for the first time.

Dress Regulations

The dates at which regulations were issued should not be confused with the dates when uniform changes were adopted as there is information from Inspection Returns that many regiments were slow in adopting the newer forms of dress and there are many instances where the regulations were anticipated. The changes in uniform that occurred between 1767 and 1768 are a particular example and many regiments still wore the older coats, and by the time of the American War of Independence, the waistcoats and lapels, which had reached only to the waist, were clearly much longer, reaching almost to the hips. The drawings by contemporary artists make it clear that the outfits worn in the field often reflected the uniforms and equipment outdated by the regulations and often what was available, while those regiments interned until the cessation of hostilities just did the best they could. While the new regulations may have been received, the ability to meet them, or even maintain the uniforms they had, was often beyond local resources, the exceptions being those new arrivals that may well have been dressed in the style prescribed by the later regulations.

Facings

Each regiment was allocated a facing colour which rarely changed but where this did occur it is shown in the plates for the regiment. The colour of dark-blue was reserved for 'Royal' regiments, or any regiment named or adopted by the Monarch or a member of his immediate family and usually had in its title, the 'King's', or the 'Queen's', etc. The facing colour was usually displayed on the coat collar, cuffs and lapels and was also used commonly as a lining to the coat before 1751, but not in every case. The long coat was worn throughout the period by all ranks. The only variations were the jackets introduced for the Light Dragoons, Highland regiments and the later light companies of 1770.

Presentation

The regimental titles used to identify the regiments are those of the Army List of the period and the index refers to regiments by both number and name. Part One addresses those items of uniform that were common to the cavalry and are more properly presented in this part rather than as a constant repetition in each illustration. Part Two considers the Household Cavalry and the Royal Horse Guards (Blues) and the other the cavalry, regiments and includes the heavy cavalry represented by the dragoon guards and dragoons, the light cavalry represented by the light dragoons regiments. Part Three addresses those items of uniform that were common to the infantry, also the tartans of the Highland regiments while Part Four gives the regiments of Foot Guards and the numbered regiments of infantry.

PART ONE

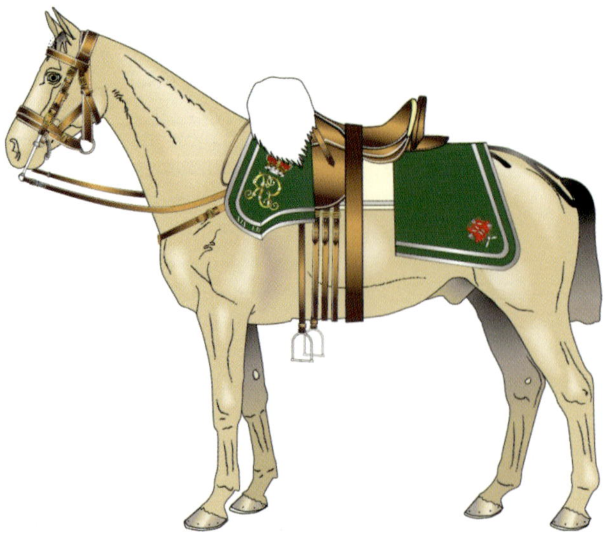

CHAPTER ONE

Cavalry Headwear

Tricorne Hat

This was the standard form of headdress for officers and enlisted men with the exception of Horse Grenadier Guards and the 2nd Dragoons who wore the mitre cap of a style similar to the infantry grenadiers. The cocked hat was made with a very wide brim that has been pinned up on three sides, giving the hat three corners, locks or points, and was popular in the seventeenth and eighteenth centuries, when it was part of civilian dress, military and naval uniforms. The hat was made from thick black felt or beaver with a central crown to take the head and a wide brim of four and a half inches wide with tape or other woven material to add strength. The main differences in the cocked hat of the period were the older style of cock adopted by the cavalry; later the front was brought to a pinch and over time the fashion changed to a shallow pinch and a piece of whalebone four inches long was stitched into the brim to form a shallower pinch. The hats were laced about with white and yellow braid one and a quarter inches wide for the rank and file and silver or gilt for the officers'; the non-commissioned officers (NCOs) wore either silver or gilt lace, while other regiments like the Life Guards wore gilt lace for all ranks. The left turn-up held a black Hanoverian cockade of woven horsehair, held in place by a gilt loop and. regimental button. The hat was worn with the front point over the left eye and the right wing thrown forward and to ensure that the hat remained in position, a cord or thong was usually attached to the linen lining and secured under the hair by a hook and eye. The cavalry also adopted the use of Hanoverian cords and tassels after 1768, each cord passing around the crown, through the loop of the other with the tassel end hanging from the two opposing locks in the hat. The cords were in gold or silver for officers and yellow or white for enlisted men, but when the regiments were converted to Light Dragoons after 1768 they wore no hat lace.

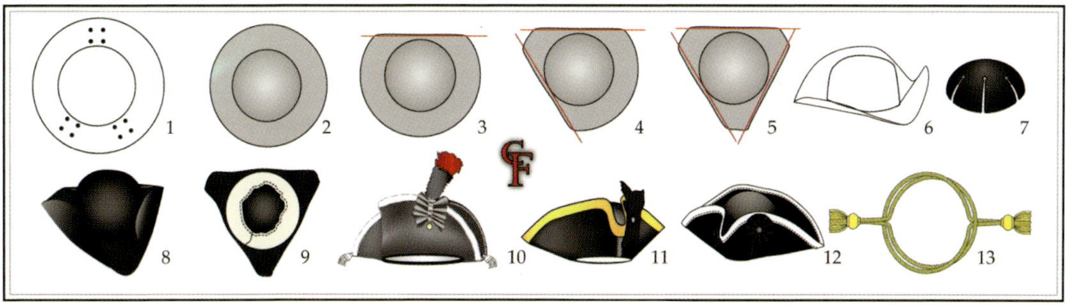

The Cocked Hat or Tricorne. The machine used to cock the hats (1). The basic form of the cocked hat with the dome at the centre (2). The rear of the Tricorne with the first fold upwards (3). The continuing folds (4). The final fold of the Tricorne (5). The basic shape (6). The metal protective plate sometimes worn under the Tricorne (7). The basic shape (8), with an under view showing the linen lining (9). The early hat of a silver laced regiment with cords at the crown (10). With the hat of a gold laced regiment (11). A similar earlier version of an enlisted man's (12) and the tasselled cords adopted by other regiments (13).

Mitre Cap of circa 1751

The mitre cap was introduced circa 1751 for the horse grenadiers of the Life Guards and the 2nd Dragoons. Originally the cap was formed from a tasseled stocking with a turnup to the front and to the rear but over time the styles evolved. At the top of the cap was a coloured woollen tuft with a centre of coloured threads. The front was covered with facing material mounted on a shaped stiffened card, or of felt, and embroidered in a way usual for each regiment. The rear of the cap had a piece of red cloth stitched to the stiffened front and two pieces of cane to retain the shape, with tape placed over the sides and back to conceal the stitching. At the rear there was a small flap of facing material at the bottom and the cap was lined with unbleached linen with a strip of regimental lace running around the bottom edge. To prevent caps from falling off they were usually fitted with tapes sewn into the lining and tied or secured with hooks and eyes, worn under the plait of the hair. Officer's caps were usually decorated with silver or gold thread and were generally much more lavish in their decoration. To cover the mitre caps during inclement weather, canvas covers, often painted with similar designs, were worn. In normal dress the cover was worn hooked into the pleat of the coat and over the left hip button.

Drum and Mitre Caps circa 1755. Drum cap of a Royal regiment (1). A rear view after Morier (2). A mitre cap as worn by the 2nd Royal North British Dragoons (3). The mitre cap of the 1st Troop Horse Grenadier Guards (4) and a similar mitre of the 2nd Troop (5).

Fur Cap of circa 1768

While other regiments are known to have worn these caps in 1763, particularly the Horse Grenadier Guards of the Life Guards. Drummers also wore them, but the 2nd Dragoons only adopted them in 1778. Each was issued with twelve-inch tall fur caps; usually shown as black, they were made from a very dark brown or black bearskin and the caps of officers were often decorated with silver or gold thread. The fur caps had the fur rising towards the top in a tapered point and the rear carried a red patch or a bag for the horse grenadiers. Fur caps were usually restricted to wear on dress occasions and formal parades with, the cocked hat more usually worn when in undress; this applied to officers, grenadiers and drummers.

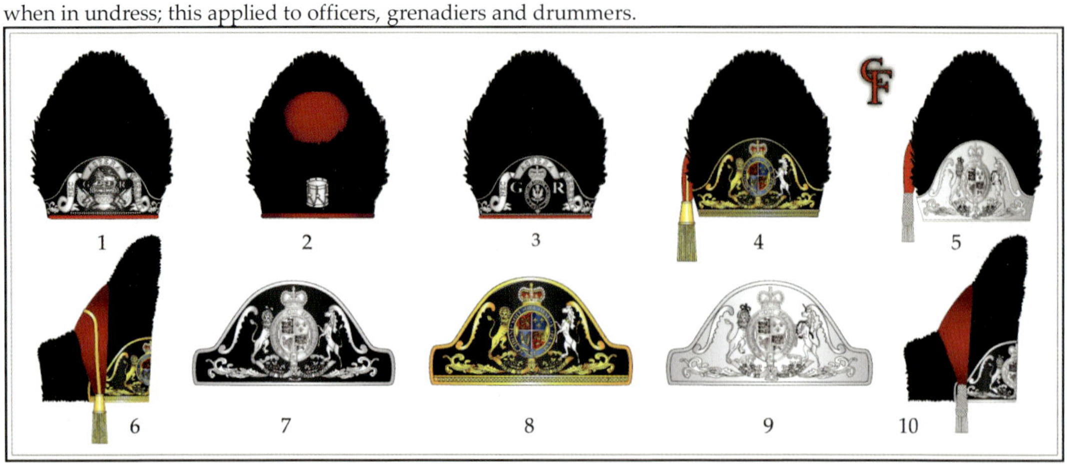

Fur caps of 1768. A drummer trooper (1). The rear of the cap of a drummer (2), and a speculative front view of the cap of the 2nd (Royal North British) Dragoons (3). A front view of the cap for an officer of the Horse Grenadier Guards (4). A front view of the cap for the 1st Troop Horse Grenadier Guards (5). The side view of an officer of the Horse Grenadiers (6). The plate of a trooper of the 2nd Troop Horse Grenadier Guards (7). The plate of an officer of the Horse Grenadier Guards (8). The plate of a trooper of the 1st Troop Horse Grenadier Guards (9) and a side view of the cap of the 2nd Troop Horse Grenadier Guards (10).

A number of different plates were worn on this cap. They were all of the same size, five inches tall by twelve inches long, but with different japanning and special versions for each. The cap was soon to be laced about with knotted white worsted cords and tassels, those of the officers being gold or silver. Later the bearskin caps also carried plumes.

Light Dragoon Caps

The caps of many Light Dragoons, and those of regiments that were ordered to form them in 1756, were required to enable the men to move about more easily, than the cocked hats worn by the rest of the cavalry. Regulations prescribed a 'GR' Cypher and the identification of the regiment together with a crest and mane and this seems to have been adhered to but there were exceptions: the light Company of the 11th Dragoons wore a red front to the cap and no mane. Later, as the Light Dragoons became an arm of the cavalry in their own right, the style of the caps became more elaborate and it seems that there was more than one style of these caps which changed over time. The metal used for the troopers was brass, copper or white metal; those of the officers were either gilt or silver.

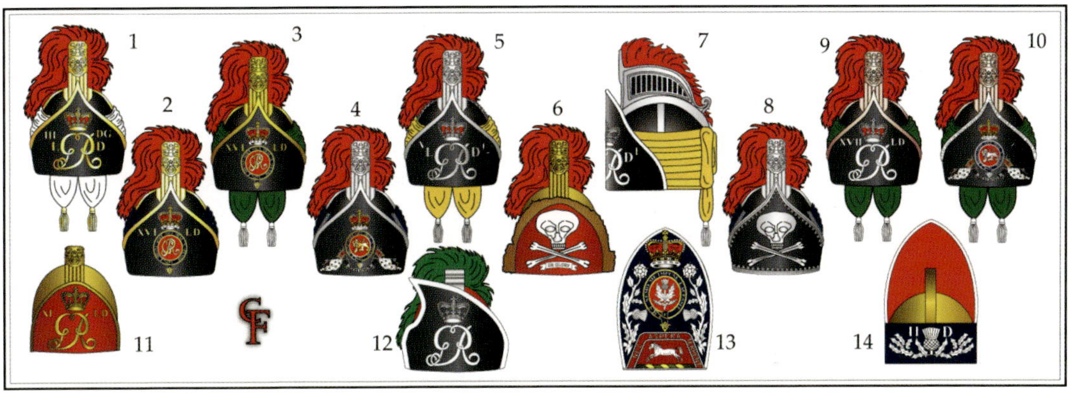

Light Dragoon Caps. A cap of an officer of a gold-laced regiment, the 3rd Dragoon Guards (1). A cap of an officer of the 16th Light Dragoons after 1769 in gilt with a blue turban (2). The cap of the 16th Light Dragoons before 1769 when the facings were green (3), and the cap of an officer of the 15th Light Dragoons (4). An officer light troop of the 6th Dragoons (5). The cap of a trooper of 17th Light Dragoons before 1759 (6). Trooper of the 6th Dragoons (7). The cap of an officer of the 17th Light Dragoons after 1775 (8). A trooper of the 15th Light Dragoons before 1759 (9). The cap of the 16th Light Dragoons after 1769 with the inscription around the rim of the helmet 'Five battalions of French defeated and taken by this regiment with their colours and nine pieces cannon on the plains of Emsdorf July the sixteenth 1760' (10). A trooper of the light troop of the 11th Dragoons (11). A cap of the Royal Foresters the original 21st Light Dragoons (12). A front view of the light troop of the 2nd Royal North British Dragoons (13) and a rear view of the same cap (14).

Tarletons

The Tarleton leather caps proved to be an attractive proposition for the light dragoons; they had been worn since the 1770s and both sides wore them during the War of Independence. They were also worn by the 16th and 17th Light Dragoons who were dismounted cavalry acting as infantry. The turbans were originally to be the colour of the facings as was also the feather, except that this applied only when the facings were white in which case they were mixed with red. Every regiment was to have the number of the dragoons regiment in silver or white metal on the front of the helmet. When many regiments were converted to light dragoons in 1783 most adopted the Tarleton as their cap. Tarletons with pianted white or white lining; this was also adopted by the 8th Light Dragoons. While it was common to wear the turban, which could be let down in bad weather, officers also adopted tassels at the rear as well as the bow for the turban. It was only much later that badges worn on the left side of the helmet became the fashion.

Cavalry Tarleton Helmets or Caps. An officer's helmet of a regiment with green facings (1), the helmet of a trooper with a leopard-skin turban of the 16th Light Dragoons (2). A right side view of a trooper's Tarleton with yellow facings (3) and an officer's Tarleton of a regiment with white facings (4).

CHAPTER TWO

Cavalry Coats

Facings

Each regiment was allocated a facing colour and this was rarely changed except if the regiment was made Royal when it adopted blue or, in the case of the Royal Horse Guards, where it was scarlet, but when it did occur it is shown in the illustrations for each regiment.

The Coat of circa 1751

The Royal Collection has a series of paintings by Morier completed about 1755 and later. These provide important detail of the uniforms of the period. In some paintings the lapels are unclear but the coats of the Dragoon Guards had half lapels; those of the Horse were lapelled all the way down while the Dragoons had no lapels at all; the light Dragoons were later lapelled to the waist and the cuff was not indented. The shape of the coat was cut to show an elaborate fullness of the extra material gathered in the side pleat below the hip button. The elaborate cuff has a vertical flap, usually laced for about officers but plain for the other ranks with a vertical cuff and chevrons of lace arranged in different groups, usually pairs or threes. In other cases the officers' swords are shown passing through a gap in the pleats, which has been stiffened to provide a greater flare to the material. The fullness given to the coat by the pleats from the hip buttons continues during this period, while each cavalry coat had two shoulder straps set back towards the point of the shoulder. Where the colour of the regimental metal was concerned the colour was either gold or silver for officers, and either yellow or white for the men; it should be noted that the Royal Horse Guards had twist buttonholes.

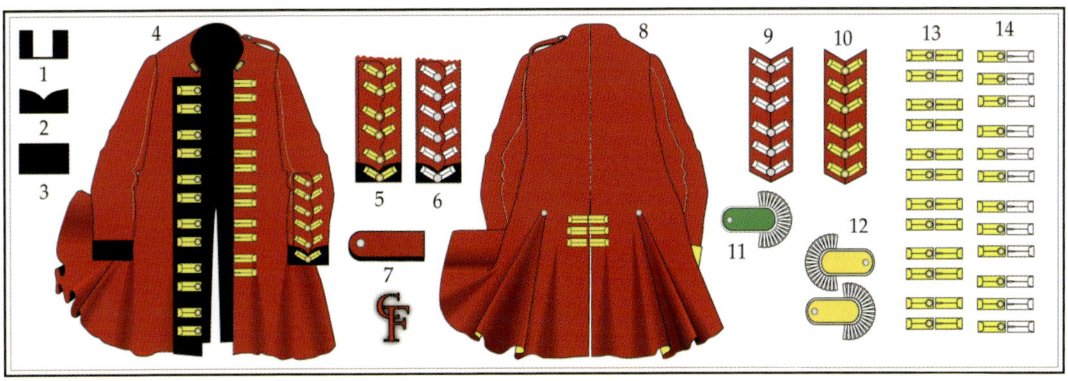

Coat of a cavalry trooper of circa 1751. The different cuff styles: that of the 2nd Royal North British Dragoons (1). The indented cuff of the Dragoons Guards, Horse and Dragoons (2). The cuff of the Light Dragoons (3). The front of the coat showing black facings with the full-length lapels of the Horse at left and those of the Dragoons on the right side (4). The chevron lace peculiar to the cuff (5). The white lace of a silver-laced regiment (6). The shoulder strap of the Horse (7) and the rear view of the coat with yellow facings set in threes (8). A pocket of a white-laced regiment set in threes (9). The vertical pocket of a yellow-laced regiment set in threes (10). The shoulder strap of the Dragoon Guards and Dragoons worn on the left shoulder only (11) and the two epaulettes worn by the Light Dragoons (12). Two views of the lacing of a regiment set in pairs (13) and those set in threes which could be either white or yellow, silver or gold (14).

The Cavalry Coat of circa 1768

This provides detailed information on the dress of this period. It illustrates considerable detail of the uniforms and is used to show the changes prior to the end of the American War of Independence. The coats of the other ranks were provided by the Colonel and were issued at nominally regular periods by contracted military tailors.

They were dyed with a madder-red for the other ranks and the lesser form of scarlet for non commissioned officers was made from a mixture of dyes, both cochineal and madder. The facing colour was worn on the collar, lapel and cuffs. The changes to the coat were significant; the skirt of the coat lost the fullness with material at the pleats and this was much reduced, but still with some fullness and the increase of a dubby. The fold-down collar of facing colour was usually worn buttoned to the top button of the lapel when worn. The cuffs of facing colour were indented for most regiments and each cuff had six vertical buttons but the sleeve of the coat was no longer slit. Initially the lapels of the coat came to the waist, but by the American Revolution had moved to the hips. The vertical pocket was retained and by 1768 the lapels on the coats were different: the coats of the Dragoon Guards, Horse and light Dragoons were to be lapelled to the waist but the Dragoons were without lapels. The buttons were to be set on the sleeve in such a way that they extended up the arm even if the lacing was in pairs or threes. Cuffs were indented for most regiments but not the Light Dragoons who retained the square cuff and, after 1768, only three chevrons above, or the 2nd Royal North British Dragoons who retained the square, cut away cuff and, according to the warrant of 1768, the Horse wore twist button buttonholes or, in modern parlance, they were unlaced.

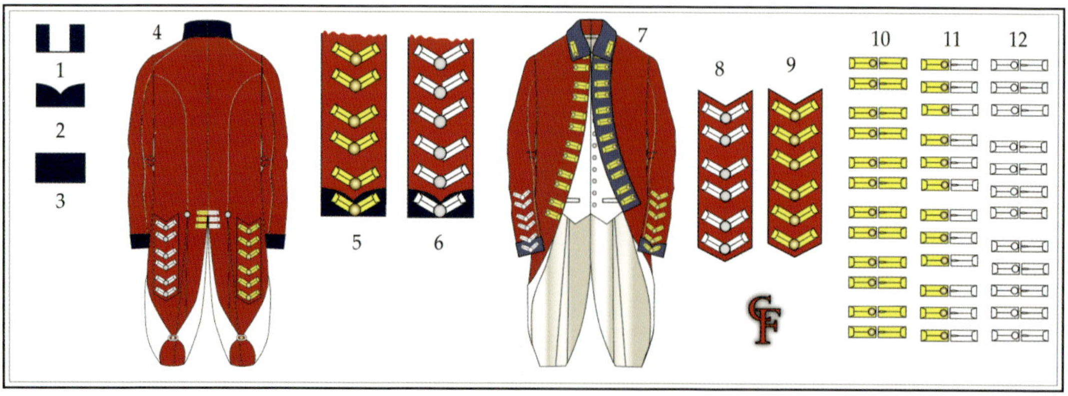

The Cavalry Coat of 1768. The different cuff styles, that of the 2nd Royal North British Dragoons (1), the indented cuff of the Dragoon Guards, Horse and Dragoons (2), the cuff of the Light Dragoons (3), a rear of the coat showing blue facings with pockets, on the left white in pairs, on the right yellow in threes, and the three laces at the rear, note also the introduction of the dubby at the coat turnbacks (4), the chevron lace of the cuff without a slash of a gold-laced regiment (5), the white lace of a silver-laced regiment in threes (6), the front view of the coat with pale blue facings showing the yellow lace of a dragoon regiment on the right, and the half lapel of dragoon guards and the cuff lace (7), the vertical pocket of a silver -laced regiment set in pairs (8), the pocket of a gold-laced regiment set in threes (9), a view of a gold-laced regiment set in pairs (10) those set in threes which could be either white or yellow (11) and those peculiar to the 10th Dragoons.

Light Dragoon Coats

Light Dragoon troops were formed in 1756, with most regiments required to form a light troop; the uniform was similar to that of the rest of the cavalry. In 1759 many regiments of Light Dragoons were formed and in most cases they wore half lapels and sleeves that were not indented; they also wore caps, and rode with a lighter saddle. The amount of lace on the coat seems to have varied: in one painting, by Morier, of the 15th Light Dragoons they are shown with eight loops on the lapel and only three loops on the cuff and pocket; in another painting Morier shows the 16th Light Dragoons with eight loops with no lapel and three on the cuff; the 17th Light Dragoons show the lapel with eight loops and only three buttons on the cuff and pocket. In his painting of the 21st Light Dragoons he shows eight loops on the lapel with a further loop below it, while the cuff has four loops and the pocket three. It is not clear who wore what and, while it may be that wore an evolving uniform, but the difference has been noted. In 1784 the Light Dragoons adopted a jacket and shell of blue cloth.

Officers' Coats

The coats of officers were scarlet, dyed with cochineal, and of much better materials and made to personal order by military tailors. In 1751 there was very little regulation of officers' dress and a variety of cuff styles was worn, most being square-ended, opened at the side of the cuff, and invariably laced about with lace to the cuff and the buttonholes of the sleeve. At the start of the period the long coats were often worn without lapels and those of 1768 were less loose but still with ample material. The linings were of different colours and usually represented the facings of the regiment, as did the waistcoat and breeches. It is clear that officers interpreted the regulations loosely and that many continued to wear the coat in styles contrary to the current regulations and officers also used decorative items to the turnbacks. The officers tended to use the chevron loop to the cuff, although other versions are known, the Colonel being the arbiter in such matters. Officers' coats were embroidered or laced in gold or silver and, in each case the men of the regiment aped the colour while NCOs often wore gilt or silver epaulettes.

Epaulettes

Officers of the Dragoon Guards and Dragoons were to wear an embroidered or laced epaulette with fringe on the left shoulder while those of the Light Dragoons were to wear one on each shoulder with the cloth of the epaulette to be of the facing colour. Officers' of Horse wore epaulettes but the men wore red shoulder straps lined with facing colour.

Farriers

The farriers were to wear blue coats with blue linings, which later became white. Cuffs and capes were to be the colour of the facing of the regiment except for the Royal regiments where the facings were to be scarlet. Buttonholes were to be the same manner as those of the men. They were to wear a small bearskin cap with a Horseshoe on the front part and a badge at the rear with the number of the regiment. They were also to wear an apron.

Coats of The War of Independence

An officer's coat of the Queen's County Troop of Horse circa 1778. This jacket shows the shorter style adopted by both the British and Continental cavalry. It is the usual scarlet with blue facings and silver lace. The original buttons are missing but the positions are clearly marked. The pleat at the rear of the coat is of interest.

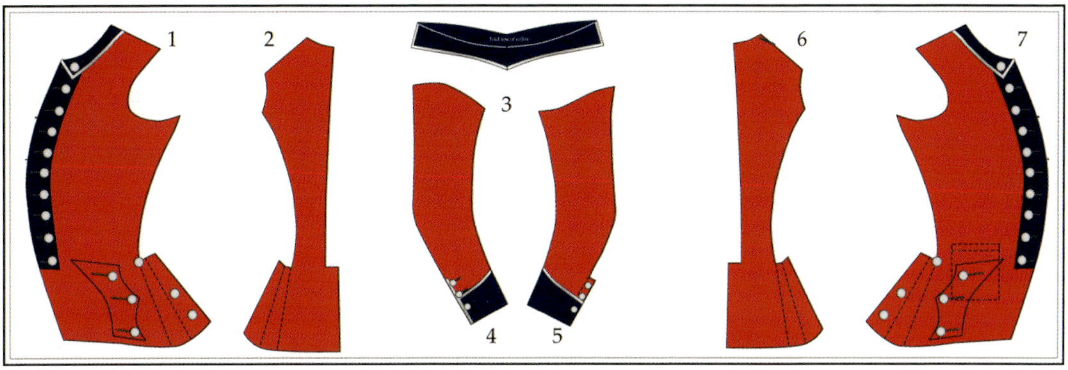

Thomas Week Coatee, circa 1778. (Courtesy of the Oyster Bay Historical Society and Henry Cooke who provided the pattern). The front of the coat with facing colour lapel, the pleats of the coat, silver braid, the opening pocket and silver buttons that are not original (1). The rear of the coat (2). The collar with silver lace and pointed at the rear (3). Outside of sleeve with cuff of facing colour (4). The cuff showing the tuck under into the sleeve (5). The rear of the coat (6) and the front of coat showing the rear of the lapel (7).

CHAPTER THREE

Cavalry Buttons and Lace

Metal

The colour of the cavalry officer buttons and lace was set by Whitehall, each regiment being allocated a colour, silver or gold, referred to as the 'metal' colour. Initially lace had been introduced to reinforce the material of the uniforms at the buttonholes and similar points of stress, but this soon developed into a method by which the regiments were identified.

Buttons

The early buttons were formed by two half shells soldered together with a wire shank hooked into the rear shell. The early buttons had no specific pattern, but by 1760, patterns and numbers were beginning to be shown by many regiments; after the regulations of 1768 each regiment was ordered to carry a distinctive number or design on the button, the dragoon guards being permitted to use their initial letters.

Officers' buttons were of gold or silver but those of the rank and file were either brass or white metal depending upon the regimental colour. By 1768 the numbered buttons of officers and enlisted men changed to a cast flat pattern with a shank set into the rear of the button. Made from a form of pewter, this inexpensive button material was known as trifle, a pewter alloy of medium hardness consisting of 83 parts of tin to 17 parts of antimony. A definition of the period states that a button of tin of a given size would weigh 182 grains; pewter plate, 183.5 grains; while that of trifle would weigh 185.5 grains. The objection to pewter was that it would not shine when polished. Sizes varied considerably due to the different manufacturers; jewellers usually made the silver or gilt buttons of the officers.

Cavalry Buttons. The joined shell (1), a similar gilt shell (2), the later flat button of 1768 (3). An officer of the 3rd Dragoons (4). An officer of the 2nd Horse (5). A trooper of the 4th Horse (6). An officer of the 7th Light Dragoons (7) and a trooper of the 14th Light Dragoons.

The cavalry used a standard size of button, except where a waistcoat was worn when it was more usually smaller. Many regiments adopted the use of Roman numerals for the officers and Arabic numerals for the other ranks, but this was not always the case. Where the buttons are known, they have been indicated on the regimental illustrations, but it is clear that there were smaller buttons on the shoulder straps from very early on.

Spacing

The next distinction was in the spacing of the loops or buttons: some were spaced in pairs; others were set in threes and in one case (the 10th Dragoons) set in threes, fours and fives.

Lace

Officers' lace was either gilt or silver while that of a private soldier was a woven worsted half-an-inch wide and arranged to form a shaped buttonhole in either yellow or white. The shape and design of the buttonholes did not vary, each having a square or diagonal loop. Where the information is known the lace has been included on the plate for that regiment, but in some cases the sergeant major wore the same braid as the officers.

Buttons and Loops. An officer of the 6th (Inniskilling) Dragoons (1). An officer of the 1st Dragoons (2). An officer of the 1st (King's) Dragoon Guards (3). A trooper of the 9th Light Dragoons (4). A trooper of the 2nd (Queen's) Dragoon Guards (5). A trooper of the 4th Dragoons (6) and a trooper of 2nd Troop of Horse Grenadier Guards (7).

CHAPTER FOUR

Cavalry Waistcoats, Shirts, Gloves, Stocks and Cloaks

Waistcoats

Generally waistcoats had sleeves but sleeveless versions are known. They were made in a variety of colours, often to match the facings of the regiment, even after 1768.

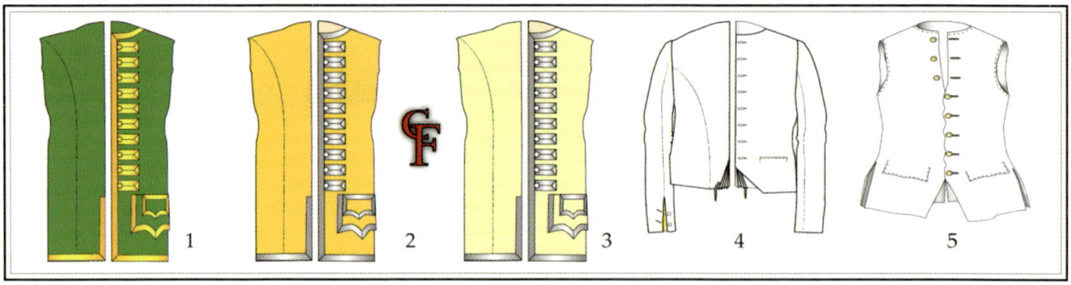

Cavalry Waistcoats. The style of waistcoat of 1751 that could be laced or unlaced. Officers often wore them in the facing colour both without lace, in this case the 13th Dragoons (1). The laced waistcoat of the 8th Dragoons (2). The 1768 and laced waistcoat of an trooper that originally reached to the waist, it was white and often with sleeves (4) and a later white officers' waistcoat (5).

Waistcoats of 1751

This was close fitting at the waist with vents at the rear and usually laced about. Many regiments at this time wore waistcoats of facing colour and profusely laced. The waistcoat had no collar but was often laced at the buttonholes the number of loops on the waistcoats of the rank and file was determined by the height of the wearer, nine loops for those under five feet eight inches, ten for those of five feet nine inches while, those above this height had eleven and grenadiers of five feet eleven inches had twelve. The waistcoats were usually fitted with horizontal pockets and those of the officers were laced about. It is known from inspection returns that some regiments after 1755 had already changed to the style of 1768 when it was ordered that waistcoats were to be without lace or embroidery.

Waistcoats of 1768

These could be either with or without sleeves and were in white, secured by a number of small buttons, without embroidery and the pockets were to be cross pocket without flaps but there is clear evidence that this was often not adhered to. They were single-breasted with the rear seam sewn down to the waistband of the breeches. The light company wore scarlet waistcoats.

Shirts

The shirts worn by officers in the early period were profusely decorated with starched and ironed frills, often with lace for dress, which were allowed to show at the neck and cuffs. Shirts of the other ranks were usually of a simpler nature but still had more simple frills. The earlier period shows shirts decorated with a nine-inch frill, puffed out and starched to show protruding between the lapels of the coat. While officers may have worn the stock for parades, in undress and walking out neck cloths are more usually shown.

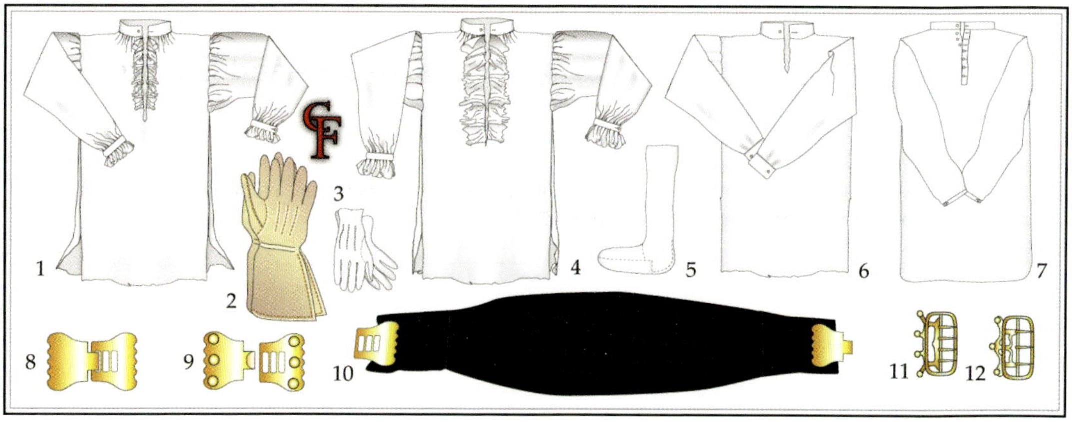

Shirts, Stocks, Buckles, Socks and Gloves. An enlisted man's dress shirt with frills at the cuff and chest (1). The gauntlet leather gloves of officers and NCOs worn by all ranks of cavalry (2). The leather gloves for officers walking out (3) and an officers shirt with lace and larger frills (4). The white or grey socks (5) and an other ranks' shirt worn earlier in 1751 (6). An enlisted mans shirt of 1775 (7). A basic stock clasp (8). A rear view showing the clasp and studs that passed through the stock (9). A stock of either horsehair or leather (10) and different versions of the stock clasps (11 & 12).

Gloves

Buff leather gauntlet gloves were worn by all ranks of cavalry, although officers and NCOs usually wore white leather gloves for walking out dress. These short gloves ended at the wrist with a slit or a small turned-back cuff.

Stocks

All ranks wore stocks, either of black woven horsehair, black leather for dress and or of white linen. The stock formed a high-stiffened neckband but allowed the ruffled shirt to be seen at the front. It was worn high, around the neck and secured by a buckle or clasp usually placed under the hair. Over the period it gradually increased in height and became most uncomfortable to wear. Officers also wore velvet stocks, fastening at the rear but later adopted white neckerchiefs.

Cloaks

The cloaks were to be red lined with the same colour as that of the facings, and secured to the back of the horse to the small pad at the rear of the saddle and held in place by three equally spaced straps.

CHAPTER FIVE

Cavalry Netherwear

Breeches of 1751

These were worn by all ranks and were made from a material similar to the coat and often in the colour of the facings. The early style had a wide angle at the crotch with a roomy but shapeless seat, while the breeches opened at a front fly and were secured by four buttons on the right side and buttonholes on the left; many were fitted with two pockets at the upper leg. The top was gathered on to a waistband, deeper at the front and closed with buttons at the waist; the legs were wide at the top, narrowed to just below the knees and fitted with a knee band and a white linen knee protector. Adjustment was by a small slit at the rear, closed by lacing to make the breeches fit. Officers often wore a strap and buckle to replace the lacing at the rear; leather breeches are also recorded for some regiments.

Breeches of 1768

The warrant introduced white breeches but some were buff or the colour of the facings. Some years before the 1768 warrant, some regiments had adopted white or buff breeches. They were made of a material to come high on the hips and below the knee-pan to the calf of the leg, the waistband was required to be wide enough to hold three large buttons and they usually had a pocket at the right side. To cover the open fly the breeches were fitted with a 'whole fall', a large flap at the front, buttoning with two large buttons at the waist. At the bottom of each leg were four small regimental buttons to secure the opening and to prevent them riding up, a woollen strap and buckle or button was also fitted. Adjustment to the waist was by tapes fed through gathers at the rear and they were marked with the trooper's name on the waistband. As the breeches became looser fitting at the waist they were held up by linen or canvas suspenders. Some breeches had horizontal pockets with flaps at the front at thigh level and were closed with a button on a corner flap to the waistband. In other cases vertical pockets were sometimes in the side seams on either side, usually there was often only one pocket on the right side. There could also be a small pocket in the waistband on either side. Breeches were worn for all occasions except fatigues and walking out.

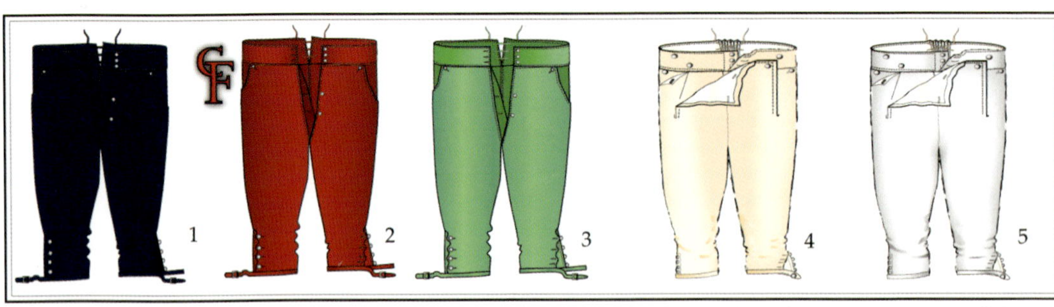

Breeches of 1751 and 1768. Generally the breeches were blue for Royal Regiments (1) but other regiments wore red (2) and the officers often wore breeches of the appropriate facing colour (3). The breeches of 1768 had a front fall and those of the 3rd (King's Own) were buff (4) but generally they were white (5).

Boot Stockings

These were worn to prevent wear of the breeches by the tops of the boots. They were usually white cloth or canvas some eight inches longs and attached below the knee by a string. They rose some four inches above the boot or gaiter tops and were fastened by a loop or other attachment to the lower buttons of the breeches. The later version was shorter, nominally some four inches tall and buttoned to the lower four buttons of the breeches.

Boots and Shoes

In 1751 these were of brown leather dyed black with squared toes, they were high heeled with soles, the instep was generally brown. The boots were straight lasted and were supposed to be worn on alternate feet every other day, a practice generally avoided, officers' had their boots made to order by boot makers and their boots were not as prone to the same problem. The boot of 1768 had the same general appearance but was rounded at the toe and 'not of the heavy sort'. The shoes were held on the feet by a strap stitched to each upper and buckled together. The buckles for the officers' and rank and file could be quite elaborate when used for walking out or dress. In undress half boots that reached just above the ankle were often worn. Pumps were worn by the fashionable officers' and were low-heeled shoes with a thin, supple sole; they were fastened with a buckle over the tongue.

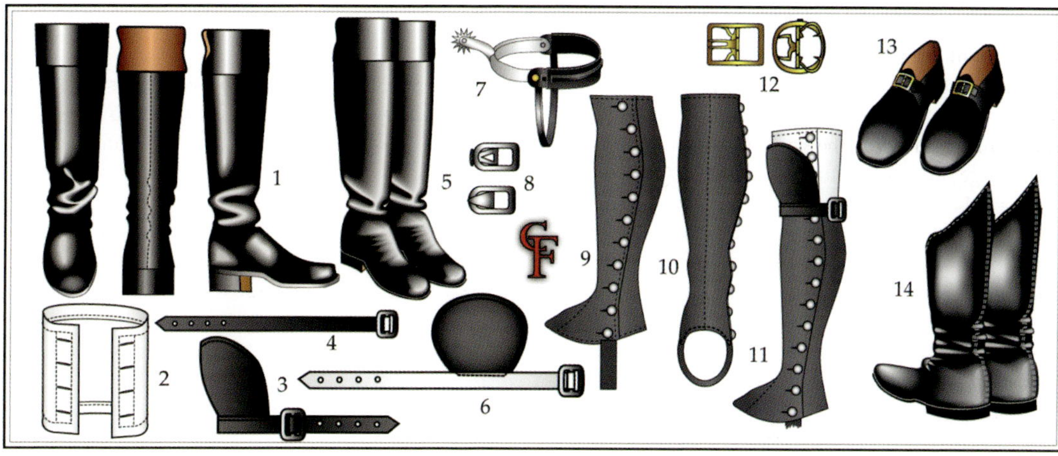

Boots and Shoes. Boots with cut-away tops and very high heels were typical of 1751 (1) and the white top that buttoned to the breeches to protect the knees (2). The 1768 black leather stiff tops and black leather garters (3), the boots of 1768 (5), a black top with a white garter (6). The spurs of the period which strapped under the foot (5). Two steel buckles for the garters (8) and the gaiters were of dark grey or black and were generally fitted with varying amounts of buttons, there was the usual extension for the foot (9). A rear view of a gaiter (10) and the black gaiters fitted with leather tops, garters and white knee protectors (11). Two brass buckles for the shoes (12), the shoes with brass buckles (13) and the half boots with pointed rear ends (14).

Spatterdashes, Gaiters and Knee Pieces

In 1751 all cavalry wore black boots but, in 1768, officers and men of the cavalry were ordered to have black linen gaiters with black buttons, the black gaiters with small stiff tops cut away behind the knee and secured by a strap or buckled garter, a practice many regiments had adopted by 1760. These tops were introduced to prevent wear at the knee and to protect the breeches, but many styles were adopted as inspection reports show; there are references to spatterdashes, half gaiters, full gaiters and, in cases, more than one type were in use. The Light Dragoons were to wear black half gaiters. Gaiters could be a variety of colours; for parade or dress black was commonly used; for campaign grey, brown or black were preferred. Another means of obtaining 'small stiff tops' was achieved by painting the gaiter. This had many advantages in that the paint acted as both a stiffener and a waterproofing. It is possible that many units wore full gaiters, painted, cut-off at the knee of the breeches, and supplemented with black leather knee-guards or any form of gaiter. Boot stockings were worn to prevent wear of the breeches by the tops of the boots or leather tops of the gaiters. These were usually white cloth or canvas eight inches long and attached below the knee by a string. They rose four inches above the boot or gaiter tops and were fastened by a loop or other attachment to the lower buttons of the breeches. The later version was shorter, nominally four inches tall and buttoned to the lower four buttons of the breeches.

Stockings and Hose

When not wearing boots, or for dress the officers wore stockings pulled over the knees and secured under the bottom of the breeches. These were made either of cotton, wool or silk. Garters were made of strips of woven material and worn with a buckle. Thicker stockings were worn inside boots over thinner stockings as protection. Officers attending levees, balls and the dining room in breeches wore white silk stockings. The rank and file were issued with knitted woollen socks.

Canes

Both officers and senior non commissioned officers carried canes. They were usually of the standard type with a head of a particular metal. Often heavily embellished or carved, they were commonly fitted with a ring to attach to a coat button.

Spurs

The spurs of 1751 were curved to fit the heel with a curved neck and a spiked rowel. They were secured to the foot by a strap around the front of the boot one-and-a-half inches tall, with a much narrower strap passing through it, to feed inside and terminate in a buttoned eye. A strap or chain held the stirrup under the instep.

CHAPTER SIX

Cavalry Accoutrements

Introduction

It should be noted that cavalry belts for the sword and bayonet, cartridge pouch and the carbine sling of light dragoons were originally three inches wide but this later decreased to two-and-a-half inches; the waist belts were three inches wide and this later decreased one-and-a-half inches. Those for heavy cavalry were three inches for the carbine belt and pouch belt with two-and-a-half inches for the waist belt for the bayonet and sword. However, where measurement, are given they must be considered purely arbitrary, as there was a huge variety of manufacturers and, in some cases, belts were made to regimental requirements.

Three-piece Sword Waist-belt

This belt became popular during the later stages of the War of Independence. It was made from three straps of white buff (buffalo) leather one-and-a-half inches to two inches wide and joined together by two rings. It had a brass buckle and a further buckle and runner on the right side to adjust the length. The first section was ten inches long; the second, which connected the two rings, nine inches; and the third sixteen inches plus the adjustment. A sword sling, one inch wide, was suspended from each ring; the front sling was eleven inches long and the rear about thirty-six inches, the slings being attached to the scabbard. This could also be fitted to carry a bayonet frog or worn hooked to the belt and the sword carried 'hooked up'. It was favoured later in the period by mounted officers of infantry as the belt could be in different colours, with some black, others buff and the usual white.

One-piece Cavalry Musket and Pouch Belt

Worn over the left shoulder, this belt allowed the carbine or musket to fall under the right arm and the length was sufficient to allow the weapon to be fired and reloaded without removing it from the belt. The width of this strap varied over the period but each had a buckle, runner and tip to the belt. The overall length could vary but more generally they were six feet long and carried a swivel to carry the carbine or musket. On the inside of the belt, were stitched two straps to carry the thirty-round cartridge pouch.

General accoutrements

The water bottle and haversack are considered in the section on infantry accoutrements.

Shoulder belts

The shoulder belt was to be forty-five inches wide, those of the light dragoons two-and-a half inches. Those regiments that had buff waistcoats were to have buff accoutrements and likewise for those who had white. The breadth of the waist belts was to be two-and-three-quarter inches except those of the light dragoons that were to be one-and-thee-quarter inches. Each was to have brass buckles and clasps. The horse was to wear cross shoulder belts, the light dragoons one, except the 8th Regiment that was authorized to wear cross belts before it became light. It should also be noted that the accoutrements of the 2nd Royal North British Dragoons were white and this regiment was considered to be the first to introduce the practice of pipe-claying buff leather equipment. The Light Dragoons' belts' were worn over the right shoulder, while those of the Dragoon Guards and Dragoons were worn round the waist.

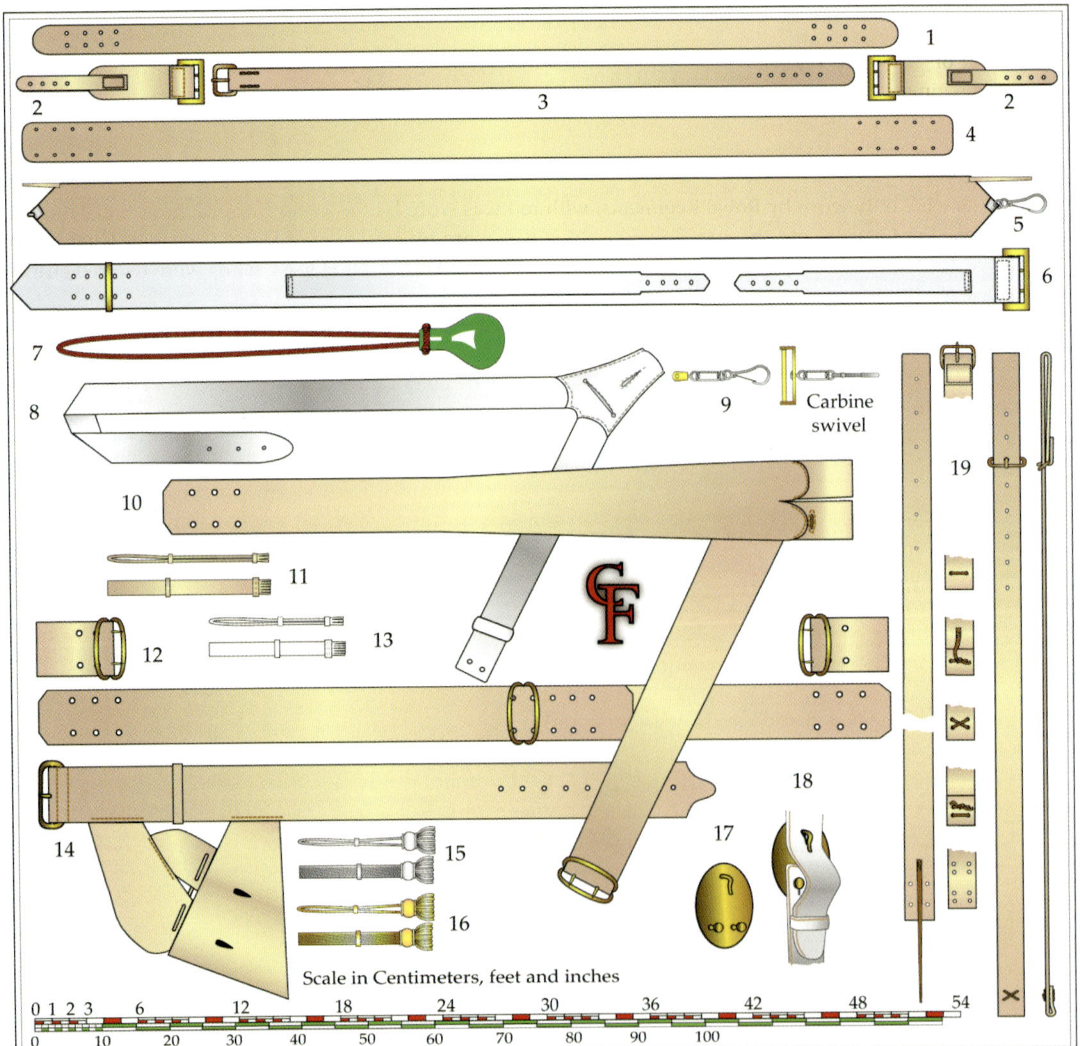

Cavalry Accoutrements. The shoulder belt for the cartridge pouch (1), the two ends that connected it to the pouch itself (2), a cavalry waist belt for the belly cartridge pouch of Light Dragoons (3), a different shoulder belt of 1751 (4), the cross belt that was used to support the musket with the attachment for the musket (5), a similar belt of 1768 used to support the musket or carbine and the two straps to connect to the cartridge pouch (6), a flask cord worn by most regiments of 1751: some came with different coloured cords (7), a one-piece sword belt of 1768 worn over the left shoulder (8) and two views of the attachment to the carbine or musket (9), a one-piece sword belt of 1751 (10), a sword knot of 1751 (11), a three-piece pouch belt of 1751 (12), an unregulated sword knot of 1768 (13), the one-piece waist belt for the sword and bayonet of 1751 (14), an unregulated sword knot of a silver-laced regiment (15) and an unregulated sword knot of a gold-laced regiment (16), a rear view of the an oval cross plate of a private soldier (17), a view of the plate hooked into the belt (18) and the different views of the variations of musket or carbine sling (19).

Sword Knots

The colour of the sword knot after 1768 was to match the colour of the waistcoat, either buff or white, but it is clear that regiments used sword knots of silver and gilt to match the colour of the metal of the regiment. The sword knot of the cavalry was gilt with a crimson centre.

Flask Cords

Flask cords were only worn by Royal Regiments, with red was worn by the Royal Horse Guards, 2nd Troop of Horse Grenadier Guards, and the 2nd Dragoons; blue was worn by 1st Troop of Horse Grenadier Guards, 1st Dragoons, 3rd Dragoons and white was worn by the 7th Dragoons. The 1st Horse Guards wore two red stripes on their carbine belts where-as the 2nd Horse Guards wore two blue.

Light Dragoons

These were formed as early as 1756. Each wore a tanned leather belt of three-and-a-half inches in breadth fitted as a sling for the carbine with a swivel; they also carried a waist belt for the sword and bayonet and a belly box of tanned leather with twenty-four cartridges with a waist belt.

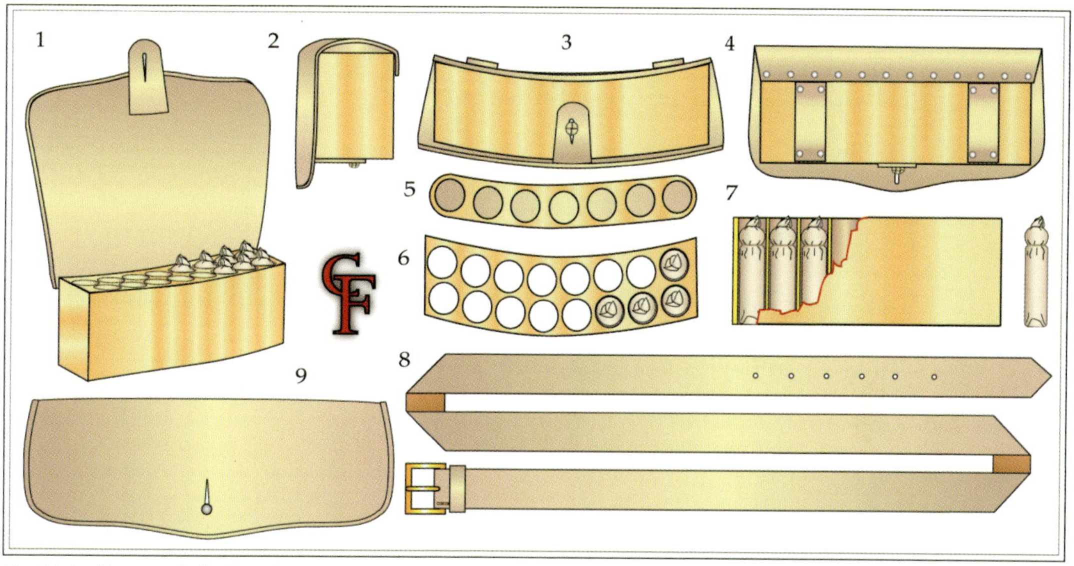

The Light Dragoon Belly Box. A perspective view (1), a side view (2), an under view (3), a rear view showing the strap holder nailed to the box to hold the strap (4); there were different blocks for the cartridges (5), a curved block to hold sixteen cartridges (6), and a sectioned front view of this block (7), the strap which held the belly box which could pass over the front or rear of the block (8) and one of the many different fronts and the different methods of retaining the flap (9)

Cartridge Pouches

There were many styles of cartridge pouch. Those most commonly associated with the cavalry are the twelve-round pouches and the thirty-round pouches, but others dated from the earlier1751 period. It is not possible to show all the variations and the many different cartridges they carried, but the main ones are mentioned below.

The Round Cartridge Pouch of 1751

These are shown worn by the different regiments of cavalry that existed in 1751. It is difficult to determine the precise size of this pouch but measurements taken from the Morier illustrations of the period suggest the sizes mentioned below.

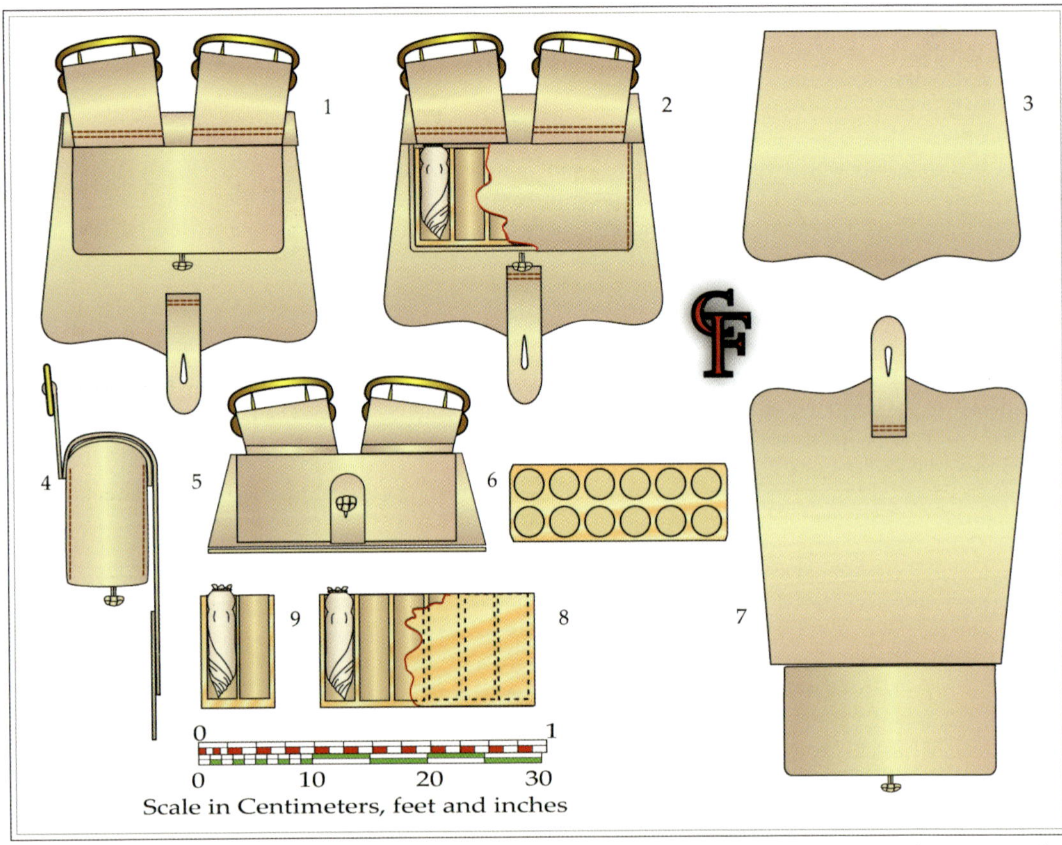

Cartridge Pouch of 1751. A rear view of the pouch showing the small box for the cartridges and the stitching securing the shoulder strap ends (1), a sectioned view of the pouch from the rear showing the method of carrying the cartridges (2), a front view of the pouch (3), a side view (4), an under view (5), the wooden block drilled to take twelve rounds (6), and a front view of the pouch with the flap open (7), a sectioned view of the front of the block (8) and a side view (9).

Twelve-round Cartridge Pouch

Both officers and NCOs carried the twelve round pouches in undress. The cartridges were stored in a drilled wooden block that had two extra holes for a picker and brush to clean the lock of the pistol. The pouch was made of leather; the pouch belt terminated at each side with a one-inch strap that passed through the keeper and buckles on the pouch. There were several patterns but in the main they were fundamentally similar each carrying twelve rounds and the tools. This pouch should not be confused with the dress order version, which was a different and far more decorative item.

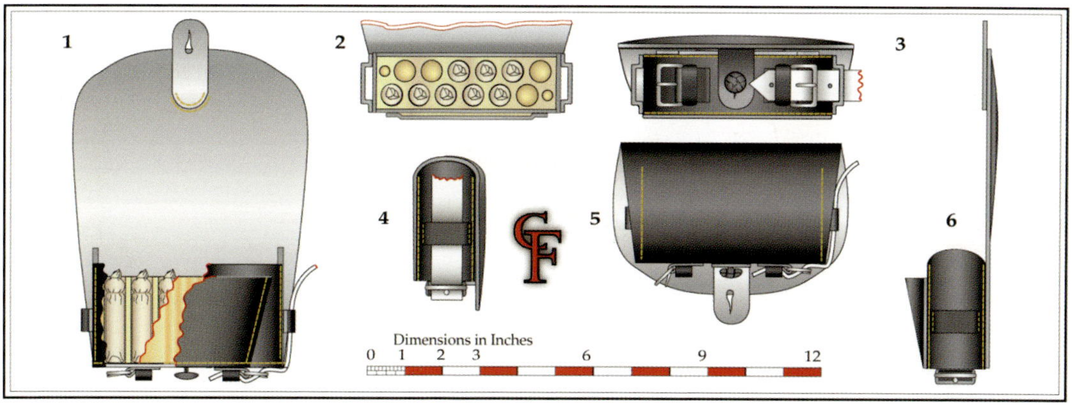

The twelve-round pouch carried by officers and NCOs of the cavalry. A sectioned view with the flap fully open (1), a top view showing the pocket on the front for the tools and flints and the wooden block drilled for cartridges; the two extra holes are for the picker and brush for the lock (2), an under view showing the keepers and buckles and one belt strap attached (3), an end view with the flap closed and a pouch strap fitted; note how the flap of the pouch is curved to fit over the pocket (4), a rear view (5) and a side view with the flap and pocket open (6), there were several patterns but in the main they were fundamentally similar, each carrying twelve rounds and the tools.

The Thirty-round Cavalry Pouch.

This cavalry cartridge pouch had a rear pocket and roller buckles. Made from leather one-fifth of an inch thick, the sizes of the pouches varied with the manufacturer, as did the exact method of construction. The cartridges were carried in a curved wooden block drilled to take thirty cartridges. The tools for the pistol and carbine were carried in the rear pocket. Fitted with the usual runners and buckles, it was more normally attached to a combined carbine sling. An asterisk stamp was used to hide the nail holes used to nail the leather to a block during assembly and it was common to find pouches where the leather had been joined to save on wastage. Stitching was usually applied at an angle to pass through the pieces of leather being stitched, but in other cases, the leather was skived, showing two raw edges.

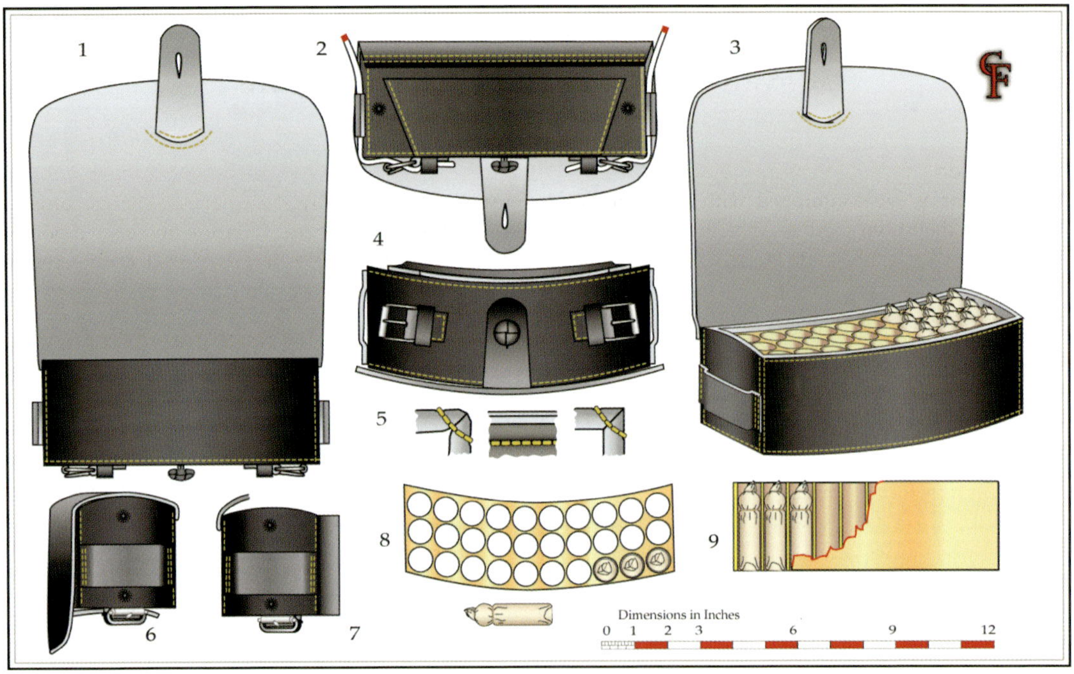

Thirty-round cavalry cartridge pouch. A front view with the flap open (1), a rear view of the pouch showing the pocket at the rear and the way the strap was fastened to the pouch (2), a perspective view showing the cartridges fitted into the curved wooden box (3), an under view showing the buckles and rear flap (4), different views of the methods of construction (5), a right side view showing the curve of the pouch (6), a left side view (7), a view of the wooden block drilled to take thirty rounds of carbine ammunition (8), and a front view (9). The colour of the stitching shown here is intended as an aid but was more normally a darker colour or was darkened when the pouch was cleaned.

CHAPTER SEVEN

Cavalry Harness and Horse Furniture

Introduction

Cavalry horses were equipped with different saddles, usually purchased by the colonel, although officers purchased their own saddles. The descriptions given are based upon extant horse furniture and contemporary illustrations. In general terms the harness was black for most arms but there is considerable variation between 1751 and 1783 to make it clear that much of the saddle and harness varied considerably over time. Horses' tails were generally short at the start of the period, but later they were grown long; since this took time, later again they were docked once more. Tails were cut to a length between the hoof and fetlock but officers in review order still preferred their horses un-docked.

Bridles

The standard bridle of the day was a bridoon or double-bridle and, while there were regimental or personal variations, this form of bridle was in general use by the British cavalry to 1751. The first part of the double-bridle consisted of a simple, two-part, bridle head, buckled on the near side and fitted with a jointed and twisted snaffle bit on loose rings. Over this was worn the more elaborate second bridle which consisted of a head-piece, brow band, nose band, throat lash, curb bit, and two cheek pieces with billots. The head piece was two inches wide, and thirty inches long, and split about eight inches at either end to form two straps, each three-quarters of an inch wide, one for the buckle of the cheek piece and the other for the buckle of the throat lash.

The brow band was one and a quarter inches wide and twelve inches between the loops; the noseband was about twenty-two inches long and one and a half inches wide; the throat lash was twenty-one inches long and three-quarters of an inch wide with a buckle at each end. The two cheek pieces were eight inches long from buckle to buckle, with seven-inch billots, three and a half inches being turned up to the buckle after passing through the eye of the bit. This formed the basic composition of the bridle; while there were regimental variations in the colours of the headbands this is very much the form of the heavy cavalry. Light Dragoons adopted a different form and a different bit.

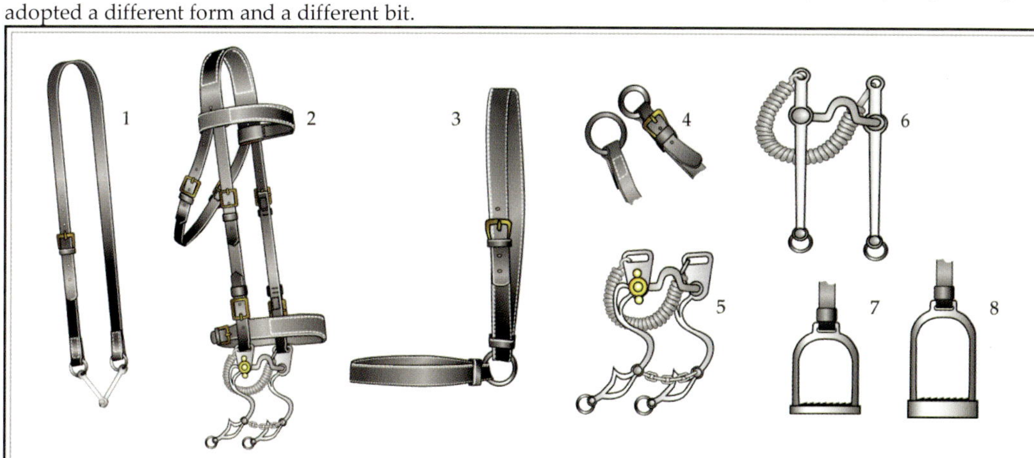

The Parts of a Bridle. The snaffle bit and bridle (1), the heavy cavalry bridle (2), the head collar (3), two different methods of attaching the reins (4), the heavy cavalry bit (5), the Light Dragoon bit (6), the Light Dragoon stirrup (7) and the heavy cavalry stirrup (8).

Reins

Reins were three-quarters of an inch wide; the curb reins were either two pieces or one piece and eight feet long with six-inch billots. The snaffle reins could be either one or two piece and were usually shorter being only seven or so feet long, again with six-inch billots. Generally, they were attached to the rings of the bit by billots but examples are known where they were stitched to the rings of the bit.

Head-collar

Under the bridle, each horse wore a leather or canvas head collar made from a throat lash and a noseband, both linked together at a ring from which a leather leading rein led to the saddle or, when not required, usually passed around the horse's neck. In stables it was mainly used on its own for watering parades and securing the horse in bivouac.

Riding Saddle

A saddle of about 1750 (an example is in The Scottish War Museum) weighed twelve pounds with the tree fixed to the saddle arch, the wood riveted to the pommel and cantle reinforced by iron bands and joined by pieces of wood to strengthen the leather. The wood had buckles to which the stirrups and flaps were fitted and it is clear that a blanket or pad was required under the saddle; a hook was used to position the pistol holster while at the rear there was a valise. Saddles used by the British cavalry depended upon the colonel of the regiment, and the patterns varied considerably, with the regulations noted that 'some Regiments have adopted the saddle of the Light Dragoons; other Regiments have saddles with burrs before, and no cantle behind; and there are still others, which have demi-peaks'. Each saddle was designed to take the various straps, and, accoutrements and the saddle was usually placed on top of a blanket folded lengthwise and breadth wise to make a pad for the horse. This was varied to suit the horse and often many folds were needed. The saddle was held in position on the horse's back by the girth, a chest strap at the front and the crupper at the rear and, usually, a surcingle to aid the girth. The advantage of the new Light Dragoon saddle was so apparent that it was quickly adopted by the heavy cavalry; the new saddle meant that the heavy cavalry rode some one hundred and seventy-five pounds.

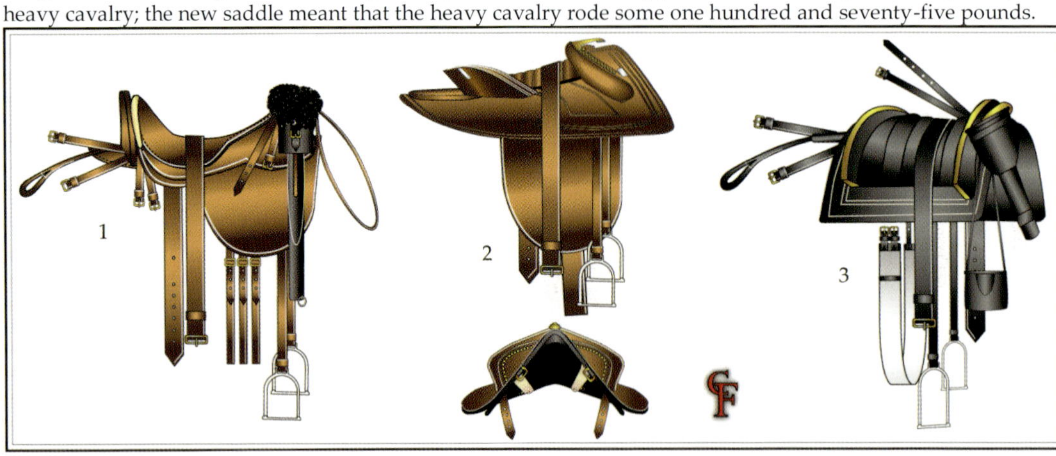

Saddles. The new saddle for Light Dragoons with surcingle (1), an eighteenth century saddle (2), the standard saddle used by the Household and Heavy cavalry that also used a surcingle (3).

Stirrup Irons

The British military rider of this period usually rode on long stirrups with the knees slightly bent. Stirrup leathers were attached to the saddle and back down to the stirrup where they were buckled. Heavy cavalry wore a runner at the stirrup iron and the leathers were adjusted so that the lower edge of the bar was two fingers above the upper edge of the heel of the boot.

Crupper

To prevent the saddle slipping forward every horse wore a crupper, consisting of a rolled leather dock at one end with a strap at the other. The dock passed under the tail of the horse and the both ends fastened to staples on the rear of the saddle.

Breast Plate or Martingale.

The breastplate prevented the saddle slipping backwards. It consisted of a leather strap joined to a billot at each end. The strap arms passed around the horse's neck to metal staples on the saddle. In several cases there is distinct evidence of a boss at the centre of the strap and while there is no evidence to support the wearing of a martingale there is some evidence to suggest they were worn at the later dates.

Surcingle

A surcingle was two inches wide and some sixty-eight inches long, and went over the saddle to keep them in place. It buckled on the near side and passed through loops on the girth. Both officers and troopers in dress wore leather surcingles and web for undress.

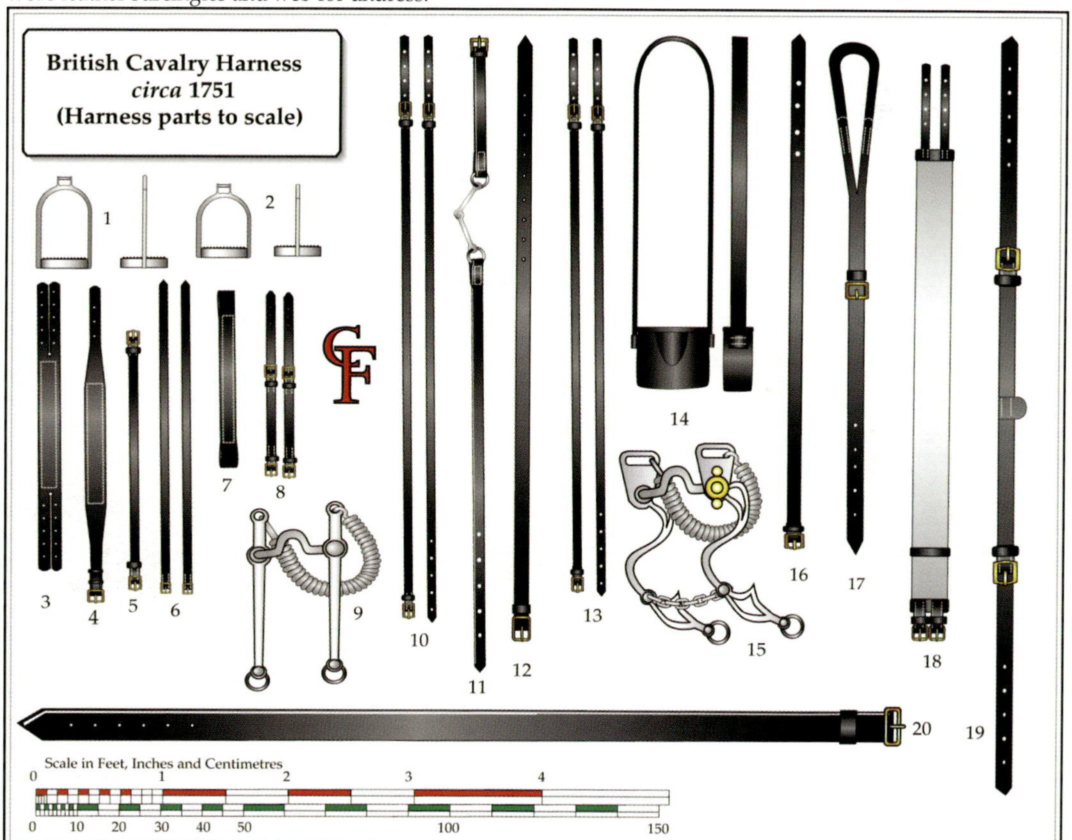

The Harness Parts. The standard heavy cavalry stirrup (1), the Light Dragoon stirrup (2). The component parts of the bridle, the head band (3), the nose band (4), the throat lash (5), two baggage straps (6), the brow band (7), the cheek pieces with their billots (8), the bit for the Light Dragoons (9), the two-part snaffle rein (10), the snaffle bit and bridle (11), the stirrup leather (12), the two-part curb rein (13), two views of the bucket to hold the musket (14), the heavy cavalry bit (15), the musket stay strap (16), the crupper (17), the girth (18), the breast plate (19) and the surcingle (20).

Light Dragoons

Formed as early as 1756, they also carried a butt bucket for the carbine while the bridle was fitted with the new bit and they carried a single rein, dispensing with the curb bit.

Valise

This was a round leather or cloth case carried behind the saddle, usually in the order of twenty-seven inches long and seven inches in diameter. It had begun to come into use in 1750 but not all units used it. Many wore the cloak at the rear of the saddle with three straps; the cloak was rolled with the facing colour to the outside.

Horse Furniture

The most practical of the horse furniture were the bearskin flounces, worn over the front of the saddle to cover the pistols and protect them from damp and moisture, although many officers adopted the skins of leopards for dress occasions. The shabraque served little useful purpose but, in the opinion of the men of the period, it improved greatly the appearance of the horseman; its main purpose was to display regimental devices. Ornamentation varied but usually consisted of a Royal or other and other such crests, badges and titles to which the regiment had an entitlement. The shape later came to represent cavalry arm but at this time those of the heavy cavalry were square or rounded with rounded holster covers, while those of Light Dragoons varied. Officers used a laced version for dress occasions and the illustrations given are taken from contemporary sources and surviving examples. The special badges worn by the regiments included those within the garter, others with the crown and yet others without. The non-royal regiments were usually surrounded with a mixed wreath of leaves, thistle and roses and carried the ranking of the regiment. In most cases the badges remained the same but in other cases they differed.

Special Badges of the Cavalry regiments of 1751 and 1768 for both the Royal and non-royal regiments. The 1st Life Guards (1), 2nd Life Guards (2), 1st Horse Grenadier Guards (3), 2nd Horse Grenadier Guards (4), 1st Dragoon Guards (5), 2nd Queen's Dragoon Guards (6), 3rd King's Own Dragoon Guards (7), 1st Royal Dragoons (8), 2nd Royal North British Dragoons (9), 3rd Dragoons (10), 4th Dragoons (11), 5th Royal Irish Dragoons (12), the second badge of the 3rd Dragoon Guards (13), 6th (Inniskilling) Dragoons (14), 1st Horse as a non-royal horse (15), 10th Dragoons and other non-royal dragoons (16), 12th Light Dragoons (17), 15th Light Dragoons (18), the later 16th Light Dragoons (19), 17th Light Dragoons (20), 21st Light Dragoons (21), 18th Light Dragoons (22) and the Cumberland Light Dragoons (23).

Mounted Officers of Infantry

The horse furniture was unregulated but often consisted of a pair of pistols, a regimental bridle with noseband, a black or white bridoon, a saddle, regimental stirrup irons, crupper, half cover with holsters and brown bear skin flounces and a regimental saddle-cloth of facing colour worn with the metal of the regiment

Housings and Holster Caps of 1768

Generally these were colour of the facings except for the King's Dragoon Guards, the Royal Dragoons, which were to be scarlet, the 4th Regiment of Horse that were to be buff, and the King's and Queen's which were to be white. The housings and holster caps were to be one broad stripe of yellow or white worsted or mohair lace with a stripe in the middle of one-third its whole breadth as specified, the lace of officers was gold or silver with the centre stripe of mohair of a similar colour to the troopers'. The ranking of the regiment was to be placed on a red ground within a wreath of leaves roses, and thistles. The crown was to appear on the top part of the hoslter cap with the King's Cypher was to be embroidered below, under it the number or rank of the regiment. Horse furniture was unregulated but often consisted of a pair of pistols, a regimental bridle with noseband, a black or white bridoon, a saddle, regimental stirrup irons, crupper, half cover with holsters and brown bear skin flounces and a regimental saddle cloth of facing colour worn with the metal of the regiment. The Prince of Wales's Light Dragoons used black cloth with strips of white goatskin. The shape of the rear furniture varied: in 1751 those of the Life Guards, Horse Guards, Horse Grenadier Guards, the regiments of Horse, 2nd, 3rd, 5th, 8th, 9th, 10th, 12th, 13th and 14th Dragoons were rounded in shape, while those of the 1st Royal, 4th, 6th, 7th Queens, 11th and 15th Light Dragoons were square.

Housings and Holster Caps. The 2nd Troop of the Horse Grenadier Guards (1), Royal Horse Guards (2), 5th King's Own Dragoons (3), 2nd Royal North British Dragoons (4), 16th Light Dragoons (5) and the 4th Dragoons (6).

CHAPTER EIGHT

Gunpowder, Carbines, Pistols and Swords

Gunpowder

The propellant used for the muskets, pistols and rifles of the period was gunpowder, the nature of which and the ratio to which it was mixed, varied from country to country. The British powder of the period was notionally composed of seventy-five parts of saltpetre, ten parts of sulphur and fifteen parts of charcoal, but different mixtures existed where the circumstances demanded. Although the main source of powder was the Royal Powder Mills, powder from civilian contractors was always needed and comparison with Royal Powder required it to be at least ninety-five percent effective to avoid being rejected. The process for the manufacture of gunpowder is well covered elsewhere, but it was mixed to the required proportions and pressed into damp cakes, which were forced through sieves to form the grain size. It was then rotated in a drum to corn the grains (round the edges) and coated with black lead to resist moisture. Gunpowder was provided from the mills in oak barrels, the largest being the 100lb whole barrel, next the 50lb half-barrel and, lastly, the 25lb quarter–barrel, each containing 90lb, 45lb and 20lb of powder respectively, the space left being to allow the powder to be 'better preserved'. The powder, made up in different forms and grades, was identified by grain size and marked on the barrels in coloured paint depending upon type. Powder deteriorated in the field; some became 'shook' while much became damp and had to be returned to be dried or re-stoved.

Powder came in three main grades with the grade identified by red lettering on the barrels:

'No ½ LG' Large grain of two to three millimeter, and the most powerful of the powders. It was used by the field ordnance and specified for use by the artillery and, later became known as 'Ordnance Powder'.

'No 2 SG' Small grain with a size of one and a half to two millimeters, it was easier to ignite but less powerful.

'No 3 FG' The finest grain of powder of a half a millimeter to one and a half millimeters, it was the easiest to ignite but less powerful and used as musket or priming powder.

'RA' Special powder for rifled arms with a larger grain size to inhibit the initial rate of burning and make the delivery of power more gradual.

When through the passage of time powder became unfit or damp it was re-stoved (dried) but since this process reduced the power, it was rarely used in its own right.

'RS No ½ LG' Painted in yellow letters inside a yellow diamond-shaped frame

'RS No 3 FG' Painted in yellow letters inside a yellow diamond-shaped frame

Re-stoved powder was mixed with good powder for those purposes where the reduced quality was considered acceptable and re-designated as white powder. In testing it was expected that two ounces of red large grain powder would give a range of 180 feet to a sixty-four pound iron ball when fired from an eight-inch mortar, a similar amount of blue large-grain would give a range of 150 feet and re-stoved powder, 107. The powder was also tested to see how much water it absorbed when exposed to the atmosphere; one hundred pounds of powder was not expected to absorb more than twelve ounces of water in seventeen or eighteen days. Each year a regiment received sufficient powder and ball for practice; this amounted to twelve full barrels and 800 pounds of ball.

There were several different charges with ball the more usual, but there was also buckshot that contained fifteen pellets of 0.32 inches and yet another with one ball and four buckshot. The standard charge for a musket was 0.165 grains. The Royal Laboratory considered that a sheet of cartridge paper twenty-one by seventeen inches would make the cartridges for twelve muskets, sixteen carbines or twenty-four pistols; the completed cartridges were then made up in barrels. During the War Of Independence the quantity of cartridges that each man carried increased significantly. One practice, used for sentry duty was a running ball loaded on a blank charge. The ball was then rolled out, and the blank charge removed, or fired off.

Flints

These came in different sizes for muskets, carbines and pistols and were usually napped to a wedge shape and wrapped in leather or lead between the two jaws of the lock. The wartime allowance varied at five per man but this depended on the quality of the flints provided.

Carbine

The term carbine is difficult to define, but in the period in question it usually meant a seventeen bore of 0.65 to 0.67 inches with the length varying from forty-two inches to under thirty-nine inches. Since the colonels of mounted units were the providers of such weapons as carbines and pistols to the units under their control, there were considerable differences between the Household Cavalry, Horse, Dragoon Guards, Dragoons and Light Dragoons. Before 1770 the carbine was a short musket with a wooden ramrod and could generally be divided into several groups: the Royal Horse Guards of 1765; the heavy Dragoon carbine with ring and bayonet of the 1770 pattern; General Eliott's Light Dragoon carbine of 1773: and the heavy Dragoon of 1796. A picker and brush to clean the carbine lock were worn on a chain that usually attached to a button on the coat or behind the cross-belt. When practicing firing drills the locks were fitted with 'wooden snappers' instead of flints.

The accuracy of these early-smooth bore carbines was not good. Cavalry carbines had no buff sling and sling swivels were rarely fitted. When they were several patterns existed: others had a lower end pierced with two holes, others four while some carried a stitched leather lace on the inside face and yet others used a separate lace. Another part that was used to protect the lock was either a full-length cover for the butt and lock or a short lock protector made of leather or other material. During this period there was a constant stream of replacement carbines and pistols.

Light Dragoons

These carried a carbine with a ring and bar fifty-three inches long, a bayonet seventeen inches long, a pistol of ten inches with a barrel of carbine bore and a straight cutting sword thirty-four inches long with a light hilt without basket.

Royal Horse Guards Carbine

Many of these models were made (at least 30,000) but the first used in America (by the 42nd Regiment) is dated as 1737. It was stocked to within four-and-a-half inches of the barrel and was retained by three blocked, semi circular brackets. Four brass pipes retained the ramrod, which could be of either wood or metal, although the wooden one was a larger diameter and the practice of wooden rammers still persisted after the American Revolution. The lock plate measured 6.75 by 1.5 inches, overall length is sixty-two inches, barrel length forty-six inches and the calibre was 0.65 inches. Many versions of this carbine included the patterns of 1748, 1756 and 1756 (Irish).

Heavy Dragoon Carbine

Originally used in 1746 as a carbine for Dragoons (over 83,000 were made of this weapon). It was stocked to within four inches of the barrel. Three unblocked, semi-circular brackets retained the barrel. There were four pipes to the to retain the metal ramrod. The lock plate measured 6.875 by 1.5 inches and was distinctive in having a double oval to the spring; overall length was fifty-eight inches, barrel length forty-two inches and the calibre was 0.65 inches. There were many versions of this carbine, which included the patterns of 1769, 1756, 1777, the Liége pattern, 1769 (Irish) and, 1779-S with a smaller S shaped side plate. A brass firelock wrist plate and bayonet socket was generally fitted and, both the firelock and bayonet were engraved with matching regimental, company, or rack number information. Markings between regiments sometimes differ considerably, with some engraved with the regimental number, company letter or rack number on the carbine wrist plate and bayonet socket.

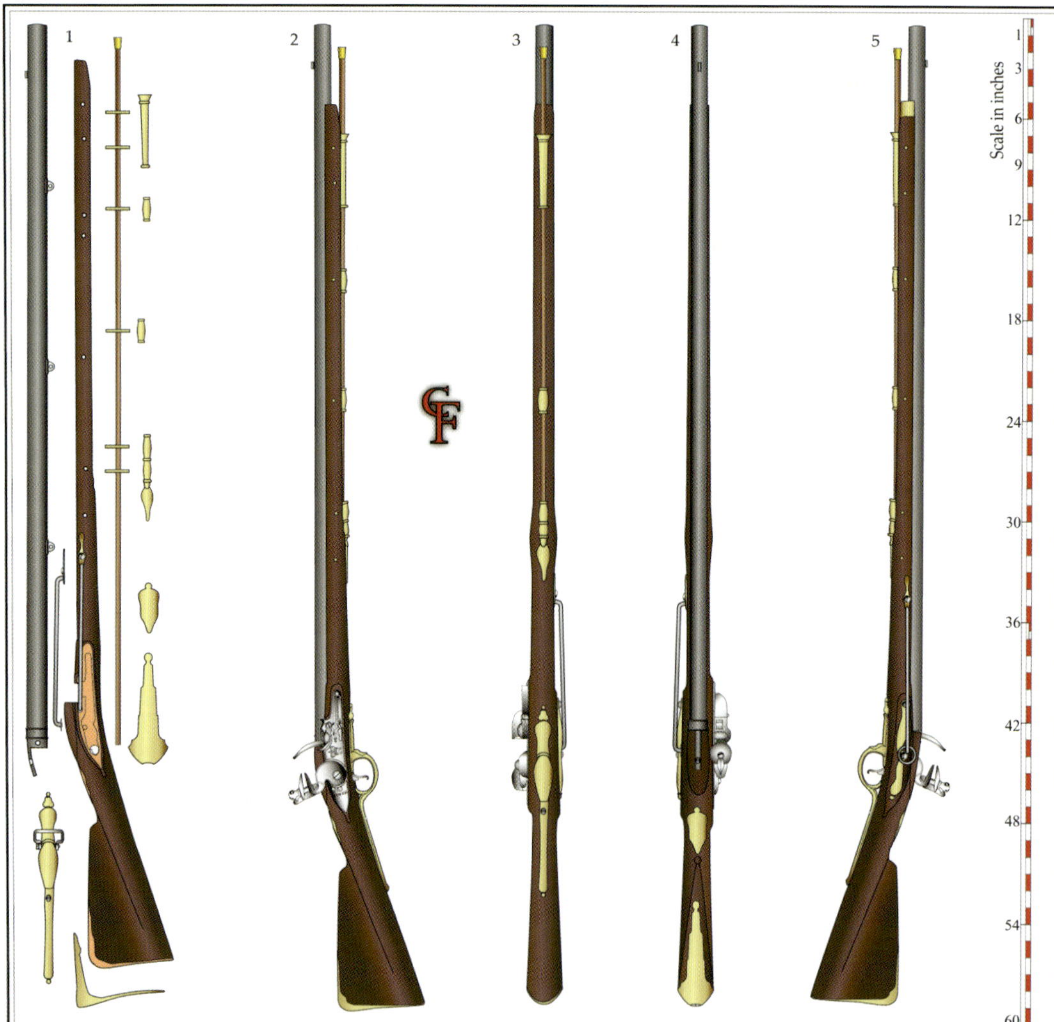

Heavy Dragoon Carbine of 1746. This carbine was fitted with a wooden ramrod and had no fore end furniture and carried a sling bar for use by cavalry (1), a right side view showing the lock, the reader should note that carbine belt swivels were rarely fitted (2), an under view with the sling bar for cavalry (3), a top view (4) and a left side view showing a ring to the carbine sling bar and a wooden ramrod (5).

Eliott Carbine

This is the earlier Eliott carbine but several were made in Ireland at Dublin Castle and differed slightly in the dimensions from this example. The upper ramrod was a different design and was fitted with the usual sling bar but certain of these carbines were also fitted with sling swivels for a bayonet belt. The lock is contemporary to the carbine. Overall length is forty-three and a half inches, the barrel length some twenty-eight inches and the calibre some 0.60 inches.

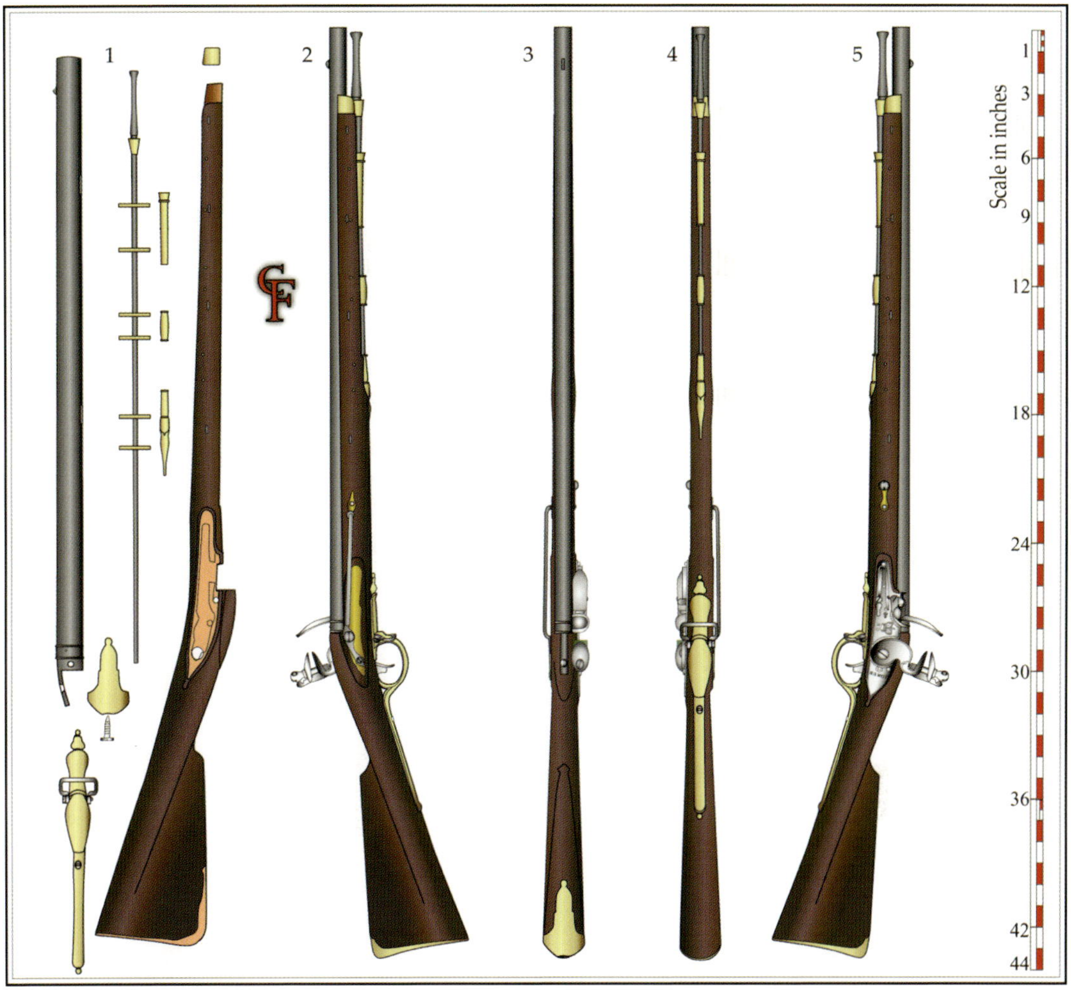

The Eliott Carbine. An exploded view showing the different parts that made up the carbine. Note this example has no upper or lower swivels for a carbine belt (1). A left side showing the sling bar (2), a view from above (3), an under view (4) and a right side view showing the lock (5).

1770 Cavalry Carbine

With the ever-increasing demands for mobility among the cavalry this carbine was lighter for weight, while the distinctive sling-bar fastener was attached to the fore end with an extension at the rear held by a screw. The Nock lock is shown with this carbine but other locks were fitted and, it should be noticed that nearly all cavalry carbines did not have carbine belts or the swivel attachments. The furniture is almost a reduced standard land pattern and was also adopted by the Horse Grenadier Guards. Overall height was fifty-seven-and-a-half inches, with the barrel length of forty-two inches and calibre of 0.65 inches.

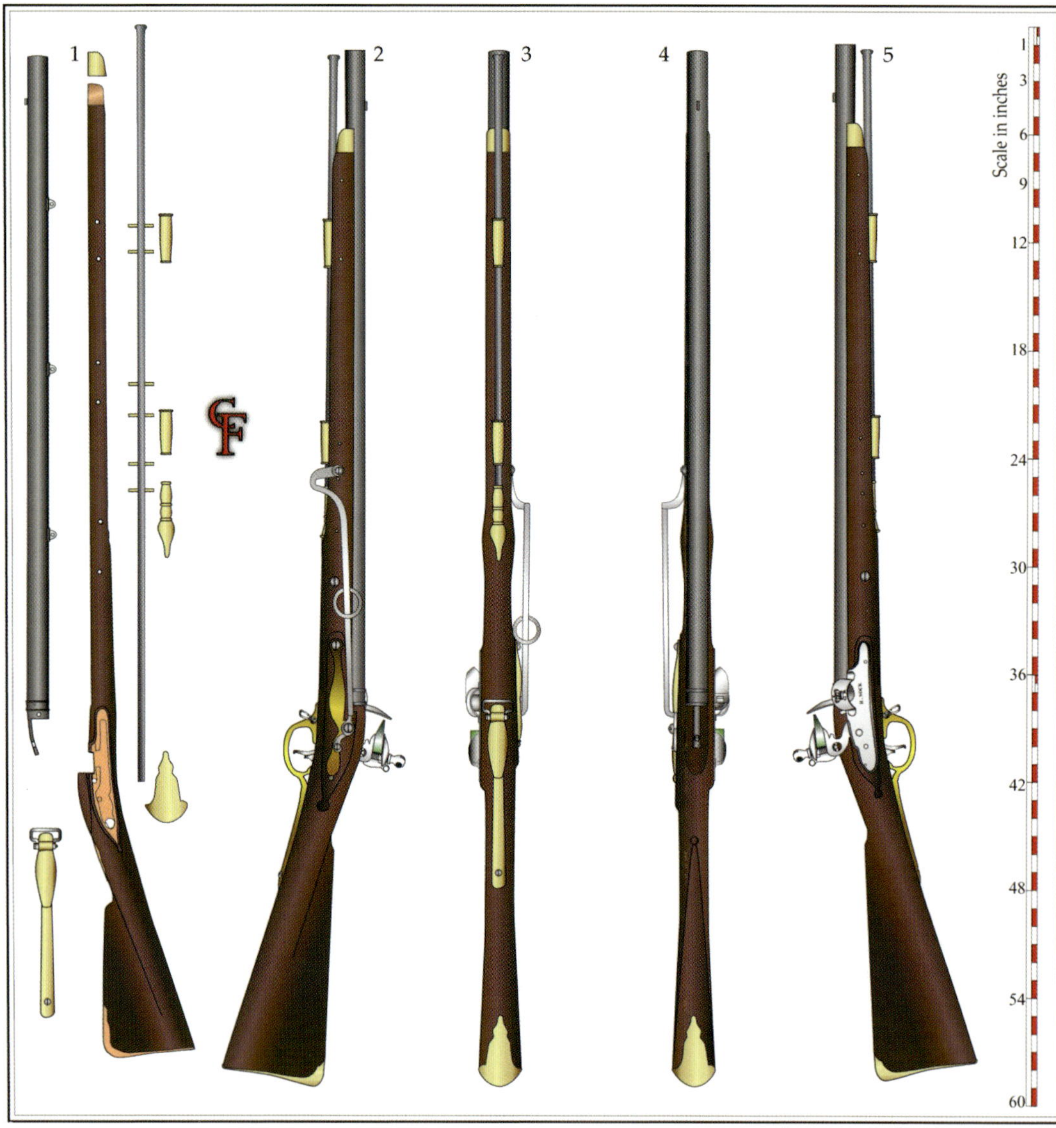

The 1770 Carbine for Cavalry. An exploded view showing the parts that made up the carbine (1), a left side view showing the sling bar (2), an under view showing the trigger and side bar (3), a similar top view (4) and a right side view showing the Nock lock (5).

Bayonets

Iron bayonets fitted with black leather bayonet scabbards and brass mountings were issued with each carbine. As there was no guarantee that bayonets could be interchanged with carbines, bayonets were generally engraved with a number corresponding with that found on the carbine to which it belonged. Bayonets were made by many manufacturers and the differences were very obvious. The Nock screw less lock came in different sizes, the five-and-a-half inch lock for muskets and carbines, and four-and-three-quarter inch for rifles and pistols; the shield for the pan was only fitted for carbines, since these locks required highly-trained craftsmen.

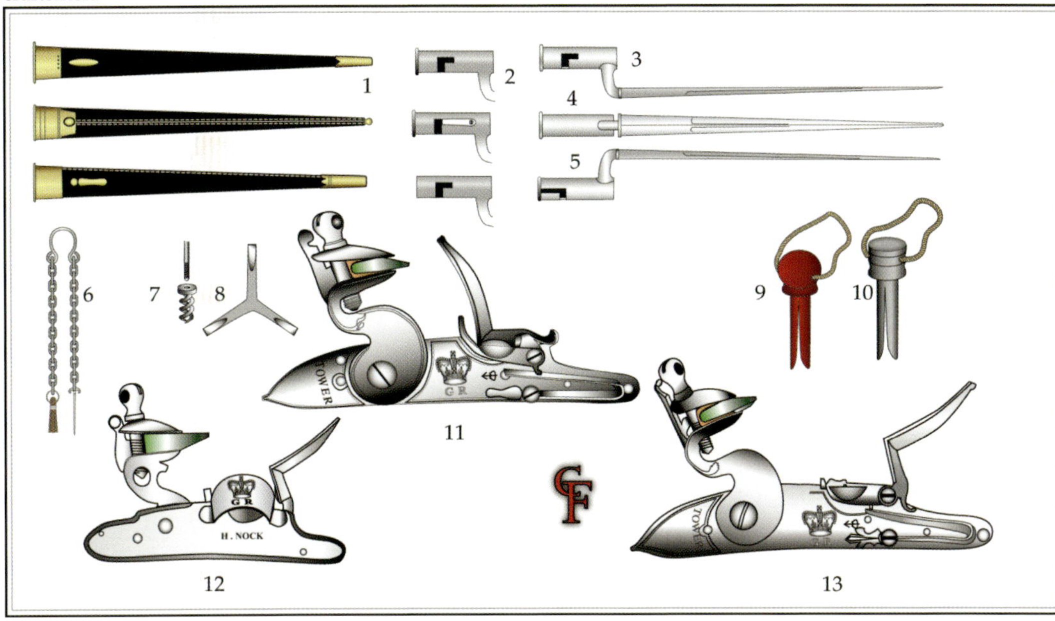

Locks, Tools and Bayonets. The different types of bayonet scabbard (1), the different types of bayonet (2), three views of a bayonet, the right side view (3), the under view (4) and the left side view (5), the picker and lock usually worn attached to a button on the coat (6), the rammer end and cartridge removal tool (7), a multipurpose tool for the carbine (8), two plugs to prevent ingress of water and damp to the barrel (9 and 10), the lock from a later version of the short Land carbine (11), the Nock lock with shield guard fitted (12) and the lock variant from a short land pattern carbine (13).

Pistols

The pistols used during this period varied in every possible way: some were carbine bore but the locks and every other aspect changed in almost every case. There were barrels of different form, but with the patterns changing as the years progressed. Eventually the standard metal ramrod made an appearance but, in the main, the cavalry used what was available from the stores, including sea service pistols.

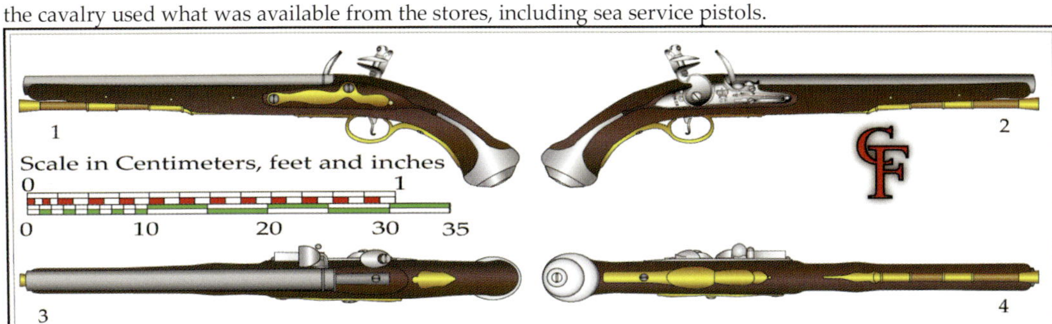

Pistols. These pistols are generic. A left side view (1), a right side view showing the lock (2), a top view (3) and an under view showing the trigger and wooden ramrod (4).

Swords

Morier shows many and varied types and each regiment seems to have adopted its own pattern and this is not surprising as the colonel chose the troopers' weapons. All were long in the reach, straight bladed and large enough to fit a gauntleted hand, often with a leather liner. Each was profusely decorated with elaborate scroll bars with a full basket hilt in either brass or steel and carried in a brass-mounted scabbard. Officers' swords were also straight bladed with a sufficient basket hilt to protect the hand and, as each purchased his own his own, the standard varied. With the introduction of Light Dragoons a smaller sword was used, some of which had a curved blade like the 17th Light Dragoons, while others like the 16th Light dragoons, had a straight blade.

It was not until 1788 that the swords of Dragoon Guards and Dragoons started to become regulated. Hilts were to be half basket in the same form as the 6th Inniskilling Dragoons (which Morier did not illustrate as the picture is from the near side). The grip from the guard to the button was to be 7.6 inches the blades to be thirty-nine inches, the breadth of the blade at the shoulder one-and-a-third inches and finish at about fourteen inches from the point. The Light Dragoons were also included, the hilt was to be five inches long, the blade to be thirty-six inches long and the curve at the centre was to be one-and-three-quarter inches, the breadth to be one-and-a-half inches at the shoulder point-three inches thick and finish at eleven inches from the bottom.

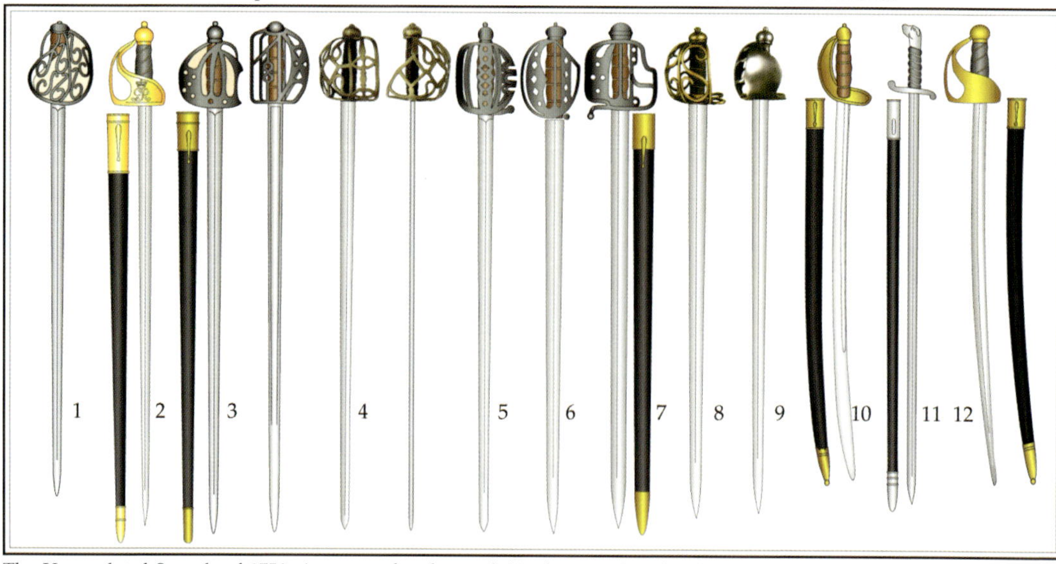

The Unregulated Swords of 1751. An unregulated sword (1), the sword and scabbard of Life Guards (2), the sword of a trooper of the Royal Horse Guards (3), other different and unregulated swords (4), a sword of a trooper of the 10th Dragoons (5), other examples of a trooper of the 7th Queen's Dragoons (6), a further unregulated sword and scabbard (7), a trooper 's sword of the 3rd Dragoons (8), an officer's sword of the Horse Grenadier Guards (9), 17th Light Dragoons (10), the sword of an officer of the 16th Light Dragoons (11) and the new sword of 1788 (12).

Part Two

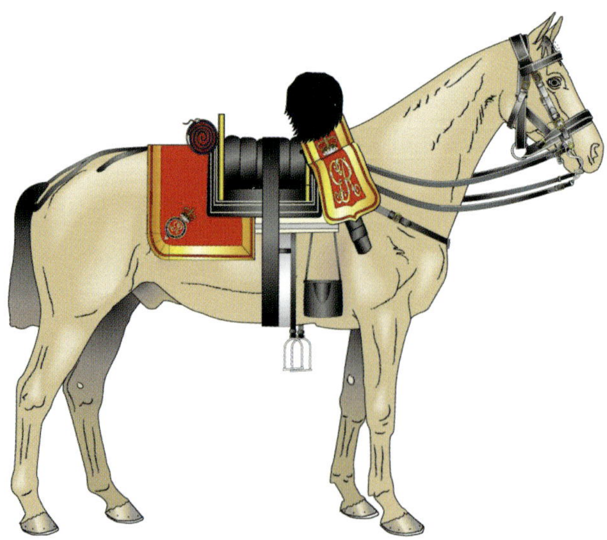

Introduction

The 1st of Horse was originally what is now known as the Royal Horse Guards. In 1746 three regiments of Horse, the 2nd, 3rd and 4th, were converted into Dragoon Guards. The remaining four regiments of Horse then became the 1st, 2nd, 3rd and 4th as the Royal Horse Guards had dropped the title of 1st Horse. In 1756 a light troop was added to each Dragoon Guard and Dragoon regiment and, in 1759, separate regiments of Light Dragoons were raised; the light troops were disbanded in 1763. In 1788 the troops of Horse Guards and Horse Grenadier Guards were reorganized as the 1st and 2nd Life Guards, and the remaining regiments of Horse were converted into the 4th, 5th, 6th and 7th Dragoon Guards. During the 1730s the shoulder knot appeared for the 31st Regiment followed by the 33rd in 1739.

In 1756 the Heavy Cavalry were ordered to raise Light Dragoons and these were raised by the 1st, 2nd and 3rd Dragoon Guards, and the 1st, 2nd, 3rd, 4th, 6th, 7th, 10th and 11th Dragoons, to be disbanded during 1767. Then in 1759 the 20th were raised; in 1760 the 21st; the 17th and 18th in 1763; the 16th in 1766, the 12th in 1768; the 15th in 1769, the 8th in 1775, the 14th in 1776, the 19th in 1779 as well as the second 20th, the second 21st and the 22nd; in 1783 the 7th, 9th, 10th, 11th and 13th; in 1786 the 23rd was renumbered as the 19th, while many others were also converted at dates outside the period.

The inspection returns show how the regiments made every effort to move away from the regulated uniform and exactly who wore what on a given occasion is impossible to show since even the portraits are somewhat speculative.

Horses' tails were cropped very short until 1764 when it was decided that they should be long, but it took time for the tails to grow. Later the tails were cropped short again.

CHAPTER NINE

Household Cavalry

Placed on the English establishment on 26 January 1661 as:
His Majesty's 1st, 2nd and 3rd Troops of Guards (also known as Life Guards of Horse)
Raised in 1658 as:
1st or His Majesty's Own Troop of Guards
Raised in 1659 as:
3rd or Duke of Albemarle's Troop of Guards
Renumbered in 1670 as:
2nd (The Queen's) Troop of Guards
Raised before 1661 as:
2nd or Duke of York's Troop of Guards
Renumbered in 1670 as:
3rd or Duke of York's Troop of Guards
This Troop was disbanded in 1746.
Raised in 1661 and disbanded in 1663
4th Troop of Guards
Raised in 1687 and disbanded in 1689:
4th Troop of Guards or Lord Dover's
Raised in 1660 and returned to Holland in 1689 the:
Dutch Troop
Raised in 1661 as a Scots Troop and renumbered in 1676 as:
4th Troop of Guards
Raised in 1664 and disbanded in 1676
5th Troop of Guards
In 1746 personnel of the 1st and 2nd Troops of Guards absorbed the 3rd Troop of Guards and 4th Troop of Guards that were effectively disbanded; three Troops of Horse Grenadiers were also attached to each Troop of Guards as:
The King's Troop of Horse Grenadiers
The Duke's Troop of Horse Grenadiers
The Queen's Troop of Horse Grenadiers
These separated from the Troops of Guards in 1687 and became:
1st Troop of Horse Grenadiers
2nd Troop of Horse Grenadiers
3rd Troop of Horse Grenadiers
Raised in 1687 and disbanded in 1689 was:
4th Troop of Horse Grenadiers
In 1693 the three Troops of Horse Grenadiers were amalgamated as:
1st Troop of Horse Grenadier Guards
They were joined in 1709 by a Scots troop raised in 1702 to become:
2nd Troop of Horse Grenadier Guards
There were two regiments of Horse Guards:
1st Troop of Horse Guards
2nd Troop of Horse Guards
In 1788 the horse Grenadier Guards were absorbed and the name was changed:

1st Regiment of Life Guards
2nd Regiment of Life Guards
Two regiments amalgamated in 1922 to form:
The Life Guards

The 1st Troop Life Guards in 1751:
• The facings for this royal regiment were dark-blue without lapels and the waistcoats and breeches were buff; linings of the cloaks and coats of all ranks were blue: Milan's list of 1749 gives the 1st Troop faced and lined blue with red furniture and gold shoulder knots; 2nd Troop faced blue, with buff furniture and gold shoulder knots; 3rd Troop faced blue with yellow furniture and gold shoulder knots; 4th Troop faced dark-blue with, dark-blue furniture and gold shoulder knots.
• Officers' lace and buttons were gold and officers' coats were laced for dress with eight pointed loops set on in pairs; the coat was laced down the front in gold. There was a blue, laced gold pointed patch at the collar.
• The coats of the private gentlemen were similarly laced and had gold edged shoulder straps.
• All ranks' coats were lined blue.
• The horizontal pocket had four buttons below and was laced on the bottom edge in gold; there were four pointed gold loops to the pocket.
• The waistcoat was buff and laced about by gold lace and breeches were buff with white tops.
• The blue cuff was square ended and laced about with gold lace and two pointed loops with a further pointed loop above the cuff; the cuff slash was laced about with three buttons and three pointed loops in gold.
• The colour of the housings and holster caps was scarlet.
• Colours of the Royal lace were red with a thin gold on the outside two millimetres wide, a stripe of red-half millimetre wide and on the inside a four-millimetre-wide stripe.
• Badges: the King's Cypher within the garter with a crown over on both the holster caps and rounded saddlecloth.
• The musket sling was gold with two scarlet stripes.
• The regiment rode black horses.

Not Included in 1768 Regulations but by 1767:
• The facings for this royal regiment were dark-blue with half lapels; the waistcoats, breeches, linings of the cloaks and coats of all ranks were white.
• The officers' lace and buttons were gold set on in four pairs and the lapel was laced about, as were the turnbacks.
• The indented cuff was not slit and was laced with four chevron loops in pairs.
• The vertical pocket was not slit and was laced with four chevron loops in pairs.
• The coats of the troopers were similar with gold lace and buttons.
• The colours of the housings and holster caps were scarlet.
• The colours of the lace remained unchanged.
• Badges: the King's Cypher within the garter with a crown over on both the holster caps and rounded saddlecloth.

The 2nd Troop of Life Guards in 1751:
• The facings for this royal regiment were dark-blue without lapels and the waistcoats and breeches were buff; linings of the cloaks and coats of all ranks were blue.
• Officers' lace and buttons were gold and officers' coats were laced for dress with eight pointed loops set on in pairs; the coat was laced down the front and round the collar in gold. There was a blue, laced gold pointed patch at the collar.
• The coats of the private gentlemen were similarly laced and had gold edged shoulder straps.

• The coats of all ranks were lined blue.
• The horizontal pocket had four buttons below and was laced on the bottom edge in gold; there were four pointed gold loops to the pocket.
• The waistcoat was buff, laced about by gold lace, and breeches were buff with white tops.
• The blue cuff was square-ended and laced about with gold lace and two pointed loops. The cuff slash was laced about with three buttons and three pointed loops in gold.
• The colour of the housings and holster caps was blue.
• The shape of the rear saddlecloth was rounded.
• Colours of the Royal lace were blue with a thin gold to the outside one millimetre wide and a broader stripe five millimetres wide, followed by a one millimetre wide stripe on the inside.
• Badges: the King's Cypher within the garter with a crown over on both the holster caps and rounded saddlecloth.
• The musket sling was gold with two blue stripes.
• The regiment rode black horses.

Not Included in 1768 Regulations but by 1767:
• The facings for this royal regiment were dark-blue with half lapels and the waistcoats, breeches, linings of the cloaks and coats of all ranks were white.
• The officers' lace and buttons were gold set in four pairs and the lapel was laced about, as were the turnbacks.
• The indented cuff was not slit and was laced with four chevron loops in pairs.
• The vertical pocket was not slit and was laced with four chevron loops in pairs.
• The coats of the Troopers were similar, with gold lace and buttons.
• The colours of the housings and holster caps were blue.
• The colours of the lace remained unchanged.
• Badges: the King's Cypher within the garter with a crown over on both the holster caps and rounded saddlecloth.

1st Troop of Horse Grenadier Guards in 1751:
• The facings for this royal regiment were dark-blue without lapels; Milan's list of 1749 gives the 1st Troop Horse Grenadier Guards faced blue with blue furniture.
• Officers' lace and buttons were gold and officers' coats were laced for dress with nine loops set on evenly.
• The private soldiers wore white lace but their coats were of madder-red.
• The coats of all ranks were lined blue with a red edge.
• The coat had no lapels and a slit cuff with six buttons and six chevrons of lace, set evenly.
• The vertical pocket was slit and had six buttons and six chevrons of lace, set evenly.
• The waistcoat and breeches were buff with white tops.
• The mitre cap of the 1st Troop had a blue front, they wore the King's Cypher doubled and reversed, within the garter with a crown over, with foliate designs on either side of leaves embroidered in white. At the rear a white tassel hung from a red ground, while the front turn-up was red with a grenade and a trophy of flags at either side. At the rear a red turn-up had a crossed musket and sword and a grenade in colour; they also wore a blue flask cord over buff cartridge pouch.
• The colour of the housings and holster caps was blue.
• Colours of the lace were gold, with a thin gold on the outside one millimetre wide, a red stripe one millimetre wide and a broader stripe two millimetres wide on the inside.
• The shape of the rear saddlecloth was rounded.
• The badge on the housings was the King's Cypher, within the garter with a crown over.
• The regiment rode black horses.
• The Horse Grenadier Guards wore fur caps from 1763.

Not Included in 1768 Regulations but by 1767:

- The facings for this royal regiment were dark-blue without lapels; the linings of the cloaks and coats of all ranks were white. The waistcoats and breeches were white.
- The officers' lace and buttons were gold and carried nine square loops.
- Other ranks were similar but of madder-red and carried white lace with silver buttons.
- The cuff was indented and had four buttons and four chevrons of lace, set in pairs.
- The vertical pocket was unslit and had six buttons and six chevrons of lace, set in pairs.
- The badge on the housings was the King's Cypher, within the garter with a crown over.
- In all other respects the housings and lace were the same, but the fur caps still differed.

2nd Troop of Horse Grenadier Guards in 1751:

- The facings for this royal regiment were dark-blue without lapels; Milan's list of 1749 gives the 2nd Troop Horse Grenadier Guards, faced blue with red furniture.
- Officers' lace and buttons were gold and officers' coats were laced for dress with nine loops set on evenly.
- The private soldier wore white lace but their coats were of madder-red.
- The coats of all ranks were lined dark-blue with a red edge.
- The coat had slit cuff with a dark-blue; with six buttons and six chevrons of lace, set evenly.
- The vertical pocket was unslit and had six buttons and six chevrons of lace, set evenly.
- The waistcoat and breeches were buff with white tops.
- The mitre cap of the 2nd Troop had a red front, they wore the King's Cypher doubled and reversed, within the garter with a crown over on a red ground inside the garter; the foliate designs on either side were of roses, thistles and leaves embroidered in gold and white. The front flap and rear turn up were blue with a thistle in full colour and either side were white thistles. The front was edged in white and carried the motto 'Nemo Me Impune Lacessit'. At the rear a white tassel hung from a red ground, the rear blue turn up had a crossed musket and sword and a thistles in full colour; they also wore a red flask cord over buff cartridge pouch.
- The colour of the housings and holster caps was red.
- Colours of the lace were gold, with a thin gold on the outside one millimetre wide, a blue stripe one millimetre wide and a broader stripe two millimetres wide on the inside.
- The colour of the housings and holster caps was scarlet.
- The shape of the rear saddlecloth was rounded.
- The regiment rode black horses.
- The Horse Grenadier Guards wore fur caps from 1763.

Not Included in 1768 Regulations but by 1767:

- The facings for this royal regiment were dark-blue without lapels; the linings of the cloaks and coats of all ranks were white. The waistcoats and breeches were white.
- The officers' lace and buttons were gold and carried nine square loops.
- The coats of the other ranks were similar but of madder-red and carried white lace with silver buttons.
- The cuff was indented and had four buttons and four chevrons of lace, set in pairs.
- The vertical pocket was unslit and had six buttons and six chevrons of lace, set in pairs.
- The badge on the housings was the King's Cypher, within the garter with a crown over.
- In all other respects the housings and lace were the same, but the fur caps still differed.

Raised in 1661 by the Earl of Oxford as:

The Royal Regiment of Horse (also known as the Oxford Blues)
Ranked as 1st Horse until 1747

And known from 1750 as:
Royal Horse Guards (Blue)
Redesignated in 1819 as:
Royal Regiment of Horse Guards (The Blues)
It was included as part of the Household Cavalry after 1687 but, being originally the 1st Horse and while not officially part of the Household Cavalry until 1820, it was usually brigaded with the Life Guards.

Royal Horse Guards in 1751:
• This royal regiment wore dark-blue coats with scarlet facings and full-length red lapels as confirmed by Milan's list of 1749.
• Officers' lace and buttons were gold and officers' coats were laced for dress.
• The coats of all ranks were lined in scarlet as were the waistcoats and breeches but officers and troopers are known to have worn buff waistcoats and breeches by 1758.
• The scarlet lapels had four buttons and loops, set in pairs. The cuff, open at the font, has four buttons set in pairs although officers are known to have worn gold braid to the square scarlet cuff.
• The vertical coat pocket was slit, and laced with chevron loops in pairs.
• The accoutrements crossed over each other with the musket sling with a red flask cord on the top and the shoulder sword belt over the right shoulder.
• The colour of the housings and holster caps was scarlet with the shape of the rear saddlecloth as rounded.
• Colours of Royal lace were red with gold on both sides, the width of the scarlet to be one-fifth of the breadth.
• Badges included the King's Cypher within the garter with a crown over.
• The regiment rode black horses.
• In July 1758 the regiment was issued with cuirasses and skullcaps.

Not Included in 1768 Regulations but by 1767:
• This royal regiment wore dark-blue coat with scarlet facings. Half-lapels, turnbacks, waistcoats and breeches were buff; linings of the cloaks and coats were scarlet.
• All ranks wore lace and buttons of gold: in dress they wore chevron loops on the skirts and cuffs, while in undress twist loops to the buttons.
• The cuff was indented, and has six chevron loops, in pairs.
• The vertical coat pocket was unslit, laced with six chevron loops, in pairs.
• Colours of Royal lace were red with gold on both sides, the width of the scarlet to be one-fifth of the breadth.
• The colours of the housings and holster caps were red.
• The badge on the housings was the King's Cypher within the garter with a crown over.

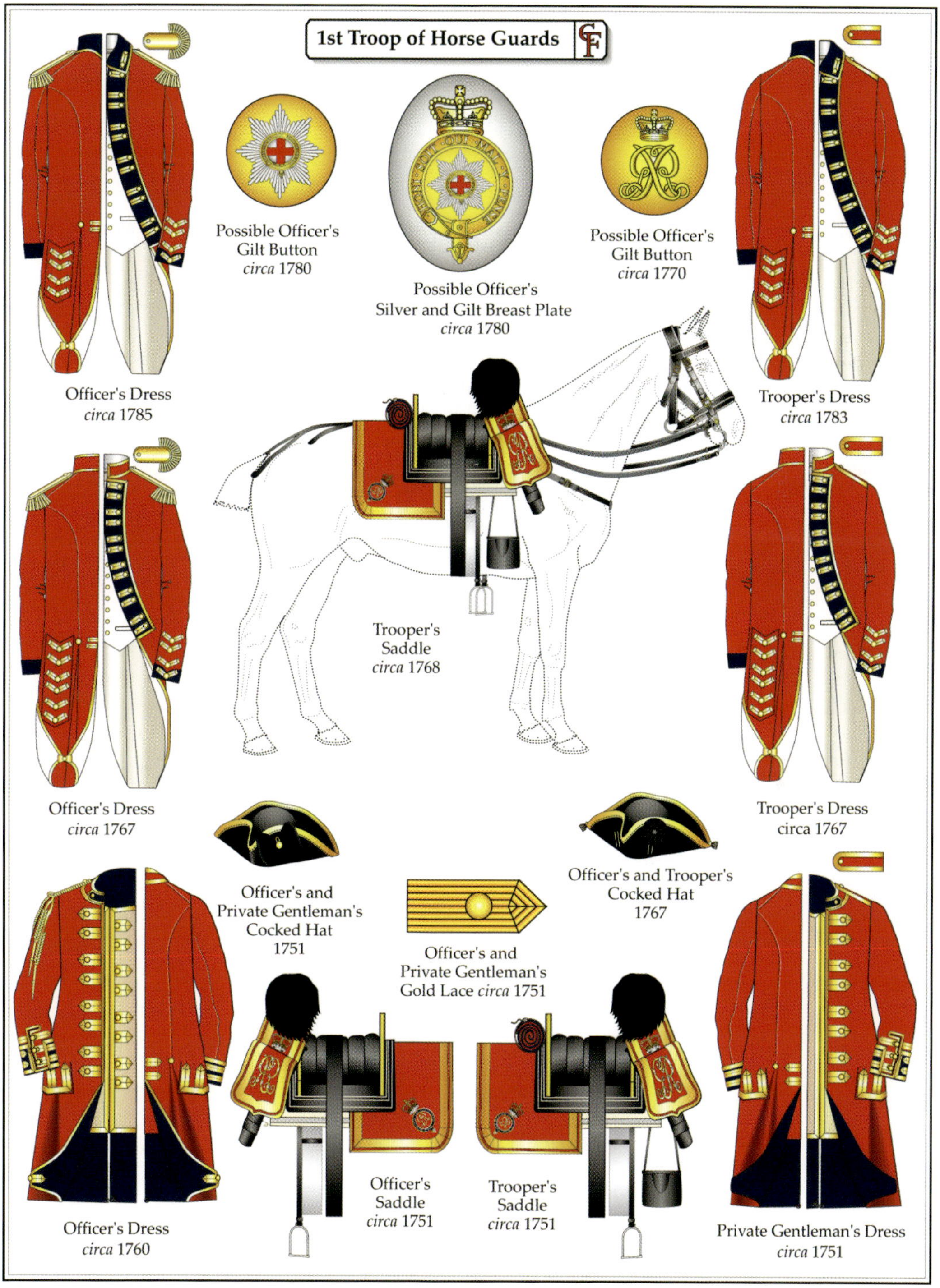
1st Troop of Horse Guards
CF
Officer's Dress
circa 1785
Possible Officer's
Gilt Button
circa 1780
Possible Officer's
Silver and Gilt Breast Plate
circa 1780
Possible Officer's
Gilt Button
circa 1770
Trooper's Dress
circa 1783
Officer's Dress
circa 1767
Trooper's
Saddle
circa 1768
Trooper's Dress
circa 1767
Officer's and
Private Gentleman's
Cocked Hat
1751
Officer's and Trooper's
Cocked Hat
1767
Officer's and
Private Gentleman's
Gold Lace circa 1751
Officer's Dress
circa 1760
Officer's
Saddle
circa 1751
Trooper's
Saddle
circa 1751
Private Gentleman's Dress
circa 1751

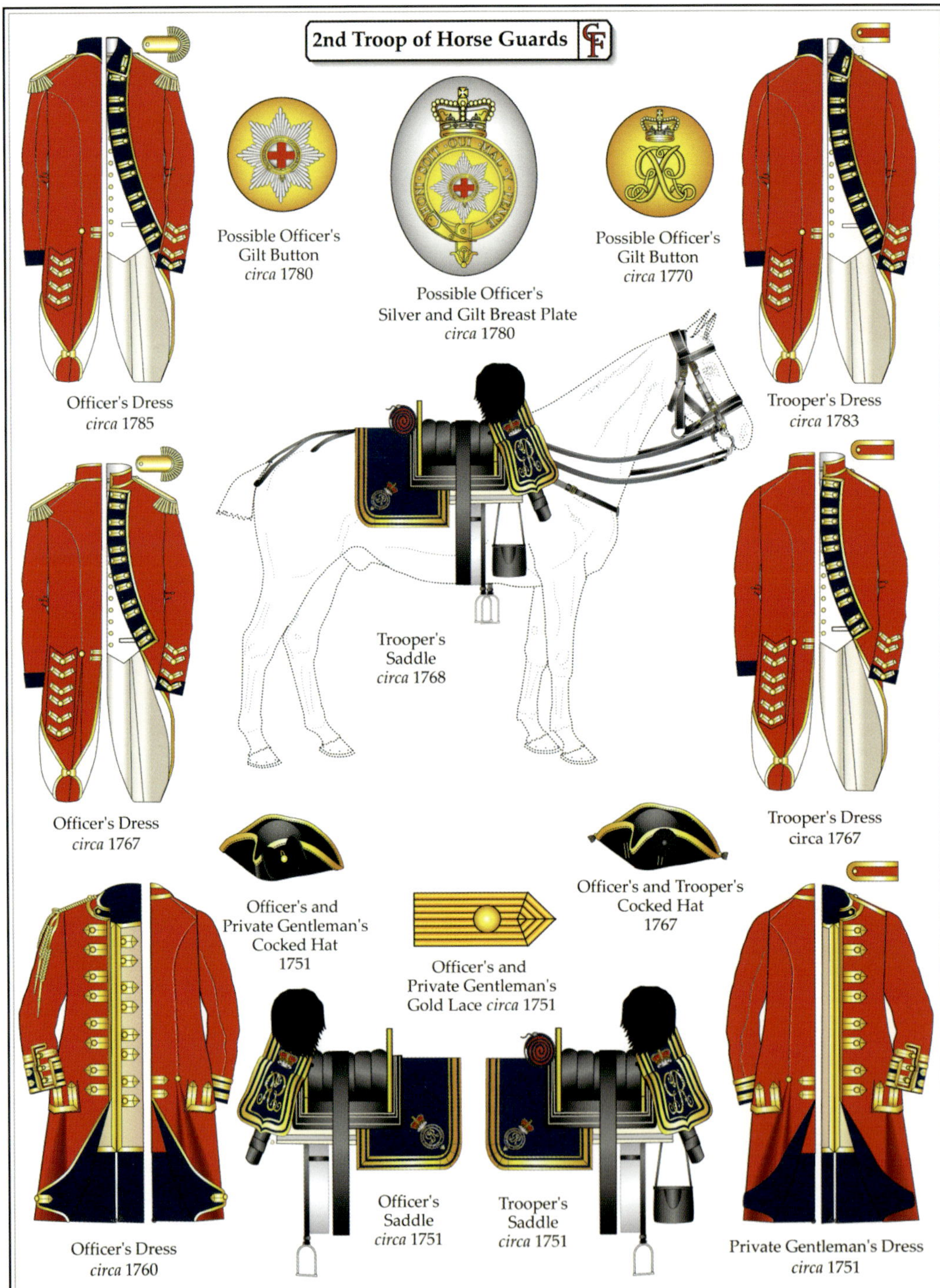
2nd Troop of Horse Guards
Officer's Dress *circa* 1785
Possible Officer's Gilt Button *circa* 1780
Possible Officer's Silver and Gilt Breast Plate *circa* 1780
Possible Officer's Gilt Button *circa* 1770
Trooper's Dress *circa* 1783
Trooper's Saddle *circa* 1768
Officer's Dress *circa* 1767
Trooper's Dress circa 1767
Officer's and Private Gentleman's Cocked Hat 1751
Officer's and Trooper's Cocked Hat 1767
Officer's and Private Gentleman's Gold Lace *circa* 1751
Officer's Dress *circa* 1760
Officer's Saddle *circa* 1751
Trooper's Saddle *circa* 1751
Private Gentleman's Dress *circa* 1751

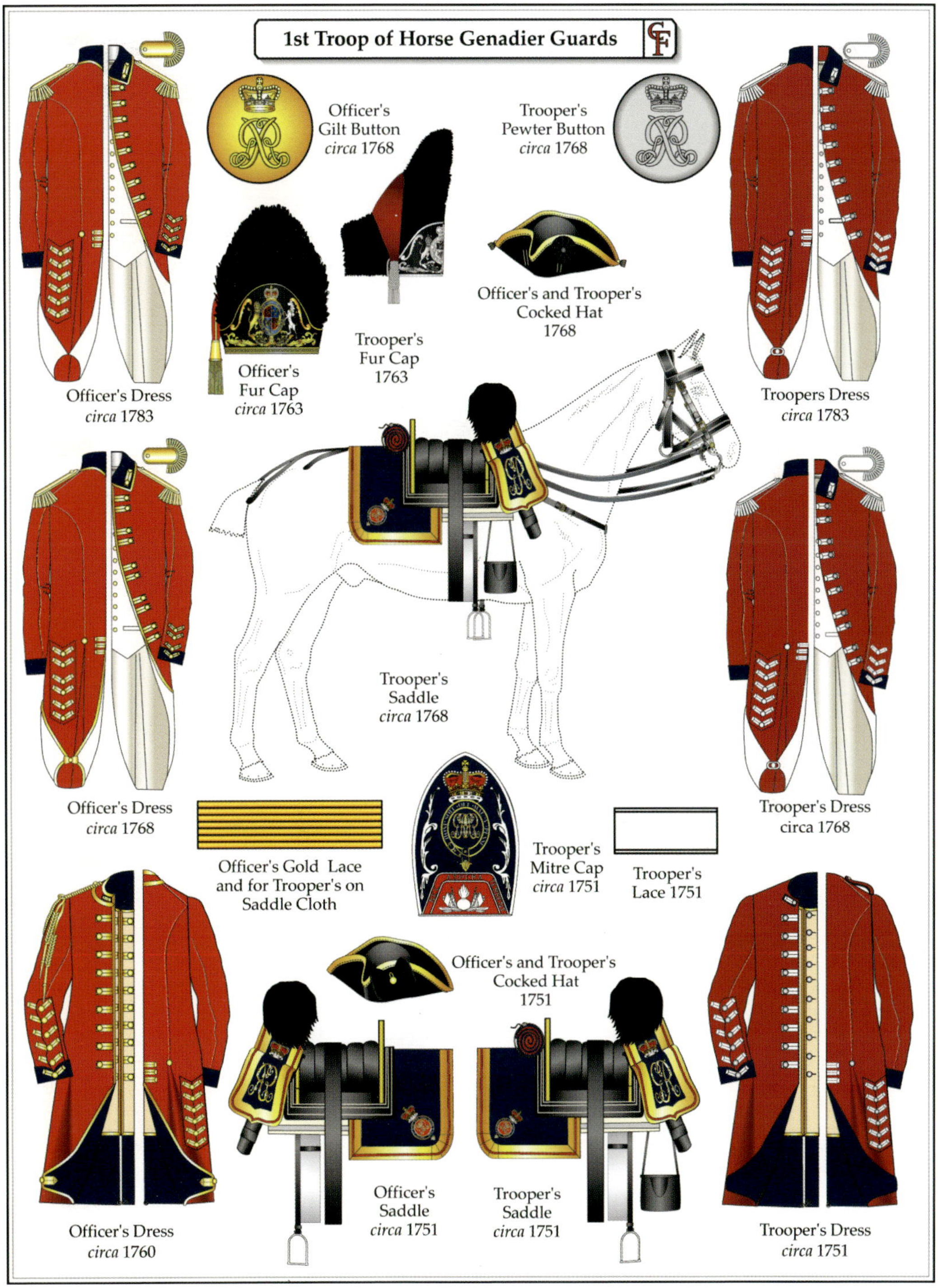

1st Troop of Horse Genadier Guards
CF
Officer's Gilt Button circa 1768
Trooper's Pewter Button circa 1768
Officer's Dress circa 1783
Officer's Fur Cap circa 1763
Trooper's Fur Cap 1763
Officer's and Trooper's Cocked Hat 1768
Troopers Dress circa 1783
Trooper's Saddle circa 1768
Officer's Dress circa 1768
Officer's Gold Lace and for Trooper's on Saddle Cloth
Trooper's Mitre Cap circa 1751
Trooper's Lace 1751
Trooper's Dress circa 1768
Officer's and Trooper's Cocked Hat 1751
Officer's Dress circa 1760
Officer's Saddle circa 1751
Trooper's Saddle circa 1751
Trooper's Dress circa 1751

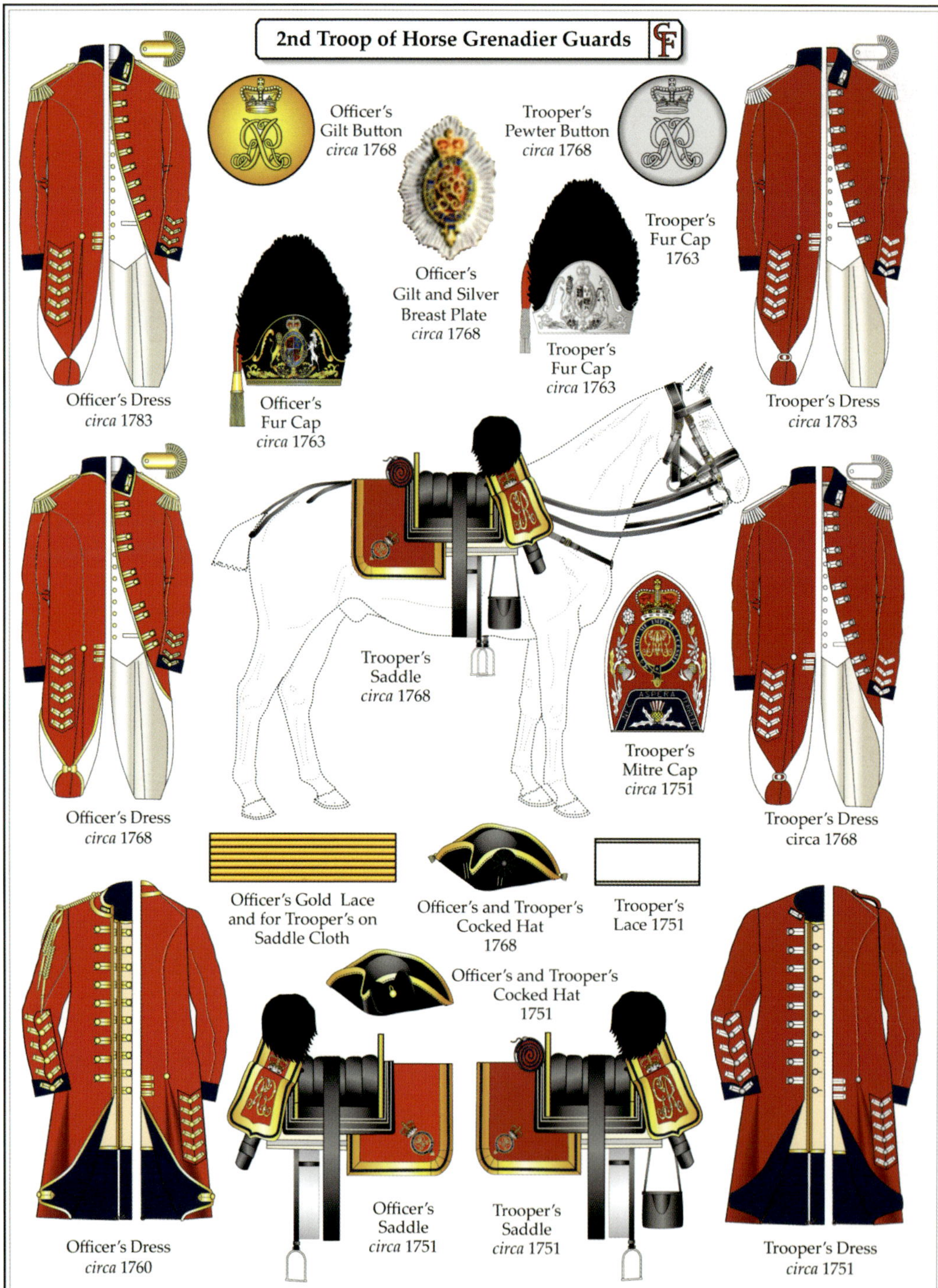
2nd Troop of Horse Grenadier Guards
CF
Officer's Gilt Button circa 1768
Trooper's Pewter Button circa 1768
Officer's Gilt and Silver Breast Plate circa 1768
Trooper's Fur Cap 1763
Trooper's Fur Cap circa 1763
Officer's Dress circa 1783
Officer's Fur Cap circa 1763
Trooper's Dress circa 1783
Trooper's Saddle circa 1768
Trooper's Mitre Cap circa 1751
Officer's Dress circa 1768
Trooper's Dress circa 1768
Officer's Gold Lace and for Trooper's on Saddle Cloth
Officer's and Trooper's Cocked Hat 1768
Trooper's Lace 1751
Officer's and Trooper's Cocked Hat 1751
Officer's Saddle circa 1751
Trooper's Saddle circa 1751
Officer's Dress circa 1760
Trooper's Dress circa 1751

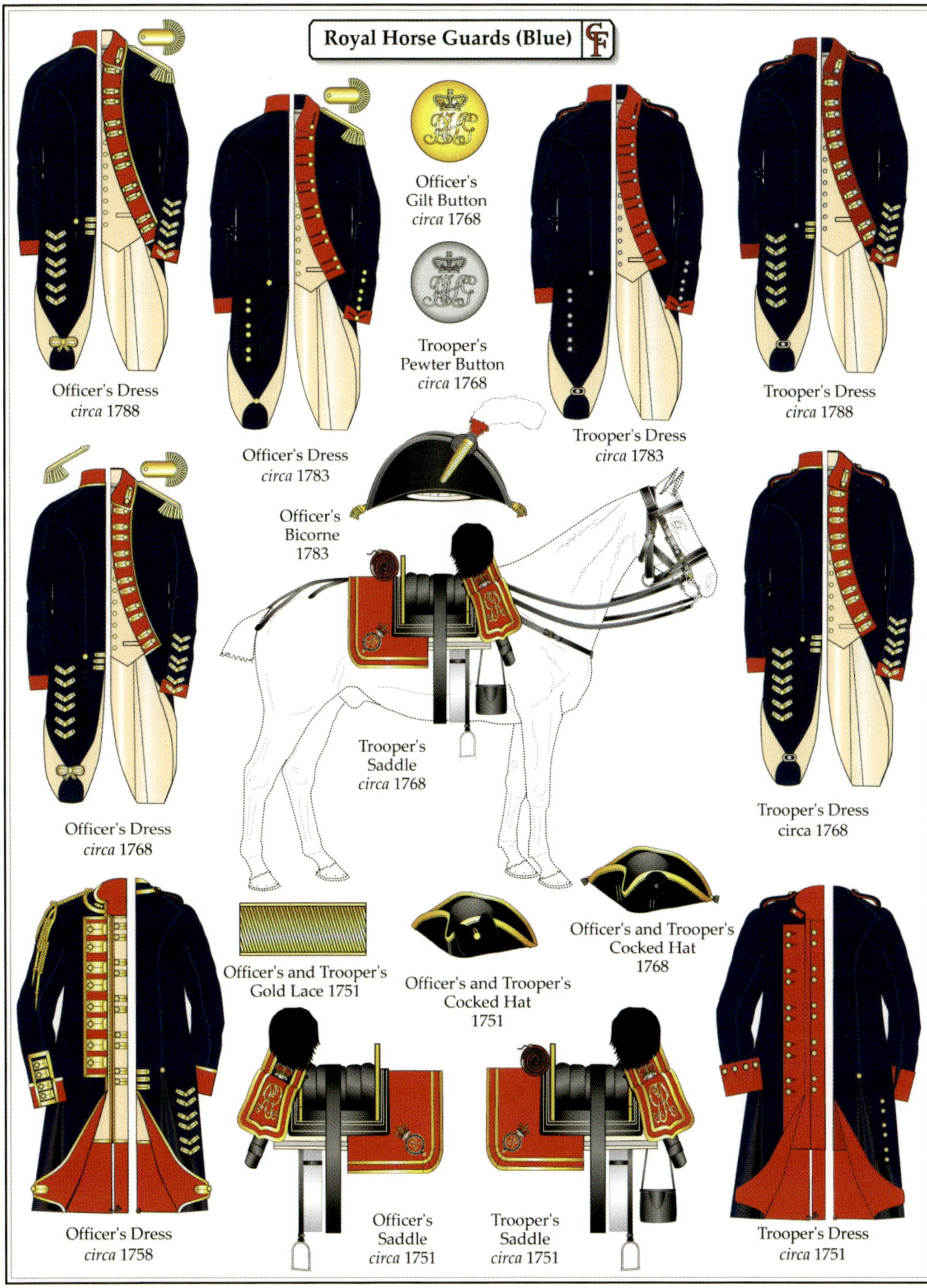
Royal Horse Guards (Blue)
CF
Officer's Gilt Button circa 1768
Trooper's Pewter Button circa 1768
Officer's Dress circa 1788
Officer's Dress circa 1783
Trooper's Dress circa 1783
Trooper's Dress circa 1788
Officer's Bicorne 1783
Trooper's Saddle circa 1768
Officer's Dress circa 1768
Trooper's Dress circa 1768
Officer's and Trooper's Gold Lace 1751
Officer's and Trooper's Cocked Hat 1751
Officer's and Trooper's Cocked Hat 1768
Officer's Dress circa 1758
Officer's Saddle circa 1751
Trooper's Saddle circa 1751
Trooper's Dress circa 1751

CHAPTER TEN

Regiments of Heavy and Light Cavalry

Raised 6 June 1685, by Sir John Lannier as:
Queen's Regiment of Horse
in 1685 as:
2nd Regiment of Horse
In 1714 it became:
The King's Own Regiment of Horse
Converted in 1746 to:
The King's Dragoon Guards
Numbered in 1751 as
1st (The King's) Regiment of Dragoon Guards.

The 1751 Warrant:
• The facings for this royal regiment were dark-blue with half lapels while the waistcoats, breeches, linings of the cloaks and coats of all ranks were blue, as confirmed Milan's list of 1749.
• The officers' lace and buttons were gold.
• Other ranks' coats were similar with yellow lace and buttons.
• The lapels had twelve square loops set in pairs.
• The vertical pocket was slit with six chevron loops.
• The indented cuff was square-ended and the cuff slashed and laced with six buttons and six chevron laced loops.
• Housings and holster caps were scarlet.
• The colour of the royal lace was blue with a yellow stripe on either side, the blue to be one third of the breadth.
• The shape of the rear saddlecloth was rounded.
• Badges included, on the holster caps, the crown over the 'GR' Cypher and, at the rear, the crest of England, within the garter with a crown over.
• The regiment wore a red flask cord.
• The regiment rode black horses.

In 1756
This regiment raised a troop of Light Dragoons who were dressed as the rest of the regiment but with caps.

In the 1768 regulations:
• The facings for this royal regiment were dark-blue with half lapels while waistcoats, breeches, linings of the cloaks and the coats of all ranks were buff.
• The officers' lace and buttons were gold set on in pairs.
• The other ranks' coats were similar with yellow lace and buttons.
• Drummers and trumpeters were dressed in reverse colours with half lapels while their waistcoats, breeches, linings of the cloaks and coats were buff. The Royal lace was blue and yellow.
• Housings and holster caps were red.
• The colour of the Royal lace was yellow on either side with a blue stripe at the centre to be one third of the breadth.
• Badges included, on the holster caps, the crown over the 'GR' Cypher and, at the rear, the crest of England, within the garter with a crown over.

Raised on 20 June 1685 as:
Earl of Peterborough's Regiment of Horse
Ranked in 1688 as:
3rd Regiment of Horse
In 1715 it became:
The Princess of Wales's Own Regiment of Horse
In 1727 it became:
The Queen's Own Regiment of Horse
In 1746 it became:
The Queen's Dragoon Guards
Numbered in 1751 as:
2nd (the Queen's) Dragoon Guards
Redesignated in 1780 as:
2nd (or the Queen's Bays) Regiment of Dragoon Guards.

The 1751 Warrant:
• The facings for this regiment were buff with half-lapels while waistcoats, breeches, linings of the cloaks and coats of all ranks were buff, as confirmed by Milan's list of 1749.
• The officers' lace and buttons were gold.
• Other ranks' coats were similar with yellow lace and buttons.
• The lapels had twelve square loops set in threes.
• The vertical pocket was slit with six chevron loops.
• The indented cuff was square-ended and the cuff slashed and laced with six buttons and six chevron laced loops.
• Housings and holster caps were buff.
• The shape of the rear saddlecloth was rounded.
• The colour of the Royal lace was blue with a yellow stripe on either side, the blue to be one third of the breadth.
• The regiment wore a blue flask cord.
• Badges included, on the holster caps, the crown over the 'GR' Cypher, and at the rear the Queen's Cypher within the garter with a crown over.

In 1756
This regiment raised a troop of Light Dragoons who were dressed as the rest of the regiment but with caps.

In the 1768 regulations:
• The facings for this regiment were buff with half lapels while the waistcoats, breeches, linings of the cloaks and coats of all ranks were buff.
• The officers' lace and buttons were gold set in threes.
• Other ranks' coats were similar with yellow lace and buttons.
• Drummers and trumpeters were dressed in reverse colours with half lapels while their waistcoats, breeches, linings of the cloaks and coats were buff. The Royal lace was blue and yellow.
• Housings and holster caps were buff.
• The colour of the Royal lace was yellow on either side with a blue stripe at the centre to be one third of the breadth.
• The badge on the housings was the Queen's Cypher within the garter.

Raised on 15 July 1685 **as the Earl of Plymouth's Regiment of Horse**
Ranked in 1688 as:
4th Horse
Retitled in 1746 as:
3rd of Dragoon Guards
Redesignated 1751 as:
3rd Regiment of Dragoon Guards
Designated in 1765 as:
3rd (The Prince of Wales's) Regiment of Dragoon Guards
renamed as:
3rd (Prince of Wales's) Regiment of Dragoon Guards

The 1751 Warrant:
• The facings for this regiment were white with half lapels while the waistcoats, breeches, linings of the cloaks and coats of all ranks were white, as confirmed by Milan's list of 1749.
• The officers' lace and buttons were gold.
• Other ranks' coats were similar with yellow lace and buttons.
• The lapels had twelve square loops set in pairs.
• The vertical pocket was slit with six chevron loops.
• The indented cuff was square-ended and the cuff slashed and laced with six buttons and six chevron laced loops.
• Housings and holster caps were white.
• The shape of the rear saddlecloth was rounded.
• The colour of the Royal lace was blue with a yellow stripe on either side, the blue to be one third of the breadth.
• Badges included, on the holster caps, the crown over the 'GR' Cypher and, at the rear, the rank of the regiment, **III DG** in a wreath of thistles, leaves and roses on a red ground.

In 1756
This regiment raised a troop of Light Dragoons who were dressed as the rest of the regiment but with caps.

In the 1768 regulations:
• The facings for this regiment were white with half-lapels while the waistcoats, breeches, linings of the cloaks and coats of all ranks were white.
• The officers' lace and buttons were gold set on in twos.
• Other ranks' coats were similar with yellow lace and buttons.
• Drummers and trumpeters were dressed in reverse colours with half lapels while their waistcoats, breeches, linings of the cloaks and coats were red. The Royal lace was blue and yellow.
• Housings and holster caps were white.
• The colour of the Royal lace was yellow on either side with a blue stripe at the centre to be one third of the breadth.
• The badge on the housings was the Prince of Wales's feathers issuing out of a coronet.

Raised on 28 July1685 as:
Earl of Arran's Regt of Cuirassiers
Ranked in 1685 as:
6th Regiment of Horse
Designated in 1691 as:
5th Regiment of Horse
Re-ranked in 1746 as:
1st Regiment of Horse (also known as the Blue Horse)
Designated in 1751 in Ireland as:
1st Regiment of Horse
Converted in 1788 to become:
4th (or the Royal Irish) Regiment of Dragoon Guards

The 1751 Warrant:

- The facings for this regiment were pale blue with full lapels while the breeches; linings of the cloaks and coats of all ranks were pale blue, as confirmed by Milan's list of 1749.
- The officers' lace and buttons were silver.
- Other ranks' coats were similar with white lace and buttons.
- The waistcoat was laced at the buttonholes with square lace loops set in pairs.
- The full-length lapels had sixteen square loops set in pairs.
- The square cuff was split at the rear and carried four vertical laces set in pairs.
- Housings and holster caps were pale blue.
- The shape of the rear saddlecloth was rounded.
- The colour of the lace was red with a white stripe on either side, the red to be one third of the breadth.
- Badges included, on the holster caps, the crown over the 'GR' Cypher and, at the rear the rank of the regiment, **I H,** in a wreath of thistles, leaves and roses on a red ground.

In the 1768 regulations:

- The facings for this regiment were changed in 1768 to a dark-blue with half lapels and the waistcoats, breeches, linings of the cloaks and coats of all ranks were white.
- The officers' twist lace and buttons were silver set on in pairs.
- Other ranks' coats were similar with twist lace and buttons.
- The square cuff was split at the rear and carried four vertical twist laces set in pairs.
- Drummers and trumpeters were dressed in reverse colours with half lapels while their waistcoats, breeches, linings of the cloaks and coats were white. The lace was white with a red stripe.
- The colour of the lace was white on either side with a red stripe at the centre to be one third of the breadth.
- Badges, the rank of the regiment, **I H**, within a red ground surrounded by roses and thistles.

Raised in 1685 **as the Duke of Shrewsbury's Regiment of Horse.**
Ranked in 1685 as:
7th of Horse,
Re-ranked 1690 as:
6th of Horse
Re-ranked in 1746 as:
2nd Horse (also known as the Green Horse)
Re-designated in 1751 as:
2nd Horse

Converted in 1788 as:
5th Regiment of Dragoon Guards

The 1751 Warrant:
• The facings for this regiment were full-green with full lapels while the breeches; linings of the cloaks and coats of all ranks were full-green, as confirmed by Milan's list of 1749.
• The officers' lace and buttons were gold.
• Other ranks' coats were similar with yellow lace and buttons.
• The waistcoat was laced at the buttonholes with square lace loops set in pairs.
• The full-length lapels had sixteen square loops set in pairs.
• The vertical pocket was slit with six chevron loops.
• The square cuff was open at the rear and laced with four vertical laced loops.
• Housings and holster caps were full-green.
• The shape of the rear saddlecloth was rounded.
• The colour of the lace was red with a white stripe on either side, the red to be one third of the breadth.
• Badges included, on the holster caps, the crown over the 'GR' Cypher and, at the rear, the rank of the regiment, **II H,** in a wreath of thistles, leaves and roses on a red ground.

In the 1768 regulations:
• The facings for this Royal regiment were a full-green with full lapels while the waistcoats, breeches, linings of the cloaks and coats of all ranks were white.
• The officers' twist lace and buttons were gold set on in pairs.
• Other ranks' coats were similar with twist lace and buttons.
• The square cuff was open at the rear and carried four vertical twist laces set in pairs.
• Drummers and trumpeters were dressed in reverse colours with half lapels while their waistcoats, breeches, linings of the cloaks and coats were white. The lace was white with a red stripe.
• The colour of the lace was white on either side with a red stripe at the centre to be one third of the breadth.
• Housings were full-green.
• Badges, the rank of the regiment, **II H,** within a red ground surrounded by leaves, roses and thistles.

Raised by Lord Lumley on 31 July 1685 as:
Queen Dowager's Regiment of Horse
Designated in 1692 as:
The King's Regiment of Carabineers
Ranked in 1688 as:
9th Regiment of Horse (also known as Lumley's Horse)
Ranked in 1690 as:
8th Regiment of Horse
Ranked in 1694 as:
7th Regiment of Horse
Ranked in 1746 as:
3rd Regiment of Horse
Designated in 1756 as:
3rd Regiment of Horse (Carabineers)
Converted in 1788 to be:

6th Regiment of Dragoon Guards (Carabineers)

The 1751 Warrant:

• The facings for this regiment were pale-yellow with full lapels while the waistcoats, breeches, linings of the cloaks and coats of all ranks were pale-yellow, as confirmed by Milan's list of 1749.
• The officers' lace and buttons were silver.
• Other ranks' coats were similar with white lace and buttons.
• The waistcoat was laced at the buttonholes with square lace loops set in pairs.
• The full-length lapels had sixteen square loops set in pairs.
• The square cuff was open at the rear and laced with four buttons and four vertical laced loops.
• Housings and holster caps were pale-yellow.
• The shape of the rear saddlecloth was rounded.
• The colour of the lace was red with a white stripe on either side, the red to be one third of the breadth.
• Badges included, on the holster caps, the crown over the 'GR' Cypher and, at the rear the rank of the regiment, **III H** in a wreath of thistles, leaves and roses on a red ground.
• In 1760 the regiment was issued with cuirasses and skullcaps.

In the 1768 regulations:

• The facings for this regiment were changed to in 1768 to white with half lapels while the waistcoats, breeches, linings of the cloaks and coats of all ranks were white.
• The officers' twist lace and buttons were silver set in pairs.
• Other ranks' coats were similar with twist lace and buttons.
• The square cuff was open at the rear and carried four vertical twist laces set in pairs.
• Drummers and trumpeters were dressed in reverse colours with half lapels while their waistcoats, breeches, linings of the cloaks and coats were red. The lace was yellow with a black stripe.
• Housings were white.
• The colour of the lace was white on either side with a black stripe at the centre to be one third of the breadth.
• Badges, the rank of the regiment, **III H**, within a red ground surrounded by roses and thistles.

Raised 31 December 1688 as **Lord Cavendish's Regiment of Horse**
Ranked in 1690 as:
9th of Horse
Re-ranked in 1694 as:
8th of Horse
Re-ranked in 1746 as the:
4th Horse (also known as the Black Horse)
Re-designated in 1751 as:
4th Regiment of Horse
Converted in 1788 as:
7th (Princess Royal's) Dragoon Guards

The 1751 Warrant:

• The facings for this regiment were black with full lapels while the waistcoats, breeches, linings of the cloaks and coats of all ranks were buff, as confirmed by Milan's list of 1749.
• The officers' lace and buttons were gold.
• Other ranks' coats were similar with yellow lace and buttons.
• The waistcoat was laced at the buttonholes with square lace loops set in pairs.

• The full-length lapels had sixteen square loops set in pairs.
• The square cuff was open at the rear and laced with four buttons and four vertical laced loops.
• Housings and holster caps were buff.
• The shape of the rear saddlecloth was rounded.
• The colour of the lace was black with a white stripe on either side, the black to be one third of the breadth.
• Badges included, on the holster caps, the crown over the 'GR' Cypher and, on the rear the rank of the regiment, **IV H** in a wreath of thistles, leaves and roses on a red ground.
• In 1760 the regiment was issued with cuirasses and skullcaps.

In the 1768 regulations:
• The facings for this regiment were black with half lapels while the waistcoats, breeches, linings of the cloaks and coats of all ranks were buff.
• The officers' twist lace and buttons were gold set on in pairs.
• Other ranks' coats were similar with twist lace and buttons.
• The square cuff was open at the rear and carried four vertical twist laces set in pairs.
• Drummers and trumpeters were dressed in buff coats with red facings with half lapels while their waistcoats, breeches, linings of the cloaks and coats were red. The lace was white with a black stripe.
• Housings were buff.
• The colour of the lace was white on either side with a black stripe at the centre to be one third of the breadth.
• Badges, the rank of the regiment, **IV H**, within a red ground surrounded by roses and thistles.

Raised in 1744 as **the Duke of Montague's Regiment of Horse:**
Ranked as:
9th of Horse
This regiment was disbanded in 1746

• Research has failed to find any details of the uniform except that they were dressed in blue coats, lined with red, and yellow buttons.

Raised in 1745 as:
Duke of Kingston's Regiment of Horse
Ranked as:
10th of Horse
This regiment disbanded in September 1748
and was concurrently reformed by Lord Robert Manners as:
15th Regiment of Light Horse (also known as Duke of Cumberland's Dragoons)
This regiment was disbanded in February 1749 for reasons unknown.

• The facings for this regiment were green without lapels while the waistcoats, breeches, linings of the cloaks and coats of all ranks were buff, as confirmed by Milan's list of 1749.
• The officers' buttons were gold and wore no lace, but the hat lace was gold with a green plume.
• Other ranks were similar but in madder-red.
• The coats had twelve buttons set in evenly.
• The vertical pocket was slit with six chevron loops.
• The cuff was square-ended and the cuff slashed and laced with six buttons.
• Housings and holster caps were green.

• The shape of the rear saddlecloth was square.
• The colour of the lace was green with a yellow stripe on either side, the green to be one third of the breadth.
• Badges included, on the holster caps, the crown over the Lion Crest of England within the garter surrounded by a wreath of thistles, roses and leaves with a crown over the top; the same was repeated on the rear saddlecloth.
• This regiment used a curved sword.

Raised in 1745 by the Duke of Montague as:
Montague's Carabineers, also known as the Derby Blues
Ranked as:
A regiment of Horse (possibly the 11th)
This regiment disbanded in September 1746

• Research has failed to find other details of the uniform other than, according to the Ipswich Journal, blue coats, lined red with yellow buttons.

Raised in 1745 by the Duke of Bolton and ranked as:
A regiment of Horse (possibly the 12th)
This regiment disbanded in September 1746

• Research has failed to find any details of the uniform.

Raised in 1745 by the Duke of Ancaster and ranked as:
A regiment of Horse (possibly the 13th)
This regiment disbanded in September 1746

• Research has failed to find any details of the uniform.

Raised in 1745 by the Marquis of Granby and ranked as:
A regiment of Horse (possibly the 14th)
This regiment disbanded in September 1746

• Research has failed to find any details of the uniform.

Raised in 1745 by the Earl of Berkeley and ranked as:
A regiment of Horse (possibly the 15th)
This regiment disbanded in September 1746

• Research has failed to find any details of the uniform.

Raised in 1745 by the Viscount Falmouth and ranked as:
A regiment of Horse (possibly the 16th)
This regiment disbanded in September 1746

• Research has failed to find any details of the uniform.

Raised in 1745 by the Viscount Harcourt and ranked as:
A regiment of Horse (possibly the 17th)
This regiment disbanded in September 1746

• Research has failed to find any details of the uniform.

The following regiments were Dragoons or Light Dragoons.
Raised in 1661 by Earl of Peterborough as:
Tangier Horse
Ranked in 1674 as:
1st of Dragoons
1683 renamed as:
The King's Own Royal Regiment of Dragoons
Retitled in 1690 as:
The Royal Regiment of Dragoons
Designated in 1751 as:
1st (Royal) Regiment of Dragoons

The 1751 Warrant:
• The facings for this royal regiment were dark-blue without lapels while the waistcoats, breeches, linings of the cloaks and coats of all ranks were blue, as confirmed by Milan's list of 1749.
• The officers' lace and buttons were gold.
• Other ranks' coats were similar with yellow lace and buttons.
• The coats had twelve square loops set in pairs.
• The vertical pocket was slit with six chevron loops.
• The indented cuff was square-ended and the cuff slashed and laced with six buttons and six chevron laced loops.
• Housings and holster caps were scarlet.
• The shape of the rear saddlecloth was square.
• The colour of Royal lace was blue with a yellow stripe on either side, the blue to be one third of the breadth.
• Badges included, on the holster caps, the crown over the 'GR' Cypher and, at the rear, the Crest of England within the garter with a crown over.
• The regiment rode black horses.
• The regiment wore a blue flask cord.

In 1756

This regiment raised a troop of Light Dragoons who were dressed as the rest of the regiment but with caps.

In the 1768 regulations:

• The facings for this royal regiment were dark-blue without lapels while the waistcoats, breeches, linings of the cloaks and coats of all ranks were white.
• The officers' lace and buttons were gold set on in pairs.
• The coats of the other ranks were similar with yellow lace and buttons.
• The drummers and trumpeters were dressed in reverse colours and the waistcoats, breeches, linings of the cloaks and coats were white.
• The colours of the housings were red.
• The colour of the Royal lace was yellow on either side with a blue stripe at the centre to be one third of the breadth.
• Badges included the Crest of England within the garter.

Raised in 1678 and regimented 25 November 1681 as:
Royal Regiment of Scots Dragoons
Ranked by 1688 as:
2nd of Dragoons
Designated in 1737 as:
Royal Regiment of North British Dragoons
Designated in 1751 as:
2nd (Royal North British) Regiment of Dragoons

The 1751 Warrant:

• The facings for this royal regiment were dark-blue without lapels awhile the waistcoats, breeches, linings of the cloaks and coats of all ranks were blue, as confirmed by Milan's list of 1749.
• The officers' lace and buttons were gold.
• Other rank's coats were similar with white lace and buttons.
• The coats had twelve square loops set in pairs.
• The vertical pocket was slit with six chevron loops.
• The indented cuff was square-ended and the cuff slashed and laced with six buttons and six chevron laced loops.
• Housings and holster caps were blue.
• The shape of the rear saddlecloth was rounded.
• The colour of Royal lace was blue with a yellow stripe on either side, the blue to be one third of the breadth.
• Badges included, on the holster caps, the crown over the 'GR' Cypher and, at the rear, the thistle and leaves within the circle of Saint Andrew.
• The regiment wore the grenadier mitre cap.
• The flask cord was red.
• The regiment rode grey horses and wore whitened leather belts.

In 1756

This regiment raised a troop of Light Dragoons who were dressed as the rest of the regiment but with caps.

In the 1768 regulations:

• The facings for this royal regiment were dark-blue without lapels while the waistcoats, breeches, linings of the cloaks and coats of all ranks were white.

• The officers' lace and buttons were gold set on in pairs.

• Other ranks' coats had white lace and buttons.

• The cuffs were square and cut away at the centre with six chevron loops arranged in pairs behind the cuff.

• Drummers and trumpeters were dressed in reverse colours while their waistcoats, breeches, linings of the cloaks and coats were white. The lace was Royal lace.

• The regiment rode grey horses and wore white leather belts

• Housings were dark-blue edged with Royal lace and ornamented with the thistle within the circle of Saint Andrew.

Raised on 2 August 1685 **as Duke of Somerset's Regiment of Dragoons**
Ranked as **3rd of Dragoons**
Designated in 1694 as:
The Queen Consort's Own Regiment of Dragoons
Designated in 1714 as:
The King's Regiment of Dragoons
Designated in 1751 as:
3rd (King's Own) Regiment of Dragoons

The 1751 Warrant:

• The facings for this regiment were light blue without lapels while the waistcoats, breeches, linings of the cloaks and coats of all ranks were light blue, as confirmed by Milan's list of 1749.

• The officers' lace and buttons were gold.

• Other ranks' coats were similar with yellow lace and buttons.

• The coats had twelve square loops set in threes.

• The vertical pocket was slit with six chevron loops.

• The indented cuff was square-ended and the cuff slashed and laced with six buttons and six chevron laced loops.

• Housings and holster caps were light blue.

• The shape of the rear saddlecloth was rounded.

• The colour of Royal lace was blue with a yellow stripe on either side, the blue to be one third of the breadth.

• Badges Included, on the holster caps, the crown over the 'GR' Cypher and, at the rear the white horse within the garter with a crown over.

• The flask cord was blue.

• The regiment rode black horses.

In 1756

This regiment raised a troop of Light Dragoons who were dressed as the rest of the regiment but with caps.

In the 1768 regulations:

• The facings for this royal regiment were dark-blue without lapels and while the waistcoats, breeches, linings of the cloaks and coats of all ranks were buff.

• The officers' lace and buttons were gold set in threes.

• The coats of the other ranks were similar with yellow lace and buttons.

• Drummers and trumpeters were dressed in reverse colours while their waistcoats, breeches, linings of the cloaks and coats were buff.
• Housings were dark-blue edged with Royal lace and ornamented with the white horse within the garter with a crown over.

Raised on 17 July 1685 as:
Princess Anne of Denmark's Regiment of Dragoons
Redesignated 1751 as:
4th Regiment of Dragoons
Redesignated 1788 as:
4th (Queen's Own) Regiment of Dragoons
Redesignated 1818 as:
4th (or the Queen's Own) Regiment of Light Dragoons

The 1751 Warrant:
• The facings for this regiment were green without lapels and the waistcoats, breeches; linings of the cloaks and coats of all ranks were green, as confirmed by Milan's list of 1749.
• The officers' lace and buttons were silver.
• Other ranks' coats were similar with white lace and buttons.
• The coats had twelve square loops set in pairs.
• The vertical pocket was slit with six chevron loops.
• The indented cuff was square-ended and the cuff slashed and laced with six buttons and six chevron laced loops.
• Housings and holster caps were green.
• The shape of the rear saddlecloth was square.
• The colour of lace was red with a white stripe on either side, the red to be one third of the breadth.
• Badges included, on the holster caps, the crown over the 'GR' Cypher and, at the rear, the rank of the regiment **IV D**, in a wreath of thistles, leaves and roses on a red ground.

In 1756
This regiment raised a troop of Light Dragoons who were dressed as the rest of the regiment but with caps.

In the 1768 regulations:
• The facings for this regiment were full-green without lapels while the waistcoats, breeches, linings of the cloaks and coats of all ranks were white.
• The officers' lace and buttons were silver set in pairs.
• Other ranks' coats were similar with white lace and buttons.
• Drummers and trumpeters were dressed in reverse colours while their waistcoats, breeches, linings of the cloaks and coats were white. The lace was white with a red stripe.
• Housings were full-green edged with white lace with a red stripe and ornamented with the rank of the regiment, **IV D**, within a red ground surrounded by roses and thistles.

Raised on 20 June 1689 as **Owen Wynne's or Ross's Regiment of Dragoons**
Ranked as **6th of Dragoons.**
Redesignated in 1690 as:
5th of Dragoons

Redesignated in 1704 as:
Royal Dragoons of Ireland
Redesignated in 1751 as:
5th Regiment of Dragoons
Redesignated in 1756 as:
5th (Royal Irish) Regiment of Dragoons
This regiment was disbanded at Chatham on 10 April 1799

The 1751 Warrant:
• The facings for this royal regiment were dark-blue without lapels while the waistcoats, breeches, linings of the cloaks and coats of all ranks were blue, as confirmed by Milan's list of 1749.
• The officers' lace and buttons were silver.
• Other ranks' coats were similar with white lace and buttons.
• The coats had twelve square loops set in threes.
• The vertical pocket was slit with six chevron loops.
• The indented cuff was square-ended and the cuff slashed and laced with six buttons and six chevron laced loops.
• Housings and holster caps were blue.
• The shape of the rear saddlecloth was rounded.
• The colour of Royal lace was blue with a yellow stripe on either side, the blue to be one third of the breadth.
• Badges included, on the holster caps, the crown over the 'GR' Cypher and, at the rear the Harp of Ireland with a crown over.
• The flask cord was buff.

In the 1768 regulations:
• The facings for this royal regiment were dark-blue without lapels while the waistcoats, breeches, linings of the cloaks and coats of all ranks were white.
• The officers' lace and buttons were silver set in threes.
• Other ranks' coats were similar with white lace and buttons.
• Drummers and trumpeters were dressed in reverse colours while the waistcoats, breeches, linings of the cloaks and coats were white. The lace was Royal lace.
• Housings were dark-blue edged with Royal lace and ornamented with the harp and crown.

Raised 20 June 1689 as **Sir Albert Cunningham's Regiment of Dragoons and**
Ranked in 1690 as:
7th of Dragoons
Re-ranked in 1691 as:
6th of Dragoons
Also known in 1715 as:
The Black Dragoons
Redesignated 1751 as:
6th (Inniskilling) Dragoons

The 1751 Warrant:
• The facings for this regiment were full yellow without lapels while the waistcoats, breeches, linings of the cloaks and coats of all ranks were full yellow, as confirmed by Milan's list of 1749.
• The officers' lace and buttons were silver.

• Other ranks' coats were similar with white lace and buttons.
• The coats had twelve square loops set in pairs.
• The vertical pocket was slit with six chevron loops.
• The indented cuff was square-ended and the cuff slashed and laced with six buttons and six chevron laced loops.
• Housings and holster caps was full yellow.
• The shape of the rear saddlecloth was square.
• The colour of the lace was blue with a white stripe on either side, the blue to be one third of the breadth.
• Badges included, on the holster caps, the crown over the 'GR' Cypher and, at the rear, the castle of Inniskilling within a blue ground surrounded by roses and thistles.

In 1756

This regiment raised a troop of Light Dragoons who were dressed as the rest of the regiment but with caps.

In the 1768 regulations:

• The facings for this regiment were full yellow without lapels while the waistcoats, breeches, linings of the cloaks and coats of all ranks were white.
• The officers' lace and buttons were silver set on in pairs.
• Other ranks' coats were similar with white lace and buttons.
• Drummers and trumpeters were dressed in reverse colours while the waistcoats, breeches, linings of the cloaks and coats were red. The lace was white with a blue stripe.
• Housings were full yellow edged with white lace and a blue stripe.
• Badges included the castle of Inniskilling within a blue ground surrounded by roses and thistles.

Raised in 1690 as:
Princess of Wales's Own Regiment of Dragoons
Redesignated 1727 as:
The Queen's Own Regiment of Dragoons
Redesignated 1751 as:
7th (The Queen's Own) Regiment of Dragoons
Redesignated 1783 as:
7th (Queen's Own) Regiment of (Light) Dragoons
This regiment was retitled on 25 December 1807 as:
7th (or the Queen's Own) Regiment of (Light) Dragoons (Hussars)

The 1751 Warrant:

• The facings for this regiment were white without lapels while the waistcoats, breeches, linings of the cloaks and coats of all ranks were white, as confirmed by Milan's list of 1749.
• The officers' lace and buttons were silver.
• Other ranks' coats were similar with white lace and buttons.
• The coats had twelve square loops set in pairs.
• The vertical pocket was slit with six chevron loops.
• The indented cuff was square-ended and the cuff slashed and laced with six buttons and six chevron laced loops.
• Housings and holster caps were white.
• The shape of the rear saddlecloth was square.
• The colour of Royal lace was blue with a yellow stripe on either side, the blue to be one third of the breadth.

• Badges included, on the holster caps, the crown over the 'GR' Cypher and, at the rear the Queen's Cypher within the garter with a crown over.
• The flask cord was white.

In 1756
This regiment raised a troop of Light Dragoons who were dressed as the rest of the regiment but with caps.

In the 1768 regulations:
• The facings for this regiment were white without lapels while the waistcoats, breeches, linings of the cloaks and coats of all ranks were white.
• The officers' lace and buttons were silver set on in threes.
• Other ranks' coats were similar with white lace and buttons.
• Drummers and trumpeters were dressed in red coats with blue facings while the waistcoats, breeches, linings of the cloaks and coats were white. The lace was Royal lace.
• Housings were white edged with Royal lace with a blue stripe, and ornamented with the Queen's Cypher within the garter.
• When the regiment converted into Light Dragoons in 1783 it adopted half lapels and the cuff was square with three chevron lace loops above it.

Raised in 1693 as **Henry Cunningham's Regiment of Dragoons**
Ranked as **8th of Dragoons.**
Redesignated 1751 as:
8th Regiment of Dragoons
Redesignated 1775 as:
8th Regiment of Light Dragoons
Redesignated 1777 as:
8th (The King's Royal Irish) Regiment of (Light) Dragoons

The 1751 Warrant:
• The facings for this Royal regiment were yellow without lapels while the waistcoats, breeches, linings of the cloaks and coats of all ranks were yellow but according, to Milan's List of 1749, the facings, waistcoat and breeches were orange.
• The officers' lace and buttons were silver.
• Other ranks' coats were similar with white lace and buttons.
• The coats had twelve square loops set in threes.
• The vertical pocket was slit with six chevron loops.
• The indented cuff was square-ended and the cuff slashed and laced with six buttons and six chevron laced loops.
• Housings and holster caps were yellow.
• The shape of the rear saddlecloth was rounded.
• The colour of lace was yellow with a white stripe on either side, the yellow to be one third of the breadth.
• Badges included, on the holster caps, the crown over the 'GR' Cypher and, at the rear, the rank of the regiment, **VIII D,** within a red ground surrounded by leaves, roses and thistles.
• By 1742 the regiment was accorded the privilege of wearing cross belts in the same manner as regiments of horse.

In the 1768 regulations:

• The facings for this regiment were full yellow without lapels while the waistcoats, breeches, linings of the cloaks and coats of all ranks were white.

• The officers' lace and buttons were silver set on in threes.

• Other ranks' coats were similar with white lace and buttons.

• Drummers and trumpeters were dressed in reversed facings while the waistcoats, breeches, linings of the cloaks and coats were red. The lace was white with a yellow stripe.

• Housings were full yellow edged with white lace and a yellow stripe and ornamented with the rank of the regiment, **VIII D**, within a red ground surrounded by roses and thistles.

• When the regiment was converted to Light Dragoons 1775 it lost the right to wear crossed shoulder belts and adopted half lapels with a square cuff with three chevron lace loops above it.

• In 1777 the regiment became Royal and wore blue facings; it also adopted the crowned harp on the saddlecloth and the Royal Cypher on the pistol housings.

Raised 22 July 1715 as **Owen Wynne's Regiment of Dragoons**
Ranked in1719 as:
9th Regiment of Dragoons
Redesignated in 1751 as:
9th Regiment of Dragoons
Redesignated in 1783 as
9th Regiment of (Light) Dragoons

The 1751 Warrant:

• The facings for this regiment were buff without lapels while the waistcoats, breeches, linings of the cloaks and coats of all ranks were buff, as confirmed by Milan's list of 1749.

• The officers' lace and buttons were silver.

• Other ranks' coats were similar with white lace and buttons.

• The coats had twelve square loops set in pairs.

• The vertical pocket was slit with six chevron loops.

• The indented cuff was square-ended and the cuff slashed and laced with six buttons and six chevron laced loops.

• Housings and holster caps were buff.

• The shape of the rear saddlecloth was rounded.

• The colour of the lace was blue with a white stripe on either side, the blue to be one third of the breadth.

• Badges included, on the holster caps, the crown over the 'GR' Cypher and, at the rear the rank of the regiment, **IX D**, within a red ground surrounded by leaves, roses and thistles.

In the 1768 regulations:

• The facings for this regiment were buff without lapels while the waistcoats, breeches, linings of the cloaks and coats of all ranks were buff.

• The officers' lace and buttons were silver set on in pairs.

• Other ranks' coats were similar with white lace and buttons.

• Drummers and trumpeters were dressed in reversed facings while the waistcoats, breeches, linings of the cloaks and coats were red. The lace was white with a blue stripe.

• Housings were white edged with white lace and a blue stripe and ornamented with the rank of the regiment, **IX D**.

• When the regiment was converted to Light Dragoons in 1783 it adopted half lapels and the cuff was square with three chevron lace loops above it.

Raised on 22 July 1715 as **Humphrey Gore's Regiment of Dragoons**
Ranked as:
10th of Dragoons
Redesignated 1751 as:
10th Regiment of Dragoons
Redesignated 1783 as:
10th (Prince of Wales's Own) Regiment of (Light) Dragoons
It was retitled in 1806 as:
10th, Prince of Wales's Own Hussars
Retitled on 18 April 1811:
10th (or the Prince of Wales's Own Royal) Regiment of (Light) Dragoons (Hussars)

The 1751 Warrant:
• The facings for this regiment were deep-yellow without lapels while the waistcoats, breeches, linings of the cloaks and coats of all ranks were deep-yellow, but Milan's list of 1749 gives yellow facings, waistcoat and breeches.
• The officers' lace and buttons were silver.
• Other ranks' coats were similar with white lace and buttons.
• The coats had twelve square loops set in three, four and five, which is recorded in Lawson's list, but the painting by Morier clearly suggests threes.
• The vertical pocket was slit with six chevron loops in threes.
• The indented cuff was square-ended and the cuff slashed and laced with six buttons and six chevron laced loops.
• Housings and holster caps were deep-yellow.
• The shape of the rear saddlecloth was rounded.
• The colours of the lace were green with a white stripe on both sides, the centre to be one third of the breadth.
• Badges included, on the holster caps, the crown over the 'GR' Cypher and, at the rear the rank of the regiment, **X D**, within a red ground surrounded by leaves, roses and thistles.
• Portrait of John Tempest, Cornet of 1741. Officers' scarlet coat, narrow silver loops on chest, buttons at outer end equally spaced. The cuff has a long turn-up, extending the length of the forearm, with five buttons and loops on the turn-up to correspond with rear of the sleeve. Silver shoulder knot on left shoulder, waistcoat of a lilac colour.

In 1756
This regiment raised a troop of Light Dragoons who were dressed as the rest of the regiment but with caps.

In the 1768 regulations:
• The facings for this regiment were deep-yellow without lapels while the waistcoats, breeches, linings of the cloaks and coats of all ranks were now white.
• Other ranks' coats were similar with white lace and buttons.
• Drummers and trumpeters were dressed in reversed facings while the waistcoats, breeches, linings of the cloaks and coats were red. The lace was white with a green stripe.
• Housings were deep-yellow edged with white lace and a green stripe and ornamented with the rank of the regiment, **X D**, within a red ground surrounded by roses and thistles.

• When the regiment was converted to Light Dragoons in 1783 it was awarded the Prince of Wales's badge and adopted half lapels.

Raised on 22 July 1715 as **Philip Honeywood's Regiment of Dragoons**
Ranked as
11th of Dragoons.
Redesignated 1751 as:
11th Regiment of Dragoons
Redesignated 1783 as:
11th Regiment of (Light) Dragoons

The 1751 Warrant:

• The facings for this regiment were buff without lapels while the waistcoats, breeches, linings of the cloaks and coats of all ranks were buff, but Milan's list of 1749 gives light buff, the waistcoat as white and the breeches red.
• The officers' lace and buttons were silver.
• Other ranks' coats were similar with white lace and buttons.
• The coats had twelve square loops set in threes.
• The vertical pocket was slit with six chevron loops.
• The indented cuff was square-ended and the cuff slashed and laced with six buttons and six chevron laced loops.
• Housings and holster caps was buff.
• The shape of the rear saddlecloth was square.
• The colours of the lace were green with a white stripe on both sides, the stripe at the centre to be one third of the breadth.
• Badges included, on the holster caps, the crown over the 'GR' Cypher and, at the rear the rank of the regiment, **XI D**, within a red ground surrounded by leaves, roses and thistles.

In 1756

This regiment raised a troop of Light Dragoons who were dressed as the rest of the regiment but with caps.

In the 1768 regulations:

• The facings for this regiment were buff without lapels while the waistcoats, breeches, linings of the cloaks and coats of all ranks were buff.
• The officers' lace and buttons were silver set on in threes.
• Other ranks' coats were similar with white lace and buttons.
• Drummers and trumpeters were dressed in reversed facings while the waistcoats, breeches, linings of the cloaks and coats were red. The lace was white with a green stripe.
• Housings were buff edged with white lace and a green stripe and ornamented with the rank of the regiment, **XI D**, within a red ground surrounded by roses and thistles.
• When the regiment was converted to Light Dragoons in 1783 it adopted half lapels and the cuff was square with three chevron lace loops above it.

Raised 22 July 1715 as **Phineas Bowles's regiment of Dragoons**
Ranked in 1759 as:
12th of Dragoons
Retitled in 1751 as:

12th Regiment of Dragoons
Retitled in 1768 as:
12th (The Prince of Wales's) Regiment of (Light) Dragoons
Redesignated in 1816 as:
12th (The Prince of Wales's) Regiment of (Light) Dragoons (Lancers)

The 1751 Warrant:

- The facings for this regiment were white without lapels while the waistcoats, breeches, linings of the cloaks and coats of all ranks were white, but Milan's list of 1749 gives red breeches.
- The officers' lace and buttons were silver.
- Other ranks' coats were similar with white lace and buttons.
- The coats had twelve square loops set in pairs.
- The vertical pocket was slit with six chevron loops.
- The indented cuff was square-ended and the cuff slashed and laced with six buttons and six chevron laced loops.
- Housings and holster caps were white.
- The shape of the rear saddlecloth was rounded.
- The colour of the lace was green with yellow stripe on either side, the green to be one third of the breadth.
- Badges included, on the holster caps, the crown over the 'GR' Cypher and, at the rear the rank of the regiment, **XII D,** within a red ground surrounded by leaves, roses and thistles.

In the 1768 regulations:

- The facings for this regiment were changed to black with half lapels as Light Dragoons and the waistcoats, breeches, linings of the cloaks and coats of all ranks were white.
- The officers' lace and buttons were silver set on in pairs, but no hat lace was worn.
- Other ranks' coats were similar with white lace and buttons.
- Drummers and trumpeters were dressed in red coats with blue facings while the waistcoats, breeches, linings of the cloaks and coats were white. The lace was now Royal lace.
- Housings were now black with strips of white goatskin edged without lace.
- The new badge has three feathers issuing from the Prince of Wales's Coronet.

Raised on 22 July 1715 as **Richard Munden's Regiment of Dragoons**
Ranked in 1715 as:
13th of Dragoons
Redesignated in 1751 as:
13th Regiment of Dragoons
Redesignated in 1783 as:
13th Regiment of (Light) Dragoons

The 1751 Warrant:

- The facings for this regiment were light green without lapels while the waistcoats, breeches, linings of the cloaks and coats of all ranks were light green, but Milan's list of 1749 gives facings as green; the waistcoat and breeches were white.
- The officers' lace and buttons were gold.
- Other ranks' coats were similar with yellow lace and buttons.
- The coats had twelve square loops set in threes.
- The vertical pocket was slit with six chevron loops.

• The indented cuff was square-ended and the cuff slashed and laced with six buttons and six chevron laced loops.
• Housings and holster caps were light green.
• The shape of the rear saddlecloth was rounded.
• The colour of the lace was yellow with a white stripe on either side, the yellow to be one third of the breadth.
• Badges included, on the holster caps, the crown over the 'GR' Cypher and, at the rear the rank of the regiment, **XIII D**, within a red ground surrounded by leaves, roses and thistles.

In the 1768 regulations:
• The facings for this regiment were changed to deep-green without lapels while the waistcoats, breeches, linings of the cloaks and coats of all ranks were buff.
• The officers' lace and buttons were gold set on in threes.
• Other ranks' coats were similar with yellow lace and buttons.
• Drummers and trumpeters were dressed in reversed facings while the waistcoats, breeches, linings of the cloaks and coats were white. The lace was white with a yellow stripe.
• The colour of the lace was white on either side, the yellow stripe at the centre to be one third of the breadth.
• Badges included, the rank of the regiment, **XIII D**, within a red ground surrounded by leaves, roses and thistles.
• When the regiment was converted to Light Dragoons in 1783 it adopted half lapels and the cuff was square with three chevron lace loops above it.

Raised 22 July 1715 as **James Dormer's Regiment of Dragoons**
Ranked in 1715 as:
14th of Dragoons
Redesignated in 1751 as:
14th Regiment of Dragoons
Redesignated in 1776 as:
14th Regiment of (Light) Dragoons
This regiment was retitled from 1798 as the:
14th (or the Duchess of York's Own) Regiment of (Light) Dragoons

The 1751 Warrant:
• The facings for this regiment were lemon without lapels while the waistcoats, breeches, linings of the cloaks and coats of all ranks were lemon, as confirmed by Milan's list of 1749.
• The officers' lace and buttons were silver.
• Other ranks' coats were similar with white lace and buttons.
• The coats had twelve square loops set in threes, but Morier shows the loops in pairs and this has been assumed.
• The vertical pocket was slit with six chevron loops.
• The indented cuff was square-ended and the cuff slashed and laced with six buttons and six chevron laced loops.
• Housings and holster caps were lemon.
• The shape of the rear saddlecloth was rounded.
• Colours of the lace were a white, red and green stripe, the red to be one third of the breadth, but Morier shows white lace with a red centre.
• Badges included, on the holster caps, the crown over the 'GR' Cypher and, at the rear the rank of the regiment, **XIV D,** within a red ground surrounded by leaves, roses and thistles.

In the 1768 regulations:

• The facings for this regiment were lemon without lapels while the waistcoats, breeches, linings of the cloaks and coats of all ranks were white.
• The officers' lace and buttons were silver set on in threes.
• Other ranks' coats were similar with white lace and buttons.
• Drummers and trumpeters were dressed in reversed facings while the waistcoats, breeches, linings of the cloaks and coats were red. The lace was white with red and green stripes.
• Housings were lemon.
• The colour of the lace was white, red and green stripes.
• The regiment adopted green facings in 1776.
• When the regiment was converted to Light Dragoons in 1776 it adopted half lapels and the cuff was square with three chevron lace loops above it.
• Badges included the rank of the regiment, **XIV D**, within a red ground surrounded by leaves, roses and thistles.

Raised 10 March 1759 as:
15th (or Light) Regiment of Dragoons also known as Eliott's Light Horse
Redesignated in 1760 as:
15th Regiment of (or Light) Dragoons
Redesignated in 1766 as:
1st (The King's) Regiment of Light Dragoons
Redesignated in 1769 as:
15th (The King's) Regiment of (Light) Dragoons
It was retitled in March 1807 as:
15th (or the King's) Regiment of (Light) Dragoons (Hussars)

The 1759 Warrant:

• The facings for this regiment were originally green with half lapels they became a royal regiment in 1766 with blue lapels while the waistcoats, breeches, linings of the cloaks and coats of all ranks were blue.
• The officers' lace and buttons were silver.
• Other ranks' coats were similar with white lace and buttons.
• The lapels had eight square loops set in pairs.
• The vertical pocket had three chevron loops.
• The cuff was square-ended and the cuff slashed and laced with three buttons and three chevron laced loops.
• Housings and holster caps were blue.
• The colour of Royal lace was blue with a yellow stripe on either side, the blue to be one third of the breadth.
• Badges included, on the holster caps, the crown over the 'GR' Cypher and, at the rear, the King's Crest of the lion within the garter with a crown over.

In the 1768 regulations:

• The facings for this royal regiment were dark-blue with half lapels while the waistcoats, breeches, linings of the cloaks and coats of all ranks were now white.
• The officers' lace and buttons were silver set in pairs; no hat lace was worn.
• Other ranks' coats were similar with white lace and buttons.
• Drummers and trumpeters were dressed in reversed facings while the waistcoats, breeches, linings of the cloaks and coats were white.
• Housings were now white.

• The colour of the Royal lace was blue with a yellow stripe on either side, the blue stripe at the centre to be one third of the breadth.
• Badges included, on the holster caps, the Crown over a 'GR' Cypher and, at the rear the King's crest within the garter with a crown over.

Raised 4 August 1759 as:
16th Regiment of (Light) Dragoons (also known as Burgoyne's Light Horse)
Not a regular unit until 18 March 1763.
Redesignated in 1766 as:
2nd (or the Queen's) Regiment of Light Dragoons
Redesignated in 1769 as:
16th (The Queen's Own) Regiment of (Light) Dragoons
Redesignated in 1816 as:
16th (The Queen's) Regiment of (Light) Dragoons (Lancers)
This regiment served in North America during the War of Independence.

The 1759 Warrant:
• The facings for this regiment were black with half lapels while the waistcoats, breeches, linings of the cloaks and coats of all ranks were white; the regiment became Royal in 1766 and the facings were changed to blue.
• The officers' lace and buttons were silver.
• Other ranks' coats were similar with white lace and buttons.
• The coat had eight square loops set in pairs.
• The vertical pocket had three chevron loops.
• The square cuff had three chevron-laced loops above it.
• Housings and holster caps were white.
• The colour of lace was black with a red stripe on either side, the black to be one third of the breadth.
• Badges included, on the holster caps, the crown over the 'GR' Cypher and, at the rear of a pointed saddlecloth, the rank of the regiment on a red ground surrounded by leaves, roses and thistles under the scroll bearing the word 'EMSDORF'.
• In 1766 the lace became Royal and at the rear of a rounded saddlecloth a badge of the Queen's Cypher within the garter with a crown over it, replaced the earlier badge.

In the 1768 regulations:
• The facings for this royal regiment were dark-blue with half lapels while the waistcoats, breeches, linings of the cloaks and coats of all ranks were white.
• The officers' lace and buttons were silver set on in pairs; no hat lace was worn.
• Other ranks' coats were similar with white lace and buttons and narrow blue shoulder straps edged with white and trimmed with white worsted fringe.
• Drummers and trumpeters were dressed in reversed facings while the waistcoats, breeches, linings of the cloaks and coats were white.
• Housings were white.
• The colour of the Royal lace was yellow on either side with a blue stripe at the centre to be one third of the breadth.
• Badges included the Queen's Cypher within the garter with the crown over.

During the War of Independence:

• Abandoning their old-pattern dragoon caps, new light cavalry leather caps of the Tarleton type were purchased in 1776 before embarking. Waist belt cartridge boxes were standard issue when mounted. Much of the regiment was detailed as an infantry escort working with a 1776 short carbine. The dismounted personnel were issued with infantry accoutrements and short brown marching gaiters and boots were naturally traded for shoes.

• The mounted section consisted of six troops, each headed by a Captain, Lieutenant, Cornet, Quartermaster, two Sergeants, two Corporals and thirty-four light dragoons. A Cornet, a Sergeant, two Corporals and thirty-eight light dragoons further augmented the mounted troops.

• The dismounted section had a Captain, Lieutenant, six Cornets, six Sergeants, twelve Corporals, two Trumpeters and 174 light dragoons.

• The peaked leather caps of the Tarleton style were trimmed with false-leopard skin turbans and had three rows of chains around the crown surmounted by a bearskin crest.

• The 16th Regiment of Light Dragoons arrived in Halifax, Nova Scotia in October 1776 after a voyage of three months. The regiment was immediately dispatched to New York 1776, where it saw action at White Plains, Trenton, Brandywine Creek, Paoli, Germantown and Monmouth Court House. The 16th Light Dragoons returned to New York in 1778, were under strength and drafted into the 17th Light Dragoons in 1778. The officers, along with the regiment's Colours, returned to England in 1779.

Raised 7 November 1759 as:

18th Regiment of (or Light) Dragoons (also known as Hale's Light Horse)

Not a regular unit until 24 July 1763.

Redesignated in 1763 as:

17th Regiment of (or corps of) Light Dragoons

Redesignated in 1766 as:

3rd Regiment of Light Dragoons

Redesignated in 1768 as:

17th Regiment of (Light) Dragoons

Redesignated in 1822 as:

17th (The Queen's) Regiment of (Light) Dragoons (Lancers)

This regiment served in North America during the War of Independence.

The 1759 Warrant:

• The facings for this regiment were white with half lapels while the waistcoats, breeches, linings of the cloaks and coats of all ranks were white.

• The officers' lace and buttons were silver with a black line through the lace.

• Other ranks' coats were similar with white lace and buttons.

• The lapels had eight square loops set in pairs.

• The vertical pocket was slit with four chevron loops.

• The square cuff was laced with four chevron-laced loops set in pairs.

• Housings and holster caps were red.

• The colour of the lace was black with a red stripe on either side, the black to be one third of the breadth.

• Badges included, on the holster caps, and at the rear of the saddle cloth, the skull below crossed bones on a red ground.

In the 1768 regulations:

- The facings for this regiment were white with half lapels while the waistcoats, breeches, linings of the cloaks and coats of all ranks were white.
- The officers' lace and buttons were silver set in pairs with a black line through the lace; no hat lace was worn.
- Other ranks' coats were similar with white lace and buttons.
- Drummers and trumpeters were dressed in reversed facings with the waistcoats, breeches, linings of the cloaks and coats were red. The lace was white with black edges.
- Housings were white.
- The colour of the lace was white with two black edges.
- Badges included, on the holster caps, the crown over the 'GR' Cypherand at the rear, the rank of the regiment, **XVIII LD**, within a red ground surrounded by leaves, roses and thistles; or the skull below crossed bones on a red ground.

During the War of Independence:

The 17th Light Dragoons facings were white. The black line through the lace is purported to have been adopted after the death of Wolfe. Officers wore silver appointments. The 17th arrived in Boston in May 1775 and took part in actions at Long Island, Fort Washington, Princeton, White Marsh, Monmouth, Cowpens and Guilford Court House. Elements served at Forts Clinton and Montgomery. After spending the summer of 1779 in New York, they were sent to the Carolinas. While in transit a storm blew up and most of the horses died. They landed at Savannah and were attached to the British Legion throughout the southern campaigns; ninety-four men of the 16th Light Dragoons were drafted to the 17th in 1778. Many of their force served as foot troops and were issued with brown overalls, infantry arms and equipment, but retained their cavalry swords. The 17th surrendered near Yorktown and left for home in 1783.

Raised on 7 December 1759 by the Earl of Drogheda as:
19th Regiment of (or Light) Dragoons
Renumbered in 1763 as:
18th Regiment of (or corps of Light) Dragoons
Redesignated in 1766 as:
4th Regiment of Light Dragoons
Redesignated in 1768 as:
18th Regiment of (Light) Dragoons
It was retitled in January 1805 as:
18th (or The King's Irish) Regiment of (Light) Dragoons
Retitled in December 1807 as:
18th (or The King's Irish) Regiment of (Light) Dragoons (Hussars)
The regiment was disbanded in September 1821.

The 1759 Warrant:

- The facings for this regiment were black with half lapels while the waistcoats, breeches, linings of the cloaks and coats of all ranks were white.
- The officers' lace and buttons were silver.
- Other ranks' coats were similar with white lace and buttons.
- The coat had eight square loops set in pairs.
- The vertical pocket had three chevron loops.
- The square cuff had three chevron-laced loops above it.

• Housings and holster caps were white.
• The colour of lace was black with a red stripe on either side, the black to be one third of the breadth.
• Badges included on the holster caps, the crown over the 'GR' Cypher and, at the rear the rank of the regiment, **XVIII LD**, within a red ground surrounded by leaves, roses and thistles.

In the 1768 regulations:
• The facings for this regiment were white with half lapels while the waistcoats, breeches, linings of the cloaks and coats of all ranks were white.
• The officers' lace and buttons were silver set in pairs and no hat lace was worn.
• Other ranks' coats were similar with white lace and buttons.
• Drummers and trumpeters were dressed in reversed facings while the waistcoats, breeches, linings of the cloaks and coats were red. The lace was red and white on either side.
• Badges included, on the holster caps, the crown over the 'GR' Cypher and, at the rear the rank of the regiment, **XVIII LD**, within a red ground surrounded by leaves, roses and thistles.

Raised in 1779 by Russell Manners and formed from light companies of the 1st and 2nd Dragoon Guards and the 4th and 10th Dragoons as:
19th Regiment of (Light) Dragoons
This regiment was disbanded in 1783

• The facings for this regiment were green with half lapels while the waistcoats, breeches, linings of the cloaks and coats of all ranks were white.
• The officers' lace and buttons were silver.
• Other ranks' coats were similar with white lace and buttons.
• The coat had eight square loops set in pairs.
• The vertical pocket had three chevron loops.
• The cuff was square with three chevron lace loops above it.
• Housings and holster caps were green.
• The colour of lace was green with white to either side.
• Badges included, on the holster caps, the crown over the 'GR' Cypher and, at the rear, the rank of the regiment **XIX LD** on a red ground surrounded by leaves, roses and thistles.

Raised 12 January 1760 in Ireland by Sir James Caldwell as:
20th Regiment of (or Corps of) Light Dragoons
also known as 20th (Inniskilling) Light Dragoons.
This regiment was disbanded in 1763

• Research has failed to find any details of the uniform.

Raised in February 1779 by R.B. Philipson from light troops attached to the dragoon guards as:
20th Regiment of (Light) Dragoons
This regiment was disbanded in 1783

• The facings for this regiment were yellow with half lapels, while waistcoats, breeches, linings of the cloaks and coats of all ranks were white.
• The officers' lace and buttons were silver and spaced in pairs.
• Other ranks' coats were similar with white lace and buttons.
• The lapel had eight square loops set in pairs.
• The vertical pocket had three chevron loops.
• The square cuff had three chevron-laced loops above it.
• Housings and holster caps were white.
• The colour of the lace was yellow with white on either side.
• Badges included, on the holster caps, the crown over the 'GR' Cypher and, at the rear the rank of the regiment, **XX LD**, within a red ground surrounded by leaves, roses and thistles.

There were two regiments with this number:

Raised in 1759 by the Marquis of Granby as:
21st (Royal Foresters) Light Dragoons
This regiment was disbanded in 1763

The 1759 Warrant:
• The facings for this royal regiment were dark-blue with half lapels and cape while, the waistcoats, breeches; linings of the cloaks and coats of all ranks were white.
• The officers' lace and buttons were silver and spaced in pairs.
• Other ranks' coats were similar with white lace and buttons.
• The lapel had eight square loops set in pairs with a further loop and button below the lapel.
• The vertical pocket had three chevron loops.
• The square cuff had four chevron-laced loops in pairs.
• This regiment wore white leather carbine sling and sword belt.
• Housings and holster caps were white.
• There was no lace to the housings.
• The badge on the white holster caps was the 'GR' Cypher with a crown foliate design round it.

The second regiment:

Raised in April 1779 by John Douglas and formed from the light companies of 2nd, 3rd, 7th, 15th, and 16th dragoons as:
21st Regiment of (Light) Dragoons
This regiment was disbanded in 1783

• The facings for this regiment were white with half lapels while, the waistcoats, breeches, linings of the cloaks and coats of all ranks were white.
• The officers' lace and buttons were gold and spaced in twos.
• Other ranks' coats were similar with yellow lace and buttons.
• The lapel had eight square loops set in twos.
• The vertical pocket had three chevron loops.
• The square cuff had three chevron-laced loops above it.
• Housings and holster caps were white.
• The colour of the lace on the housings was black on red.

• Badges included, on the holster caps, the crown over the 'GR' Cypher and, at the rear, the rank of the regiment, **XXI LD**, within a red ground surrounded by leaves, roses and thistles.

Raised on 14th December 1779 by Lord John Sheffield as:
22nd Regiment of (Light) Dragoons, also known as the Sussex Dragoons
This regiment was disbanded in 1783

• The coat of this regiment was green with a green pelisse without lapels the while waistcoats, breeches, linings of the cloaks and coats of all ranks were white.
• This regiment wore a Tarleton cap with a turned-up peak.
• The officers' lace and buttons were silver and spaced in twos.
• Other ranks' coats were similar with white lace and buttons.
• The coat had eight square loops set in twos.
• The vertical pocket had three chevron loops.
• The square cuff had three chevron-laced loops above it.
• Housings and holster caps were green.
• The colour of the lace on the housings was green on white.
• Badges included, on the holster caps, the crown over the 'GR' Cypher and, at the rear, the rank of the regiment, **XXII LD**, within a red ground surrounded by leaves, roses and thistles.

Raised by Sir John Burgoyne in September 1781 for service in India as:
23rd Regiment of (Light) Dragoons
Renumbered in 1786 as:
19th Regiment of (Light) Dragoons
Renamed in 1816 as:
19th Regiment of (Light) Dragoons (Lancers)
This regiment was disbanded in 1821
This regiment served in Canada during the War of 1812.

• The coats of this regiment were green without lapels until 1784 when they adopted green facings with half lapels; the waistcoats, breeches, and linings of the cloaks of all ranks were white.
• The officers' lace and buttons were silver and spaced in pairs.
• Other ranks' coats were similar with white lace and buttons.
• The lapel had eight square loops set in pairs.
• The vertical pocket had three chevron loops.
• The square cuff had three chevron-laced loops above it.
• Housings and holster caps were white.
• The colour of the lace is not known.
• Badges included, on the holster caps, the crown over the 'GR' Cypher and, at the rear, the rank of the regiment, **XXIII LD**, within a red ground surrounded by leaves, roses and thistles.

There were no other light regiments raised during the period.

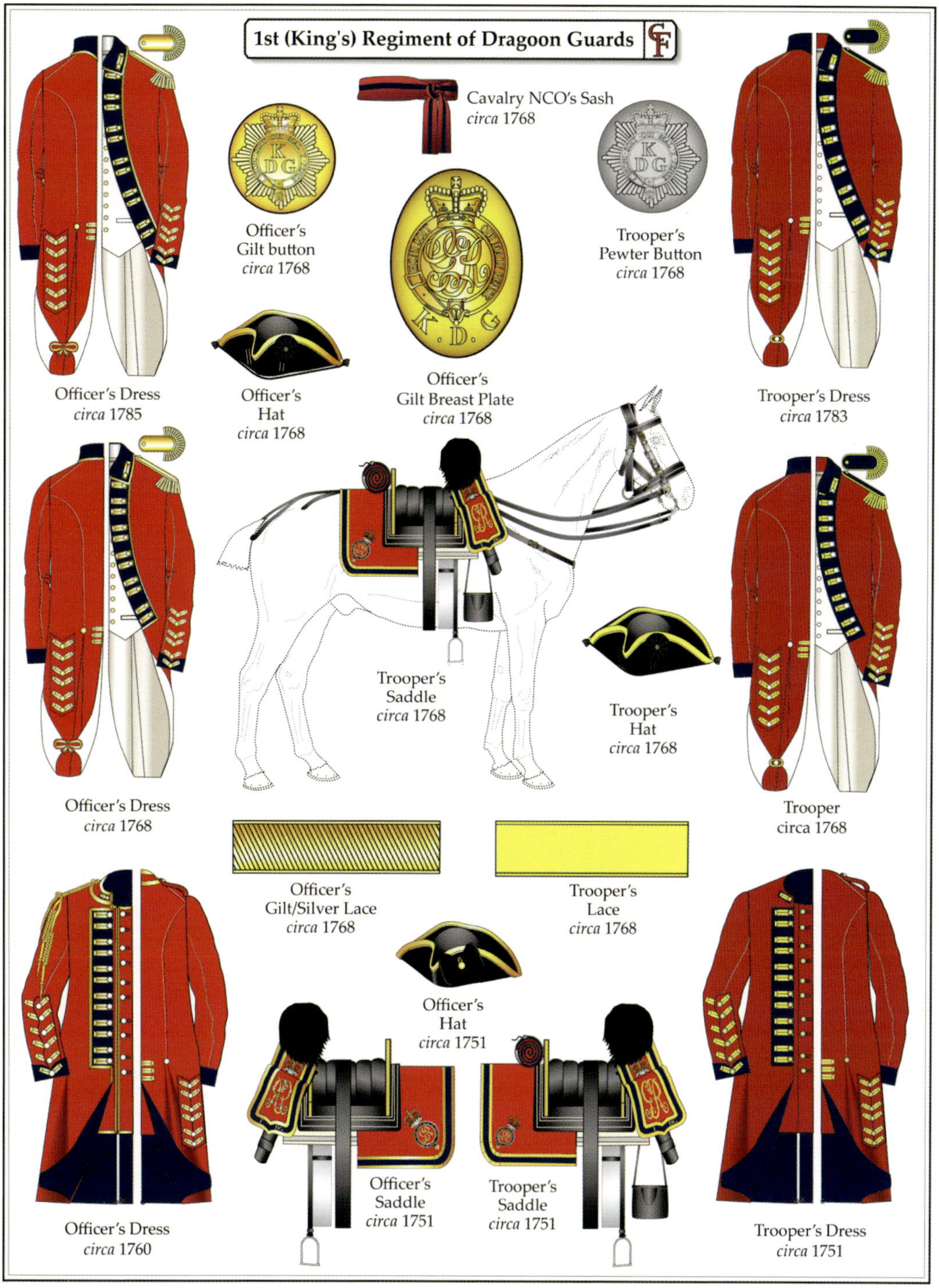
1st (King's) Regiment of Dragoon Guards
Officer's Dress
circa 1785
Officer's
Gilt button
circa 1768
Cavalry NCO's Sash
circa 1768
Officer's
Gilt Breast Plate
circa 1768
Trooper's
Pewter Button
circa 1768
Trooper's Dress
circa 1783
Officer's
Hat
circa 1768
Officer's Dress
circa 1768
Trooper's
Saddle
circa 1768
Trooper's
Hat
circa 1768
Trooper
circa 1768
Officer's
Gilt/Silver Lace
circa 1768
Trooper's
Lace
circa 1768
Officer's
Hat
circa 1751
Officer's Dress
circa 1760
Officer's
Saddle
circa 1751
Trooper's
Saddle
circa 1751
Trooper's Dress
circa 1751

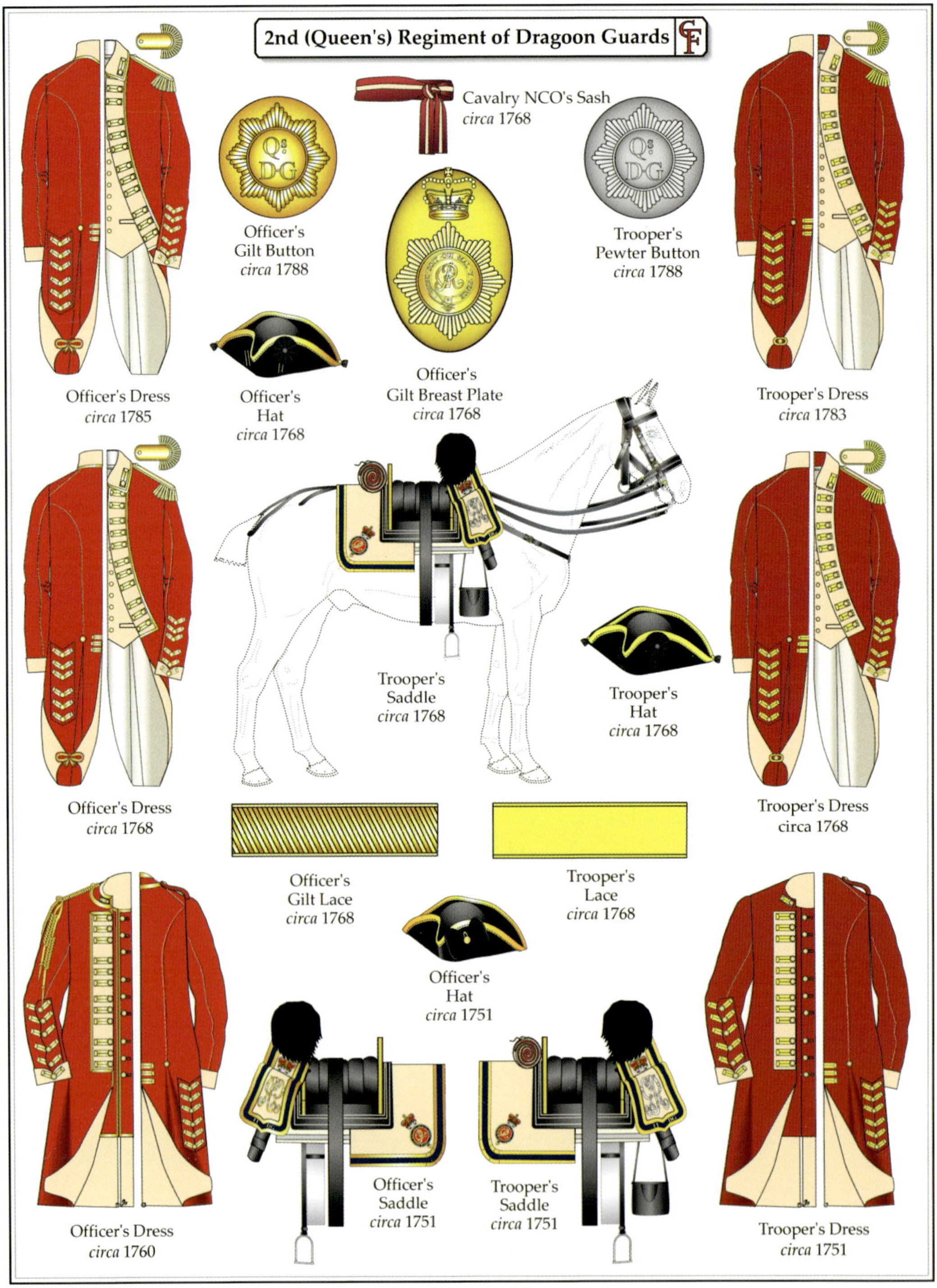
2nd (Queen's) Regiment of Dragoon Guards
Cavalry NCO's Sash circa 1768
Officer's Gilt Button circa 1788
Trooper's Pewter Button circa 1788
Officer's Dress circa 1785
Officer's Hat circa 1768
Officer's Gilt Breast Plate circa 1768
Trooper's Dress circa 1783
Trooper's Saddle circa 1768
Trooper's Hat circa 1768
Officer's Dress circa 1768
Trooper's Dress circa 1768
Officer's Gilt Lace circa 1768
Trooper's Lace circa 1768
Officer's Hat circa 1751
Officer's Saddle circa 1751
Trooper's Saddle circa 1751
Officer's Dress circa 1760
Trooper's Dress circa 1751

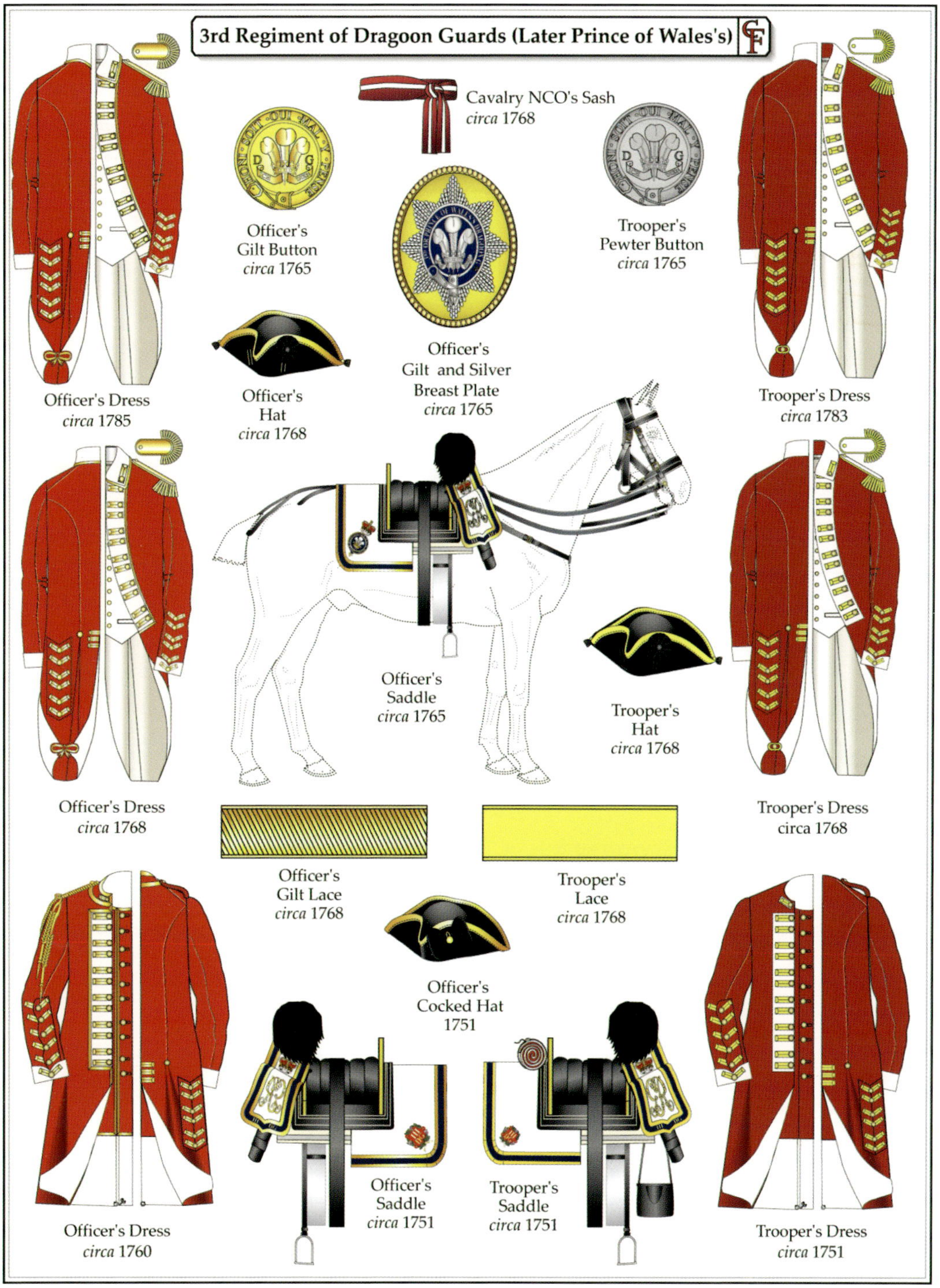
3rd Regiment of Dragoon Guards (Later Prince of Wales's)
CF
Cavalry NCO's Sash
circa 1768
Officer's
Gilt Button
circa 1765
Trooper's
Pewter Button
circa 1765
Officer's
Gilt and Silver
Breast Plate
circa 1765
Officer's Dress
circa 1785
Officer's
Hat
circa 1768
Trooper's Dress
circa 1783
Officer's
Saddle
circa 1765
Trooper's
Hat
circa 1768
Officer's Dress
circa 1768
Trooper's Dress
circa 1768
Officer's
Gilt Lace
circa 1768
Trooper's
Lace
circa 1768
Officer's
Cocked Hat
1751
Officer's
Saddle
circa 1751
Trooper's
Saddle
circa 1751
Officer's Dress
circa 1760
Trooper's Dress
circa 1751

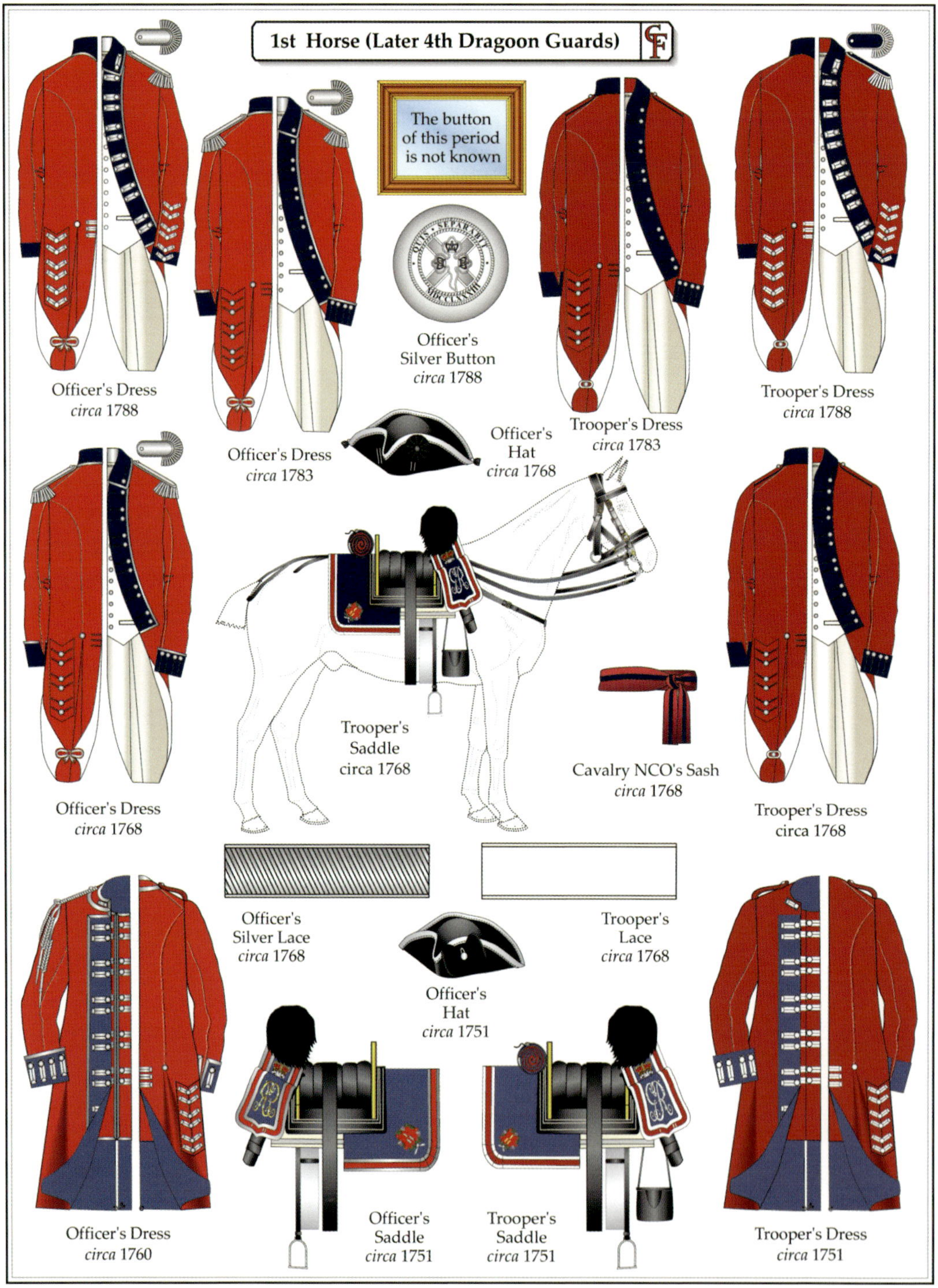
1st Horse (Later 4th Dragoon Guards)
The button of this period is not known
Officer's Silver Button circa 1788
Officer's Dress circa 1788
Officer's Dress circa 1783
Trooper's Dress circa 1783
Trooper's Dress circa 1788
Officer's Hat circa 1768
Officer's Dress circa 1768
Trooper's Saddle circa 1768
Cavalry NCO's Sash circa 1768
Trooper's Dress circa 1768
Officer's Silver Lace circa 1768
Trooper's Lace circa 1768
Officer's Hat circa 1751
Officer's Dress circa 1760
Officer's Saddle circa 1751
Trooper's Saddle circa 1751
Trooper's Dress circa 1751

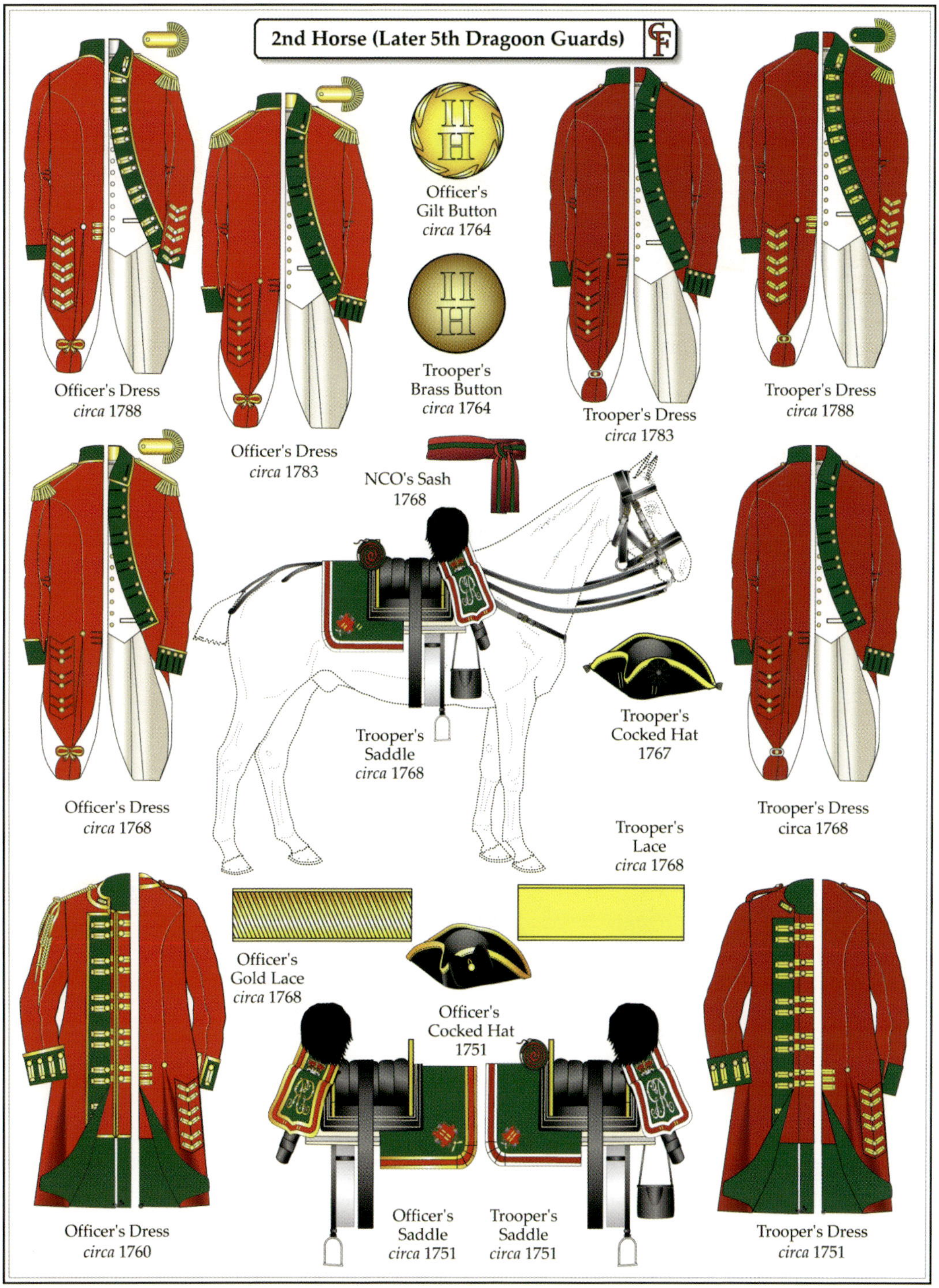
2nd Horse (Later 5th Dragoon Guards)
Officer's Dress
circa 1788
Officer's Dress
circa 1783
Officer's Gilt Button
circa 1764
Trooper's Brass Button
circa 1764
Trooper's Dress
circa 1783
Trooper's Dress
circa 1788
NCO's Sash
1768
Officer's Dress
circa 1768
Trooper's Saddle
circa 1768
Trooper's Cocked Hat
1767
Trooper's Dress
circa 1768
Trooper's Lace
circa 1768
Officer's Gold Lace
circa 1768
Officer's Cocked Hat
1751
Officer's Dress
circa 1760
Officer's Saddle
circa 1751
Trooper's Saddle
circa 1751
Trooper's Dress
circa 1751

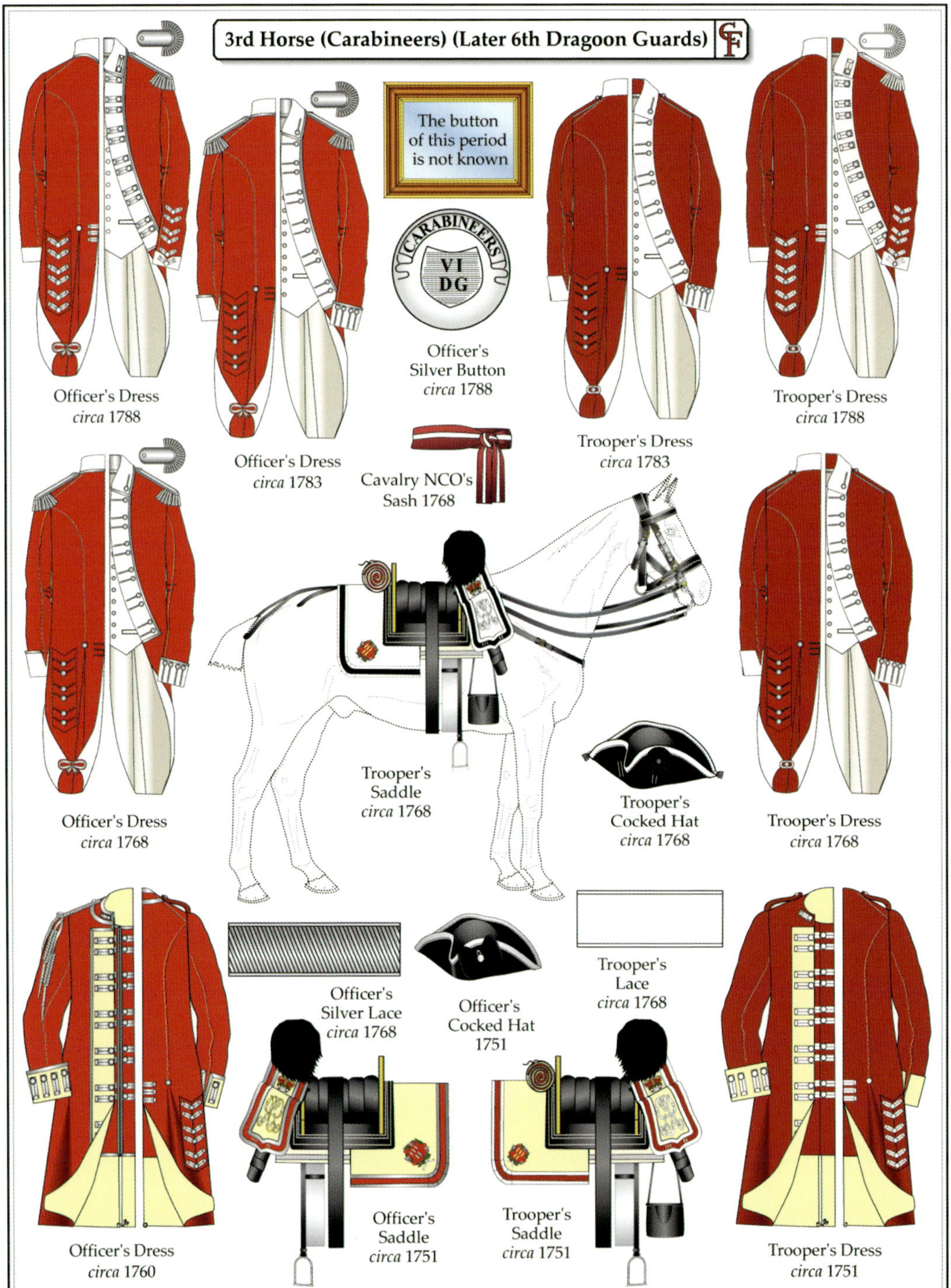
3rd Horse (Carabineers) (Later 6th Dragoon Guards)
The button of this period is not known
CARABINEERS
VI DG
Officer's Dress circa 1788
Officer's Dress circa 1783
Officer's Silver Button circa 1788
Trooper's Dress circa 1783
Trooper's Dress circa 1788
Cavalry NCO's Sash 1768
Officer's Dress circa 1768
Trooper's Saddle circa 1768
Trooper's Cocked Hat circa 1768
Trooper's Dress circa 1768
Officer's Silver Lace circa 1768
Officer's Cocked Hat 1751
Trooper's Lace circa 1768
Officer's Dress circa 1760
Officer's Saddle circa 1751
Trooper's Saddle circa 1751
Trooper's Dress circa 1751

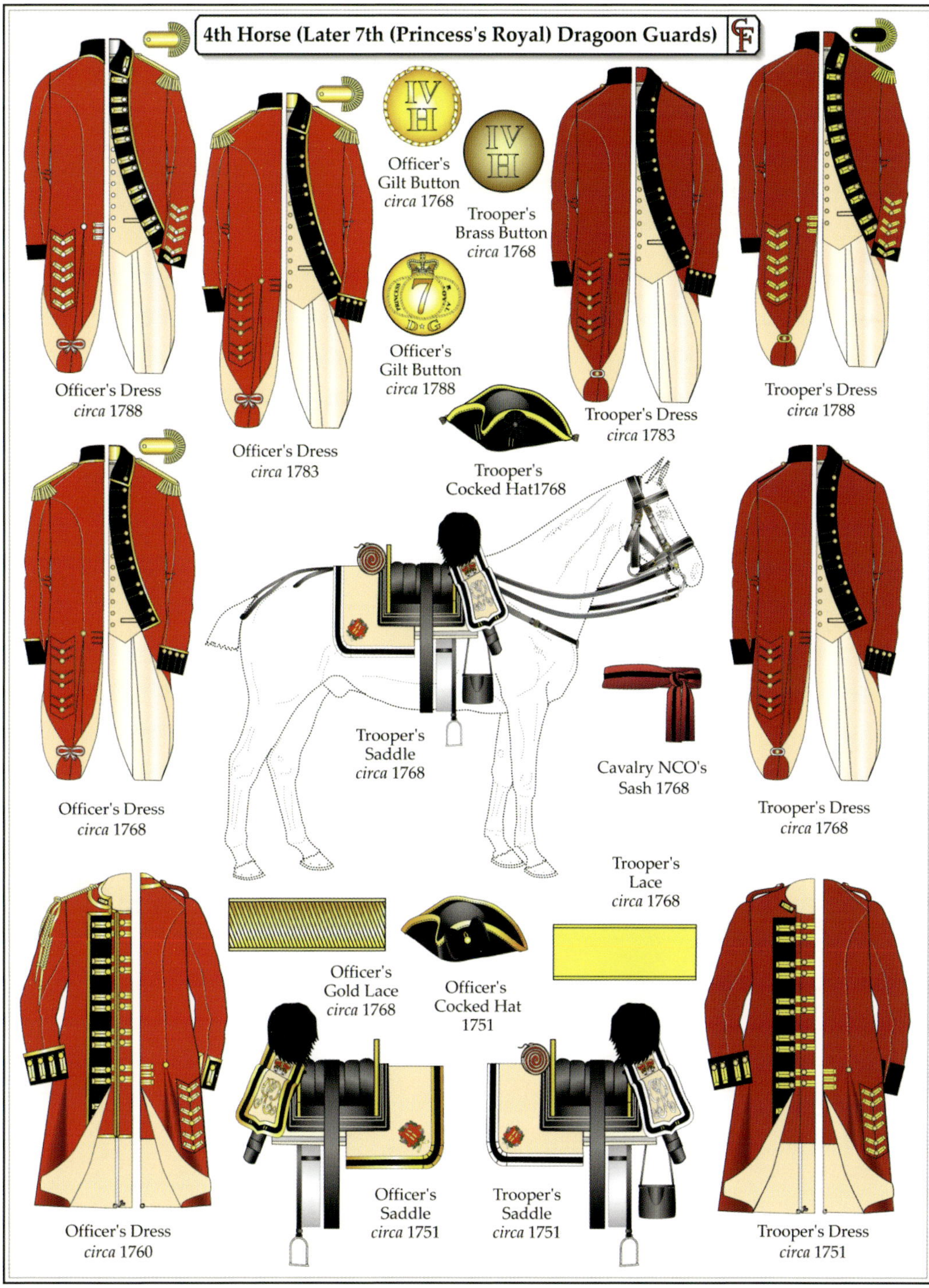
4th Horse (Later 7th (Princess's Royal) Dragoon Guards)
Officer's Dress circa 1788
Officer's Dress circa 1783
Officer's Gilt Button circa 1768
Trooper's Brass Button circa 1768
Officer's Gilt Button circa 1788
Trooper's Dress circa 1783
Trooper's Dress circa 1788
Trooper's Cocked Hat1768
Officer's Dress circa 1768
Trooper's Saddle circa 1768
Cavalry NCO's Sash 1768
Trooper's Dress circa 1768
Trooper's Lace circa 1768
Officer's Gold Lace circa 1768
Officer's Cocked Hat 1751
Officer's Dress circa 1760
Officer's Saddle circa 1751
Trooper's Saddle circa 1751
Trooper's Dress circa 1751

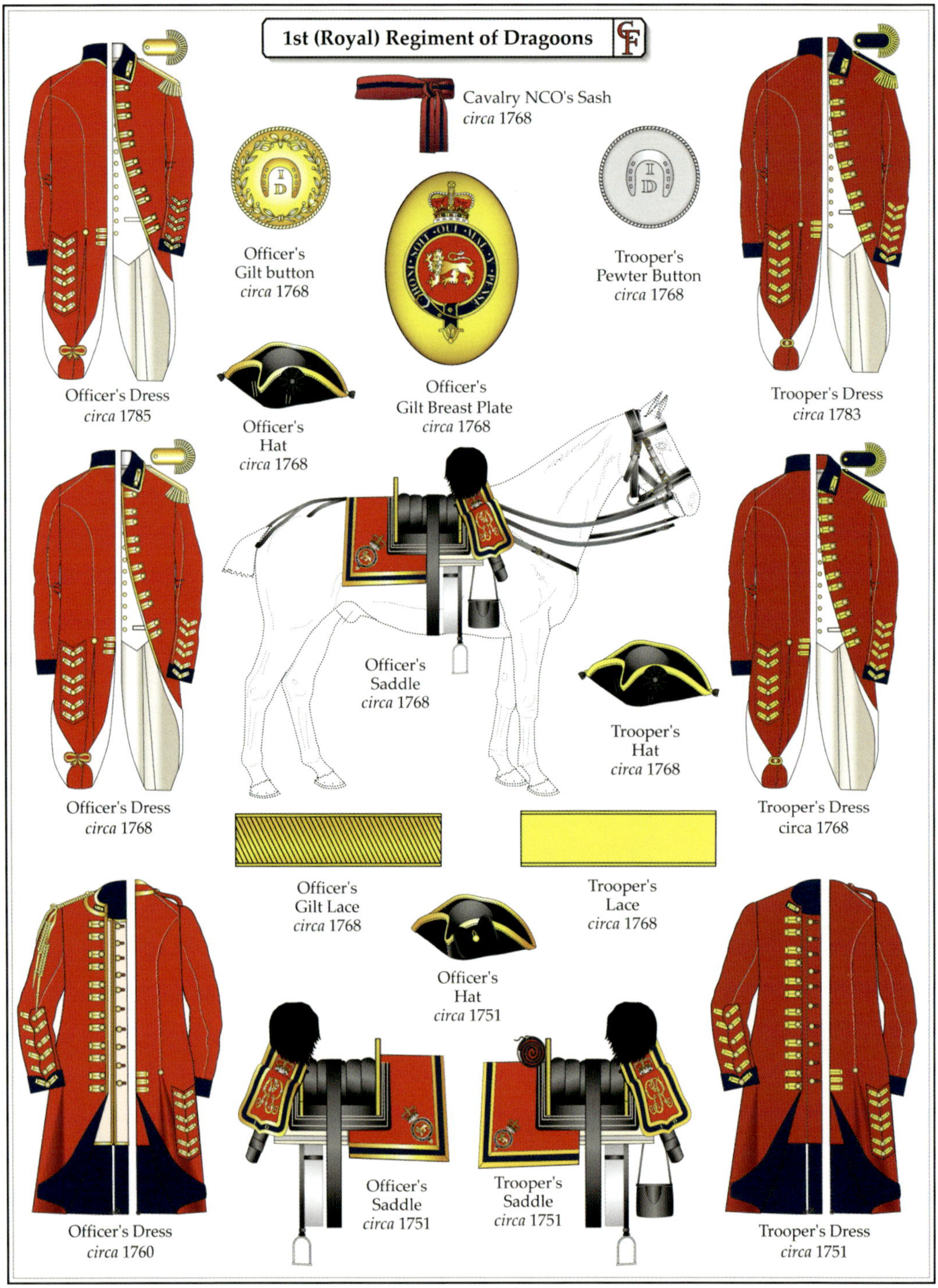
1st (Royal) Regiment of Dragoons
CF
Cavalry NCO's Sash
circa 1768
Officer's Gilt button
circa 1768
Trooper's Pewter Button
circa 1768
Officer's Dress
circa 1785
Officer's Hat
circa 1768
Officer's Gilt Breast Plate
circa 1768
Trooper's Dress
circa 1783
Officer's Saddle
circa 1768
Trooper's Hat
circa 1768
Officer's Dress
circa 1768
Trooper's Dress
circa 1768
Officer's Gilt Lace
circa 1768
Trooper's Lace
circa 1768
Officer's Hat
circa 1751
Officer's Dress
circa 1760
Officer's Saddle
circa 1751
Trooper's Saddle
circa 1751
Trooper's Dress
circa 1751

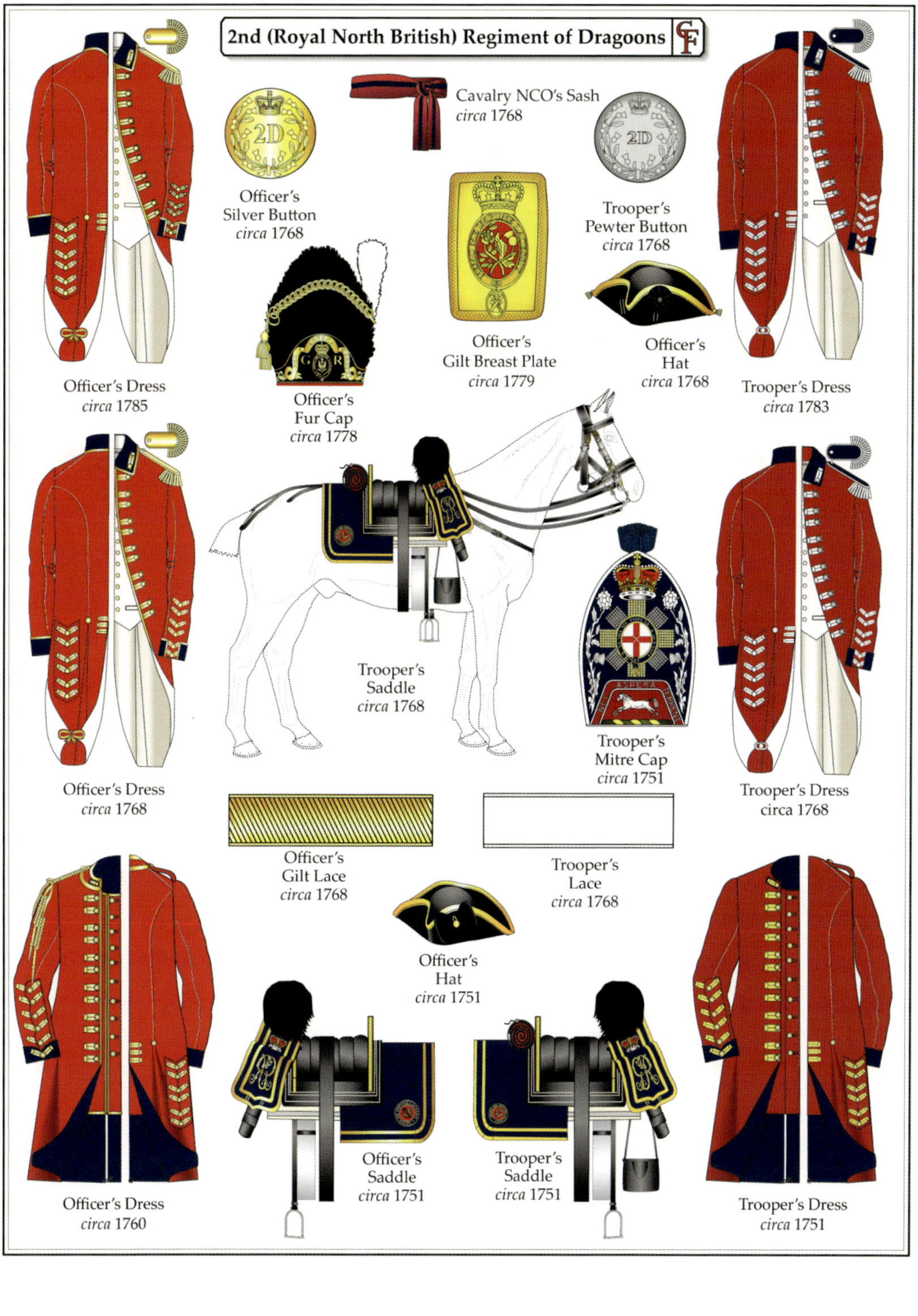
2nd (Royal North British) Regiment of Dragoons
CF
Cavalry NCO's Sash
circa 1768
2D
Officer's
Silver Button
circa 1768
2D
Trooper's
Pewter Button
circa 1768
Officer's Dress
circa 1785
Officer's
Fur Cap
circa 1778
Officer's
Gilt Breast Plate
circa 1779
Officer's
Hat
circa 1768
Trooper's Dress
circa 1783
Trooper's
Saddle
circa 1768
Trooper's
Mitre Cap
circa 1751
Officer's Dress
circa 1768
Trooper's Dress
circa 1768
Officer's
Gilt Lace
circa 1768
Trooper's
Lace
circa 1768
Officer's
Hat
circa 1751
Officer's Dress
circa 1760
Officer's
Saddle
circa 1751
Trooper's
Saddle
circa 1751
Trooper's Dress
circa 1751

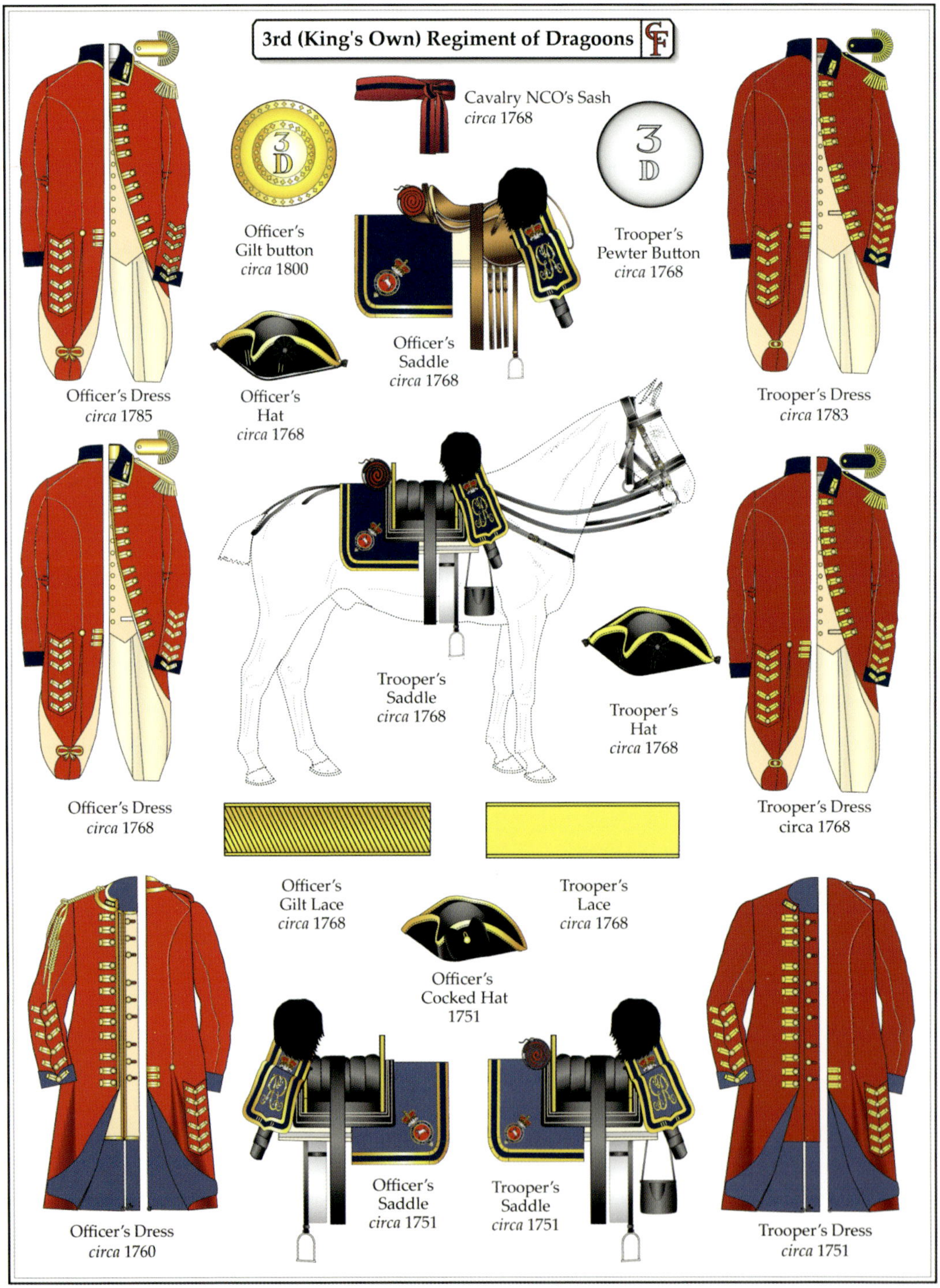
3rd (King's Own) Regiment of Dragoons
Officer's Dress circa 1785
Officer's Gilt button circa 1800
Cavalry NCO's Sash circa 1768
Officer's Saddle circa 1768
Trooper's Pewter Button circa 1768
Trooper's Dress circa 1783
Officer's Hat circa 1768
Officer's Dress circa 1768
Trooper's Saddle circa 1768
Trooper's Hat circa 1768
Trooper's Dress circa 1768
Officer's Gilt Lace circa 1768
Trooper's Lace circa 1768
Officer's Cocked Hat 1751
Officer's Dress circa 1760
Officer's Saddle circa 1751
Trooper's Saddle circa 1751
Trooper's Dress circa 1751

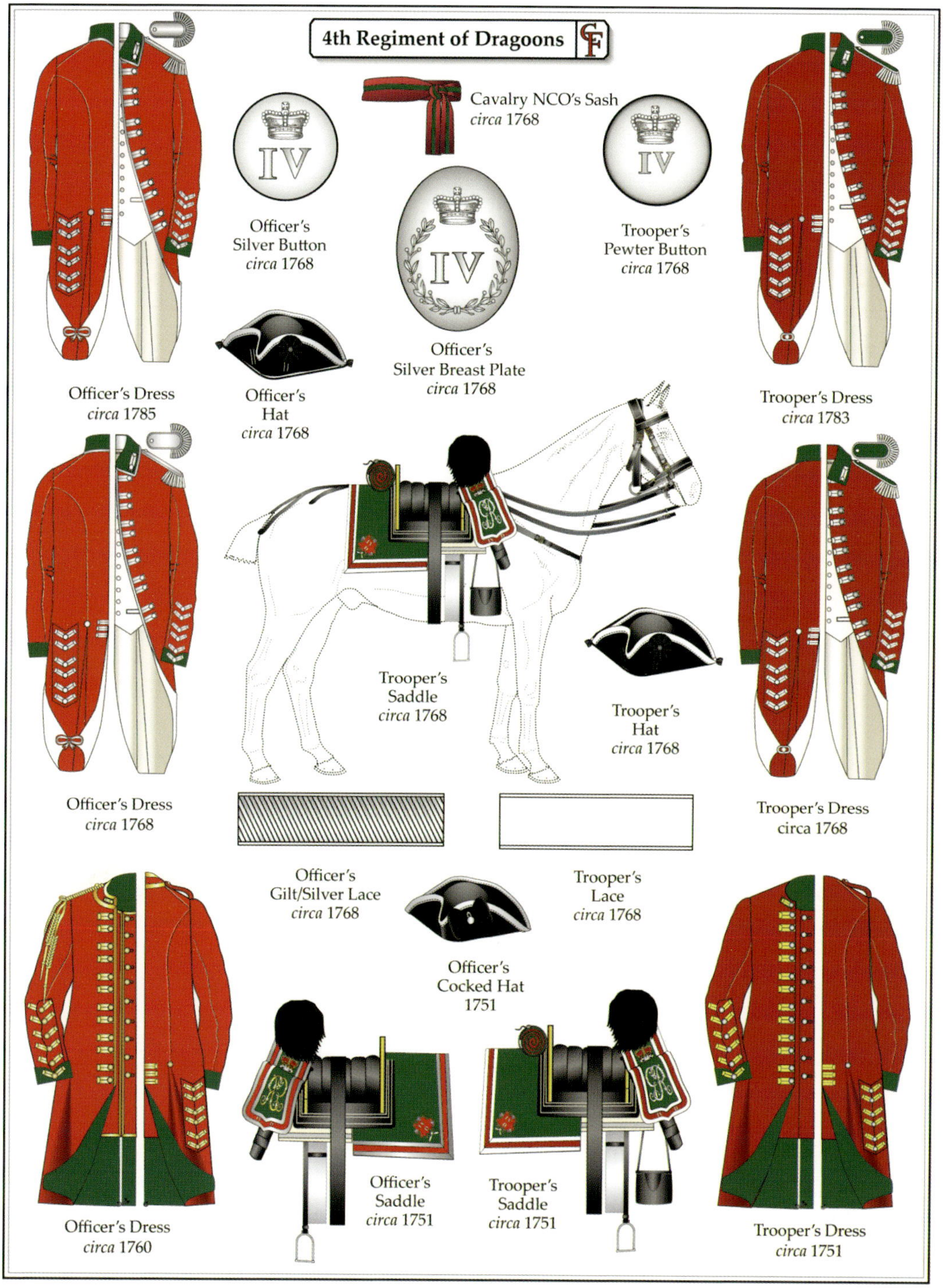
4th Regiment of Dragoons
CF
Officer's Dress circa 1785
Officer's Silver Button circa 1768
Cavalry NCO's Sash circa 1768
Officer's Silver Breast Plate circa 1768
Trooper's Pewter Button circa 1768
Trooper's Dress circa 1783
Officer's Hat circa 1768
Officer's Dress circa 1768
Trooper's Saddle circa 1768
Trooper's Hat circa 1768
Trooper's Dress circa 1768
Officer's Gilt/Silver Lace circa 1768
Trooper's Lace circa 1768
Officer's Cocked Hat 1751
Officer's Dress circa 1760
Officer's Saddle circa 1751
Trooper's Saddle circa 1751
Trooper's Dress circa 1751

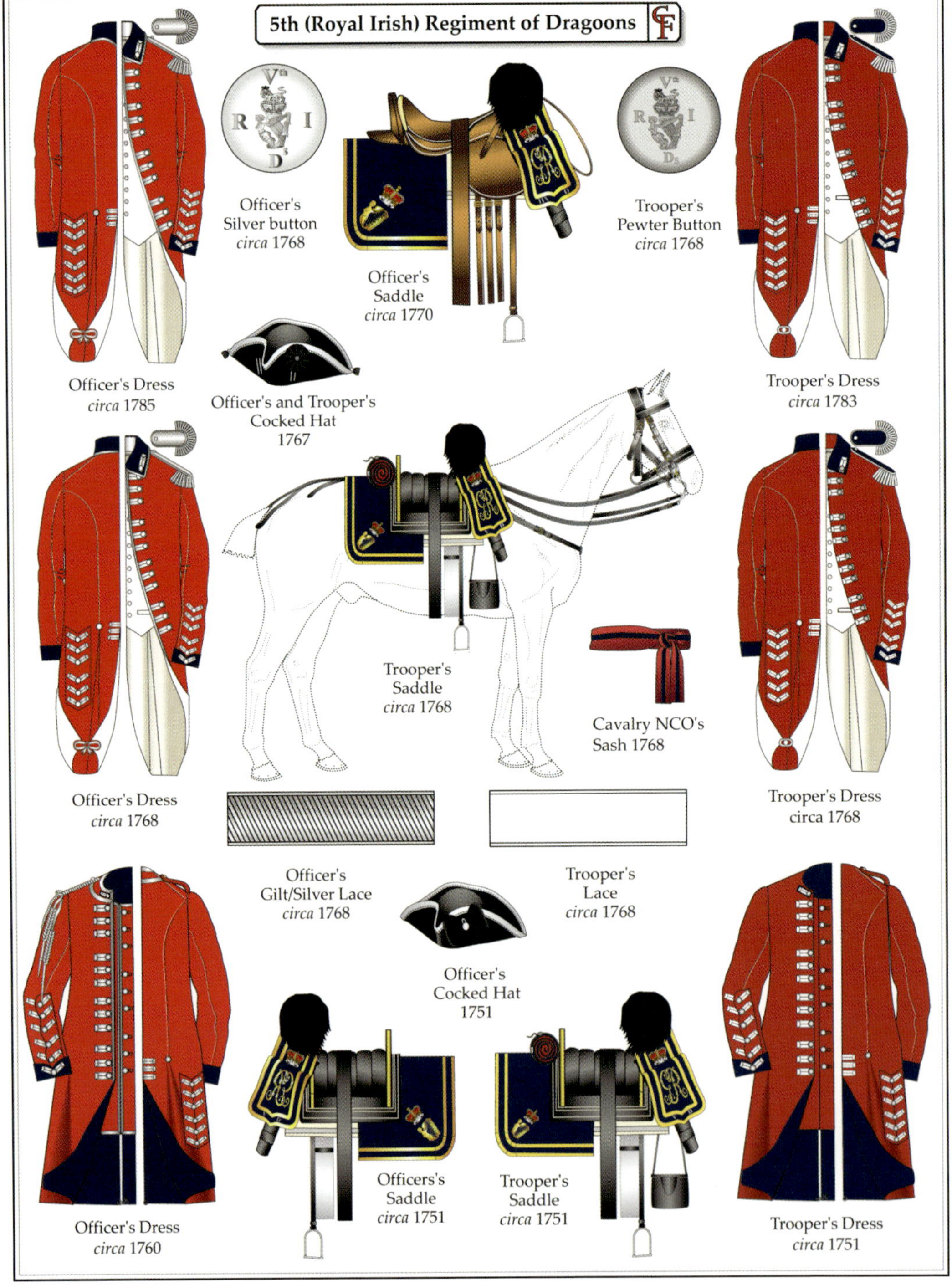
5th (Royal Irish) Regiment of Dragoons
CF
R I
V[th] D[s]
Officer's Silver button circa 1768
Officer's Saddle circa 1770
Trooper's Pewter Button circa 1768
Officer's Dress circa 1785
Officer's and Trooper's Cocked Hat 1767
Trooper's Dress circa 1783
Trooper's Saddle circa 1768
Cavalry NCO's Sash 1768
Officer's Dress circa 1768
Trooper's Dress circa 1768
Officer's Gilt/Silver Lace circa 1768
Trooper's Lace circa 1768
Officer's Cocked Hat 1751
Officers's Saddle circa 1751
Trooper's Saddle circa 1751
Officer's Dress circa 1760
Trooper's Dress circa 1751

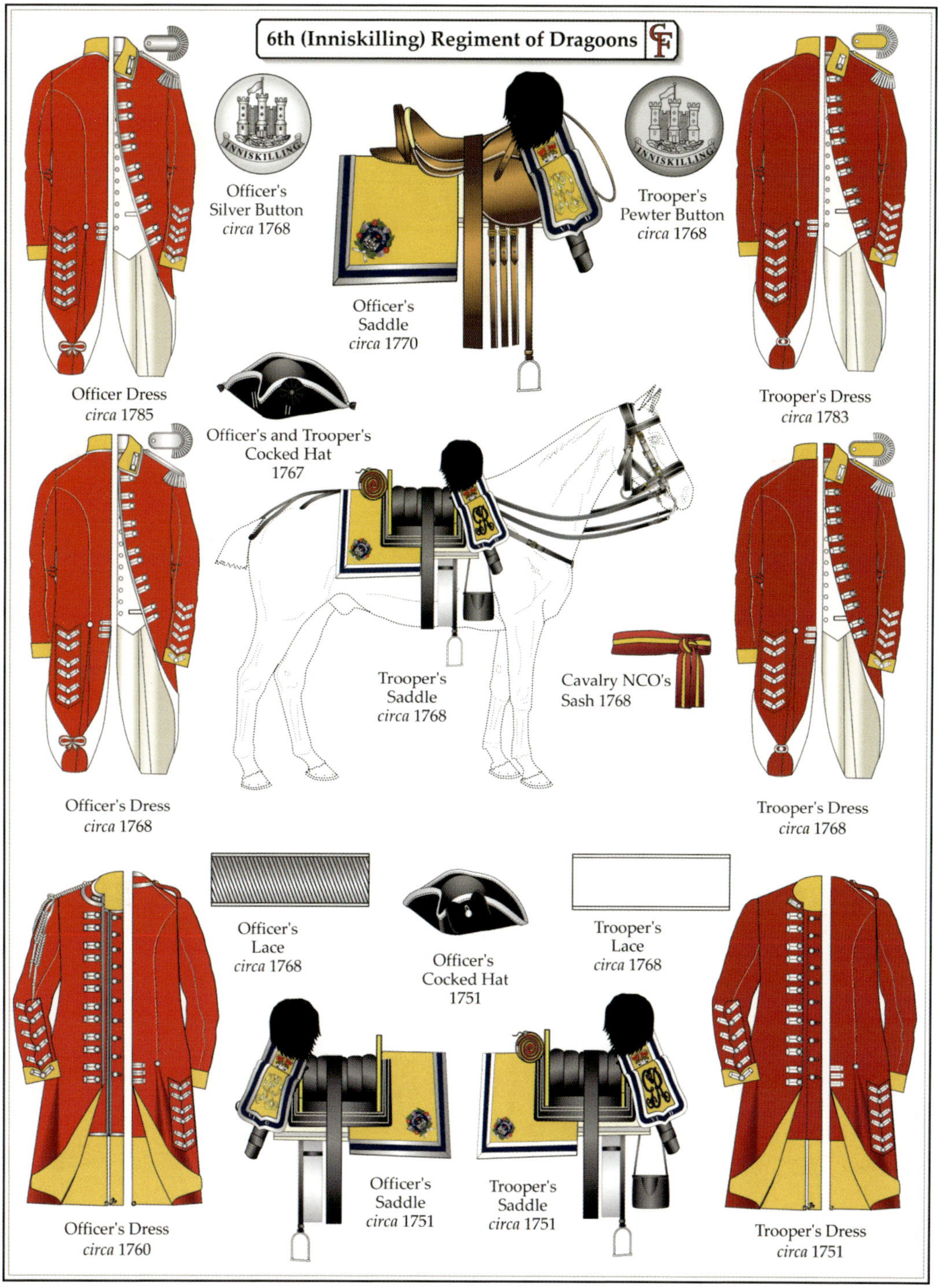
6th (Inniskilling) Regiment of Dragoons
CF
INNISKILLING
Officer's Silver Button circa 1768
Officer's Saddle circa 1770
INNISKILLING
Trooper's Pewter Button circa 1768
Officer Dress circa 1785
Officer's and Trooper's Cocked Hat 1767
Trooper's Dress circa 1783
Trooper's Saddle circa 1768
Cavalry NCO's Sash 1768
Officer's Dress circa 1768
Trooper's Dress circa 1768
Officer's Lace circa 1768
Officer's Cocked Hat 1751
Trooper's Lace circa 1768
Officer's Saddle circa 1751
Trooper's Saddle circa 1751
Officer's Dress circa 1760
Trooper's Dress circa 1751

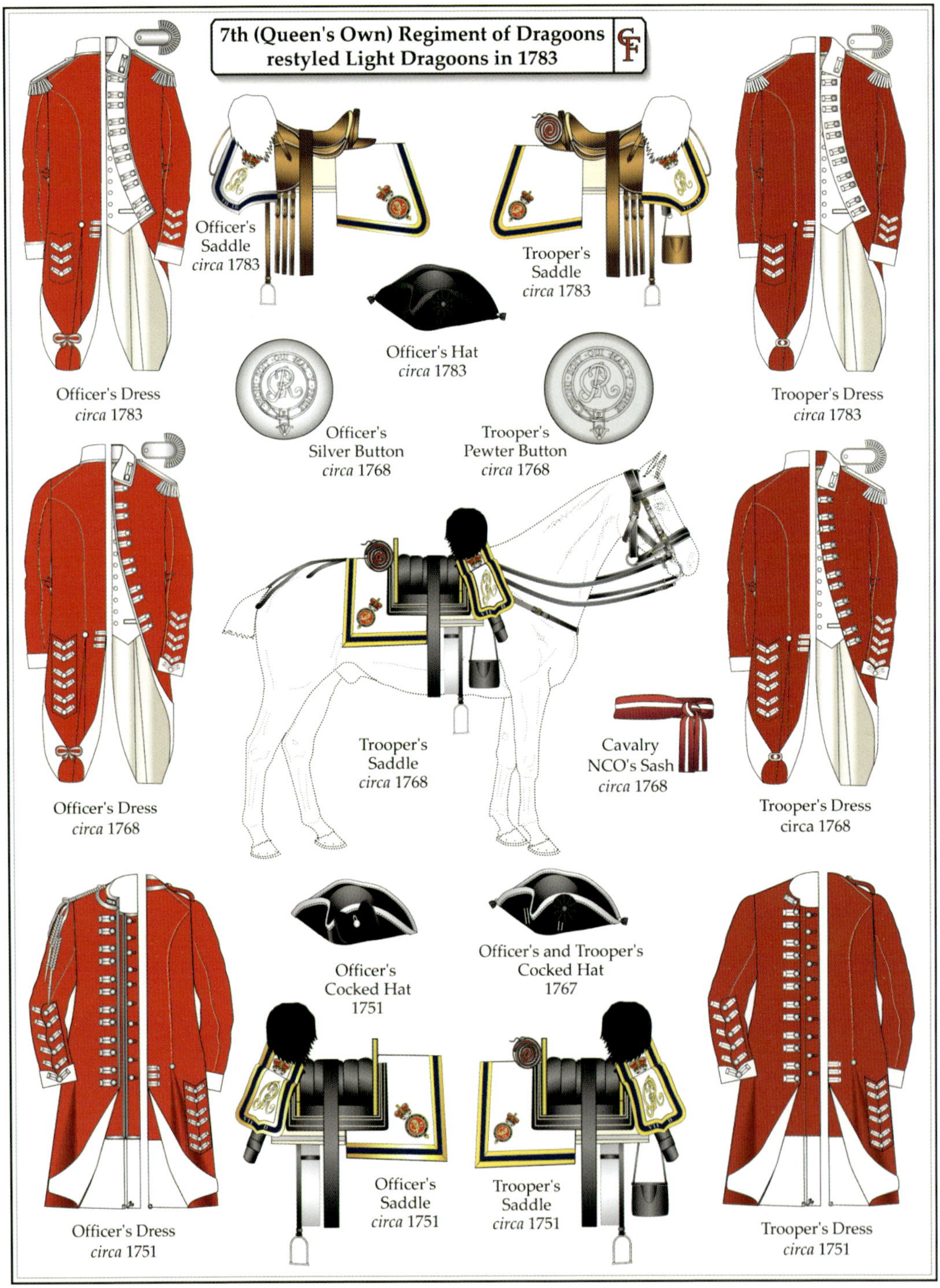
7th (Queen's Own) Regiment of Dragoons
restyled Light Dragoons in 1783
CF
Officer's Saddle circa 1783
Trooper's Saddle circa 1783
Officer's Hat circa 1783
Officer's Dress circa 1783
Trooper's Dress circa 1783
Officer's Silver Button circa 1768
Trooper's Pewter Button circa 1768
Trooper's Saddle circa 1768
Cavalry NCO's Sash circa 1768
Officer's Dress circa 1768
Trooper's Dress circa 1768
Officer's Cocked Hat 1751
Officer's and Trooper's Cocked Hat 1767
Officer's Saddle circa 1751
Trooper's Saddle circa 1751
Officer's Dress circa 1751
Trooper's Dress circa 1751

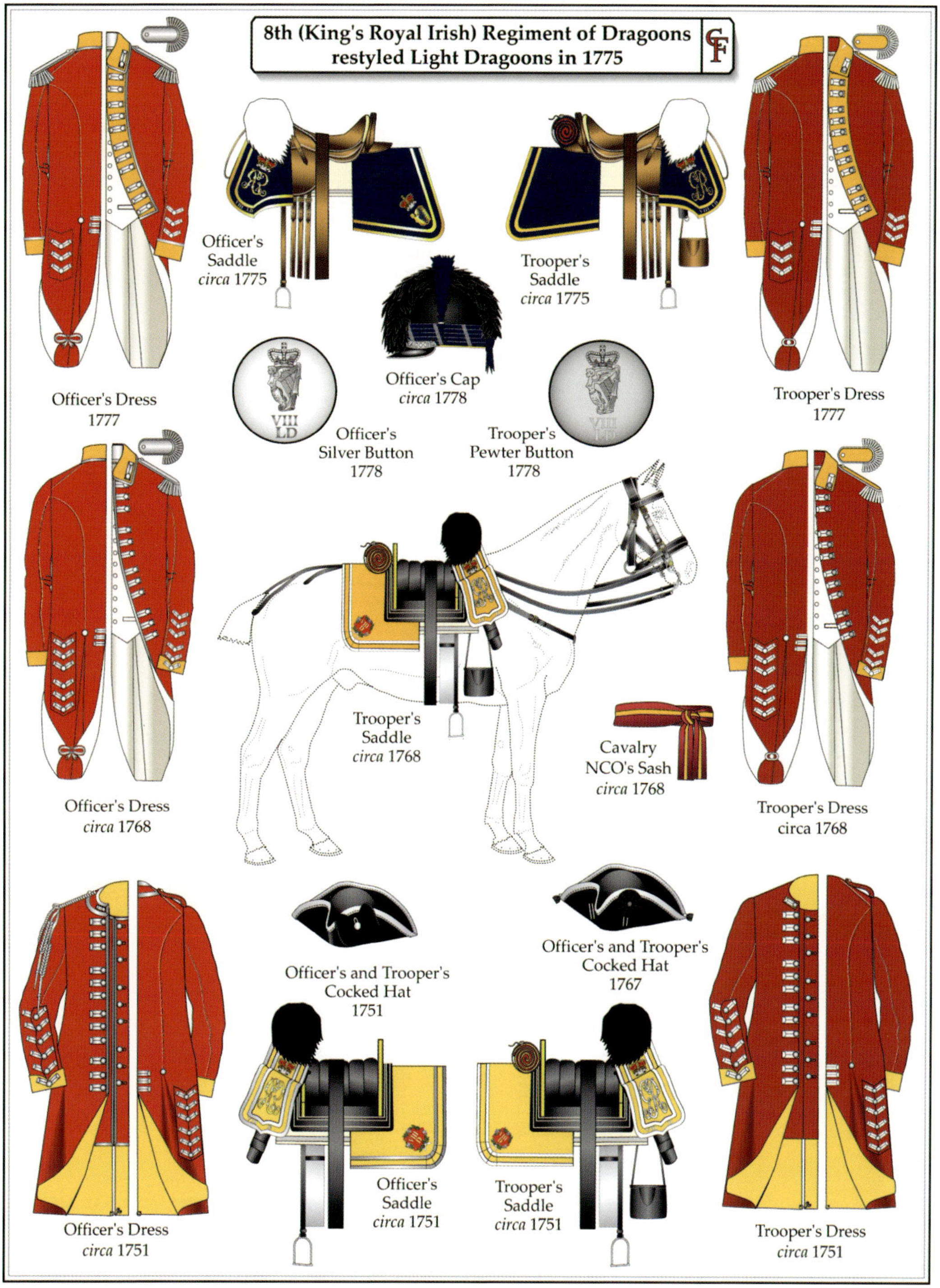
8th (King's Royal Irish) Regiment of Dragoons
restyled Light Dragoons in 1775
CF
Officer's Dress
1777
Officer's Saddle
circa 1775
Trooper's Saddle
circa 1775
Officer's Cap
circa 1778
Trooper's Dress
1777
VIII LD
Officer's Silver Button
1778
Trooper's Pewter Button
1778
Officer's Dress
circa 1768
Trooper's Saddle
circa 1768
Cavalry NCO's Sash
circa 1768
Trooper's Dress
circa 1768
Officer's and Trooper's Cocked Hat
1751
Officer's and Trooper's Cocked Hat
1767
Officer's Dress
circa 1751
Officer's Saddle
circa 1751
Trooper's Saddle
circa 1751
Trooper's Dress
circa 1751

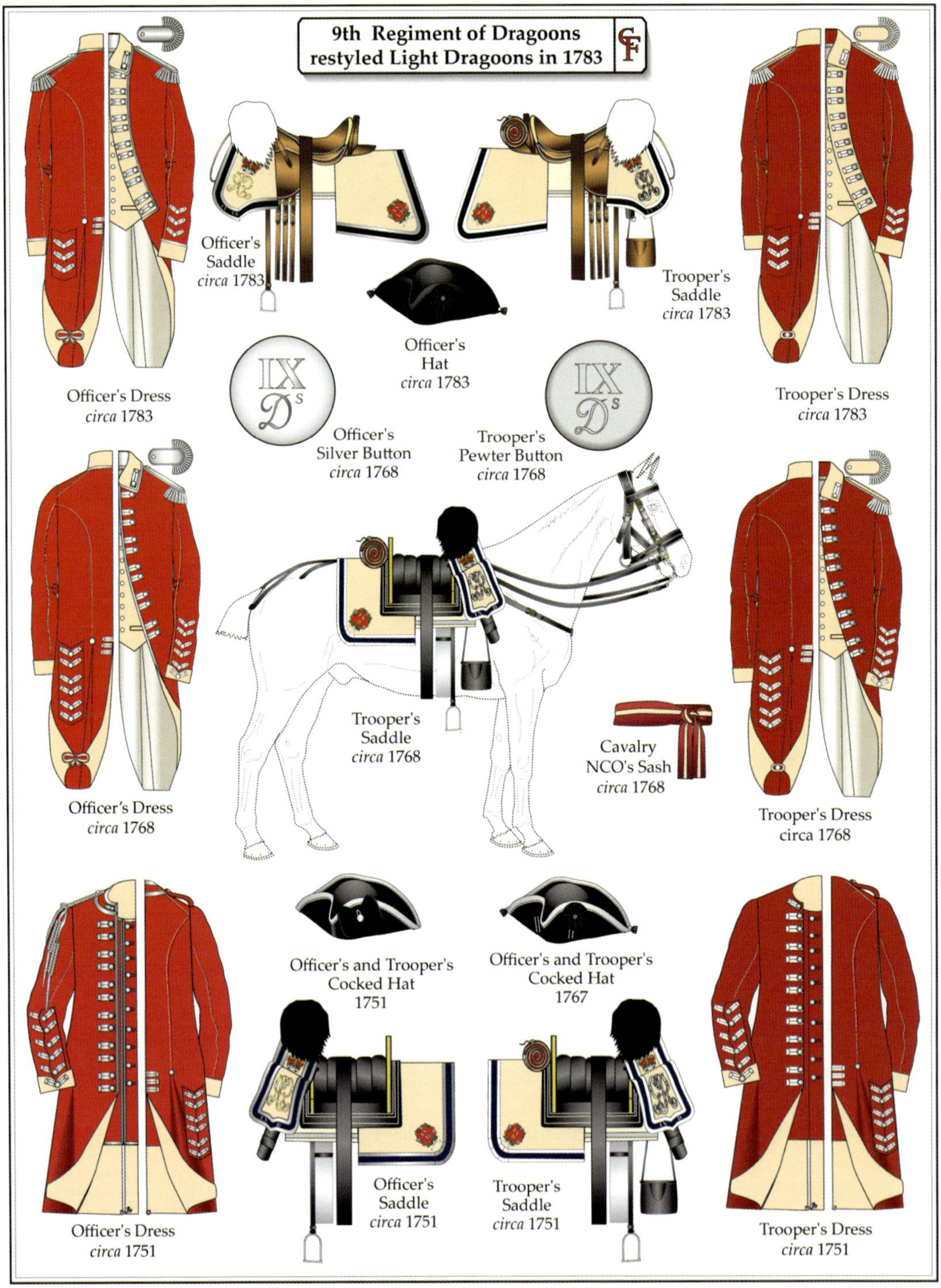
9th Regiment of Dragoons
restyled Light Dragoons in 1783
CF
Officer's Dress
circa 1783
Officer's Saddle
circa 1783
Officer's Hat
circa 1783
Trooper's Saddle
circa 1783
Trooper's Dress
circa 1783
IX
Ds
Officer's Silver Button
circa 1768
Trooper's Pewter Button
circa 1768
Officer's Dress
circa 1768
Trooper's Saddle
circa 1768
Cavalry NCO's Sash
circa 1768
Trooper's Dress
circa 1768
Officer's and Trooper's Cocked Hat
1751
Officer's and Trooper's Cocked Hat
1767
Officer's Dress
circa 1751
Officer's Saddle
circa 1751
Trooper's Saddle
circa 1751
Trooper's Dress
circa 1751

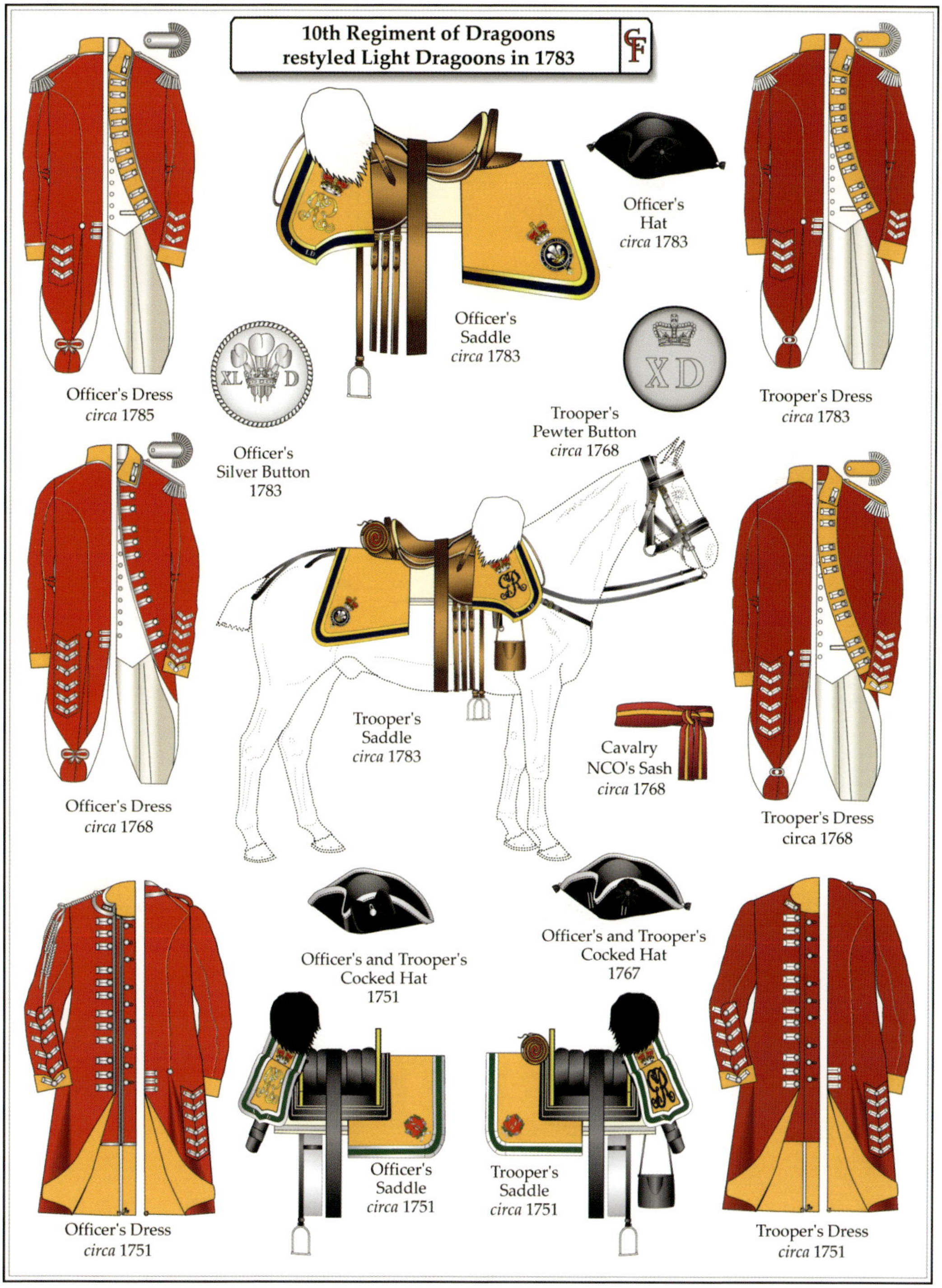
10th Regiment of Dragoons
restyled Light Dragoons in 1783
CF
Officer's Dress
circa 1785
Officer's Saddle
circa 1783
Officer's Hat
circa 1783
Trooper's Dress
circa 1783
XL D
Officer's Silver Button
1783
XD
Trooper's Pewter Button
circa 1768
Officer's Dress
circa 1768
Trooper's Saddle
circa 1783
Cavalry NCO's Sash
circa 1768
Trooper's Dress
circa 1768
Officer's and Trooper's Cocked Hat
1751
Officer's and Trooper's Cocked Hat
1767
Officer's Dress
circa 1751
Officer's Saddle
circa 1751
Trooper's Saddle
circa 1751
Trooper's Dress
circa 1751

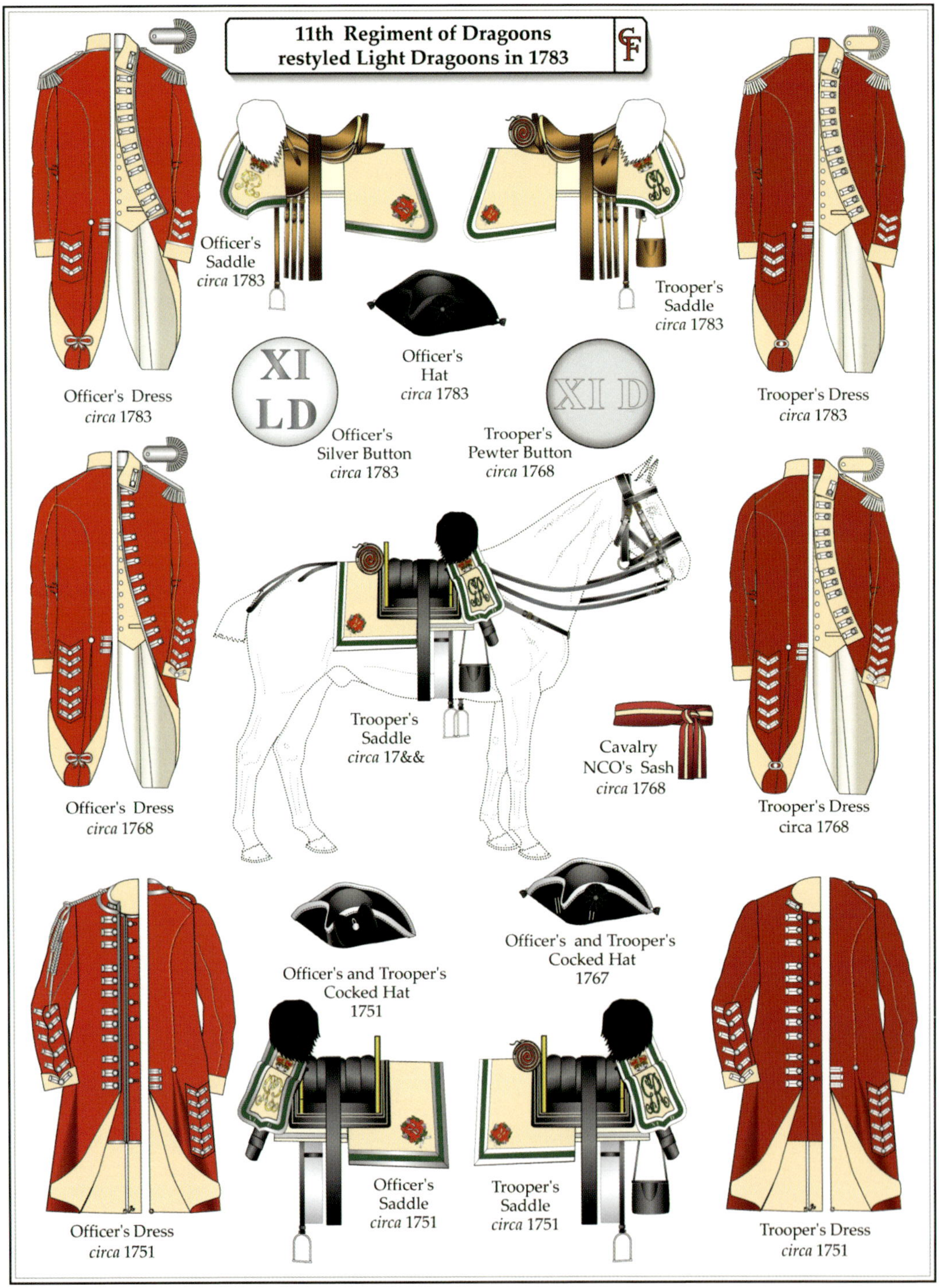
11th Regiment of Dragoons
restyled Light Dragoons in 1783
CF
Officer's Saddle circa 1783
Trooper's Saddle circa 1783
Officer's Hat circa 1783
XI LD
XI D
Officer's Dress circa 1783
Officer's Silver Button circa 1783
Trooper's Pewter Button circa 1768
Trooper's Dress circa 1783
Trooper's Saddle circa 17&&
Cavalry NCO's Sash circa 1768
Officer's Dress circa 1768
Trooper's Dress circa 1768
Officer's and Trooper's Cocked Hat 1767
Officer's and Trooper's Cocked Hat 1751
Officer's Saddle circa 1751
Trooper's Saddle circa 1751
Officer's Dress circa 1751
Trooper's Dress circa 1751

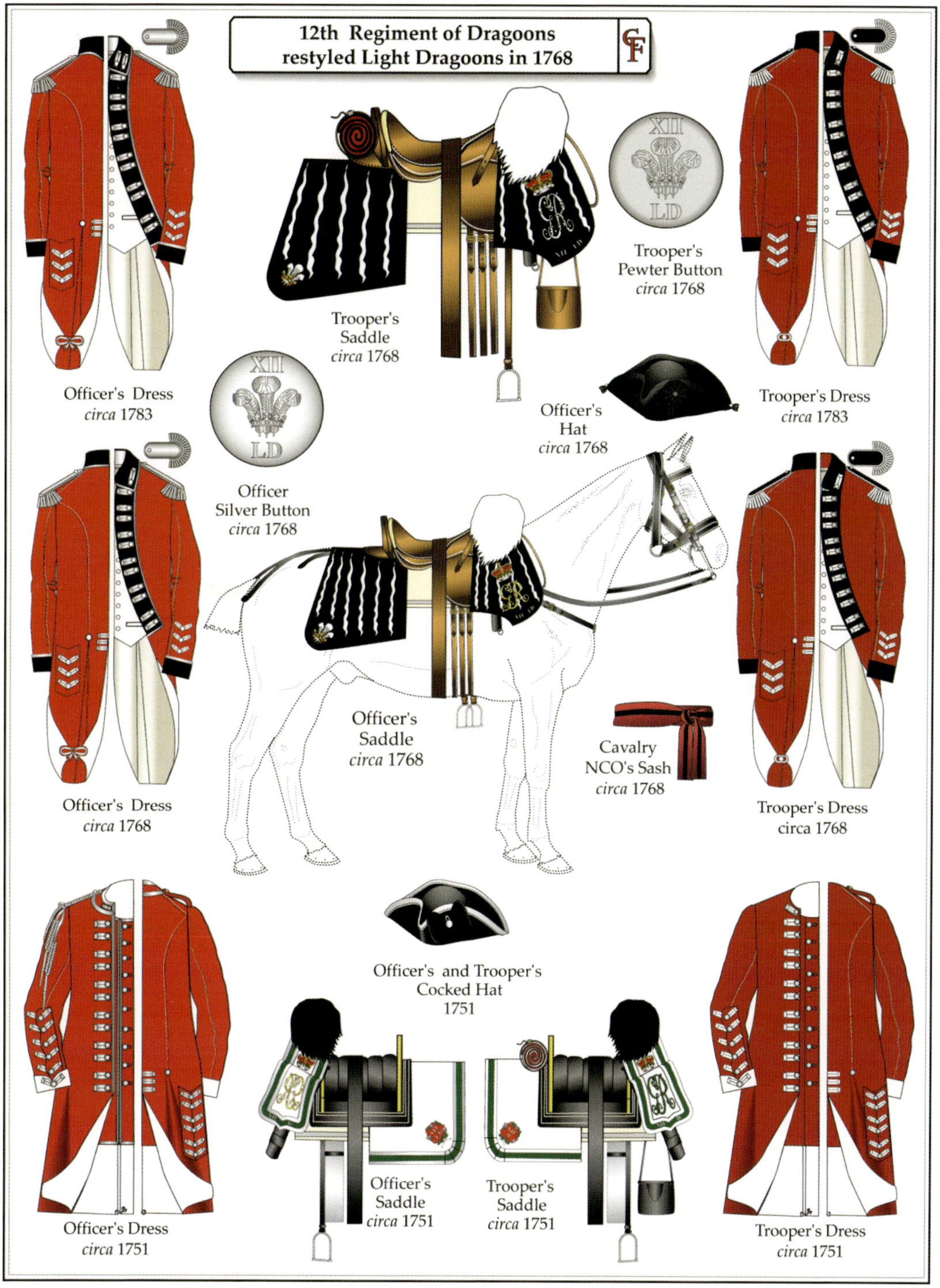
12th Regiment of Dragoons
restyled Light Dragoons in 1768
CF
Officer's Dress
circa 1783
Trooper's Saddle
circa 1768
Trooper's Pewter Button
circa 1768
XII
LD
Trooper's Dress
circa 1783
Officer Silver Button
circa 1768
Officer's Hat
circa 1768
Officer's Dress
circa 1768
Officer's Saddle
circa 1768
Cavalry NCO's Sash
circa 1768
Trooper's Dress
circa 1768
Officer's and Trooper's Cocked Hat
1751
Officer's Dress
circa 1751
Officer's Saddle
circa 1751
Trooper's Saddle
circa 1751
Trooper's Dress
circa 1751

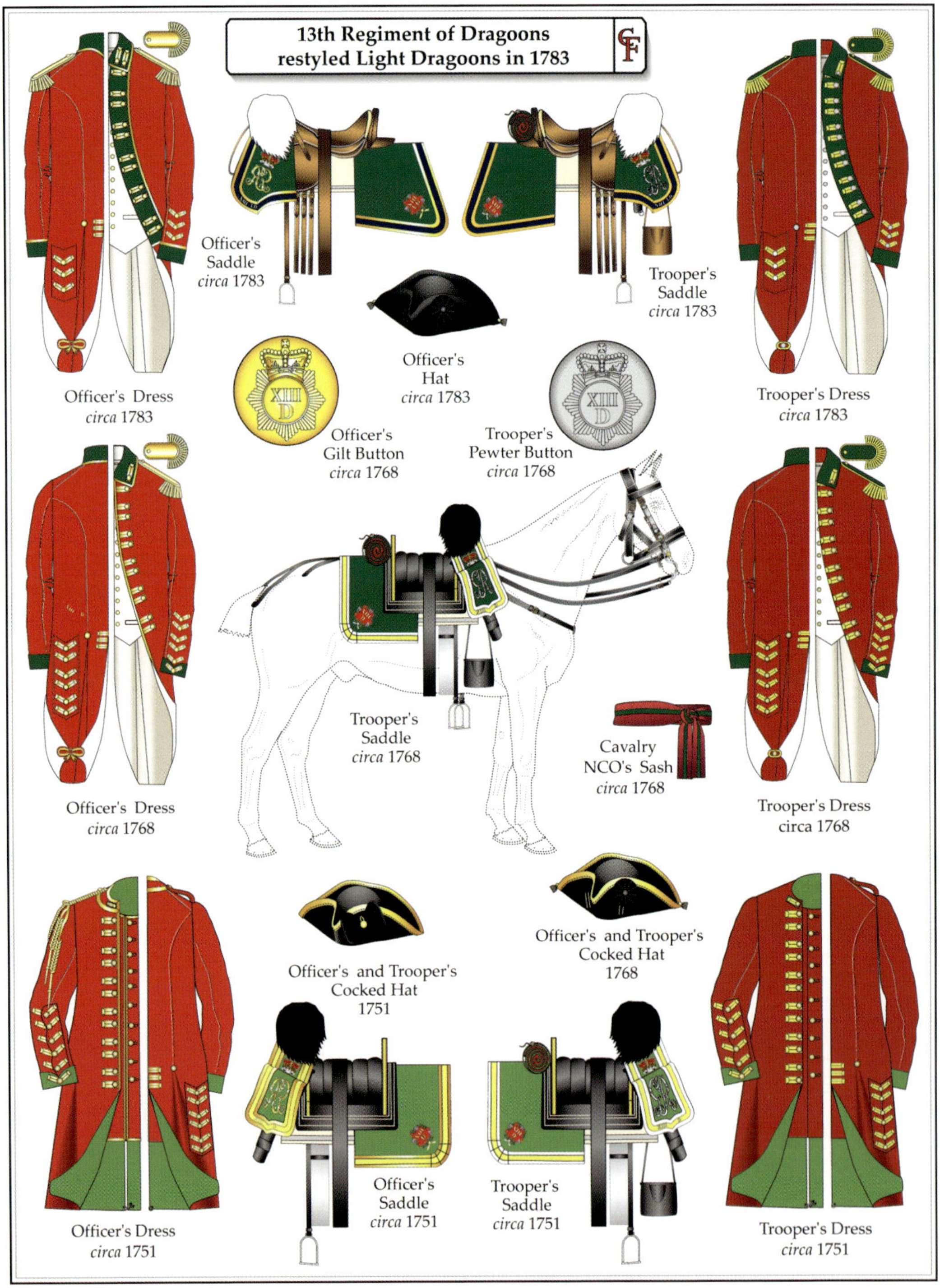
13th Regiment of Dragoons
restyled Light Dragoons in 1783
Officer's Saddle circa 1783
Trooper's Saddle circa 1783
Officer's Dress circa 1783
Officer's Hat circa 1783
Trooper's Dress circa 1783
Officer's Gilt Button circa 1768
Trooper's Pewter Button circa 1768
Officer's Dress circa 1768
Trooper's Saddle circa 1768
Cavalry NCO's Sash circa 1768
Trooper's Dress circa 1768
Officer's and Trooper's Cocked Hat 1768
Officer's and Trooper's Cocked Hat 1751
Officer's Dress circa 1751
Officer's Saddle circa 1751
Trooper's Saddle circa 1751
Trooper's Dress circa 1751

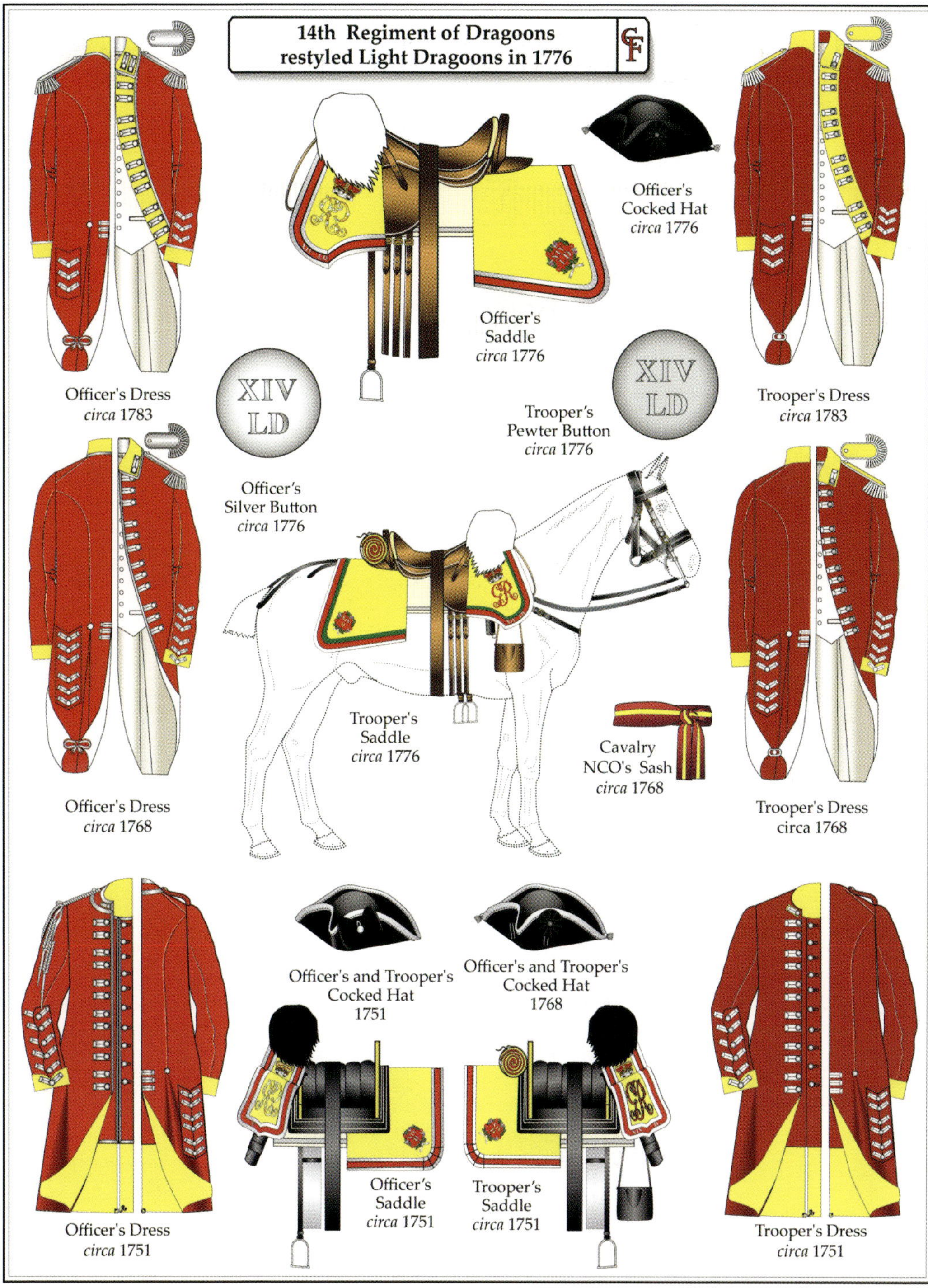
14th Regiment of Dragoons
restyled Light Dragoons in 1776
CF
Officer's Dress
circa 1783
Officer's Saddle
circa 1776
Officer's Cocked Hat
circa 1776
Trooper's Dress
circa 1783
XIV
LD
Officer's Silver Button
circa 1776
XIV
LD
Trooper's Pewter Button
circa 1776
Officer's Dress
circa 1768
Trooper's Saddle
circa 1776
Cavalry NCO's Sash
circa 1768
Trooper's Dress
circa 1768
Officer's and Trooper's Cocked Hat
1751
Officer's and Trooper's Cocked Hat
1768
Officer's Dress
circa 1751
Officer's Saddle
circa 1751
Trooper's Saddle
circa 1751
Trooper's Dress
circa 1751

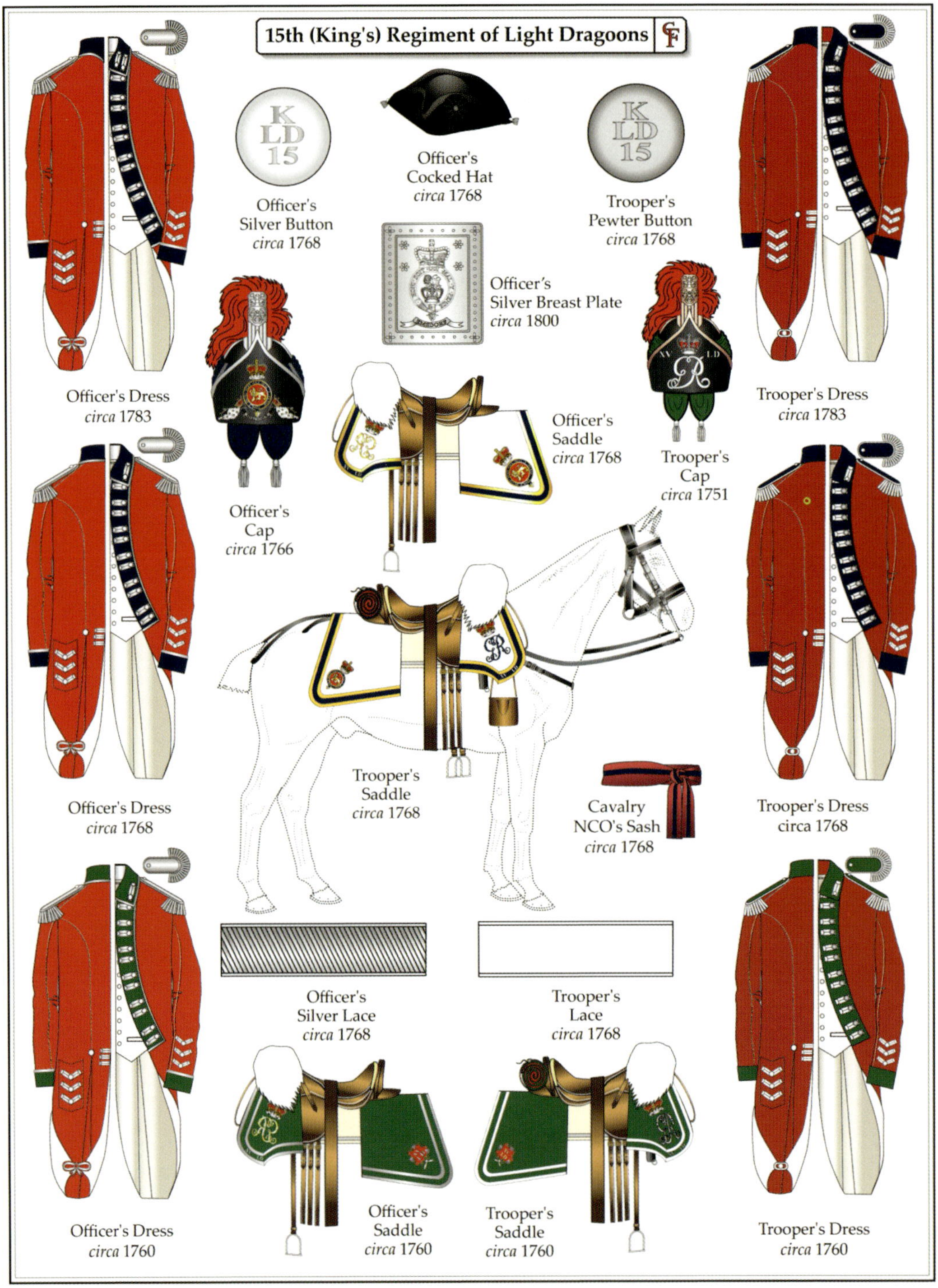
15th (King's) Regiment of Light Dragoons
CF
K LD 15
Officer's Silver Button circa 1768
Officer's Cocked Hat circa 1768
K LD 15
Trooper's Pewter Button circa 1768
Officer's Silver Breast Plate circa 1800
Officer's Dress circa 1783
Trooper's Dress circa 1783
Officer's Cap circa 1766
Officer's Saddle circa 1768
Trooper's Cap circa 1751
Officer's Dress circa 1768
Trooper's Saddle circa 1768
Cavalry NCO's Sash circa 1768
Trooper's Dress circa 1768
Officer's Silver Lace circa 1768
Trooper's Lace circa 1768
Officer's Dress circa 1760
Officer's Saddle circa 1760
Trooper's Saddle circa 1760
Trooper's Dress circa 1760

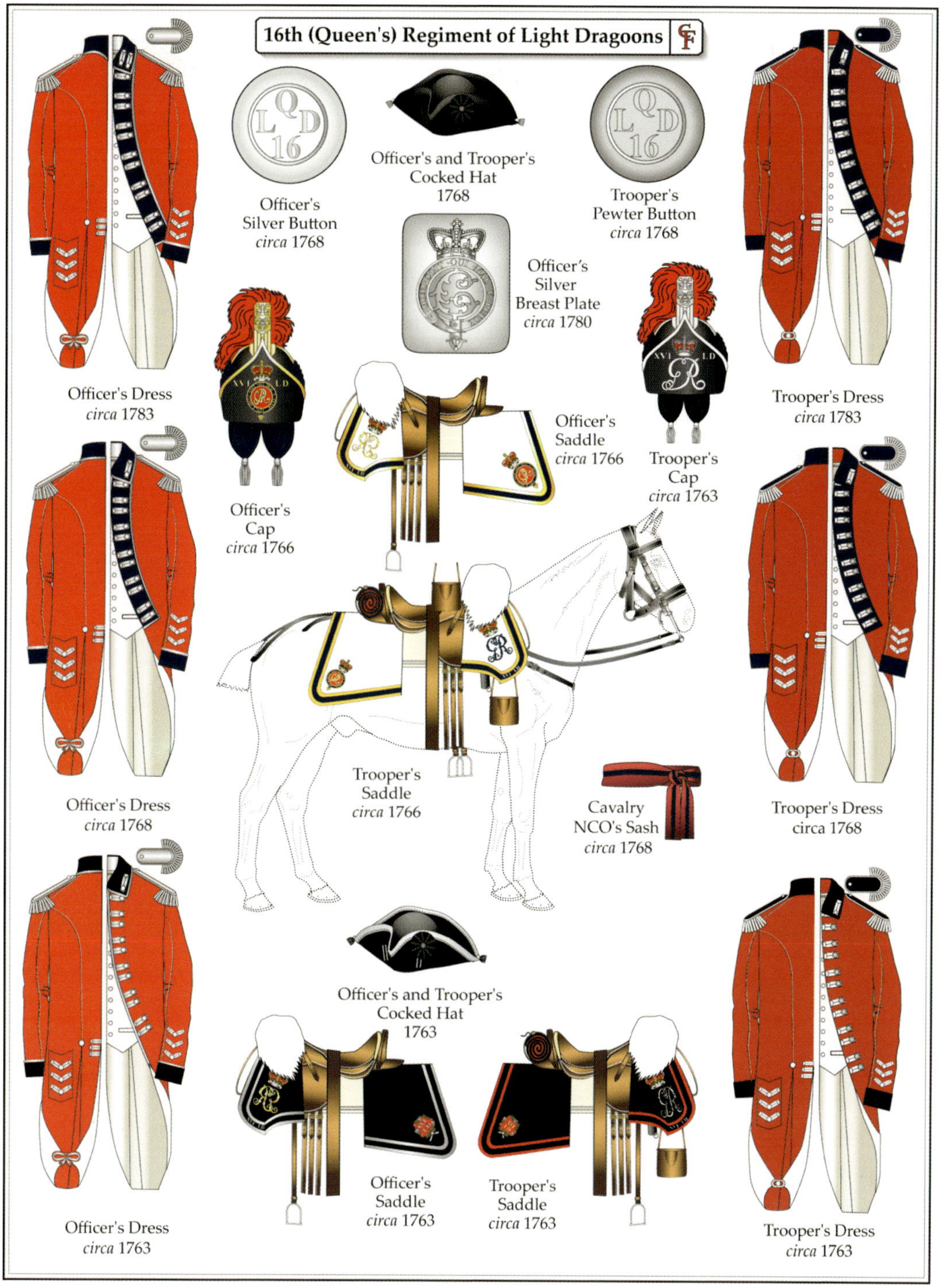
16th (Queen's) Regiment of Light Dragoons
CF
Officer's Silver Button circa 1768
Officer's and Trooper's Cocked Hat 1768
Trooper's Pewter Button circa 1768
Officer's Silver Breast Plate circa 1780
Officer's Dress circa 1783
Trooper's Dress circa 1783
Officer's Cap circa 1766
Officer's Saddle circa 1766
Trooper's Cap circa 1763
Officer's Dress circa 1768
Trooper's Saddle circa 1766
Cavalry NCO's Sash circa 1768
Trooper's Dress circa 1768
Officer's and Trooper's Cocked Hat 1763
Officer's Dress circa 1763
Officer's Saddle circa 1763
Trooper's Saddle circa 1763
Trooper's Dress circa 1763

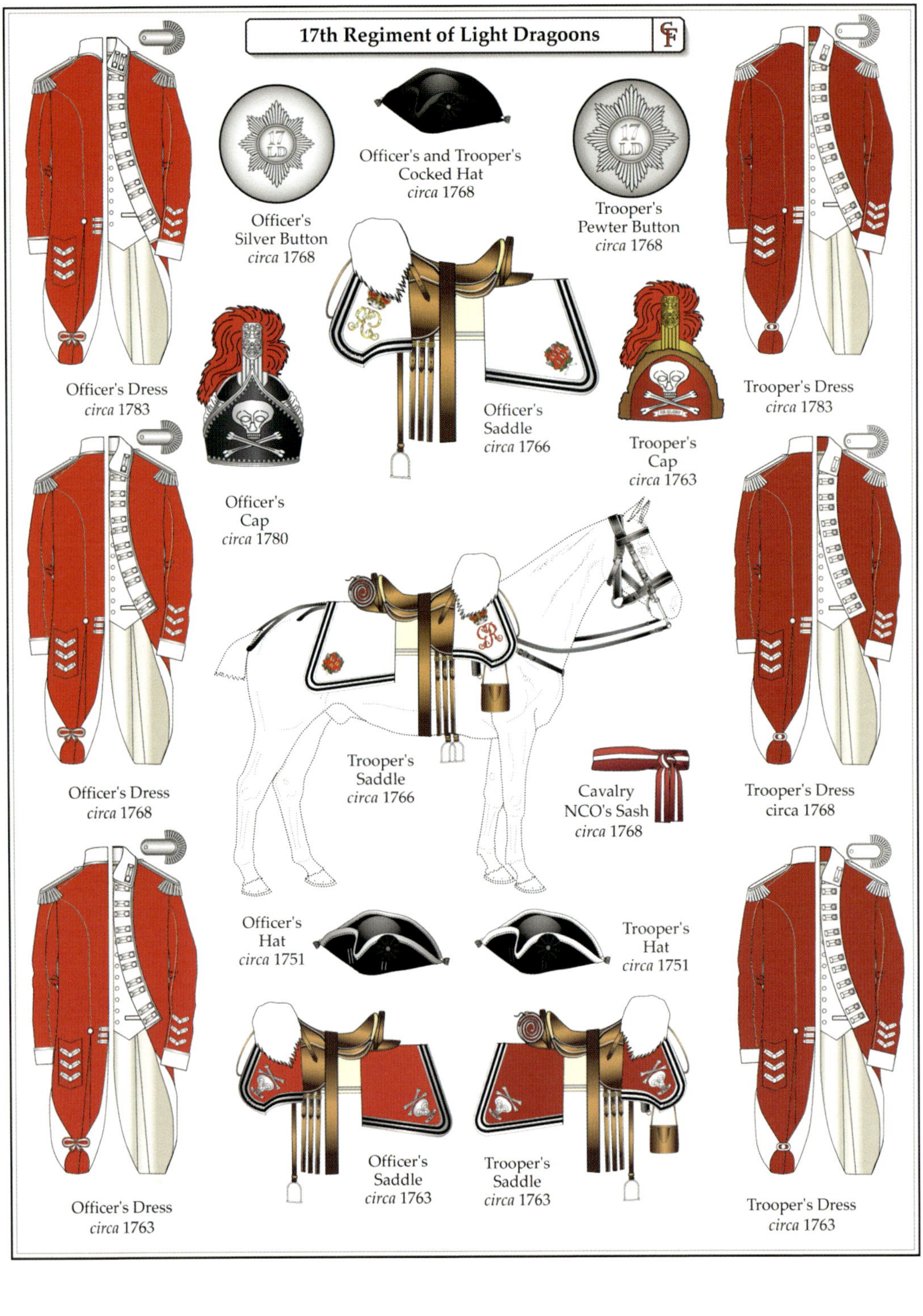
17th Regiment of Light Dragoons
CF
Officer's Dress circa 1783
Officer's Silver Button circa 1768
Officer's and Trooper's Cocked Hat circa 1768
Trooper's Pewter Button circa 1768
Trooper's Dress circa 1783
Officer's Cap circa 1780
Officer's Saddle circa 1766
Trooper's Cap circa 1763
Officer's Dress circa 1768
Trooper's Saddle circa 1766
Cavalry NCO's Sash circa 1768
Trooper's Dress circa 1768
Officer's Hat circa 1751
Trooper's Hat circa 1751
Officer's Dress circa 1763
Officer's Saddle circa 1763
Trooper's Saddle circa 1763
Trooper's Dress circa 1763

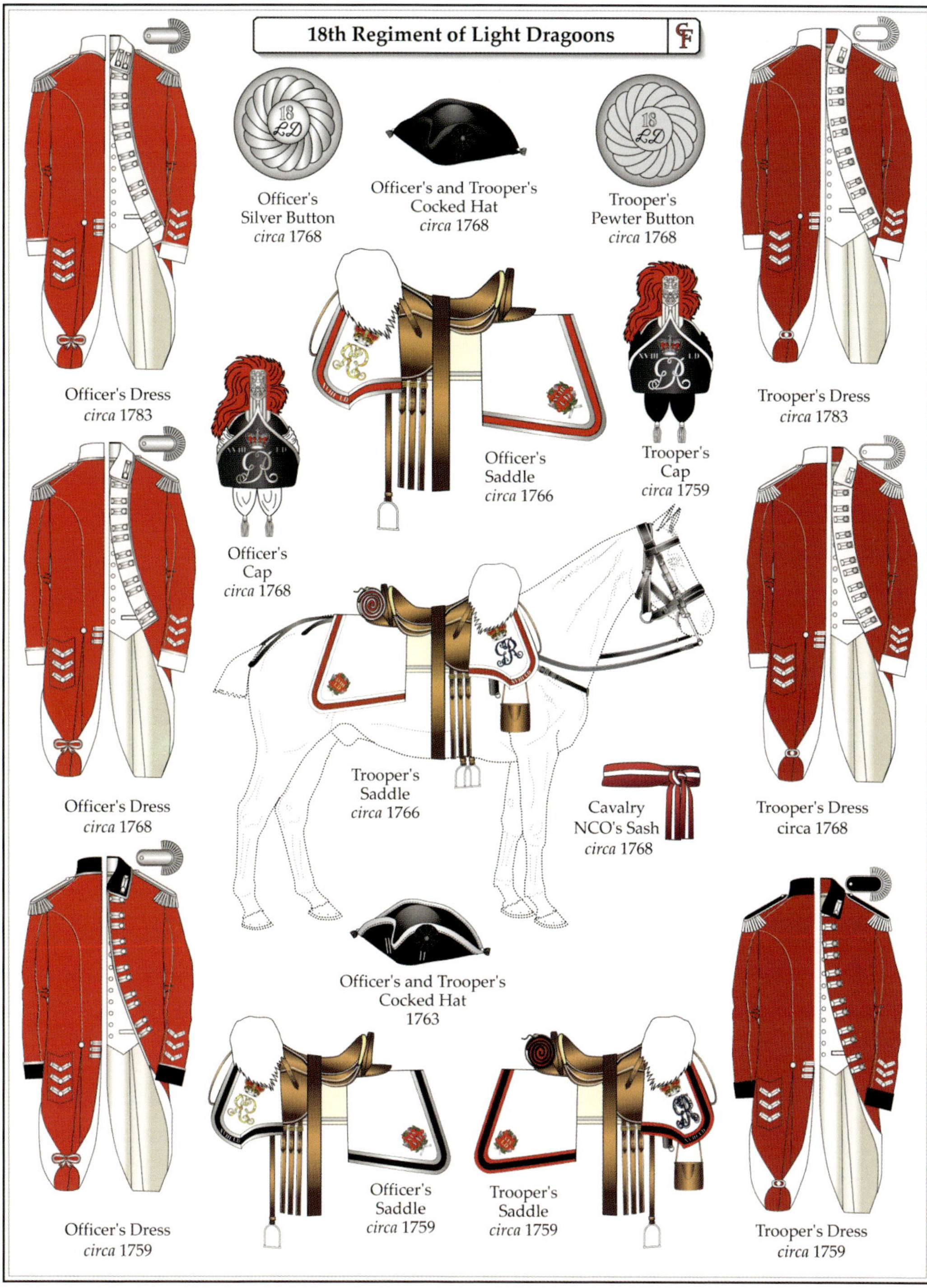
18th Regiment of Light Dragoons
Officer's Silver Button circa 1768
Officer's and Trooper's Cocked Hat circa 1768
Trooper's Pewter Button circa 1768
Officer's Dress circa 1783
Trooper's Dress circa 1783
Officer's Saddle circa 1766
Trooper's Cap circa 1759
Officer's Cap circa 1768
Officer's Dress circa 1768
Trooper's Saddle circa 1766
Cavalry NCO's Sash circa 1768
Trooper's Dress circa 1768
Officer's and Trooper's Cocked Hat 1763
Officer's Saddle circa 1759
Trooper's Saddle circa 1759
Officer's Dress circa 1759
Trooper's Dress circa 1759

21st (Royal Foresters) Regiment of Light Dragoons

Officer's
Cap 1759
(Assumed)

Trooper's
Cap 1759

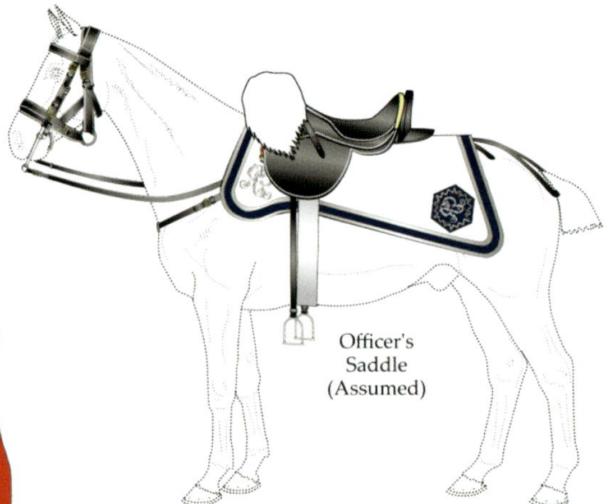

Officer's
Saddle
(Assumed)

Officer's Dress
circa 1763

Trooper's Dress
circa 1763

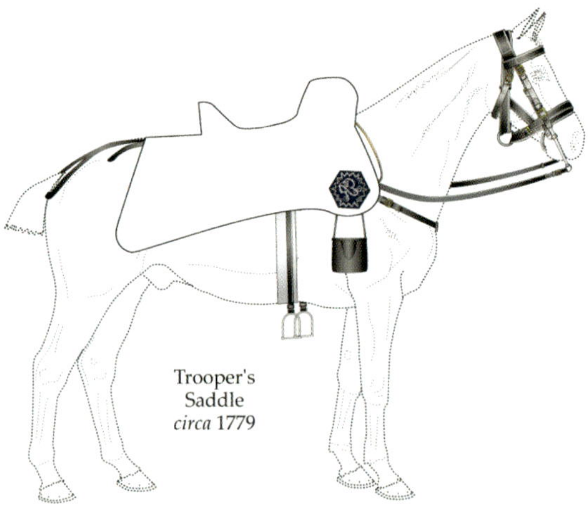

Trooper's
Saddle
circa 1779

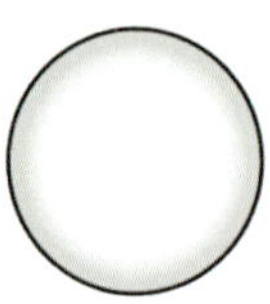

Officer's
Silver Button
circa 1759

Trooper's
Button
circa 1759

This regiment only
existed between
1759 and 1763

20th Regiment of Light Dragoons

Officer's Dress
circa 1783

Officer's and Trooper's
Cocked Hat
circa 1779

Trooper's
Cap
circa 1779

Trooper's Dress
circa 1783

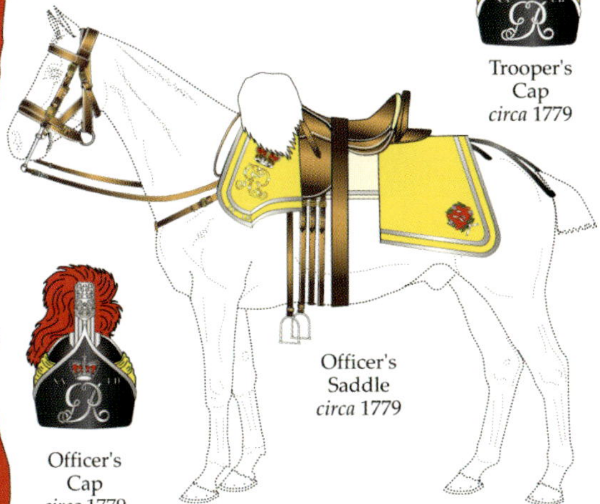

Officer's
Saddle
circa 1779

Officer's
Cap
circa 1779

Officer's Dress
circa 1779

Trooper's Dress
circa 1779

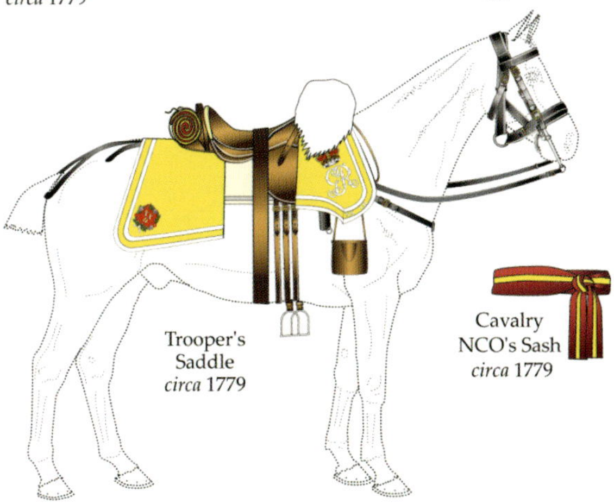

Trooper's
Saddle
circa 1779

Cavalry
NCO's Sash
circa 1779

Officer's
Silver Button
circa 1779

Trooper's
Pewter Button
circa 1779

This regiment only existed between 1779 and 1783

21st (Royal Foresters) Regiment of Light Dragoons

Officer's
Cap 1759
(Assumed)

Trooper's
Cap 1759

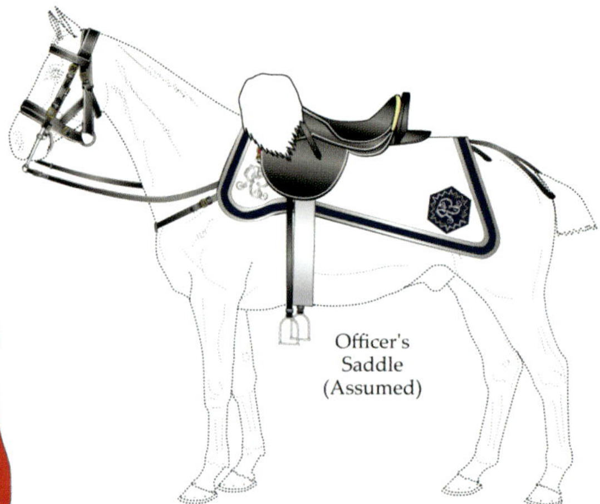

Officer's
Saddle
(Assumed)

Officer's Dress
circa 1763

Trooper's Dress
circa 1763

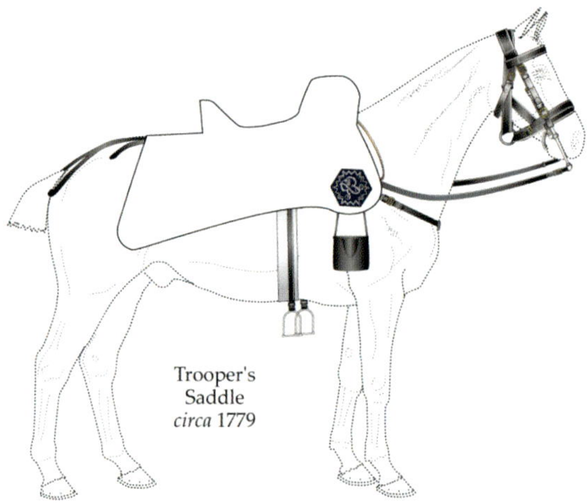

Trooper's
Saddle
circa 1779

Officer's
Silver Button
circa 1759

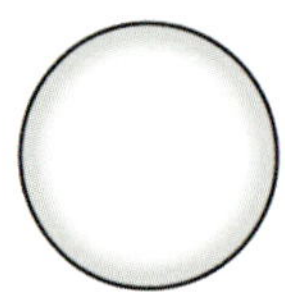

Trooper's
Button
circa 1759

This regiment only
existed between
1759 and 1763

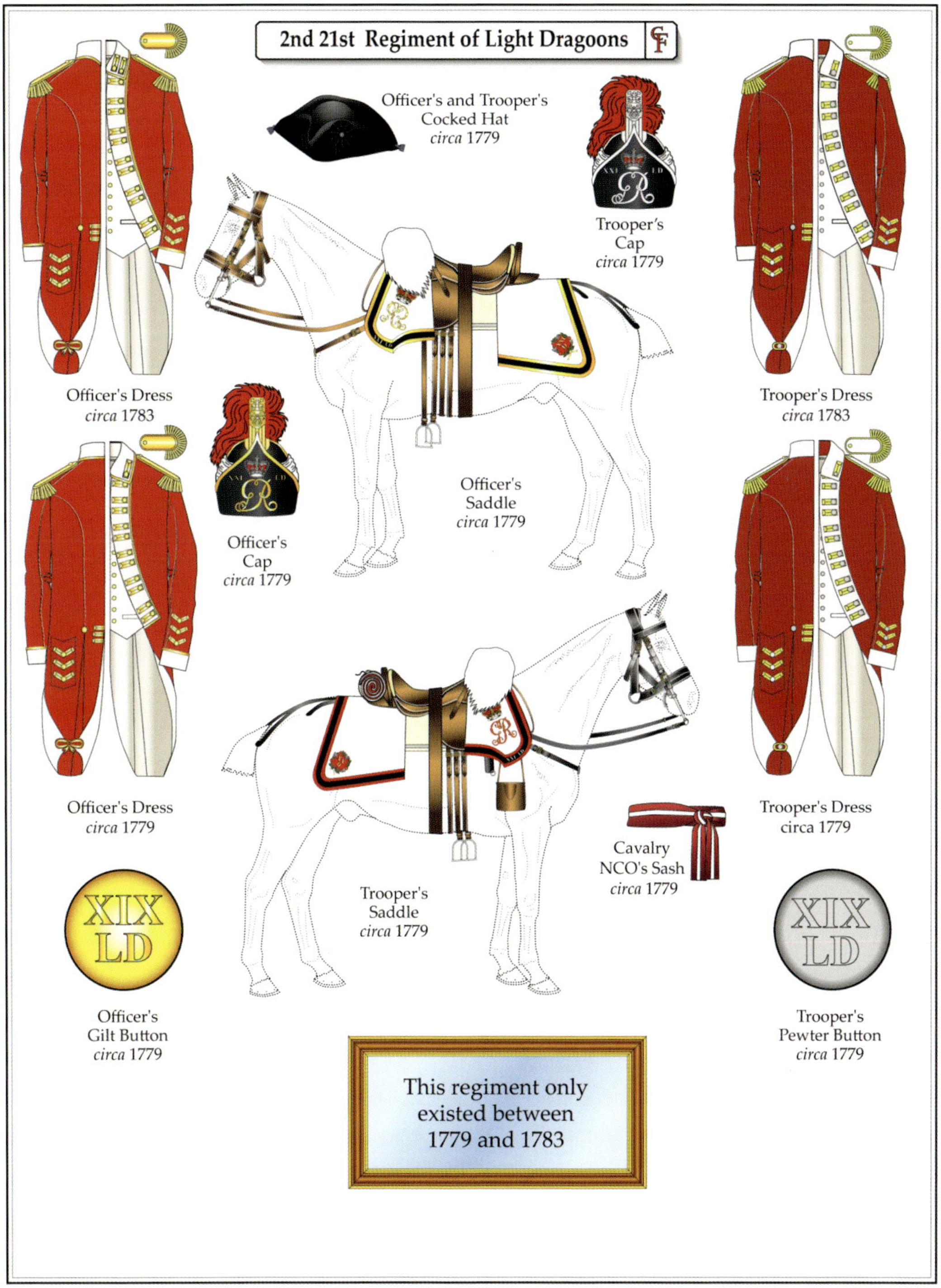
2nd 21st Regiment of Light Dragoons
CF
Officer's and Trooper's
Cocked Hat
circa 1779
Trooper's
Cap
circa 1779
Officer's Dress
circa 1783
Trooper's Dress
circa 1783
Officer's
Saddle
circa 1779
Officer's
Cap
circa 1779
Officer's Dress
circa 1779
Trooper's Dress
circa 1779
Cavalry
NCO's Sash
circa 1779
Trooper's
Saddle
circa 1779
XIX
LD
Officer's
Gilt Button
circa 1779
XIX
LD
Trooper's
Pewter Button
circa 1779
This regiment only
existed between
1779 and 1783

22nd Regiment of Light Dragoons

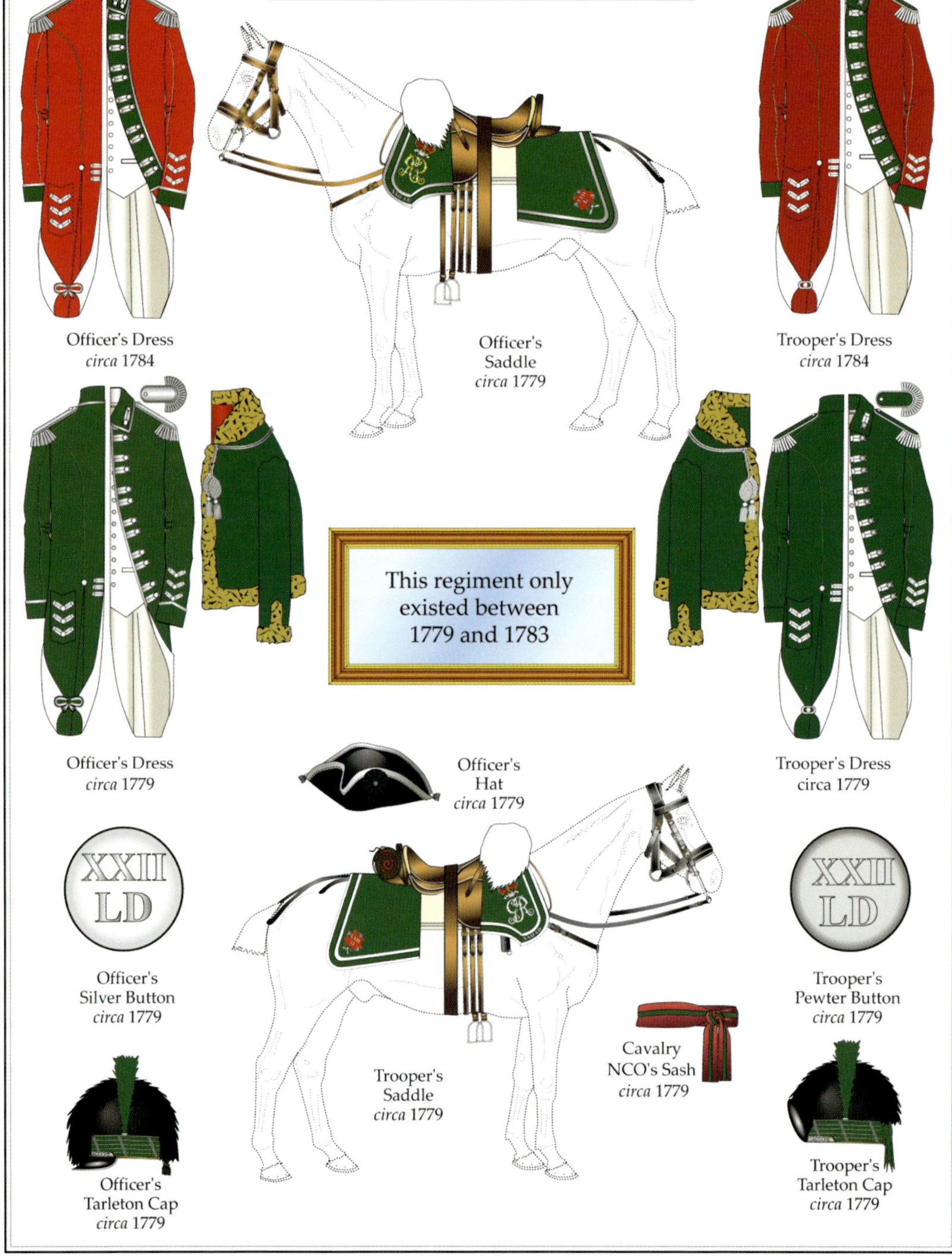

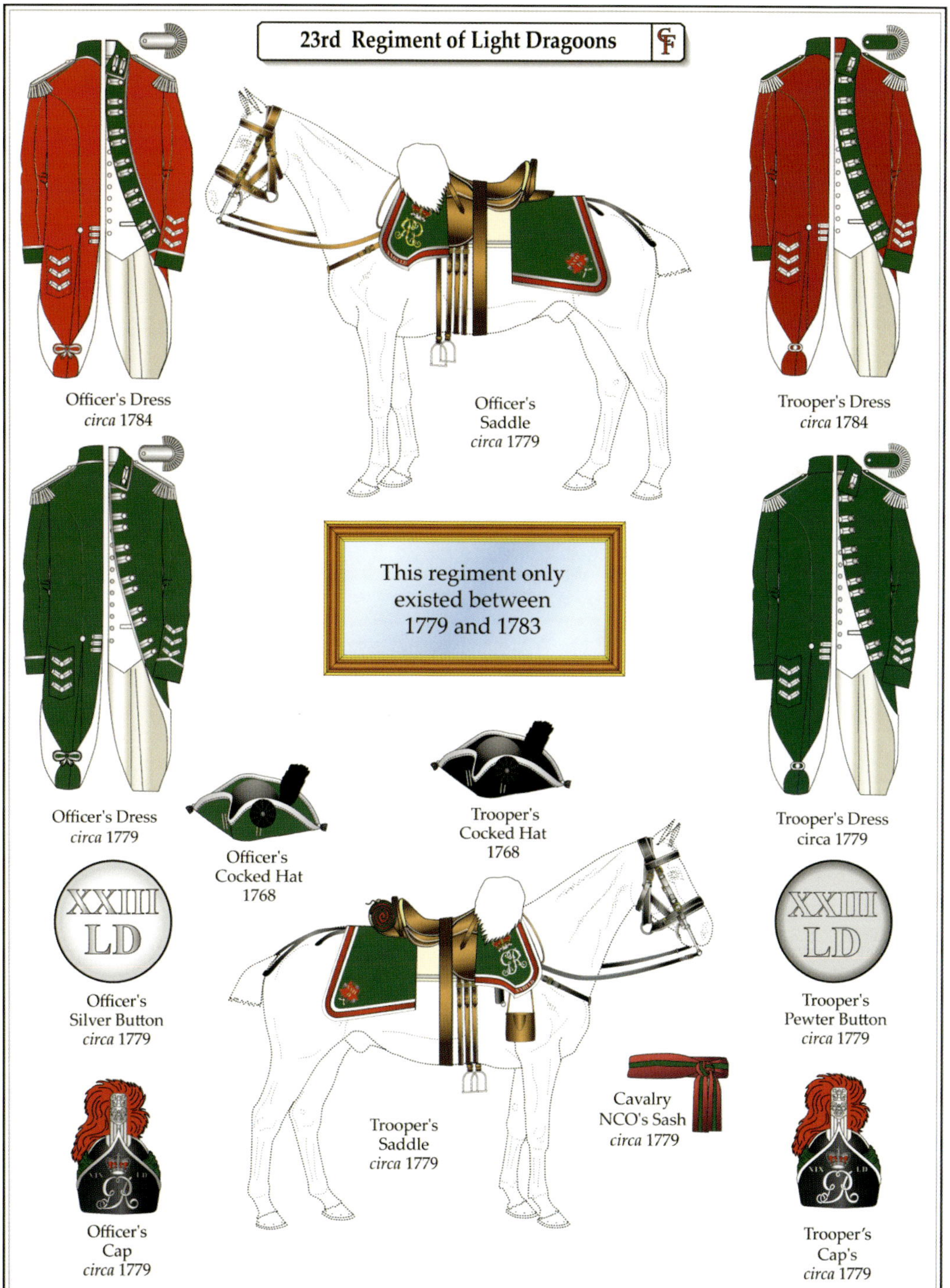
23rd Regiment of Light Dragoons
Officer's Dress
circa 1784
Officer's Saddle
circa 1779
Trooper's Dress
circa 1784
This regiment only existed between 1779 and 1783
Officer's Dress
circa 1779
Officer's Cocked Hat
1768
Trooper's Cocked Hat
1768
Trooper's Dress
circa 1779
XXIII
LD
Officer's Silver Button
circa 1779
XXIII
LD
Trooper's Pewter Button
circa 1779
Trooper's Saddle
circa 1779
Cavalry NCO's Sash
circa 1779
Officer's Cap
circa 1779
Trooper's Cap's
circa 1779

PART THREE

CHAPTER ELEVEN

Infantry Headwear

Tricorne Hat

This hat is more fully discussed under cavalry headwear in Chapter 1 but most of the general description still applies although in the infantry there were obvious differences; it became common practice in some regiments after the 1768 warrant to wear small and oddly cocked hats and to wear the Hanoverian cords and tassels. Each cord now passed around the crown, passing through the loop of the other, with the tassel end hanging from the lock in the hat. The cords were in gold or silver for the officers and yellow or white for enlisted men; the hats were still laced about with white and yellow braid one and a quarter inches wide for the rank and file and silver or gilt for the officers. The non commissioned officers (NCOs) wore either silver or gilt lace while the 42nd Highland NCOs wore silver lace. Other regiments like the Foot Guards wore gilt lace for all ranks. The left turn-up held a black Hanoverian cockade of woven horsehair, held in place for officers by a loop of the regimental metal and regimental button and, for the private men, a similar cockade with a black loop and regimental button.

The Cocked Hat or Tricorne. The early hat of a gold-laced regiment (1). The early round hat worn by troops serving abroad (2). The later version with the bearskin crest (3). The later hat of an enlisted man with tassels (4) and the later hat of an enlisted man without tassels (5).

Mitre Cap of the Grenadiers, Drummers and Fusiliers circa 1751

Grenadiers had been introduced into the Army in 1678 and the mitre cap was introduced to prevent knocking off the Tricorne when throwing grenades. Originally the cap was formed from a tasseled stocking with a turn-up to the front and to the rear. Over time the styles evolved but was regulated in 1749, when the practice of regimental or family crests was abandoned. At the top of the cap was a white woolen tuft with a centre of coloured threads. The front was covered with facing material mounted on a shaped stiffened card, or of felt, and embroidered with the Royal Cypher (Georges Rex) surmounted by a crown and other foliate designs. At the bottom of the front face was a small red flap embroidered with 'Nec Aspera Terrent' ('difficulties taunt us not') with the white horse of Hanover underneath, mounted over a ground of green and yellow. Those regiments with special badges and distinctions, including the six old corps were permitted to wear them. The rear of the cap had a piece of red cloth stitched to the stiffened front and two pieces of cane to retain the shape, with coloured tape placed over the sides and back to conceal the stitching. At the rear there was a small flap of facing material at the bottom with the number of the regiment, a flaming grenade and, often, other foliate designs. The cap was lined with unbleached linen with a strip of regimental lace running around the bottom edge. To prevent caps from falling off they were usually fitted with tapes sewn into the lining and tied or secured with hooks and eyes, worn under the pleat of the hair. The caps of officers were usually decorated with silver or gold thread and were generally much more lavish in their decoration. To cover these mitre caps during inclement weather canvas covers, often painted with similar designs, were worn. In normal dress the cover was worn hooked into the pleat of the coat and over the left hip button. Drummers wore caps similar to the grenadiers, but the bag hung down at the back with a tassel at the end and the rear carried an embroidered drum. The stiffened front was of facing colour and carried a trophy of drums and arms.

Grenadier and Fusilier mitre caps of 1742 and 1755. A front and rear view of the early grenadier cap of the 49th Regiment in 1742 (1). The cap according to the 1749 regulations showing the side and front view for the 10th Regiment (2). The rear view of caps for the 67th and 19th Regiments (3). The rear view of an officer's cap of the 64th Regiment but the caps of both officers and men were often decorated at the rear with foliate designs.

Drummer Caps circa 1755. Drummer's cap of a Royal regiment (1). The rear view after Morier (2). The rear view of a later drummer mitre cap of a green-faced regiment (3). The rear view of a yellow-faced regiment (4) and the front view of a drummer mitre cap of a bright-yellow-faced regiment (5).

Fur Cap of Grenadiers of the 42nd, circa 1751

This was the only regiment to wear a fur cap during the period; the others all wore the mitre, although it is considered that some other regiments followed the pattern. It was the pattern for highland grenadier regiments in the blackest colour available and only five inches tall. The helmet plate at the front was of red and white painted copper. It was worn without plumes or tassels.

Fur Cap of Grenadiers, Drummers and Fusiliers, circa 1768

Some regiments are known to have worn these caps before the introduction of the 1768 Warrant, and others like the 30th were wearing fur caps in 1755. Where inspection returns are known to have recorded these events they are entered under the respective regiment. Grenadiers and drummers were all eventually issued with twelve-inch-tall fur caps. Usually shown as black they were made from a very dark brown or black bearskin, while others are recorded as wearing white fur and the caps of officers were usually decorated with silver or gold thread; those used by the fusiliers are recorded as being shorter in height. The fur caps of 1768 had the fur rising towards the top in a tapered point and the rear carried a red patch often embroidered with a regimental number or some other distinction, particularly for the six old corps and it quickly became practice to use cords and tassels to decorate them when in full dress. The caps of the grenadiers had a grenade at the rear; the drummers had a drum, both with the number of the regiment upon it. Fur caps were often worn in dress but the grenadiers and drummers often wore the cocked hat when on campaign, as did the officers, although there is clear evidence that fusiliers wore the hat on most occasions.

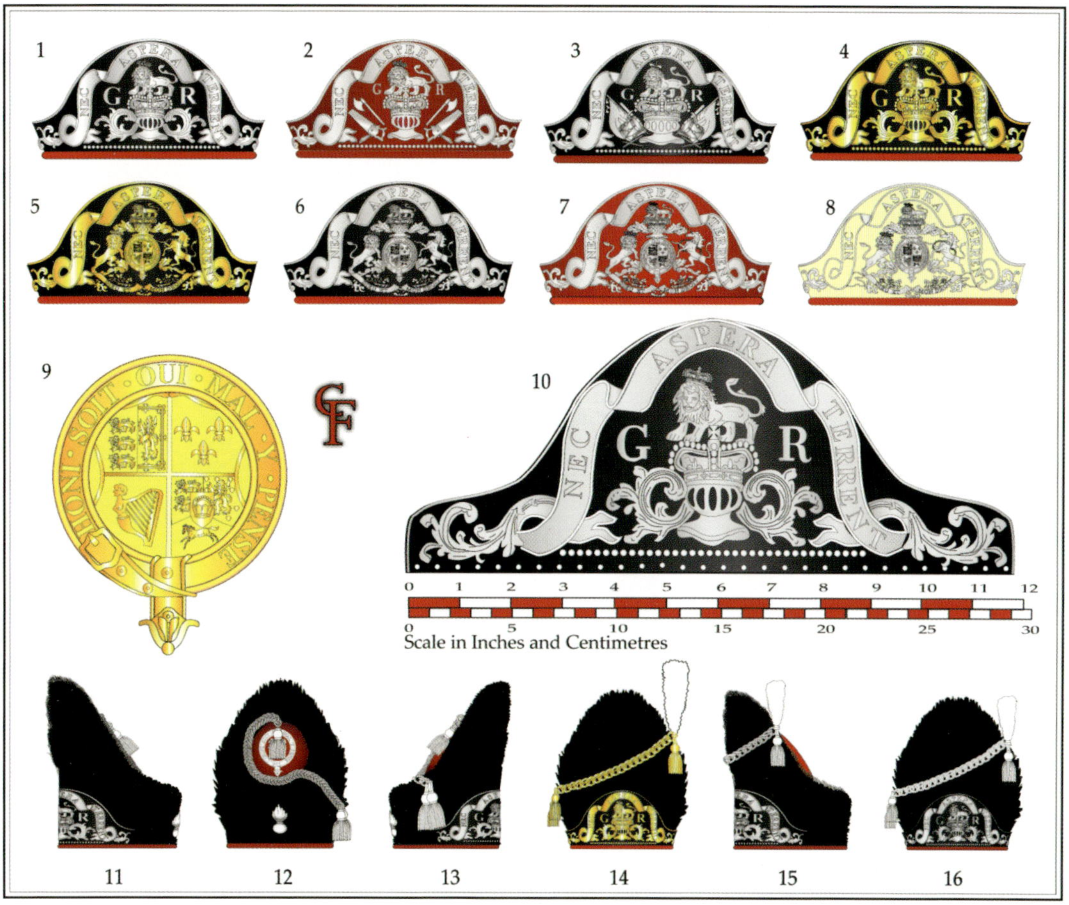

Grenadier and fusilier fur caps of 1768. The grenadier plate of an officer of a silver-laced regiment (1). The plate for a pioneer (2). The plate of a drummer (3). The plate of an officer of a gold-laced regiment (4). The plate of an officer of Foot Guards (5). The plate of an enlisted man of the 1st Foot Guards (6). The enlisted man of the Coldstream Guards (7). The plate of an enlisted man of the 3rd Foot Guards (8). The enlarged view of the centre of the plate of the Foot Guards (9). The scaled view of the plate of an enlisted man (10). The early view of the left-side of an enlisted man of grenadiers (11). The rear view (12). The a right-side view (13). The later cap of a gold-laced fusilier regiment (14). The side view of an enlisted man of a fusilier regiment (15) and a front view of the later cap (16).

Several different plates were worn on this cap, all of the same size, five inches tall by twelve inches long, but with different japanning and special versions for each; the officers usually wore a plate to match the regimental metal. The enlisted men of the 1st Foot Guards wore a black plate with white metal. The Coldstream wore a red plate with white metal and the 3rd Foot Guards, after 1768, wore a white plate with white metal.

The cap was quickly laced about with knotted white worsted cords and tassels, those of the officers being gold or silver as the painting of the 25th at Minorca show. The cap carried a drum at the back for drummers and a grenade, with the regimental number on the ball, for grenadiers. The Foot Guards wore special plates with the Royal Arms and the NCOs wore gilt cords and brass plates. Originally only the 5th Regiment was authorized to wear a plume, but later the grenadiers and fusiliers adopted plumes, though it is clear that some regiments stayed with the old cords and tassels. Drummers retained bearskin caps for parade and dress but usually wore cocked hats on campaign. The cap was soon to be laced about with knotted white worsted cords and tassels, those of the officers being gold or silver; later the bearskin caps adopted plumes.

Originally only the twelve 'old corps' were allowed to wear special badges on their colours and the front of the grenadier's mitre cap; these were the 1st to 8th, the 18th, 21st, 23rd and 27th. Eventually other regiments joined these. The list below gave status to fifteen regiments who were allowed to wear them. In 1768 these were placed at the rear of their fur caps on the red patch and were worn in full colour by the officers and mounted on the red patch at the rear of the fur cap, but there are cases where the most senior of the NCOs also wore them in colour. Those of the rank and file were usually in white, although the 7th Fusiliers also wore them in colour at a later period.

The badges adopted in 1768 by the fifteen regiments that were now entitled to wear them. They were worn on the red or scarlet patch at the rear and are shown above. Those of the officers were in full colour but those of the enlisted men were in white.

Highland Bonnets

The highland bonnet was of heavy blue wool and took several forms. Later around each bonnet was a three-inch chequered band of white, red and green dicing. The feather ornamentation gradually increased so that by the end of the century there were more feathers than bonnet. The hackle was of cock's feathers, clipped and fastened on a stem and worn with a black cockade and a regimental button at the centre. The later hackle was white for the grenadier company, white over red for the battalion companies and, after 1770, green for the light company. Hackles were eight and a half inches for the battalion companies and twelve inches tall for the flank companies, but there were exceptions to this rule. The practice of using ostrich feathers to enhance the bonnet was a common feature: some wore only a single feather while others wore a profusion of feathers; the difference when worn without feathers are considered to be the definition of the 'hummel bonnet'. The 42nd wore the bonnet with feathers but are shown wearing a plain blue Kilmarnock bonnet in undress. Others wore flat blue bonnets in undress. The 'tourie' or tuft on the top was white for grenadiers, green for the light company and red for battalion companies. The grenadier companies of the highland regiments usually wore the grenadier fur cap in full dress.

Highland Bonnets. The early wool cap (1). The different variants worn by officers (2). The wool cap with a chequered band (3). The wool cap of a private soldier with plume (4). The Kilmarnock bonnets with chequered band and plumes (5) and one with no plumes (6).

Light Company Caps

The caps adopted by the light companies were in a variety of styles with each regiment adopting the style they considered most appropriate. Although light companies were approved in November 1770, their implementation did not take place much before September 1771. Philip de Loutherbourg drew sketches of these caps in 1800; they were of black leather with three chains round the crown. At the front was a plate that carried the 'GR' Cypher surmounted by a crown, underneath was the number of the regiment.

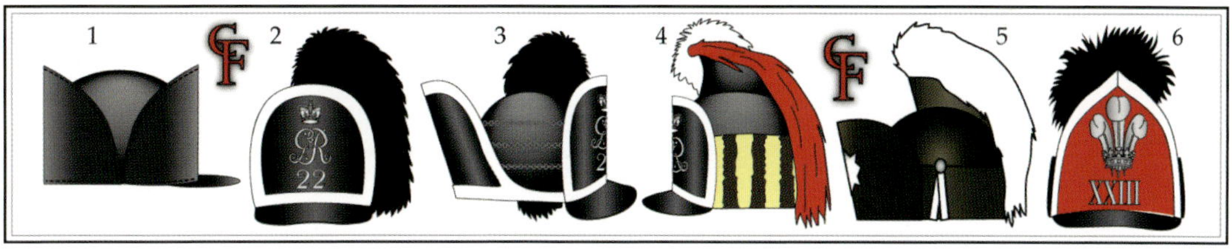

Introduced into the British Army in 1770 the light infantry adopted a wide variety of caps of different patterns: one form of a simple leather cap as shown by Philip de Loutherbourg in 1780 (1). The front view showing the crown and 'GR' Cypher with the regimental number underneath (2). The a side view showing the three chains around the crown (3). Another shown by Philip de Loutherbourg in 1778 (4). The light company cap of 62nd Regiment (5) and one of the 23rd Royal Welch Fusiliers (6).

Tarletons

The Tarleton helmets proved to be an attractive proposition for the light companies and were worn by during the War of Independence by both sides, the British and the opposing Congress. They were also worn by the 16th and 17th Light Dragoons who were dismounted cavalry acting as infantry.

Introduced into the British Army in 1770 by the light infantry who adopted a wide variety of caps of different patterns, one of which was the Tarleton Helmet. An officer's helmet of silver-metalled regiment (1). The helmet of an enlisted man with leopard skin turban (2) and an officer's Tarleton with a red turban and a white-over-red plume (3).

CHAPTER TWELVE

Infantry Coats and Jackets

Facings

Each regiment was allocated a facing colour and this was rarely changed but when this did occur it is shown in the plates for the regiment.

The Coat of circa 1751

The Royal Collection has a series of painting by Morier completed about 1755 and later. These provide important detail of the uniforms of the period of George II. In some paintings, particularly where the lapels are buttoned over each other, the shape continues to be shown rounded at the lower edge but in those cases where the lapels are folded back the lower edge is clearly straighter which is also seen on the coats of officers of the period. It was generally cut to show an elaborate fullness of extra material gathered at the side pleat below the hip button, and in many cases acted more as a greatcoat than a coat. In other cases the officers' swords are shown passing through a gap in the pleats, which has been stiffened to provide a greater flare to the material. The fullness given to the coat by the pleats from the hip buttons continues during this period and there is now clear evidence to show a buttoned strip of lace included within the pleats, at least for the rank and file. The length of the coat was altered to each man so that it ended just above the knees when kneeling. A reconstruction of a tailor's drawing of a coat, circa 1755, and 'cut to the new fashion' retains the lapels and the pockets in the lining of the pleat, but still weighs five and a half pounds. The shoulder straps were originally of red cloth and worn only on the left shoulder to secure the cartridge pouch. The shape seems to have been with a rounded end, but it is noted that some of the paintings show a lace edge to the shoulder strap which may suggest that the 31st, 34th, 37th, 39th, 45th and 48th regiments anticipated the later regulation. The number of loops on the turnback lapel varied from four to seven, and could be either square or pointed in shape.

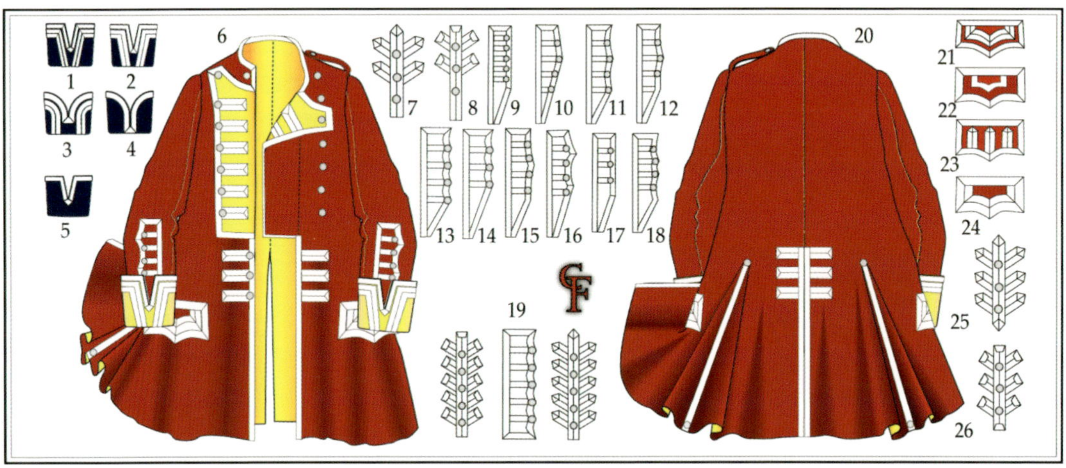

The coat of 1751 (after Morier). The different cuff styles (1 to 5). A front view of the 1751 coat (6). The different styles of cuff lace shown by Morier, (7 to 18), but there well may have been a standard pattern (19). A rear view of the 1751 coat (20) and the different styles of horizontal and vertical pockets shown by Morier (21 to 26).

In 1750 an order stated that 'six points of lapels to be tacked down in such a manner as to be easily undone and the back pleat sewn down to the lower of three loops'. In 1751 the coat was made two inches shorter than before and the length of the loops of the Foot Guards were to 2.65 inches and the distance between each loop a quarter of an inch.

Throughout the Morier paintings much of the detail is not shown clearly and, where it is, there are often variations in style. This applied particularly to the shape of the cuff, the lace to the cuff flap, the pockets and the number of loops. In each case the relevant detail is shown on the corresponding plate for that regiment. It has not been possible to say if these variances are due to the artist's interpretation or a regimental distinction but, it may well be that there was a distinct number of buttons to the lace of the cuff flap although it is difficult to be certain and in those cases where the detail is uncertain they have been assumed.

There are cases where the shoulder straps are laced and this applies to the 31st, 39th, 45th and 48th. It may well be that, over time, shoulder straps were laced, but this may have not been the case.

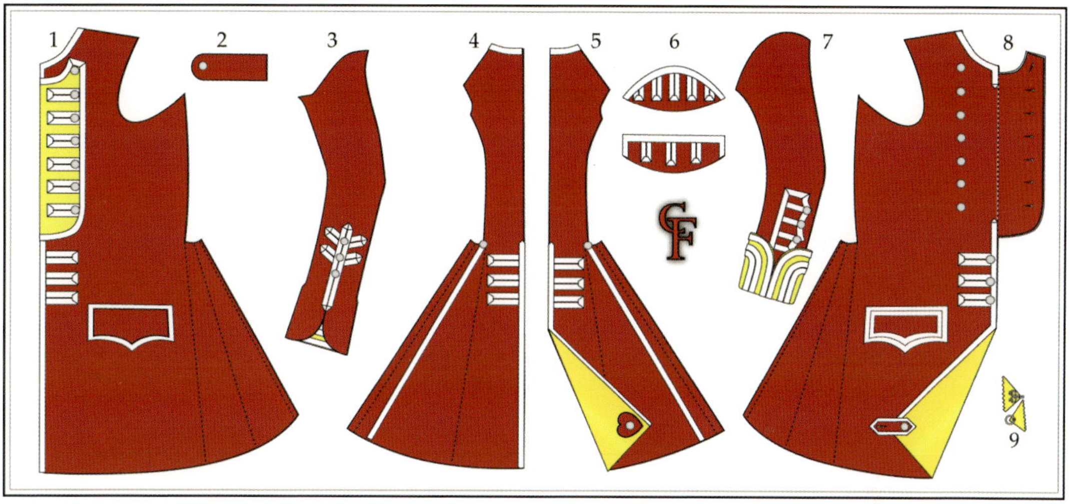

Coat of an enlisted man of the 1755 period. The front of the coat with facing colour lapel, the very large pleats of the coat and the button loops as shown (1). The shoulder strap, worn on the left shoulder only (2). The inside of sleeve with the cuff folded down showing one version of the lace (3). The rear of the coat with lacing and the very large pleat (4). The rear panel of the coat showing the turnbacks and a form of dubby ornament (5). The wings worn by grenadiers (6). The outside of sleeve with the fold-back cuff and elaborate lace ladder, which took different forms (7). The front of the coat showing the lacing, and the rear of the lapel, an alternative pocket and turnbacks with an alternative form of dubby (8) and hooks and eyes often used to join the turnbacks (9).

The Battalion and Grenadier Coat of circa 1768

Regulations issued by George III in the warrant of December 1768 for the marching regiments of foot provide detailed information on the dress of this period. It gives considerable detail of the uniforms and this is used to show the changes prior to the end of the American War of Independence. The Foot Guards were not included in the 1768 warrant; they changed in dress in November 1770 for the 1st Foot Guards, November 1773 for the Coldstream Foot Guards and April 1768 and July 1774 for the 3rd Foot Guards.

The coats of the other ranks were provided by the colonel and were issued at nominally regular periods by contracted military tailors. They were dyed with a madder-red for the other ranks and the lesser form of scarlet for non-commissioned officers was made from a mixture of dyes, both cochineal and madder. The regimental facing colour was worn on the collar, lapel and cuffs. The changes to the coat were significant; the skirt of the coat lost the fullness with material at the pleats was much reduced, but still with a certain fullness. The skirts were turned back and secured with turn-back ornaments or dubby, which could be heart-shaped, diamond or square in shape. The turn-backs and linings to the skirts were white with the exception of those regiments with buff or buff-toned facings who wore matching turn-backs, waistcoats and linings. While private soldiers wore brass turn-back ornaments and the grenadiers used grenades, but the use of thistles is not unknown by those regiments with such an association.

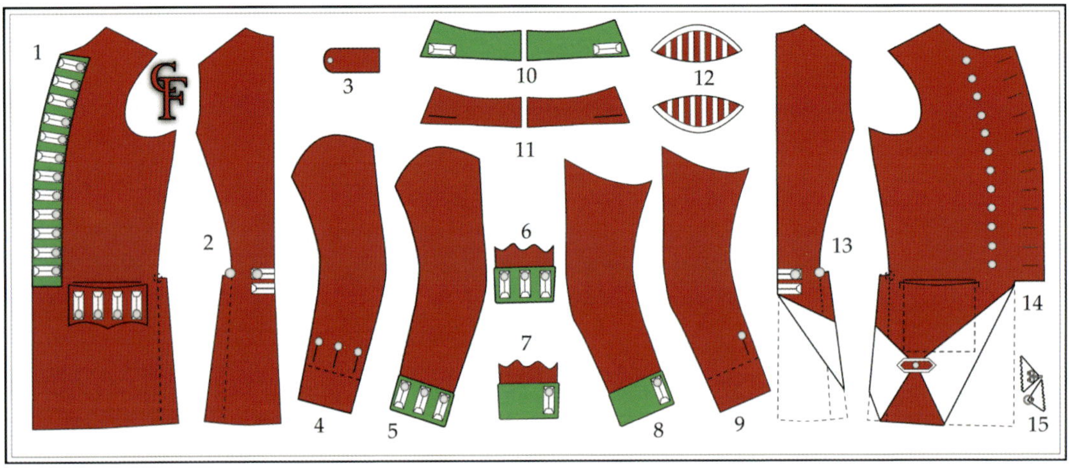

1768 Coat, (Courtesy of Henry Cooke who provided the pattern). The front of the coat with facing lapel, the pleats of the coat, the stitched-down pocket and pocket opening welt (1). The rear of the coat with buttons and lacing (2). The shoulder strap, worn only on the left side (3). The outside of sleeve of 1768 made to unbutton and fold down (4). The sleeve with the later integral cuff (5). The 1768 turn-back cuff (6). The turn-back cuff of the inside of the sleeve (7). An inside sleeve with the later integral cuff (8) and an inside sleeve of 1768 made to unbutton and fold down (9). The two-piece collar (10). The lining of madder-red (11). The grenadier wings, worn on both shoulders (12). The rear of coat with turn-backs (13). The front of coat showing the rear of the lapel, turn-backs with dubby, pocket opening, the internal bag and pocket position (14) and hooks and eyes often used to join the turn-backs (15).

Regarding the length of the coat, Cuthbertson noted in 1768 that they should show 'two of the lower buttons of the breeches knee, exclusive of that upon the band', but at a later date in 1777 Simes noted that, 'the bottom of every man's coat to be six inches, except the men of the Light Infantry, which is to be made nine inches from the ground when kneeling upon both knees, and hang of an equal length quite round' but it is clear that regiments adopted shorter coats. The coats were worn for dress, hooked together at the chest and the upper part left undone so that the cambric shirt-frill could be pulled out to resemble a cock's comb while the lower part was cut away to show the waistcoat. The lapels of the enlisted men could be buttoned across in either direction, often dependent upon which way the wind blew and, as the waist moved lower during the period this acted to maintain body warmth. The front of the coat sloped away to reveal the chest and carried a three-inch wide lapel to the waist of facing colour backed with madder-red cloth. This had ten buttons, originally evenly spread but later some regiments adopted buttons and lace in pairs. The rank and file had the square-bastion-or flowerpot shaped loops to decorate the front of the coat and strengthen the buttonholes.

The madder-red pockets of grenadier and battalion companies were horizontal and sewn shut at the waist and each pocket had four buttons and loops. They had a welted opening to a pocket bag contained on the inside of the coat. The fold-down collar of facing colour was usually worn buttoned to the top button of the lapel. Cuthbertson notes that the collar was only 'three fingers deep at the rear' but examples are shown curved to a point at the rear. The front where it buttoned to the lapel was at least three and a half inches wide but it should be remembered that the collar could be turned up in bad weather. The shoulder strap was originally of red cloth and worn only on the left shoulder to secure the cartridge pouch; the shape seems to have been with a rounded end. Later, after the introduction of two shoulder straps for the Foot Guards it seems they were adopted by most line regiments and edged about by the appropriate regimental lace. They were sewn to the shoulder seam of the jacket, tapered at the centre and pointed at the other end, where they were secured, close to the collar, by a small regimental button. In 1784 facing colour shoulder straps edged with regimental lace were introduced officially but long before this date some regiments had already changed to this pattern. The cuffs were of facing colour, three and a half inches deep. Each cuff had four buttons and four laced loops with the front pair astride the front seam of the sleeve. Originally they could be unbuttoned and folded down when the wearer was cold, the lace loops being on the inside of the cuff but it seems that the fold-down cuff was replaced before the end of the century by the integral cuff. An analysis of the distance between the bottoms of the knees of the figures to the bottoms of their coats yields a proportional distance much greater than the prescribed six inches, particularly after 1775.

With the introduction of laced edged shoulder straps for the Foot Guards, it may well be that other regiments followed suit, but there is evidence during the American Revolution a general trend towards this pattern which had become practice by 1793.

Officers Coats

The coats of circa 1751 for the officers were scarlet, dyed with cochineal, and of much better materials and made to personal order by military tailors with the same fullness at the pleats associated with the enlisted men, and, at the start of the period, the long coats were often worn without lapels. The coats of circa 1768 were worn sloped away to the waist; the turn-backs and linings to the skirts were white with the exception of those regiments with buff-toned facings who wore appropriate turn-backs, waistcoats and linings. It is clear that officers loosely interpreted the regulations and many continued to wear the coat in styles contrary to the current regulations and officers more commonly used a bow-shaped decoration to the turnbacks while the grenadiers used grenades. The officers tended to use the square loop although other versions are known, but some regiments used unlaced twist buttonholes, particularly in undress. The colonel was the arbiter in such matters, but there is very little information regarding which regiment wore what.

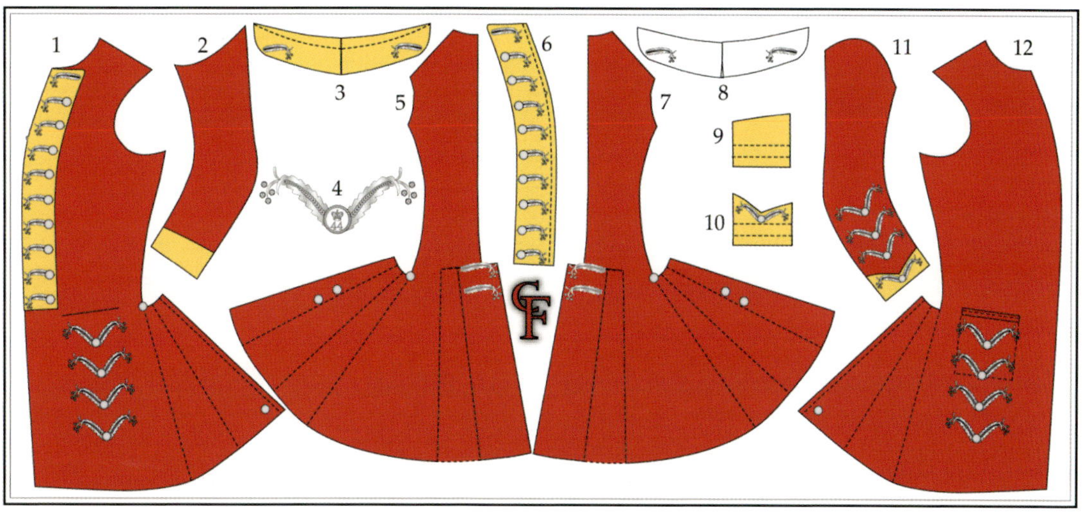

Lieutenant Eli Dagworthy as an officer of the 44th Regiment of Foot, circa 1768, (Courtesy of Henry Cooke who provided the pattern). The front of the coat with facing colour lapel, the eyelet, pleats of the coat, the elaborate silver lace, the buttons and entrance to the pocket bag (1). The inside of the sleeve with the integral cuff (2). The collar with silver lace showing the fold line of the collar (3). The enlarged silver lace and button (4) and the rear of the coat with silver lacing with the inverted pleat at the rear (5). The lapel with the cloth overlap to cover the scarlet material (6). The rear of the coat with silver lacing and the inverted pleat at the rear (7). The collar lining with embroidered silver lace (8). The cuff showing the tuck-under into the sleeve and the lining line (9). The outside of sleeve cuff with elaborate silver lace with the tuck-under into the sleeve and the lining line (10). The outside of sleeve and cuff with elaborate silver lace (11) and the front of the coat with lacing and turnbacks and the pocket welt and bag (12).

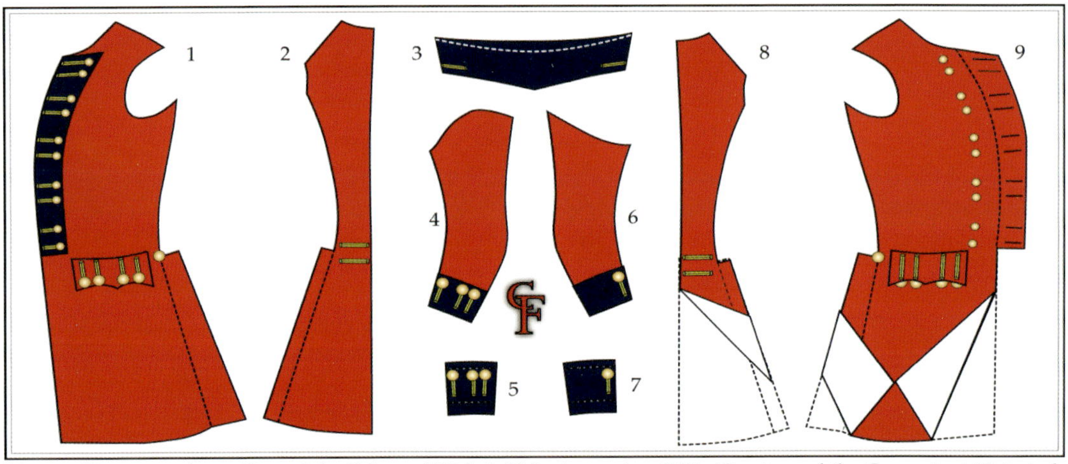

Munson Hoyt coat of an officer of the Prince of Wales's Volunteers, circa 1782, (Courtesy of the Connecticut Historical Society and Henry Cooke who provided the pattern). The front of the coat with facing colour turnbacks, lapel, the pleats of the coat, gilt braid, the opening pocket and plain brass buttons (1). The rear of the coat with gilt lacing (2). The collar with silver lace and pointed at the rear (3). The outside of sleeve with integral cuff (4). The cuff showing the tuck-under into the sleeve and the top fold line (5). The inside of sleeve with integral cuff (6). The cuff showing the tuck-under into the sleeve and the top fold line (7). The rear of the coat with lacing and turnbacks (8) and the front of coat showing the rear of the lapel, the pocket often shown with the buttons undone and the turnbacks (9).

Highland Jackets

The early jackets of highland regiments were quite different to the coats of the line regiments. They had short skirts to allow the wearing of the full plaid but still had the fullness at the pleats with horizontal pockets and a deep falling collar. Officers often wore blue lapels to the waist laced in gold bastion-shaped loops with matching gold, laced white waistcoats. They also carried three bastion loops to the skirt, pocket and cuffs.

The highland jacket of 1768 had a lapel, collar and pleats, and was very similar to the light company jacket after it was introduced, later resembling the light company jacket of 1780 with the tommy and lace triangle at the rear. The officers usually wore gold, square, regularly spaced loops.

Light Company Jackets

Light companies had been formed among those regiments that served in North America during the Seven Years' War as early as 1757, but it was not until November 1770 that a tenth company was added to each regiment to serve as a light company. It took time before the clothing was finally resolved and the pockets eventually became oblique. Even the Foot Guards who did not possess light companies before 1793 were ordered in 1776 to select suitable men for service in America and dress them to 'the coats cut in accordance with the pattern in the orderly room'.

> Simes, Thomas. A Military Course for the Government and Conduct of a Battalion (London: 1777): the bottom of every man's coat to be six inches, except the men of the Light Infantry, which is to be made nine inches from the ground when kneeling upon both knees, and hang of an equal length quite round.

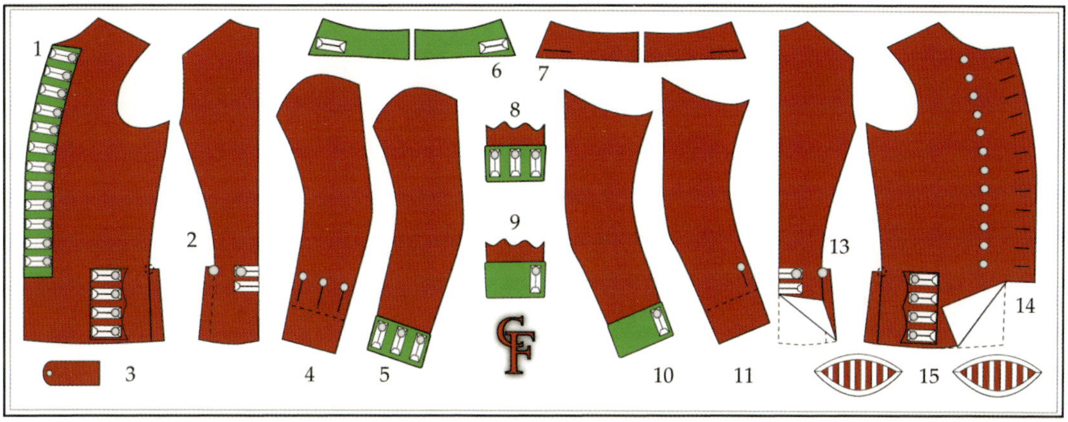

1770 Light Infantry Jacket. The front of the coat with facing lapels to the waist, the pleats of the coat, the stitched down pocket and pocket opening pleat (1). The rear of the coat with tommy and lace loops (2). The shoulder strap only worn on the shoulder left shoulder (3). The outside of sleeve of 1770 made to unbutton and fold down (4). The sleeve with the later integral cuff (5). The two-piece collar of facing colour circa 1770 (6) and the collar lining of madder-red (7). The 1770 turn-back cuff (8). Turn-back cuff of the inside of the sleeve (9). The inside sleeve with the later integral cuff (10). The inside sleeve of 1770 made to unbutton and fold down (11). The rear of coat with the turnbacks as shown (13). The front of coat showing the rear of the lapel, the turnbacks and the sealed pocket opening in the pleats (14) and the light infantry wing worn on both shoulders (15).

In 1770 the light companies wore turnbacks to the rear and front skirts with the standard loops at the top of the skirts that are still full with the pleats at the waist. The pockets were vertical and sewn shut with the entrance in the pleat, although these eventually became oblique, but it took time before the clothing was finally resolved. Those regiments serving abroad were rarely able to adopt the shorter coat, a case in point being the 36th who were still wearing the long tailcoats while in India. The light companies soon adopted a red waistcoat and the collar was quite narrow at the rear. The use of the bugle horn by the light companies seems to have become the fashion soon after they were adopted.

In 1778, Philip de Loutherbourg sketched several soldiers in preparation for his painting 'The Review at Warley Camp', including sketches of the 6th and 69th's light companies with a tommy to the rear and a triangle of lace above. The skirt is still full with the pleats at the waist, but the pockets were vertical with four loops to either side. The rear of the collar is much wider and taken to a point at the centre of the back. The light companies had begun to wear the bugle horn as a badge before 1782.

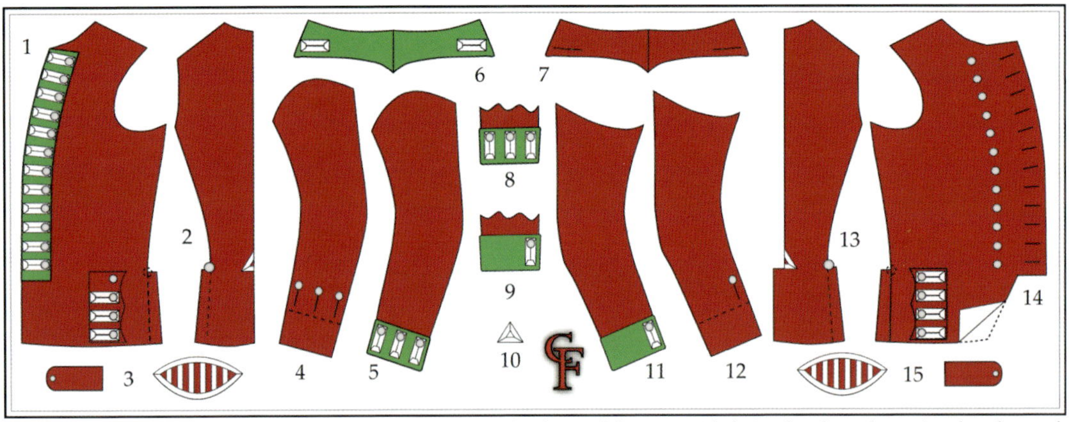

1780 Light Infantry Jacket, (after Philip de Loutherbourg). The front of the coat with facing lapels to the waist, the pleats of the coat, the stitched down pocket and pocket opening pleat (1). The rear of the coat with tommy and lace triangle (2). The shoulder strap and light infantry wing worn on each shoulder (3). The outside of sleeve of 1770 made to unbutton and fold down (4). The sleeve with the later integral cuff (5). The two-piece collar of facing colour with pointed rear circa 1780 (6). The collar lining of madder-red (7). The 1770 turn back cuff (8). Turn back cuff of the inside of the sleeve (9) and the lace triangle (10). An inside sleeve with the later integral cuff (11). The inside sleeve of 1770 made to unbutton and fold down (12). The rear of coat with tommy and lace triangle (13). The front of coat showing the rear of the lapel, the turn backs and the sealed pocket opening in the pleats (14) and the shoulder strap and light infantry wing worn on both shoulders (15).

Drummers circa 1751

The warrant of 1751 noted that drummers of royal regiments wore red, lined and faced in blue and laced with royal lace. The drummers of other regiments were to wear coats of the facing colour lined and faced in red and laced as the colonel 'thought fit for distinction sake', but the lace was to be of the colour of that worn by the rank and file. There is no record, which I can find, of the drummer lace of this period of 1751.

Drummers circa 1768

Drummers usually wore reversed colours with red collars and cuffs. The drummers of the Foot Guards and those of royal regiments wore scarlet jackets, faced with royal blue and 'royal' lace, 'considerably raised above the common lace'. Lace for drummers of other regiments was 'to be raised in the same manner' and 'in such manner as the Colonel shall think fit'. However, there is no record of the lace for the period, apart from the books of J. B .& N. Pearse that are later, during the Napoleonic War.

Drummers of regiments serving in the East or West Indies (and India) wore unlined jackets with the turn backs faced in the appropriate colour. The waistcoats, breeches and linings were white except for those regiments with buff-toned facings.

Bands of Music

Bands of music came into fashion in British regiments after the Seven Years' War. While it is known that many regiments maintained bands, there is not a great deal of information about them, but there are details of British regimental bands that served in the War of Independence. The 22nd Regiment musicians wore red coats with buff facings, waistcoats, linings and with black cocked hats trimmed with silver lace; this band of music was formed in 1767, and new clothing was purchased every second year, at least until 1774. These men were musicians, not drummers and fifers, for whom the reversed colours were typical. Bands were not a part of a regimental establishment, but some accompanied their regiments to the War of Independence: the 21st who apparently wore reversed colours, but as a royal regiment did not need to do so, including the 22nd, 59th and

64th who did wear reversed colours. Several regiments that included bands during the period were the 2nd, 10th, 13th, 12th, 15th, 34th, 36th, 39th, 43rd, 57th, 58th and 101st.

CHAPTER THIRTEEN

Metal, Lace and Buttons

Metal

The colour of officers' buttons and lace was set by Whitehall with each regiment allocated a colour, silver or gold, which is often referred to as the 'metal' colour. Initially lace had been introduced to reinforce the material of the uniforms at the buttonholes and similar points of stress, but this soon developed into a method by which the regiments were identified. The colonel of each regiment could decide if the officers wore lace on the buttonholes or not. In other regiments it was custom and practice for officers not to use lace on the jacket, just a silk twist edging the buttonhole; these are usually referred to as 'unlaced regiments'.

Buttons

The early buttons were formed by two half-shells soldered together with a wire shank hooked into the rear shell. The early buttons had no specific pattern but by 1760 patterns and numbers were beginning to be shown by some regiments and after the regulations of 1768 each regiment was ordered to carry a distinctive number or design on the button, the dragoon guards being permitted to use their initial letters.

The buttons of officers were of gold, silver or brass but those of the rank and file were either brass or white metal depending upon the regimental colour. By 1768 the numbered buttons of officers and enlisted men changed to a cast, flat pattern with a shank set into the rear of the button; made from a form of pewter, this inexpensive button material was known as 'trifle', a pewter alloy of medium hardness consisting of eighty-three parts of tin to seventeen parts of antimony. A definition of the period states that a button of tin of a given size would weigh 182 grains; pewter plate, 183.5 grains; while that of trifle would weigh 185.5 grains. The objection to pewter was that it would not shine when polished. Sizes varied considerably due to the different manufacturers. Jewellers usually made the silver or gilt buttons for the officers.

Buttons. The shell form of a silver button (1). The larger gilt button (2). The later flat button (3). The smaller buttons of the 44th (4). The enlisted man's button of the 5th (5). The larger button of an enlisted man of the 31st (6) and an officer's button of the 5th (7).

The use of large and small buttons had already begun to be adopted by 1728. Records of the 29th Regiment of Foot note brass buttons on the breast smaller than the others. The use of small buttons and oblique pockets to differentiate the light companies began to appear as early as 1771 and eventually became standard practice. Many regiments adopted the use of roman numerals for the officers and Arabic numerals for the other ranks, but this was not always the case. Where the buttons are known, they have been indicated on the regimental illustrations, but it is clear that there were smaller buttons on the shoulder straps from very early on. Coats of the battalion and grenadier companies had ten large buttons on the lapel, four on the cuff, and four on the pocket and at the waist two large buttons; in each case there were twenty large buttons and two smaller on the shoulder strap. It is not known when the smaller buttons were adopted by the light companies; it may well have been a case of fashion, but it is clear from the inspection returns that they very quickly adopted them for their jackets when they wore twenty-eight small buttons.

Spacing

The next distinction was in the spacing of the loops or buttons, some of which were evenly or regularly spaced while others were set in pairs or in a few cases set in threes, but the use of this spacing was restricted to the 3rd Foot Guards and some heavy cavalry regiments. At the time the 1751 Warrant was enacted almost all British infantry coat lapel buttons were placed singly.

Lace

The lace of the private soldiers was a woven worsted some half an inch wide and arranged to form a shaped buttonhole according to the regimental pattern. The shape and design of the buttonholes varied with the regiment: there were bastion, flowerpot, Jew's Harp, a plain square or double-headed and a Coldstream scallop pointed loop. Each regiment was allocated a particular style and pattern of lacing, but it is clear that some regiments changed the loop pattern if the regiment changed its name or role, and the NCOs and officers often adopted a different style of loop. The lace of NCOs was normally white but silver was specified for the 42nd, and gold for the Foot Guards. The lace of the rank and file of the Foot Guards was plain white, but those of the rank and file of other regiments were plain white with coloured threads running through it, often to form a particular shape or pattern. It is clear some that regiments changed their lace often as the title changed. The position of these coloured threads, together with the facings and button spacing, enabled the rank and file of a regiment to be identified. Where the information is known the lace has been included on the plate for that regiment.

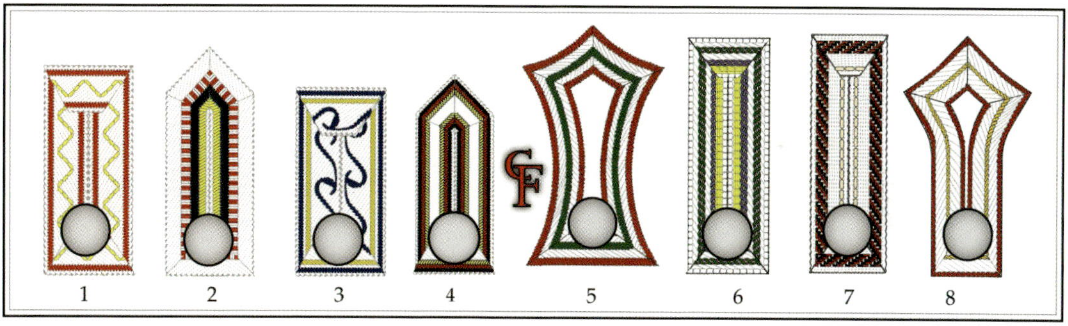

The different types of buttonhole loops used in 1751. A square loop of the 16th Regiment (1). The pointed loop of the 23rd (2). The square loop of the 34th (3). The lace of the 3rd (4). The lace of 1768, a flowerpot loop of the 49th Regiment (5) which some refer to as a Jew's Harp loop, a square or double-headed loop from the 67th Regiment (6). The second square loop illustrates the 14th Regiment (7) and the bastion loop of the 38th Regiment (8).

CHAPTER FOURTEEN

Waistcoats, Shirts, Gloves and Stocks

Waistcoats

Initially those of the enlisted were made from the same material as the coat, and often made from them. Generally waistcoats had sleeves but sleeveless versions are known. They were made in a variety of colours but the most usual was red. The waistcoats of officers followed the same general practice but were made from scarlet or a variety of colours, often that of the facings.

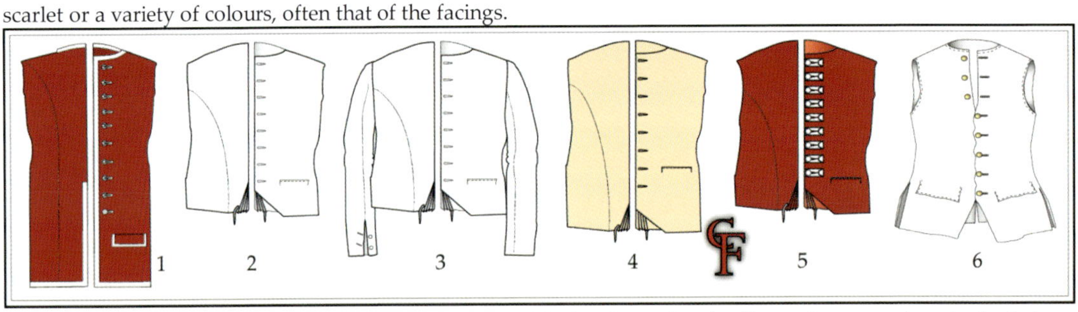

Infantry waistcoats. The style of waistcoat of 1751 that could be laced or unlaced, officers often wore them in the facing colour both with and without lace (1). The waistcoat of 1768 of an enlisted man that originally reached to the waist, it was white and normally sleeveless (2). The waistcoat with sleeves (3). The later waistcoat of a buff-faced regiment circa 1775 that reaches to the hips (4). The madder-red waistcoat of a light infantry company enlisted man, normally sleeveless it could have braided loops to the buttonholes in either white or buff according to the regiment (4) and an officer's waistcoat that could be either white or buff (6).

Waistcoats of 1751

This pattern was close fitting at the waist with vents at the rear and usually laced about. It had no collar but was often laced at the buttonholes, the number of loops on the waistcoats of the rank and file determined by the height of the wearer, nine loops for those under five feet eight inches, ten for those of five feet nine inches; those above this height had eleven and grenadiers of five feet eleven inches had twelve. The waistcoats were usually fitted with laced about, horizontal pockets were laced and fastened with the appropriate number of buttons, smaller than, but matching, those of the coat. It is known from inspection returns that some regiments after 1755 had already changed to the style of 1768.

Waistcoats of 1768

The sleeveless waistcoats were plain, secured by a number of small buttons, without embroidery and either white or buff-toned for those regiments with buff-toned facings. They were single-breasted with the rear seam sewn down to the waistband of the breeches. Cuthbertson notes 'the short front skirts some nine inches long, open from the lower button'. They also had horizontal pockets with no flaps, but later pocket flaps were common, but Simes in 1777 notes 'the waistcoat for the front and rear rank of Grenadiers to have twelve holes and buttons' and 'the front and rear rank to have eleven holes and buttons, the centre rank of the battalion ten'. Some regiments with black facings are known to have worn a matching trim to the waistcoats.

Light Infantry Waistcoats

On 4 March 1771 a recommendation was made by a Committee of the Board of General Officers regarding the clothing and accoutrements best adapted for the use of the Light Company belonging to each of the Marching Regiments of Foot on the British Establishment. It was approved by the King, the waistcoat to be red and laced. In 1778 Phillip de Loutherburg sketched several soldiers in preparation for his painting 'The Mock Battle' at

Warley Camp, including sketches of the 6th and 69th light companies. The soldier of the 6th light company has the waistcoat in the picture is partially obscured by the belly box and ball bag he wears around his waist. However, it does not appear to have tails. The picture of the 69th Light is much the same. Officers of the light companies were expected to wear uniforms similar to those of the men. In June 1772, the following inspection return was reported for the 40th Regiment: 'The Officers of the Light Companies have their pockets of the same form as the men, and likewise their waistcoats of same form and colour, but without lace', while an inspection report of the 54th noted that both the pockets and waistcoats were 'looped with silver lace', but it is known that officers of the 19th and 4th wore white waistcoats.

Shirts

The shirts worn by officers in the early period were profusely decorated with starched and ironed frills, often with lace for dress, which were allowed to show at the neck and cuffs. Shirts of the other ranks were usually of a simpler nature but still had more simple frills. The earlier period shows shirts decorated with a nine-inch frill, puffed out and starched to show protruding between the lapels of the coat. While officers may have worn the stock for parades, in undress and walking out neck-cloths are usually shown.

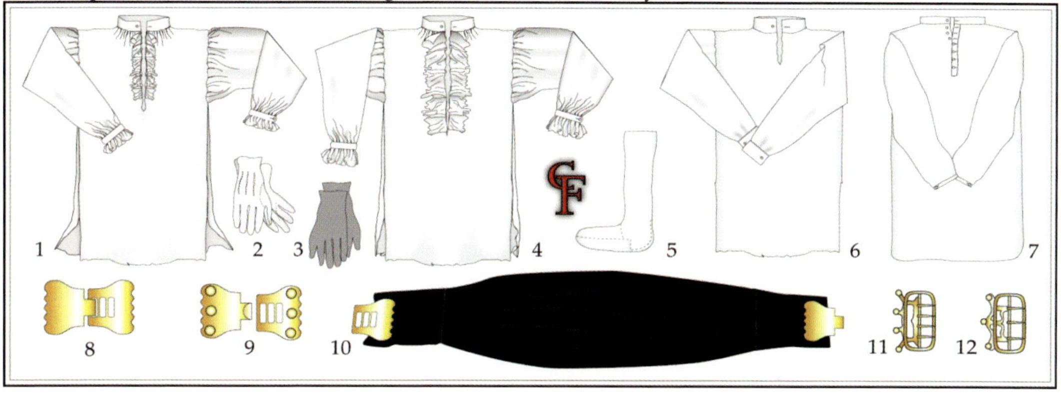

Shirts, Stocks, Buckles, Socks and Gloves. An enlisted man's dress shirt with frills at the cuff and chest (1). The leather gloves of officers and NCOs worn by all ranks when in dress (2). The worsted or woollen gloves for the other ranks (3). The officer's shirt with lace and larger frills (4). The white or grey socks (5) and other rank's shirt worn earlier in 1751 (6). The enlisted mans shirt of 1775 (7). The basic stock clasp (8). The rear view showing the clasp and studs that passed through the stock (9). The stock of either horsehair or leather (10) and two further stock clasps (11 & 12).

Gloves

Leather, worsted or woollen gloves of battalion pattern were issued to all other ranks. Officers and NCOs usually wore white leather gloves for dress. The short gloves ended at the wrist with a slit or a small turned back cuff.

Stocks

The enlisted men wore stocks, either of black woven horsehair, black leather for dress or of white linen. The stock formed a high neckband, stiffened but allowing the ruffled shirt to be seen at the front. It was worn high, around the neck, and secured by a buckle or clasp usually placed under the hair. Over the period it gradually increased in height and became most uncomfortable to wear. Officers also wore velvet stocks; fastening at the rear with a false turndown white collar they also wore black or white neck clothes tied to puff out under the chin.

CHAPTER FIFTEEN

Infantry Netherwear

Breeches of 1751

These were worn by all ranks and were made from a similar material to the coat, or often made from it. The early breeches were in many colours: red for line regiments, blue for royal regiments or for the officers often the colour of the facings. The early style had a wide angle at the crotch with a roomy but shapeless seat, the breeches opened at a front fly and were secured by four buttons on the right side and buttonholes on the left and some were fitted with two pockets at the upper leg. The top was gathered on to a waistband, deeper at the front and closed with buttons, the legs were wide at the top, narrowed to just below the knees and were fitted with a knee band, the lower part of the outer seam being closed with three or four buttons and secured by a strap and buckle to prevent them riding up the leg. Adjustment was by a small slit at the rear, closed by lacing to make the breeches fit. Officers often wore a strap and buckle to replace the lacing at the back.

Breeches of 1768

The warrant introduced white breeches but those regiments with buff, or a tone of buff, wore breeches of the appropriate colour. Some regiments had adopted white or buff breeches some years before the 1768 warrant, and these were made of a white material to come high on the hips and below the knee-pan to the calf of the leg. The waistband was required to be wide enough to hold three large buttons and the breeches usually had a pocket at the right side. To cover the open fly, the breeches were fitted with a 'whole fall', a large flap at the front, buttoning with two large buttons at the waist. At the bottom of each leg were four small regimental buttons to secure the opening and, to prevent them riding up, a woollen strap and buckle or button was also fitted. Adjustment to the waist was by tapes fed through gathers at the rear and they were marked with the soldier's name on the waistband. As the breeches became looser fitting at the waist they were held up by 'gallowses' or linen or canvas braces. Some breeches had horizontal pockets with flaps at the front at thigh level and were closed with a button on a corner flap to the waistband. Vertical pockets were sometimes in the side seams on either side, although there was often only one pocket on the right side. There could also be a small pocket in the waistband on either side. Breeches were worn for all occasions except fatigues and walking out.

Pantaloons

Pantaloons were close fitting and usually skin-tight fastening either below the calf or at the foot, and were worn in different colours but usually white or buff, and could be made of white kerseymere or stocking material. They were buttoned or laced up the outside of the leg and pulled tight around the ankle with a cord or some such device and were usually fitted with a large fall. Officers often wore pantaloons for dress and walking out, with the bottom ten inches of each leg open with several lace loops passing through holes to interlace down the outside of the leg to a button at the bottom. These were also known as gaiter-trousers; these buttoned at the foot and strapped under the boot and this form of trouser can be traced back to the West Indies where they were often referred to as 'mosquito' trousers.

Breeches of 1751 and 1768. Generally the breeches were blue for Royal regiments and red for non-royal regiments (1). The officers' often wore breeches of the appropriate facing colour (2). The breeches of 1768 had a front fall, generally they were white (3) but those regiments with buff facings or buff toned wore the same colour breeches (2).

Spatter-dashes, Gaiters, Knee-pieces and Boot Stockings

In 1751 all infantry wore spatter-dashes in white cloth for dress or on campaign: black or brown, they reached to mid thigh and carried buckled garters of black cloth or leather. Each was fitted with a cloth insert stitched into the leg to cover the shoe. Gaiters were similar but reached only to the knee and also had a stitched insert to cover the shoe. They were made from two pieces of material with some twenty-eight buttons down the outer face, with a loop passing under the foot, being secured by a buttonhole at the lower button. Gaiters could be a variety of colours: for parade or dress black was commonly; used, for campaign grey, brown or black were preferred.

In 1768 the warrant stipulated black gaiters with small stiff tops cut away behind the knee and secured by a strap or buckled garter, but many regiments had adopted the practice by 1760. These tops were introduced to prevent wear at the knee and to protect the breeches, but many styles were adopted as inspection reports show: there are references to spatter-dashes, half gaiters, full gaiters and in some cases more than one type were in use. Boot stockings were usually white cloth or canvas some eight inches long and attached below the knee by a string. They rose some four inches above the boot or gaiter tops and were fastened by a loop or other attachment to the lower buttons of the breeches. The later version was shorter, nominally some four inches tall, and buttoned to the lower four buttons of the breeches.

> Cuthbertson notes
> Gaiters were designed to prevent dirt and gravel from getting into the shoes. To answer this purpose, the gaiters must be shaped to the leg without wrinkles and they must come down low on the quarters of the shoe, the tongues large enough to cover the buckle, without rising at every motion of the foot. Stout gray linen makes the best gaiters for blackening. They do not require being made longer than to meet the knee band of the breeches, as a leather top which buckles above the calf entirely covers the knee pan, defends it when kneeling in the firings, and is an addition to the good appearance of the leg: small horn or metal buttons without shanks are best as they contribute to the fit of the gaiter. There should be a double leather strap to pass under the shoe, white tops, like those of the cavalry, preserve the breeches from being soiled. They must button tight upon the knee;

rise (some four inches) above the leather tops, and sink (two inches) below the top of the gaiters, so as to cover the stockings.

Another means of obtaining 'small stiff tops' was achieved by painting the gaiter. This had some advantages in that the paint acted as a stiffener and as waterproofing. It is possible that some units wore full gaiters, painted, cut-off at the knee of the breeches, and supplemented with black leather knee-guards or any form of gaiter.

Footwear

These were black and made of dyed leather with round toes, leather heels and soles. They were straight-lasted and were supposed to be worn on alternate feet every other day, a practice apparently avoided. The shoes were held on the feet by a strap stitched to each upper and buckled together. The buckles for the officers and rank and file could be quite elaborate when used for walking out or dress. In undress, half boots that reached just above the ankle were often worn. Pumps were mainly worn by the fashionable officers and were low-heeled shoes with thin, supple soles; they were fastened with a buckle over the tongue.

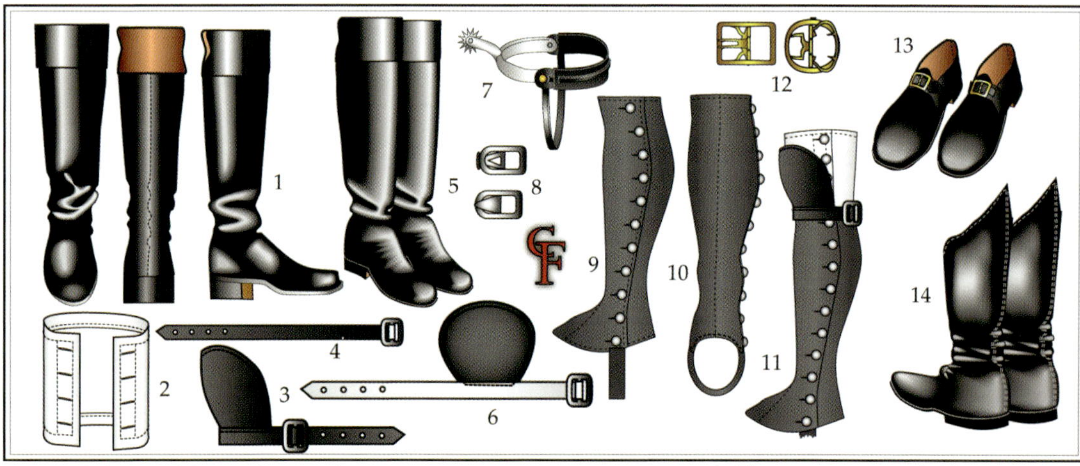

Boots and Shoes and Gaiters. Boots with cut-away tops and the high heel of 1751(1). The boot stockings (2). The stiff tops with garter (3). The boots of 1768 (5). The knee pieces with white garter (6). The spur of 1751 (7). The garter buckles (8). The gaiter side view (9). The gaiter rear view (10). The gaiter with stiff top, garter and boot stocking (11). The shoe buckles (12). The shoes (13) and the half boots with pointed rear ends (14).

Stockings and Hose

When not wearing boots, or for dress, the officers wore stockings. These were pulled over the knees and secured under the bottom of the breeches. They were made either of cotton, wool or silk. Garters were made of strips of woven material and worn with a buckle. Thicker stockings were worn inside boots over thinner stockings as protection. Officers when attending levees, balls and the dining room in breeches wore white silk stockings. The rank and file were issued with knitted woollen socks.

Canes

Both officers and senior non-commissioned officers carried canes. They were usually of the standard type with a head of a particular metal and often heavily embellished or carved. They were commonly fitted with a ring to attach to a coat button.

Spurs

Only mounted infantry officers wore spurs. These were plated spurs strapped over the boot, each with long straight necks and a spiked revolving rowel.

CHAPTER SIXTEEN

Tartans of the Highland Regiments

Belted Plaid

The belted plaid began to be replaced for undress by the kilt as early as 1750 and, by 1785, the belted plaid was effectively an obsolete item although it was still considered to be appropriate dress for formal parades, until discontinued in 1816. The full plaid was made up of some five or more yards of material for officers; grenadiers wore three and three-quarters and the other ranks some three and a half yards of material, all of doubled width, some twenty-seven inches wide. To dress in a belted plaid, the belt was first laid upon the ground and the plaid laid over it such that the plaid on the lower half would reach to about the knee. The plaid was then folded to form pleats but the first and last two feet were left unfolded to form the apron. The wearer then lay down on the plaid and after folding over the two unpleated sections the belt was buckled and the person rose to the standing position with the upper part of the plaid almost reaching to the ankles. The lower half of the plaid formed a kilt, the two unpleated sections were folded over to form the apron and the corners of the lower part were often secured by a leather strap, buckle, button or pin. The two upper corners of the plaid were then raised and, in inclement weather, used to wrap round the body or, in fine weather, attached to the left shoulder, with some form of attachment, or to the shoulder strap.

The Kilt

The kilt was formed from the lower part of the belted plaid with the now redundant upper part removed. It had seen service during the Seven Years' War and had become a practicable form of highland dress with the box seams stitched into place. The kilt was to replace the belted plaid, except for full dress occasions, by the latter part of the century.

Breeches or Trousers

Many of the kilts or plaids worn during the period were often unavailable with breeches, trousers or gaiters being worn when the supply of kilts were no longer available. There are instances where any material that could be made available was made into trousers or breeches, in some cases made of plaid or kilts themselves.

Tartans

The tartan used were coloured with vegetable dyes and produced a variety of softer tones than those of the later aniline dyes; the older tartan shows much paler colours and a much smaller sett than that associated with the later setts and while the thread counts varied they resulted in similar sett sizes. There were different thread counts for the plaids and kilts of the different ranks, officers wearing the finest, then the NCO and lastly the private soldier. The thread count is given for the government sett and has been taken to the point of pivot where the pattern would be repeated and, as each sett had both horizontal threads, the thread count was repeated accordingly. The sett took two forms, the twenty and a half inches fine and the coarse kilt with a small sett with seven green turns and a full repeat every six and one eighths inches and the larger sett with four green turns and a full repeat every ten and three quarter inches. The MacKenzie sett was based upon the government sett with a buff line with two black guards replacing the single black line of the green turns, and a red line with two black guards replacing the central single line of the alternate blue turns. It followed the same sizes as the Government sett.

1 2 3 4

The Government tartan worn by the 42nd Highlanders and upon which nearly all of the military setts were based (1). It was listed by Wilson's for drummers, musicians and the grenadier companies and had a modified sett comprising a red line without guards replacing the single black line of the green turns (2). The tartan of the 73rd Highlanders, also known as the MacKenzie (3) and the tartan of the 1st 105th (Queen's Own Royal Highlanders) (4).

The pattern or design of a tartan is known as the sett and is made up from a series of different coloured threads. The main sett used during this early period was the basic government sett; this had a two and four bar black over-stripes on alternate blue turns with a black stripe on the green turns. This formed the basis of the tartan for most of the highland regiments with varying thread counts. The thread count for the plaid of a private soldier was:

> Blue twenty, black ten, blue ten, black ten, blue ten, black sixty-four, green sixty-four, black ten, green sixty-four, black sixty-four, blue sixty-two, black ten and blue five. The sett was then repeated about the pivot point.

The other popular sett was the government tartan with a red overstripe. This was used by the 42nd when wearing the kilt, but they maintained the ordinary government set for full dress. The 77th Atholl Highlanders and 84th Royal Highland Emigrants also used the red overstripe. The thread count for the plaid of a private soldier was:

> Blue twenty, black ten, blue ten, black ten, blue ten, black sixty-four, green twenty-seven, red ten, green twenty-seven, black ten, green sixty-four, black sixty-four, blue sixty-two, black ten and blue five. The sett was then repeated about the pivot point.

The other tartan worn during this period was that of the 73rd Highlanders. While based upon the government sett this had a buff stripe replacing the black stripe of the green turns and a red stripe replacing the central blue stripe of the alternate blue turns, such that it appeared to have two black guards. It had a different thread count and that for the plaid of a private soldier was:

> Blue twenty, black six, blue six, black six, blue six, black forty-two, green thirty-eight, black four, buff six, black four, green thirty-eight, black forty-two, blue thirty-eight, black four and red three. The sett was then repeated about the pivot point.

The 42nd are considered to have worn a red overstripe (without guards) replacing the single black line of the green turns during this period. Lawson considers that it was worn by the whole regiment when wearing the kilt, but only by the grenadiers when wearing the belted plaid. There were considerable variations for the pipers and drummers of the regiments. In the 42nd the pipers are attributed with two further red stripes to replace the blue between the double black lines of the alternate blue turns. The drummers of regiments wearing the government sett usually had a stripe of the facing colour added.

Most highland regiments were disbanded between 1763 and 1765, with the exception of the 42nd Royal Highlanders, but some were reformed during the period of the War of Independence and these are listed below:

Table of tartans worn by the different regiments.	
Regiment and title	Sett and overstripe
42nd Royal Highland Regiment	Government
42nd Royal Highland Regiment	Drummer, government with red overstripe on the green ways
42nd Royal Highland Regiment	Grenadier, government with red overstripe on the green ways
71st Regiment Fraser's Highlanders	Government
73rd McLeod's Highlanders	Government with red with guards on the green ways and buff with guards
74th Argyllshire Highlanders	Government
76th MacDonald's Highlanders	Government
77th Atholl Highlanders	Government with red overstripe on the green ways
78th Seaforth Highlanders	Government
81st Aberdeen Highlanders	Government
84th Royal Highland Emigrants	Government with red overstripe on the green ways
1st 105th (Queen's Own Royal Highlanders)	A red and blue sett.

Sporrans

The purse, when worn, was made from almost any animal skin usually with the hair to the outside, but plain leather versions are known. There was often some form of metal fitting to the top and leather thongs or tassels placed on the face.

Highland Hose

The hose of all ranks was cut from the red and white check tartan cloth and sewn up the back. Some regiments, particularly the 42nd, had a black edging to the checks. Footless half-hose was worn with socks and began to be used in marching order as the cloth hose often 'galled' the feet. The rosettes and garters were scarlet, often worn with the long end showing after the top of the hose had been turned over the garter.

CHAPTER SEVENTEEN

Infantry Accoutrements

Introduction

At the start of the period the belts of regiments of the Foot Guards and line regiments were pipe-clayed, the highland regiments wore black leather straps and introduced the light companies in 1770, generally wore tan shoulder straps, but inspection reports clearly indicate these general rules were commonly not adhered to. The term 'buff' applied to accoutrements usually means they were made from buffalo leather, not the colour.

Musket Slings

Slings were considered accoutrements and were the property of the colonel of the regiment, at least until 1793. Hence there was no universal musket sling. The infantry muskets were fitted with a white (buffalo) sling one and three quarter inches wide and up to forty-five inches long. There were several patterns, some with a lower end pierced with two holes, others four and some carried a stitched leather lace on the inside face, while yet others used a separate lace. The upper end could be fitted with a leather loop, a single buckle or double buckle. The lace end of the sling was passed through the back of the upper swivel, down through the loop or buckle and then to the front of the lower swivel. It was then passed through the swivel and the lace tied, from the back, through the holes to secure it. The sling was adjusted by moving the loop or buckle.

One-piece Sword Shoulder belt of 1750

This sword belt was made up of several pieces: firstly there was the waist belt itself, next the bayonet frog, and, finally the sword frog. Both the sword and bayonet were retained in place by loops of leather and the whole belt was some three inches wide with curved buckles to fasten it together. The wearing of swords by the enlisted men was abolished in 1763. The manufacture varied and there were many versions of these belts.

One-piece Sword Shoulder belt of 1768

This sword belt was made up of three pieces: firstly there was the waist belt itself, next the bayonet frog and, finally, the sword frog. Both the sword and bayonet were retained in place by shaped openings and the whole belt was some two inches wide. The wearing of sword by the grenadiers was abolished in 1784. Those regiments with buff facing wore buff-coloured belts. Once again there were many versions of this belt, particularly as regiments adopted their own style of buckle; evidence is clear that the Foot Guards used them, as did many other regiments.

One-piece Sword Shoulder belt

Infantry officers and NCOs usually wore the sword on a one-piece cross belt worn over the right shoulder, the sword being carried in a frog, secured by a shaped oval on the scabbard. The belt was made of white buff (buffalo) leather some two inches wide and consisted of a sword frog sewn to a short, seventeen inch, front strap with a longer forty-six inch rear strap. Normally the two belt straps were clipped together by the studs and hook on the rear of the belt plate. It became common practice for officers to wear the bayonet in America and it was worn in the sword frog pointing outwards.

Three-part Sword Waist-belt

Just becoming popular during the American Revolution was the belt of three pieces. It was made from three straps of white buff (buffalo) leather some one and a half inches wide, joined together by one or more rings. It had a brass buckle and a further buckle and runner on the right side to adjust the length. The first section was about ten inches long; the second, which connected the two rings, about nine inches; and the third about sixteen inches plus the adjustment. A sword sling, an inch wide, was suspended from each ring; the front sling was some eleven inches long and the rear about thirty-six inches.

One-piece and three-piece Cartridge Pouch Belt

The cartridge belt was made of white buff leather, the width changing with time and the regiments concerned. The belts were some fifty-four inches long, with two one-inch straps, six inches long, stitched to each end; these were secured under buckles on the cartridge pouch. The Foot Guards had their own thee-piece version; this consisted of a fifty-inch strap with metal tips at both ends and was passed into the buckles of two short straps with the usual one-inch pouch straps stitched to each end.

Four-part Grenadier Shoulder Strap and Match Case.

The styles varied over the years, with some as illustrated above, as shown by Morier in his paintings of grenadiers, while others changed over the years until they were dispensed with until officially abolished in 1784 although the Foot Guards continued to wear them for some time. The 29th Regiment only discarded them when they returned from Foreign Service in 1838.

Bayonet Belt

The bayonet belt was made of white leather some two and one tenth inches wide, later reduced to two inches. The cross-belt consisted of a short seventeen-inch front and a longer forty-six inch rear strap, both stitched to the bayonet frog. When dressing, the cartridge belt was put on over the left shoulder and the flap on the rear of the cartridge pouch; next the bayonet belt went over the right shoulder. The two belts were then clipped between the plate and strap of the bayonet belt. In this way the equipment was secured together and to the jacket.

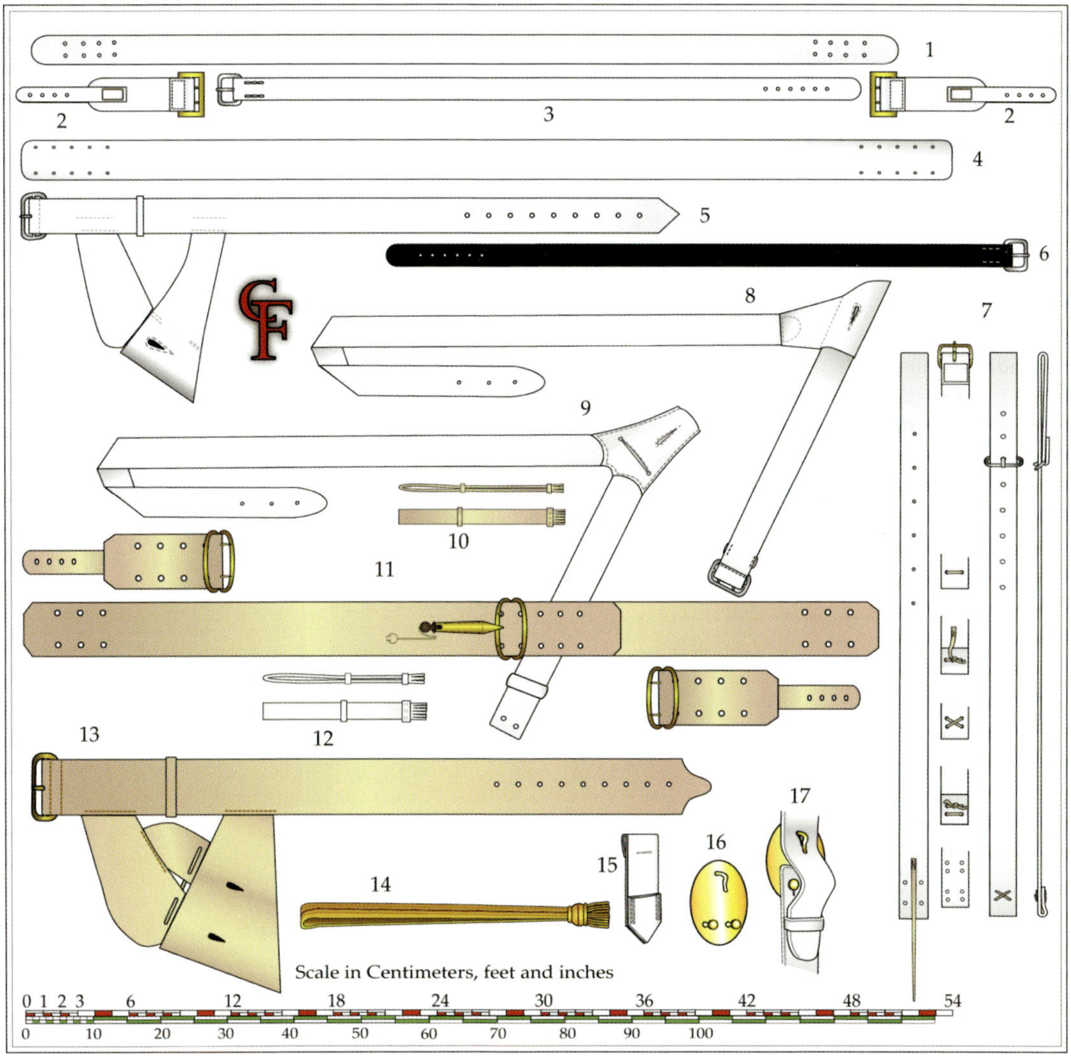

Accoutrements. The double-ended pouch strap (1). The buckles to secure it to the cartridge pouch (2). The belt to hold the belly box (3). The different size pouch belt (4). The sword belt of 1768 (5). The black belly strap of the cartridge box (6). The different musket straps of the period (7). The bayonet belt of 1768 (8). The one-piece sword frog (9). The sword sling of 1750 (10). The grenadier belt of 1750 and the two ends that buckled to the cartridge pouch (10). The sword sling of an enlisted man in 1768 (12). The sword and bayonet belt of 1750 (13). The infantry sword sling of gold and crimson (14). The bayonet attachment for the belly box (15). The rear of an oval gilt breast plate (16) and the method by which the two straps were connected together (17).

Camp Equipment

The Board of Ordnance issued troops engaged in active service with these stores. They were issued out of public funds and only charged to the regiment in cases of negligent loss. Each man received a canteen and strap, a haversack and a blanket. Also issued were forage cords, picquet ropes and leather water buckets.

Water Bottle and Haversack

The bottle was standard water container and was two different sizes. The first some seven inches tall and three inches deep held four pints, while the second, found during the American Revolution, held some three pints, and were six inches tall and two inches deep. They all of tinplate with soldered seems and were carried on a knotted cord. The haversack was designed to carry three days of rations; the haversack was made of light canvas or coarse, unbleached linen. It was about twenty inches wide, twelve inches deep and worn on a two-inch wide strap three feet long, and secured by a buckle and runner. The flap was fastened with buttons with the exact style varying from maker to maker. The colour seems to have varied between fawn to off-white. On the march it carried three days, bread or biscuit, salt beef or whatever the owner considered appropriate. This was a standard item of equipment issued to all other ranks.

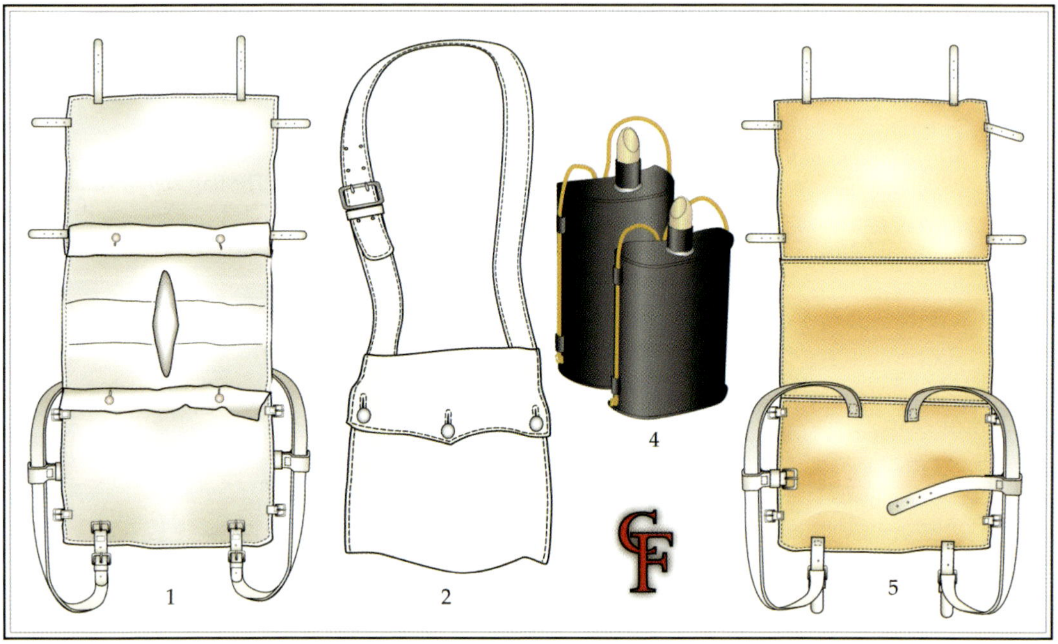

The knapsacks, water bottle, haversack. An inside view of the 'Envelope' pack showing the two ends and the central pocket (1), an overall view of the haversack (2), a view of the water bottles (4) and an outside view of the knapsack showing the securing buckles and straps (5).

Knapsacks

The ubiquitous, and unpopular, British infantry pack had been in service for many years and some regiments adopted a goatskin covering during the War of Independence. The early issue was made of canvas or coarse linen with the outside usually painted to make it weatherproof and the rear face embellished with a regimental badge or other identity. The interior had two main pockets fourteen inches tall, with buttoned flaps and a central hollow compartment of eight inches that usually held shoes and brushes; when folded out flat it was about eighteen inches wide and three feet inches long. When packed it was folded over and the two ends strapped together at the sides and the bottom forming a pack eighteen inches wide and fourteen inches high. It had no stiffening or rigidity and was usually worn over the cross belts and shoulder straps. The shoulder straps of the knapsack were secured across the chest by a cross strap that often accorded acute discomfort to the wearer. Several variations in pattern are known and these are probably due to the different manufacturers and the modifications applied by the battalions or personnel in the field.

Cartridge Pouches

The final component to a soldier's stand of arms was the black eighteen-hole cartridge box, detachable bayonet frog and waist belt assembly. After he came to his regiment the new recruit was eventually issued a regimental cartridge pouch with shoulder belt and a regimental waist belt to hold the bayonet scabbard. Originally, the pouch and box were intended to be worn together, with the pouch over the shoulder and the box around the waist. This may be seen in a majority of the early 1750s paintings of British grenadiers executed by David Morier housed in the Royal Collection. The unpopularity of the cartridge box was infamous, as the construction was of very poor design as it was attached to the soldier around the waist by the thin leather strap and the box was prone to turning upon itself and dumping the load of cartridges. While the cartridge boxes may not have been commonly used in peacetime, they were used during the early days of American Revolution in 1775. The Battle of Bunker Hill in June demonstrated all too well the faults of the cartridge box design. According to the 3 August 1775 general order issued by the Commander-in-Chief of British forces in North America, Lieutenant General the Hon. Thomas Gage, the soldiers were 'to wear their Cartouche Boxes Over their Shoulders and not round their waists'.

Infantry Cartridge Pouch of 1750.

The paintings by Morier in the Royal Collection give many views of the Infantry cartridge pouch and it is noted that that of the 33rd Regiment had a buff flap and a black body to the pouch itself. The flap appears quite long, about seven inches, but the pouch is quite small being, about three inches deep. Inside this was a wooden block with eighteen cartridges arranged in pairs. The iron buckles were placed so that they could pierce the strap; the width of the cartridge belt was approximately three inches.

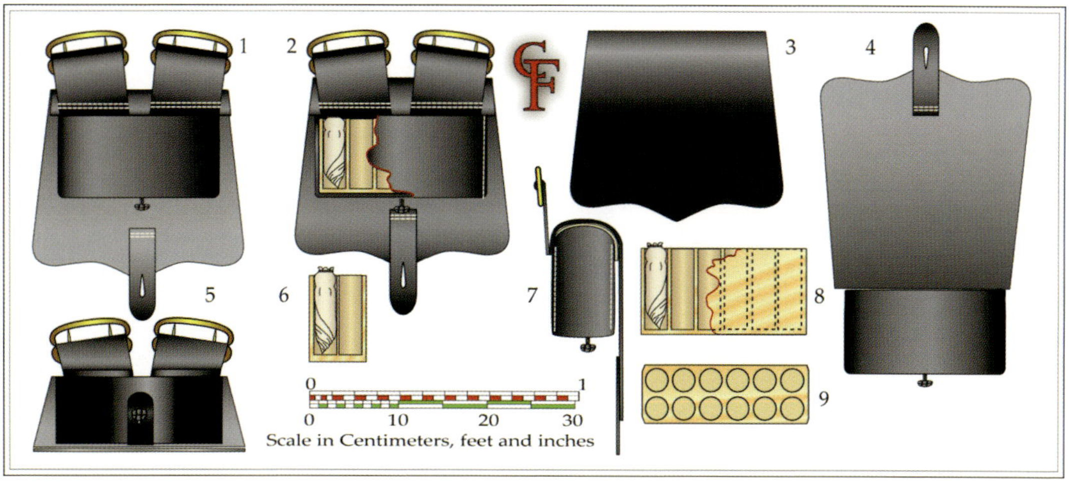

Cartridge Pouch of 1751. A rear view of the pouch showing the small box for the cartridges and the stitching securing the shoulder strap ends (1), a sectioned view of the pouch from the rear showing the method of carrying the cartridges (2), a front view of the pouch (3), a further front view with the pouch open (4), an under view (5), the side view of the wooden block drilled to take twelve rounds (6), a side view of the pouch (7), a sectioned view of the front of the block (8) and a top view (9).

Belly Box, Nine to Twenty-Eight Rounds

The cartridge pouches were fitted with curved wooden blocks drilled to take the cartridges. There were several different versions with as many as twenty-eight holes in two rows, others with as few as six in one row, dependent upon the version of the pouch. The strap could be passed behind the box in front. The construction varied with some in a leather container while others held just a wooden block, which could be square-ended or curved. The example shown below seems to conform to the normal method of construction.

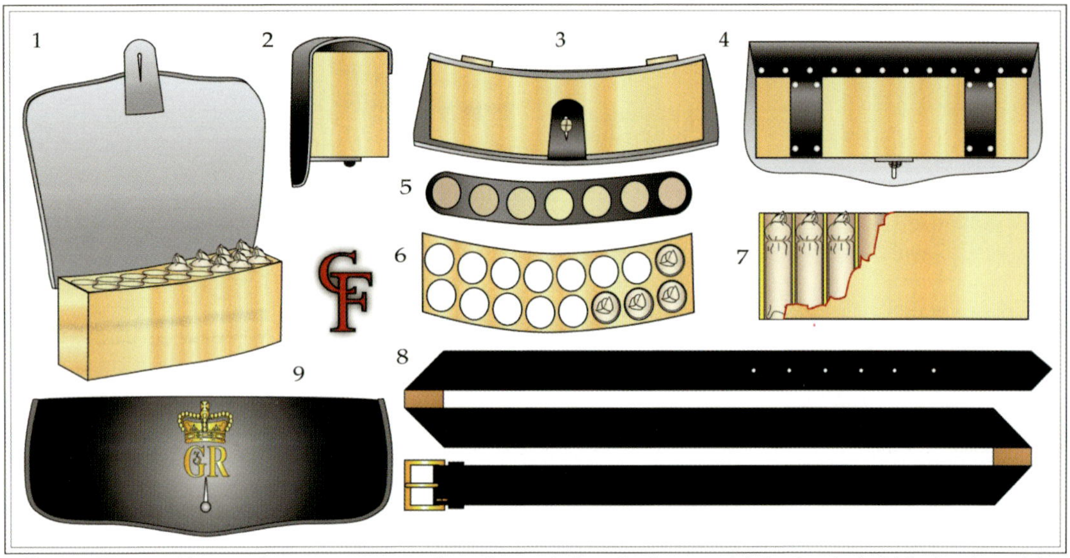

Belly Box. This cartridge pouch was worn across the waist, made from leather one eighth of an inch thick, the sizes of the pouches varied with the manufacturer, as did the exact method of construction. A perspective view (1). The side view (2). The under view showing the securing flap and button (3). The rear view of the pouch (4). The different quantities of cartridge were carried (5). This block held sixteen cartridges (6). The sectioned view of the same block (7). The strap used the keep belly box in place (8) and the front view of the belly box and the different methods of construction (9).

Thirty-Six Round, Reversible Block Cartridge Pouch.

This pouch, illustrated below, came back into general use until other more practical pouches replaced it. The reversible block pouch was never fully successful as it had the reputation of dropping the lower cartridges to the ground. The construction was quite complex including, a wooden block drilled to take thirty-six rounds; this was double ended and had two flaps of leather to protect the cartridges. The sides of the block were bevelled to facilitate removal, which are a pinch fit into the pouch; the Y-shaped strap extended over the block and was used to pull out the block and reverse it to gain access to the ammunition on the underside, which were placed as to enable the block to be reversed when the first eighteen cartridges were expended. The belt straps passed through keepers to buckles positioned beneath the pouch. These were arranged so that the tongue protruded below the buckle to engage with the narrower straps stitched to the main strap; an asterisk stamp is used to hide the holes nailing the pouch to a wooden block for assembly. When the leather could be saved it usually was and pouches with different pieces of leather were common, the user often stamping letters into the leather of the pouch as regimental identifiers. The inside of the flap was of finished leather and the outer side unfinished leather blackened with wax.

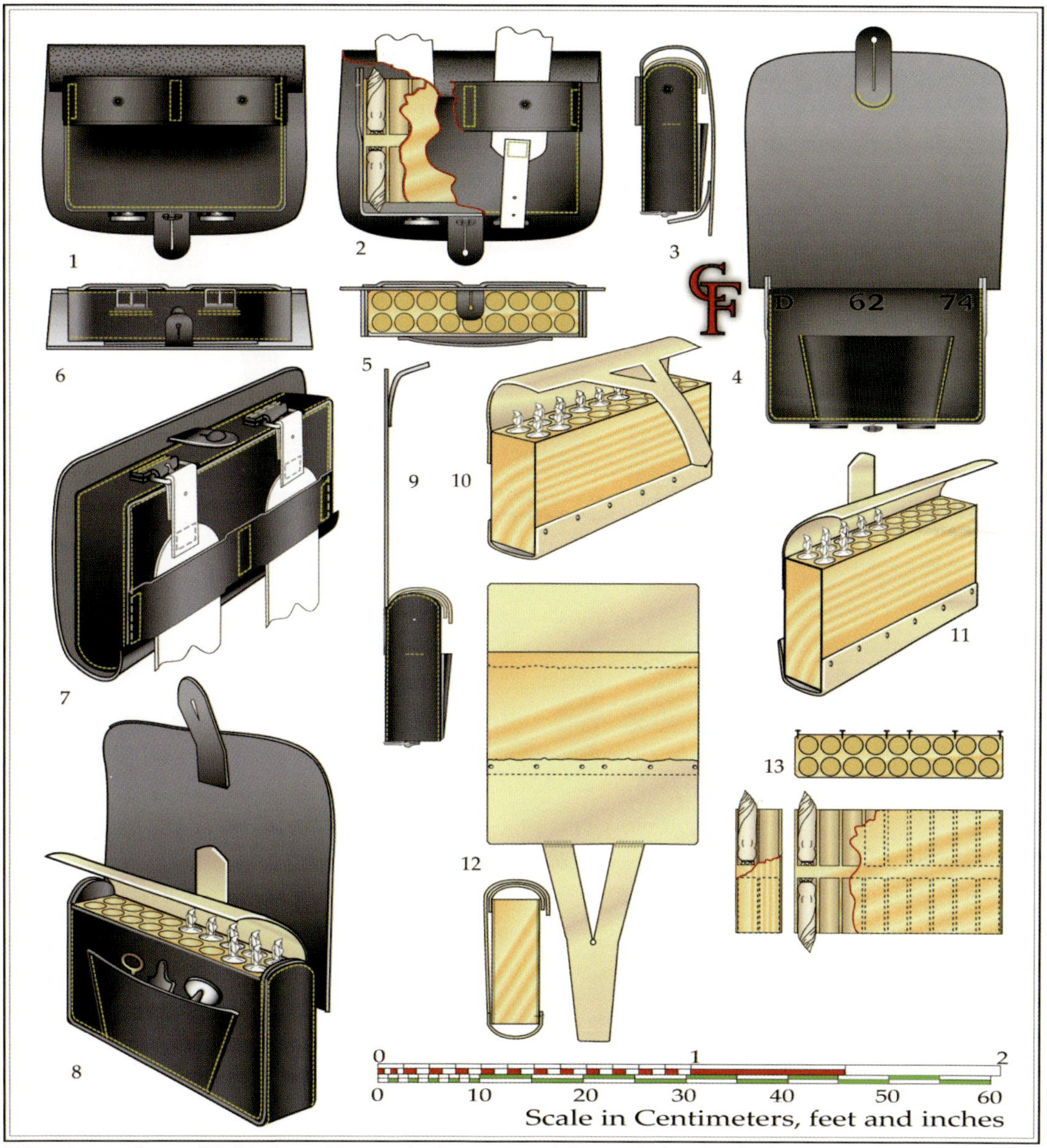

Thirty-six round reversible block cartridge pouch. A rear view of the pouch showing the keepers (1). The sectioned view showing the internal construction (2). The end view with the pouch flap closed (3). The front view of the pouch showing the pocket for the tools and spare flints (4). The top view (5). The under-view shows the buckles with the tongue underneath, the cross belt strap buckles through, under itself (6), a perspective view of the underside of the pouch and buckles (7). The perspective top view showing the wooden block and front pocket for the flints or tools (8). The end view with the flap open (9). The two perspective views to show contents of the block, the first showing the strap to reverse the block (10). The second showing the wooden block in the normal position (11). The internal wooden block with the two flaps used to remove and reverse the block (12). The three views of the block with thirty-six holes, in two rows of nine drilled into the top and bottom (13).

Twenty-nine Round Cartridge Pouch

This type of pouch is typical of the sort used during the War of Independence. Here again the buckles securing the belt ends were passed underneath the buckle. This sort of cartridge pouch was common to the period and this particular example was drilled to take twenty-nine cartridges. The use of badges on cartridge pouches was officially withdrawn in 1784 but the evidence is that they were still used by some regiments. An asterisk stamp was used to hide the holes nailing the pouch to a wooden block for assembly.

A twenty-nine round cartridge pouch attributed to the grenadier company of the 50th Regiment circa 1775, the rear view (1) has the letter 'G', believed to stand for 'Grenadier', stamped into the leather of both the keeper and the rear face of the pouch. A side view (2), with the flap closed showing the nails and screws used to retain the block and the plain buckles with the tongue underneath so that the cross belt strap buckles through, under itself. The badge worn on the pouch (3). The alternative badge carried on the pouch (4). The front view showing the method of retaining the badge by three split pins on the inside of the flap and a view of the pocket used to gain access underneath the wooden block (5). The part view (6) showing the pouch belt attached to the buckle and an under-view (7) showing the keepers and buckles. A sectioned front view to show the wooden block secured in position, the front pocket flap to allow access to the void underneath the block where flints and tools would have been stored (8). The top view shows the wooden block drilled to take twenty-nine cartridges and nailed into position in the pouch, which has a flap opening at the front (9). The sectioned view showing internal details of pouch (10) and a side view with the pocket extended and the flap fully open (11).

Light Companies

A small twenty-eight round pouch was worn over left shoulder, as well as a powder horn, bags for ball, hatchets and carbines. A waist-belt was also worn, with an added bayonet frog. Like their battalion and grenadier soldier counterparts, light infantry soldiers received eighteen-hole cartridge box assemblies with their firelocks. In addition, according to the light infantry uniform regulations of 4 March 1771, light infantry soldier accoutrements provided by the colonels of regiments were to consist of 'a small cartridge box to contain nine rounds in one row, to be worn before with a belt of tanned leather round the waist,' and a powder horn and leather ball-bag for 'running ball' firing. Of course, both cartridge boxes could not be worn around the waist; the eighteen-hole government issue box was worn over the right shoulder, to rest on the left side. Alternate views of this soldier, and similar views of a light infantry private of the 6th Regiment from the same encampment, show that the nine-hole box was worn around the waist. The light infantry companies carried a variety of cartridge boxes worn over the left shoulder which could vary in the number of cartridges from as few as nine to as many as twenty-eight. They also carried a bag for shot, a powder horn and hatchet and were armed with shortened arms.

General

Although it was originally expected that British infantry soldiers carried either the around the waist pouch or the new over the shoulder cartridge box during the American War for Independence, this was not always the case. It was probably no accident that, of the two British commissioners assigned by Burgoyne to hammer out the details of the convention with their rebel counterparts before the surrender, one was Captain James Henry Craig (47th Regiment), Burgoyne's head judge advocate. Craig was no doubt careful to ensure that only the term 'arms' would find its way into the Convention, and that neither clothing nor military accoutrements were to be included. None the less, chaos soon ensued. An inventory of the military articles surrendered by Burgoyne's entire army on 17 October 1777 included the following arms: 4,647 muskets, 3,477 bayonets without scabbards and 638 cartouche boxes. Of great concern to the congress was the fact that the number of firelocks was not equal to the number of soldiers surrendered, the number of bayonets was significantly less than the number of firelocks, none had their surrendered scabbards and the number of 'cartridge boxes' surrendered was significantly less than everything else. The Congress saw this as a contravention of the Treaty of War.

CHAPTER EIGHTEEN

Infantry Weapons

Muskets

The musket in use was the ubiquitous Brown Bess of which there was a multiplicity of designs and variations. The examples considered in this appendix represent only a sample of the many varieties that existed. It had an effective range of about 200 yards and its weight with the bayonet was over eleven pounds. The barrel was over three feet long, the calibre of the bore was three-quarters inches (effectively a twelve bore shot-gun firing a solid shot) and the bullet weighed 490 grains or just under twelve to the pound. A picker and brush to clean the musket lock were worn on a chain that usually attached to a button on the coat or behind the cross belt. When practising firing drills the locks were fitted with 'wooden snappers' instead of flints.

The infantry muskets were fitted with a white buff sling about one and three-quarter inches wide and up to forty-five inches long. There were several patterns, some with a lower end pierced with two holes, others with four while others carried a stitched leather lace on the inside face; others used a separate lace. The upper end could be fitted with a buckle or double buckle. The lace end of the sling was passed through the back of the upper swivel, and down through the loop or buckle to the front of the lower swivel. It was then passed through the swivel and the lace tied, from the back, through the holes to secure it. The sling was adjusted by moving the buckle. Another part that was used to protect the lock was either a full-length cover for the butt and lock or a short lock protector made out of leather or other material. During the period there was a constant stream of replacement muskets, carbines and pistols.

The accuracy of these early smoothbore muskets was not good. In a series of tests carried out to determine the effects of the smoothbore musket a target three feet wide and eleven and a half feet high was set up at a range of 150 yards. At this range, only three-quarters of the rounds fired hit the target. The chances of hitting at 250 yards were so poor that the width of the target was increased to six feet, but not one in ten rounds hit and, at 300 yards, although many rounds were fired, none actually hit the target.

Long Land Pattern Musket

Over 30,000 of this model were made. The first used in used in America, by the 42nd Regiment, is dated as 1737. It was stocked to within four and a half inches; three blocked, semi-circular brackets retained the barrel. There were brass pipes to retain the ramrod which could be either wood or metal, although the wooden was of a larger diameter; the use of wooden rammers still persisted after the American Revolution. The lock plate measured six and five eighth inches by one and a half inches, overall length was sixty-two inches, barrel length forty-six inches and the calibre was 0.78 inch. There were many versions of this musket, which included the patterns of 1748, 1756 and the 1756 (Irish).

Short Land Pattern Musket

Over 83,000 were made. This musket was originally used in 1746 as a carbine for dragoons. It was stocked to within four inches of the barrel; three unblocked, semi-circular brackets retained the barrel. There were four pipes to the to retain the metal ramrod. The lock plate measures six and five and-a-half inches, but is distinctive in that it had a double oval to the spring. Overall length was fifty-eight and one eighth inches, barrel length forty-two inches and the calibre was 0.78 inches. There were many versions of this musket, which included the patterns of 1756, 1769, 1777, the Liége pattern, the 1769 (Irish) and 1779-S with a smaller S shaped side plate.

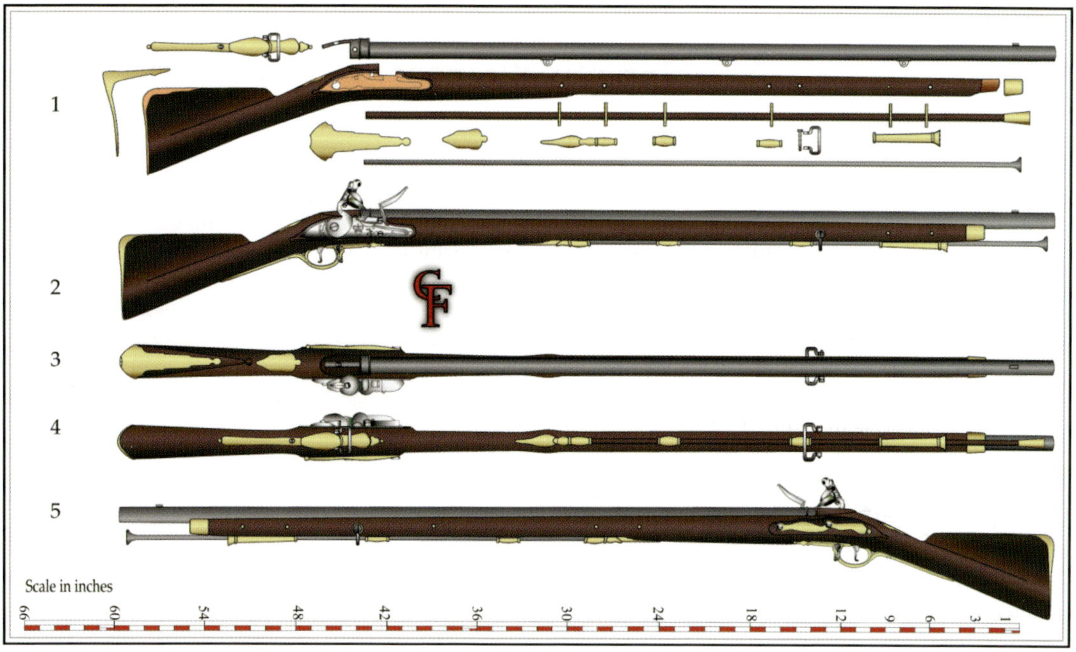

Long Land Pattern Musket. An exploded view of the Long Land pattern Musket with the different parts shown with a steel rammer (1). The right side view showing the lock mechanism ((2). The top view showing the barrel and lock mechanism (3). The under view showing a wooden rammer which was used in many muskets (3) and a left side view showing a metal rammer (5).

Carbines

Carbines usually have a calibre of between 0.65 and 0.67 inches to take a ball of 0.615 inches. The barrel length varied from forty-two inches to thirty-nine inches.

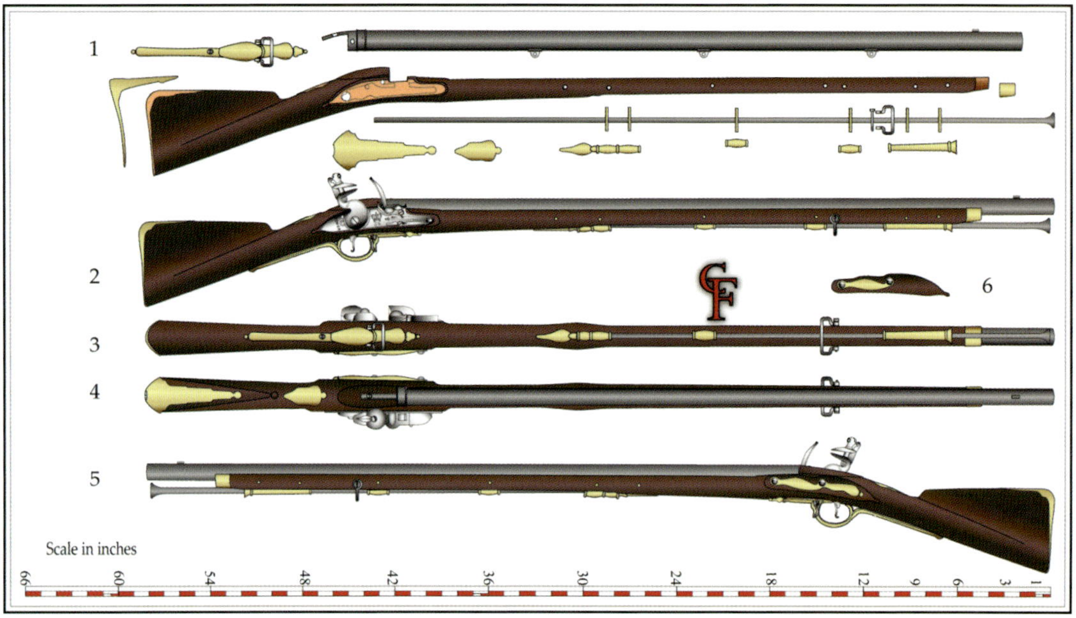

Short Land Pattern Musket. A sectioned view showing the assembly of the pins, barrel, and separate trigger guard, butt plate and metal ramrod (1). The right side view of the musket (2). The under view of the musket showing the lock mechanism (3). The top view showing the escutcheon plate and butt (4). The left side view showing the double curved side-plates (5) and a view of the different side-plate of the 1779 S-model (6).

Generally, both the firelock and bayonet were engraved with matching regimental, company, or rack number information but markings between regiments sometimes differed considerably. Arms of regiments on the Irish Establishment were engraved with the regimental number or company letter rack number on the musket wrist-plate and bayonet socket.

Fusils

Officers commonly adopted the fusil, which were often privately commissioned from gun-makers, while enlisted men who received the standard issue. Fusils were also issued to fusilier regiments, highland officers and, in many cases, the light companies. Some were equipped with wooden rammers and not metal rammers as may be imagined.

Bayonets

Seamed iron bayonets fitting black leather bayonet scabbards with brass mountings were issued with each musket. As there was no guarantee for interchangeability between bayonets and muskets, bayonets were generally engraved with a numbering system corresponding with that found on the muskets to which they belonged. Many different manufacturers, including Thomas Helier, William Higgins, William & Edwards, among others, made the triangular bayonet. It was four inches long in the shank and seventeen inches long in the blade. The black leather scabbard was eighteen and a half inches long with brass fittings but there were many variations. After 1776 the men of 62nd served the rest of the campaign, with their eastern timber rattlesnake skin covering the bayonet scabbards.

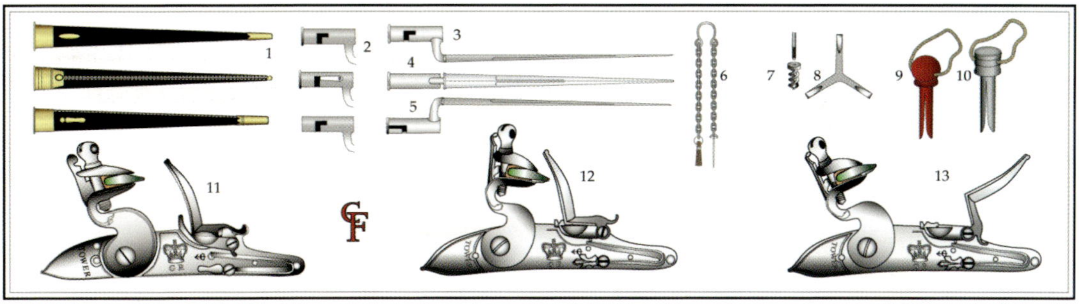

Locks, Tools and Bayonets. The different types of bayonet scabbard (1). The different types of Bayonet (2). The three views of a bayonet, the right side view (3), the under view (4) and the left side view (5). The picker and lock usually worn attached to a button on the coat (6). The rammer end and cartridge removal tool (7). The multipurpose tool for the musket (8). The two plugs to prevent ingress of water and damp to the barrel (9 and 10). The lock from a later version of the Short Land musket (11). The two views of the lock from a long land musket (12) and the lock variant from a Short Land Pattern musket (13)

Ferguson Rifle

The story begins with Ferguson's service in Germany and Flanders at the end of the Seven Years' War. He had come into contact with a few of Britain's German allies who were armed with clumsy rifles. He learned the value of light infantry for counterinsurgency, and the advantages of aimed fire. While in the West Indies he had rifles made to his specifications in England for use against Black Carib insurgents. A breechloader on John Warsop's system was the best. Using a separate wrench, its vertical plug could be unscrewed perpendicularly from the bottom of the barrel, exposing the chamber for loading. The rifle shot well and accurately. Its oversized ball completely sealed the rifled bore. However, because it loaded from the bottom, it was slow and complicated to use. Major Patrick Ferguson took an existing idea the screw breech, and built it into a practical military firearm, or at least as practical as technology of the 1770 would permit. His major innovation was to incorporate the screw breech into the trigger guard with a handle that didn't detach and become lost, and stayed out of the way when not being used. Screw breech rifles of the time usually had a detachable handle that protruded from the side of the rifle. This alteration made the rifle into a practical weapon that could be operated in the field without fear of losing parts. Ferguson added another refinement: he used a multistart tapered screw for the breech plug. Multiple threads allowed more movement per turn, which allowed the breech to be completely opened with one turn of the handle. By adding a gentle, inward taper on the plug, it would loosen up very quickly after a slight rotation, yet be tight enough when locked to maintain a good gas seal. These were features not found on any previous breechloader. Nor were they simple tasks, given the machine tools of the time. Machining out a screw with multiple threads, adding a taper, and then machining the same multithread taper into the breech itself was quite a feat in the late 1700.

This rifle was used during the War of Independence; it now consisted of a screw plug at the breech, which could be unscrewed by rotating the trigger guard. The user would tilt it forward and initially load in a lead ball of a slightly larger diameter than the barrel. The lead ball would roll forward and be stopped by the onset of the grooves in the barrel. The calibre was 0.645 inches and, the ball diameter 0.648 inches. Unlike most muzzleloaders, the ball did not have to be wrapped in a cloth or paper patch to provide a tight seal, since it was a slightly larger diameter than the barrel. Then the user would pour in some gunpowder to fill the loading chamber in the rear of the breech rotating the trigger guard the other way to screw the plug back in. The screw plug rising back up would clear any excess gunpowder in the breech, and the user could then cock the flintlock mechanism and be ready to fire. Upon firing, the lead ball would deform slightly and keep the tight seal as it made its way through the barrel. The twelve start separate threads spiralled from the top to the bottom. It was only necessary to turn the screw plug once on a Ferguson rifle. The screw threads were interrupted by vertical slots cut into them; some excess powder would fall into these gaps between the screw threads when the plug was screwed back in, and the remaining excess fouling could simply be wiped off. The top of the screw plug was of a slightly larger diameter than the screw hole. What this meant was that the screw plug could not be removed from the rifle even if it was fully unscrewed. This was done so that it was not possible to drop the screw plug even in the heat of combat.

Setting up a target 200 yards from his position, Ferguson fired for four or five minutes continuously at it, at a steady rate of four shots per minute. In one 'mad minute' of extra rapid fire he managed to fire six shots. He then advanced on the target, reloading and firing as he walked at a steady rate of four shots per minute. To prove the impossible, and ignoring the rain which was heavy enough, to disable most flintlock weapons, he poured a bottle of water into the firing pan and down the weapon's barrel, so that all the powder was wet, and within half a minute he had the rifle firing again as well as before. In 1776 Viscount Barrington took charge of the Ferguson Rifle project from the Master of Ordnance. Immediately detaching Ferguson from his regiment, he ordered the recruiting of a special corps of one hundred men, mostly drawn from the 6th and 14th Regiments of Foot. By the end of March 1777, the new unit was ready to sail for America and the war under command of Patrick Ferguson himself, and armed with his rifle. The only identifiable original Ferguson rifle from the first one hundred made is in the Morristown National Park Museum. The rifle is forty-nine inches long overall and is stocked to four and a half inches of the barrel, it has a thirty-four inch barrel and a calibre 0.68 inches. The rifle had a hexagonal barrel with eight square grooves and made one turn in sixty inches, the rear rifle sling swivel is at the left side of the breech.

The Ferguson Rifle was easy to use and the rate of fire was far higher than could be achieved with a normal flintlock musket. It was never taken into service and there are reasons to suggest the matter was not properly handled in the normal manner. The main reason for the quick and accurate fire came from the screw thread; the handle at the rear was to rotate the trigger guard and thread for quick and easy loading.

Highland Pistols

Almost all highland infantry carried pistols of this generic type with the typical ram's horn butts. Each Colonel issued the pistols and evidence is clear that they were issued to almost every highland regiment of the period. Many were made in Birmingham and London but others in Scotland and they were evident during the War of Independence. It was only after 1795 that the Board of Ordnance declined to support the issue of pistols to highland regiments but there is clear evidence that they were still issued to all ranks during the period.

Highland Pistols. The illustrations show a pair of typical pistols with the lock mechanism (1). The reverse side shows the clip used to secure the pistol to the clothing or belt (2) and the absence of a trigger mechanism is particularly noticeable.

Swords

A weapon with a long blade sharp on one or both edges and often referred to as a hanger where the blade curved. Before the days of regulation swords the colonel of the regiment usually dictated which should be used and the example of the 35th officer's sword is a classic example. It was not until after 1786 regulation that swords were issued. In many cases officers carried the sword and general officers carried the same weapon in a lightened form. The early swords were basket-hilted, based on the older patterns that were in many cases very similar to the swords carried by highland officers. Over time the length of the sword increased, the blade being just less than three feet, with a weight of about twenty-six ounces. Never-the-less the colonels of regiments picked the swords for their men while the hilts varied from regiment to regiment with some in brass, others in iron. The sword cutlers of Birmingham made most of them.

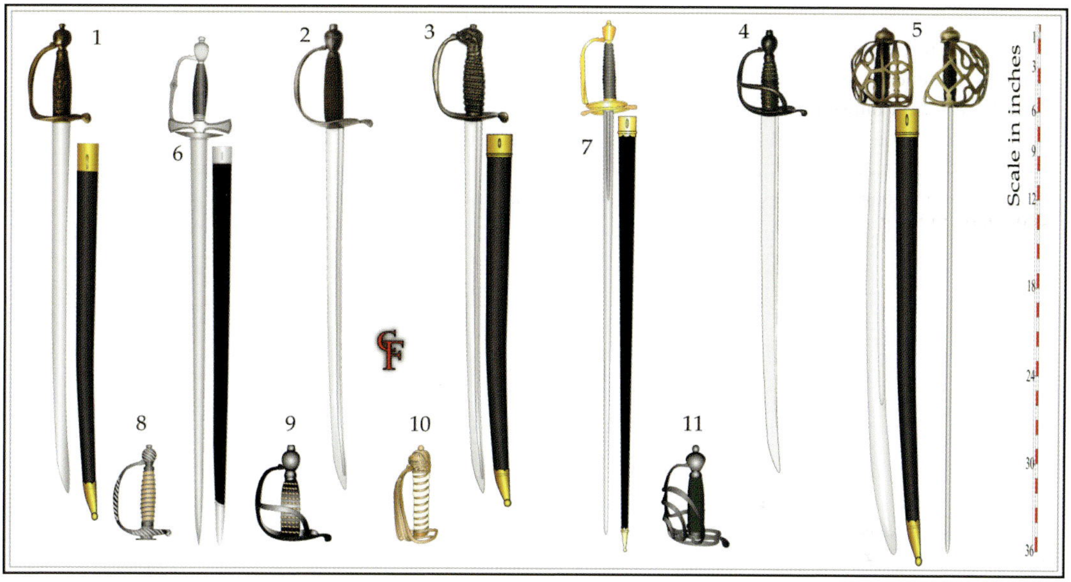

Swords of the period. The fusilier sword of the 23rd Regiment is some 30.85 inches overall with a blade length of 24.61 inches (1). There is no detail of the length (2). The dog-headed sword of 1755 is 32.13 inches 3 with a blade of twenty-six inches (3). The length of this sword is not known (4). The basket hilted grenadier sword is 36.13 inches overall with a blade length of thirty-and-a-half inches (5). The 35th Regiment sword is thirty-five inches overall with a twenty-nine inch blade (6). The general officers sword is thirty-five inches overall with a blade length of twenty and a half inches (7). The hilts of 1775 to 1783 have no measurements (8 to 11).

In 1776 corporals and private soldiers of the 42nd (Royal Highland) Regiment of Foot ceased to carry broadswords, dirks and pistols. The background of the painting from Minorca shows the prevalent British practice of 'piling' (stacking) arms in groupings of three. This is how British infantry surrendered their firelocks at Saratoga on 17 October 1777.

Losses of Weapons

The main loss was during the War of Independence. In 1774 the capture of Fort William lost a mixed collection of 1,500 weapons; the capture of the Ordnance stores in Boston from HMS *Hope*, 1,600 carbines; capture of the Ordnance stores in Boston from the HMS *Nancy* 20,001. Long land pattern muskets, surrendered at Saratoga were 1,065 muskets and forty-three fusils. In 1780 sinking of the HMS *Russia Merchant* lost a further 3,125 muskets and, at the surrender at Yorktown, 6,658 mixed muskets, carbines and pistols were lost This is apart from those arms lost during campaign overall the British Army lost more than 34,000 weapons.

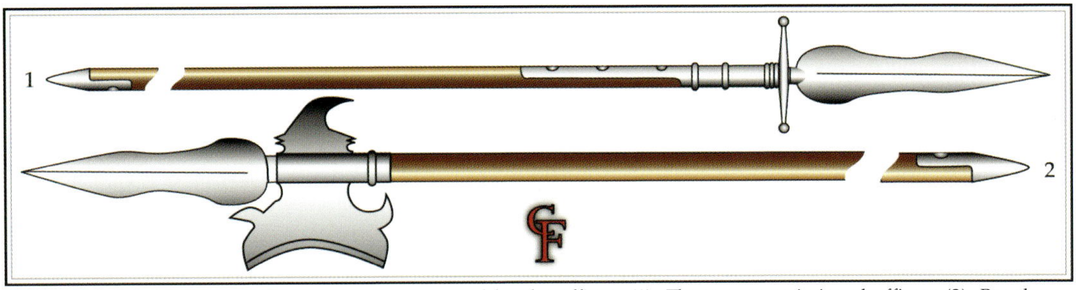

The espontoon and halberd. These weapons were used by the officers (1). The non-commissioned officers (2). But these ceased to be used in North America after about 1776 or so when fusils were more usually used.

Espontoon and Halberds

The officers carried the espontoon and NCOs the halberd. Each had an ash shaft nine feet long with a steel butt. The officer's espontoon had a steel blade screwed into a ringed socket four and a half inches deep securing the crosspiece that prevented the point penetrating too far. The blade was some twelve and three-quarter inches long and the cross bar five and a half inches wide. Two shaft supports extended down from the socket to give added strength. These ceased to be used in America by about 1776 and eventually went out of use in April 1786. The halberd resembled a spear with a sharp pointed edge and a hatchet head below, although patterns varied. It was mounted on a pole of about five to seven feet.

PART FOUR

Introduction to Foot Guards and Infantry Regiments.

The regiments included on the following pages represent those raised between 1730 and 1815; the practice of indicating the precedence by number of the regiments in the British Army was common after 1751. Regiments listed below refer to those that are known to have existed during the period but each includes their titles to a later date. In the British Army the establishment of 1755 was: ten companies, each consisting of one captain, one lieutenant, one ensign, three sergeants, three corporals, two drummers and seventy private soldiers. The equivalent Irish establishment was the same number of officers but only two sergeants, two corporals, one drummer and twenty-nine private men.

In each case the regiment is referred to in the list by the lowest number allocated and, thus, any renumbered regiment appears under the lower, or later, number. In 1782 infantry regiments were allocated county titles and the lineage charts in Appendix D should be consulted in order to understand the changing numbers of regiments over the period and indicate the way the regiments were renumbered. In this book the uniforms of 1751 from the paintings by Morier, 1758 warrant, 1768 warrant and most of the information gleaned from the American War of Independence has been included. At the time the 1751 Warrant was enacted almost all British infantry coat lapel buttons were placed singly but, as time progressed and fashion changed, button pairing started to develop in some regiments as early as the late 1760s. Throughout the 1770s and 1780s, the number of regiments employing paired buttons increased so much so, that by the 1790s, regiments displaying paired buttons were more common than those which did not. It is difficult to track when those regiments which changed to the style of pairing buttons did so; however, all regiments which employed paired buttons made the change at one point or during this time another although none of the pre-American Revolutionary War marching regiments of Foot utilized paired coat lapel buttons or loops. Dating officer portraiture is generally the only way to determine the trend, although such representations are usually limited.

The 1768 warrant lists the seventy regiments that made up the British infantry at that time. It excludes the Foot Guards who had their dress changed after 1771. Light companies had been formally introduced into the line regiments on 30 November 1770 when it was ruled that a tenth company was to be added to each regiment as a left flank, or light, company. Each was to consist of one captain, two lieutenants, three sergeants, three corporals and sixty-two private men. Officers in dress retained the long coat, but in undress wore a jacket similar to the men. One aspect of the painting of the 25th at Minorca is that there was a wide variety of dress; this is apparent in the hats and a combination of shoulder knots and epaulettes. All foot regiments in America had an increased establishment of eighteen men to each company. Although this was ordered in 1775 it took some time for all the drafts to arrive. The main dates of involvement in the battles of the War of Independence are given below. They do not cover every incident, only those where significant engagements took place between the British Army and the Continental Army.

The following regiments formed the garrisons before the war:
7th Regiment of Foot in Quebec, 8th Regiment of Foot in Quebec, 26th Regiment of Foot in Quebec, 14th Regiment of Foot in Boston, 29th Regiment of Foot in Boston, 64th Regiment of Foot in Boston and the 60th Regiment of Foot in the West Indies.

The following regiments were added during 1774:
4th Regiment of Foot, 5th Regiment of Foot, 18th Regiment of Foot, 38th Regiment of Foot, 43rd Regiment of Foot, 47th Regiment of Foot, 52nd Regiment of Foot, 59th Regiment of Foot and the 65th Regiment of Foot.

The following regiments were added during 1775:
17th Light Dragoons, 10th Regiment of Foot, 17th Regiment of Foot, 22nd Regiment of Foot, 35th Regiment of Foot, 40th Regiment of Foot, 44th Regiment of Foot, 45th Regiment of Foot, 49th Regiment of Foot, 55th Regiment of Foot, 63rd Regiment of Foot and the 84th Regiment of Foot.

The following regiments were added during 1776:
16th Light Dragoons, Guards Composite Battalion, 6th Regiment of Foot, 9th Regiment of Foot, 15th Regiment of Foot, 16th Regiment of Foot, 20th Regiment of Foot, 24th Regiment of Foot, 28th Regiment of Foot, 31st Regiment of Foot, 33rd Regiment of Foot, 34th Regiment of Foot, 37th Regiment of Foot, 42nd Regiment of Foot, 46th Regiment of Foot, 50th Regiment of Foot, 53rd Regiment of Foot, 54th Regiment of Foot, 57th Regiment of Foot, 62nd Regiment of Foot and the 71st Regiment of Foot.

The following regiment was added during 1777:
77th Regiment of Foot.

The following regiments were added during 1778:
70th Regiment of Foot, 74th Regiment of Foot, 80th Regiment of Foot, 82nd Regiment of Foot, 105th Regiment of Foot, 3rd Battalion of the 60th Regiment of Foot and 4th Battalion of the 60th Regiment of Foot.

No regiments were added during 1779 and 1780.

The following regiments were added during 1781:
3rd Regiment of Foot, 19th Regiment of Foot, 30th Regiment of Foot and the 69th Regiment of Foot.

The main engagements between the British Army and the Continental Army.
In 1775:
Concord, 19 April; Lexington, 19 April; Bunker Hill also known as Breed's Hill, 17 June; St John's, 4 September; Chambley, 17 October; Montreal, 13 November; Quebec, 4 December; Great Bridge, 9 December.

In 1776:
Moiré's Greek, 27 February; Boston, 17 March; Cedars, 16 May; Brooklyn Heights, 22 August; Long Island, 27 August; Harlem Heights or the Hollow Way, 16 September; Pell's Point, 18 October; White Plains, 28 October; Fort Washington, 16 November; Trenton, 25 December.

In 1777:
Princeton, 3 January; Ticonderoga, 5 July; Hubbardston, 7 July, Brandywine Creek; 11 September; Freeman's Farm, 19 September; Paoli, 20 September; Germantown, 4 October;

In 1778:
Monmouth, 28 June; Newport; Savannah 29 December.

In 1779:
Stony Point, 15 July; Penobscot Bay, 13 August; Paulus Hook, 19 August.

In 1780:
Charleston, 12 May; Springfield, 23 June; Camden, 16 August.

In 1781:
Cowpens, 17 January 1781; Guilford Courthouse, 15 March; Relief of Ninety-Six, 22 June; Eutaw Springs, 8 September; Yorktown, 19 October.

The following represented the regiments captured by the Continental Army:

Two companies of the 71st were captured at Boston in 1776.

Saratoga
The following regiments were surrendered by General Burgoyne: the Composite Battalion of grenadiers and light companies together with the battalion companies of the 9th, 20th, 21st, 24th, 31st, 47th and 62nd, together with the flank companies of the 29th, 34th and 53rd; in all this totaled 5,791 officers and men.

Yorktown
General Cornwallis surrendered 7,000 officers and men: the Composite Foot Guards, twenty-three officers and 504 men; an alleged number of the 7th Regiment; 17th Regiment, seventeen officers and 227 men; a number of the 19th Regiment; 23rd Regiment, twelve officers and 221 men; 33rd Regiment, eleven officers and 259 men; 43rd Regiment, fourteen officers and 354 men; 71st Regiment (2nd Battalion), twenty-two officers and 272 men; 76th Regiment, thirty-one officers and 684 men; 80th, thirty-two officers and 657 men; plus some companies of the 82nd and 84th. The flank companies of the 22nd, 57th, 38th, thirty-one officers and 640 men; the light company of the 22nd Regiment; and Royal Artillery, thirteen officers and 198 men; there is also a possibility that the flank companies of the 49th were captured.

The following regiments were surrendered in other battles:
One company (forty men) of the 8th Regiment at Fort Sackville in February 1779.
Fifty men of the 49th Regiment and six companies of the 17th Regiment at Stony Point in July 1779.
1st Battalion 60th and 16th Regiment (less light company) at Pensacola in May 1781.
Nine companies of the 7th Regiment and their colours at Fort Chambley and Fort St John in October 1775.

State of the British Army during the War of Independence						
	On Duty	Other duties	Prisoner	Sick	Wounded	Total
March 1776						
Boston	8,150	419	31	236	358	9,194
December 1776						
New York	7,536	88	0	5	112	7,741
July 1777						
New York	12,270	572	47	157	38	13,084
Rhode Island	1,203	36	15	159		1,413
May 1778						
Philadelphia	12,050	645	814	1,504	?	15,013
New York	1,727	42	129	349	?	2,247
Rhode Island	1,425	31	13	135	?	1,604
December 1779						
New York	10,162	984	544	2,473	9	14,172
Georgia	427	10	34	124	0	595
Florida	1,264	206	7	170	0	1,647
March 1780						
New York	6,311	933	469	1,101	314	9,128
Carolina	4,415	461	66	221	4	5,167
Georgia	621	83	53	133	20	910
West Florida	362	33	168	42	3	608
November 1781						
New York	4,953	606	103	579	55	6,296
Virginia	3,573	152	358	1,220	262	5,565
South Carolina	4,077	289	233	545	61	5,205
East Florida	514	12	22	24	0	572
West Florida	42	26	253	8	3	332

CHAPTER NINETEEN

Regiments of Foot Guards

Raised in 1656 and placed on the English establishment in 1660 as:
Lord Wentworth's Regiment
Amalgamated in 1665 with:
King's Royal Regiment of Guards to form:
1st Regiment of Foot Guards
Redesignated in 1815 as:
1st, (or Grenadier) Regiment Of Foot Guards

In the Morier Paintings of 1751:

• The facings for this Household royal regiment were dark-blue.
• Officers' lace and buttons were gold and officers' coats were laced for dress with square loops, set evenly.
• Other ranks' coats were scarlet lined blue. The lapels were laced about with seven, square loops, set evenly with three further square loops below. The coat pocket carried three buttons and was laced about.
• The red waistcoat was laced about and had nine square loops.
• Breeches for this regiment were dark-blue.
• Lace of the rank and file was a plain white.
• The outer braid of the cuff was rounded with a square end. The cuff slash was laced about with four buttons and two points to the ladder lace.
• The pocket was horizontal and laced about with three buttons.
• Grenadier cap had a blue front and rear turn-up and was laced in white. The front carried a crown over the Garter Star inside which was the blue garter belt inscribed 'Honi Soit Qui Mal Y Pense'. This had a blue centre and a red cross of Saint George over a white cross of Saint Andrew. Either side of this were foliate designs in white. The tassel was white with a red centre.
• Wings were not worn until after 1752.
• The sword hilt was of steel.

The Foot Guards were not covered by the general Royal Warrant of July 1768 for Regiments of Foot, but the 1st Regiment of Foot Guards was in the Royal Warrant of June 1771:

• The facings for this Household royal regiment were dark-blue while the linings, breeches and waistcoats of all ranks were white.
• The officers' lace and buttons were gold, for dress they wore pointed loops by two and buff waistcoats.
• Other ranks' coats were laced about with ten diamond-shaped loops and shoulder straps to both shoulders.
• The dark-blue cuff had four diamond headed loops.
• The lace of the rank and file was plain white.
• The sergeants wore gilt buttons and braid.
• The buttons were flat instead of domed.
• Corporals wore a silk epaulette instead of a worsted shoulder knot.
• Drummers wore white silk and tinsel stripes in the lace instead of the orange colour. The collar and wings were trimmed in white silk fringe.
• The Grenadiers wore blue wings and the fur caps had black plates with white embellishments.

During the War of Independence:

On 13 February 1776 orders were issued from Guards Headquarters in London forming a detachment from the three Regiments of Foot Guards for service in North America. The detachment was to consist of fifteen privates from each of the sixty-four companies that made up the three regiments of Foot Guards. The detachment consisted of thirty officers, eighty-two non-commissioned officers, fourteen drummers, six fifers and 960 private men. Three officers, five additional staff and drummer were added to the strength prior to embarkation. They were to be organized into ten companies; the 120 drafts from the existing grenadier companies formed a composite grenadier company. The fifty-six regular infantry companies contributed 840 privates of whom ninety-six were allocated to the composite light company (the Foot Guards had no light companies at this time). The remaining 744 men were divided into eight companies of ninety-three men each. The first to third companies were composed of officers, NCOs and men of the 1st Foot Guards, the fifth and sixth were similarly composed from the 3rd Foot Guards and the seventh and eighth were from the Coldstream Foot Guards of which there whom nine officers and 298 other ranks. The fourth or brigade company was staffed by officers of the 1st Foot Guards but consisted of NCOs and men from all three regiments. Over the period of the war they were re-organized several times, particularly as new drafts arrived from home.

The bulk of each regiment remained in the British Isles while the composite unit embarked for America in March 1776, arriving in New York in August 1776. They saw action at Long Island, White Plains, Brooklyn, New York, Brandywine, Germantown, Guilford Courthouse, Springfield and Yorktown. General Cornwallis surrendered over 6,000 men including some 500 Foot Guards, after this battle in October 1781. They returned to England in two detachments, one arriving in January 1783 and the other in July 1783.
• The regiment used a shoulder bayonet belt while serving in North America.
• In March 1778, gold lace was removed from officers' and NCOs' coats and replaced with white lace like that of the private men of the 1st Foot Guards but other reports give no lace.
• The officers and NCOs were to be armed with fusils.
• The light infantry company was to have the coats cut in accordance with the pattern in the orderly room, but this order applied to current clothing only.

Raised in 1650 as George Monk's Regiment
Designated in 1660 as:
Duke of Albemarle's Regiment of Foot
Designated in 1661 as:
Lord General's Regiment of Foot Guards
Redesignated in 1661 as:
Coldstream Regiment of Foot Guards

In the Morier Paintings of 1751:
• The facings for this Household royal regiment were dark-blue.
• Officers' lace and buttons were gold and officers' coats were laced for dress with, square loops, set evenly.
• Other ranks' coats were scarlet, lined dark-blue. The lapels were laced about with nine pointed loops, set evenly, with three further pointed loops below. The vertical coat pocket carried twelve pointed loops with six buttons.
• The red waistcoat was laced about and had nine pointed loops.
• Breeches for this regiment were dark-blue.
• Lace of the rank and file was a plain white.
• The outer braid of the cuff was square with a pointed end. The cuff slash was laced about with five buttons and a six-ladder lace.
• The pocket to the skirt was vertical and lined about by thirteen pointed loops.
• Grenadier cap had a blue front and rear turn-up and was laced in white. The front carried a crown over the Garter Star inside which was the blue garter belt inscribed 'Honi Soit Qui Mal Y Pense'. This had a blue centre and a red cross of Saint George over a white cross of Saint Andrew. Either side of this were foliate designs in white. The tassel was white with a red centre.
• Wings were not worn until after 1752.

• The sword hilt was of steel.

The Foot Guards were not covered by the general Royal Warrant of July 1768 for Regiments of Foot, but the Coldstream or 2nd Regiment of Foot Guards was in the Royal Warrant of June 1774:

• The facings for this Household royal regiment were dark-blue and the linings, breeches and waistcoats of all ranks were white.

• The officers' lace and buttons were gold. They were laced about with ten scallop-headed loops in pairs, with large buttons instead of pointed loops in pairs with small buttons. There were two to each cuff and ten to each lapel.

• Other ranks' coats were laced about with ten scallop-headed loops in pairs, with large buttons instead of pointed loops in pairs with small buttons.

• The blue cuff had four scallop-headed loops in pairs.

• The pocket was horizontal with four scallop-headed loops in pairs and large buttons and laced about instead of the original small cuff and branch, pointed loops four and four to answer by twos lengthways up the arm with small buttons.

• The lace on the hips and back was scalloped instead of pointed.

• The lace of the rank and file was plain white.

• Sergeants wore gilt buttons, braid and gold epaulette.

• Corporals wore a silk epaulette instead of a worsted shoulder knot.

• Drummers wore six laces upon the sleeves, which were regular and pointed downwards. The cuffs were the same as the private soldier. The collar and wings were trimmed in white silk fringe, the wings having six pointed loops in pairs.

• Grenadiers wore blue wings with six pointed loops in pairs instead of six pointed loops set evenly and two shoulder straps; the fur caps had red plates.

During the War of Independence:

See notes above relating to the 1st Foot Guards

• The regiment used a waist belt with the letters 'CG'.

• In March 1778, gold lace was removed from officers' and NCOs' coats and replaced with white lace like that of the private men of the 1st Foot Guards.

• The officers and NCOs were to be armed with fusils.

• The light infantry company was to have the coats cut in accordance with the pattern in the orderly room, but this order applied to current clothing only.

Raised in 1660 as independent companies:
Designated in 1661 as:
Scots Regiment of Foot Guards
Numbered in 1713 as:
3rd Regiment of Foot Guards
This regiment served in North America during the War of Independence.

In the Morier Paintings of 1751:

• The facings for this Household royal regiment were dark-blue.

• Officers' lace and buttons were gold and officers' coats were laced for dress with pointed loops, set in pairs.

• Other ranks' coats were scarlet, lined dark-blue.

• The lapels were laced about with nine pointed loops, set evenly with three further, pointed loops, below.

• The red waistcoat was laced about with thin white loops.

• Breeches for this regiment were dark-blue.

• Lace of the rank and file was a plain white.

• The outer braid of the cuff was square with a pointed end. The cuff slash was laced about with five buttons and six-ladder lace.
• The horizontal coat pocket carried three buttons and was laced about with a thin inner lace.
• Grenadier cap had a blue front and rear turn-up and was laced in white. The front carried a crown over the Garter Star inside which was the blue garter belt inscribed 'Honi Soit Qui Mal Y Pense'. This had a blue centre and a red cross of Saint George over a white cross of Saint Andrew. Either side of this was foliate designs in white. The tassel was white with a red centre.
• Wings were not worn until after 1752.
• The sword hilt was of steel.

The Foot Guards were not covered by the general the general Royal Warrant of July 1768 for Regiments of Foot, but the 3rd Regiment of Foot Guards were re-clothed by the Royal Warrant in April 1768 and for the Royal Warrant issued in July 1774:
• The facings for this Household royal regiment were dark-blue and the linings, breeches and waistcoats of all ranks were white. The buttons on the waistcoats were in pairs.
• The officers' lace and buttons were gold, the coat lapels with ten scallop-headed loops in pairs, four in pairs on the pocket and cuff.
• Other ranks' coats had ten, scallop-headed loops in pairs instead of twelve pointed loops in pairs.
• The blue cuff was bound was edged in white lace and four loops in pairs.
• The pocket was horizontal with four scallop-headed loops in pairs and large buttons.
• The lace on the hips and back was scalloped instead of pointed.
• The lace of the rank and file was plain white.
• Sergeants wore a scarlet cloth, gold lace and ten pointed loops in pairs with the skirt of the coat one-pleat only, with gold epaulette, grenadiers wore two epaulettes.
• Corporals wore the collar, cuffs and epaulettes laced in silver, waistcoats of scarlet cloth buttoned in pairs and, hats laced silver. Grenadier corporals wore two silver epaulettes.
• Private men were dressed as the corporals but with plain white lace and no epaulettes; grenadiers wore two worsted epaulettes.
• Drummers wore white coats lined blue, with dark-blue cuffs, lapels, collar and wings trimmed in white silk fringe, the wings having six pointed loops in pairs. They wore white fur caps with yellow plates. Coats were laced at the seams, sleeves, sides and skirts. Waistcoats were red, bound with lace. The cuffs were the same as the private soldier.
• Grenadiers wore black fur caps with white plates, blue wings with six pointed loops in pairs instead of six pointed loops, set evenly, and a shoulder strap. Officers wore black plate faced gilt with gilt cords and epaulettes. Sergeants and drummer wore brass plates.

The 3rd Regiment of Foot Guards were further amended in the 1774 Warrant for issue in June 1775:
• The lapels to be scalloped-headed, looped in threes, with nine loops to each lapel. The cuffs, pockets and back of the skirts were to have three loops each.

During the War of Independence:
See notes above relating to the 1st Foot Guards
• The regiment used a waist belt with the letters 'Gds 3' stamped at the top and bottom.
• In March 1778, gold lace was removed from officers' and NCOs' coats and replaced with white lace like that of the private men of the 1st Foot Guards.
• The officers and NCOs were to be armed with fusils.
• The light infantry company was to have the coats cut in accordance with the pattern in the orderly room, but this order applied to current clothing only.

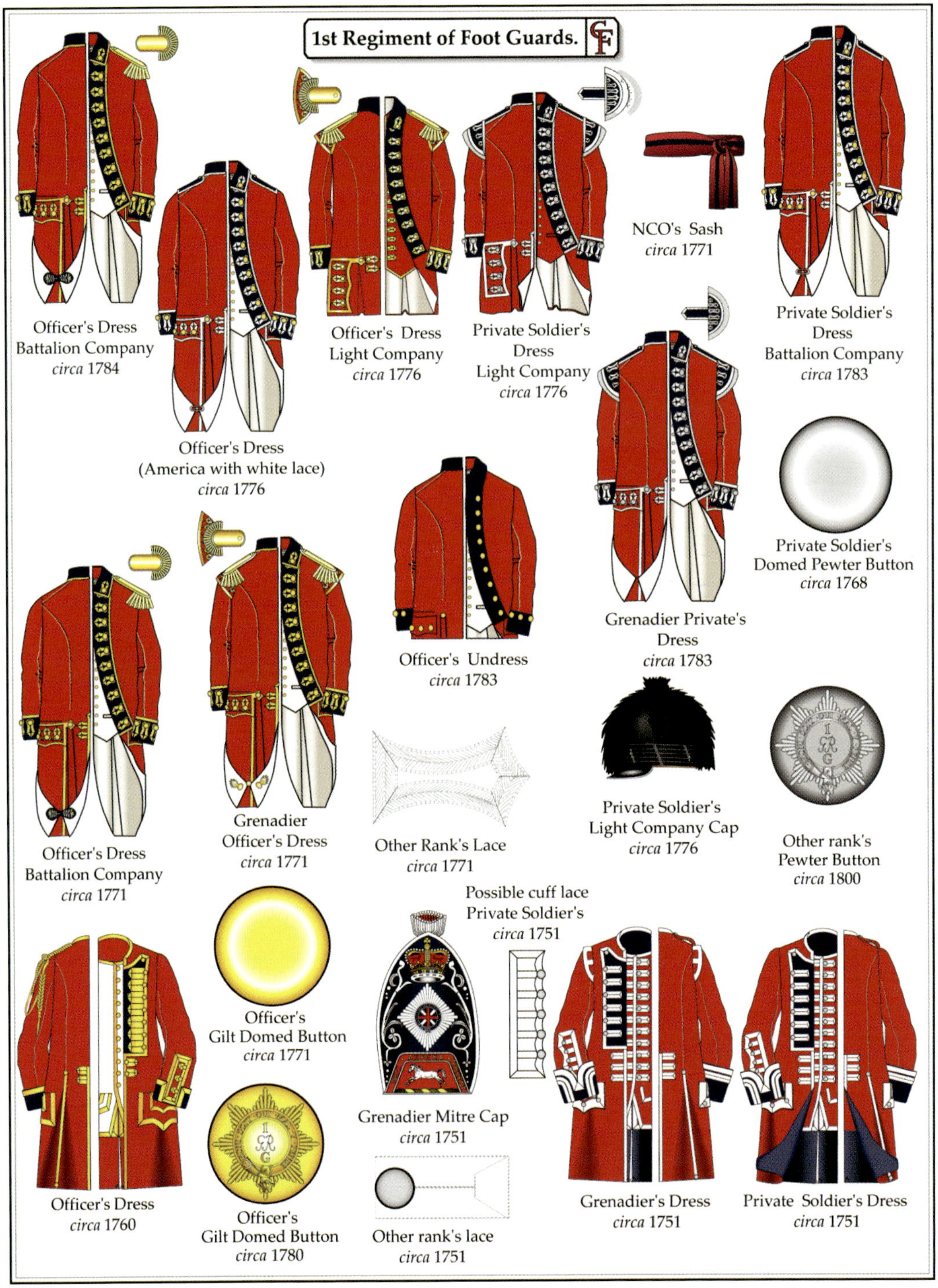
1st Regiment of Foot Guards.
Officer's Dress
Battalion Company
circa 1784
Officer's Dress
(America with white lace)
circa 1776
Officer's Dress
Light Company
circa 1776
Private Soldier's
Dress
Light Company
circa 1776
NCO's Sash
circa 1771
Private Soldier's
Dress
Battalion Company
circa 1783
Private Soldier's
Domed Pewter Button
circa 1768
Grenadier Private's
Dress
circa 1783
Officer's Undress
circa 1783
Officer's Dress
Battalion Company
circa 1771
Grenadier
Officer's Dress
circa 1771
Other Rank's Lace
circa 1771
Private Soldier's
Light Company Cap
circa 1776
Other rank's
Pewter Button
circa 1800
Possible cuff lace
Private Soldier's
circa 1751
Officer's
Gilt Domed Button
circa 1771
Grenadier Mitre Cap
circa 1751
Officer's Dress
circa 1760
Officer's
Gilt Domed Button
circa 1780
Other rank's lace
circa 1751
Grenadier's Dress
circa 1751
Private Soldier's Dress
circa 1751

2nd (Coldstream) Regiment of Foot Guards.
Officer's Dress
Battalion Company
circa 1785
Officer's Dress
(While in America with white lace)
circa 1776
Officer's Dress
Light Company
circa 1776
Private Soldier's
Dress
Light Company
circa 1776
Private Soldier's
Dress
Battalion Company
circa 1783
NCO's Sash
circa 1774
Officer's Undress
circa 1784
Grenadier Private's
Dress
circa 1768
Other Rank's
Pewter Button
circa 1774
Officer's
Light Company Hat
circa 1780
Officers's
Gilt Domed Button
circa 1773
Grenadier
Officer's Dress
circa 1774
Other rank's lace
(Set in pairs)
circa 1774
Other Rank's
Pewter Button
circa 1770
Grenadier Mitre Cap
circa 1751
Officer's
Small Gilt
Domed Button
circa 1770
Officer's Dress
circa 1751
Other Rank's Lace
(Set in pairs)
circa 1751
Grenadier's Dress
(Wings were not worn until 1753)
circa 1755
Private Soldier's Dress
circa 1751

3rd Regiment of Foot Guards.
Officer's Dress
Battalion Company
circa 1774
Officer's Dress
(America, white lace)
circa 1776
Officer's Dress
Light Company
circa 1776
Private Soldier's
Dress
Light Company
circa 1776
Grenadier Private's
Dress
circa 1774
Private Soldier's
Dress
Battalion Company
circa 1774
Officer's Undress
circa 1780
Grenadier
Officer's Dress
circa 1774
NCO's Sash
circa 1768
Other rank's
Pewter Button
circa 1800
Officer's Dress
Battalion Company
circa 1768
Grenadier
Officer's Dress
circa 1768
Other Rank's Lace
(Set in Pairs in 1768
after 1774 set in three)
Grenadier Private's
Dress
circa 1768
Private Soldier's
Dress
Battalion Company
circa 17768
Officer's Dress
circa 1760
Officer's
Gilt Button
circa 1780
Genadier's Mitre Cap
circa 1751
Other Rank's Lace
circa 1751
Grenadier Private's
Dress
(Wore no wings until 1753)
circa 1751
Private soldier's
Dress
circa 1751

CHAPTER TWENTY

Regiments of Foot

Raised in 1625 by Sir John Hepburn as a Scots regiment for French service.
It became part of the British establishment in 1670.
Retitled in 1684 as:
His Majesty's Royal Regiment of Foot
Ranked in 1747 as:
1st Regiment of Foot
Retitled in 1751 as:
1st (Royal) Regiment of Foot
In 1812 this regiment was retitled as the:
1st Regiment of Foot (the Royal Scots)

In the Morier Paintings of 1751:

- The facings for this royal regiment were dark-blue; this is confirmed by Milan's List of 1749.
- Officers' lace and buttons were gold and officers' coats were laced for dress with square loops, set evenly.
- Other ranks' coats were lined blue.
- The lapels were laced about and had seven square loops, set evenly, with three further square loops below.
- The horizontal coat pocket appears to be fully laced.
- The red waistcoat was laced about and had nine pointed loops.
- Breeches for this regiment were blue.
- Lace of the rank and file was a plain white.
- The outer braid of the rounded cuff was square ended and the cuff slash was laced about with four buttons and four points to the lace.
- Grenadier cap had a blue front and rear turn-up and was laced in yellow, the 'GR' Cypher was yellow on a blue ground within a green belt of Saint Andrew inscribed 'Nemo Me Impune Lacessit' with a white foliate design either side. The tassel was mixed white, red and blue.
- Wings were not worn until after 1752.
- The sword hilt was yellow metal.

In the 1768 regulations:

- The facings for this royal regiment were a dark-blue; while the linings, breeches the waistcoats of all ranks were white.
- The officers' lace and buttons were gold and their coats were laced for dress with ten embroidered loops, in undress they were laced with square loops, set evenly.
- The coat of the other ranks was laced about and had ten square loops, spaced evenly with the lace of the rank and file being white with a blue central chain stitch.
- The *Grenadier Book* at The Prince Consort's Library shows this regiment with loops spaced evenly.

Raised in 1661, by the Earl of Peterborough as the:
Tangier Regiment of Foot
Retitled in 1684 as:
The Queen Dowager's Regiment of Foot
Retitled in 1703 as:
The Queen's Royal Regiment of Foot

Retitled in 1715 as:
The Princess of Wales's Own Regiment of Foot
Retitled in 1727 as:
The Queen's Own Royal Regiment of Foot
Ranked in 1747 as:
2nd (The Queen's Own Royal) Regiment of Foot
In 1751 retitled as the:
The 2nd (Queen's Royal) Regiment of Foot

In the Morier Paintings of 1751:

- The facings for this regiment were sea-green; this is confirmed by Milan's List of 1749.
- Officers' lace and buttons were silver and officers' coats were laced for dress with seven, square loops, set evenly.
- Other ranks' coats were lined sea-green.
- The lapels were laced about and had seven pointed loops, set evenly, with three further loops below, but the coat is folded over and the lacing is not clear. The horizontal coat pocket was laced about and had three pointed loops.
- The red waistcoat was laced about, the coat was shown buttoned over but no further details are known.
- Breeches for this regiment were red.
- Lace of the rank and file was white with sea-green and white diagonal stripes to the outer edge.
- The top braid of the square cuff was pointed and the cuff slash was laced about with four buttons and four points to the lace.
- Grenadier cap was laced in white with a sea-green front and rear turn-up. The vertical Cypher of a small 'A' over 'GR' with a small 'A' below was in yellow on a red ground within a garter belt without buckle. The garter belt was inscribed 'Honi Soit Qui Mal Y Pense' with a white foliate design either side. The tassel was mixed white, red and sea-green.
- Wings were not worn until after 1752.
- The sword hilt was steel.

In the 1768 regulations:

- The facings for this royal regiment were sea-green until November 1768 when they were changed to dark-blue. The linings, breeches and waistcoats of all ranks were white.
- The officers' lace and buttons were silver. Their coats were laced for dress with ten square loops, set evenly.
- Other ranks' coats were similar with ten square loops, spaced evenly with the lace of the rank and file being white with a blue outer stripe.
- The *Grenadier Book* at The Prince Consort's Library shows this regiment with loops spaced evenly.

Raised in 1665 by Colonel Robert Sydney as:
Holland Regiment
Retitled in 1689 as:
Prince George of Denmark's Regiment of Foot
Retitled in 1708 as:
The Buffs
Ranked in 1749 as:
3rd Regiment of Foot
Retitled in 1751 as:
3rd Regiment of Foot, or the Buffs
In 1782 retitled as the:

3rd (or the East Kent) Regiment of Foot (The Buffs).

In the Morier Paintings of 1751:

- The facings for this regiment were buff; this is confirmed by Milan's List of 1749.
- Officers' lace and buttons were silver and officers' coats were laced and bound for dress with square loops , set evenly. They wore buff waistcoats.
- Other ranks' coats were lined buff. The lapels were laced about and had seven pointed loops, set evenly with three further loops below, but the coat is folded over and the lacing is not clear. The horizontal coat pocket was laced about and had three pointed loops.
- The red waistcoat was laced about, the coat was shown buttoned over but no further details are known.
- Breeches for this regiment were red.
- Lace of the rank and file was white with stripes of black, red and yellow to each edge.
- The top braid of the square cuff was pointed and the cuff slash was laced about with four buttons and two points to the lace.
- Grenadier cap was laced in white with a buff front and rear turn-up. The badge was a red-tongued, green dragon with a white foliate design either side. The tassel was mixed white, red and buff.
- Wings were not worn until after 1752.
- The sword hilt was steel.

In the 1768 regulations:

- The facings for this regiment were buff and the linings, breeches and waistcoats of all ranks were buff.
- The officers' lace and buttons were silver. Their coats were laced for dress with ten square loops, set evenly, during the period they were changed to ten square loops set in pairs.
- Other ranks' coats had ten square loops set, evenly; during the period they were changed to ten square loops set in pairs. The lace of the rank and file was white with a red outer stripe, a black outer-centre stripe and a yellow center stripe.
- The *Grenadier Book* at The Prince Consort's Library shows this regiment with loops spaced evenly, but Lawson considered that the loops were set in pairs.

During the War of Independence:

The 3rd Regiment served in North America between 1781 and 1782. They embarked from Ireland in March 1781 and arrived in Charleston 1781. They served in South Carolina and saw action at the Relief of Ninety-Six and Eutaw Springs, escaping the Yorktown capitulation while in garrison at Charleston. The regiment was posted to Jamaica in December 1782, remaining there until 1790.

- Officers and men purchased black feathers for their hats.

Raised in 1680 as:
2nd Tangier Regiment
Renamed in 1684 as:
The Duchess of York and Albany's Regiment
Renamed in 1685 as:
Queen's Regiment of Foot
Renamed in 1688 as:
The Queen Consort's Regiment of Foot
Renamed in 1702 as:
The Queen's Regiment of Foot
Renamed in 1715 as:
The King's Own Regiment of Foot

Ranked in 1747 as:
4th (The King's Own) Regiment of Foot
In 1751 retitled as the:
4th (or King's Own) Regiment of Foot

In the Morier Paintings of 1751:

• The facings for this regiment were sea-green and changed in November 1768 to a Royal regiment with dark-blue, as confirmed by Milan's List of 1749.
• Officers' lace and buttons were silver, changed to gold officially in 1758. The officers' coats were laced for dress with square loops, set evenly.
• Other ranks' coats were lined blue. The lapels were laced about and had seven pointed loops, set evenly, with three further loops below, but the coat is folded over and the lacing is not clear. The horizontal coat pocket was laced about and had three pointed loops.
• The red waistcoat was laced about, the coat was shown buttoned over and no further details are known.
• Breeches for this regiment were blue.
• Lace of the rank and file was white with a central blue zigzag.
• The top braid of the square cuff was pointed and the cuff slash was laced about with three buttons and one point to the lace, which slopes to the cuff.
• Grenadier cap was laced in white with a blue front and rear turn-up. The 'GR' Cypher was yellow on a red ground within a garter belt with buckle. The garter belt was inscribed 'Honi Soit Qui Mal Y Pense' with a white foliate design either side. The tassel was mixed white and blue.
• Grenadier wings were rounded.
• The sword hilt was steel.
• In 1765 white linings and breeches were adopted by this regiment while pioneers wore black bearskin caps with plates and grenadier officers carried fusils.

In the 1768 regulations:

• The facings for this royal regiment were dark-blue, while the linings, breeches and waistcoats of all ranks were white.
• The officers' lace and buttons were silver. Their coats were laced for dress with ten square loops, set evenly.
• Other ranks' coats had ten square loops, spaced evenly with the lace of the rank and file being white with a blue center stripe.
• The *Grenadier Book* at The Prince Consort's Library shows this regiment with loops spaced evenly.

During the War of Independence:

The 4th Regiment served in North America, arriving in Boston in June 1774 and serving until October 1778 when it was posted to Barbados. The regiment saw action at Lexington and Concord, Bunker Hill, Long Island, Fort Washington and Brandywine Creek. In 1778 it left New York for the West Indies, returning home in 1780.

• Some officers' wore silver lace on their hats while other ranks are reported as wearing scalloped lace.
• Light company distinctions in North America included bugle and cords.
• The other ranks wore a brass shoulder belt plate bearing the numeral 'IV'.

Raised in 1674 as:
The Irish Regiment
Brought into the English establishment in 1688.
Ranked in 1747 as:
5th Regiment of Foot

In 1782 retitled as the:
5th (or the Northumberland) Regiment of Foot.

In the Morier Paintings of 1751:
• The facings for this regiment were gosling-green; this is confirmed by Milan's List of 1749, which gives pale green.
• Officers' coats lined, faced and lapelled pale-green with silver binding.
• Other ranks' coats were lined gosling-green. The lapels were laced about and had six pointed loops, set evenly, with three further loops below, but the coat is folded over and the lacing is not clear. The vertical coat pocket was laced about and had seven pointed loops.
• The red waistcoat was laced about, the coat was shown buttoned over and no further details are known.
• Breeches for this regiment were red.
• Lace of the rank and file was plain white, but an Inspection Return of October 1755, lists white with pale-green.
• The outer braid of the square cuff was pointed. The cuff slash had three buttons and forms five pointed loops.
• Grenadier cap was laced in white with a pale-green front and rear turn-up. The badge was of a gilt Saint George mounted on a white horse, slaying a green dragon with a red tongue. The decorative flourishes either side included green leaves. The tassel was mixed white and pale green.
• Grenadier wings were rounded.
• The sword hilt was steel.

In the 1768 regulations:
• The facings for this regiment were gosling-green and the linings, breeches and waistcoats of all ranks were white.
• The officers' lace and buttons were silver. Their coats were laced for dress with ten square loops, set evenly, during the American Revolution period they were placed in pairs.
• Other ranks' coats had had ten bastion loops, spaced evenly with the lace of the rank and file being white with a red outer stripe and a red inner stripe.
• The *Grenadier Book* at The Prince Consort's Library shows this regiment with loops spaced evenly, Lawson noted the facing colour as a dull green.
• After defeating the French at St Lucia in 1778, the regiment adopted a white plume.

During the War of Independence:
The 5th Regiment left Ireland on 7 May 1774 and arrived in Boston in July 1774.The regiment's light companies saw action at Concord and the regiment at Lexington, Bunker Hill, Long Island, White Plains, Fort Washington, Brandywine Creek, Germantown and Monmouth Court House. Once back in New York, the regiment remained until 3 November 1778 when it left America for the West Indies, returning home in 1780.
• There is an extant 5th Regiment officer's light infantry cap. It shows the regimental badge of St George slaying the Dragon and a ribbon bearing a light infantry horn and Arabic numeral. Its crest has a lion in relief and red horsehair plume and a red turban at its base.
• The officers and NCOs were armed with fusils.

Raised in 1673 as:
Sir Walter Vane's Regiment
Brought into the English establishment in 1688.
Ranked in 1747 as:
6th Regiment of Foot
In 1782 retitled as the:

6th (or the 1st Warwickshire) Regiment of Foot

In the Morier Paintings of 1751:

- The facings for this regiment were deep-yellow; this is confirmed by Milan's list of 1749.
- Officers' lace and buttons were silver and officers' coats were laced for dress with square loops, set evenly.
- Other ranks' coats were lined deep-yellow. The lapels were laced about and had six pointed loops, set evenly, with three further loops below but the coat is folded over and the lacing is not clear. The horizontal coat pocket was laced about and has a further lace to the inside.
- The red waistcoat was laced about, the coat was shown buttoned over and no further details are known.
- Breeches for this regiment were red.
- Lace of the rank and file was white with a central red zigzag, to the outer edge only are placed further red arrow type decoration.
- The top braid of the square cuff was pointed and the cuff slash was laced about with three buttons and one point to the lace, which slopes to the cuff.
- Grenadier cap was laced in white with a deep-yellow front and rear turn-up. The badge was of a white goat with gold chains. The decorative flourishes either side include red leaves. The tassel was mixed white and deep-yellow.
- Grenadier wings were not worn until 1752.
- The sword hilt was steel.

In the 1768 regulations:

- The facings for this regiment were deep-yellow; while the linings, breeches and waistcoats of all ranks were white.
- The officers' lace and buttons were silver. Their coats were laced for dress with ten square loops, set evenly; during the American Revolution period they were placed in pairs.
- Other ranks' coats had ten square loops set evenly; the lacing followed the pattern of the officers'. The lace of the rank and file was white with a red outer stripe and a yellow inner stripe.
- The *Grenadier Book* at The Prince Consort's Library shows this regiment with loops spaced evenly, Lawson noted the facing colour as a brownish raw sienna.

During the War of Independence:

The 6th Foot arrived in New York from the West Indies in October 1776. Being seriously reduced in numbers by sickness from service in the West Indies, the surviving men were drafted into other regiments, while the officers and the colours returned to England in December 1776. After the experimental rifle companies were returned to England they were converted to the light companies of the 6th and 14th regiments.

Raised in 1685 as:
The Ordnance Regiment
Ranked in 1747 as:
7th Regiment of Foot
In 1751 retitled as the:
7th (Royal Fusiliers) Regiment of Foot
In 1782 retitled as the:
7th (or the Derbyshire) Regiment of Foot
The regiment effectively never used this title.

In the Morier Paintings of 1751:

- The facings for this royal regiment were dark-blue; this is confirmed by Milan's List of 1749.

• Officers' lace and buttons were gold and officers' coats were laced for dress with square loops, set evenly, officers wore buff waistcoats and breeches in 1755.
• Other ranks' coats were lined blue. The lapels were laced about and had six pointed loops, set evenly with three further loops below, but the coat as folded over and the lacing is not clear. The horizontal coat pocket was laced about and had three pointed loops.
• The red waistcoat was laced about but the coat was shown buttoned over and no further details are known.
• Breeches for this regiment were blue, but red breeches were noted in 1755.
• Lace of the rank and file was white with a blue outer stripe.
• The top braid of the cuff was not shown and the cuff slash was laced about with four buttons; the shape of the flap is assumed.
• Grenadier cap was laced in white with a blue front and rear turn-up. The blue centre carries a red rose with green leaves within a garter belt without buckle. The garter belt was inscribed 'Honi Soit Qui Mal Y Pense' with a white foliate design either side. The tassel was mixed white and blue.
• Grenadier wings were not worn until 1752.
• The sword hilt was gilt.

In the 1768 regulations:
• The facings for this royal regiment of fusiliers were dark-blue, while the linings, breeches and waistcoats of all ranks were white.
• The officers' lace and buttons were gold. Their coats were laced for dress with ten square loops, set evenly, during the American Revolution period they were placed in pairs.
• Other ranks' coats had ten square loops set evenly; the lace followed the pattern of the officer's. The lace of the rank and file was white with a blue outer worm.
• The *Grenadier Book* at The Prince Consort's Library shows this regiment with loops spaced evenly.

During the War of Independence:
The 7th Regiment was posted to Upper Canada in July 1773, and saw duty at Montreal, Quebec and the Great Lakes. Nine companies were captured at Fort St John's and Fort Chambley where they surrendered and were released in 1776. The tenth company formed part of the garrison of Quebec during the siege of 1775 and 1776. The regiment was reformed in New York during 1777 and saw action at Monmouth Court House. In December 1779 it set sail for South Carolina and saw action at Charleston and Cowpens. The colours of this regiment were captured twice during the War, once at the surrender of Fort St John and again after the Battle of Cowpens. The regiment suffered heavily at Cowpens and was sent to New York in August 1782 and never fully reformed until returned to England in 1783. It is claimed that some minor elements of the regiment were part of the surrender at Yorktown on 19 October 1781.
• The officers and NCOs were armed with fusils.

Raised in 1685 as:
Princess Anne of Denmark's Regiment of Foot Regiment
Retitled in 1702 as:
The Queen's Regiment of Foot
Retitled in 1716 as:
The King's Regiment of Foot
Ranked in 1747 as:
8th (The King's) Regiment of Foot
In 1751 retitled as the:
8th (or the King's) Regiment of Foot.

In the Morier Paintings of 1751:

- The Morier painting shows a royal regiment with dark-blue facings but Milan's list of 1749 still gives yellow.
- Officers' lace and buttons were gold and officers' coats were laced for dress with square loops, set evenly.
- Other ranks' coats were lined blue. The lapels were laced about and had six pointed loops, set evenly, with three further loops below. The horizontal coat pocket was laced about but the pockets are not shown; they probably had three pointed loops.
- The red waistcoat was laced about, but the buttonholes had very narrow white lace.
- Breeches for this regiment were blue.
- In 1751 the lace of the rank and file was changed, as it too closely resembled that of the 4th Regiment; the new lace was white with a broad outer yellow stripe.
- The top braid of the cuff was not shown and the cuff slash was laced about with four buttons; the shape of the flap was not shown and has been assumed.
- Grenadier cap was laced in white with a blue front and rear turn-up. The red centre carried a white horse on a green ground within a garter belt without buckle. The garter belt was inscribed 'Honi Soit Qui Mal Y Pense' with a white foliate design either side. The tassel was mixed white and blue.
- Grenadier wings were square.
- The sword hilt was gilt.

In the 1768 regulations:

- The facings for this royal regiment were dark-blue, while the linings, breeches and waistcoats of all ranks were white.
- The officers' lace and buttons were gold. Their coats were laced for dress with ten square loops, set evenly.
- Other ranks' coats had had ten square loops, spaced evenly. The lace of the rank and file was white with a yellow outer stripe and a blue outer-centre stripe.
- The *Grenadier Book* at The Prince Consort's Library shows this regiment with loops spaced evenly.

During the War of Independence:

The 8th Regiment served in Canada during the summer of 1768 and was stationed at the major posts of Quebec, Montreal, Niagara, Detroit and Michimackinac. The regiment took part in operations and conflicts throughout the Mohawk Valley, Ohio Valley, Great Lakes and St Laurence regions. Between 1776 and 1782 the regiment saw action at the Cedars, Fort Stanwix, Cherry Valley, Grand Portage, Vincennes, Fort Laurens, Newtown, St Joseph, Martin and Ruddle Station, Schoharie Valley, Hannastown, and Cahoki (St Louis). One company surrendered at Fort Sackville, the remainder being posted to garrison border forts.

- The duties in Canada altered the 8th's uniform and, regimental coats gave way to the blanket coat.
- The officers and NCOs were armed with fusils.

Raised in 1685 as:

Henry Cornewall's Regiment of Foot

Ranked in 1747 as:

9th Regiment of Foot

In 1782 retitled as the:

9th (or the East Norfolk) Regiment of Foot.

In the Morier Paintings of 1751:

- The facings for this regiment were originally bright-green but they changed to light-orange in 1733 and were yellow in 1751; this is confirmed by Milan's List of 1749.
- Officers' lace and buttons were silver and officers' coats were laced for dress with square loops, set evenly.

• Other ranks' coats were lined yellow. The lapels were laced about and had six pointed loops, set evenly, with three further loops below, but the coat was folded over and the lacing is not clear. The horizontal coat pocket was laced about with three pointed loops.
• The red waistcoat was laced about but, the coat was shown buttoned over and no further details are known.
• Breeches for this regiment were red.
• Lace of the rank and file was white with a black outer, a red centre and a black inner stripe.
• The top braid of the cuff was not shown and the cuff slash was laced about with four buttons; the shape of the flap was not shown and has been assumed.
• Grenadier cap was laced in white with a yellow front and rear turn-up. The white 'GR' Cypher had white foliate designs on either side. The tassel was mixed white and yellow.
• Grenadier wings were not worn until 1752.
• The sword hilt was steel.

In the 1768 regulations:
• The facings for this regiment were yellow; while the linings, breeches and waistcoats of all ranks were white.
• The officers' lace and buttons were silver. Their coats were laced for dress with ten square loops, set evenly.
• Other ranks' coats had had ten square loops, evenly spaced, with the lace of the rank and file being white with a black outer stripe and a black inner stripe.
• The *Grenadier Book* at The Prince Consort's Library shows this regiment with loops spaced evenly, Lawson noted the facing colour as a bright-yellow.

During the War of Independence:
The 9th Regiment served in Canada, arriving in Quebec in May 1776 from Ireland. It saw action at Ticonderoga and Freeman's Farm. The regiment was surrendered at Saratoga and was interned in October 1777. It left North America after three years of internment returning home in 1781.
• The officers and NCOs were armed with fusils.

Raised in 1685 as:
Earl of Bath's Regiment of Foot
Ranked in 1747 as:
10th Regiment of Foot
In 1782 retitled as the:
10th (or the North Lincolnshire) Regiment of Foot.

In the Morier Paintings of 1751:
• The facings for this regiment were bright-yellow; this is confirmed by Milan's List of 1749.
• Officers' lace and buttons were silver and officers' coats were laced for dress with square loops, set evenly.
• Other ranks' coats were lined bright-yellow. The lapels were laced about and had six pointed loops, set evenly, with three further loops below, but the coat was folded over and the lacing is not clear. The horizontal coat pocket was laced about with two further loops inside it.
• The red waistcoat was laced about, the coat was shown buttoned over and no further details are known.
• Breeches for this regiment were red.
• Lace of the rank and file was white with two black zigzags, a yellow inner-centre and a red inner stripe.
• The top braid of the square cuff was pointed and the cuff slash was laced about with four buttons; the shape of the flap had two points and sloped to the cuff.
• Grenadier cap was laced in white with a bright-yellow front and rear turn-up. The white 'GR' Cypher had white foliate designs on either side. The tassel was mixed white and yellow.
• Grenadier wings were not worn until 1752.

• The sword hilt was steel.

In the 1768 regulations:

• The facings for this regiment were bright-yellow, while the linings, breeches and waistcoats of all ranks were white.

• The officers' lace and buttons were silver. Their coats were unlaced for dress with ten square loops, set evenly.

• Other ranks' coats had ten square loops, spaced evenly, with the lace of the rank and file being white with a blue outer stripe.

• The *Grenadier Book* at The Prince Consort's Library shows this regiment with loops spaced evenly, Lawson noted the facing colour as a bright-yellow.

During the War of Independence:

The 10th Regiment sailed from Cork Haven, Ireland in June 1767, arriving at Port Levi in August. It garrisoned the Great Lakes forts until October 1774 when it embarked for Boston, arriving in late 1774. The grenadier company and the light company took part in the actions at Concord and the entire regiment at Lexington Green. The regiment saw action at Bunker's Hill, Long Island, Brandywine, Germantown, Manhattan Island, Monmouth, Rhode Island, Newport and Quaker Hill. The other ranks were drafted into other regiments in September 1778, while the officers, colours, sergeants and drummers returned home in December 1778.

Raised in 1685 as:

Duke of Beaufort's Regiment of Foot

Ranked in 1747 as:

11th Regiment of Foot

In 1782 retitled as the:

11th (or the North Devonshire) Regiment of Foot

In the Morier Paintings of 1751:

• The facings for this regiment were full-green; this is confirmed by Milan's List of 1749.

• Officers' lace and buttons were gold and officers' coats were laced for dress with square loops, set evenly.

• Other ranks' coats were lined full-green. The lapels were laced about and had six pointed loops, set evenly, with three further loops below, but the coat was folded over and the lacing is not clear. The horizontal coat pocket was laced about with two further loops inside it.

• The red waistcoat was laced about but the coat was shown buttoned over and no further details are known.

• Breeches for this regiment were red.

• Lace of the rank and file was white with a red outer, a green outer-centre, a green inner-centre and a red inner stripe.

• The top braid of the cuff was pointed and the cuff slash was laced about with four buttons; the shape of the flap has three points.

• Grenadier cap was laced in white with a full-green front and rear turn-up. The white 'GR' Cypher had white foliate designs on either side. The tassel was mixed white and green.

• Grenadier wings were not worn until 1752.

• The sword hilt was steel.

In the 1768 regulations:

• The facings for this regiment were full-green; while the linings, breeches and waistcoats of all ranks were white.

• The officers' lace and buttons were gold. Their coats were laced for dress with ten square loops, set evenly.

• Other ranks' coats had ten flowerpot loops, spaced evenly, with the lace of the rank and file being white with a red outer stripe, a green outer-centre stripe, a green inner-centre stripe and a red inner stripe.
• The *Grenadier Book* at The Prince Consort's Library shows this regiment with loops spaced evenly, Lawson noted the facing colour as a dark or full-green.

Raised in 1685 as:
Duke of Norfolk's Regiment of Foot
Ranked in 1747 as:
12th Regiment of Foot
In 1782 retitled as the:
12th (or the East Suffolk) Regiment of Foot

In the Morier Paintings of 1751:
• The facings for this regiment were yellow; this is confirmed by Milan's list of 1749.
• Officers' lace and buttons were gold and officers' coats were laced for dress with pointed loops, set evenly. Sergeants wore gold lace to hats.
• Other ranks' coats were lined yellow. The lapels were laced about and had six pointed loops, set evenly, with three further loops below, but the coat was folded over and the lacing is not clear. The horizontal coat pocket was laced about with two further loops inside it.
• The red waistcoat was laced about but the coat was shown buttoned over and no further details are known.
• Breeches for this regiment were red.
• Lace of the rank and file was white with a broad yellow centre stripe.
• The top braid of the cuff was pointed and the cuff slash was laced about with four buttons; the shape of the cuff slash has two points.
• Grenadier cap was laced in white with a yellow front and rear turn-up. The white 'GR' Cypher had white foliate designs on either side. The tassel was mixed white and yellow. Grenadiers wore a brass grenade on their pouch.
• Grenadier wings were not worn until 1752.
• The sword hilt was steel.

In the 1768 regulations:
• The facings for this regiment were yellow, while the linings, breeches and waistcoats of all ranks were white.
• The officers' lace and buttons were gold. Their coats were unlaced for dress with ten square loops, set evenly.
• Other ranks' coats had ten flowerpot loops, spaced evenly with the lace of the rank and file being white with a black outer stripe, a yellow centre stripe and a red inner stripe.
• The *Grenadier Book* at The Prince Consort's Library shows this regiment with loops spaced evenly, Lawson noted the facing colour as a pale-yellow.

Raised in 1685 as:
Earl of Huntingdon's Regiment of Foot
Ranked in 1747 as:
13th Regiment of Foot
In 1782 retitled as the:
13th (or the 1st Somersetshire) Regiment of Foot

In the Morier Paintings of 1751:
• The facings for this regiment were deep-yellow until 1757 when they changed to philemot yellow; this is confirmed by Milan's list of 1749.

• Officers' lace and buttons were silver and officers' coats were laced for dress with square loops, set evenly.
• Other ranks' coats were lined deep-yellow until 1757 after which philemot yellow was used. The lapels were laced about and had six pointed loops, , set evenly, with three further loops below, but the coat was folded over and the lacing is not clear. The horizontal coat pocket was laced about with two further loops inside it.
• The red waistcoat was laced about but the coat was shown buttoned over although the Baillie engravings show square loops to the waistcoats.
• Breeches for this regiment were red.
• Lace of the rank and file was white with a single blue zigzag near the outer edge and a single red zigzag near the inner edge.
• The top braid of the square cuff was pointed and the cuff slash was laced about with four buttons; the shape of the flap was not shown and has been assumed.
• Grenadier cap was laced in white with a deep-yellow front and rear turn-up. The white 'GR' Cypher had white foliate designs on either side. The tassel was mixed white and deep-yellow.
• Grenadier wings were not worn until 1752 when square wings were adopted according to Baillie.
• The sword hilt was steel.

In the 1768 regulations:
• The facings for this regiment were philemot yellow or 'Feuille mort', a dead-leaf shade; the linings, breeches and waistcoats of all ranks were white.
• The officers' lace and buttons were silver. Their coats were laced for dress with ten square loops, set evenly; during the period they were later set in pairs.
• Other ranks' coats had ten square loops, set evenly; during the period they were later set in pairs. The lace of the rank and file was white with a yellow centre stripe.
• The *Grenadier Book* at The Prince Consort's Library shows this regiment with loops spaced evenly, but Lawson considered that the loops were set in pairs and noted the facing colour as yellow ochre.

Raised in 1685 as:
Sir Edward Hale's Regiment of Foot
Ranked in 1747 as:
14th Regiment of Foot
In 1782 retitled as the:
14th (or the Bedfordshire) Regiment of Foot
Retitled in May 1809 and became:
14th (or the Buckinghamshire) Regiment of Foot
The old county title 'Bedfordshire' was passed to the 16th Regiment.

In the Morier Paintings of 1751:
• The facings for this regiment were buff; this is confirmed by Milan's list of 1749.
• Officers' lace and buttons were silver and officers' coats were laced for dress with square loops, set evenly.
• Other ranks' coats were lined buff. The lapels were laced about and had six square loops, set evenly, with three further square loops below, but the coat was folded over and the lacing is not clear. The horizontal coat pocket was laced about with two further loops inside it.
• The red waistcoat was laced about but the coat was shown buttoned over and no further details are known.
• Breeches for this regiment were red.
• Lace of the rank and file was white with a red outer stripe, a blue zigzag and a yellow mid-inner and a blue inner stripe.
• The top braid of the cuff was not shown and the cuff slash was laced about with four buttons, the shape of the flap was not shown. The cuff and cuff slash have been assumed.

• Grenadier cap was laced in white with a buff front and rear turn-up. The white 'GR' Cypher had white foliate designs on either side. The tassel was mixed white and buff.
• Grenadier wings were not worn until 1752.
• The sword hilt was steel.

In the 1768 regulations:
• The facings for this regiment were buff, while the linings, breeches and waistcoats of all ranks were buff.
• The officers' lace and buttons were silver. Their coats were unlaced for dress with ten square loops, set evenly, until the end of the century when they were placed in pairs.
• Other ranks' coats had ten square loops, spaced evenly, with the lace of the rank and file being white with a red and blue outer worm and a buff inner stripe.
• The *Grenadier Book* The Prince Consort's Library shows this regiment with loops spaced evenly, Lawson noted the facing colour as a pale-buff.

During the War of Independence:
The 14th Regiment arrived in Boston in September 1768 from Halifax. In 1776 'not less than sixty men' were taken from the detachments at St Augustine and saw action at Great Bridge for service in America. The regiment was sent to Virginia in 1775 and New York in 1776. The other ranks were drafted to other regiments, the officers and colours returning to England in December 1776. After recruiting in 1777, and while in training in England, one company of the 14th Regiment was placed under the command of Colonel Patrick Ferguson and sent to America to test the new Ferguson Rifle. The rifle companies fought well in the Battle of Brandywine. After the experimental rifle companies were returned to England they were converted to the light companies of the 6th and 14th regiments.

Raised in 1685 as:
Sir William Clifton's Regiment of Foot
Ranked in 1747 as:
15th Regiment of Foot
In 1782 it was retitled as the:
15th (or the Yorkshire East Riding) Regiment of Foot.

In the Morier Paintings of 1751:
• The facings for this regiment were deep-yellow; this is confirmed by Milan's list of 1749.
• Officers' lace and buttons were silver and officers' coats were laced for dress with square loops, set evenly.
• Other ranks' coats were lined deep-yellow. The lapels were laced about and had six square loops, set evenly, with three further square loops below, but the coat is folded over and the lacing is not clear. The horizontal coat pocket was laced about with two further loops inside it.
• The red waistcoat was laced about but the coat was shown buttoned over and no further details are known.
• Breeches for this regiment were red.
• Lace of the rank and file was white with a deep-yellow and black diagonal outer stripe with a similar, but opposite, inner stripe.
• The top braid of the cuff was not shown and the cuff slash was laced about with four buttons; the shape of the flap was not shown. The cuff and cuff slash have been assumed.
• Grenadier cap was laced in white with a deep-yellow front and rear turn-up. The white 'GR' Cypher had white foliate designs on either side. The tassel was mixed white and deep-yellow.
• Grenadier wings were not worn until 1752.
• The sword hilt was steel.

In the 1768 regulations:

• The facings for this regiment were yellow; while the linings, breeches and waistcoats of all ranks were white.

• The officers' lace and buttons were silver. Their coats were laced for dress with ten square loops, set evenly.

• Other ranks' coats had ten square loops, spaced evenly, with the lace of the rank and file being white with a yellow and black outer worm and a thin red inner stripe.

• The *Grenadier Book* at The Prince Consort's Library shows this regiment with loops spaced evenly, Lawson noted the facing colour as a philemot yellow.

During the War of Independence:

The 15th Regiment served in North America between 1776. It departed from Ireland in 1775 and arrived at Cape Fear in May 1776 and saw action at Brandywine, Charleston, New York, Long Island, Fort Washington, Brandywine and Germantown, it returned to New York in 1776. The regiment was sent to the West Indies in November 1778 with the 28th, 46th and 55th regiments and saw action seizing St Lucia and St Eustatius from the French where it was captured and later exchanged. It returned to England in March 1782

• This regiment was fitted with simple jackets with yellow collar and cuffs while in America. The hats were cut down and turned up but still retained the white tape.

• Brass, eight-pointed-star cap plates with an engraved number '15' were used.

• The officers and NCOs were armed with fusils.

Raised in 1688 as:

Archibald Douglas's Regiment of Foot

Ranked in 1747 as:

16th Regiment of Foot

In 1782 it was retitled as the:

16th (or the Buckinghamshire) Regiment of Foot

Retitled in May 1809 to become:

16th (or the Bedfordshire) Regiment of Foot

The old county title 'Buckinghamshire' passed to the 14th Regiment.

In the Morier Paintings of 1751:

• The facings for this regiment were yellow; this is confirmed by Milan's list of 1749.

• Officers' lace and buttons were silver and officers' coats were laced for dress with square loops, set evenly.

• Other ranks' coats were lined yellow. The lapels were laced about and had six square loops, set evenly, with three further square loops below. The horizontal coat pocket was not shown and has been assumed as vertical with eight square loops.

• The red waistcoat was laced about with plain buttonholes.

• Breeches for this regiment were red.

• Lace of the rank and file was white with a red outer stripe, a yellow zigzag at the centre and a red inner stripe.

• The braid of the cuff formed five square loops and the cuff slash had three buttons.

• Grenadier cap was laced in white with a yellow front and rear turn-up. The red 'GR' Cypher had white foliate designs on either side. The tassel was mixed white and yellow.

• Grenadier wings were square.

• The sword hilt was not shown.

In the 1768 regulations:

• The facings for this regiment were yellow, while the linings, breeches and waistcoats of all ranks were white.

• The officers' lace and buttons were silver. Their coats were laced for dress with ten square loops, set evenly.

• Other ranks' coats had ten square loops, spaced evenly, with the lace of the rank and file being white with a red outer stripe.
• The *Grenadier Book* at The Prince Consort's Library shows this regiment with loops spaced evenly, Lawson noted the facing colour as a philemot yellow.

During the War of Independence:
The 16th Regiment of Foot left Ireland and arrived in Florida in 1767. It saw action at the defence of Savannah. One company was detached to Port Royal. The regiment withdrew from Florida and arrived in New York in 1776 but was sent back to Florida in 1777 where it remained largely as detachments. In 1779 it saw action at Baton Rouge and the siege of Pensacola where the regiment was captured and later exchanged but the clothing was taken at Pensacola and the soldiers arrived almost naked. This did not include the light companies, which had formed part of the composite light company battalion who saw further action at Pensacola in 1781. The regiment returned to England in March 1782.

Raised in 1688 as:
Solomon Richards's Regiment of Foot
Ranked in 1747 as:
17th Regiment of Foot
In 1782 it was retitled as the:
17th (or the Leicestershire) Regiment of Foot.

In the Morier Paintings of 1751:
• The facings for this regiment were greyish-white but, this is not confirmed by Milan's list of 1749, which states light grey.
• Officers' lace and buttons were silver and officers' coats were laced for dress with square loops, set evenly.
• Other ranks' coats were lined greyish-white. The lapels were laced about and had six pointed loops, set evenly, with three further pointed loops below. The vertical coat pocket was assumed to have eight pointed loops.
• The red waistcoat was laced about and had pointed loops to the buttonholes.
• Breeches for this regiment were red.
• Lace of the rank and file was white with a dark grey outer stripe, a central dark grey zigzag and a dark grey inner stripe.
• There was limited detail for the cuff but a five-pointed cuff slash with three buttons has been assumed.
• Grenadier cap was laced in white with a light-grey front and rear turn-up. The dark-green 'GR' Cypher had a green leaved and yellow foliate design on either side. The tassel was mixed white and dark-blue.
• Grenadier wings were round.
• The sword hilt was steel.

In the 1768 regulations:
• The facings for this regiment were greyish-white, while the linings, breeches and waistcoats of all ranks were white.
• The officers' lace and buttons were silver. Their coats were laced for dress with ten square loops, set evenly.
• Other ranks' coats had ten square loops, spaced evenly, with the lace of the rank and file being white with a blue outer stripe, a yellow outer-centre stripe and a blue centre stripe.
• The *Grenadier Book* at The Prince Consort's Library shows this regiment with loops spaced evenly, Lawson noted the facing colour as practically white.

During the War of Independence:
The 17th Regiment left Ireland and arrived in Boston in December 1775. The regiment saw action in the battles for New York, Philadelphia Campaign, Princeton, Brandywine, Germantown and Monmouth Courthouse. On two occasions the regiment was surrendered and later exchanged: the first was at Stony Creek in 1779 and the 2nd was at Yorktown under General Cornwallis. The regiment was later exchanged and left America in 1783 for Nova Scotia where it served for many years.
• The regiment wore its buttons in pairs.

Raised in 1684 as:
Earl of Granard's Regiment of Foot
Ranked in 1747 as:
18th (or the Royal Irish) Regiment of Foot
In 1782 it was retitled as the:
18th (or the Royal Irish) Regiment of Foot.

In the Morier Paintings of 1751:
• The facings for this royal regiment were blue; this is confirmed by Milan's list of 1749.
• Officers' lace and buttons were gold and officers' coats were laced for dress with square loops, set evenly.
• Other ranks' coats were lined dark-blue. The lapels were laced about and had six square loops, set evenly, with three further square loops below. The horizontal coat pocket was not shown and has been assumed.
• The red waistcoat was laced about with plain pockets and no loops to the buttonholes.
• Breeches for this regiment were dark-blue.
• Lace of the rank and file was white with a central dark-blue curved worm.
• The top braid of the square cuff was also square and the cuff slash is laced about with four buttons; the shape of the flap was not shown and has been assumed.
• Grenadier cap was laced in white with blue front and rear turn-up. A gilt Irish harp decorated the front between the white foliate designs. The tassel was mixed white and dark-blue.
• Grenadier wings were rounded.
• The sword hilt was gilt.

In the 1768 regulations:
• The facings for this royal regiment were blue, while the linings, breeches and waistcoats of all ranks were white.
• The officers' lace and buttons were gold. Their coats were laced for dress with ten square loops, set evenly.
• Other ranks' coats had ten square loops, spaced evenly. The lace of the rank and file was white with a blue inner stripe.
• The *Grenadier Book* at The Prince Consort's Library shows this regiment with loops spaced evenly.

During the War of Independence:
The 18th Regiment of Foot arrived in Philadelphia in July 1767 and, in May 1768, was sent to replace the 34th at Fort Pitt. It garrisoned the frontier and arrived in Boston in October 1774 from Nova Scotia. It took part in the fighting at Concord and Lexington, Bunker Hill and Charleston Heights. The 18th left Boston for Nova Scotia in July 1776 where the men were drafted into other regiments and the officers and colours returned to England. The regiment was reformed at Dover Castle in 1777 and was routed to the Channel Islands where it suppressed a mutiny of a local militia on Guernsey in 1783.
• The regiment wore its buttons in pairs.

Raised in 1688 as:

Francis Lutterell's Regiment of Foot
Ranked in 1747 as:
19th Regiment of Foot
In 1782 it was retitled as the:
19th (or the 1st Yorkshire North Riding) Regiment of Foot.

In the Morier Paintings of 1751:
• The facings for this regiment were yellowish-green; this is contrary to Milan's list of 1749, which gives pale green.
• Officers' lace and buttons were gold and officers' coats were laced for dress with square loops, set evenly.
• Other ranks' coats were lined yellowish-green. The lapels were laced about and had five square loops, set evenly, with three further square loops below. The vertical coat pocket formed eight square loops and had three buttons.
• The red waistcoat was laced about but shown with no pockets or loops to the buttonholes.
• Breeches for this regiment were red.
• Lace of the rank and file was white with a black outer, a red mid-outer, a red mid-inner and a black inner stripe.
• The braid of the cuff slash formed five square loops with three buttons.
• Grenadier cap was laced in white with a yellowish-green front and rear turn-up. The white 'GR' Cypher had white foliate designs on either side. The tassel was mixed white and pale green.
• Grenadier wings were square.
• The sword hilt was steel.

In the 1768 regulations:
• The facings for this regiment were pale green but changed to full-green in January 1769. The linings, breeches and waistcoats of all ranks were white.
• The officers' lace and buttons were gold. Their coats were laced for dress with ten square loops, set evenly.
• Other ranks' coats had ten square loops, spaced evenly. The lace of the rank and file was white with a red outer, a green outer-centre and a mixed green and red, thin inner stripe.
• The *Grenadier Book* at The Prince Consort's Library shows this regiment with loops spaced evenly. Lawson noted the facing colour as a dark brownish green.

During the War of Independence:
The 19th Regiment left Ireland and arrived in Charleston in June 1781. Flank companies saw action at Eutaw Springs and the regiment was employed in harassing actions throughout South Carolina, primarily in the affair at Monk's Corner, the relief of Fort Ninety-Six and Eutaw Springs. In December 1782 the regiment moved to Barbados.
• Buttons were worn in pairs.
• The officers and NCOs were armed with fusils.

Raised in 1688 as:
Sir Richard Peyton's Regiment of Foot
Ranked in 1747 as:
20th Regiment of Foot
In 1782 it was retitled as the:
20th (or the East Devonshire) Regiment of Foot.

In the Morier Paintings of 1751:

- The facings for this regiment were pale-yellow; this is confirmed by Milan's list of 1749.
- Officers' lace and buttons were silver and officers' coats were laced for dress with square loops, set evenly.
- Other ranks' coats were lined pale-yellow. The lapels were laced about and had six square loops, set evenly, with three further square loops below. The horizontal coat pocket was laced about with two further loops inside it.
- The red waistcoat was laced about but shown with no pockets or loops to the buttonholes.
- Breeches for this regiment were red.
- Lace of the rank and file was white with a black outer, a red outer-centre, a red inner-centre and a black inner stripe.
- The top braid of the square cuff was pointed and the cuff slash was laced about with four buttons and one point.
- Grenadier cap was laced in white with a pale-yellow front and rear turn-up. The white 'GR' Cypher had white foliate designs on either side. The tassel was mixed white and pale-yellow.
- Grenadier wings were square.
- The sword hilt was steel.

In the 1768 regulations:

- The facings for this regiment were pale-yellow, while the linings, breeches and waistcoats of all ranks were white.
- The officers' lace and buttons were silver. Their coats were laced for dress with ten square loops, set in pairs.
- Other ranks' coats had ten square loops, spaced in pairs. The lace of the rank and file was white with a black outer stripe and a red inner stripe.
- The *Grenadier Book* at The Prince Consort's Library shows this regiment with loops spaced evenly, but Lawson considered that the loops were set in pairs.

During the War of Independence:

The 20th Regiment of Foot arrived in Canada reaching Quebec in May 1776. The regiment was among the troops sent to the relief of Quebec in May 1776, and served under General Burgoyne for the remainder of the Canadian Campaign. The regiment was surrendered at Saratoga in October 1771 and remained interned until returning to England in 1781.

- The regiment wore buttons in pairs.

Raised in 1678 as:
Earl of Mar's Regiment of Foot
In 1686 retitled as:
Scots Fusiliers Regiment of Foot
In 1707 retitled as a Royal Regiment:
Royal North British Fusiliers
Ranked in 1747 as:
21st Regiment of Foot (Royal North British Fusiliers)
In 1782 it was retitled as the:
21st Regiment of Foot (or the Royal North British Fusiliers).

In the Morier Paintings of 1751:

- The facings for this royal regiment were dark-blue; this is confirmed by Milan's list of 1749.
- Officers' lace and buttons were gold and officers' coats were laced for dress with square loops, set evenly.

• Other ranks' coats were lined dark-blue. The lapels were laced about and had five square loops, set evenly, with three further square loops below. The horizontal coat pocket was not shown and is assumed.
• The red waistcoat was laced about but shown with no pockets or loops to the buttonholes.
• Breeches for this regiment were dark-blue.
• Lace of the rank and file was white with a black outer curved worm and a yellow inner stripe.
• The top braid of the cuff was not shown and the cuff slash was laced about with four buttons; the flap was not shown and is assumed.
• Grenadier cap was laced in white with a dark-blue front and rear turn-up. The dark-blue centre carries a purple thistle with green leaves within a gold garter belt without buckle. The garter belt was inscribed 'Honi Soit Qui Mal Y Pense'. The tassel was mixed white and dark-blue.
• Grenadier wings were not worn until 1752.
• The sword hilt was steel.

In the 1768 regulations:
• The facings for this royal fusilier regiment were dark-blue, while the linings, breeches and waistcoats of all ranks were white.
• The officers' lace and buttons were gold. Their coats were laced for dress with ten square loops, set evenly.
• Other ranks' coats had ten square loops, spaced evenly. The lace of the rank and file was white with a blue outer edge.
• The *Grenadier Book* at The Prince Consort's Library shows this regiment with loops spaced evenly.

During the War of Independence:
The 21st Regiment sailed from Cork in 1776 and was present at the relief of Quebec in May 1776. It saw action at Fort Ticonderoga, Hubbardston and Freeman's Farm. The regiment was surrendered at Saratoga in October 1777 and eventually returned home after internment in 1783.
• The regiment was dressed to the 1768 regulations but did not take their fusilier caps with them.
• Coats were cut short and vertical pockets replaced the horizontal ones.
• The musket was of the Long Land pattern.

Raised in 1688 as the:
Duke of Norfolk's Regiment of Foot
Ranked in 1747 as:
22nd Regiment of Foot
In 1782 it was retitled as the:
22nd (or the Cheshire) Regiment of Foot.

In the Morier Paintings of 1751:
• The facings for this regiment were pale-buff but Milan's List of 1749 gives reddish-buff.
• Officers' lace and buttons were gold and officers' coats were laced for dress with square loops, set evenly.
• Other ranks' coats were lined pale-buff. The lapels were laced about and had six square loops, set evenly, with three further square loops below. The horizontal coat pocket was laced about with two further loops inside it.
• The red waistcoat was laced about but shown with no pockets or loops to the buttonholes.
• Breeches for this regiment were red.
• Lace of the rank and file was white with an alternate red and dark-blue diagonal outer stripe with a corresponding and matching inner stripe.
• The top braid of the square cuff was pointed and the cuff slash was laced about with four buttons, has one point and slopes to the cuff.

• Grenadier cap was laced in white with a pale-buff front and rear turn-up. The white 'GR' Cypher had white foliate designs on either side with brown leaves. The tassel was mixed white and pale-buff.
• Grenadier wings were rounded.
• The sword hilt was steel.

In the 1768 regulations:
• The facings for this regiment were pale-buff, while the linings, breeches and waistcoats of all ranks were pale-buff.
• The officers' lace and buttons were gold. Their coats were laced for dress with ten square loops set, in pairs.
• Other ranks' coats had ten flowerpot loops, spaced in pairs. The lace of the rank and file was white with a blue outer stripe and a red outer-centre stripe.
• The *Grenadier Book* at The Prince Consort's Library shows this regiment with loops spaced evenly, but Lawson considered that the loops were set in pairs.

During the War of Independence:
The 22nd Regiment was sent from England and arrived in Boston in May 1775. In March 1776, during the evacuation of Boston, the regiment left for Halifax, Nova Scotia. Returning to America in June of 1776, the regiment garrisoned in and around New York City. It saw action at the siege of Boston, Bunker Hill, Long Island, Rhode Island, Monmouth and Springfield. The grenadier and light companies saw action in Pennsylvania and Monmouth. The light company was part of the army surrendered at Yorktown. In 1783 the regiment evacuated New York and returned home.

Raised in 1689 as:
Lord Herbert's Regiment of Foot
Designated in 1714 as the:
Prince of Wales's Own Regiment of Welch Fusiliers
Designated in 1723 as the:
Royal Regiment of Welch Fusiliers
Ranked in 1747 as:
23rd Regiment of Foot (Royal Welch Fusiliers)
In 1751 it was retitled as the:
23rd Regiment of Foot (or the Royal Welch Fusiliers).

In the Morier Paintings of 1751:
• The facings for this royal regiment were dark-blue; this is confirmed by Milan's list of 1749.
• Officers' lace and buttons were gold and officers' coats were laced for dress with square loops, set evenly.
• Other ranks' coats were lined dark-blue. The lapels were laced about and had six pointed loops, set evenly, with three further pointed loops below. The horizontal coat pocket was laced about with two further loops inside it.
• The red waistcoat was laced about but shown with no pockets or loops to the buttonholes.
• Breeches for this regiment were dark-blue but an Inspection Return of 1745 gives red.
• Lace of the rank and file was white with an alternate red and white central stripe, with a black inner-centre and a yellow inner stripe.
• The top braid of the square cuff was pointed and the cuff slash was laced about with four buttons, is square and sloped to the cuff.
• Grenadier cap was laced in white with a dark-blue front and rear turn-up. The badge shows the Prince of Wales's three white feathers issuing from a gilt coronet with white foliate designs on either side. The tassel was all white.

• Grenadier wings were not issued until 1752.
• The sword hilt was steel.

In the 1768 regulations:
• The facings for this royal regiment of fusiliers were dark-blue, while the linings, breeches and waistcoats of all ranks were white.
• The officers' lace and buttons were gold. Their coats were laced for dress with ten square loops, set evenly.
• Other ranks' coats had ten loops, spaced evenly but this was changed after the period to ten flowerpot loops evenly spaced. The lace of the rank and file was white with a red centre stripe, a blue inner-centre and a yellow inner stripe.
• The *Grenadier Book* at The Prince Consort's Library shows this regiment with loops spaced evenly.
• All ranks wore the fusilier cap with the exception of the light company in North America, but there are records to show that cocked hats were the only headwear available.

During the War of Independence:
The 23rd, Royal Welch Fusiliers, arrived in New York in June 1773 and moved to Boston in 1774. The regiment's flank companies saw action at Lexington and Concord with battalion reinforcements later in the day. The regiment saw action at Bunker Hill, Long Island, White Plains, Brooklyn Heights, Harlem Heights, and Fort Washington, New York and then served as marines in 1778. The 23rd saw further action at Brandywine Creek, Germantown, and the capture of Philadelphia. Arriving in Charleston in 1780, they saw further action, participating in the siege of the city, Guilford Court House and Camden. The regiment was surrendered at Yorktown by General Cornwallis and interned until 1783 when it returned home.
• As a fusilier regiment all ranks wore the fur cap but by war's close their cap-maker had 'disappointed' them. As a substitute it was ordered that a spray of three white feathers was to be worn in the cocked hat in imitation of the PoW's badge. A unique feature of this regiment is the wearing of the 'Flash', a spray of five black ribbons worn at the back of the collar to prevent the powdered queue bag from soiling the coat. At the time of the Revolution all officers commonly wore it.

Raised in 1689 as:
Sir Edward Dering's Regiment of Foot
Ranked in 1747 as:
24th Regiment of Foot
In 1782 it was retitled as the:
24th (or the 2nd Warwickshire) Regiment of Foot.

In the Morier Paintings of 1751:
• The facings for this regiment were willow-green; this is contrary to Milan's list of 1749, which gives green.
• Officers' lace and buttons were silver and officers' coats were laced for dress with square loops, set evenly.
• Other ranks' coats were lined and faced willow-green; they were lined white after 1757. The lapels were laced about and had six square loops, set evenly, with three further square loops below. The horizontal coat pocket was not shown and is assumed.
• The red waistcoat was laced about but shown with no pockets or loops to the buttonholes.
• Breeches for this regiment were red.
• Lace of the rank and file was white with a willow-green outer stripe.
• The top braid of the square cuff was square and the cuff slash was laced about with four buttons; the flap has two points and sloped to the cuff.
• Grenadier cap was laced in white with a willow-green front and rear turn-up. The white 'GR' Cypher had white foliate designs on either side with green leaves. The tassel was mixed white and willow-green.

• Grenadier wings were not issued until 1752.
• The sword hilt was steel.

In the 1768 regulations:
• The facings for this regiment were willow-green, while the linings, breeches and waistcoats of all ranks were white.
• The officers' lace and buttons were silver. Their coats were laced for dress with ten square loops, set evenly.
• Other ranks' coats had ten square loops, spaced evenly. The lace of the rank and file was white with a green centre stripe and a red inner stripe.
• The *Grenadier Book* at The Prince Consort's Library shows this regiment with loops spaced evenly. Lawson noted the facing colour as a very dark bluish green.

During the War of Independence:
The 24th Regiment was part of the reinforcements sent to Canada and arrived for the relief of Quebec in May 1776, serving on operations on Lake Champlain. The regiment served in Burgoyne's advance corps. It saw action at Fort Ticonderoga, Hubbardston and Freeman's Farm. General Burgoyne surrendered the regiment at Saratoga in October 1771. It was later exchanged and returned home in 1783.

Raised in 1689 as:
The Earl of Leven's (or Edinburgh) Regiment of Foot
Ranked in 1747 as:
25th Regiment of Foot
In 1751 it was retitled as the:
25th (Edinburgh) Regiment of Foot
In 1782 retitled as the:
25th (or the Sussex) Regiment of Foot
This regiment was retitled in 1805 and became:
25th (or the King's Own Borderers) Regiment of Foot
The old county title 'Sussex' was passed to the 35th Regiment.

In the Morier Paintings of 1751:
• The facings for this regiment were deep-yellow; this is confirmed by Milan's list of 1749.
• Officers' lace and buttons were gold and officers' coats were laced for dress with square loops, set evenly.
• Other ranks' coats were lined deep-yellow. The lapels were laced about and had seven square loops, set evenly, with three further loops below. The pocket was not fully shown and has been assumed.
• The red waistcoat was laced about, with very narrow square loops.
• Breeches for this regiment were red.
• Lace of the rank and file was white with a black outer stripe, a yellow centre worm and a red inner stripe.
• The top braid of the square cuff was also square and the cuff slash was laced about with four buttons, one point and sloped to the cuff.
• Grenadier cap was laced in white with a deep-yellow front and rear turn-up. The white 'GR' Cypher had white foliate designs on either side with brown leaves. The tassel was mixed white and deep-yellow.
• Grenadier wings were rounded.
• The sword hilt was steel.

In the 1768 regulations:
• The facings for this regiment were deep-yellow, while the linings, breeches and waistcoats of all ranks were white.

• The officers' lace and buttons were gold. Their coats were laced for dress with ten square loops, set evenly; later they were changed to pairs probably during the War of Independence or shortly thereafter.
• Other ranks' coats had ten flowerpot loops, spaced evenly. The lace of the rank and file was white with a blue outer stripe, a yellow outer-centre stripe and a red centre stripe.
• The *Grenadier Book* at The Prince Consort's Library shows this regiment with loops spaced evenly. Lawson noted the facing colour as yellow ochre.

Raised in 1688 as:
Earl of Angus's Regiment of Foot
Taken on the English establishment in 1689 and known as the 'Cameronians'
Ranked in 1751 as:
26th Regiment of Foot
Designated in 1786 as the:
26th (or the Cameronian) Regiment of Foot
The regiment was converted to light infantry in 1815 to become:
26th (or the Cameronian) Regiment of Foot (Light Infantry).

In the Morier Paintings of 1751:
• The facings for this regiment were pale-yellow, but Milan's list of 1749 states yellow.
• Officers' lace and buttons were silver and officers' coats were laced for dress with square loops, set evenly, and they are recorded as wearing pale-yellow waistcoats.
• Other ranks' coats were lined pale-yellow. The lapels were laced about and had seven square loops, set evenly, with three further loops below. The pocket was not fully shown and has been assumed.
• The red waistcoat was laced about, with narrow square loops.
• Breeches for this regiment were red.
• Lace of the rank and file was white with a yellow outer stripe and a yellow inner stripe.
• The top braid of the square cuff was also square and the cuff slash was laced about with four buttons, and two points.
• Grenadier cap was laced in white with a pale-yellow front and rear turn-up. The white 'GR' Cypher had white foliate designs on either side with brown leaves. The tassel was mixed white and pale-yellow.
• Grenadier wings were rounded.
• The sword hilt is not shown.

In the 1768 regulations:
• The facings for this regiment were pale-yellow, while the linings, breeches and waistcoats of all ranks were white.
• The officers' lace and buttons were silver. Their coats were laced for dress with ten square loops, set evenly.
• Other ranks' coats had ten square loops, set evenly. The lace of the rank and file was white with a yellow outer stripe, a blue centre stripe and a yellow inner stripe.
• The *Grenadier Book* at The Prince Consort's Library shows this regiment with loops spaced evenly.

During the War of Independence:
The 26th Foot arrived in New Jersey in the summer of 1767. In 1775 the regiment was sent to Canada where individual companies served all along the frontier from Ticonderoga to Three Rivers. They left Montreal to take part in the successful defence of Quebec and were part of the surrendered garrisons of Fort Chambley and Fort St Johns, exchanged in December 1776. The regiment was reformed in New York in 1777 and saw action at Monmouth Court House. In December 1779 the men were drafted into other regiments and the officers and colours returned to England to recruit a new regiment.

Raised in 1689 as:
Zachariah Tiffin's Regiment of Foot
Ranked in 1751 as:
27th Regiment of Foot
In 1751 retitled as the:
27th (or the Inniskilling) Regiment of Foot.

In the Morier Paintings of 1751:
- The facings for this regiment were buff; this is confirmed by Milan's list of 1749.
- Officers' lace and buttons were silver and officers' coats were laced for dress with square loops, set evenly, and they are recorded as wearing buff waistcoats and breeches.
- Other ranks' coats were lined buff. The lapels were laced about and had six pointed loops, set evenly, with three further loops below, but the coat was folded over and the lacing is not clear. The pocket was laced about with two inner laces.
- The red waistcoat was laced about, the coat was shown buttoned over and no further details are known.
- Breeches for this regiment were red.
- Lace of the rank and file was white with an outer blue zigzag, a yellow centre stripe and an opposing inner black zigzag.
- The top braid of the square cuff was pointed and the cuff slash was laced about with four buttons, and one point to the lace.
- Grenadier cap was laced in white with a buff front and rear turn-up. A blue circle carried the Castle of Inniskilling with white foliate designs on either side with brown leaves. The tassel was mixed white buff.
- Grenadier wings were square.
- The sword hilt was steel.

In the 1768 regulations:
- The facings for this regiment were buff, while the linings, breeches and waistcoats of all ranks were buff.
- The officers' lace and buttons were gold. Their coats were laced for dress with ten square loops, set evenly; later they were set in pairs.
- Other ranks' coats had ten square loops; set evenly, later they were set in pairs. The lace of the rank and file was white with a blue outer edge and a red inner stripe.
- The *Grenadier Book* at The Prince Consort's Library shows this regiment with loops spaced evenly, but Lawson considered that the loops were set in pairs.

During the War of Independence:
The 27th Regiment arrived in Boston in October of 1775. Taking part in the New York campaign of 1776, the regiment saw action at Long Island, White Plain, Fort Washington, Brandywine and Germantown. In November 1778 it was sent to East Florida and thence to St Lucia in the West Indies until the end of the war.

Raised in 1694 as:
Sir John Gibson's Regiment of Foot
Ranked in 1751 as:
28th Regiment of Foot
In 1782 it was retitled as the:
28th (or the North Gloucestershire) Regiment of Foot.

In the Morier Paintings of 1751:

- The facings for this regiment were bright-yellow, but Milan's list of 1749 gives yellow.
- Officers' lace and buttons were gold and officers' coats were laced for dress square loops, set evenly.
- Other ranks' coats were lined bright-yellow. The lapels were laced about and had with seven square loops, set evenly, with three further loops below. The pocket was laced about with two inner laces.
- The red waistcoat was laced about, with narrow square loops.
- Breeches for this regiment were red.
- Lace of the rank and file was white with an outer yellow stripe, a black zigzag and an opposing black zigzag with central black dots.
- The top braid of the square cuff was pointed and the cuff slash was laced about with three buttons, and one point.
- Grenadier cap was laced in white with a bright-yellow front and rear turn-up. The blue 'GR' Cypher had white foliate designs on either side. The tassel was mixed white and bright-yellow.
- Grenadier wings were not issued until 1752.
- The sword hilt was steel.

In the 1768 regulations:

- The facings for this regiment were bright-yellow, while the linings, breeches and waistcoats of all ranks were white.
- The officers' lace and buttons were silver. Their coats were unlaced for dress with ten square loops, set evenly.
- Other ranks' coats had ten square loops, spaced evenly. The lace of the rank and file was white with a black outer stripe, a yellow centre stripe and a black inner stripe.
- The *Grenadier Book* at The Prince Consort's Library shows this regiment with loops spaced evenly.

During the War of Independence:

The 28th Regiment arrived at Cape Fear in May 1776 from Ireland. Sent to New York in 1776, the regiment saw action at the first siege of Charleston, Long Island, White Plains, Brooklyn Heights and Brandywine Creek. In 1778 the regiment sailed, in company with the 15th, 46th and 55th Foot, for the West Indies and participated in the seizure of St Lucia. It spent the next three years at St Kitts and at Antigua, returning home in 1783.

Raised in 1694 as:
Thomas Farrington's Regiment of Foot
Ranked in 1751 as:
29th Regiment of Foot
In 1782 it was retitled as the:
29th (or the Worcestershire) Regiment of Foot.

In the Morier Paintings of 1751:

- The facings for this regiment were yellow; this is confirmed by Milan's list of 1749.
- Officers' lace and buttons were silver and officers' coats were laced for dress with square loops, set evenly, and they are recorded as wearing yellow waistcoats and breeches.
- Other ranks' coats were lined yellow. The lapels were laced about and had seven square loops, set evenly, with three further loops below. The pocket was laced about with two inner laces.
- The red waistcoat was laced about, with very narrow square loops.
- Breeches for this regiment were red.
- Lace of the rank and file was white with an outer blue stripe, a yellow centre stripe and a curved blue worm.
- The top braid of the square cuff was pointed and the cuff slash was laced about with three buttons and one point.

• Grenadier cap was laced in white with a yellow front and rear turn-up. The blue 'GR' Cypher had white foliate designs on either side. The tassel was mixed white and yellow.
• Grenadier wings were not issued until 1752.
• The sword hilt was steel.

In the 1768 regulations:
• The facings for this regiment were yellow, while the linings, breeches and waistcoats of all ranks were white.
• The officers' lace and buttons were silver. Their coats were laced for dress with ten square loops, set evenly.
• Other ranks' coats had ten flowerpot loops, spaced evenly, but this changed in 1788 to ten loops, spaced in pairs. The lace of the rank and file was white with a blue outer stripe, a yellow centre stripe and a blue inner stripe.
• In 1788 the shape of the loop changed to a square loop; the spacing and lace remaining unchanged.
• The *Grenadier Book* at The Prince Consort's Library shows this regiment with loops spaced evenly; Lawson noted the facing colour as yellow ochre.

During the War of Independence:
The 29th Regiment arrived in Boston in September 1768. On the evening of 5 March 1770 their patrol was attacked in an incident that was to become known as the 'Boston Massacre'. The regiment returned to England in 1773 but was back in Quebec in May 1776 and saw action in the defence of Quebec; during October 1776 they acted as marines. The regiment's grenadier and light companies served under General Burgoyne and were surrendered at Saratoga; these flank companies remained imprisoned until rejoining the regiment in 1783. The headquarters and battalion companies remained in Canada until 1787 when they returned home to Worcestershire.
• This regiment had received the uniforms of the 1768 warrant shortly before 1770. The older uniforms were worn on campaign during the war.

Raised in 1702, as:
Colonel Thomas Sanderson's Regiment of Marines.
Ranked in 1747 as:
30th Regiment of Foot
In 1782 it was retitled as the:
30th (or Cambridgeshire) Regiment of Foot.

In the Morier Paintings of 1751:
• The facings for this regiment were pale-yellow, but Milan's List of 1749 gives bright-yellow.
• Officers' lace and buttons were silver and officers' coats were laced for dress with square loops, set evenly, and they are recorded as wearing pale-yellow waistcoats.
• Other ranks' coats were lined pale-yellow. The lapels were laced about and had seven square loops, set evenly, with three further loops below. The pocket was laced about with two inner laces.
• The red waistcoat was laced about, with no loops.
• Breeches for this regiment were red.
• Lace of the rank and file was white with an outer blue stripe and a blue inner stripe.
• The top braid of the square cuff was pointed and the cuff slash was laced about with three buttons and one point.
• Grenadier cap was laced in white with a pale-yellow front and rear turn-up. The blue 'GR' Cypher had white foliate designs on either side. The tassel was mixed white and pale-yellow.
• Grenadier wings were not issued until 1752.
• The sword hilt was steel.

In the 1768 regulations:

- The facings for this regiment were pale-yellow, while the linings, breeches and waistcoats of all ranks were white.
- The officers' lace and buttons were silver. Their coats were laced for dress with ten square loops, set evenly.
- Other ranks' coats had ten flowerpot loops, spaced evenly. The lace of the rank and file was white with a pale blue outer worm.
- The *Grenadier Book* at The Prince Consort's Library shows this regiment with loops spaced evenly.

During the War of Independence:

The 30th Regiment was stationed in Ireland and sailed from Cork with other reinforcements, arriving in Charleston in June 1781 and saw service in the campaigns in Carolina. In December 1782 the regiment was sent to Jamaica where it remained until 1800 after which it returned to the United Kingdom.

Raised in 1702 by:

Colonel George Villiers as a regiment of Marines.

Ranked in 1747 as:

31st Regiment of Foot, also known as the Young Buffs.

In 1782 it was retitled as the:

31st (or the Huntingdonshire) Regiment of Foot.

In the Morier Paintings of 1751:

- The facings for this regiment were buff; this is confirmed by Milan's list of 1749.
- Officers' lace and buttons were silver and officers' coats were laced for dress with square loops, set evenly, and they are recorded as wearing buff waistcoats and breeches.
- Other ranks' coats were lined buff. The lapels were laced about and had five pointed loops, set evenly, with three further loops below. The vertical pocket had three buttons and eight pointed loops.
- The red waistcoat was laced about, with narrow square loops.
- Breeches for this regiment were red.
- Lace of the rank and file was white with a blue outer stripe. The shoulder strap is shown laced about.
- The top braid of the square cuff was also square and the cuff slash was laced with three buttons and five pointed loops.
- Grenadier cap was laced in white with a buff front and rear turn-up. The white 'GR' Cypher had white foliate designs on either side with brown leaves. The tassel was mixed white and buff.
- The grenadier wings were square.
- The sword hilt was steel.

In the 1768 regulations:

- The facings for this regiment were buff, while the linings, breeches and waistcoats of all ranks were buff.
- The officers' lace and buttons were silver. Their coats were laced for dress with ten square loops, spaced evenly, they were spaced in pairs around 1780.
- Other ranks' coats had ten square loops, spaced evenly The lace of the rank and file was white with a mixed blue and yellow outer worm and a thin red inner stripe.
- The *Grenadier Book* at The Prince Consort's Library shows this regiment with loops spaced evenly.

During the War of Independence:

The 31st Foot arrived in America in 1765 and was stationed in Pensacola until August 1772 when it was sent to the island of St Vincent in the Caribbean where the regiment suffered heavy losses due to disease. The regiment disembarked at Sheerness in May 1773 and was stationed in England until November 1775. Ordered north to

Scotland it embarked for Cork and was eventually transferred back to North America, arriving in Quebec in May 1776 where the battalion companies formed part of the garrison. The regiment's Grenadier and Light Infantry companies served under General Burgoyne during the Canadian Campaign and were with the force that surrendered at Saratoga. These companies remained imprisoned until rejoining the regiment in 1783. The regiment returned home from Canada in 1787.

Raised in 1702 by Colonel Edward Fox as a regiment of Marines.
Converted in 1714 to a Regiment of Foot
Ranked in 1747 as:
32nd Regiment of Foot
In 1782 it was retitled as the:
32nd (or the Cornwall) Regiment of Foot

In the Morier Paintings of 1751:

- The facings for this regiment were white; this is confirmed by Milan's list of 1749.
- Officers' lace and buttons were silver and officers' coats were laced for dress with square loops, set evenly, and they are recorded as wearing white waistcoats and breeches.
- Other ranks' coats were lined white. The lapels were laced about and had six pointed loops, set evenly, with three further loops below. The pocket was laced about with two further laces inside.
- The red waistcoat was laced about, with bastion loops.
- Breeches for this regiment were red.
- Lace of the rank and file was white with an outer black stripe, a central black zigzag and a black inner stripe.
- The top braid of the square cuff was pointed and the cuff slash laced about with four buttons and two points to the lace.
- Grenadier cap was laced in white with a white front and rear turn-up. The red 'GR' Cypher had green foliate designs on either side with roses and green leaves. The tassel was white.
- The grenadier wings were square.
- The sword hilt was not shown.

In the 1768 regulations:

- The facings for this regiment were white, while the linings, breeches and waistcoats of all ranks were white.
- The officers' lace and buttons were gold. Their coats were unlaced for dress with ten square loops, set evenly.
- Other ranks' coats had ten square loops, spaced evenly. The lace of the rank and file was white with a black outer arrowhead worm with a black inner stripe.
- The *Grenadier Book* at The Prince Consort's Library shows this regiment with loops spaced evenly.

Raised in 1702 as:
Earl of Huntingdon's Regiment of Foot
Ranked in 1747 as:
33rd Regiment of Foot
In 1782 it was retitled as the:
33rd (or the 1st Yorkshire West Riding) Regiment of Foot.

In the Morier Paintings of 1751:

- The facings for this regiment were red; this is confirmed by Milan's list of 1749.
- Officers' lace and buttons were silver and officers' coats were laced for dress square loops, set evenly, and they are recorded as wearing red waistcoats and breeches.

• Other ranks' coats were lined white. The lapels were laced about and had seven pointed loops, set evenly, with three further loops below. The pocket was not fully shown and has been assumed as laced about with two further interior laces.
• The red waistcoat was laced about, with pointed loops.
• Breeches for this regiment were red.
• Lace of the rank and file was a plain white.
• The top braid of the cuff was not shown and the cuff slash was laced about with four buttons and two points to the lace.
• Grenadier cap was laced in white with a red front and rear turn-up. The white 'GR' Cypher had white foliate designs on either side. The tassel was mixed white and red.
• The grenadier wings were square.
• The sword hilt was steel.

In the 1768 regulations:
• The facings for this regiment were red, while the linings, breeches and waistcoats of all ranks were white.
• The officers' facings were scarlet, lace and buttons were silver. Their coats were laced for dress with ten square loops, set evenly; later, about 1780, they were changed to pairs.
• Other ranks' coats had ten flowerpot loops; spaced evenly, later they were mounted in pairs. The lace of the rank and file was white with a red centre stripe.
• The *Grenadier Book* at The Prince Consort's Library shows this regiment with loops spaced evenly.

During the War of Independence:
The 33rd Regiment left Cork in February 1776 and arrived at Cape Fear in May the same year. It saw action at Charleston, Long island, Brooklyn Heights, White Plains, Fort Washington, Brandywine, Germantown, Freehold, Charleston, Camden and Guilford Court House. It was part of the army surrendered by General Cornwallis at Yorktown where the regiment was interned. The regiment was exchanged and sent to Halifax in September 1783.

Raised in 1702 as:
Lord Lucas's Regiment of Foot
Ranked in 1747 as:
34th Regiment of Foot
In 1782 it was retitled as the:
34th (or the Cumberland) Regiment of Foot.

In the Morier Paintings of 1751:
• The facings for this regiment were yellow; this is confirmed by Milan's list of 1749.
• Officers' lace and buttons were silver and officers' coats were laced for dress square loops, set evenly, and they are recorded as wearing yellow waistcoats.
• Other ranks' coats were lined yellow. The lapels were laced about and had six square loops, set evenly, with three further loops below, but the coat is folded over and the lacing is not clear. The pocket was fully shown and was laced about with two inner laces showing a gap between them and the outer lace.
• The red waistcoat was not shown.
• Breeches for this regiment were red.
• Lace of the rank and file was white with an outer blue curved worm with an inner-centre yellow stripe and a blue inner stripe. The shoulder strap was shown laced about.
• The top braid of the square cuff was pointed and the cuff slash laced about with three buttons, with one point to the lace.

• Grenadier cap was laced in white with a yellow front and rear turn-up. The blue 'GR' Cypher had white foliate designs on either side. The tassel was mixed white and yellow.
• The grenadier wings were square.
• The sword hilt was steel.

In the 1768 regulations:
• The facings for this regiment were bright-yellow, while the linings, breeches and waistcoats of all ranks were white.
• The officers' lace and buttons were silver. Their coats were laced for dress with ten square loops, set evenly, later they were spaced in pairs.
• Other ranks' coats had ten square loops, set evenly, later they were spaced in pairs. The lace of the rank and file was white with a mixed blue and yellow outer worm and a thin red inner stripe.
• The *Grenadier Book* at The Prince Consort's Library shows this regiment with loops spaced evenly, but Lawson considered that the loops were set in pairs.

During the War of Independence:
The 34th Regiment arrived in Quebec in May 1776. The grenadier and light companies were detached for service with General Burgoyne and were surrendered after Saratoga and exchanged in 1781 when they rejoined the battalion companies, remaining in Canada until 1786 when they returned home.

Raised in 1701 in Belfast as:
Earl of Donegal's (also known as The Belfast) Regiment of Foot
Ranked in 1747 as:
35th Regiment of Foot
In 1774 it became:
The Prince of Orange's Own Regiment
In 1782 it was retitled as the:
35th (or the Dorsetshire) Regiment of Foot
The regiment was retitled in 1804, when it took the old county title of the 25th Regiment to become:
35th (Sussex) Regiment of Foot
The county title 'Dorsetshire' was passed to the 39th Regiment.

In the Morier Paintings of 1751:
• The facings for this regiment were orange; this is confirmed by Milan's list of 1749.
• Officers' lace and buttons were silver and officers' coats were laced for dress with square loops, set evenly, and they are recorded as wearing orange waistcoats.
• Other ranks' coats were lined orange. The lapels were laced about and had six square loops, set evenly, with three further loops below. The pocket was not fully it appears to be laced about with two inner laces.
• The red waistcoat was laced about, with very narrow square loops.
• Breeches for this regiment were red.
• Lace of the rank and file was white with an outer yellow stripe, a central yellow zigzag and a red inner stripe.
• The top braid of the cuff was not shown and the cuff slash was laced about with three buttons with five square loops to the lace. This was the only regiment with a five-branch pointed lace to the cuff and a horizontal pocket.
• Grenadier cap was laced in white with an orange front and rear turn-up. The white 'GR' Cypher had white foliate designs on either side. The tassel was mixed white and orange.
• Grenadier wings were not worn before 1752.
• The sword hilt was steel.

In the 1768 regulations:

• The facings for this regiment were orange, while the linings, breeches and waistcoats of all ranks were white.
• The officers' lace and buttons were silver. Their coats were laced for dress with ten square loops, set evenly.
• Other ranks' coats had ten square loops, spaced evenly. The lace of the rank and file was white with an orange-yellow inner stripe.
• The *Grenadier Book* at The Prince Consort's Library shows this regiment with loops spaced evenly, Lawson noted the facing colour as a brownish yellow.

During the War of Independence:

The 35th Foot arrived in Boston in June 1775. It saw action at Bunker Hill, New York, Long Island, Staten Island, Brooklyn, White Plains, and Fort Washington. The regiment left America for the West Indies in November 1778 and arrived at St Lucia in December 1778 where it forced the French to surrender and remained there until 1786.
• In 1776 the regiment was issued with the Long Land pattern musket.

Raised in 1701 from the 2nd Battalion of 29th Regiment as:
Thomas Allnut's Regiment of Foot
Ranked in 1751 as:
36th Regiment of Foot
In 1782 it was retitled as the:
36th (or the Herefordshire) Regiment of Foot.

In the Morier Paintings of 1751:

• The facings for this regiment were green; this is confirmed by Milan's list of 1749.
• Officers' lace and buttons were silver and officers' coats were laced for dress with square loops, set evenly.
• Other ranks' coats were lined green. The lapels were laced about and had seven square loops, set evenly, with three further loops below. The pocket was not fully shown and has been assumed.
• The red waistcoat was laced about, with very narrow square loops.
• Breeches for this regiment were red.
• Lace of the rank and file was white with an outer green stripe.
• The top braid of the square cuff was pointed and the cuff slash laced about with three buttons, and one point to the lace.
• Grenadier cap was laced in white with a green front and rear turn-up. The white 'GR' Cypher had white foliate designs on either side. The tassel was mixed white and green.
• Grenadier wings were not worn until 1752.
• The sword hilt was steel.

In the 1768 regulations:

• The facings for this regiment were green, while the linings, breeches and waistcoats of all ranks were white.
• The officers' lace and buttons were gold. Their coats were laced for dress with ten square loops, set evenly, but by 1775 they were in pairs.
• Other ranks' coats had ten square loops, spaced evenly, but followed the practice of the officers. The lace of the rank and file was white with a red outer stripe and a green centre stripe.
• By 1775 the flank companies wore black plumes with red centres and white tops.
• The *Grenadier Book* at The Prince Consort's Library shows this regiment with loops spaced evenly. Lawson noted the facing colour as willow-green, a dull dark-green.

Raised in 1702 as:
Thomas Meridith's Regiment of Foot

Ranked in 1747 as:
37th Regiment of Foot
In 1782 it was retitled as the:
37th (or the North Hampshire) Regiment of Foot.

In the Morier Paintings of 1751:

- The facings for this regiment were yellow; this is confirmed by Milan's list of 1749.
- Officers' lace and buttons were gold and officers' coats were laced for dress square loops, set evenly, and they are recorded as wearing yellow waistcoats.
- Other ranks' coats were lined yellow. The lapels were laced about and had with six square loops, set evenly, with three further loops below. The vertical pocket had three buttons and was laced with eight square loops.
- The red waistcoat was laced about, with pointed and laced loops; the pocket is shown as laced with three loops.
- Breeches for this regiment were red.
- Lace of the rank and file was white with an outer blue zigzag, two yellow central stripes and an inner red zigzag. The shoulder strap was shown laced about.
- The top braid of the square cuff was pointed and the cuff slash laced about with three buttons and five square loops.
- Grenadier cap was laced in white with a yellow front and rear turn-up. The black 'GR' Cypher had white foliate designs on either side. The tassel was mixed white and black and yellow.
- Grenadier wings were worn after 1752.
- The sword hilt was steel.

In the 1768 regulations:

- The facings for this regiment were yellow, while the linings, breeches and waistcoats of all ranks were white.
- The officers' lace and buttons were silver. Their coats were laced for dress with ten square loops, set evenly.
- Other ranks' coats had ten square loops, spaced evenly. The lace of the rank and file was white with a red outer stripe and a yellow outer-centre stripe.
- The *Grenadier Book* at The Prince Consort's Library shows this regiment with loops spaced evenly. Lawson noted the facing colour as bright-yellow.

During the War of Independence:
The 37th Regiment was ordered to America from Cork in Ireland, arriving at Cape Fear in May 1776. The regiment saw action at the first siege of Charleston, Brandywine, Delaware, Monmouth Court House and New York. Three companies were sent to St Augustine while the rest were sent to Nova Scotia in September 1779.

Raised in 1705 as:
Luke Lillington's Regiment of Foot
Ranked in 1747 as:
38th Regiment of Foot
In 1782 it was retitled as the:
38th (or Staffordshire) Regiment of Foot

In the Morier Paintings of 1751:

- The facings for this regiment were yellow; this is confirmed by Milan's list of 1749, which gives the linings as brown linen for service in the Windward Islands.
- Officers' lace and buttons were silver and officers' coats were laced for dress square loops, set evenly, and they are recorded as wearing yellow waistcoats.

• Other ranks' coats were lined yellow. The lapels were laced about and had with six square loops, set evenly, with three further loops below. The pocket was laced about with two laces inside it.
• The red waistcoat was laced about, with very narrow square loops. The pocket was laced about.
• Breeches for this regiment were red.
• Lace of the rank and file was white with an outer blue stripe, a central yellow stripe and a blue inner stripe.
• The top braid of the square cuff was pointed and the cuff slash was laced about with three buttons and one point to the lace.
• Grenadier cap was laced in white with a yellow front and rear turn-up. The blue 'GR' Cypher had white foliate designs on either side. The tassel was mixed white and blue.
• Grenadier wings were worn after 1752.
• The sword hilt was steel.

In the 1768 regulations:
• The facings for this regiment were yellow and the linings, breeches and waistcoats of all ranks were white.
• The officers' lace and buttons were silver. Their coats were laced for dress with ten square loops, set evenly.
• Other ranks' coats had ten bastion loops, spaced evenly. The lace of the rank and file was white with a red outer edge, a yellow centre stripe and a red inner edge.
• The *Grenadier Book* at The Prince Consort's Library shows this regiment with loops spaced evenly. Lawson noted the facing colour as bright-yellow.

During the War of Independence:
The 38th Regiment left Ireland, arriving in Boston in July 1774. The regiment saw action in New York, Newport, Rhode Island, Lexington and Concord, Bunker Hill, Long Island, Fort Lee, Chestnut Neck, Brandywine, Germantown and Monmouth Court House. It left New York in 1783 and moved to Nova Scotia where it remained for some years. The flank companies were surrendered with General Cornwallis at Yorktown and were interned and later exchanged.

Raised in 1702 as:
Richard Coote's Regiment of Foot
Ranked in 1747 as:
39th Regiment of Foot
In 1782 it was retitled as the:
39th (or the East Middlesex) Regiment of Foot
This regiment absorbed the 104th Regiment (Royal Manchester Volunteers) in 1795 and was retitled in 1807 as the:
39th (or the Dorsetshire) Regiment of Foot
The old county title 'East Middlesex' passed to the 77th Regiment.

In the Morier Paintings of 1751:
• The facings for this regiment were green, but Milan's list of 1749 gives pale green.
• Officers' lace and buttons were silver and officers' coats were laced for dress square loops, set evenly, the waistcoats were white and carried silver braid.
• Other ranks' coats were lined green. The lapels were laced about and had with six square loops, set evenly, with three further loops below. The pocket was laced about with two inner laces.
• The red waistcoat was laced about, without loops.
• Breeches for this regiment were red.
• Lace of the rank and file was white with a central blue curved worm. The shoulder strap is shown laced about.

• The top braid of the square cuff was pointed and the cuff slash laced about with three buttons and one point to the lace.
• Grenadier cap was laced in white with a green front and rear turn-up. The white 'GR' Cypher had white foliate designs on either side. The tassel was mixed white and green.
• Grenadier wings were worn after 1752.
• The sword hilt was steel.

In the 1768 regulations:
• The facings for this regiment were green while the linings, breeches and waistcoats of all ranks were white.
• The officers' lace and buttons were gold. Their coats were laced for dress with ten square loops, set evenly.
• Other ranks' coats had ten square loops, spaced evenly. The lace of the rank and file was white with a green outer worm.
• The *Grenadier Book* at The Prince Consort's Library shows this regiment with loops spaced evenly. Lawson noted the facing colour as willow-green, a dull lightish green.
• In 1784 this regiment adopted a lighter green for their facings.

Raised in 1717 as:
Richard Philips's Regiment of Foot
Ranked in 1747 as:
40th Regiment of Foot
In 1782 it was retitled as the:
40th (or the 2nd Somersetshire) Regiment of Foot.

In the Morier Paintings of 1751:
• The facings for this regiment were buff; this is confirmed by Milan's list of 1749.
• Officers' lace and buttons were silver and officers' coats were laced for dress with square loops, set evenly, and they are recorded as wearing buff waistcoats and breeches.
• Other ranks' coats were lined buff. The lapels were laced about and had six square loops, set evenly, with three further loops below, but the coat was folded over and the lacing is not clear. The pocket was laced about with two loops inside it leaving a clear red light to the outer lace.
• The red waistcoat was laced about but the coat is buttoned over and no further details are known.
• Breeches for this regiment were red.
• Lace of the rank and file was white with a black outer-centre stripe with a buff stripe either side of it.
• The top braid of the square cuff was pointed and the cuff slash is laced about with three buttons and one point to the lace.
• Grenadier cap was laced in white with a buff front and rear turn-up. The black 'GR' Cypher had white foliate designs on either side. The tassel was mixed white and black.
• Grenadier wings were worn after 1752.
• The sword hilt was steel.

In the 1768 regulations:
• The facings for this regiment were buff while the linings, breeches and waistcoats of all ranks were buff.
• The officers' lace and buttons were gold. Their coats were laced for dress with ten square loops, set evenly.
• Other ranks' coats had ten square loops, spaced evenly. The lace of the rank and file was white with a black outer edge and a red inner edge.
• The *Grenadier Book* at The Prince Consort's Library shows this regiment with loops spaced evenly.

During the War of Independence:

The 40th Regiment sailed from Ireland and arrived in Boston in June 1775 and saw action at Long Island, New York, Brooklyn, Princeton, Brandywine Creek, Paoli, Germantown, Monmouth Court House and New London. In November 1778 six companies were sent to Antigua and in July 1778 the remainder were sent to Barbados but returned to New York in September 1781 where they remained as garrison until departing for England in 1783.

• They are shown wearing short roundabout jackets without facings, officers having plain buff facings. The light company wore black belts; battalion men had white leather.

Raised in 1719 from companies of invalids and designated as:

Colonel Edmund Fielding's Regiment of Foot

Ranked in 1747 as:

41st (Royal Invalids) Regiment of Foot.

In 1782 retitled as

41st (Royal Invalids) Regiment of Foot.

In 1787 it was converted to a marching regiment and retitled as the:

41st Regiment of Foot

In the Morier Paintings of 1751:

• The facings for this royal regiment were dark-blue; this is confirmed by Milan's list of 1749.
• Officers' lace and buttons were gold and officers' coats were laced for dress with square loops, set evenly.
• Other ranks' coats were lined dark-blue with thirteen buttons. There were no lapels and the pocket was plain with three buttons below.
• The waistcoat was not shown.
• Breeches for this regiment were dark-blue.
• The rank and file wore no lace to the coat.
• The cuff was square with one button.
• Grenadier cap had a dark-blue front and rear turn-up and was laced in white. The front carried a crown over the Garter Star inside which was the blue garter belt inscribed 'Honi Soit Qui Mal Y Pense' with a red centre. Either side of this were foliate designs in white. The tassel was white with a red centre.
• Wings were not worn until after 1752.
• The sword hilt was steel.

In the 1768 regulations:

• The facings for this royal regiment were dark-blue and the linings, breeches and waistcoats of all ranks were blue while the lace was originally silver but changed to gold in September 1768 although the regiment was allowed to wear silver until the old epaulettes wore out. Their coats were unlaced for dress. This was changed to silver in 1787 when the regiment was converted to a marching regiment.
• Other ranks' coats had blue twist buttonholes with no loops before 1787. It was only after this period that evenly spaced loops were authorized.
• The *Grenadier Book* at The Prince Consort's Library shows this regiment with loops spaced evenly.

Raised in 1662 by the Earl of Athol from independent companies, the regiment formed in 1739.

Ranked in 1747 as:

43rd Regiment of Foot

Renumbered in 1749 as the:

42nd Regiment of Foot

In 1751 retitled as the:

42nd (Royal Highland) Regiment of Foot
Retitled In November 1758:
42nd (or the Royal Highland) Regiment of Foot (also known as the Black Watch)

In the Morier Paintings of 1751:
• The facings for this regiment were buff; this is confirmed by Milan's list of 1749. In July 1758 the facings were changed to those of a royal regiment with dark-blue.
• Officers' lace and buttons were gold and officers' coats were laced for dress with square loops, set evenly, and they are recorded as wearing buff waistcoats and breeches and often wore the bastion pattern of gold lace.
• The short coat or jacket had eleven pointed loops, set evenly, and the shoulder strap was on the right allowing the wearing of the belted plaid. The pocket was not fully shown and has been assumed to have three pointed loops.
• The red waistcoat was laced about; it has no loops and the pocket was not shown.
• This regiment wore the government sett and the grenadiers wore a red overstripe; a plaid was twelve yards of cloth folded and belted.
• Lace of the rank and file was white with a red outer stripe and a red inner stripe.
• The cuff was of the mariner type and laced about; the cuff slash was laced about with four buttons. The shape of the cuff-flap was square with five rungs.
• Grenadier cap after 1747 was bearskin with a red plate and white foliate designs.
• Grenadier wings were not worn before 1752.
• The sword hilt was steel.

In the 1768 regulations:
• The facings for this royal regiment were dark-blue; the linings and waistcoats were white and when breeches were worn they were white.
• This regiment was more commonly dressed in the full plaid of the government sett with the grenadier company wearing a red overstripe replacing the single black line of the blue way.
• The officers' lace and buttons were gold. Their coats were laced for dress with ten square loops, set evenly.
• Other ranks' coats had ten bastion loops, spaced evenly. The lace of the rank and file was white with a red outer stripe.
• The *Grenadier Book* at The Prince Consort's Library shows this regiment with loops spaced evenly.
• Sergeants and senior NCOs wore silver lace on their tunics.
• The rank and file wore badgerskin purses.

During the War of Independence:
The 42nd Regiment returned from New York to Cork in October 1767. The regiment embarked from Greenock in May 1776 and arrived in Staten Island in August 1776 and then moved to New York in July 1776. It saw action at Long Island, White Plains, Brooklyn, Harlem Heights, Fort Washington, Brandywine, Germantown, Monmouth Court House, Paoli, Billingsport, Whitemarsh and Stony Point. Returning to New York in 1778, it then saw action at Monmouth Court House and was also present at the relief of Newport 1778 before relocating to East Florida November 1778. It saw further action at the second Siege of Charleston and the raid on Portsmouth in 1780. The regiment left for Halifax in Nova Scotia in October 1783 where it was disbanded and those who chose were offered a land grant in Canada, the rest returning to Glasgow in 1790.
• The kilt was rarely worn after 1777.
• The grenadiers are noted as wearing bonnets like the men when on campaign.
• Each man was issued with a new Short Land pattern musket and bayonet.
• The broadswords and pistols were left in store in 1775.

Raised in 1741 as:
Thomas Fowke's Regiment of Foot
Ranked in 1747 as:
54th Regiment of Foot
Renumbered in 1751 as the:
43rd Regiment of Foot
In 1782 it was retitled as the:
43rd (or Monmouthsire) Regiment of Foot
It changed role on 10 July 1803 and became:
43rd (or Monmouthshire) Regiment of Foot (Light Infantry).

In the Morier Paintings of 1751:
• The facings for this regiment were white; this is confirmed by Milan's list of 1749.
• Officers' lace and buttons were silver and officers' coats were laced for dress with square loops, set evenly, and they are recorded as wearing white waistcoats and breeches.
• Other ranks' coats were lined white. The lapels were laced about and had five pointed loops, set evenly, with three further loops below. The vertical pocket carried three buttons and eight pointed loops.
• The red waistcoat was laced about, with no loops.
• Breeches for this regiment were red.
• Lace of the rank and file was white with an outer red stripe and a six-pointed central blue star and a red inner stripe.
• The top braid of the round cuff was square and had no lace below it. The cuff slash was laced about with three buttons; the shape of the cuff-flap was shown with a five-branch pointed lace to the cuff.
• Grenadier cap was laced in white with a white front and rear turn-up. The blue 'GR' Cypher had white foliate designs on either side. The tassel was mixed white and blue.
• Grenadier wings were rounded.
• The sword hilt was steel.

In the 1768 regulations:
• The facings for this regiment were white while the linings, breeches and waistcoats of all ranks were white.
• The officers' lace and buttons were silver. Their coats were unlaced for dress with ten square loops, set evenly.
• Other ranks' coats had ten square loops, spaced evenly. The lace of the rank and file was white with a red outer stripe and a black inner stripe.
• The *Grenadier Book* at The Prince Consort's Library shows this regiment with loops spaced evenly.

During the War of Independence:
The 43rd Regiment of Foot arrived in Boston in July of 1774 and saw action at Lexington, Bunker Hill, New York, the Battles of Long Island, Kiap's Bay and White Plains, and the capture of Fort Washington. In August 1778 the 43rd arrived in Rhode Island where it remained in 'occupation' until October 1779. The regiment was part of the surrender by General Cornwallis at Yorktown, leaving America in November of 1783 when the companies were brought home.

Raised in 1741 as:
James Long's Regiment of Foot
Ranked in 1747 as:
55th Regiment of Foot
Renumbered in 1751 as the:

44th Regiment of Foot
In 1782 it was retitled as the:
44th (or East Essex) Regiment of Foot.

In the Morier Paintings of 1751:
• The facings for this regiment were yellow; but Milan's list of 1749 gives deep-yellow.
• Officers' lace and buttons were silver and officers' coats were laced for dress with square loops, set evenly, and they are recorded as wearing yellow waistcoats.
• Other ranks' coats were lined yellow. The lapels were laced about and had six pointed loops, set evenly, with three further loops below. The pocket was not fully shown and has been assumed to have three pointed loops.
• The red waistcoat was laced about, with narrow square loops.
• Breeches for this regiment were red.
• Lace of the rank and file was white with an outer back zigzag and a yellow centre stripe and a blue inner and opposing zigzag.
• The top braid of the curved cuff was square with no lace below it. The cuff slash was laced about with four buttons; the cuff flap had two curved points.
• Grenadier cap was laced in white with a yellow front and rear turn-up. The black 'GR' Cypher had white foliate designs on either side. The tassel was mixed white and yellow.
• Grenadier wings were not worn before 1752.
• The sword hilt was steel.

In the 1768 regulations:
• The facings for this regiment were yellow while the linings, breeches and waistcoats of all ranks were white.
• The officers' lace and buttons were silver. Their coats were unlaced for dress with ten square loops, set evenly.
• Other ranks' coats had ten square loops, spaced evenly. The lace of the rank and file was white with a black outer stripe, a yellow centre stripe and a blue inner stripe.
• The *Grenadier Book* at The Prince Consort's Library shows this regiment with loops spaced evenly, Lawson noted the facing colour as bright-yellow.

During the War of Independence:
The 44th Regiment embarked at Cork and arrived in Boston in July 1775. During the battles in 1776 the flank companies saw action at the first siege of Charleston and the regiment saw action at New York, Brooklyn, White Plains, Danbury, Brandywine, Paoli, and Germantown, seeing action again the following year at Monmouth Court House. In September 1779, the regiment was sent to Quebec where it remained until returning to England in 1786.

Raised in 1741 as:
Daniel Houghton's Regiment of Foot
Ranked in 1747 as:
56th Regiment of Foot
Renumbered in 1751 as the:
45th Regiment of Foot
In 1782 it was retitled as the:
45th (or Nottinghamshire) Regiment of Foot.

In the Morier Paintings of 1751:
• The facings for this regiment were deep-green; Milan's list of 1749 gives green. The figure for this regiment has been re-touched to a blue colour for which no authority is known; the shoulder strap is shown edged with lace.

• Officers' lace and buttons were silver and officers' coats were laced for dress with square loops, set evenly.
• Other ranks' coats were lined deep-green. The lapels were laced about and had six pointed loops, set evenly, with three further loops below. The pocket was fully shown and was laced about with a single inside lace.
• The red waistcoat was laced about, with no loops.
• Breeches for this regiment were red.
• Lace of the rank and file was white with an outer blue stripe and; a central blue six-pointed star. The shoulder strap was shown laced about.
• The cuff has been painted out in blue leaving only a single lace but there is clear evidence that the cuff was originally square with a further set of lace below. The top braid of the square cuff was pointed. The cuff slash was laced about with three buttons; cuff-flap had one curved point at the centre.
• Grenadier cap was laced in white with a deep-green front and rear turn-up. The white 'GR' Cypher had white foliate designs on either side. The tassel was mixed white and deep-green.
• Grenadier wings were not worn before 1752.
• The sword hilt was steel.

In the 1768 regulations:
• The facings for this regiment were deep-green while the linings, breeches and waistcoats of all ranks were white.
• The officers' lace and buttons were silver. Their coats were laced for dress with ten square loops, set evenly.
• Other ranks' coats had ten bastion loops spaced evenly. The lace of the rank and file was white with a centre green leaf design of worm.
• The *Grenadier Book* at The Prince Consort's Library shows this regiment with loops spaced evenly. Lawson noted the facing colour as a dark bluish green.
• During 1780 it was noticed by Inspecting Officers that the officers' buttonholes were at equal distance and not like the men, which were in pairs.

During the War of Independence:
Returning to America, the 45th Regiment arrived in Boston in July 1775. In 1776, during the battles for New York, the regiment saw action at Long Island, Philadelphia, Brandywine and Germantown. In November 1778 as the regiment were under strength, the soldiers were drafted into other regiments while the officers and colours returned to England. After the war the surviving one hundred men returned to Nottingham.
• This regiment wore their bastion lace in pairs.

Raised in 1741 from the 2nd Battalion of 32nd Regiment of Foot and designated as:
James Price's Regiment of Foot
Ranked in 1747 as:
57th Regiment of Foot
Renumbered in 1751 as the:
46th Regiment of Foot
In 1782 it was retitled as the:
46th (or South Devonshire) Regiment of Foot.

In the Morier Paintings of 1751:
• The facings for this regiment were yellow; this is confirmed by Milan's list of 1749.
• Officers' lace and buttons were silver and officers' coats were laced for dress with square loops, set evenly, and they are recorded as wearing yellow waistcoats.

• Other ranks' coats were lined yellow. The lapels were laced about and had six pointed loops, set evenly, with three further loops below. The vertical pocket carried three buttons and eight pointed loops.
• The red waistcoat was laced about, with no loops.
• Breeches for this regiment were red.
• Lace of the rank and file was white with a yellow outer worm and a red stripe inside it, with two inner blue zigzags.
• The top braid of the round cuff was square and had no lace below it. The cuff slash was laced about with three buttons; the cuff-flap was shown with a five-branch pointed lace to the cuff.
• The front of the grenadier cap was not shown. It was laced in white with a yellow front and rear turn-up. The tassel was mixed white, red, blue and yellow. It is assumed that the front carried a white, blue or black 'GR' Cypher with white foliate designs on either side.
• Grenadier wings were rounded.
• The sword hilt was steel.

In the 1768 regulations:
• The facings for this regiment were yellow while the linings, breeches and waistcoats of all ranks were white.
• The officers' lace and buttons were silver. Their coats were laced for dress with ten square loops, set evenly.
• Other ranks' coats had ten square loops, spaced evenly. The lace of the rank and file was white with a red stripe and a purple stripe placed about the centre of the lace with the red to the outside.
• The *Grenadier Book* at The Prince Consort's Library shows this regiment with loops spaced evenly, Lawson noted the facing colour as a pale-yellow.
• In 1769 it was noted that the officers clothing, had the pleats taken out

During the War of Independence:
The 46th left Ireland and landed at Cape Fear in 1776, seeing action at the first siege of Charleston. The light company was detailed to a composite Light Infantry Battalion. The regiment saw further action at Paoli, Long Island, Brandywine, and Germantown and then returned to New York in 1778. More action was experienced at Monmouth Court House, Quinton's Bridge, Rhode Island. The 46th served as marines with Admiral Byron's fleet during 1778 and was sent to the West Indies in November 1779 with the 15th, 28th and 55th Regiments seizing St Lucia and St Eustatius from the French. It returned to England in March 1782 and was stationed at Plymouth.
• The Light Battalion dyed their cap feathers red as a distinctive mark after the action at Paoli. The light company of the 46th retained this for many years.

Raised in 1741 as:
John Mordaunt's Regiment of Foot
Ranked in 1747 as:
58th Regiment of Foot
Renumbered in 1751 as the:
47th Regiment of Foot
In 1782 it was retitled as the:
47th (or Lancashire) Regiment of Foot

In the Morier Paintings of 1751:
• The facings for this regiment were white.
• Officers' lace and buttons were silver and officers' coats were laced for dress with square loops, set evenly.
• Other ranks' coats were lined white. The lapels were laced about and had six pointed loops, set evenly, with three further loops below. The pocket was laced about with a further lace inside it leaving a clear red light.

• The red waistcoat was laced about, with very narrow square loops.
• Breeches for this regiment were red.
• Lace of the rank and file was white with an outer black zigzag and a yellow inner zigzag with a black central dot and a further opposed yellow and black zigzag.
• The top braid of the cuff was not clear. It could be round or square with a square end and no lace inside it. The cuff slash was laced about with three buttons; the cuff-flap had one point.
• Grenadier cap was laced in white with a white front and rear turn-up. The blue 'GR' Cypher had white, buff and blue foliate designs on either side. The tassel was mixed white, buff and blue.
• Grenadier wings were not worn before 1752.
• The sword hilt was steel.

In the 1768 regulations:
• The facings for this regiment were white while the linings, breeches and waistcoats of all ranks were white.
• The officers' lace and buttons were silver. Their coats were unlaced for dress with ten square loops, set evenly.
• Other ranks' coats had ten square loops, spaced evenly. The lace of the rank and file was white with a black outer edge, a thin red centre stripe and a black inner edge.
• The *Grenadier Book* at The Prince Consort's Library shows this regiment with loops spaced evenly.

During the War of Independence:
The 47th Foot arrived in 1773, landing at New Jersey. The regiment was sent to Boston in October of 1774, where it saw action at Bunker Hill and the defence of Quebec in 1776. Serving with the force under General Burgoyne on the Great Lake the regiment was surrendered at Saratoga and was later exchanged, returning home in 1781.

Raised in 1741 as:
James Cholmondeley's Regiment of Foot
Ranked in 1747 as:
59th Regiment of Foot
Renumbered in 1751 as the:
48th Regiment of Foot
In 1782 it was retitled as the:
48th (or Northamptonshire) Regiment of Foot.
This regiment was originally in America but was posted to the West Indies, and served there throughout the period of the War of Independence.

In the Morier Paintings of 1751:
• The facings for this regiment were buff; this is confirmed by Milan's list of 1749.
• Officers' lace and buttons were gold and officers' coats were laced for dress with square loops, set evenly, and they are recorded as wearing buff waistcoats and breeches.
• Other ranks' coats were lined buff. The lapels were laced about and had six square loops, set evenly, with three further loops below. The pocket was fully shown and was laced about with a further lace inside it showing a clear red light.
• The red waistcoat was laced about, with eleven bastion shape loops.
• Breeches for this regiment were red.
• Lace of the rank and file was white with a blue outer, a yellow outer-centre and a blue curved worm. The shoulder strap was shown laced about.
• The top braid of the curved cuff was square with no lace inside it. The cuff slash was laced about with three buttons; the cuff-flap had one point at the centre.

• Grenadier cap was laced in white with a buff front and rear turn-up. The blue 'GR' Cypher had white foliate designs on either side. The tassel was mixed white and blue.
• Grenadier wings were rounded.
• The sword hilt was steel.

In the 1768 regulations:
• The facings for this regiment were buff while linings, breeches and waistcoats of all ranks were buff.
• The officers' lace and buttons were gold. Their coats were laced for dress with ten square loops, set evenly; by 1782 they were unlaced.
• Other ranks' coats had ten square loops, spaced evenly. The lace of the rank and file was white with a red outer stripe and a black inner stripe.
• The *Grenadier Book* at The Prince Consort's Library shows this regiment with loops spaced evenly.

Raised in 1743 as:
Edward Trelawney's Regiment of Foot
Ranked in 1747 as:
63rd Regiment of Foot
Renumbered in 1751 as the:
49th Regiment of Foot
In 1782 it was retitled as the:
49th (or Hertfordshire) Regiment of Foot.

In the Morier Paintings of 1751:
• The facings for this regiment were full-green; this is confirmed by Milan's list of 1749.
• Officers' lace and buttons were silver and officers' coats were laced for dress with square loops, set evenly, and they are recorded as wearing full-green waistcoats.
• Other ranks' coats were lined full-green. The lapels were laced about and had seven square loops, set evenly, with three further loops below. The pocket was not fully shown and has been assumed.
• The red waistcoat was laced about, with very narrow square loops.
• Breeches for this regiment were red.
• Lace of the rank and file was white with an outer blue curved worm, a yellow centre stripe and an opposing blue curved worm.
• The top braid of the cuff was square with no lace inside it. The cuff slash was not shown in the Morier paintings and is assumed laced about with three buttons, with one point to the lace.
• Grenadier cap was laced in white with a full-green front and rear turn-up. The white 'GR' Cypher had white foliate designs on either side. The tassel was mixed white and full-green. A surviving example of a Grenadier mitre has a green 'GR' Cypher with green foliate designs on either side.
• Grenadier wings were not worn before 1752
• The sword hilt was steel.

In the 1768 regulations:
• The facings for this regiment were full-green while the linings, breeches and waistcoats of all ranks were white.
• The officers' lace and buttons were gold. Their coats were laced for dress with ten square loops, set evenly.
• Other ranks' coats had ten flowerpot loops, spaced evenly. The lace of the rank and file was white with a red outer stripe, a green centre stripe and a red inner stripe.
• The *Grenadier Book* at The Prince Consort's Library shows this regiment with loops spaced evenly. Lawson noted the facing colour as a very dark-blue green.

During the War of Independence:
The 49th Regiment left Ireland and landed in Boston June 1775. It saw action at Brooklyn, Long Island, White Plains, Brandywine and Germantown. The battalion companies went with the regiment to the West Indies in 1778. In 1803 the regiment embarked for Quebec.
• The light company also wore red feathers. This action continued to be commemorated by the wearing of the red 'Brandywine Flash' behind the cap badge by the Royal Berkshire Regiment.

Raised in 1690 were two regiments of:
Marines
These were disbanded in May 1699.
On the 1st June 1701 a further six regiments were raised and six others for sea service which were taken into the line in 1713.
In October 1739 six regiments were raised as:
Marines
Followed by four more during November and December 1740; these were ranked as the 44th to the 53rd Regiment of Foot but were taken under Admiralty Control on 28 February 1747 and no longer ranked with the Line Regiments; they were disbanded by November 1748.
In 1755 fifty companies of marines were raised and split into the three divisions of Chatham, Portsmouth and Plymouth. These were formed as:
Marines
Retitled on 29 April 1802 as:
Royal Marines
This regiment is placed 49th in the order of precedence.

In the Morier Paintings of 1751:
• The facings for this regiment were white.
• Officers' coats lined, faced and lapelled white with gold binding.
• Other ranks' coats were lined white. The lapels were laced about and had six square loops, set evenly, with three further loops below; the horizontal coat pocket was laced about.
• The red waistcoat was laced about.
• Breeches for this regiment were red.
• Lace of the rank and file was plain white, with a blue outer, a red centre and a blue inner worm.
• Grenadier cap was laced in white with a white front and rear turn-up. The badge was of silver and the foliate designs on either side were white as were the tassel.
• Grenadier wings were rounded.

In the 1768 regulations:
• The facings for this regiment were white while the linings, breeches and waistcoats of all ranks were white.
• The officers' lace and buttons were gold. Their coats were laced for dress with ten square loops, set evenly, during the American Revolution period they were placed in pairs.
• Other ranks' coats had ten loops, spaced evenly. The lace of the rank and file was white with a red outer stripe and a blue inner stripe.
• In April 1802 the regiment was made royal and adopted blue facings.
• This regiment originally had loops spaced evenly, but by 1783 they were spaced on pairs for the officers.

During the War of Independence:
The 1st and 2nd Battalions of Marines saw action at Concord, Boston, Charlestown and Bunker Hill. The Marines left for Halifax in Nova Scotia during 1777. They returned home in 1778.

• There were four Battalions during the War of Independence; each had one Grenadier Company, who wore the fur cap in America, eight centre companies, and one light company who wore the light cap in America. These were reduced by losses to 460 men by which time they had two Majors, ten Captains, twenty-seven subalterns, twenty-eight Sergeants, twenty-five Corporals, twenty-nine Drummers and 600 private soldiers to form two Battalions.

Raised in September 1754 by Thomas Shirley for service in North America as the:
American Provincials
Also known as:
50th Regiment of Foot
This regiment was lost at Fort Oswego and disbanded in December 1756.

In the Frederick Aubert paintings of circa 1755:
• The facings for this regiment were red.
• Officers' lace and buttons were silver and officers' coats were laced for dress with square loops, set evenly.
• Other ranks' coats were lined madder-red. The lapels were laced about and had six square loops, set evenly, with three further loops below. The pocket was laced about.
• The red waistcoat was laced about.
• Breeches for this regiment were red.
• Lace of the rank and file was white with one black outer stripe.
• The top braid of the cuff was pointed with no lace inside it. The cuff slash was laced about with four buttons.
• Grenadier cap was laced in white with a red front and rear turn-up. The large white 'GR' Cypher had white foliate designs on either side. The tassel was mixed white and red.
• Grenadier wings were rounded.

Raised in September 1754 by Sir William Pepperel for service in North America as the:
Cape Breton Regiment
Also known as:
51st Regiment of Foot
This regiment was lost at Fort Oswego and disbanded in December 1756.

In the Frederick Aubert paintings of circa 1755:
• The facings for this regiment were red.
• Officers' lace and buttons were gold and officers' coats were laced for dress with square loops, set evenly.
• Other ranks' coats were lined madder-red. The lapels were laced about and had with six square loops, set evenly, with three further loops below. The pocket was laced about.
• The red waistcoat was laced about.
• Breeches for this regiment were red.
• Lace of the rank and file was plain white.
• The top braid of the cuff was pointed with no lace inside it. The cuff slash was laced about with four buttons.
• Grenadier cap was laced in white with a red front and rear turn-up. The white 'GR' Cypher had white foliate designs on either side. The tassel was mixed white and red.
• Grenadier wings were rounded.

Raised in December 1755 by Colonel James Abercromby as the:
52nd Regiment of Foot
Renumbered in 1757, after the existing 50th and 51st had been lost at Fort Oswego and were disbanded in December 1755, as the:

50th Regiment of Foot
In 1782 it was retitled as the:
50th (or West Kent) Regiment of Foot.

In December 1755:
• The facings for this regiment were black.
• Officers' lace and buttons were silver and officers' coats were laced for dress with square loops, set evenly, and they are recorded as wearing white waistcoats and breeches.
• Other ranks' coats were lined black, by 1758 white. The lapels were laced about and had six square loops.
• The red waistcoat was laced about with narrow loops.
• Breeches for this regiment were red.
• Lace of the rank and file was white and black.
• The braid of the cuff was not shown and has been assumed.
• Grenadier cap was laced in white with a black front and rear turn-up. The white 'GR' Cypher had white foliate designs on either side. The tassel was mixed white and black.

In the 1768 regulations:
• The facings for this regiment were black while the linings, breeches and waistcoats of all ranks were white.
• The officers' lace and buttons were silver. Their coats were unlaced for dress with ten square loops, set evenly, later they were set in pairs.
• Other ranks' coats had ten square loops, set evenly, later they were set in pairs. The lace of the rank and file was white with a red centre stripe.
• The *Grenadier Book* at The Prince Consort's Library shows this regiment with loops, spaced evenly, but Lawson considered that the loops were set in pairs.

During the War of Independence:
Personnel of the 50th Foot arrived in New York from Jamaica in July 1776 with many sick. The fit men were drafted to other regiments in August 1776 and the officers, colours and the sick men returned to Salisbury in November 1776. After recruiting at home, the regiment returned to America, serving as marines with the fleet until 1778, when the officers, NCOs and men returned home.

Raised in December 1755 as the:
53rd Regiment of Foot
Renumbered in 1757, after the existing 50th and 51st had been lost at Fort Oswego and were disbanded in December 1755, as the:
51st Regiment of Foot
In 1782 it was retitled as the:
51st (or 2nd Yorkshire West Riding) Regiment of Foot
It was retitled in 1808 as:
51st (or 2nd Yorkshire West Riding) Regiment of Foot (Light Infantry).

In December 1755:
• The facings for this regiment were sea-green.
• Officers' lace and buttons were gold and officers' coats were laced for dress with square loops, set evenly, and they are recorded as wearing white waistcoats and breeches.
• Other ranks' coats were lined sea-green. The lapels were laced about and had six square loops.
• The red waistcoat was laced about.
• Breeches for this regiment were red.

• Lace of the rank and file was white with a green worm.
• The braid of the cuff is not known.
• Grenadier cap was laced in white with a sea-green front and rear turn-up. The white 'GR' Cypher had white foliate designs on either side. The tassel was mixed white and sea-green.

In the 1768 regulations:
• The facings for this regiment were deep-green while the linings, breeches and waistcoats of all ranks were white.
• The officers' lace and buttons were gold. Their coats were laced for dress with ten square loops, set evenly.
• Other ranks' coats had ten bastion loops, spaced evenly. The lace of the rank and file was white with a green outer worm.
• The *Grenadier Book* at The Prince Consort's Library shows this regiment with loops spaced evenly. Lawson noted the facing colour as an olive green.

Raised in December 1755 from the 2nd Battalion of 43rd Regiment of Foot and designated as the:
54th Regiment of Foot
Renumbered in 1757, after the existing 50th and 51st had been lost at Fort Oswego and were disbanded in December 1755, as the:
52nd Regiment of Foot
In 1782 it was retitled as the:
52nd (or Oxfordshire) Regiment of Foot
In 1803 is was retitled as:
52nd (or Oxfordshire) Regiment of Foot (Light Infantry).

In December 1755:
• The facings for this regiment were buff.
• Officers' lace and buttons were gold and officers' coats were unlaced for dress and they were recorded as wearing buff waistcoats and breeches.
• Other ranks' coats were lined buff. The lapels were laced about and had six pointed loops.
• The red waistcoat was laced about.
• Breeches for this regiment were red.
• The vertical pocket carried three buttons and eight pointed loops.
• Lace of the rank and file was white with red and orange stripe.
• The top braid of the round cuff was square and had no lace below it. The cuff slash was laced about with three buttons, the cuff-flap was shown with a five-branch pointed lace to the cuff.
• Grenadier cap was laced in white with a buff front and rear turn-up. The red 'GR' Cypher had white foliate designs on either side. The tassel was mixed white and buff.

In the 1768 regulations:
• The facings for this regiment were buff while the linings, breeches and waistcoats of all ranks were buff.
• The officers' lace and buttons were silver. Their coats were laced for dress with ten square loops, set evenly.
• Other ranks' coats had ten square loops, spaced evenly. The lace of the rank and file was white with a red arrowhead worm outer and an orange inner stripe.
• The *Grenadier Book* at The Prince Consort's Library shows this regiment with loops spaced evenly.

During the War of Independence:
The 52nd Foot arrived in Boston in October 1774. The flank companies saw action at Concord, the regiment at Lexington Green. The regiment was effectively destroyed at Bunker Hill but saw further action at Long Island,

Fort Washington, the New Jersey campaign and the relief of Newport. The 52nd returned to New York where the men were drafted to other regiments and the officers and colours returned to England in August 1778 to recruit.

Raised in 1755 as the:
55th Regiment of Foot
Renumbered in 1757 as the:
53rd Regiment of Foot
In 1782 it was retitled as the:
53rd (or Shropshire) Regiment of Foot.

In December 1755:
• The facings for this regiment were red.
• Officers' lace and buttons were silver and officers' coats were laced for dress with square loops, set evenly, and they are recorded as wearing buff waistcoats and breeches.
• Other ranks' coats were lined red. The lapels were laced about and had six square loops.
• The red waistcoat was laced about.
• Breeches for this regiment were red.
• Lace of the rank and file had a red centre stripe.
• The braid of the square cuff was pointed and lined about by a ladder of lace with two points.
• Grenadier cap was laced in white with a red front and rear turn-up. The white 'GR' Cypher had white foliate designs on either side. The tassel was mixed white and red.

In the 1768 regulations:
• The facings for this regiment were red while the linings, breeches and waistcoats of all ranks were white.
• The officers' lace and buttons were gold. Their coats were laced for dress with ten square loops, set evenly.
• Other ranks' coats had ten square loops, spaced evenly. The lace of the rank and file was white with a red centre stripe.
• The *Grenadier Book* at The Prince Consort's Library shows this regiment with loops spaced evenly.

During the War of Independence:
The 53rd Regiment sailed from Minorca to Canada in May 1776 as reinforcement for Quebec. The battalion companies of the regiment were dispersed among the border garrisons in Canada, but General Burgoyne surrendered the Grenadier and Light Companies of the regiment at Saratoga in October 1771. They remained interned until 1783 when they returned home.

Raised in 1755 from the 2nd Battalion of the 39th Regiment of Foot and designated as the:
56th Regiment of Foot
Renumbered in 1757, after the existing 50th and 51st had been lost at Fort Oswego and were disbanded in December 1755, as the:
54th Regiment of Foot
In 1782 it was retitled as the:
54th (or West Norfolk) Regiment of Foot.

In December 1755:
• The facings for this regiment were popinjay-green.
• Officers' lace and buttons were silver and officers' coats were laced for dress with square loops, set evenly, and they are recorded as wearing buff waistcoats and breeches.

• Other ranks' coats were lined white. The lapels were laced about and had six pointed loops; the cuff lace was six pointed loops.
• The red waistcoat was laced about.
• Breeches for this regiment were red.
• The vertical pocket carried three buttons and eight pointed loops.
• Lace of the rank and file was yellow.
• Grenadier cap was laced in white with a popinjay-green front and rear turn-up. The white 'GR' Cypher had white foliate designs on either side. The tassel was mixed white and green.

In the 1768 regulations:
• The facings for this regiment were popinjay-green while the linings, breeches and waistcoats of all ranks were white.
• The officers' lace and buttons were silver. Their coats were laced for dress with ten square loops, set evenly.
• Other ranks' coats had ten square loops, spaced evenly. The lace of the rank and file was white with a green centre stripe.
• The *Grenadier Book* at The Prince Consort's Library shows this regiment with loops spaced evenly. Lawson noted the facing colour as a dull yellowish-green.

During the War of Independence:
The 54th Regiment embarked from Cork and landed at Cape Fear in May 1776. It was posted to the New York garrison in 1776 and saw action at the first siege of Charleston and Newport. It then returned to New York in August 1781 losing many items of five companies on the way to Rhode Island. In September 1782 the regiment moved to Halifax in Canada where it remained for several years.
• Grenadiers' swords and match cases were not taken to America
• Cartridge boxes not taken to America.

Raised in 1755 in Stirling from the 2nd Battalion of the 34th Regiment of Foot by George Perry Esq and designated as the:
57th Regiment of Foot
Renumbered in America 1757, after the existing 50th and 51st had been lost at Fort Oswego and were disbanded in December 1755, as the:
55th Regiment of Foot
In 1782 it was retitled as the:
55th (or Northumberland) Regiment of Foot.

In December 1755:
• The facings for this regiment were dark-green.
• Officers' lace and buttons were gold and officers' coats were laced for dress with square loops, set evenly, and they are recorded as wearing buff waistcoats and breeches.
• Other ranks' coats were lined white. The lapels were laced about and had six square loops.
• The red waistcoat was laced about.
• Breeches for this regiment were red.
• Lace of the rank and file was a yellow square loop.
• The braid of the square cuff was pointed and lined about by a ladder of lace with two points.
• Grenadier cap was laced in white with a dark-green front and rear turn-up. The white 'GR' Cypher had white foliate designs on either side. The tassel was mixed white and dark-green.

In the 1768 regulations:

• The facings for this regiment were dark-green while the linings, breeches and waistcoats of all ranks were white.

• The officers' lace and buttons were gold. Their coats were laced for dress with ten square loops, set evenly.

• Other ranks' coats had ten square loops, spaced evenly. The lace of the rank and file was white with a green outer stripe and a green inner stripe.

• The *Grenadier Book* at The Prince Consort's Library shows this regiment with loops spaced evenly. Lawson noted the facing colour as a very dark-blue green.

During the War of Independence:

The 55th Regiment of Foot arrived in Boston during December 1775. It saw action at New York, in 1776, Long Island, Philadelphia, Brandywine and Germantown. It returned New York in 1778 and was sent to St Lucia and St Kitts in November 1778 with the 15th, 28th and 46th Regiments. The officers and colours returned home in 1783, followed by the men.

Raised in 1755 from the 2nd Battalion of the 44th Regiment of Foot as the:

58th Regiment of Foot

Renumbered in 1757, after the existing 50th and 51st had been lost at Fort Oswego and were disbanded in December 1755, as the:

56th Regiment of Foot

In 1782 it was retitled as the:

56th (or West Essex) Regiment of Foot.

In December 1755:

• The facings for this regiment deep-crimson or pompadour; these were changed to purple in 1764.

• Officers' lace and buttons were gold and officers' coats were laced for dress with square loops, set evenly, and they are recorded as wearing buff waistcoats and breeches.

• Other ranks' coats were lined red. The lapels were laced about and had six square loops.

• The red waistcoat was laced about; by 1764 the waistcoat, breeches and linings were white.

• Breeches for this regiment were red.

• Lace of the rank and file was white with pink stripe.

• The braid of the square cuff was pointed and lined about by a ladder of lace with two curved points.

• Grenadier cap was laced in white with a pompadour front and rear turn-up. The white 'GR' Cypher had white foliate designs on either side. The tassel was mixed white and pompadour.

In the 1768 regulations:

• The facings for this regiment were purple while the linings, breeches and waistcoats of all ranks were white.

• The officers' lace and buttons were silver. Their coats were laced for dress with ten square loops, set evenly.

• Other ranks' coats had ten square loops, spaced evenly. The lace of the rank and file was white with a purple centre stripe.

• The *Grenadier Book* at The Prince Consort's Library shows this regiment with loops spaced evenly. Lawson noted the facing colour as a very dark violet.

Raised in 1755 as:

59th Regiment of Foot

Renumbered in 1757, after the existing 50th and 51st had been lost at Fort Oswego and were disbanded in December 1755, as the:

57th Regiment of Foot

In 1782 it was retitled as the:
57th (or West Middlesex) Regiment of Foot.

In December 1755:
• The facings for this regiment were bright-yellow.
• Officers' lace and buttons were gold and officers' coats were laced for dress with square loops, set evenly, and they are recorded as wearing buff waistcoats and breeches.
• Other ranks' coats were lined buff. The lapels were laced about and had six square loops.
• The red waistcoat was laced about.
• Breeches for this regiment were red.
• Lace of the rank and file was yellow.
• The braid of the cuff was on the top edge only and was pointed. The ladder of lace carried four buttons and came to a point.
• Grenadier cap was laced in white with a bright-yellow front and rear turn-up. The white 'GR' Cypher had white foliate designs on either side. The tassel was mixed white and yellow.

In the 1768 regulations:
• The facings for this regiment were yellow while the linings, breeches and waistcoats of all ranks were white.
• The officers' lace and buttons were gold. Their coats were unlaced for dress with ten square loops, set evenly.
• Other ranks' coats had ten square loops, spaced evenly. The lace of the rank and file was white with a black centre stripe.
• The *Grenadier Book* at The Prince Consort's Library shows this regiment with loops spaced evenly. Lawson noted the facing colour as bright-yellow.

During the War of Independence:
The 57th Regiment of Foot received orders for North America in October 1775, embarked from Cork in May 1776 and landed at Cape Fear in April of the same year. It saw action at the first siege of Charleston, Brooklyn, Long Island and was then posted to the New York garrison where it remained. The light company had been detached to the 2nd Battalion of Light Infantry and was part of the surrender at Yorktown on 19 October 1781. In September 1783 the regiment moved to Halifax in Nova Scotia with 357 effective men and NCOs. The 57th returned home to the British Isles in 1791.

Raised in December 1755 from the 2nd Battalion of the 48th Regiment of Foot and designated as the:
60th Regiment of Foot
Renumbered in 1757, after the existing 50th and 51st had been lost at Fort Oswego and were disbanded in December 1755, as the:
58th Regiment of Foot
In 1782 it was retitled as the:
58th (or Rutlandshire) Regiment of Foot.

In December 1755:
• The facings for this regiment were black.
• Officers' lace and buttons were gold and officers' coats were laced for dress with square loops, set evenly, and they are recorded as wearing buff waistcoats and breeches.
• Other ranks' coats were lined buff and faced in black. The lapels were laced about and had six square loops.
• The red waistcoat was laced about.
• Breeches for this regiment were red.
• Lace of the rank and file was plain yellow.

• The braid of the rounded cuff was square-ended with a ladder of lace with four buttons and one point.
• Grenadier cap was laced in white with a black front and rear turn-up. The white 'GR' Cypher had white foliate designs on either side. The tassel was mixed white and black.
• Grenadier wings were round.

In the 1768 regulations:
• The facings for this regiment were black while the linings, breeches and waistcoats of all ranks were white.
• The officers' lace and buttons were gold. Their coats were laced for dress with ten square loops, set evenly.
• Other ranks' coats had ten square loops, spaced evenly. The lace of the rank and file was white with a red centre stripe.
• The *Grenadier Book* at The Prince Consort's Library shows this regiment with loops spaced evenly.

Raised in December 1755 from the 2nd Battalion of the 30th Regiment of Foot and designated as the:
61st Regiment of Foot
Renumbered in 1757, after the existing 50th and 51st had been lost at Fort Oswego and were disbanded in December 1755, as the:
59th Regiment of Foot
In 1782 it was retitled as the:
59th (or 2nd Nottinghamshire) Regiment of Foot.

In December 1755:
• The facings for this regiment were rose-pompadour.
• Officers' lace and buttons were gold and officers' coats were laced for dress with square loops, set evenly.
• Other ranks' coats were lined red. The lapels were laced about and had seven square loops.
• The red waistcoat was laced about.
• Breeches for this regiment were red.
• Lace of the rank and file was yellow.
• The braid of the cuff was on the top edge only and was pointed. The ladder of lace carried four buttons and came to a point.
• Grenadier cap was laced in white with a rose pompadour front and rear turn-up. The white 'GR' Cypher had white foliate designs on either side. The tassel was mixed white and rose pompadour.
• Grenadier wings were rounded.

In the 1768 regulations:
• The facings for this regiment were rose-pompadour, but in 1776 the facings changed to white. The linings breeches and waistcoats of all ranks were white.
• The officers' lace and buttons were silver. Their coats were laced for dress with ten square loops, set evenly.
• Other ranks' coats had ten square loops, spaced evenly. The lace of the rank and file was white with a red stripe and a yellow stripe, both placed at the centre of the lace with the red to the outside.
• The *Grenadier Book* at The Prince Consort's Library shows this regiment with loops spaced evenly. Lawson noted the facing colour as a pinkish crimson.
• In 1776 the facing colour changed to white.

During the War of Independence:
The 59th Regiment arrived at Halifax in 1765; it moved to Boston from Nova Scotia in 1774. Its flank companies were engaged at Concord and the regiment at Lexington Green and Bunker Hill. In 1776 the men were drafted to other regiments, the officers and colours returning to England to recruit. The new regiment was posted to Gibraltar in 1782.

Raised in 1755 in America as the:

62nd (Royal American) Regiment of Foot

Renumbered in 1757, after the existing 50th and 51st had been lost at Fort Oswego and were disbanded in December 1755, as the:

60th (Royal American) Regiment of Foot

It was retitled in 1815 and became:

60th (Royal American) Regiment of Foot (Light Infantry).

In December 1755:

- The facings for this royal regiment were dark-blue.
- Officers' lace and buttons were silver and officers' coats were laced for dress with square loops, set evenly.
- Other ranks' coats were madder-red. The lapels were laced about and had seven square loops.
- The red waistcoat was laced about.
- Breeches for this regiment were dark-blue.
- No lace worn by rank and file in undress, but when worn consisted of a blue outer worm and a blue inner stripe.
- The square cuff was laced about with full lace, the end was pointed and the ladder of lace carried four buttons and was scalloped.
- Grenadier cap was laced in white with a dark-blue front and rear turn-up. The white 'GR' Cypher had white foliate designs on either side. The tassel was mixed white and dark-blue.
- Grenadier wings were not recorded.

In the 1768 regulations:

- The facings for this royal regiment were dark-blue while the linings, breeches and waistcoats of all ranks were white.
- The officers' lace and buttons were silver. Their coats were laced for dress with ten square loops, set evenly; later they were spaced in pairs.
- Other ranks' coats had ten square loops spaced evenly, later they were spaced in pairs. The lace of the rank and file was white with a blue outer worm and a blue inner stripe.
- The *Grenadier Book* at The Prince Consort's Library shows this regiment with loops spaced evenly.

During the War of Independence:

Various contingents of the 60th Regiment were involved during the War of Independence, both in the West Indies and in the southern campaigns. During 1775 and 1776, companies of the 2nd and 4th Battalions were in East Florida, while others of the 2nd and 1st Battalions were in the Caribbean at Antigua and Jamaica. By 1778 and 1779 the situation had changed: companies of the 2nd Battalion remained at St Vincent where upwards of 400 men surrendered to the French in June 1779. The 2nd, 3rd and 4th Battalions served in Florida and Georgia and saw action at Brown's Creek, Huston Ford, Fort Morris, and the Siege of Savannah (4th Battalion). In 1780 companies of the 4th Battalion safought at the Siege of Mobile and the 3rd Battalion at Baton Rouge. The 1st Battalion saw action at Fort St Juan in Nicaragua. Eight companies of the 2nd Battalion served in both Carolina and West Florida and saw action at Pensacola remaining sections of the 2nd and 3rd Battalions continued to garrison St Augustine, while remnants of the 1st and 2nd Battalions were sent to New York where other officers were employed in an espionage capacity. The light company of the 2nd Battalion was at Grenada and St Vincent in 1784, while companies of the 1st and 2nd Battalions were sent to Jamaica and Halifax in 1787.

Raised in 1756 as the 2nd Battalion of the 3rd Regiment of Foot and designated in 1758 as the:

61st Regiment of Foot

In 1782 it was retitled as the:
61st (or South Gloucestershire) Regiment of Foot

In the warrant of 1758:
• The facings for this regiment were buff (as the 3rd Regiment).
• Officers' lace and buttons were silver and officers' coats were laced for dress with square loops, set evenly, and they are recorded as wearing buff waistcoats and breeches.
• Other ranks' coats were lined buff. The lapels were laced about and had six pointed loops.
• Lace of the rank and file was white with an outer stripe of blue.
• The square cuff was laced on the top edge and the end was pointed. The ladder of lace carried four buttons and was scalloped.
• Grenadier cap was laced in white with a buff front and rear turn-up. The blue 'GR' Cypher had white foliate designs on either side. The tassel was mixed white and buff.

In the 1768 regulations:
• The facings for this regiment were buff while the linings, breeches and waistcoats of all ranks were buff.
• The officers' lace and buttons were silver. Their coats were unlaced for dress with ten square loops, set evenly, and they wore a silver buckle, slider and tip to the shoulder belt.
• Other ranks' coats had ten square loops, spaced evenly. The lace of the rank and file was white with a blue outer stripe.
• The *Grenadier Book* at The Prince Consort's Library shows this regiment with loops spaced evenly.

Raised in 1756 as the 2nd Battalion of the 4th Regiment of Foot and designated in 1758 as:
62nd Regiment of Foot
In 1782 it was retitled as the:
62nd (or Wiltshire) Regiment of Foot

In the warrant of 1758:
• The facings for this regiment were buff.
• Officers' lace and buttons were silver and officers' coats were laced for dress with square loops, set evenly.
• Other ranks' coats were lined yellowish-buff. The lapels were laced about and had six pointed loops.
• Lace of the rank and file was white with two black and two yellowish buff stripes.
• The square cuff was laced on the top edge and the end was pointed. The ladder of lace carried four buttons and was scalloped.
• Grenadier cap was laced in white with a yellowish-buff front and rear turn-up. The green 'GR' Cypher had no foliate designs on either side. The tassel was mixed white and buff.

In the 1768 regulations:
• The facings for this regiment were yellowish-buff while the breeches and waistcoats of all ranks were yellowish-buff.
• The officers' lace and buttons were silver. Their coats were laced for dress with ten square loops, set evenly.
• Other ranks' coats had ten square loops, spaced evenly. The lace of the rank and file was white with a blue outer stripe, a yellowish buff centre stripe and a blue inner stripe.
• The *Grenadier Book* at The Prince Consort's Library shows this regiment with loops spaced evenly; Lawson noted the facing colour as a pale-yellowish buff.
• Corporals of this regiment wore a white epaulette on the right shoulder and all ranks are noted for short coats.

During the War of Independence:
The 62nd Regiment of Foot arrived in Quebec during May 1776 from Cork. During the Canadian Campaign of 1776 the regiment saw action at the relief of Quebec. It was stationed at New York and was part of the surrender by General Burgoyne at Saratoga in October 1771. It was interned for most of the war at Cambridge in November 1777, Rutland in November 1778, Charlottesville to June 1781 and Lancaster until April 1783 over a difference between cartridge pouches and boxes. The regiment eventually returned home in 1783.
• This regiment was noted for the coats being too short and the hats too small.
• Officers carried fusils and cartridge pouches.

Raised in 1756 as the 2nd Battalion of the 8th Regiment of Foot and designated in 1758 as the:
63rd Regiment of Foot
In 1782 it was retitled as the:
63rd (or West Suffolk) Regiment of Foot.

In the warrant of 1758:
• The facings for this regiment were very deep-green.
• Officers' lace and buttons were silver and officers' coats were laced for dress with square loops, set evenly.
• Other ranks' coats were lined buff. The lapels were laced about and had six pointed loops.
• Lace of the rank and file was white with green and white diagonal stripes to the outer edge.
• The square cuff was laced on the top edge and the end was pointed. The ladder of lace carried four buttons and was scalloped.
• Grenadier cap was laced in white with a very deep-green front and rear turn-up. The white 'GR' Cypher had white foliate designs on either side. The tassel was mixed white and very deep-green.

In the 1768 regulations:
• The facings for this regiment were very deep-green while the breeches and waistcoats of all ranks were white.
• The officers' lace and buttons were silver. Their coats were laced for dress with ten square loops, set evenly.
• Other ranks' coats had ten square loops, spaced evenly, with the lace of the rank and file being white with a green inner edge.
• The *Grenadier Book* at The Prince Consort's Library shows this regiment with loops spaced evenly. Lawson noted the facing colour as a very dark-green.

During the War of Independence:
The 63rd Regiment arrived at Boston in June 1775. The flank companies saw action at Bunker Hill and Fort Washington, the regiment saw action at Long Island, and the relief of Newport in November 1776. The 63rd Regiment returned to New York in May 1777 and was posted to Philadelphia. It returned to the New York garrison in 1778 and saw further action at Brandywine, Germantown, Monmouth Court House, the second siege of Charleston, Fishdam Ford, Blackstock's Hill, Hob Kirk's Hill, and at Eutaw Springs. It is known that certain companies were mounted and served as light dragoons. The regiment left Charleston in 1782 but, instead of being sent home, it was posted to the West Indies, returning home in 1783.

Raised in 1756 as the 2nd Battalion of the 11th Regiment of Foot and designated in 1758 as the:
64th Regiment of Foot
In 1782 it was retitled as the:
64th (or 2nd Staffordshire) Regiment of Foot.

In November 1758:
• The facings for this regiment were black.

• Officers' lace and buttons were gold and officers' coats were laced for dress with pointed square loops, set evenly, and they are recorded as wearing white waistcoats and breeches. The officers wore no hat lace.
• Other ranks' coats were lined white. The lapels were laced about and had six pointed loops.
• Lace of the rank and file was white with one yellow stripe.
• The square cuff was laced on the top edge and the end was pointed. The ladder of lace carried four buttons and was scalloped.
• Sergeants wore yellow lace.
• Grenadier cap was laced in white with a black front and rear turn-up. The white 'GR' Cypher had white foliate designs on either side. The tassel was mixed white and black.
• Grenadier wings were curved.

In the 1768 regulations:
• The facings for this regiment were black while the breeches and waistcoats of all ranks were white.
• The officers' lace and buttons were gold. Their coats were laced for dress with ten square loops, set evenly.
• Other ranks' coats had ten square loops, spaced evenly, with the lace of the rank and file being white with a black outer stripe and, a red centre stripe.
• The *Grenadier Book* at The Prince Consort's Library shows this regiment with loops spaced evenly.

During the War of Independence:
The 64th Regiment arrived in Boston Halifax, Nova Scotia during January 1769. The regiment saw action at Long Island, Brandywine, Germantown, Monmouth Court House, Danbury, and Newport and returned to New York in 1778. It saw further action at Stony Point, Paulus Hook, the relief of the Ninety-Six and was then posted south and served at the siege of Charleston, South Carolina and Eutaw Springs. The regiment left Charleston for Jamaica in October of 1782 where it remained for two years.

Raised in 1756 as the 2nd Battalion of the 12th Regiment of Foot and designated in 1758 as the:
65th Regiment of Foot
In 1782 it was retitled as the:
65th (or 2nd Yorkshire North Riding) Regiment of Foot.

In November 1758:
• The facings for this regiment were white.
• Officers' lace and buttons were silver and officers' coats were laced for dress with square loops, set evenly, and they are recorded as wearing white waistcoats and breeches.
• Other ranks' coats were lined white. The lapels were laced about and had six pointed loops.
• Lace of the rank and file was white with three stripes of deep-yellow, blue and red and one blue worm.
• The square cuff was fully laced about and the end was pointed. The ladder of lace carried four buttons and was scalloped.
• Grenadier cap was laced white with a white front and rear turn-up and a blue Cypher. The cap was laced about with buff foliate designs and had a white tassel.

In the 1768 regulations:
• The facings for this regiment were white while the breeches and waistcoats of all ranks were white.
• The officers' lace and buttons were silver. Their coats were laced for dress with ten square loops, set evenly.
• Other ranks' coats had ten square loops, spaced evenly. The lace of the rank and file was white with a red and black outer worm, and a black inner stripe.
• The *Grenadier Book* at The Prince Consort's Library shows this regiment with loops spaced evenly.

During the War of Independence:
The 65th Foot arrived in Boston in January 1769. The flank companies saw action at Bunker Hill but, in May 1776, the regiment was considered under strength and the men were drafted to other regiments while the officers and colours were sent home.

Raised in 1756 as the 2nd Battalion of the 19th Regiment of Foot and designated in 1758 as the:
66th Regiment of Foot
In 1782 it was retitled as the:
66th (or Berkshire) Regiment of Foot.

In November 1758:
- The facings for this regiment were yellowish-green (as the 19th Regiment).
- Officers' lace and buttons were gold and officers' coats were laced for dress with square loops, set evenly, and they are recorded as wearing red waistcoats and breeches.
- Other ranks' coats were lined yellowish-green. The lapels were laced about and had five square loops.
- Lace of the rank and file was white with two crimson stripes.
- The square cuff was laced on the top edge and the end was pointed. The ladder of lace carried four buttons and was scalloped at two points.
- Grenadier cap was laced in white with a yellowish-green front and rear turn-up. The white 'GR' Cypher had white foliate designs on either side. The tassel was mixed white and yellowish-green.
- Grenadier wings were rounded.

In the 1768 regulations:
- The facings for this regiment were yellowish-green while the breeches and waistcoats of all ranks were white.
- The officers' lace and buttons were gold but they adopted silver laced buttonholes in 1778. Their coats were laced for dress with ten square loops, set evenly.
- Other ranks' coats had ten square loops, spaced evenly with the lace of the rank and file being white with a crimson outer stripe, a green outer-centre stripe and a crimson inner stripe.
- The *Grenadier Book* at The Prince Consort's Library shows this regiment with loops spaced evenly.

Raised in 1756 as the 2nd Battalion of the 20th Regiment of Foot and was designated in 1758 as the:
67th Regiment of Foot
In 1782 it was retitled as the:
67th (or South Hampshire) Regiment of Foot.

In November 1758:
- The facings for this regiment were pale-yellow (as the 20th Regiment).
- Officers' lace and buttons were silver and officers' coats were laced for dress with square loops, set evenly.
- Other ranks' coats were lined pale-yellow. The lapels were laced about and had five square loops.
- Lace of the rank and file was white with one stripe of yellowish-green.
- The square cuff was fully laced about and the end was pointed. The ladder of lace carried four buttons and one point.
- Grenadier cap was laced in white with a pale-yellow front and rear turn-up. The green 'GR' Cypher had white foliate designs on either side. The tassel was mixed white and pale-yellow.
- Grenadier wings were rounded.

In the 1768 regulations:
- The facings for this regiment were pale-yellow while the breeches and waistcoats of all ranks were white.

• The officers' lace and buttons were silver. Their coats were laced for dress with ten square loops, set evenly; later they were set in pairs.
• Other ranks' coats had ten square loops, set evenly, later they were set in pairs. The lace of the rank and file was white with a red centre stripe.
• The *Grenadier Book* at The Prince Consort's Library shows this regiment with loops spaced evenly, but Lawson considered that the loops were set in pairs.

Raised in 1756 as the 2nd Battalion of the 23rd Regiment of Foot and designated in 1758 as the:
68th Regiment of Foot
In 1782 it was retitled as the:
68th (or Durham) Regiment of Foot
Retitled on 10th September 1808 as:
68th (or Durham) Regiment of Foot (Light Infantry).

In the Morier Paintings of 1751:
• The facings for this regiment were deep-green.
• Officers' lace and buttons were silver and officers' coats were laced for dress with square loops, set evenly.
• Other ranks' coats were lined deep-green. The lapels were laced about and had six pointed loops.
• Lace of the rank and file was white with a yellow inner, a black centre and a yellow outer stripe.
• The square cuff was fully laced about and the end was pointed. The ladder of lace carried four buttons.
• Grenadier cap was laced in white with a deep-green front and rear turn-up. The white 'GR' Cypher had white foliate designs on either side. The tassel was mixed white and deep-green.
• Grenadier wings were rounded.

In the 1768 regulations:
• The facings for this regiment were deep-green while the breeches and waistcoats of all ranks were white.
• The officers' lace and buttons were silver. Their coats were laced for dress with ten square loops, set evenly.
• Other ranks' coats had ten square loops, spaced evenly, with the lace of the rank and file being white with a black outer worm and a yellow inner stripe.
• The *Grenadier Book* at The Prince Consort's Library shows this regiment with loops spaced evenly. Lawson noted the facing colour as a very dark-green.

Raised in 1756 as the 2nd Battalion of the 24th Regiment of Foot and designated in 1758 as the:
69th Regiment of Foot
In 1782 it was retitled as the:
69th (or South Lincolnshire) Regiment of Foot.

In November 1758:
• The facings for this regiment were willow-green (as the 24th Regiment).
• Officers' lace and buttons were silver and officers' coats were laced for dress with square loops, set evenly.
• Other ranks' coats were lined white. The lapels were laced about and had six square loops.
• The red waistcoat was laced about.
• Lace of the rank and file was white with one red, one yellow stripe and a green worm, or two yellow and black stripes.
• The square cuff was laced about and the end was square. The ladder of lace carried four buttons and was scalloped at two points.
• Grenadier cap was laced in white with a willow-green front and rear turn-up. The white 'GR' Cypher had white foliate designs on either side. The tassel was mixed white and willow-green.

• Grenadier wings were rounded.

In the 1768 regulations:
• The facings for this regiment were willow-green while the breeches and waistcoats of all ranks were white.
• The officers' lace and buttons were gold. Their coats were laced for dress with ten square loops.
• Other ranks' coats had ten square loops, spaced evenly, with the lace of the rank and file being white with a green outer stripe, a red centre stripe and a green inner stripe.
• The *Grenadier Book* at The Prince Consort's Library shows this regiment with loops spaced evenly. Lawson noted the facing colour as a dark dull green.

During the War of Independence:
The 69th Regiment arrived in New York in September 1781 where it remained docked. In 1782 the regiment was deployed as marines in Hood's division of Admiral Rodney's fleet, and saw action off the Island of Dominica, in April 1782. The Battle of the Saintes ended the rule of the French fleet in the West Indies.

Raised in 1756 as the 2nd Battalion of 31st the Regiment of Foot and designated in 1758 as the:
70th Regiment of Foot
In 1782 it was retitled as the:
70th (or Surrey) Regiment of Foot
It was retitled on 22 October 1810 as the:
70th (or Glasgow Lowland) Regiment of Foot.

In November 1758:
• The facings for this regiment were grey (but deeper than the 79th Regiment).
• Officers' lace and buttons were silver and officers' coats were laced for dress with square loops, set evenly.
• Other ranks' coats were lined white. The lapels were laced about and had six pointed loops.
• Lace of the rank and file was white with one blue centre stripe.
• The square cuff was laced on the top only and the end was square.
• The red waistcoat was laced about.
• Breeches for this regiment were red.
• The cuff lace had six pointed loops.
• The vertical pocket carried three buttons and eight pointed loops.
• Grenadier cap was laced in white with a deep grey front and rear turn-up. The white 'GR' Cypher had white foliate designs on either side. The tassel was mixed white and deep grey.
• Grenadier wings were rounded.

In the 1768 regulations:
• The facings for this regiment were black while the breeches and waistcoats of all ranks were white.
• The officers' lace and buttons were gold. Their coats were laced for dress with ten square loops, set evenly.
• Other ranks' coats had ten square loops, spaced evenly, with the lace of the rank and file being white with a black centre stripe.
• The *Grenadier Book* at The Prince Consort's Library shows this regiment with loops spaced evenly.

During the War of Independence:
The 70th Regiment arrived in Halifax in August 1778. Battalion companies remained there throughout the War of Independence. The composite flank companies saw action at Little Egg Harbour and returned to Halifax. The regiment remained in Canada until returning home in 1782.

There were four regiments numbered the 71st:

The first was raised in August 1756 as the 2nd Battalion 32nd Regiment, commanded by William Petitot:
Redesignated 15 June 1758 as:
71st Regiment of Foot
This regiment was disbanded in 1763.

In 1756:

- The facings for this regiment were white.
- Officers' lace and buttons were silver and officers' coats were laced for dress with square loops, set evenly.
- Other ranks' coats were lined white. The lapels were laced about and had five pointed loops.
- The coat pocket was laced about.
- The red waistcoat was laced about.
- Lace of the rank and file was white with a red outer, a black centre and red inner stripe.
- The square cuff was laced on the tope edge and the end was pointed. The ladder of lace carried four buttons and was scalloped at two points.
- Grenadier cap was laced in white with a red 'GR' Cypher with red foliate designs on either side. The tassel was mixed white and red.
- Grenadier wings were rounded.

The second was raised in 1757 by Lord Lindores from invalids for service on Guernsey and numbered as:
81st Regiment of Foot (Invalids)
This regiment was renumbered in June 1758 as the:
71st Regiment of Foot (Invalids)
This regiment was disbanded during 1769.

From the Morier painings of circa 1751 it is assumed that this regiment was royal:

- The facings for this royal regiment were dark-blue.
- Officers' lace and buttons were gold and officers' coats were laced for dress with square loops, set evenly.
- Other ranks' coats were lined dark-blue with thirteen buttons. There were no lapels and the pocket was plain with three buttons below.
- The waistcoat was not shown.
- Breeches for this regiment were dark-blue.
- The rank and file wore no lace.
- The cuff was square with one button.
- Grenadier cap had a dark-blue front and rear turn-up and was laced in white. The front carried a crown over the Garter Star inside which was the blue garter belt inscribed 'Honi Soit Qui Mal Y Pense' with a red centre; either side of this were foliate designs in white. The tassel was white with a red centre.

The third was raised in October 1775 by Colonel Simon Fraser in Scotland for service in America as the:
71st Regiment of (Highland) Foot, also known as Fraser's Highlanders.
This regiment was disbanded in Perth during 1783.

When raised in 1775:

- The facings for this regiment were white while the waistcoats of all ranks were white.
- The officers' lace and buttons were silver. Their coats were laced for dress with ten square loops, set evenly, later in pairs.
- Other ranks' coats had ten square loops originally placed evenly but later spaced in pairs. The lace of the rank and file was white with a red centre worm.
- All ranks wore the kilt or belted plaid of the government sett in full dress; they also wore a red hackle after 1777.
- Recruiting sergeants wore yellow ribbons.

During the War of Independence:

The 71st Regiment or Fraser's Highlanders sailed from Scotland, arriving in New York in July 1776. The regiment saw action at Long Island, Fort Washington, Brandywine, Cowpens, Savannah, Briar Creek, Camden, Charlestown, Yorktown and Guilford Court House. The Light Companies were initially allocated to the 2nd Light Battalion but later became a semi-independent light company in the Carolinas. The 1st Battalion saw action at Cowpens where it was captured in 1776 and left America in 1782. The 2nd Battalion was part of the General Cornwallis surrender at Yorktown in October 1781.

- The 71st regiment was re-formed in Scotland in September 1778 and redesignated the second 71st but was disbanded at Stirling in October 1783.
- The kilt was rarely worn after 1777.

The furth regiment was raised in the highlands by Lord MacLeod between 1775 to 1777 for service in North America as:

73rd (Highland) Regiment of Foot, also known as MacLeod's Highlanders

renumbered in 1786 as:

71st (Highland) Regiment of Foot

There were two Battalions to this regiment. The first was formed in 25 October 1775 for service in America and was disbanded in 1784 and this Battalion survived and now form the regiment. The second was formed at the same time. It was reconstructed in Scotland on 24 September 1778 and redesignated in 13 February 1782 as the second 71st Regiment. It was disbanded in 3 October 1783 at Stirling.

Retitled in June 1808 as:

71st (Glasgow Highland) Regiment of Foot

On the loss of highland distinctions in April 1808 and a change of role, it became:

71st (or the Glasgow Highland Light Infantry) Regiment of Foot

It was retitled in 1810 as the:

71st (Highland) Regiment of Foot (Light Infantry)

Between 1775 and 1777:

- The facings for this regiment were buff while the linings and waistcoats were buff.
- The officers' lace and buttons were silver. Their coats were laced for dress with ten square loops, set evenly.
- Other ranks' coats had ten square loops, spaced evenly, with the lace of the rank and file being white with a red inner stripe.
- All ranks wore the kilt or belted plaid in full dress initially of the government tartan, but later the early MacKenzie.

There were three regiments numbered the 72nd:

The first was raised in September 1756 as the 2nd Battalion 33rd Regiment, commanded by the Duke of Richmond.
Redesignated in June 1758 as:
72nd Regiment of Foot
This regiment was disbanded in 1763.

In 1756:
- The facings for this regiment were red.
- Officers' lace and buttons were gold and officers' coats were laced for dress with square loops, set evenly.
- Other ranks' coats were lined white. The lapels were laced about and had five pointed loops.
- The coat pocket was laced about with a red centre.
- The red waistcoat was laced about.
- Lace of the rank and file was white with a red and black inner and outer stripe.
- The square cuff was fully laced about and the end was pointed. The ladder of lace carried four buttons and was scalloped at two points.
- Grenadier cap was laced in white with a red 'GR' Cypher and had red foliate designs on either side. The tassel was mixed white and red.
- Grenadier wings were rounded.

The second was raised in 1757 from invalids by John Parker for service in Germany as:
82nd Regiment of Foot (Invalids)
Renumbered in 1764 as:
72nd Regiment of Foot (Invalids)
This regiment was disbanded in 1768.

From the Morier painings of circa 1751 it is assumed that this regiment was royal:
- The facings for this royal regiment were dark-blue.
- Officers' lace and buttons were gold and officers' coats were laced for dress with square loops, set evenly.
- Other ranks' coats were lined dark-blue with thirteen buttons. There were no lapels and the pocket is plain with three buttons below.
- The waistcoat was not shown.
- Breeches for this regiment were dark-blue.
- The rank and file wore no lace.
- The cuff was square with one button.
- Grenadier cap had a dark-blue front and rear turn-up and was laced in white. The front carried a crown over the Garter Star inside which was the blue garter belt inscribed 'Honi Soit Qui Mal Y Pense' with a red centre. Either side of this were foliate designs in white. The tassel was white with a red centre.

The third was raised in 16 December 1777 for service at Gibraltar by Charles Mawhood as the:
72nd Regiment of Foot (Royal Manchester Volunteers)
This regiment was disbanded in 1783.

- The facings for this royal regiment were dark-blue, while the linings, waistcoats and breeches were white.

• The officers' lace and buttons were gold. Their coats were laced for dress with ten square loops, set evenly.
• Other ranks' coats were madder-red and were laced for dress with ten square loops, spaced evenly.
• The lace of the other ranks is not known.
• An inspection return of 1781 at Gibraltar noted that the men were provided with white jackets, grenadiers had no swords, whole regiment in white waistcoats, and long linen trousers.

The fourth was raised in 29 December 1777 by Lord Seaforth as the:
Seaforth (Highland) Regiment of Foot
Designated in 1778 as the:
78th (Highland) Regiment of Foot, or the Seaforth Highlanders
Was designated in 1786 as the:
72nd (Highland) Regiment of Foot
On the loss of highland distinctions in 1809 it became
72nd Regiment of Foot.
This regiment did not serve in North America during the War of Independence but served to reinforce Jersey and later embarked for India.

In 1777:
• The facings for this regiment were yolk yellow or orange while the linings and waistcoats of all ranks were white.
• The officers' lace and buttons were silver. Their coats were laced for dress with ten bastion loops, set evenly.
• Other ranks' coats had ten bastion loops, spaced evenly. The lace of the rank and file was white with a blue-green outer stripe.
• All ranks wore the kilt or belted plaid in full dress of the government sett.

There were two regiments numbered the 73rd:

The first was raised in 1756 as the 2nd Battalion 34th Regiment.
Redesignated in 1758 as:
73rd Regiment of Foot
This regiment was disbanded in 1763.

In 1756:
• The facings for this regiment were full-green.
• Officers' lace and buttons were gold and officers' coats were laced for dress with square loops, set evenly.
• Other ranks' coats were lined white. The lapels were laced about and had six pointed loops.
• The coat pocket was laced about with a red centre.
• The red waistcoat was laced about.
• Lace of the rank and file was white but there is difficulty in the description of the lace: two forms are given one with a curved central worm of white, yellow and black or a central worm as shown.
• The square cuff was fully laced about and the end was pointed. The ladder of lace carried four buttons and was scalloped at two points.
• Grenadier cap had a full-green front and rear turn-up and was laced in white with a white 'GR' Cypher and white foliate designs on either side. The tassel was mixed white and full-green.

• Grenadier wings were rounded.

The second was raised in 1757 from invalids by Major Robert Ackland as:
116th Regiment of Foot (Invalids)
Renumbered in 1763 as:
73rd Regiment of Foot (Invalids)
This regiment was disbanded in 1768.

From the Morier painings of circa 1751 it is assumed that this regiment was royal:
• The facings for this royal regiment were dark-blue.
• Officers' lace and buttons were gold and officers' coats were laced for dress with square loops, set evenly.
• Other ranks' coats were lined dark-blue with thirteen buttons. There were no lapels and the pocket is plain with three buttons below.
• The waistcoat is not shown.
• Breeches for this regiment were dark-blue.
• The rank and file wore no lace.
• The cuff was square with one button.
• Grenadier cap had a dark-blue front and rear turn-up and was laced in white. The front carried a crown over the Garter Star inside which was the blue garter belt inscribed 'Honi Soit Qui Mal Y Pense' with a red centre, either side of this were foliate designs in white. The tassel was white with a red centre.

There were three regiments numbered the 74th:

The first was raised in August 1756 as the 2nd Battalion 36th Regiment.
Redesignated in July 1758 as:
74th Regiment of Foot
This regiment was disbanded in 1763.

In 1758:
• The facings for this regiment were grass green.
• Officers' lace and buttons were gold and officers' coats were laced for dress with square loops, set evenly.
• Other ranks' coats were lined grass green. The lapels were laced about and had six square loops.
• The coat pocket was laced about with a red centre.
• The red waistcoat was laced about.
• Lace of the rank and file was white with a red outer, a yellow centre and a red inner stripe.
• The square cuff was laced on the top edge and the end was pointed. The ladder of lace carried four buttons and was scalloped at one point.
• Grenadier cap had a grass green front and rear turn-up and was laced in white with a white 'GR' Cypher and white foliate designs on either side. The tassel was mixed white and grass green.
• Grenadier wings were rounded.

• Research has failed to find any details of the uniform other that this regiment had grass green facings, and white lace with two red and one yellow stripe.

The second was raised in March 1762 from invalids by Major Loftus Cliffe as:

117th Regiment of Foot (Invalids)
Renumbered in 1763 as:
74th Regiment of Foot (Invalids)
This regiment was disbanded in 1768.

From the Morier painings of circa 1751 it is assumed that this regiment was royal:
- The facings for this royal regiment were dark-blue.
- Officers' lace and buttons were gold and officers' coats were laced for dress with square loops, set evenly.
- Other ranks' coats were lined dark-blue with thirteen buttons. There were no lapels and the pocket is plain with three buttons below.
- The waistcoat is not shown.
- Breeches for this regiment were dark-blue.
- The rank and file wore no lace.
- The cuff was square with one button.
- Grenadier cap had a dark-blue front and rear turn-up and was laced in white. The front carried a crown over the Garter Star inside which was the blue garter belt inscribed 'Honi Soit Qui Mal Y Pense' with a red centre, either side of this were foliate designs in white. The tassel was white with a red centre.

The third was raised in1777 for service in North America by Colonel John Campbell of Barbrick as the:
74th (Highland) Regiment of Foot, also known as Campbell's or Argyllshire Highlanders
This regiment was disbanded in 1783.

- The facings for this regiment were yellow or bright-yellow while the waistcoats of all ranks were white.
- The officers' lace and buttons were silver. Their coats were laced for dress with ten square loops set, in pairs.
- Other ranks' coats had ten square loops, spaced in pairs with the lace of the rank and file being white with a single red centre stripe.
- All ranks wore the kilt or belted plaid in full dress with the government sett.

During the War of Independence:
The 74th Regiment of Foot, the Argyllshire Highlanders, arrived in Halifax in August 1778. The battalion companies saw action at Penobscot in July 1779 and then returned to Halifax. In 1779 it was sent to New York and the flank companies were sent south and saw action at the siege of Charleston. They returned to Canada and the regiment returned home to Scotland and was disbanded at Stirling in 1783.

There were three regiments numbered the 75th:

The first was raised in 28 August 1756 as the 2nd Battalion 37th Regiment.
Redesignated in 23 April 1758 as:
75th Regiment of Foot
This regiment was disbanded in 1763.

In 1758:
- The facings for this regiment were red.
- Officers' lace and buttons were gold and officers' coats were laced for dress with square loops, set evenly.
- Other ranks' coats were lined buff. The lapels were laced about and had six square loops.
- Lace of the rank and file was white with a green outer, two yellow centre stripes and one green inner stripe.

• The square cuff was laced about and the end was pointed.
• The red waistcoat was laced about.
• Breeches for this regiment were red.
• The cuff lace had six square loops.
• The vertical pocket carried three buttons and eight square loops.
• Grenadier cap was laced in white with a red front and rear turn-up. The white 'GR' Cypher has white foliate designs on either side. The tassel was mixed white and red.
• Grenadier wings were rounded.

The second was raised in March 1762 from invalids by John Lind as:
118th Regiment of Foot (Invalids)
Renumbered in 1763 as:
75th Regiment of Foot (Invalids)
This regiment was disbanded in 1768.

From the Morier paintings of circa 1751 it is assumed that this regiment were royal:
• The facings for this royal regiment were dark-blue.
• Officers' lace and buttons were gold and officers' coats were laced for dress with square loops, set evenly.
• Other ranks' coats were lined dark-blue with thirteen buttons. There were no lapels and the pocket was plain with three buttons below.
• The waistcoat is not shown.
• Breeches for this regiment were dark-blue.
• The rank and file wore no lace.
• The cuff was square with one button.
• Grenadier cap had a dark-blue front and rear turn-up and was laced in white. The front carried a crown over the Garter Star inside which was the blue garter belt inscribed 'Honi Soit Qui Mal Y Pense' with a red centre, either side of which were foliate designs in white. The tassel was white with a red centre.

The third was raised in January 1778 by the Earl of Lincoln as the:
75th (Prince of Wales's) Regiment of Foot
This regiment was disbanded in 1783.

In 1778:
• The facings for this royal regiment were dark-blue while the breeches and waistcoats of all ranks were white.
• The officers' lace and buttons were gold. Their coats were laced for dress with ten square loops, set evenly.
• Other ranks' coats had ten square loops, spaced evenly, with the lace of the rank and file being white with a blue inner and outer stripe.

There were two regiments numbered the 76th:

The first regiment was raised in, Ireland in 1756 by Lord Forbes as a light infantry corps.
Redesignated as:
61st Regiment of Foot
Renumbered in 1758 as the:
76th Regiment of Foot

This regiment was disbanded in 1763; a 2nd Battalion was raised in 1758 and redesignated as the 86th regiment.

In 1756:
- The facings for this regiment were deep-green.
- Officers' lace and buttons were gold and officers' coats were laced for dress with square loops, set evenly.
- Other ranks' coats were laced about and had six square loops. The pocket was laced about with white lined red.
- The waistcoat was laced about and was red.
- Breeches for this regiment were red.
- The rank and file wore white lace with a black centre stripe.
- Grenadier cap had a deep-green front and rear turn-up and was laced in white. The front carried a crown over the white GR Cypher, either side of whichwere foliate designs in white. The tassel was white with deep-green.

The second regiment was raised in December 1777 by Lord Macdonald for service in North America as the:
76th (Highland) Regiment of Foot, also known as Macdonald's Highlanders
The regiment was disbanded in 1783.

In 1777:
- The facings for this regiment were deep-green while the waistcoats of all ranks were white.
- The officers' lace and buttons were gold. Their coats were laced for dress with ten square loops, set in pairs.
- Other ranks' coats was probably set in pairs, with the lace of the rank and file being white with an outer green stripe, a central blue stripe and an inner red stripe.
- All ranks wore the kilt or belted plaid of the government sett in full dress.

During the War of Independence:
The 76th Regiment of Foot, Macdonald's Highlanders, arrived in New York in August 1779. The light company was attached to the 2nd Light Infantry Battalion, the grenadiers remaining in New York. Sent to Virginia, and the regiment fought mostly as mounted infantry in 1781 at Petersburg (light company), Osborne's and Green Spring. The regiment was part of the surrender at Yorktown by General Cornwallis in October 1781 and marched as prisoners to different parts of Virginia. Later exchanged, it sailed to New York and then home to Scotland where it was disbanded in March 1784 at Stirling Castle.

There were two regiments numbered the 77th:

The first regiment was raised in 1757 by Archibald Montgomery as the 1st Highland Battalion, later designated as:
62nd Regiment of Foot
Renumbered in 1758 as the:
77th (Montgomery Highlanders) Regiment of Foot
This regiment was disbanded in 1763

In 1757:
- The facings for this regiment were red until *circa* 1757 and then changed to green in the following year.
- Officers' lace and buttons were silver and officers' coats were laced for dress with square loops, set evenly.
- Other ranks' coats were lined red and then green. The lapels were laced about and had thirteen pointed loops.
- Lace of the rank and file was white with a red central worm.

• The cuff was of the mariner type and had a ladder of lace with four rungs and buttons.
• The red waistcoat was laced about.
• The tartan worn by this regiment was the government sett.
• The horizontal pocket carried three buttons and pointed loops.
• Grenadier cap had a green front and rear turn-up and was laced in white. The front carried a crown over the black GR Cypher, either side of this were foliate designs in white. The tassel was white with green.
• Grenadier wings were rounded.

The second regiment was raised in December 1777 by the Duke of Atholl for service in Ireland as the:
77th (Highland) Regiment of Foot, also known as Atholl Highlanders
It mutinied after refusing to go to India and was disbanded in 1783.

In 1777:
• The facings for this regiment were red in 1778 but were later changed to green while the waistcoats of all ranks were white.
• The officers' lace and buttons were silver and their coats were laced for dress with ten square loops set, in pairs.
• Other ranks' coats were madder-red with ten square loops, set in pairs.
• The rank and file wore plain white lace, they wore fringed wings and red and black feathers.
• All ranks wore the same kilt, or belted plaid in full dress, as did the 42nd Highlanders.

There was one regiment numbered the 78th:

The first regiment was raised in 1757 as the 2nd Highland Battalion originally designated as:
62nd Regiment of Foot
Renumbered in 1757 as the:
63rd Regiment of Foot
Renumbered in 1758 as the:
78th (Highland) Regiment of Foot (or Fraser's Highlanders)
This regiment was disbanded in North America in 1763

In 1757:
• The facings for this regiment were pale-buff.
• Officers' lace and buttons were gold and officers' coats were laced for dress with six square loops, set evenly.
• Other ranks' coats were lined buff. The lapels were laced about and had thirteen pointed loops.
• Lace of the rank and file is not known.
• The cuff was of the mariner type and had a ladder of lace with four rungs and three buttons.
• The red waistcoat was laced about.
• The tartan worn by this regiment was the government sett, but one authority gives what could be a government tartan with red overstripe.
• The horizontal pocket carried three buttons and pointed loops.
• Grenadier wings were rounded and officers and men wore two black feathers in their hats.
• Research has failed to find any details of the uniform other than white or pale-buff, government sett, two black feathers in hat, numbered buttons with cuff flap three buttons and, gold lace.

There were two regiments numbered the 79th:

The first regiment was raised in 1757 by Sir William Draper as the:
64th Regiment of Foot
Renumbered in 1758 as the:
79th Regiment of Foot
This regiment was disbanded in 1763

• Research has failed to find any details of the uniform.

The second regiment was raised in January 1778 for service afloat as the:
79th Regiment of Foot (Royal Liverpool Volontiers), also known as Royal Lancashire Volunteers or the Liverpool Blues.
This regiment was disbanded in 1789.

• The facings for this royal regiment were dark-blue while the breeches and waistcoats of all ranks were white.
• The officers' lace and buttons were gold. Their coats were laced for dress with ten square loops, set evenly.
• Other ranks' coats had ten square loops, spaced evenly, with the lace of the rank and file being white with a blue centre worm.

There were two regiments numbered the 80th:

The first was raised by Thomas Gage as an experimental unit in 1757 as:
80th Regiment of Light-armed Foot
This regiment was disbanded in 1763

• The officer's coats were scarlet while the other rank's of this regiment were madder-red both and lined dark brown.
• Officers' lace was gold in dress.
• Other ranks' coats had black buttons, and the short coat had no lapels.
• The rank and file wore no lace.
• No grenadier cap was worn.
• Very little is known about this regiment. It is not known if the coats were short or long.

The second regiment was raised at Edinburgh in January 1778 by Sir William Erskin for service in North America as:
80th Regiment of Foot (Royal Edinburgh Volunteers)
This regiment was disbanded in 1783 or 1784.

In 1778:
• The facings for this regiment were yellow while the breeches and waistcoats of all ranks were white.
• The officers' lace and buttons were silver. Their coats were laced for dress with ten square loops, set evenly.
• Other ranks' coats had ten, square loops, spaced evenly. The lace of the rank and file was white with a black outer stripe, a red centre stripe and a black inner stripe.

During the War of Independence:
The 80th Regiment arrived in New York in August 1779. It was sent to Virginia and was surrendered at Yorktown by General Cornwallis in October 1781. The regiment returned home to Scotland in 1783 where it was disbanded.

Raised in March 1777 by the Honourable William Gordan of Fyvie for service in Ireland as:
81st (Highland) Regiment of Foot, also known as Aberdeenshire Highlanders
This regiment was disbanded in 1783.

In 1777:
• The facings for this regiment were white and waistcoats of all ranks were white.
• The officers' lace and buttons were silver and the coats were unlaced for dress.
• Other ranks' coats had ten square loops, spaced in pairs, with the lace of the rank and file white with a blue-black centre stripe.
• All ranks wore the kilt or belted plaid of the government sett in full dress.

Raised in December 1777 by the Duke of Hamilton for service in North America as:
82nd Regiment of Foot, also known as Hamilton's Regiment
This regiment was disbanded in 1783 or 1784.

• The facings for this regiment were black while the breeches and waistcoats of all ranks were white.
• The officers' lace and buttons were gold. Their coats were laced for dress with ten square loops, set evenly.
• Other ranks' coats had had ten square loops, spaced evenly, with the lace of the rank and file being white with a black centre stripe.

During the War of Independence:
The 82nd Regiment sailed for Halifax in August 1778. It was posted to New York in August 1779 and saw action at Penobscot in July 1779. It next deployed to Wilmington in April 1781. The bulk of the regiment were at Charleston in October 1781 and then removed to Halifax where it was disbanded in 1783. There is some confusion regarding the flank companies: one source considers they were at Yorktown, while others consider that there 'were some companies' at Yorktown and that the flank companies were lost on the coast of New Jersey before the regiment arrived in New York.

Raised in December 1777 by George Scott as:
83rd (Royal Glasgow Volontiers) Regiment of Foot
This regiment was disbanded in 1783.

• The facings for this royal regiment were dark-blue while the linings, breeches and waistcoats of all ranks were white.
• The officers' lace and buttons were gold. Their coats were laced for dress with ten square loops, set evenly.
• Other ranks' coats had ten square loops, spaced evenly, with the lace of the rank and file being plain white; a new pattern loop was approved in 1778.

During the War of Independence:
The 83rd Regiment of Foot arrived in New York in 1783. It then returned home to Scotland and was disbanded in the same year. This regiment only served in North America for a very limited time.
• The officers were armed with fusils.

There were two regiments numbered the 84th:

The first was raised in December 1758 by Eyre Coote for service in India and designated as:
84th Regiment of Foot
This regiment was disbanded in 1764.

•Research has failed to find any details of the uniform other than black facings, gold lace and tanned leather accoutrements.

The second regiment was raised by Colonel Allan MacLean from Scottish immigrants in Canada and discharged men of the 42nd, Fraser's and Montgomery's Highlanders for service in North America
It was numbered into the line in 1779 as:
84th (Royal Highland Emigrants) Regiment of Foot
It served in New York until 1783 and was disbanded in Canada in 1784.

• The facings for this royal regiment were dark-blue while waistcoats of all ranks were white.
• The officers' lace and buttons were gold. Their coats were laced for dress with ten square loops, set evenly, but later in pairs.
• Other ranks' coats had ten square loops, spaced evenly, later in pairs. The lace of the rank and file was white with a red outer stripe, blue centre stripe and a red inner stripe.
• Full kilt or belted plaid in full dress highland dress as with the 42nd but the rank and file had no dicing to the bonnets.

During the War of Independence:
The 84th Regiment of Foot, or the Royal Highland Emigrants, was raised in Canada. The 1st Battalion was chiefly engaged in raiding on the Canadian border and into New York. General Cornwallis surrendered part of the regiment at Yorktown. The 2nd Battalion was posted to Charleston and saw action at Eutaw Springs. It then returned to New York in April 1782. The 1st battalion was disbanded at Ontario and the 2nd battalion at Halifax in 1784.
• The regiment had racoon-skin sporrans.

There were two regiments numbered the 85th:

The first regiment was raised by Colonel John Craufurd as a light infantry in 1759 as:
85th Regiment of Foot (Royal Volontiers)
This regiment was disbanded in 1763

Research has failed to find any details of the uniform other than coats without lapels, dark-blue collar and cuffs, silver lace for officers, white lace for the men. The coats were lined white with white double-breasted waistcoats and breeches. Hats with white feathers, short black gaiters, waist-belt worn over shoulder, officers, sashes; at waist or not worn; buff-cross belts were worn.

The second regiment was raised in Scotland in February 1777 by William Dalrymple for service in Jamaica as:
85th (Westminster Volontiers) Regiment of Foot
This regiment was disbanded at Dover Castle in 1783.

• The facings for this regiment were yellow while the breeches and waistcoats of all ranks were white.
• The officers' lace and buttons were silver. Their waistcoats were white and the coats were laced for dress with ten square loops, set in pairs.
• Other ranks' coats had ten square loops, spaced in pairs, with the lace of the rank and file being white with yellow centre stripe.

There were two regiments numbered the 86th:

The first was raised in 1758 by Lord Forbes as the the 2nd Battalion 76th regiment.
Redesignated in July 1758 as:
86th Regiment of Foot
This regiment received drafts from other regiments and saw service in Senegal and was disbanded in 1763.

In 1756
• The facings for this regiment were orange.
• Officers' lace and buttons were silver and officers' coats were laced for dress with square loops, set evenly.
• Other ranks' coats were lined brown. The lapels were laced about and had six square loops.
• Lace of the rank and file was white with a black centre stripe.
• The cuff was square and laced on the top edge and had a ladder of lace with four rungs and buttons and two scallops.
• The red waistcoat was laced about.
• The horizontal pocket was laced about with a red centre.
• Grenadier cap had an orange front and rear turn-up and was laced in white, either side of which were foliate designs in white. The tassel was white and orange.
• Grenadier wings were rounded.

The second regiment was raised in September 1779 by Antony St Leger as:
86th Regiment of Foot, also known as the Rutland Regiment
This regiment was disbanded in 1784, after spending much of its time in the Leeward Islands.

• The facings for this regiment were yellow while the breeches and waistcoats of all ranks were white.
• The officers' lace and buttons were silver; their coats were laced for dress with ten square loops, set in pairs.
• Other ranks' coats had ten square loops, spaced in pairs, with the lace of the rank and file being unknown.

There were two regiments numbered the 87th:

The first regiment was raised as a light infantry unit from a cadre of three companies of the 42nd Highlanders on 20th August 1759 by Robert Murray Keith as:
87th (Highland Volunteers) Regiment of Foot, also known as Keith's Highlanders
This regiment was disbanded in 1763

• The facings for this regiment were green and the linings were white.
• The officers' lace and buttons were gold. Their coats were laced for dress with alternate bastion and rounded loops with a particular arrangement for the cuff lace.
• Other ranks' coats were madder-red with eleven pointed loops, set evenly, and the pattern of lace was white with a red centre stripe.
• All ranks wore the kilt or belted plaid of government sett in full dress of the.

The second was raised in 1778 by Viscount Chewton as:
87th Regiment of Foot
This regiment was disbanded in 1784.

• The facings for this regiment were white while the breeches and waistcoats of all ranks were white.
• The officers' lace and buttons were silver for dress. Their coats were laced for dress with ten twist loops, set in pairs. The cuff at the front was pointed with three buttons at each corner and the officers' wings were fringed.
• Other ranks' coats had ten square loops, spaced in pairs, with the lace of the rank and file being plain white.

There were two regiments numbered the 88th:

The first regiment was raised in September 1759 from the 87th Highlanders by John Campbell of Dunoon as:
88th Regiment of Foot (Highland Volontiers), also known as Campbell's Highlanders
This regiment was disbanded in 1763

• Research has failed to find any details of the uniform, other than that it probably had green facings, gold lace and wore the government sett.

The second was raised in October 1779 by Thomas Keating as:
88th Regiment of Foot
This regiment was disbanded in 1783.

• The facings for this regiment were pale-yellow while the breeches and waistcoats of all ranks were white.
• The officers' lace and buttons were silver. Their coats were laced for dress with ten square loops, set pairs.
• Other ranks' coats had ten square loops, spaced in pairs, but the lace of the rank and file is not known

---

There were two regiments numbered the 89th:

The first was raised in October 1759 by Staates Long Morris from the Clan Gordon as:
89th (Gordon or Morris's Highlanders) Regiment of Foot
This regiment was disbanded in 1763 or 1765.

• The facings for this regiment were light yellow while the linings were white.
• The officers' lace and buttons were silver. Their coats were laced for dress with square loops, spaced evenly.
• Other ranks' coats were madder-red with eleven pointed loops but the pattern of lace remains unknown.
• All ranks wore the kilt or belted plaid of the government sett in full dress.

The second regiment was raised in October 1779 as:
89th Regiment of Foot, also known as the Worcestershire Volunteers.
This regiment was disbanded in 1784.

• The facings for this regiment were black while the breeches and waistcoats of all ranks were white.
• The officers' lace and buttons were gold. Their coats were laced for dress with ten square loops, set in pairs.
• Other ranks' coats had ten square loops, spaced in pairs, with the lace of the rank and file being white with a blue inner stripe and a red outer stripe.

There were two regiments numbered the 90th:

The first was raised in Ireland in 1759 by Hugh Morgan as a light infantry corps as:
90th (Irish Light Infantry) Regiment of Foot
This regiment was disbanded in 1763

• Scarlet coat, green facings, turndown collar, narrow gold loops, white breeches and waistcoat. Black leather cap, the front decorated with a crown, harp and curved scrolls to either side with a turban of red silk.

The second regiment was raised in October 1779 by Anthony Tottenham as:
90th Regiment of Foot, also known as the Perthshire Volunteers.
This regiment was disbanded in 1784.

• The facings for this regiment were buff while the breeches and waistcoats of all ranks were buff.
• The officers' lace and buttons were gold. Their coats were laced for dress with ten square loops, set in pairs.
• Other ranks' coats had ten square loops, spaced in pairs, with the lace of the rank and file being white with a blue outer stripe.
• An Inspection Return in 1779 noted that the officers appeared in white cloth jackets with scarlet cuffs and facings, white waistcoats and breeches and plain hats. The men wore white jackets and red facings and cuff, white caps, white breeches and half gaiters.

The third regiment was raised was raised in Wakefield during the during the American Rebellion as:
90th Regiment of Foot.
It was disbanded in 1783.

• Research has failed to find any details for this regiment.

There were two regiments numbered the 91st:

The first was raised in Ireland in 1759 by Cadwallader Blayney as:
91st Regiment of Foot
This regiment was disbanded in 1763.

• Research has failed to find any details of the uniform, other that than it had black facings and silver lace. There was no record of the lace for the rank and file.

The second regiment was raised in December 1779 by Dudley Ackland for service in India as:
91st Regiment of Foot, also known as Shropshire Volunteers
This regiment was disbanded in 1784.

• The facings for this regiment were green while the breeches and waistcoats of all ranks were white.
• The officers' lace and buttons were gold. Their coats were laced for dress with ten square loops, set evenly.
• Other ranks' coats had ten square loops, spaced evenly, with the lace of the rank and file being white with a black centre stripe.
• Inspection Return of 1779: officers faced with green and with narrow gold lace, white waistcoats and breeches; men dressed in white jackets with green facings, white waistcoats, leather breeches and hats cocked on one side only.

There were two regiments numbered the 92nd:

The first was raised in 1760 by Sir Ralph Gore, Earl of Ross, for service in Ireland as:
92nd Regiment of Foot (Donegal Light Infantry)
This regiment was disbanded in 1763.

• Research has failed to find any details of the uniform, other than that it had black facings and silver lace. There was no record of the lace for the rank and file.

The second regiment was raised in December 1779 by the Honourable James Stuart as:
92nd Regiment of Foot, also known as the British Rangers
This regiment was disbanded in 1783.

• The facings for this regiment were buff while the breeches and waistcoats of all ranks were buff.
• The officers' lace and buttons were silver. Their coats were laced for dress with ten square loops, set in pairs.
• Other ranks' coats had ten square loops, spaced in pairs, with the lace of the rank and file being unknown.
• Inspection Return of 1779: fusils and espontoons shown for officers; the men of this regiment had buff jackets with red collars and cuffs, breeches and trousers in one piece and leather caps.

There were two regiments numbered the 93rd:

The first was raised in Ireland in August 1752 by the Earl of Sutherland as:
93rd (Highland) Regiment of Foot

This regiment was numbered just before it disbanded in 1763.

• The facings for this regiment were grey and the linings were grey.
• The officers' lace and buttons were silver. Their coats were laced for dress with evenly spaced, square loops.
• Other ranks' coats were madder-red with eleven pointed loops and the pattern of lace was white with a centre grey stripe.
• All ranks wore the kilt or belted plaid in full dress of the government sett.

The second regiment was raised in February 1780 at Fort George by William McCarmick as:
93rd Regiment of Foot
This regiment was disbanded in Ireland between 1783 and 1785.

• The facings for this regiment were yellow while the breeches and waistcoats of all ranks were white.
• The officers' lace and buttons were silver. Their coats were laced for dress with ten square loops, set in pairs.
• Other ranks' coats had ten square loops, spaced in pairs, with the lace of the rank and file being white with a central yellow stripe.
• Inspection Return of 1780: this regiment had the officers' jackets of scarlet faced with yellow and fusils, the men had received no issue of clothing and were dressed in blue jackets with red collars and cuffs, white waistcoats and leather breeches.

There were two regiments numbered the 94th:

The first was raised in January 1760 by John Vaughan as a light infantry corps for service in North America as:
94th Regiment of Foot (Royal Welsh Volontiers)
This regiment was disbanded in 1763.

• Research has failed to find any details of the uniform, other than that it had dark-blue facings and gold lace.

The second regiment was raised in October 1780 by Robert Prescott at Colchester as:
94th Regiment of Foot
This regiment went to Jamaica in 1780; but was disbanded in Ireland in 1783.

• The facings for this regiment were white while the breeches and waistcoats of all ranks were white.
• The officers' lace and buttons were silver. Their coats were laced for dress with ten square loops, set evenly.
• Other ranks' coats had ten square loops, spaced evenly. The lace of the rank and file was white but research suggests that it may have been square with a red outer, a green centre and a red inner.

There were two regiments numbered the 95th:

The first was raised in America in June 1760 by Ralph Burton as:
95th Regiment of Foot
Personnel drafted to other regiments and disbanded in 1763.

• This regiment had light grey facings and gold lace. The rank and file lace was white and green.

The second regiment was raised in America in April 1780 by John Reid as:

95th Regiment of Foot

This regiment was disbanded in 1784.

• The facings for this regiment were buff while the breeches and waistcoats of all ranks were buff.
• The officers' lace and buttons were silver. Their coats were laced for dress with ten square loops, set in evenly.
• Other ranks' coats had ten square loops, spaced evenly, with the lace of the rank and file being plain white.
• All ranks wore fringed wings.

There were two regiments numbered the 96th:

The first regiment was raised in 1760 by Lieutenant Colonel George Monson for service in India as:

96th Regiment of Foot

This regiment was disbanded in 1763.

• Research has failed to find any details of the uniform, only that it had buff facings and silver lace. It wore no lace while in the Indies.

The second regiment was raised in April 1780 by Richard Whyte as:

96th (British Musketeers) Regiment of Foot

This regiment was disbanded in 1784.

• The facings for this regiment were pale-yellow while the breeches and waistcoats of all ranks were white.
• The officers' lace and buttons were silver. Their coats were laced for dress with ten square loops, set evenly.
• Other ranks' coats had ten square loops, spaced evenly. There are no details of the lace of the private soldier
• Inspection Return of 1780: the men were dressed in white jackets faced pale-yellow.

There were two regiments numbered the 97th:

The first was raised in August 1760 by James Stuart as:

97th Regiment of Foot

This regiment was disbanded in 1763.

• Research has failed to find any details of the uniform, other than that it had gosling-green facings and silver lace. The lace for the rank and file was white and black.

The second regiment was raised in April 1780 by Samuel Stanton as:

97th Regiment of Foot

This regiment was disbanded in 1784.

• Research has failed to find any details of the uniform.

There were two regiments numbered the 98th:

The first regiment was raised in 1761 by Lieutenant Colonel Grey as:
98th Regiment of Foot
This regiment was disbanded in 1763.

• Research has failed to find any details of the uniform, other than that it had full-green facings and silver lace. There was no record of the lace for the rank and file, other than that it was white.

The second regiment was raised in May 1780 by Lieutenant Colonel Fullarton for service in India as:
98th Regiment of Foot
This regiment was lost at Bednore in 1783 and disbanded.

• The facings for this regiment were yellow while the breeches and waistcoats of all ranks were white.
• The officers' lace and buttons were silver. Their coats were laced for dress with ten square loops, set evenly.
• Other ranks' coats had ten flowerpot loops, spaced evenly, with the lace of the rank and file being white with three yellow stripes.

There were two regiments numbered the 99th:

The first was raised in January 1761 by George Byng as:
99th Regiment of Foot
This regiment was disbanded in 1763.

• Research has failed to find any details of the uniform.

The second regiment was raised in June 1780 by Charles Rainsforth for service in Jamaica as:
99th (Jamaica) Regiment of Foot
The regiment was disbanded in 1783, after spending much of its time in Jamaica.

• The facings for this regiment were light green while the breeches and waistcoats of all ranks were white.
• The officers' lace and buttons were gold. Their coats were laced for dress with ten square loop, set evenly.
• Other ranks' coats had ten square loops, spaced evenly, with the lace of the rank and file being white with a red outer edge and green inner edge.
• Inspection Return of 1780: an alligator was approved for the buttons, grenadier and light company caps.

There were two regiments numbered the 100th:

The first regiment was raised in 1760 by Colin Campbell for service in the West Indies as:
100th (Highland) Regiment of Foot, also known as Campbell's Highlanders

This regiment was disbanded in 1763

• Research has failed to find any details of this uniform, other than that the facings were a pale-yellowish buff.

The second regiment was raised in 1780 by Lieutenant Colonel Humberston for service in India as:
100th Regiment of Foot, Loyal Lincolnshire Regiment.
This regiment was lost at Bednore and disbanded in 1783.

• The facings for this regiment were black while the breeches and waistcoats of all ranks were white.
• The officers' lace and buttons were silver. Their coats were laced for dress with ten square loops, set evenly.
• Other ranks' coats had ten square loops, spaced evenly, with the lace of the rank and file being white with a black and green outer worm and a black inner edge.
• The officers carried fusils and bayonets as well as their swords.

There were two regiments numbered the 101st:

The first was raised in October 1760 by Sir James Johnstone of Westerhall from independent companies as:
101st (Highland) Regiment of Foot, also known as Johnstone's Highlanders
This regiment was disbanded in 1763

• Research has failed to find any details of the uniform, only that the facings were pale-yellowish buff and the regiment wore the government sett.

The second regiment was raised in September 1781 for service in the Indies by Robert Sandford as:
101st Regiment of Foot
This regiment was disbanded in 1785.

• The facings for this regiment were deep buff while the breeches and waistcoats of all ranks were white.
• The officers' lace and buttons were silver. Their coats were laced for dress with ten square loops, set in pairs.
• Other ranks' coats had ten square loops, spaced in pairs, while the lace of the rank and file had a scarlet figure and a sky blue stripe.
• The coat was lined with brown linen.

There were two regiments numbered the 102nd:

The first was raised in October 1760 from independent companies as:
102nd Regiment of Foot (Queen's Own Royal Volontiers)
This regiment was disbanded in 1763.

• Research has failed to find any details of the uniform.

The second regiment was raised in September 1781 for service in India by William Rowley as:
102nd Regiment of Foot
This regiment was lost at Bednore and disbanded in 1783.

• The facings for this regiment were pale-yellow while the breeches and waistcoats of all ranks were white.
• The officers' lace and buttons were silver. Their coats were laced for dress with ten square loops set in pairs.
• Other ranks' coats had ten square loops, set in pairs. The lace of the rank and file had a red outer stripe, a yellow centre stripe and a red inner stripe.
• The grenadiers were to have hats as the battalion men.

There were two regiments numbered the 103rd:

The first was raised in October 1760 by Thomas Oswald from independent companies as:
103rd Regiment of Foot (Volontier Hunters)
This regiment was disbanded in 1763.

• Research has failed to find any details of the uniform.

The second regiment was raised in November 1781 by Ralph Abercrombie as:
103rd (King's Irish Infantry) Regiment of Foot
This regiment was disbanded in 1784.

• The facings for this royal regiment were dark-blue while the breeches and waistcoats of all ranks were white.
• The officers' lace and buttons were gold. Their coats were laced for dress with ten square loops, set evenly.
• Other ranks' coats had ten square loops, spaced evenly, with the lace of the rank and file being white with central blue worm.

There were two regiments numbered the 104th:

The first was raised in March 1760 by Patrick Tonyn from independent companies as:
104th Regiment of Foot (King's Volontiers)
This regiment was disbanded in 1763.

• The facings were dark-blue; buttons were gold, coats lined white; no other details are known

---

The second regiment was raised in February 1780 by Stuart Douglas as:
104th Regiment of Foot
This regiment was disbanded in 1784.

• The facings were yellow, buttons were silver, and all ranks wore the cocked hat with a white plume. No other details are known.

There were two regiments numbered the 105th:

The first was raised in October 1760 by David Graeme from independent companies as:
105th Regiment of Foot (Queen's Own Royal Regiment of Highlanders)
The two battalions were disbanded in 1763.

• The facings were dark-blue, and the lace gold. The regiment is recorded as wearing buff waistcoats but no other details are known.

The second regiment was raised in America at Philadelphia in 1776 by Lord Rawdon as:
Volunteers of Ireland.
Designated on 25 December 1782 as:
105th Regiment of Foot
This regiment was transferred to the Irish establishment in 1783 and disbanded in 1784.

• The facings for this regiment were green without lapels while the breeches and waistcoats of all ranks were white.
• The officers' lace and buttons were gold.
• Other ranks' coats were laced for dress with five pointed green loops edged in white and decorated with white tassels. The pointed cuff was edged white.
• It is assumed that the officers and enlisted men served as both grenadiers and light companies.

During the War of Independence:
The 105th arrived in New York in April 1778 and saw action at Charleston (in December 1779), Camden, Hob Kirk's Hill and relief of the Ninety-Six. After Yorktown it left South Carolina and retrned to New York. The regiment left for England in April 1783, and was sent to Nova Scotia and 'officially' moved to England in April 1783.

There were other numbered regiments up to the 124th during the early period. Most were disbanded by 1763, but these have been included in the list below, although in many cases little is known of the uniform.

Raised in 1761 from independent companies in Ireland by Barre as:
106th Regiment of Foot (Black Musqueteers)
This regiment was disbanded in 1763

• There is little detail for this uniform, only that it was faced black, with black belts, black caps with brass plate with rampant lion over the motto 'Steady'.

Raised in 1761 from independent companies as:
107th Regiment of Foot (Queen's Own Royal Regiment of British Volontiers)
This regiment was disbanded in 1763

• There is little detail for this uniform, only that it was faced dark-blue with gold lace. There was no record of the lace for the rank and file.

Raised in 1761 by Lieutenant Colonel Patrick M'Duall as:
108th Regiment of Foot
This regiment was disbanded in 1763

• Research has failed to find any details of the uniform.

Raised in 1761 by Major John Narne as:
109th (London Volunteers) Regiment of Foot
This regiment was disbanded in 1763

• Research has failed to find any details of the uniform.

Raised in 1761 by Major John Deakin as:
110th (Queen's Royal Musketeers) Regiment of Foot
This regiment was disbanded in 1763

• There is little detail for this uniform, only that it was faced dark-blue.

Raised in 1761 from independent companies by Thomas Ogle as:
111th Regiment of Foot
This regiment was disbanded in 1763

• The facings for this regiment were pompadour; this is confirmed by the Army List. The colour was not that of the purple of the 56th nor the rose-colour of the 59th. The lace was silver but no other details are known.

Raised in 1761 from independent companies by Major Enoch Markham as:
112th (Royal Musqueteers) Regiment of Foot
This regiment was disbanded in 1763

• There is little detail for this uniform, only that it was faced dark-blue.

Raised in 1761 from independent companies by Major James Hamilton as:
113th (Royal Highlanders) Regiment of Foot
This regiment was disbanded in 1763

• Research has failed to find any details of the uniform other than that it probably had dark-blue facings, silver braid for the officers and that the tartan was the government sett.

Raised in 1761 from independent companies by Sir Allan MacLean as:
114th (King's Royal Highland Volontiers) Regiment of Foot, also known as MacLean's Highlanders
This regiment was disbanded in 1763

• Details for this regiment are not known other than that the facings were dark-blue and the lace silver.

Raised in 1762 as an Invalid regiment by Cliffe as:
117th Regiment of Foot (Invalids)
Renumbered in 1764 as:
74th Regiment of Foot (Invalids)
This regiment was disbanded in1770.

• Details for this regiment are not known.

Raised in 1762 as an Invalid regiment by Linde as:
118th Regiment of Foot (Invalids)
Renumbered in 1764 as:
75th Regiment of Foot (Invalids)
This regiment was disbanded in1770.

• Details for this regiment are not known.

Raised in 26th May 1716 two companies of 100 men in each:
Royal Artillery
They were joined in 1722 by the Gibraltar and Minorca Batteries to become:
Royal Regiment of Artillery
In 1801 they absorbed the:
Royal Irish Artillery
to form100 companies.

Circa 1751:
• The coats of this royal regiment were dark-blue with scarlet facings.
• Officers' coats were lined, faced and lapelled scarlet with gold binding.
• Other ranks' coats were lined scarlet. Lapels were laced about and had six square loops set evenly with three further loops below, while the horizontal coat pocket was laced about.
• The red waistcoat was laced about.
• Breeches for this regiment were red.
• Lace of the rank and file was plain yellow.

In the 1768 regulations:
The coats of this royal regiment were dark-blue with scarlet facings, while the linings, breeches and waistcoats of all ranks were white.
• The officers' lace and buttons gold. Their coats were laced for dress with ten square loops, set evenly.
• Other ranks' coats had ten loops, spaced evenly, with the lace of the rank and file being yellow.

During the War of Independence:

The Royal Artillery saw action at almost every encounter during the American War of Independence as well as service in Canada. Personnel were drawn from a number of different battalions but mainly from the 4th, although there was also support from Scott's Company of the 1st Battalion, and 6 Company of the 3rd Battalion. It is not clear if other batteries were involved. Most were surrendered at either Saratoga or Yorktown and were interned, returning home after 1783.

• The first arrival was by Captain Jones's Company which sailed on1 April 1777. After losses in artillery the America the men were integrated with 411 men, plus 154 from the 33rd Regiment of Foot detailed for artillery duties.

• Men integrated into the Royal Artillery also represented the Royal Irish Artillery.

• The Royal Artillery was divided into Battalions each of ten companies, numbering 100 men apiece. There were no specific roles and each company was posted to whatever duty was required.

• The ordnance used in America were the 6-pounder and 3-pounder guns on bracket carriages, for further information *'British Napoleonic Field Artillery, ISBN 978-1-86227-373-3'* History Press, 2008.

1st (Royal) Regiment of Foot.
Officer's Gilt button circa 1768
NCO's Sash circa 1768
Private Soldier's Pewter button circa 1768
Officer's Dress Battalion Company circa 1785
Officer's Dress Light Company circa 1785
Private Soldier's Dress Light Company circa 1785
Private Soldier's Dress Battalion Company circa 1783
Grenadier Officer's Dress circa 1785
Officer's Undress circa 1785
Grenadier Private's Dress circa 1783
Other rank's Brass Breast Plate circa 1768
Officer's Dress Light Company circa 1771
Private Soldier's Dress Light Company circa 1771
Other Rank's Lace circa 1768
Officer's Dress Battalion Company circa 1768
Grenadier Officer's Dress circa 1768
Grenadier Private's Dress circa 1768
Private Soldier's Dress Battalion Company circa 1768
Possible cuff lace Private Soldier's circa 1751
Grenadier Mitre Cap circa 1751
Officer's Gilt Breast Plate circa 1775
Officer's Dress circa 1760
Other Rank's Lace circa 1751
Grenadier's Dress circa 1755
Private Soldier's Dress circa 1755

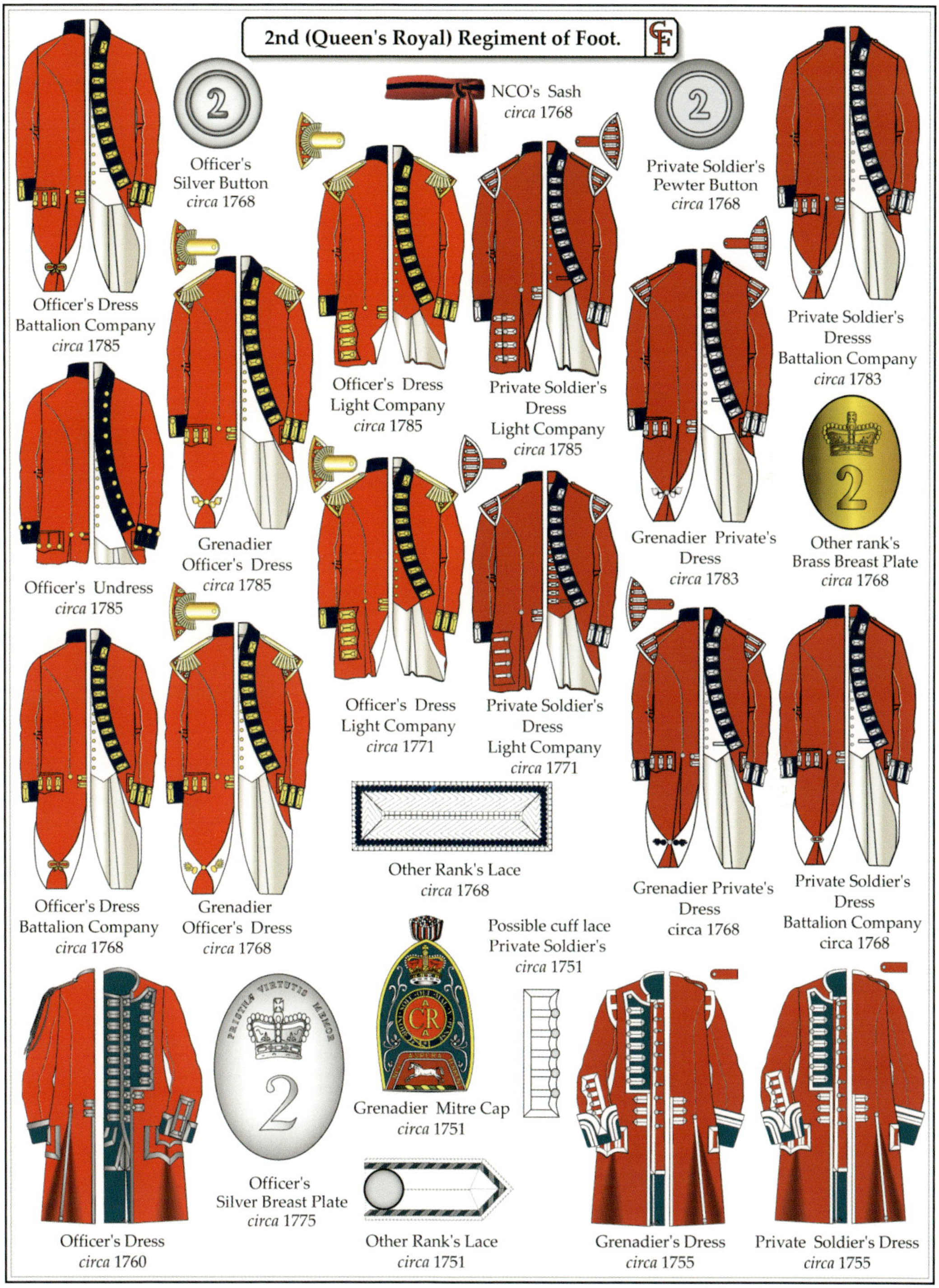
2nd (Queen's Royal) Regiment of Foot.
Officer's Dress Battalion Company *circa* 1785
Officer's Silver Button *circa* 1768
NCO's Sash *circa* 1768
Private Soldier's Pewter Button *circa* 1768
Private Soldier's Dresss Battalion Company *circa* 1783
Officer's Dress Light Company *circa* 1785
Private Soldier's Dress Light Company *circa* 1785
Officer's Undress *circa* 1785
Grenadier Officer's Dress *circa* 1785
Grenadier Private's Dress *circa* 1783
Other rank's Brass Breast Plate *circa* 1768
Officer's Dress Light Company *circa* 1771
Private Soldier's Dress Light Company *circa* 1771
Officer's Dress Battalion Company *circa* 1768
Grenadier Officer's Dress *circa* 1768
Other Rank's Lace *circa* 1768
Grenadier Private's Dress circa 1768
Private Soldier's Dress Battalion Company circa 1768
Possible cuff lace Private Soldier's *circa* 1751
Grenadier Mitre Cap *circa* 1751
Officer's Dress *circa* 1760
Officer's Silver Breast Plate *circa* 1775
Other Rank's Lace *circa* 1751
Grenadier's Dress *circa* 1755
Private Soldier's Dress *circa* 1755

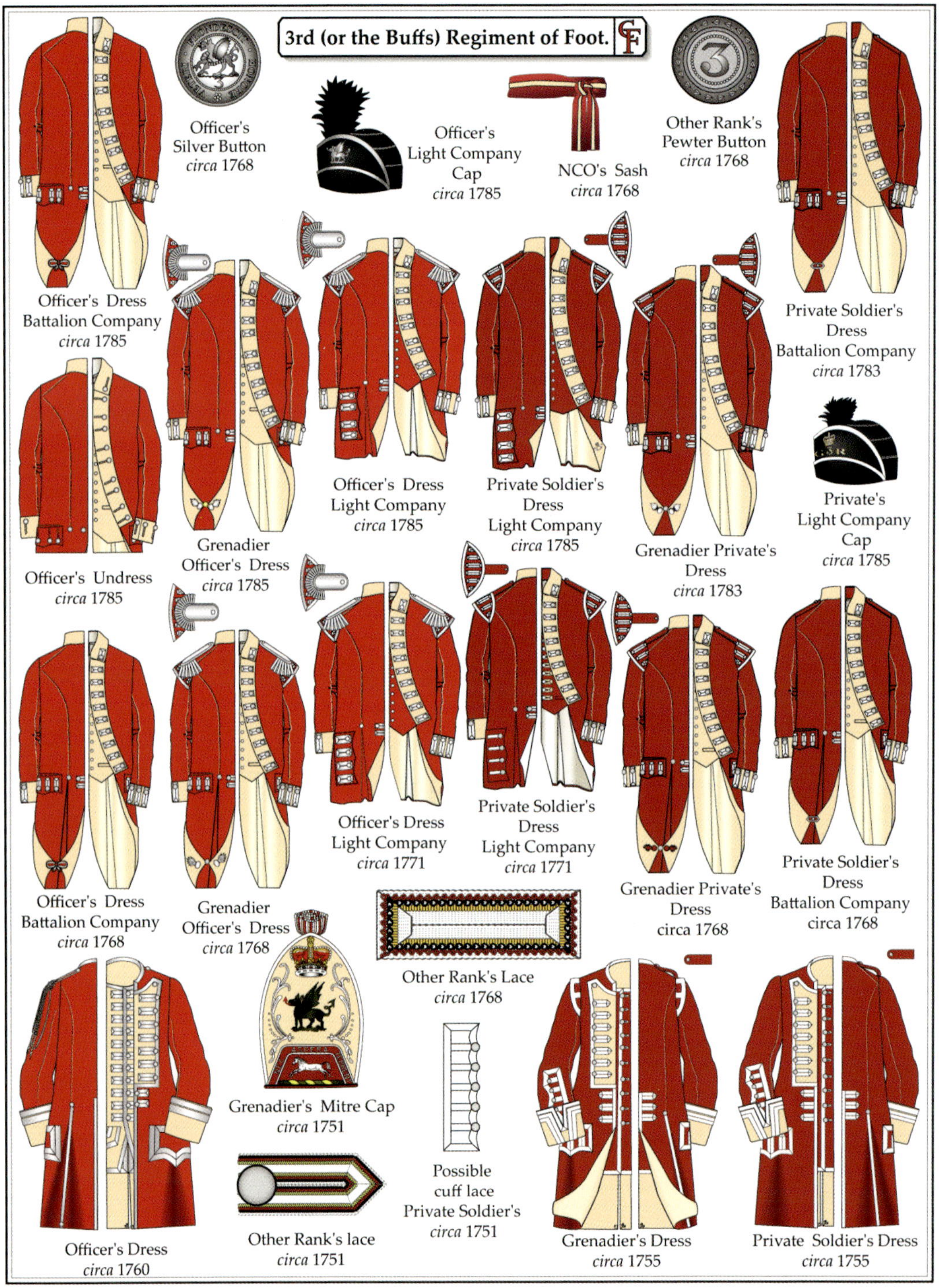
3rd (or the Buffs) Regiment of Foot.
Officer's Silver Button circa 1768
Officer's Light Company Cap circa 1785
NCO's Sash circa 1768
Other Rank's Pewter Button circa 1768
Officer's Dress Battalion Company circa 1785
Private Soldier's Dress Battalion Company circa 1783
Officer's Dress Light Company circa 1785
Private Soldier's Dress Light Company circa 1785
Grenadier Private's Dress circa 1783
Private's Light Company Cap circa 1785
Officer's Undress circa 1785
Grenadier Officer's Dress circa 1785
Officer's Dress Light Company circa 1771
Private Soldier's Dress Light Company circa 1771
Grenadier Private's Dress circa 1768
Private Soldier's Dress Battalion Company circa 1768
Officer's Dress Battalion Company circa 1768
Grenadier Officer's Dress circa 1768
Other Rank's Lace circa 1768
Grenadier's Mitre Cap circa 1751
Possible cuff lace Private Soldier's circa 1751
Officer's Dress circa 1760
Other Rank's lace circa 1751
Grenadier's Dress circa 1755
Private Soldier's Dress circa 1755

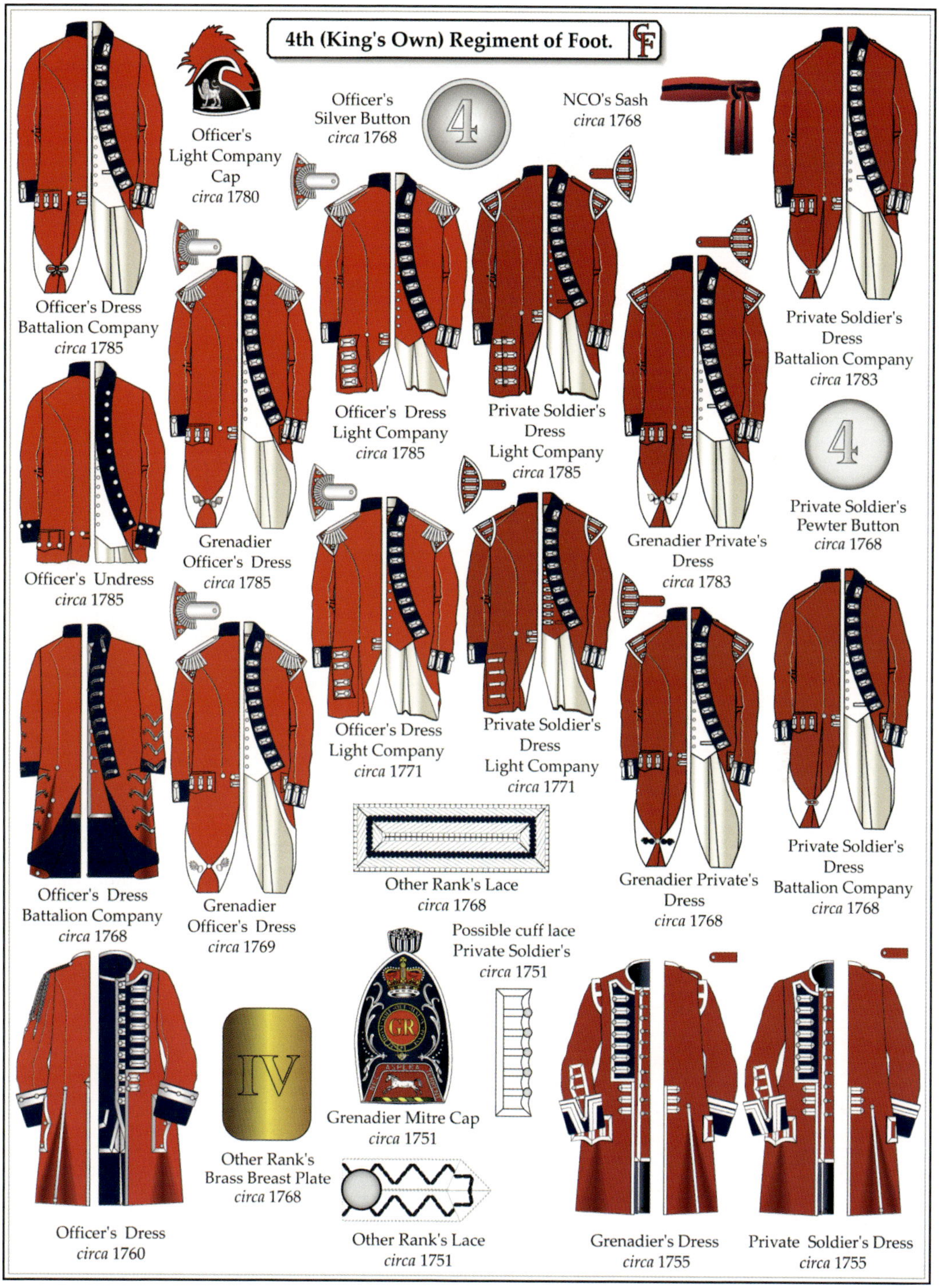
4th (King's Own) Regiment of Foot.
Officer's Light Company Cap circa 1780
Officer's Silver Button circa 1768
NCO's Sash circa 1768
Officer's Dress Battalion Company circa 1785
Officer's Dress Light Company circa 1785
Private Soldier's Dress Light Company circa 1785
Private Soldier's Dress Battalion Company circa 1783
Private Soldier's Pewter Button circa 1768
Officer's Undress circa 1785
Grenadier Officer's Dress circa 1785
Grenadier Private's Dress circa 1783
Officer's Dress Light Company circa 1771
Private Soldier's Dress Light Company circa 1771
Officer's Dress Battalion Company circa 1768
Grenadier Officer's Dress circa 1769
Other Rank's Lace circa 1768
Grenadier Private's Dress circa 1768
Private Soldier's Dress Battalion Company circa 1768
Possible cuff lace Private Soldier's circa 1751
IV
GR
Grenadier Mitre Cap circa 1751
Other Rank's Brass Breast Plate circa 1768
Officer's Dress circa 1760
Other Rank's Lace circa 1751
Grenadier's Dress circa 1755
Private Soldier's Dress circa 1755

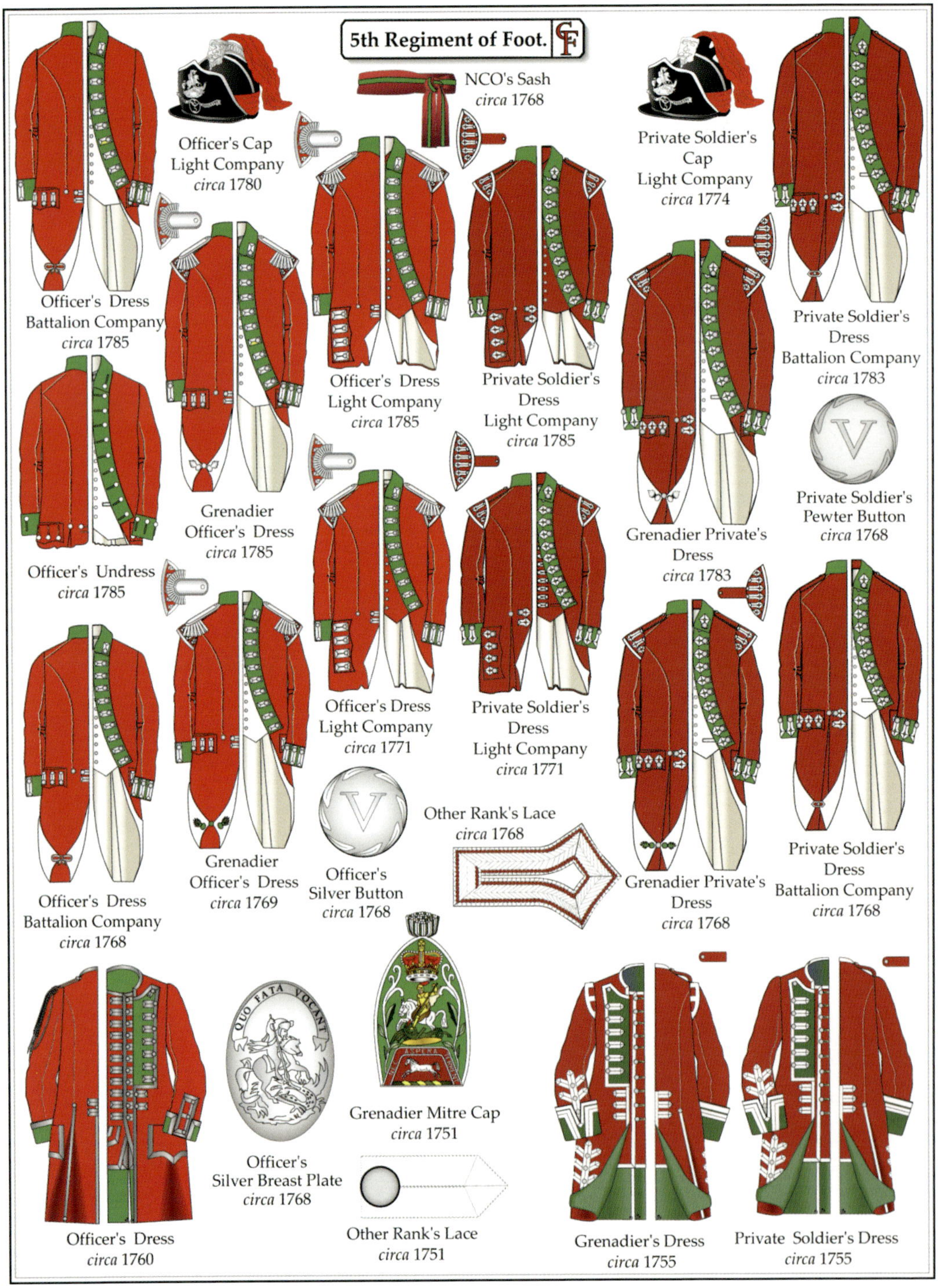
5th Regiment of Foot.
NCO's Sash circa 1768
Officer's Cap Light Company circa 1780
Private Soldier's Cap Light Company circa 1774
Officer's Dress Battalion Company circa 1785
Officer's Dress Light Company circa 1785
Private Soldier's Dress Light Company circa 1785
Private Soldier's Dress Battalion Company circa 1783
Officer's Undress circa 1785
Grenadier Officer's Dress circa 1785
Grenadier Private's Dress circa 1783
Private Soldier's Pewter Button circa 1768
Officer's Dress Light Company circa 1771
Private Soldier's Dress Light Company circa 1771
Officer's Dress Battalion Company circa 1768
Grenadier Officer's Dress circa 1769
Officer's Silver Button circa 1768
Other Rank's Lace circa 1768
Grenadier Private's Dress circa 1768
Private Soldier's Dress Battalion Company circa 1768
QUO FATA VOCANT
Officer's Dress circa 1760
Officer's Silver Breast Plate circa 1768
Grenadier Mitre Cap circa 1751
Other Rank's Lace circa 1751
Grenadier's Dress circa 1755
Private Soldier's Dress circa 1755

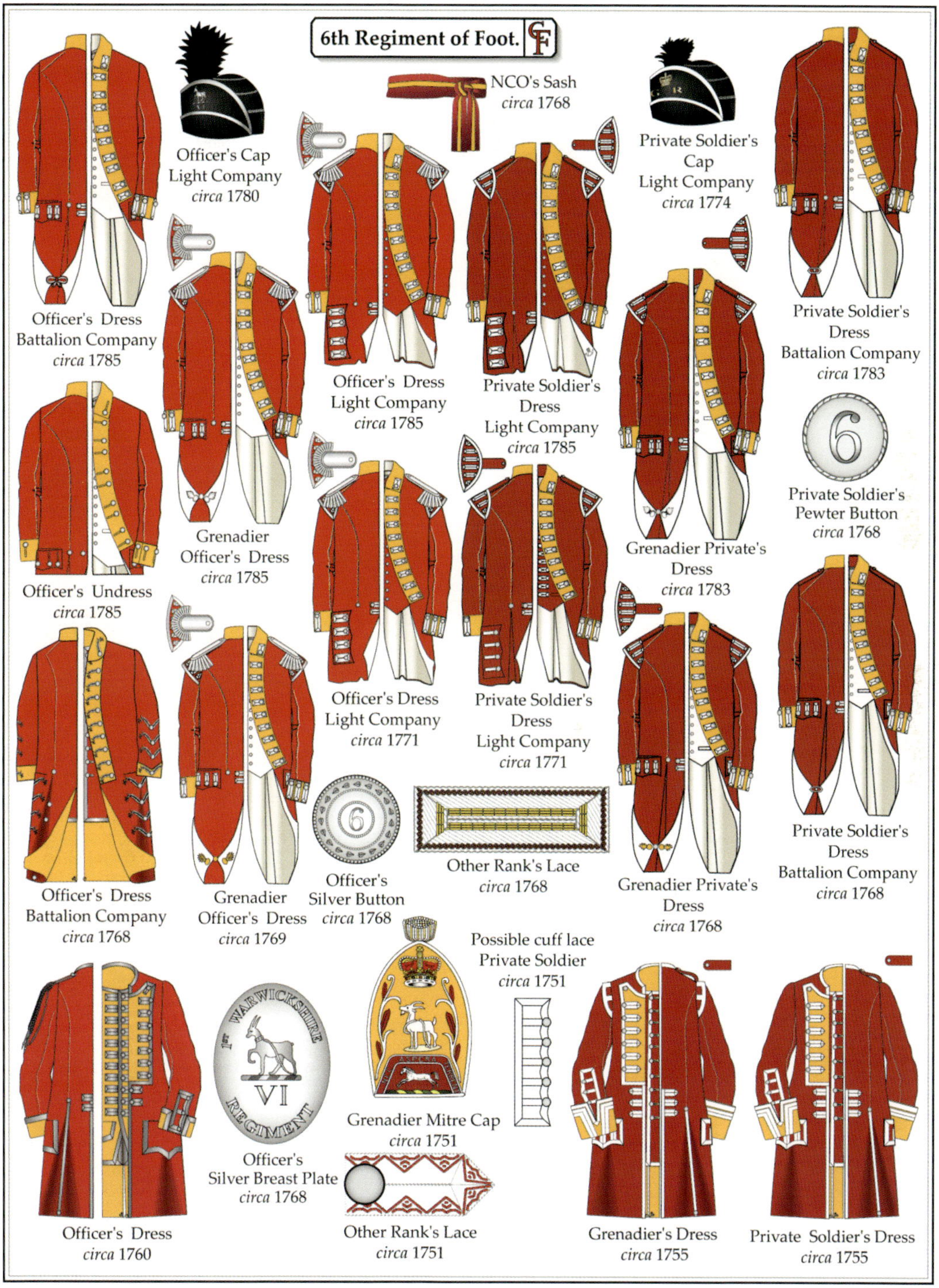
6th Regiment of Foot.
NCO's Sash circa 1768
Officer's Cap Light Company circa 1780
Private Soldier's Cap Light Company circa 1774
Officer's Dress Battalion Company circa 1785
Officer's Dress Light Company circa 1785
Private Soldier's Dress Light Company circa 1785
Private Soldier's Dress Battalion Company circa 1783
Private Soldier's Pewter Button circa 1768
Grenadier Officer's Dress circa 1785
Officer's Undress circa 1785
Grenadier Private's Dress circa 1783
Officer's Dress Light Company circa 1771
Private Soldier's Dress Light Company circa 1771
Officer's Dress Battalion Company circa 1768
Grenadier Officer's Dress circa 1769
Officer's Silver Button circa 1768
Other Rank's Lace circa 1768
Grenadier Private's Dress circa 1768
Private Soldier's Dress Battalion Company circa 1768
Possible cuff lace Private Soldier circa 1751
1st WARWICKSHIRE VI REGIMENT
Officer's Dress circa 1760
Officer's Silver Breast Plate circa 1768
Grenadier Mitre Cap circa 1751
Other Rank's Lace circa 1751
Grenadier's Dress circa 1755
Private Soldier's Dress circa 1755

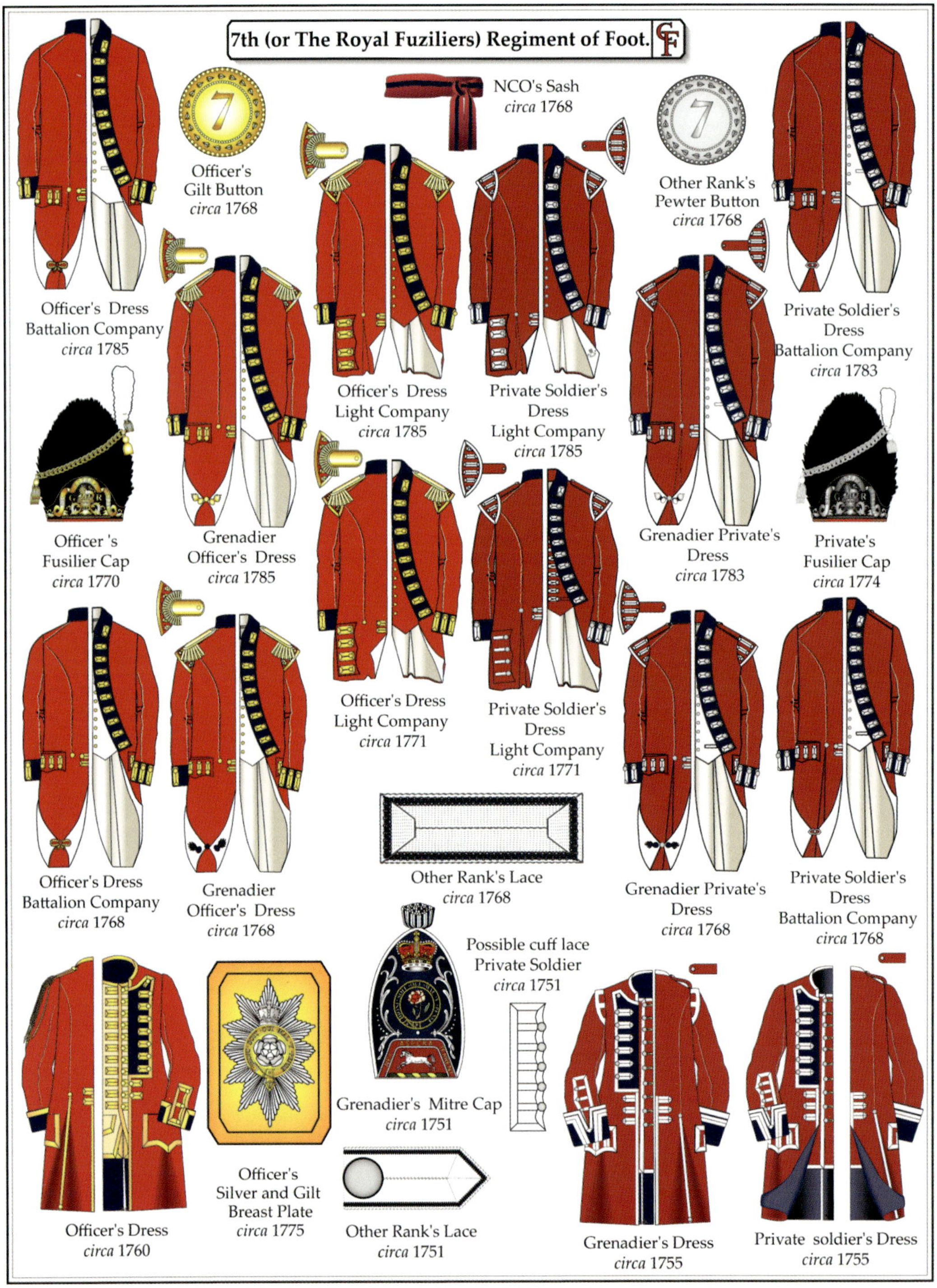
7th (or The Royal Fuziliers) Regiment of Foot.
Officer's Dress Battalion Company circa 1785
Officer's Gilt Button circa 1768
NCO's Sash circa 1768
Other Rank's Pewter Button circa 1768
Private Soldier's Dress Battalion Company circa 1783
Officer's Dress Light Company circa 1785
Private Soldier's Dress Light Company circa 1785
Officer 's Fusilier Cap circa 1770
Grenadier Officer's Dress circa 1785
Grenadier Private's Dress circa 1783
Private's Fusilier Cap circa 1774
Officer's Dress Light Company circa 1771
Private Soldier's Dress Light Company circa 1771
Officer's Dress Battalion Company circa 1768
Grenadier Officer's Dress circa 1768
Other Rank's Lace circa 1768
Grenadier Private's Dress circa 1768
Private Soldier's Dress Battalion Company circa 1768
Possible cuff lace Private Soldier circa 1751
Grenadier's Mitre Cap circa 1751
Officer's Dress circa 1760
Officer's Silver and Gilt Breast Plate circa 1775
Other Rank's Lace circa 1751
Grenadier's Dress circa 1755
Private soldier's Dress circa 1755

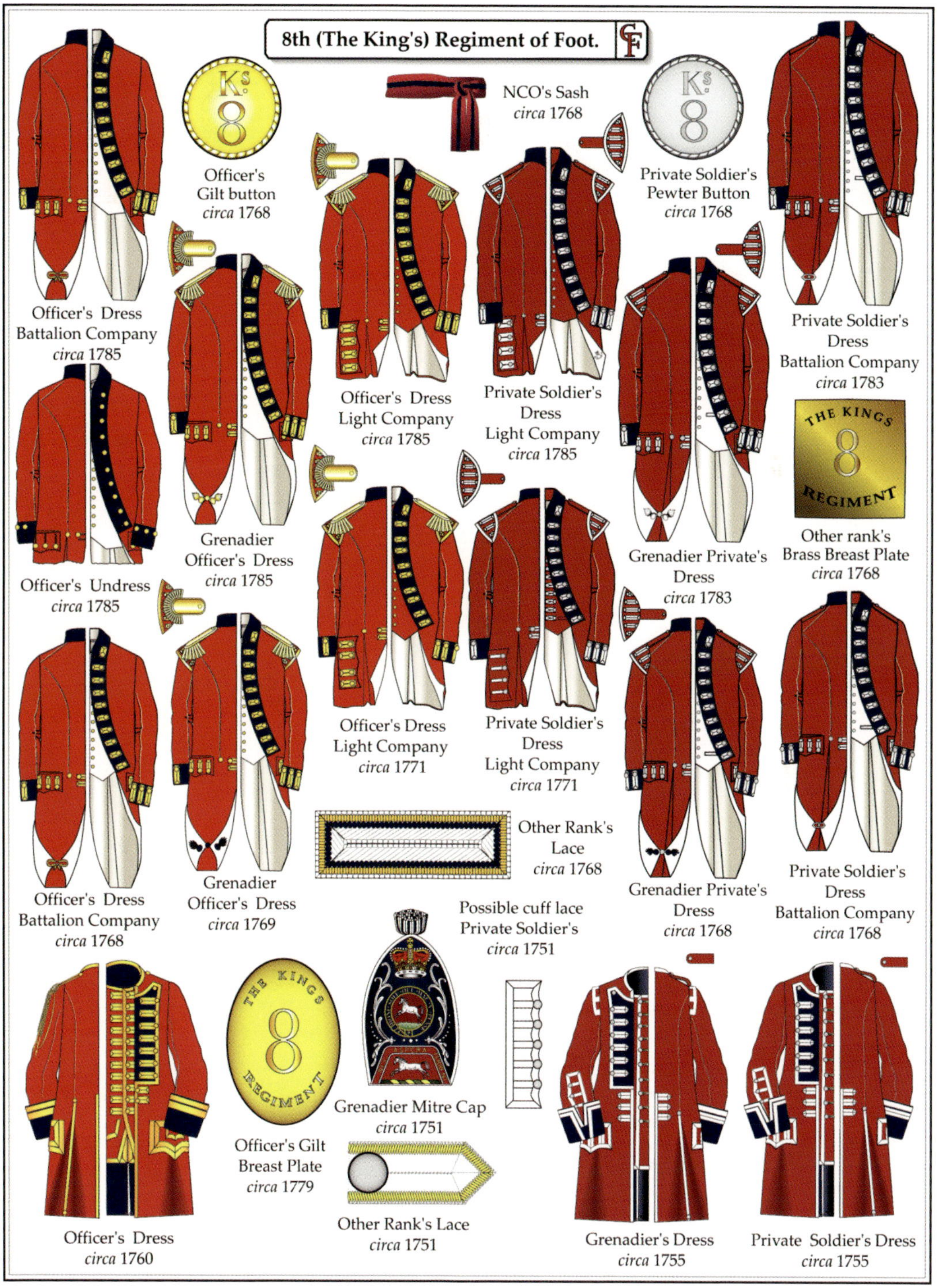
8th (The King's) Regiment of Foot.
Officer's Dress Battalion Company circa 1785
Officer's Gilt button circa 1768
NCO's Sash circa 1768
Private Soldier's Pewter Button circa 1768
Private Soldier's Dress Battalion Company circa 1783
Officer's Dress Light Company circa 1785
Private Soldier's Dress Light Company circa 1785
Officer's Undress circa 1785
Grenadier Officer's Dress circa 1785
THE KINGS 8 REGIMENT
Other rank's Brass Breast Plate circa 1768
Grenadier Private's Dress circa 1783
Officer's Dress Light Company circa 1771
Private Soldier's Dress Light Company circa 1771
Officer's Dress Battalion Company circa 1768
Grenadier Officer's Dress circa 1769
Other Rank's Lace circa 1768
Grenadier Private's Dress circa 1768
Private Soldier's Dress Battalion Company circa 1768
Possible cuff lace Private Soldier's circa 1751
THE KINGS 8 REGIMENT
Officer's Dress circa 1760
Officer's Gilt Breast Plate circa 1779
Grenadier Mitre Cap circa 1751
Other Rank's Lace circa 1751
Grenadier's Dress circa 1755
Private Soldier's Dress circa 1755

9th Regiment of Foot.
CF
Officer's Dress
Battalion Company
circa 1785
1X
Officer's
Silver Button
circa 1768
NCO's Sash
circa 1768
1X
Private Soldier's
Pewter Button
circa 1768
Private Soldier's
Dress
Battalion Company
circa 1783
Officer's Dress
Light Company
circa 1785
Private Soldier's
Dress
Light Company
circa 1785
Officer's Undress
circa 1785
Grenadier
Officer's Dress
circa 1785
Grenadier Private's
Dress
circa 1783
Other rank's
Brass Breast Plate
circa 1768
Officer's Dress
Light Company
circa 1771
Private Soldier's
Dress
Light Company
circa 1771
Officer's Dress
Battalion Company
circa 1768
Grenadier
Officer's Dress
circa 1769
Other Rank's Lace circa 1768
Grenadier Private's
Dress
circa 1768
Private Soldier's
Dress
Battalion Company
circa 1768
9 Regt
Officer's
Silver Breast Plate
circa 1768
Grenadier Mitre Cap
circa 1751
Possible cuff lace
Private Soldier
circa 1751
Other Rank's Lace
circa 1751
Officer's Dress
circa 1760
Grenadier's Dress
circa 1755
Private Soldier's Dress
circa 1755

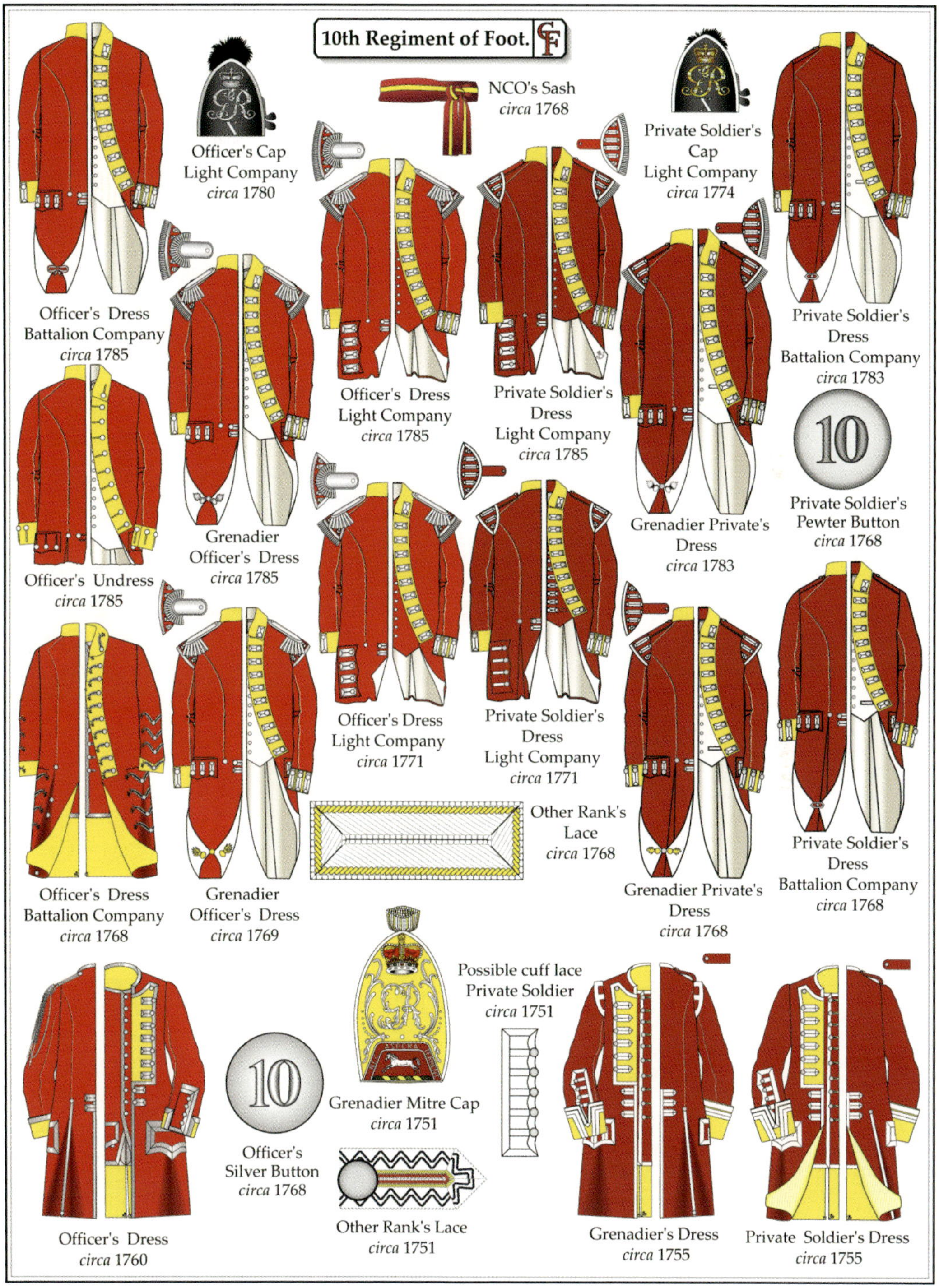
10th Regiment of Foot.
Officer's Dress Battalion Company circa 1785
Officer's Cap Light Company circa 1780
NCO's Sash circa 1768
Officer's Dress Light Company circa 1785
Private Soldier's Dress Light Company circa 1785
Private Soldier's Cap Light Company circa 1774
Private Soldier's Dress Battalion Company circa 1783
Officer's Undress circa 1785
Grenadier Officer's Dress circa 1785
Grenadier Private's Dress circa 1783
10
Private Soldier's Pewter Button circa 1768
Officer's Dress Light Company circa 1771
Private Soldier's Dress Light Company circa 1771
Officer's Dress Battalion Company circa 1768
Grenadier Officer's Dress circa 1769
Other Rank's Lace circa 1768
Grenadier Private's Dress circa 1768
Private Soldier's Dress Battalion Company circa 1768
Officer's Dress circa 1760
10
Officer's Silver Button circa 1768
Grenadier Mitre Cap circa 1751
Other Rank's Lace circa 1751
Possible cuff lace Private Soldier circa 1751
Grenadier's Dress circa 1755
Private Soldier's Dress circa 1755

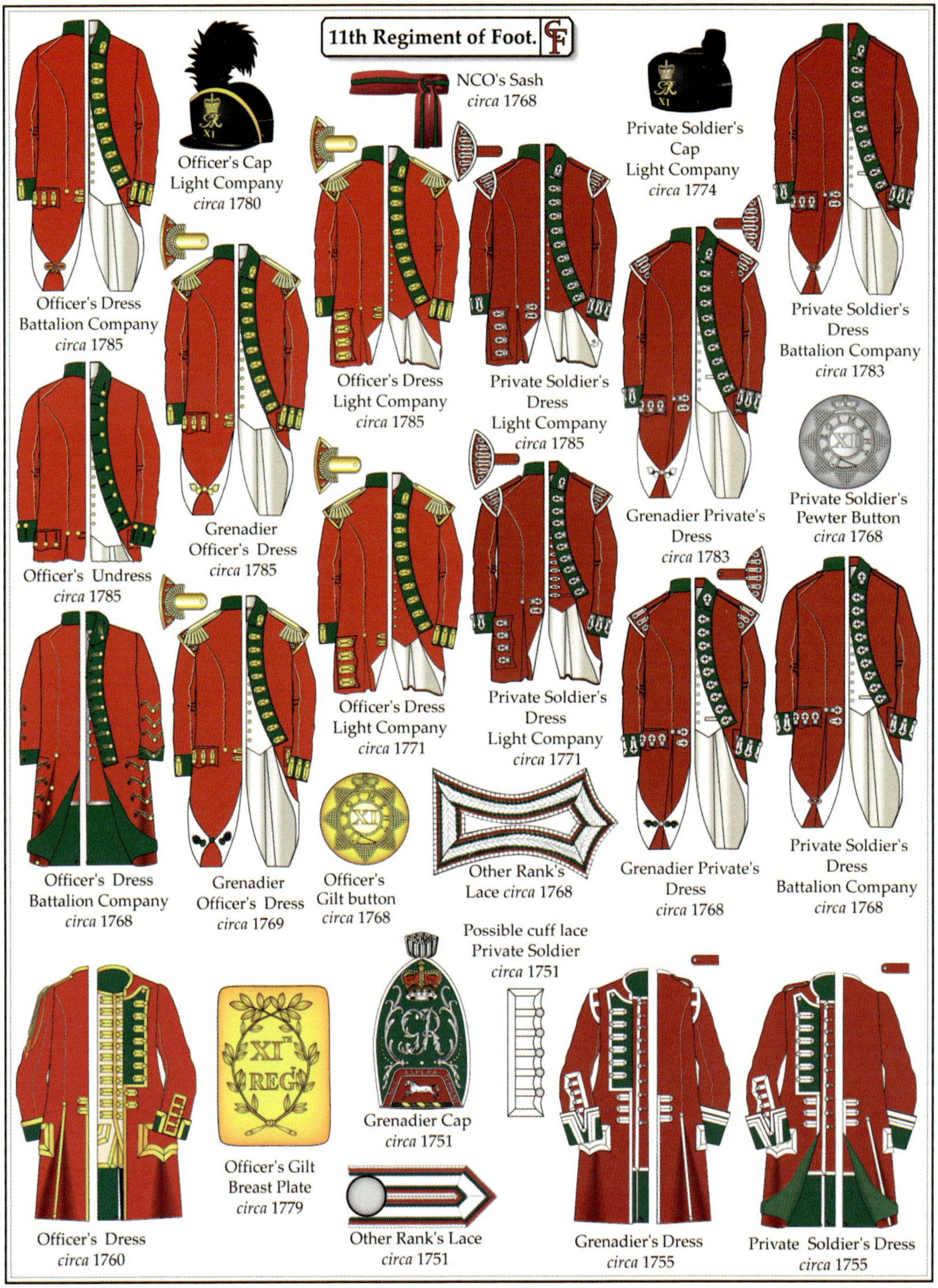
11th Regiment of Foot.
Officer's Cap
Light Company
circa 1780
NCO's Sash
circa 1768
Private Soldier's
Cap
Light Company
circa 1774
Officer's Dress
Battalion Company
circa 1785
Officer's Dress
Light Company
circa 1785
Private Soldier's
Dress
Light Company
circa 1785
Private Soldier's
Dress
Battalion Company
circa 1783
Grenadier
Officer's Dress
circa 1785
Officer's Undress
circa 1785
Grenadier Private's
Dress
circa 1783
Private Soldier's
Pewter Button
circa 1768
Officer's Dress
Light Company
circa 1771
Private Soldier's
Dress
Light Company
circa 1771
Officer's Dress
Battalion Company
circa 1768
Grenadier
Officer's Dress
circa 1769
Officer's
Gilt button
circa 1768
Other Rank's
Lace circa 1768
Grenadier Private's
Dress
circa 1768
Private Soldier's
Dress
Battalion Company
circa 1768
Possible cuff lace
Private Soldier
circa 1751
Officer's Dress
circa 1760
Officer's Gilt
Breast Plate
circa 1779
Grenadier Cap
circa 1751
Other Rank's Lace
circa 1751
Grenadier's Dress
circa 1755
Private Soldier's Dress
circa 1755

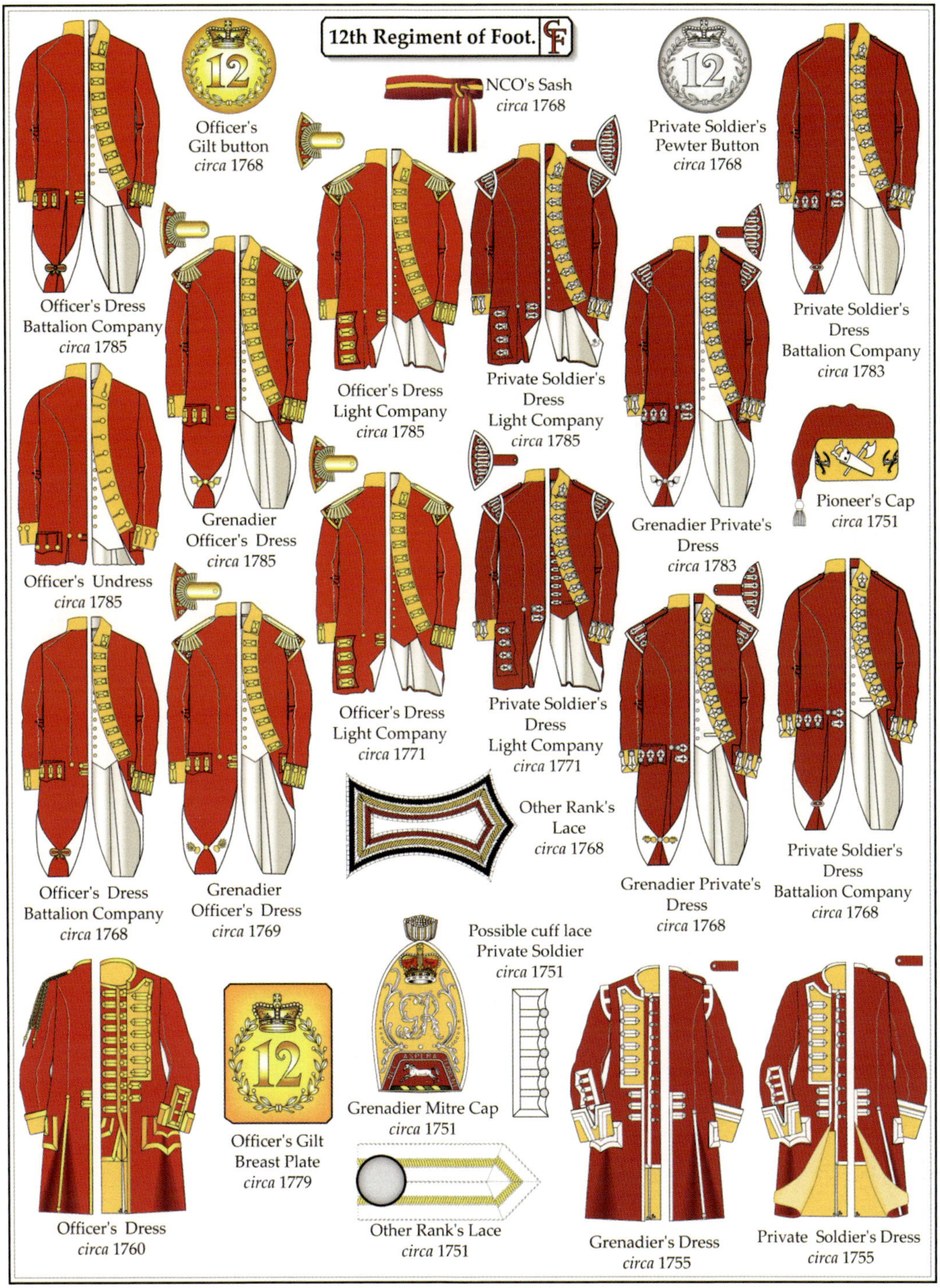
12th Regiment of Foot.
Officer's Gilt button circa 1768
NCO's Sash circa 1768
Private Soldier's Pewter Button circa 1768
Officer's Dress Battalion Company circa 1785
Officer's Dress Light Company circa 1785
Private Soldier's Dress Light Company circa 1785
Private Soldier's Dress Battalion Company circa 1783
Grenadier Officer's Dress circa 1785
Grenadier Private's Dress circa 1783
Pioneer's Cap circa 1751
Officer's Undress circa 1785
Officer's Dress Light Company circa 1771
Private Soldier's Dress Light Company circa 1771
Other Rank's Lace circa 1768
Officer's Dress Battalion Company circa 1768
Grenadier Officer's Dress circa 1769
Grenadier Private's Dress circa 1768
Private Soldier's Dress Battalion Company circa 1768
Possible cuff lace Private Soldier circa 1751
Officer's Dress circa 1760
Officer's Gilt Breast Plate circa 1779
Grenadier Mitre Cap circa 1751
Other Rank's Lace circa 1751
Grenadier's Dress circa 1755
Private Soldier's Dress circa 1755

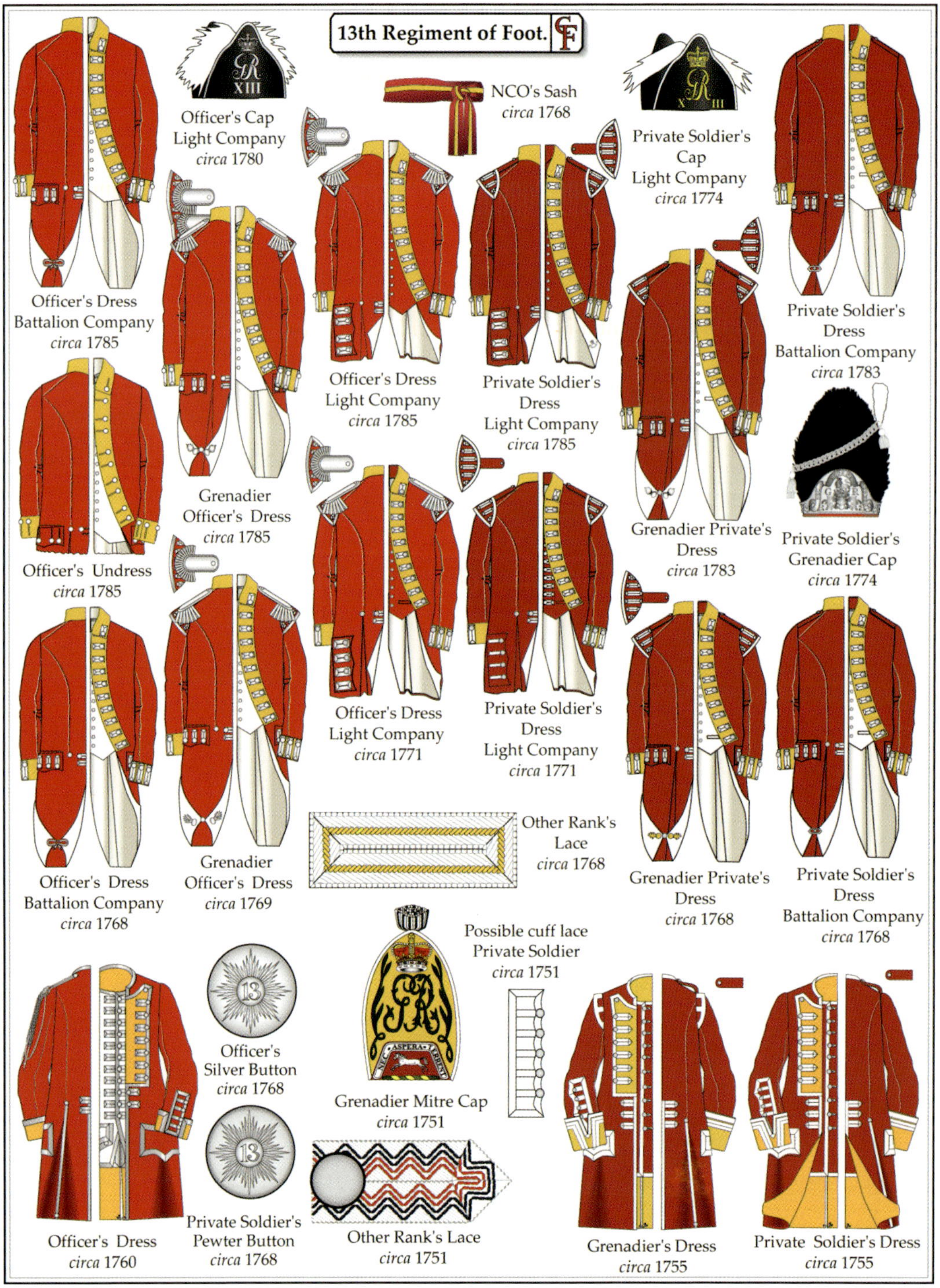
13th Regiment of Foot.
Officer's Cap
Light Company
circa 1780
NCO's Sash
circa 1768
Private Soldier's
Cap
Light Company
circa 1774
Officer's Dress
Battalion Company
circa 1785
Officer's Dress
Light Company
circa 1785
Private Soldier's
Dress
Light Company
circa 1785
Private Soldier's
Dress
Battalion Company
circa 1783
Grenadier
Officer's Dress
circa 1785
Officer's Undress
circa 1785
Grenadier Private's
Dress
circa 1783
Private Soldier's
Grenadier Cap
circa 1774
Officer's Dress
Light Company
circa 1771
Private Soldier's
Dress
Light Company
circa 1771
Other Rank's
Lace
circa 1768
Officer's Dress
Battalion Company
circa 1768
Grenadier
Officer's Dress
circa 1769
Grenadier Private's
Dress
circa 1768
Private Soldier's
Dress
Battalion Company
circa 1768
Possible cuff lace
Private Soldier
circa 1751
Officer's
Silver Button
circa 1768
Grenadier Mitre Cap
circa 1751
Private Soldier's
Pewter Button
circa 1768
Other Rank's Lace
circa 1751
Officer's Dress
circa 1760
Grenadier's Dress
circa 1755
Private Soldier's Dress
circa 1755

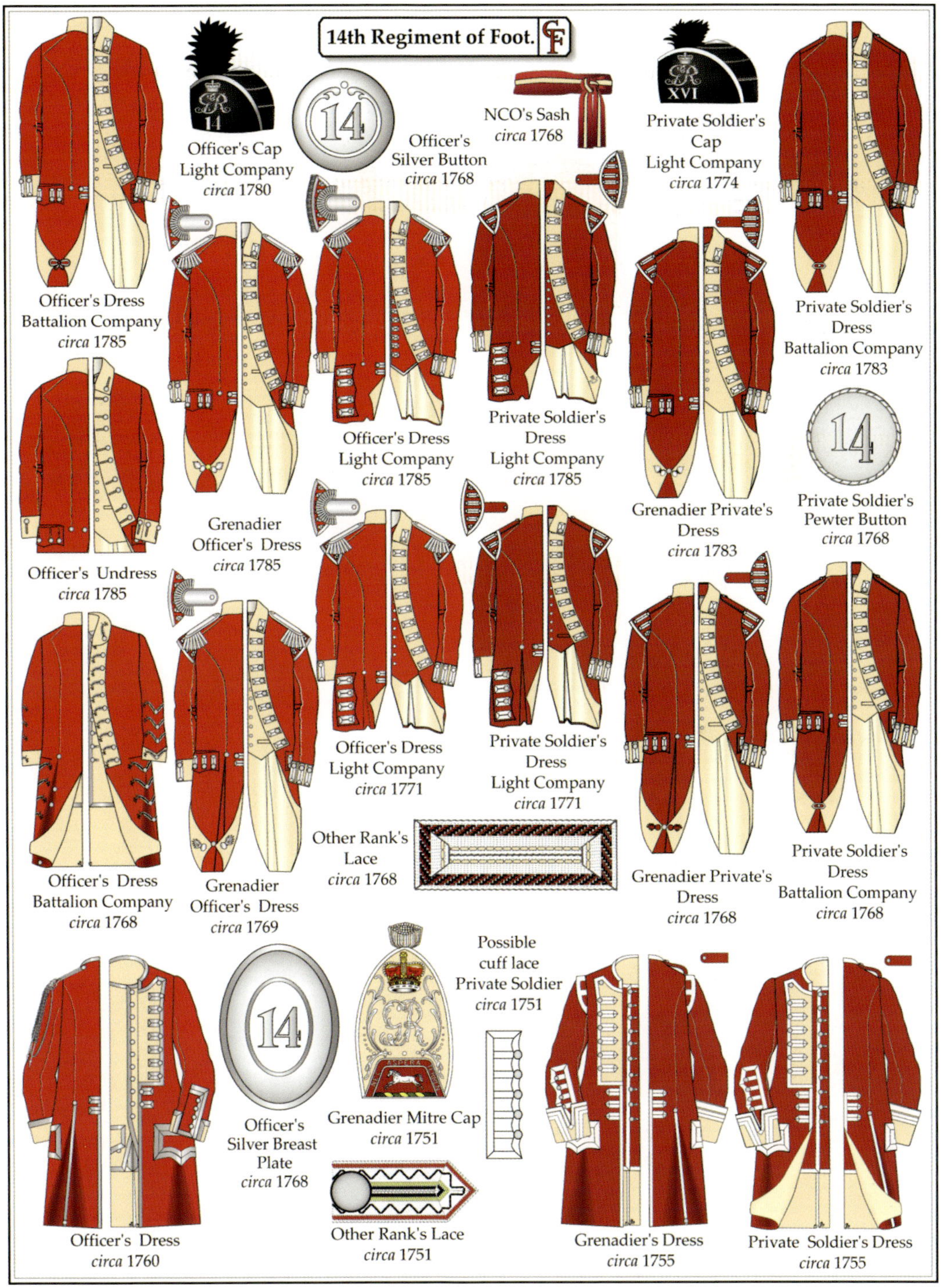
14th Regiment of Foot.
Officer's Dress Battalion Company circa 1785
Officer's Cap Light Company circa 1780
Officer's Silver Button circa 1768
NCO's Sash circa 1768
Private Soldier's Cap Light Company circa 1774
Private Soldier's Dress Battalion Company circa 1783
Officer's Undress circa 1785
Grenadier Officer's Dress circa 1785
Officer's Dress Light Company circa 1785
Private Soldier's Dress Light Company circa 1785
Grenadier Private's Dress circa 1783
Private Soldier's Pewter Button circa 1768
Officer's Dress Battalion Company circa 1768
Grenadier Officer's Dress circa 1769
Officer's Dress Light Company circa 1771
Private Soldier's Dress Light Company circa 1771
Other Rank's Lace circa 1768
Grenadier Private's Dress circa 1768
Private Soldier's Dress Battalion Company circa 1768
Possible cuff lace Private Soldier circa 1751
Officer's Dress circa 1760
Officer's Silver Breast Plate circa 1768
Grenadier Mitre Cap circa 1751
Other Rank's Lace circa 1751
Grenadier's Dress circa 1755
Private Soldier's Dress circa 1755

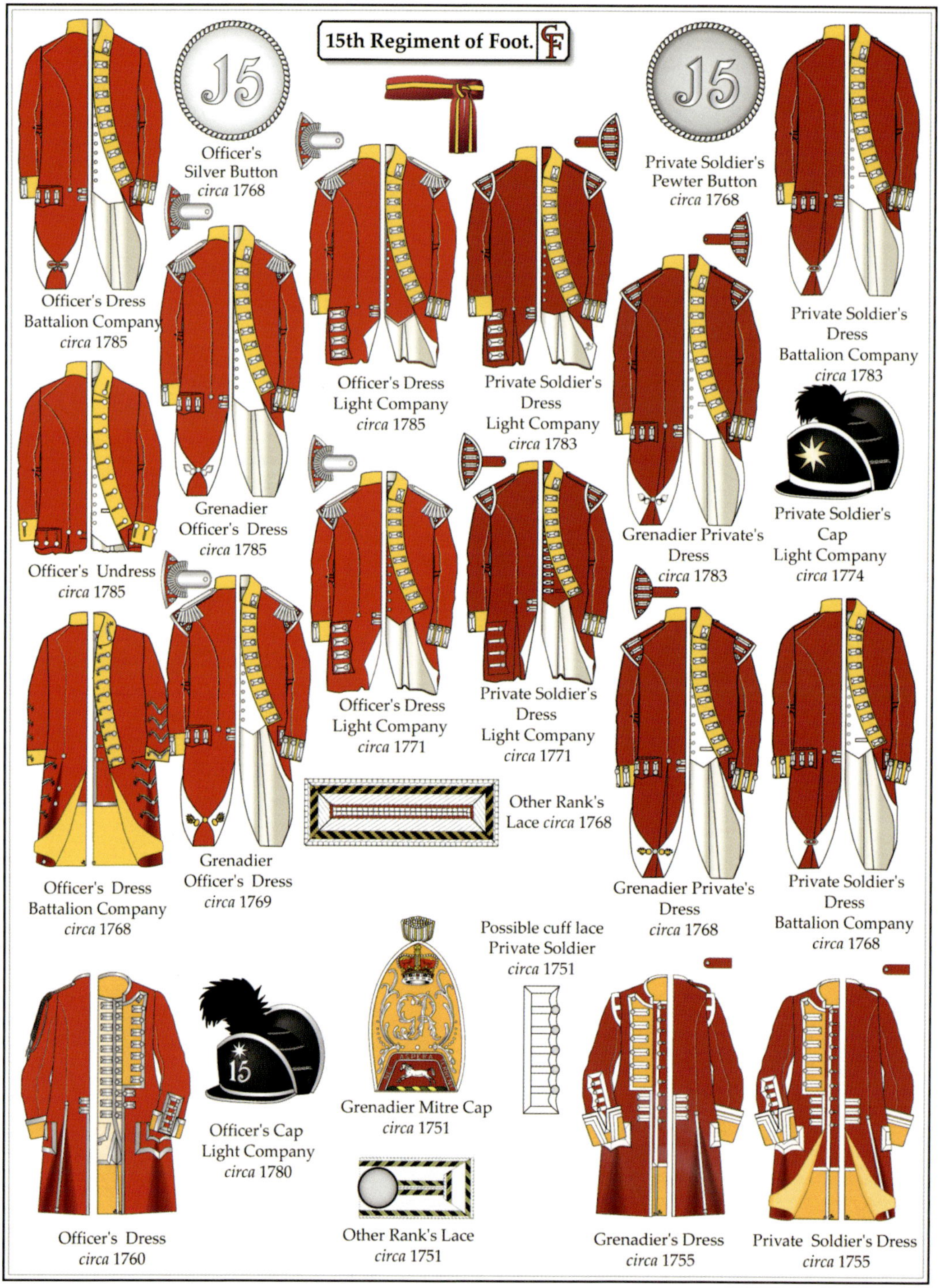
15th Regiment of Foot.
Officer's Silver Button circa 1768
Private Soldier's Pewter Button circa 1768
Officer's Dress Battalion Company circa 1785
Officer's Dress Light Company circa 1785
Private Soldier's Dress Light Company circa 1783
Private Soldier's Dress Battalion Company circa 1783
Grenadier Officer's Dress circa 1785
Grenadier Private's Dress circa 1783
Private Soldier's Cap Light Company circa 1774
Officer's Undress circa 1785
Officer's Dress Light Company circa 1771
Private Soldier's Dress Light Company circa 1771
Officer's Dress Battalion Company circa 1768
Grenadier Officer's Dress circa 1769
Other Rank's Lace circa 1768
Grenadier Private's Dress circa 1768
Private Soldier's Dress Battalion Company circa 1768
Possible cuff lace Private Soldier circa 1751
Officer's Dress circa 1760
Officer's Cap Light Company circa 1780
Grenadier Mitre Cap circa 1751
Other Rank's Lace circa 1751
Grenadier's Dress circa 1755
Private Soldier's Dress circa 1755

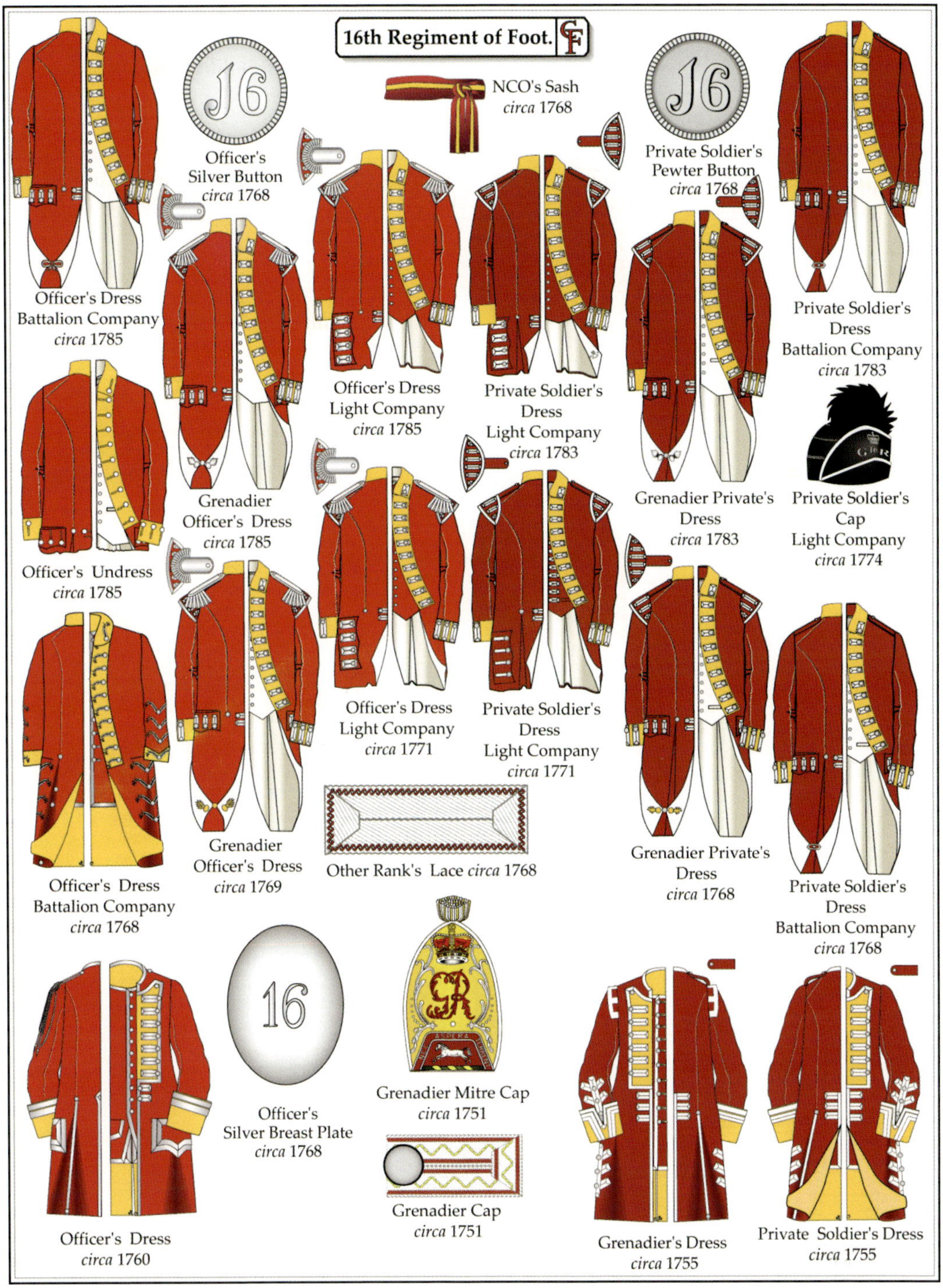
16th Regiment of Foot.
NCO's Sash circa 1768
Officer's Silver Button circa 1768
Private Soldier's Pewter Button circa 1768
Officer's Dress Battalion Company circa 1785
Officer's Dress Light Company circa 1785
Private Soldier's Dress Light Company circa 1783
Private Soldier's Dress Battalion Company circa 1783
Grenadier Officer's Dress circa 1785
Grenadier Private's Dress circa 1783
Private Soldier's Cap Light Company circa 1774
Officer's Undress circa 1785
Officer's Dress Light Company circa 1771
Private Soldier's Dress Light Company circa 1771
Officer's Dress Battalion Company circa 1768
Grenadier Officer's Dress circa 1769
Other Rank's Lace circa 1768
Grenadier Private's Dress circa 1768
Private Soldier's Dress Battalion Company circa 1768
Officer's Silver Breast Plate circa 1768
Grenadier Mitre Cap circa 1751
Grenadier Cap circa 1751
Officer's Dress circa 1760
Grenadier's Dress circa 1755
Private Soldier's Dress circa 1755

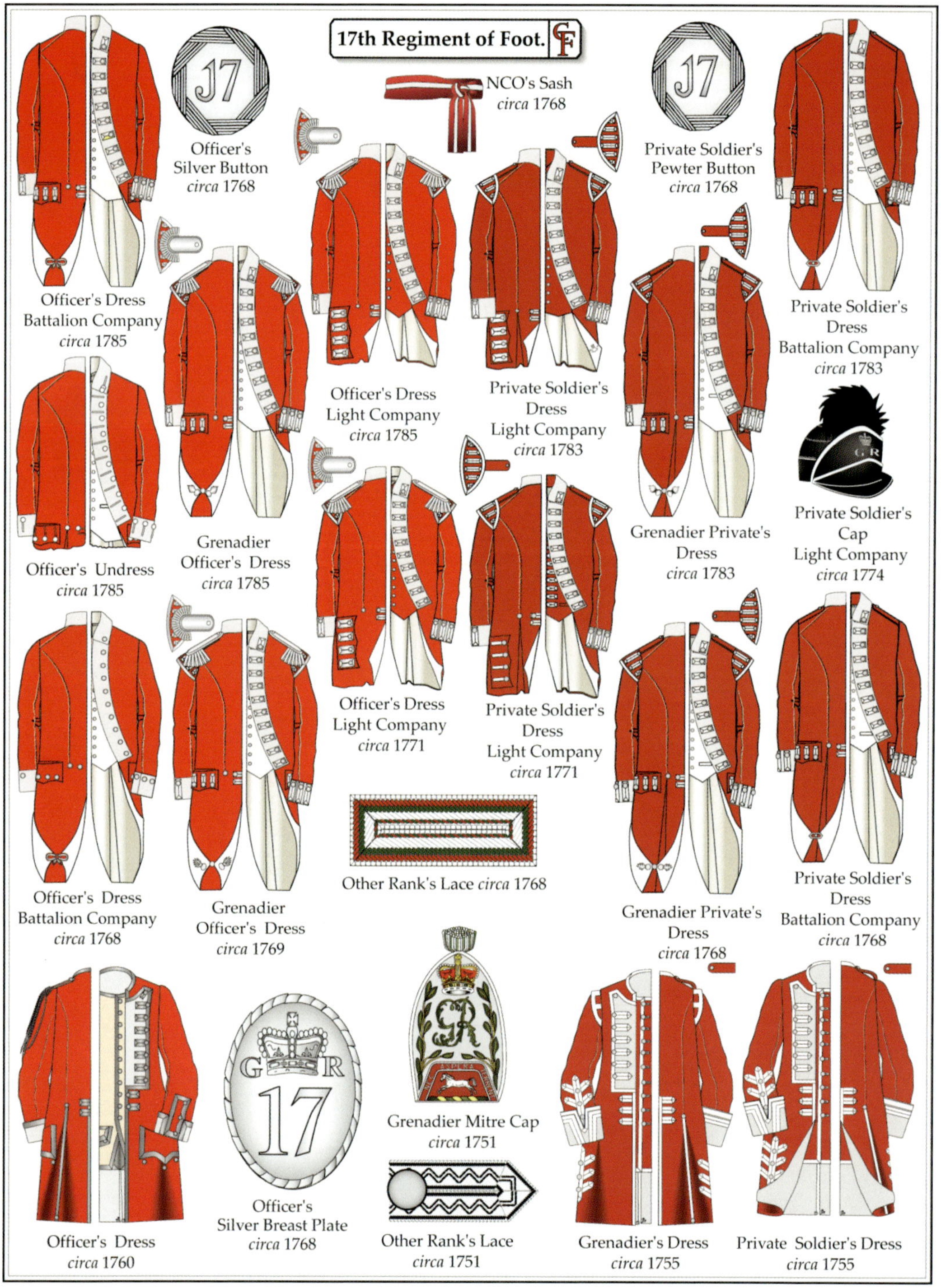
17th Regiment of Foot.
Officer's Silver Button circa 1768
NCO's Sash circa 1768
Private Soldier's Pewter Button circa 1768
Officer's Dress Battalion Company circa 1785
Officer's Dress Light Company circa 1785
Private Soldier's Dress Light Company circa 1783
Private Soldier's Dress Battalion Company circa 1783
Officer's Undress circa 1785
Grenadier Officer's Dress circa 1785
Grenadier Private's Dress circa 1783
Private Soldier's Cap Light Company circa 1774
Officer's Dress Light Company circa 1771
Private Soldier's Dress Light Company circa 1771
Officer's Dress Battalion Company circa 1768
Grenadier Officer's Dress circa 1769
Other Rank's Lace circa 1768
Grenadier Private's Dress circa 1768
Private Soldier's Dress Battalion Company circa 1768
Grenadier Mitre Cap circa 1751
Officer's Dress circa 1760
Officer's Silver Breast Plate circa 1768
Other Rank's Lace circa 1751
Grenadier's Dress circa 1755
Private Soldier's Dress circa 1755

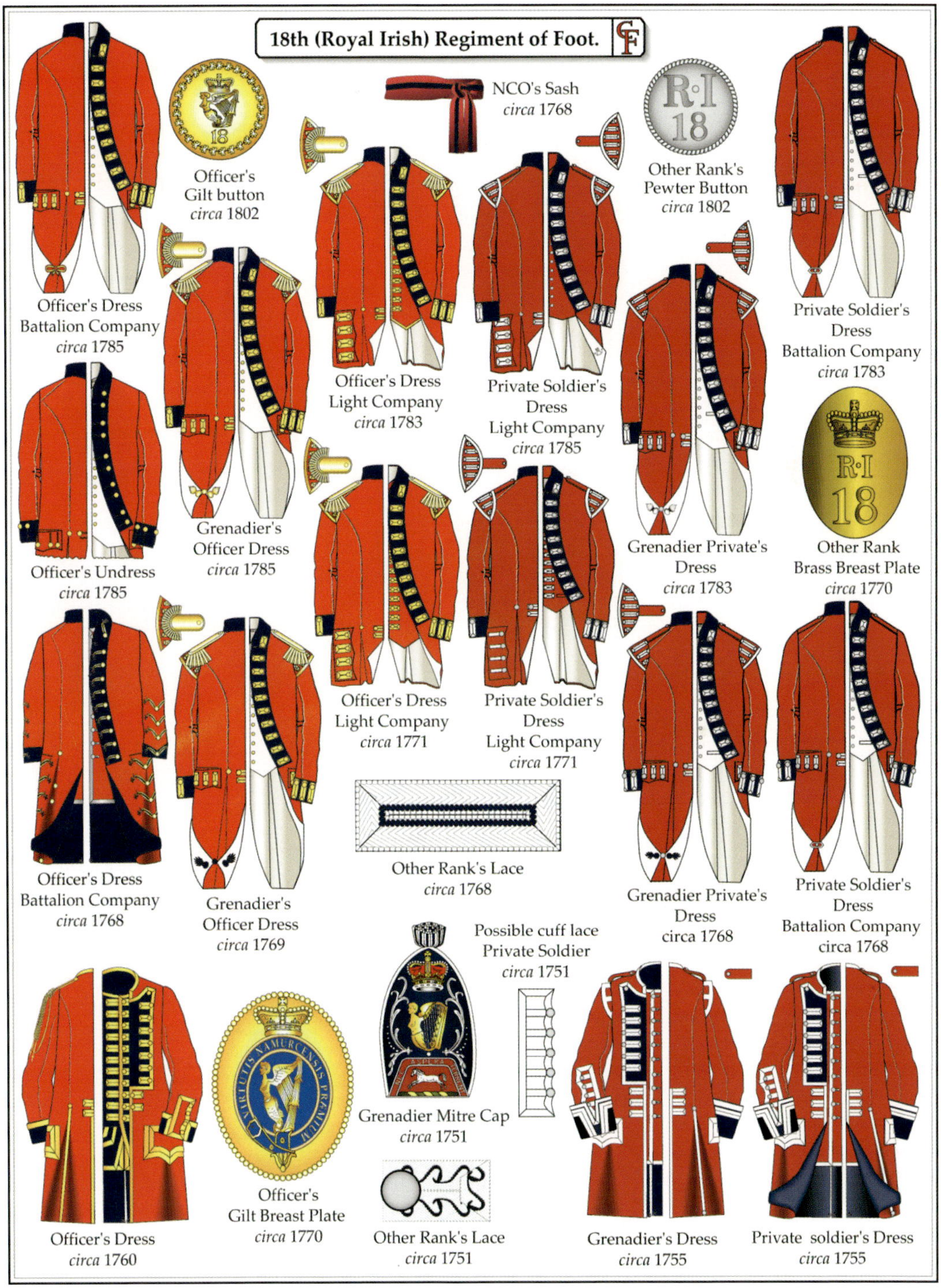
18th (Royal Irish) Regiment of Foot.
CF
Officer's Dress
Battalion Company
circa 1785
Officer's
Gilt button
circa 1802
NCO's Sash
circa 1768
R·I
18
Other Rank's
Pewter Button
circa 1802
Private Soldier's
Dress
Battalion Company
circa 1783
Officer's Dress
Light Company
circa 1783
Private Soldier's
Dress
Light Company
circa 1785
Officer's Undress
circa 1785
Grenadier's
Officer Dress
circa 1785
Grenadier Private's
Dress
circa 1783
R·I
18
Other Rank
Brass Breast Plate
circa 1770
Officer's Dress
Light Company
circa 1771
Private Soldier's
Dress
Light Company
circa 1771
Officer's Dress
Battalion Company
circa 1768
Grenadier's
Officer Dress
circa 1769
Other Rank's Lace
circa 1768
Grenadier Private's
Dress
circa 1768
Private Soldier's
Dress
Battalion Company
circa 1768
Possible cuff lace
Private Soldier
circa 1751
Officer's Dress
circa 1760
VIRTUTIS NAMURCENSIS PRÆMIUM
Officer's
Gilt Breast Plate
circa 1770
Grenadier Mitre Cap
circa 1751
Other Rank's Lace
circa 1751
Grenadier's Dress
circa 1755
Private soldier's Dress
circa 1755

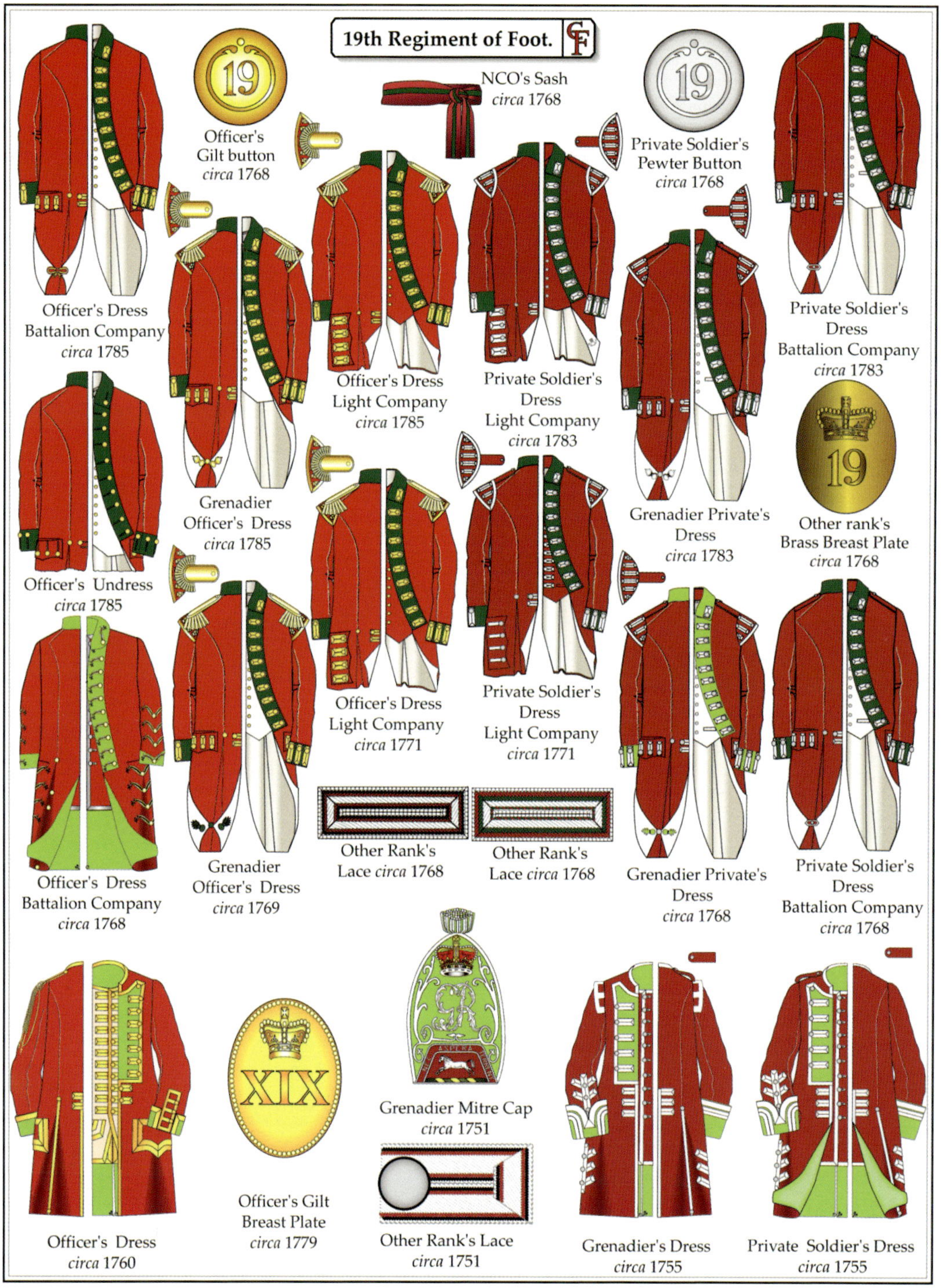
19th Regiment of Foot.
CF
Officer's Gilt button circa 1768
NCO's Sash circa 1768
Private Soldier's Pewter Button circa 1768
19
Officer's Dress Battalion Company circa 1785
Officer's Dress Light Company circa 1785
Private Soldier's Dress Light Company circa 1783
Private Soldier's Dress Battalion Company circa 1783
Grenadier Officer's Dress circa 1785
Grenadier Private's Dress circa 1783
Other rank's Brass Breast Plate circa 1768
Officer's Undress circa 1785
Officer's Dress Light Company circa 1771
Private Soldier's Dress Light Company circa 1771
Officer's Dress Battalion Company circa 1768
Grenadier Officer's Dress circa 1769
Other Rank's Lace circa 1768
Other Rank's Lace circa 1768
Grenadier Private's Dress circa 1768
Private Soldier's Dress Battalion Company circa 1768
XIX
Grenadier Mitre Cap circa 1751
Officer's Dress circa 1760
Officer's Gilt Breast Plate circa 1779
Other Rank's Lace circa 1751
Grenadier's Dress circa 1755
Private Soldier's Dress circa 1755

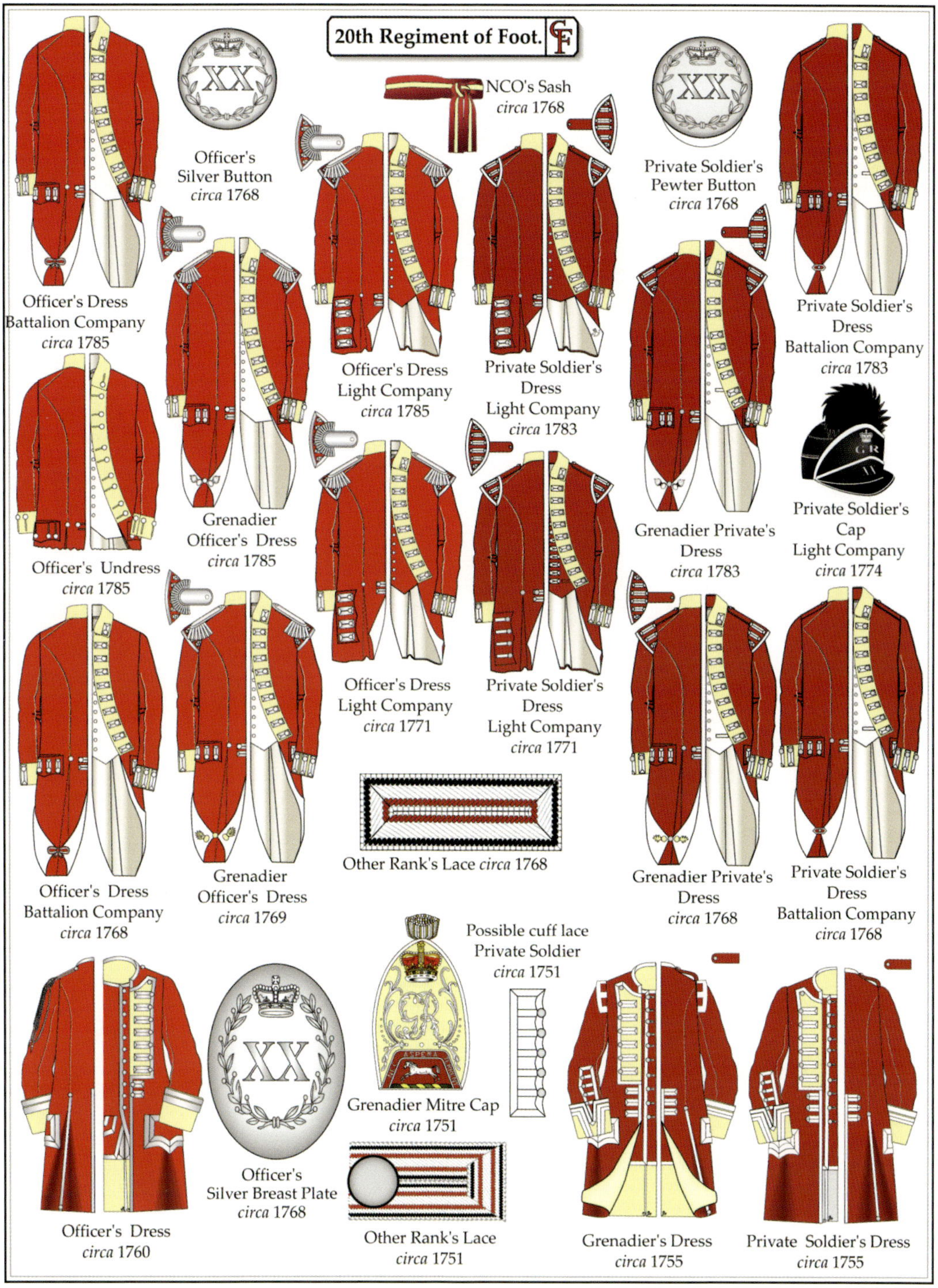
20th Regiment of Foot.
NCO's Sash circa 1768
Officer's Silver Button circa 1768
Private Soldier's Pewter Button circa 1768
Officer's Dress Battalion Company circa 1785
Officer's Dress Light Company circa 1785
Private Soldier's Dress Light Company circa 1783
Private Soldier's Dress Battalion Company circa 1783
Officer's Undress circa 1785
Grenadier Officer's Dress circa 1785
Grenadier Private's Dress circa 1783
Private Soldier's Cap Light Company circa 1774
Officer's Dress Light Company circa 1771
Private Soldier's Dress Light Company circa 1771
Other Rank's Lace circa 1768
Officer's Dress Battalion Company circa 1768
Grenadier Officer's Dress circa 1769
Grenadier Private's Dress circa 1768
Private Soldier's Dress Battalion Company circa 1768
Possible cuff lace Private Soldier circa 1751
Grenadier Mitre Cap circa 1751
Officer's Dress circa 1760
Officer's Silver Breast Plate circa 1768
Other Rank's Lace circa 1751
Grenadier's Dress circa 1755
Private Soldier's Dress circa 1755

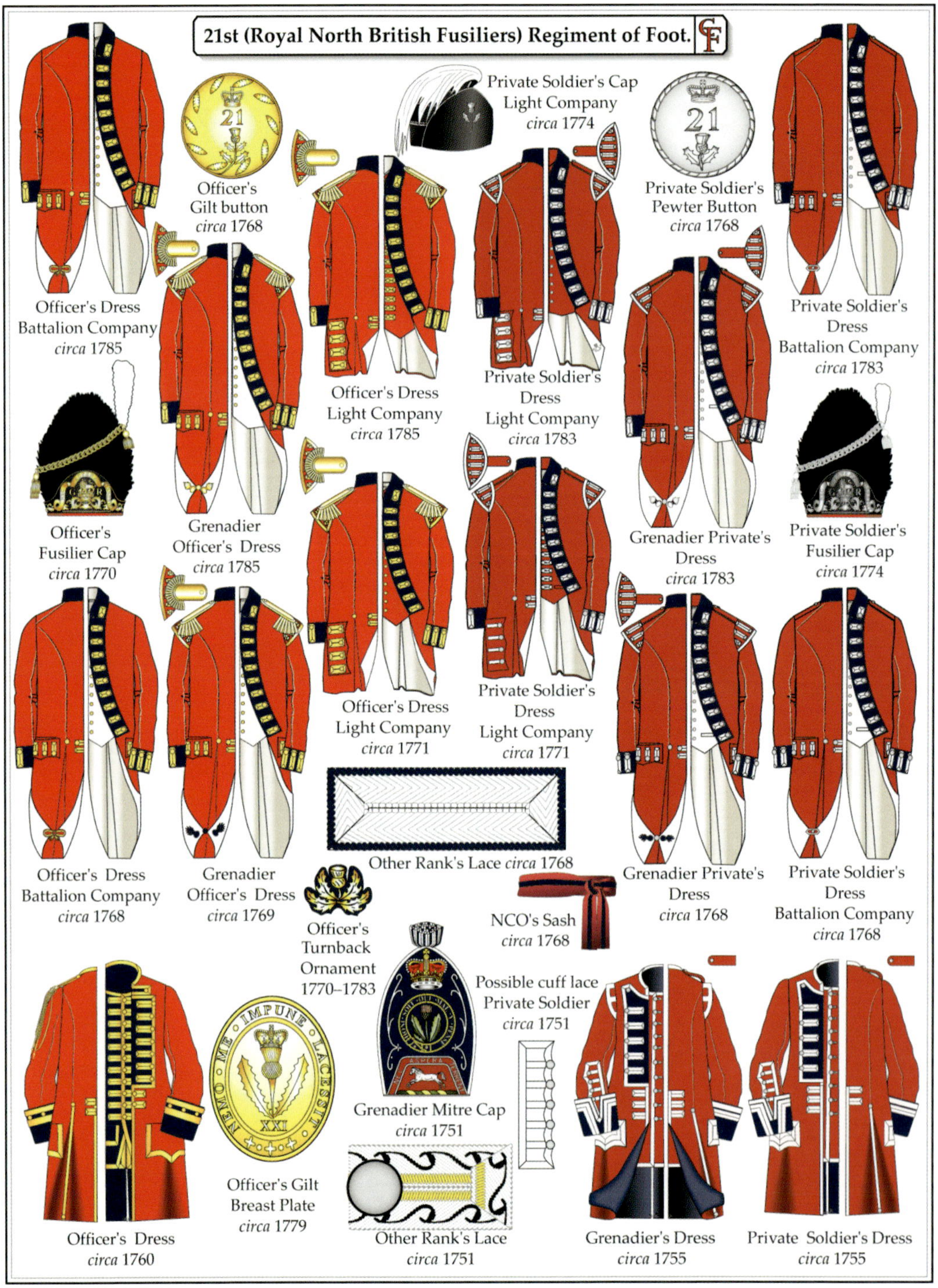
21st (Royal North British Fusiliers) Regiment of Foot.
CF
Officer's Dress
Battalion Company
circa 1785
21
Officer's
Gilt button
circa 1768
Private Soldier's Cap
Light Company
circa 1774
21
Private Soldier's
Pewter Button
circa 1768
Private Soldier's
Dress
Battalion Company
circa 1783
Officer's Dress
Light Company
circa 1785
Private Soldier's
Dress
Light Company
circa 1783
Officer's
Fusilier Cap
circa 1770
Grenadier
Officer's Dress
circa 1785
Grenadier Private's
Dress
circa 1783
Private Soldier's
Fusilier Cap
circa 1774
Officer's Dress
Light Company
circa 1771
Private Soldier's
Dress
Light Company
circa 1771
Officer's Dress
Battalion Company
circa 1768
Grenadier
Officer's Dress
circa 1769
Other Rank's Lace *circa* 1768
Officer's
Turnback
Ornament
1770–1783
NCO's Sash
circa 1768
Grenadier Private's
Dress
circa 1768
Private Soldier's
Dress
Battalion Company
circa 1768
Possible cuff lace
Private Soldier
circa 1751
NEMO ME IMPUNE LACESSIT
XXI
Grenadier Mitre Cap
circa 1751
Officer's Dress
circa 1760
Officer's Gilt
Breast Plate
circa 1779
Other Rank's Lace
circa 1751
Grenadier's Dress
circa 1755
Private Soldier's Dress
circa 1755

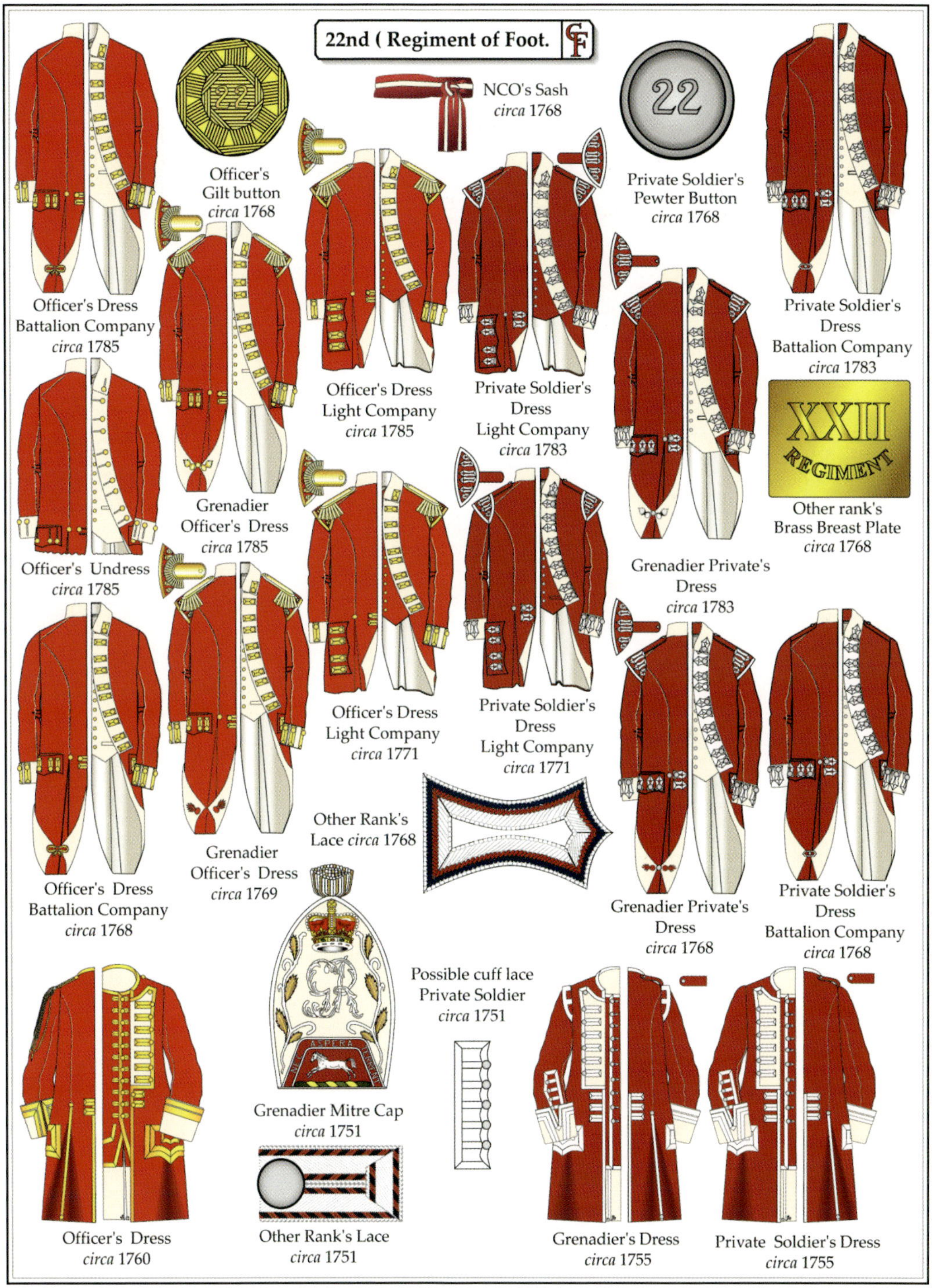
22nd (Regiment of Foot.
Officer's Dress Battalion Company circa 1785
Officer's Gilt button circa 1768
NCO's Sash circa 1768
Private Soldier's Pewter Button circa 1768
Private Soldier's Dress Battalion Company circa 1783
Grenadier Officer's Dress circa 1785
Officer's Dress Light Company circa 1785
Private Soldier's Dress Light Company circa 1783
XXII REGIMENT
Other rank's Brass Breast Plate circa 1768
Officer's Undress circa 1785
Grenadier Private's Dress circa 1783
Officer's Dress Light Company circa 1771
Private Soldier's Dress Light Company circa 1771
Officer's Dress Battalion Company circa 1768
Grenadier Officer's Dress circa 1769
Other Rank's Lace circa 1768
Grenadier Private's Dress circa 1768
Private Soldier's Dress Battalion Company circa 1768
Possible cuff lace Private Soldier circa 1751
Grenadier Mitre Cap circa 1751
Officer's Dress circa 1760
Other Rank's Lace circa 1751
Grenadier's Dress circa 1755
Private Soldier's Dress circa 1755

23rd (Royal Welch Fusiliers) Regiment of Foot.
Officer's Dress Battalion Company circa 1785
Officer's Gilt button circa 1768
Officer's Undress Hat circa 1782
Private Soldier's Pewter Button circa 1768
Private Soldier's Dress Battalion Company circa 1783
Officer's Dress Light Company circa 1785
Private Soldier's Dress Light Company circa 1783
Officer's Fusilier Cap circa 1770
Grenadier Officer's Dress circa 1785
Grenadier Private's Dress circa 1783
Private's Fusilier Cap circa 1783
Officer's Dress Light Company circa 1771
Private Soldier's Dress Light Company circa 1771
Other Rank's Lace circa 1768
Officer's Dress Battalion Company circa 1768
Grenadier Officer's Dress circa 1769
Private's Light Company Cap circa 1780
NCO's Sash Circa 1768
Grenadier Private's Dress circa 1768
Private Soldier's Dress Battalion Company circa 1768
Officer's Turnback Ornament 1770–1783
XXIII
Grenadier Mitre Cap circa 1751
Officer's Dress circa 1760
Officer's Gilt and Silver Breast Plate circa 1775
Other Rank's Lace circa 1751
Possible cuff lacePrivate Soldier circa 1751
Grenadier's Dress circa 1755
Private Soldier's Dress circa 1755

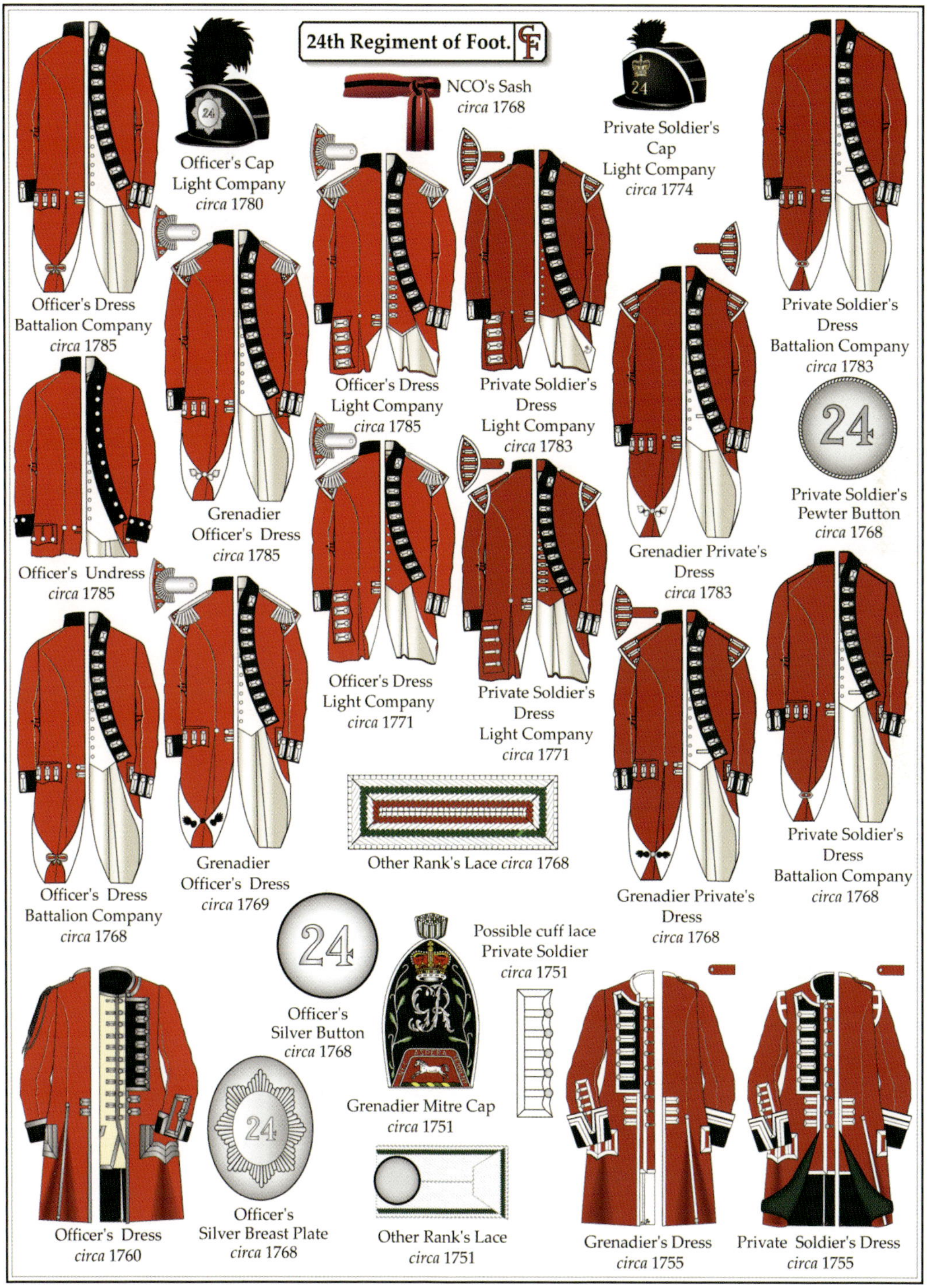
24th Regiment of Foot.
Officer's Dress
Battalion Company
circa 1785
Officer's Cap
Light Company
circa 1780
NCO's Sash
circa 1768
Private Soldier's
Cap
Light Company
circa 1774
Private Soldier's
Dress
Battalion Company
circa 1783
Officer's Dress
Light Company
circa 1785
Private Soldier's
Dress
Light Company
circa 1783
Grenadier
Officer's Dress
circa 1785
Officer's Undress
circa 1785
24
Private Soldier's
Pewter Button
circa 1768
Grenadier Private's
Dress
circa 1783
Officer's Dress
Light Company
circa 1771
Private Soldier's
Dress
Light Company
circa 1771
Officer's Dress
Battalion Company
circa 1768
Grenadier
Officer's Dress
circa 1769
Other Rank's Lace circa 1768
Grenadier Private's
Dress
circa 1768
Private Soldier's
Dress
Battalion Company
circa 1768
24
Officer's
Silver Button
circa 1768
Possible cuff lace
Private Soldier
circa 1751
Grenadier Mitre Cap
circa 1751
24
Officer's
Silver Breast Plate
circa 1768
Officer's Dress
circa 1760
Other Rank's Lace
circa 1751
Grenadier's Dress
circa 1755
Private Soldier's Dress
circa 1755

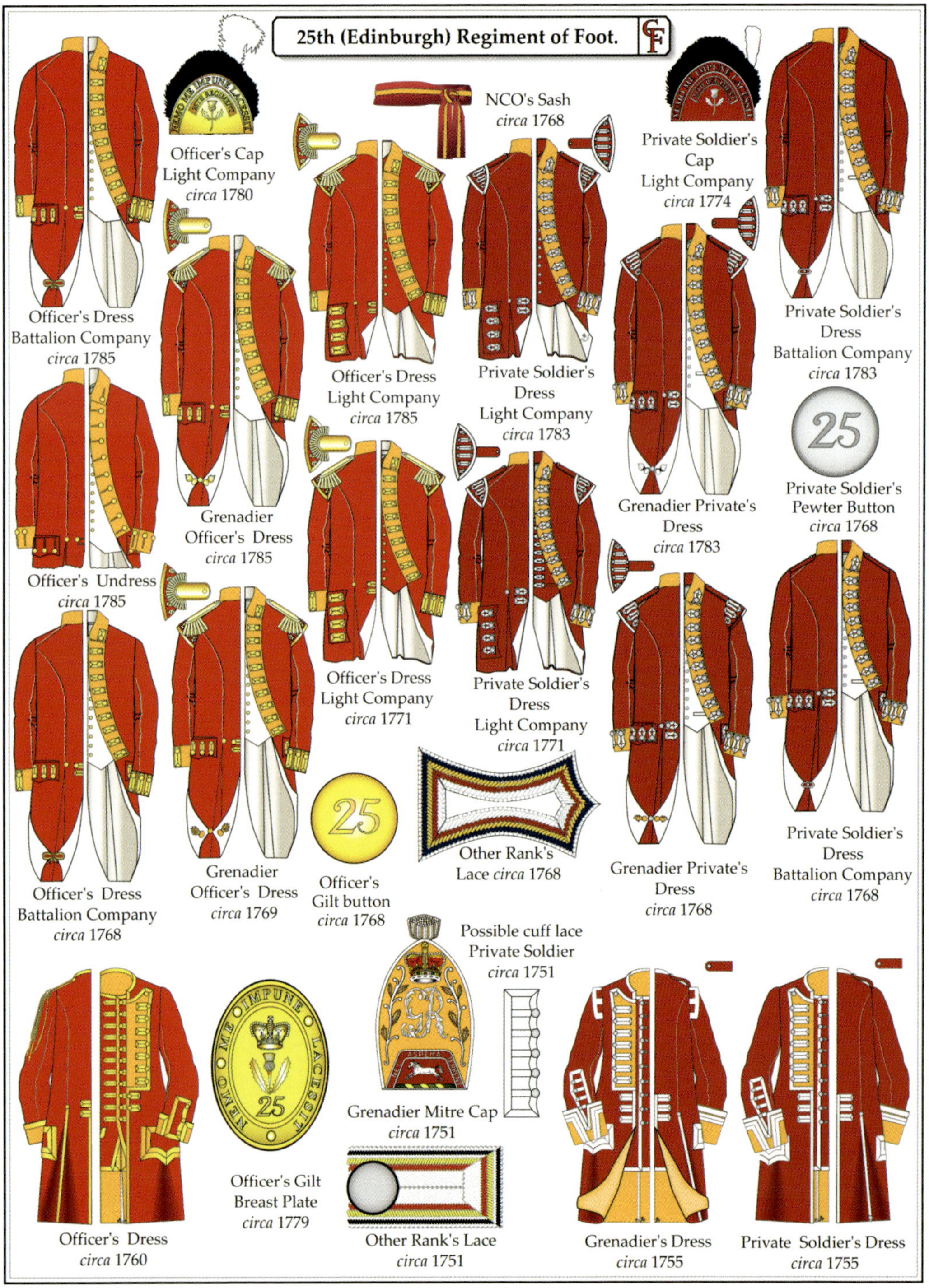
25th (Edinburgh) Regiment of Foot.
CF
Officer's Dress Battalion Company circa 1785
Officer's Cap Light Company circa 1780
NEMO ME IMPUNE LACESSIT
NCO's Sash circa 1768
Private Soldier's Cap Light Company circa 1774
Private Soldier's Dress Battalion Company circa 1783
Grenadier Officer's Dress circa 1785
Officer's Dress Light Company circa 1785
Private Soldier's Dress Light Company circa 1783
Grenadier Private's Dress circa 1783
25
Private Soldier's Pewter Button circa 1768
Officer's Undress circa 1785
Officer's Dress Light Company circa 1771
Private Soldier's Dress Light Company circa 1771
Officer's Dress Battalion Company circa 1768
Grenadier Officer's Dress circa 1769
25
Officer's Gilt button circa 1768
Other Rank's Lace circa 1768
Grenadier Private's Dress circa 1768
Private Soldier's Dress Battalion Company circa 1768
Possible cuff lace Private Soldier circa 1751
NEMO ME IMPUNE LACESSIT
25
Grenadier Mitre Cap circa 1751
Officer's Dress circa 1760
Officer's Gilt Breast Plate circa 1779
Other Rank's Lace circa 1751
Grenadier's Dress circa 1755
Private Soldier's Dress circa 1755

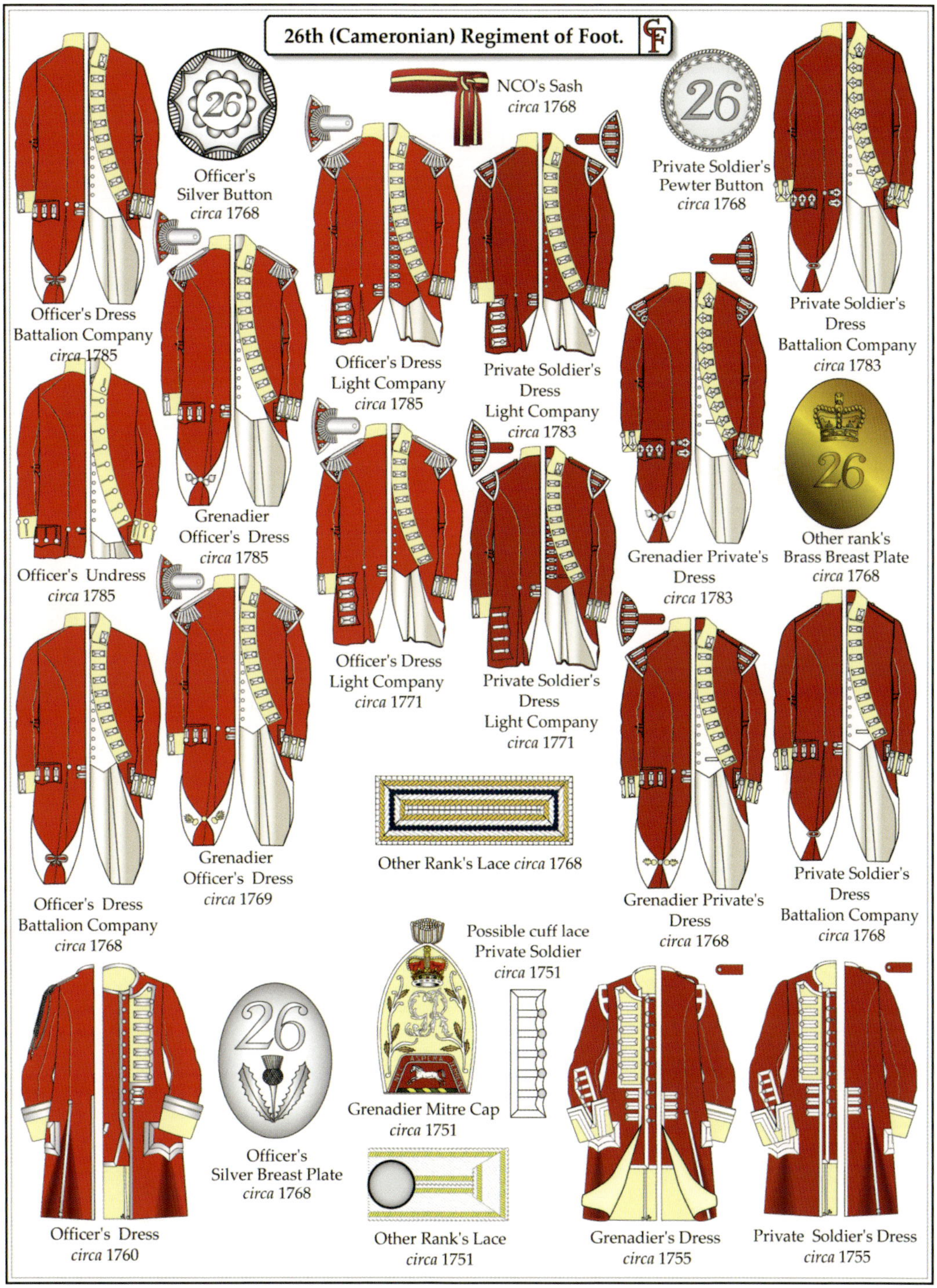
26th (Cameronian) Regiment of Foot.
CF
26
Officer's Silver Button circa 1768
NCO's Sash circa 1768
26
Private Soldier's Pewter Button circa 1768
Officer's Dress Battalion Company circa 1785
Officer's Dress Light Company circa 1785
Private Soldier's Dress Light Company circa 1783
Private Soldier's Dress Battalion Company circa 1783
Officer's Undress circa 1785
Grenadier Officer's Dress circa 1785
Grenadier Private's Dress circa 1783
26
Other rank's Brass Breast Plate circa 1768
Officer's Dress Light Company circa 1771
Private Soldier's Dress Light Company circa 1771
Officer's Dress Battalion Company circa 1768
Grenadier Officer's Dress circa 1769
Other Rank's Lace circa 1768
Grenadier Private's Dress circa 1768
Private Soldier's Dress Battalion Company circa 1768
Possible cuff lace Private Soldier circa 1751
Grenadier Mitre Cap circa 1751
26
Officer's Dress circa 1760
Officer's Silver Breast Plate circa 1768
Other Rank's Lace circa 1751
Grenadier's Dress circa 1755
Private Soldier's Dress circa 1755

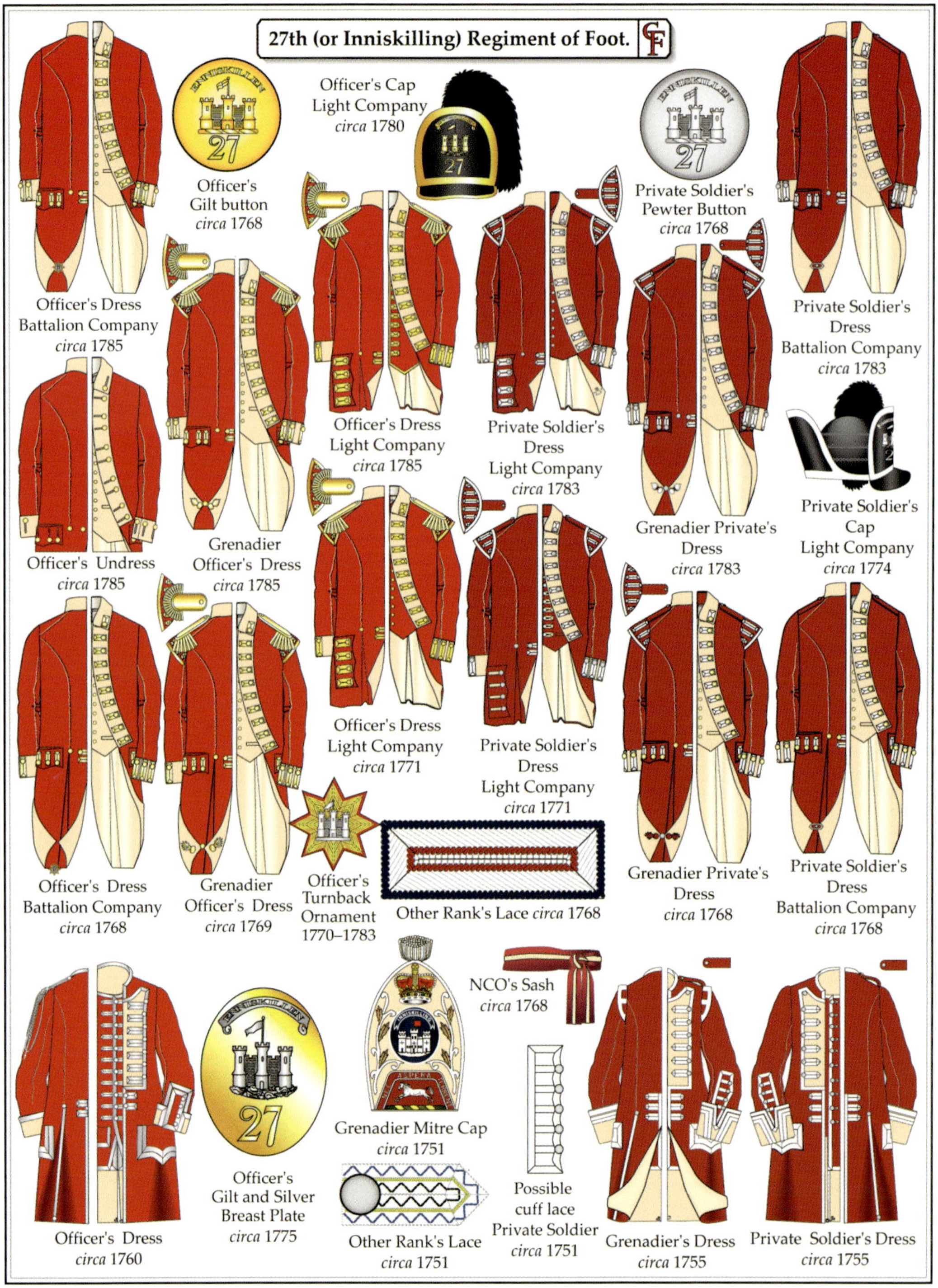
27th (or Inniskilling) Regiment of Foot.
Officer's Dress Battalion Company circa 1785
Officer's Gilt button circa 1768
Officer's Cap Light Company circa 1780
Private Soldier's Pewter Button circa 1768
Private Soldier's Dress Battalion Company circa 1783
Officer's Dress Light Company circa 1785
Private Soldier's Dress Light Company circa 1783
Officer's Undress circa 1785
Grenadier Officer's Dress circa 1785
Grenadier Private's Dress circa 1783
Private Soldier's Cap Light Company circa 1774
Officer's Dress Light Company circa 1771
Private Soldier's Dress Light Company circa 1771
Officer's Dress Battalion Company circa 1768
Grenadier Officer's Dress circa 1769
Officer's Turnback Ornament 1770–1783
Other Rank's Lace circa 1768
Grenadier Private's Dress circa 1768
Private Soldier's Dress Battalion Company circa 1768
NCO's Sash circa 1768
Grenadier Mitre Cap circa 1751
Officer's Dress circa 1760
Officer's Gilt and Silver Breast Plate circa 1775
Other Rank's Lace circa 1751
Possible cuff lace Private Soldier circa 1751
Grenadier's Dress circa 1755
Private Soldier's Dress circa 1755

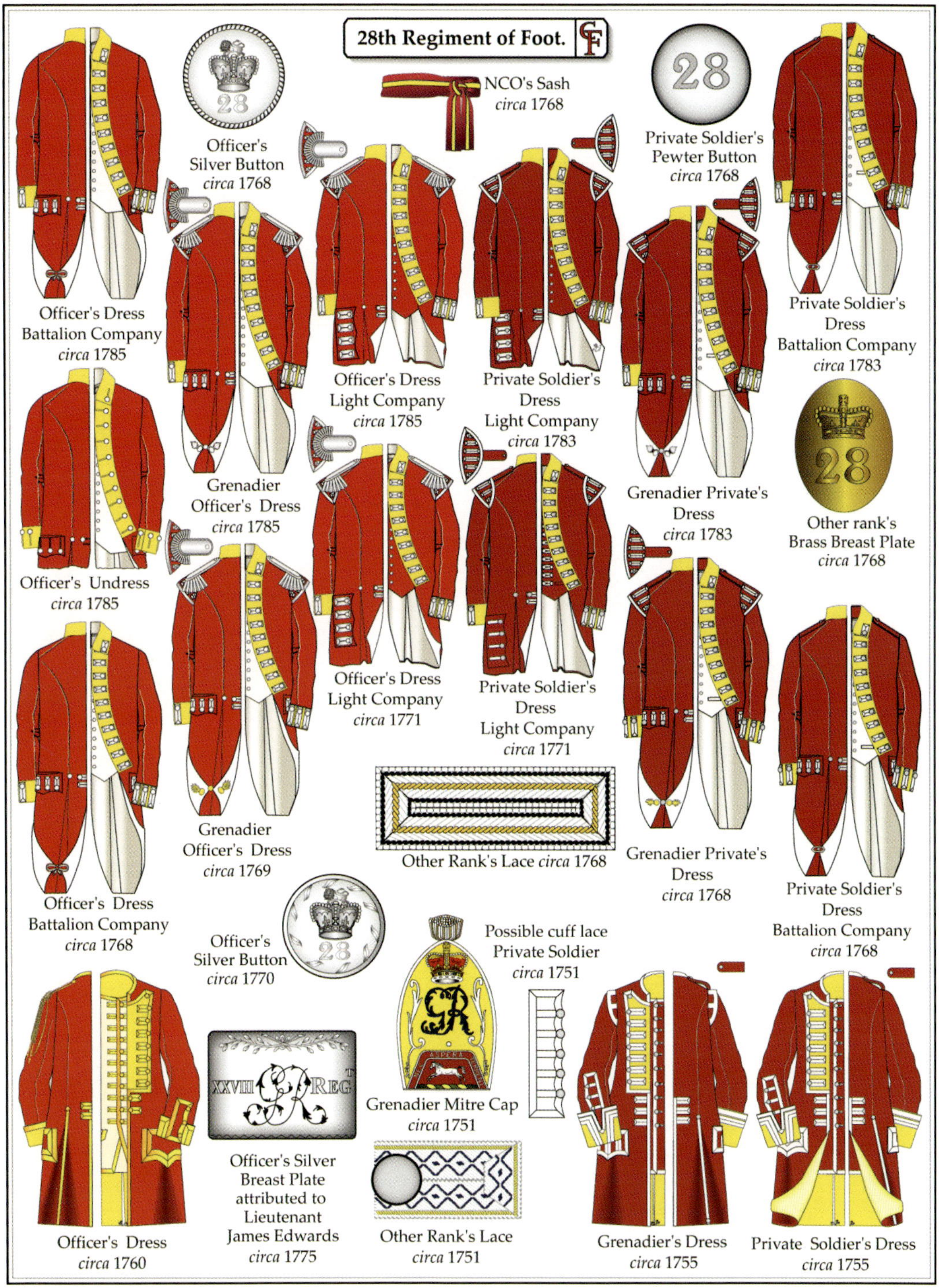
28th Regiment of Foot.
NCO's Sash circa 1768
Officer's Silver Button circa 1768
Private Soldier's Pewter Button circa 1768
Officer's Dress Battalion Company circa 1785
Officer's Dress Light Company circa 1785
Private Soldier's Dress Light Company circa 1783
Private Soldier's Dress Battalion Company circa 1783
Grenadier Officer's Dress circa 1785
Grenadier Private's Dress circa 1783
Other rank's Brass Breast Plate circa 1768
Officer's Undress circa 1785
Officer's Dress Light Company circa 1771
Private Soldier's Dress Light Company circa 1771
Officer's Dress Battalion Company circa 1768
Grenadier Officer's Dress circa 1769
Other Rank's Lace circa 1768
Grenadier Private's Dress circa 1768
Private Soldier's Dress Battalion Company circa 1768
Officer's Silver Button circa 1770
Possible cuff lace Private Soldier circa 1751
Grenadier Mitre Cap circa 1751
XXVIII
REG
Officer's Dress circa 1760
Officer's Silver Breast Plate attributed to Lieutenant James Edwards circa 1775
Other Rank's Lace circa 1751
Grenadier's Dress circa 1755
Private Soldier's Dress circa 1755

29th Regiment of Foot.
Officer's Silver Button *circa* 1768
NCO's Sash *circa* 1768
Private Soldier's Pewter Button *circa* 1768
Officer's Dress Battalion Company *circa* 1785
Grenadier Officer's Dress *circa* 1785
Officer's Dress Light Company *circa* 1785
Private Soldier's Dress Light Company *circa* 1783
Grenadier Private's Dress *circa* 1783
Private Soldier's Dress Battalion Company *circa* 1783
Other rank's Brass Breast Plate *circa* 1768
Officer's Undress *circa* 1785
Grenadier Officer's Dress *circa* 1769
Officer's Dress Light Company *circa* 1771
Private Soldier's Dress Light Company *circa* 1771
Grenadier Private's Dress *circa* 1768
Officer's Dress Battalion Company *circa* 1768
Other Rank's Lace *circa* 1768
Private Soldier's Dress Battalion Company *circa* 1768
Possible cuff lace Private Soldier *circa* 1751
Grenadier Mitre Cap *circa* 1751
Officer's Dress *circa* 1760
Officer's Silver Breast Plate *circa* 1768
Other Rank's Lace *circa* 1751
Grenadier's Dress *circa* 1755
Private Soldier's Dress *circa* 1755

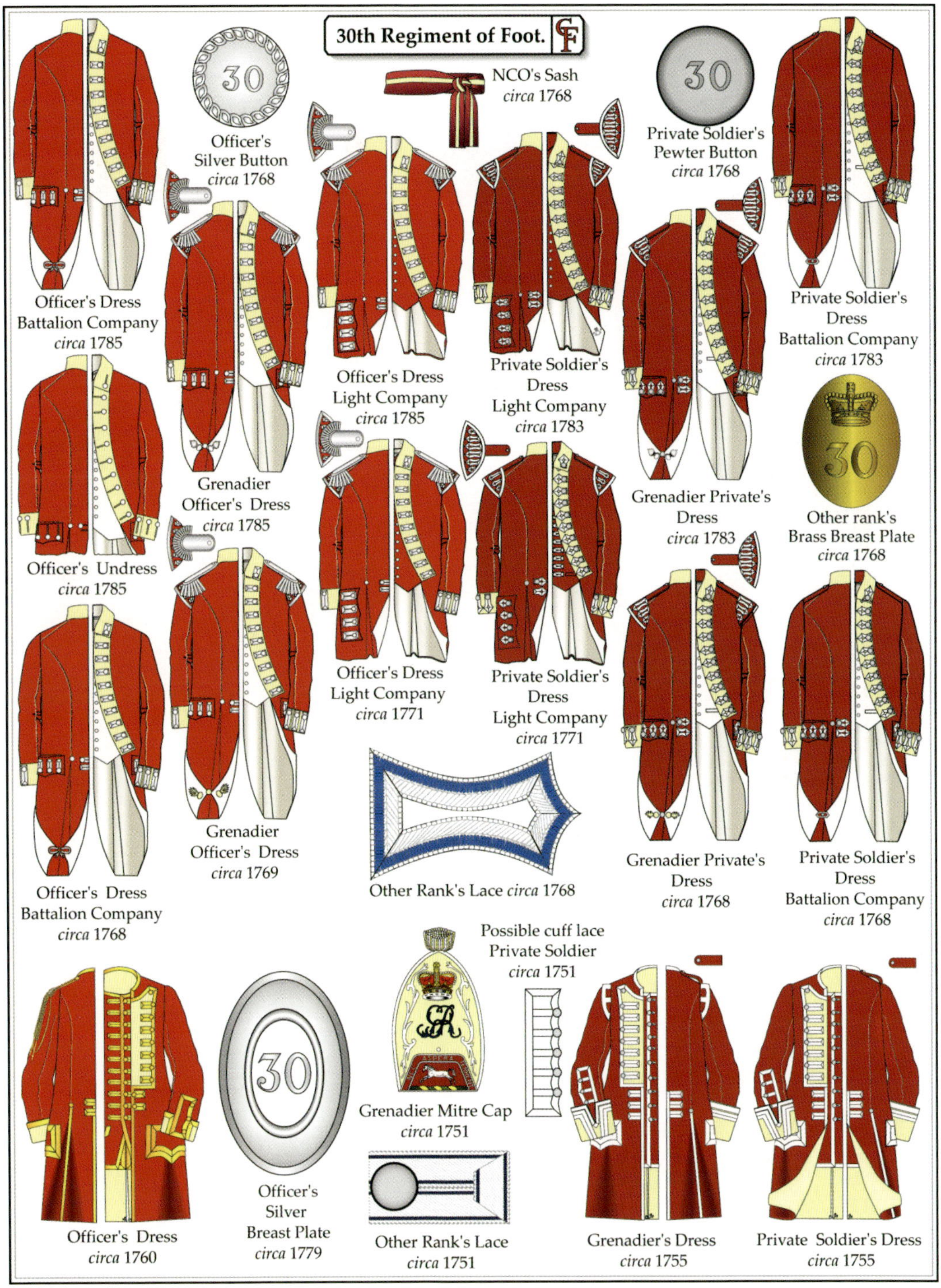
30th Regiment of Foot.
CF
Officer's Dress Battalion Company circa 1785
Officer's Silver Button circa 1768
NCO's Sash circa 1768
Private Soldier's Pewter Button circa 1768
Private Soldier's Dress Battalion Company circa 1783
Grenadier Officer's Dress circa 1785
Officer's Dress Light Company circa 1785
Private Soldier's Dress Light Company circa 1783
Grenadier Private's Dress circa 1783
Other rank's Brass Breast Plate circa 1768
Officer's Undress circa 1785
Officer's Dress Light Company circa 1771
Private Soldier's Dress Light Company circa 1771
Officer's Dress Battalion Company circa 1768
Grenadier Officer's Dress circa 1769
Other Rank's Lace circa 1768
Grenadier Private's Dress circa 1768
Private Soldier's Dress Battalion Company circa 1768
Possible cuff lace Private Soldier circa 1751
Officer's Dress circa 1760
Officer's Silver Breast Plate circa 1779
Grenadier Mitre Cap circa 1751
Other Rank's Lace circa 1751
Grenadier's Dress circa 1755
Private Soldier's Dress circa 1755

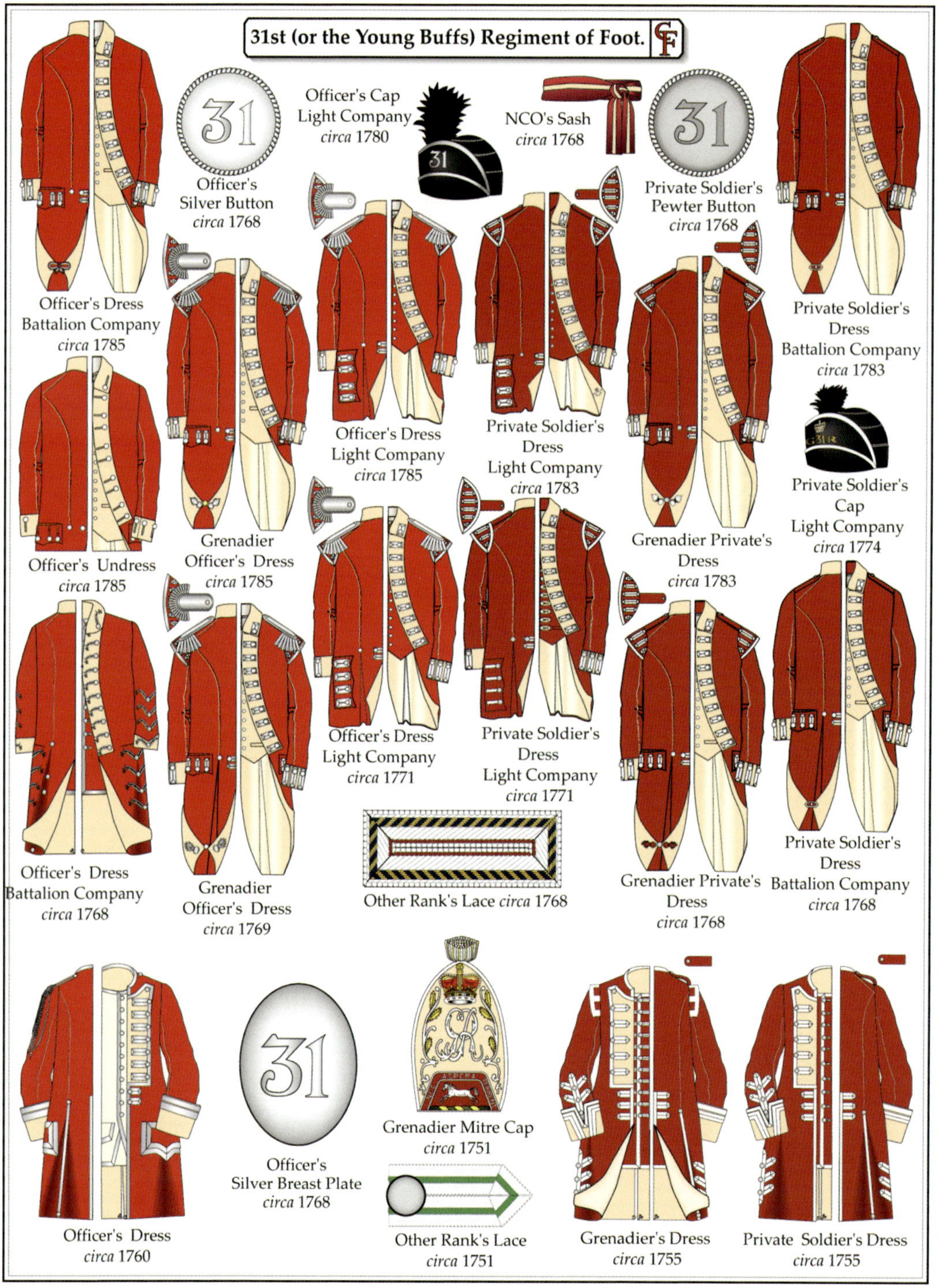
31st (or the Young Buffs) Regiment of Foot.
CF
Officer's Silver Button circa 1768
Officer's Cap Light Company circa 1780
NCO's Sash circa 1768
Private Soldier's Pewter Button circa 1768
Officer's Dress Battalion Company circa 1785
Private Soldier's Dress Battalion Company circa 1783
Officer's Dress Light Company circa 1785
Private Soldier's Dress Light Company circa 1783
Officer's Undress circa 1785
Grenadier Officer's Dress circa 1785
Grenadier Private's Dress circa 1783
Private Soldier's Cap Light Company circa 1774
Officer's Dress Light Company circa 1771
Private Soldier's Dress Light Company circa 1771
Officer's Dress Battalion Company circa 1768
Grenadier Officer's Dress circa 1769
Other Rank's Lace circa 1768
Grenadier Private's Dress circa 1768
Private Soldier's Dress Battalion Company circa 1768
Officer's Dress circa 1760
Officer's Silver Breast Plate circa 1768
Grenadier Mitre Cap circa 1751
Other Rank's Lace circa 1751
Grenadier's Dress circa 1755
Private Soldier's Dress circa 1755

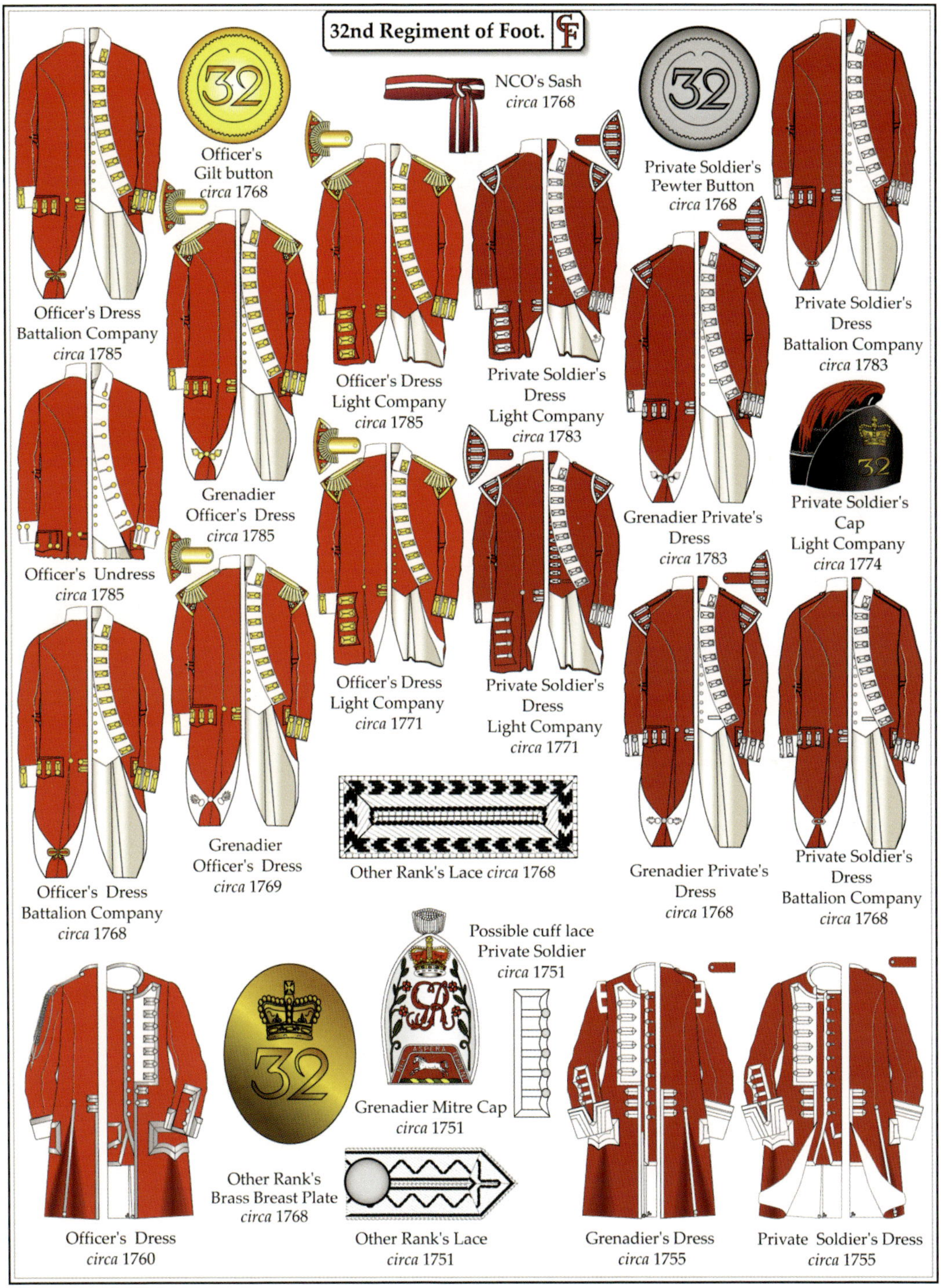
32nd Regiment of Foot.
CF
Officer's Gilt button circa 1768
NCO's Sash circa 1768
32
Private Soldier's Pewter Button circa 1768
Officer's Dress Battalion Company circa 1785
Officer's Dress Light Company circa 1785
Private Soldier's Dress Light Company circa 1783
Private Soldier's Dress Battalion Company circa 1783
Grenadier Officer's Dress circa 1785
Grenadier Private's Dress circa 1783
Private Soldier's Cap Light Company circa 1774
Officer's Undress circa 1785
Officer's Dress Light Company circa 1771
Private Soldier's Dress Light Company circa 1771
Other Rank's Lace circa 1768
Grenadier Officer's Dress circa 1769
Officer's Dress Battalion Company circa 1768
Grenadier Private's Dress circa 1768
Private Soldier's Dress Battalion Company circa 1768
Possible cuff lace Private Soldier circa 1751
GR
Grenadier Mitre Cap circa 1751
Officer's Dress circa 1760
Other Rank's Brass Breast Plate circa 1768
Other Rank's Lace circa 1751
Grenadier's Dress circa 1755
Private Soldier's Dress circa 1755

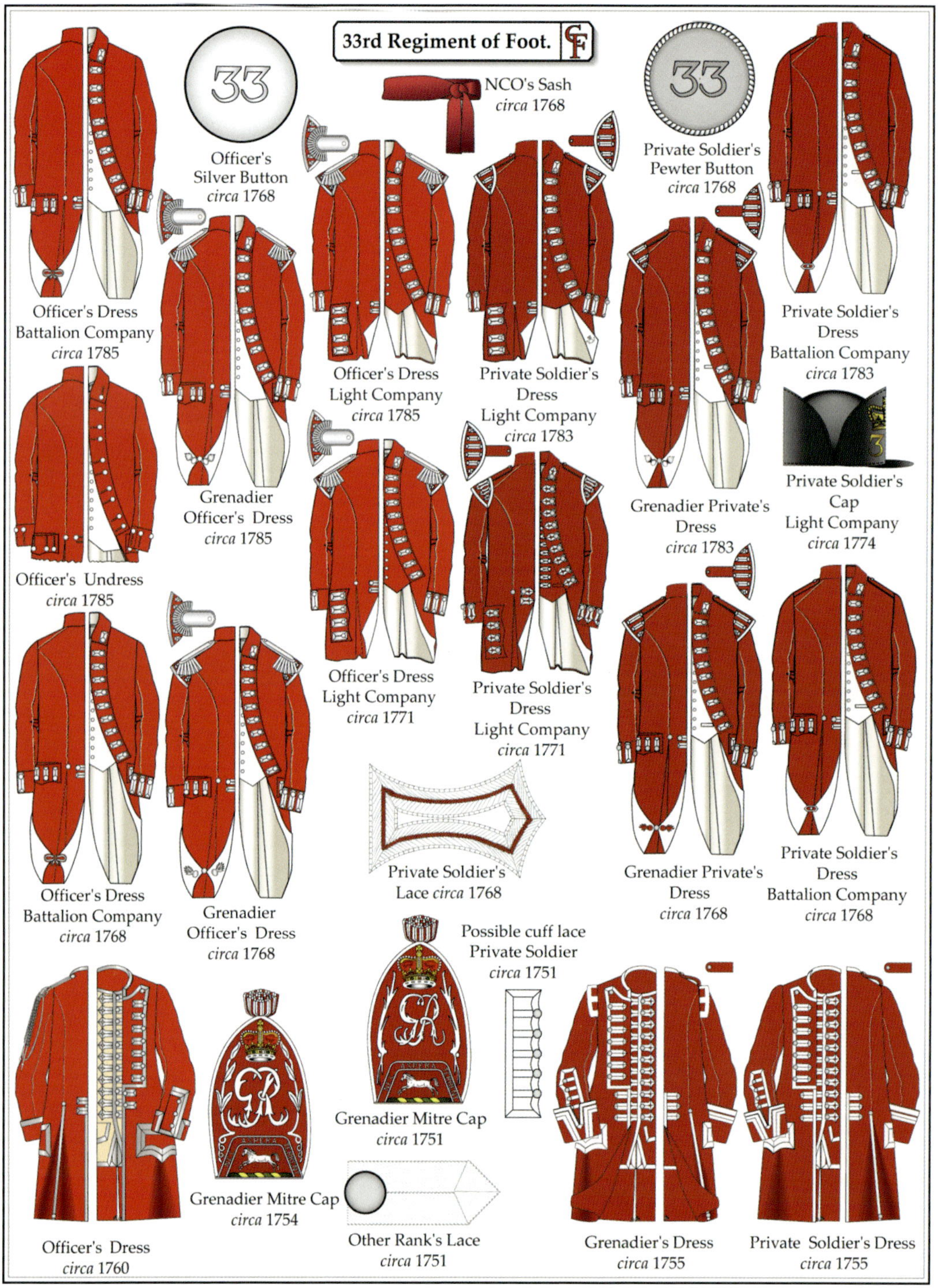
33rd Regiment of Foot.
Officer's Silver Button circa 1768
NCO's Sash circa 1768
Private Soldier's Pewter Button circa 1768
Officer's Dress Battalion Company circa 1785
Grenadier Officer's Dress circa 1785
Officer's Dress Light Company circa 1785
Private Soldier's Dress Light Company circa 1783
Grenadier Private's Dress circa 1783
Private Soldier's Dress Battalion Company circa 1783
Private Soldier's Cap Light Company circa 1774
Officer's Undress circa 1785
Officer's Dress Light Company circa 1771
Private Soldier's Dress Light Company circa 1771
Officer's Dress Battalion Company circa 1768
Grenadier Officer's Dress circa 1768
Private Soldier's Lace circa 1768
Grenadier Private's Dress circa 1768
Private Soldier's Dress Battalion Company circa 1768
Possible cuff lace Private Soldier circa 1751
Grenadier Mitre Cap circa 1751
Officer's Dress circa 1760
Grenadier Mitre Cap circa 1754
Other Rank's Lace circa 1751
Grenadier's Dress circa 1755
Private Soldier's Dress circa 1755

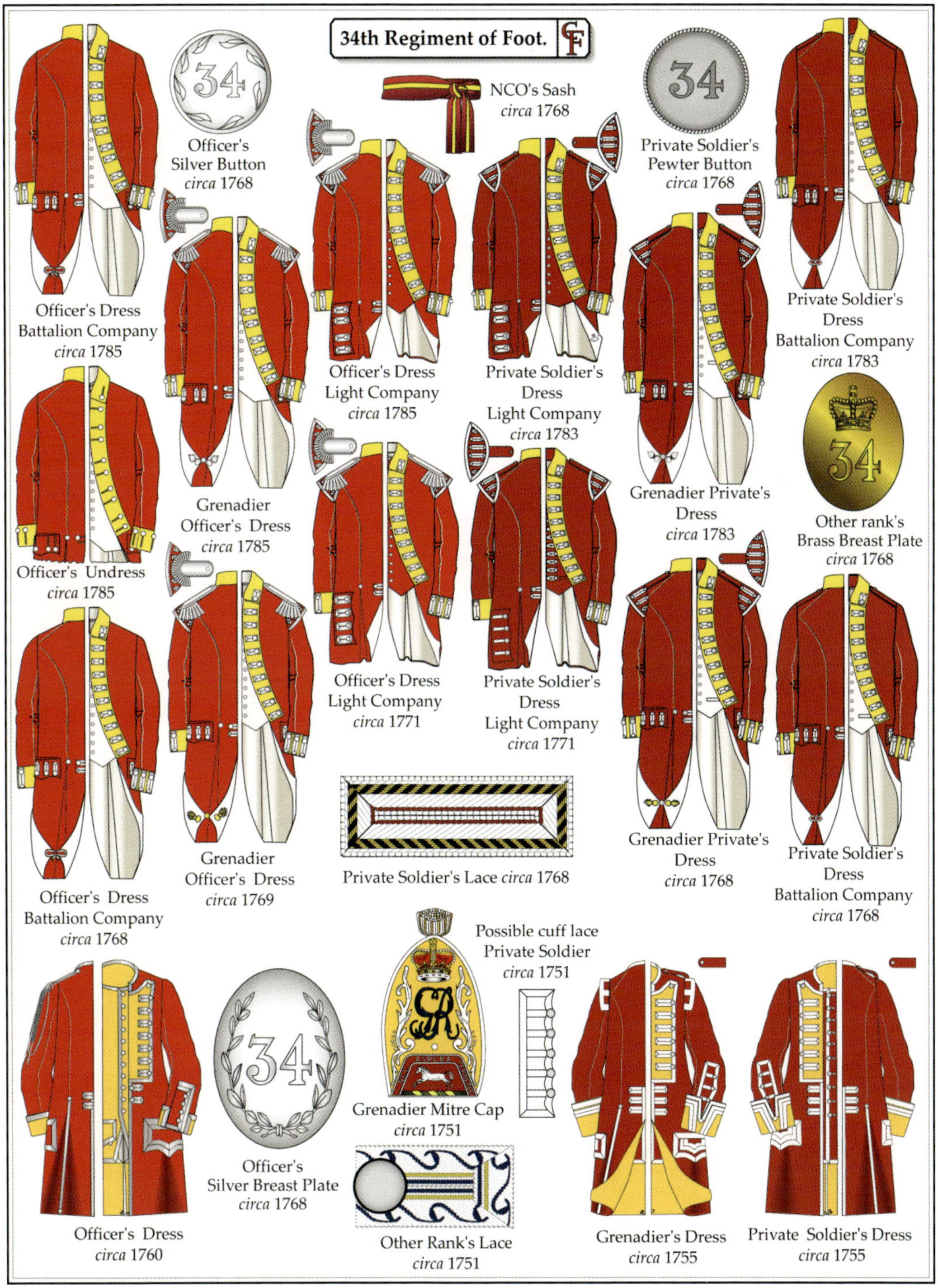
34th Regiment of Foot.
CF
Officer's Silver Button circa 1768
NCO's Sash circa 1768
Private Soldier's Pewter Button circa 1768
Officer's Dress Battalion Company circa 1785
Officer's Dress Light Company circa 1785
Private Soldier's Dress Light Company circa 1783
Private Soldier's Dress Battalion Company circa 1783
Grenadier Officer's Dress circa 1785
Grenadier Private's Dress circa 1783
Other rank's Brass Breast Plate circa 1768
Officer's Undress circa 1785
Officer's Dress Light Company circa 1771
Private Soldier's Dress Light Company circa 1771
Officer's Dress Battalion Company circa 1768
Grenadier Officer's Dress circa 1769
Private Soldier's Lace circa 1768
Grenadier Private's Dress circa 1768
Private Soldier's Dress Battalion Company circa 1768
Possible cuff lace Private Soldier circa 1751
Officer's Dress circa 1760
Officer's Silver Breast Plate circa 1768
Grenadier Mitre Cap circa 1751
Other Rank's Lace circa 1751
Grenadier's Dress circa 1755
Private Soldier's Dress circa 1755

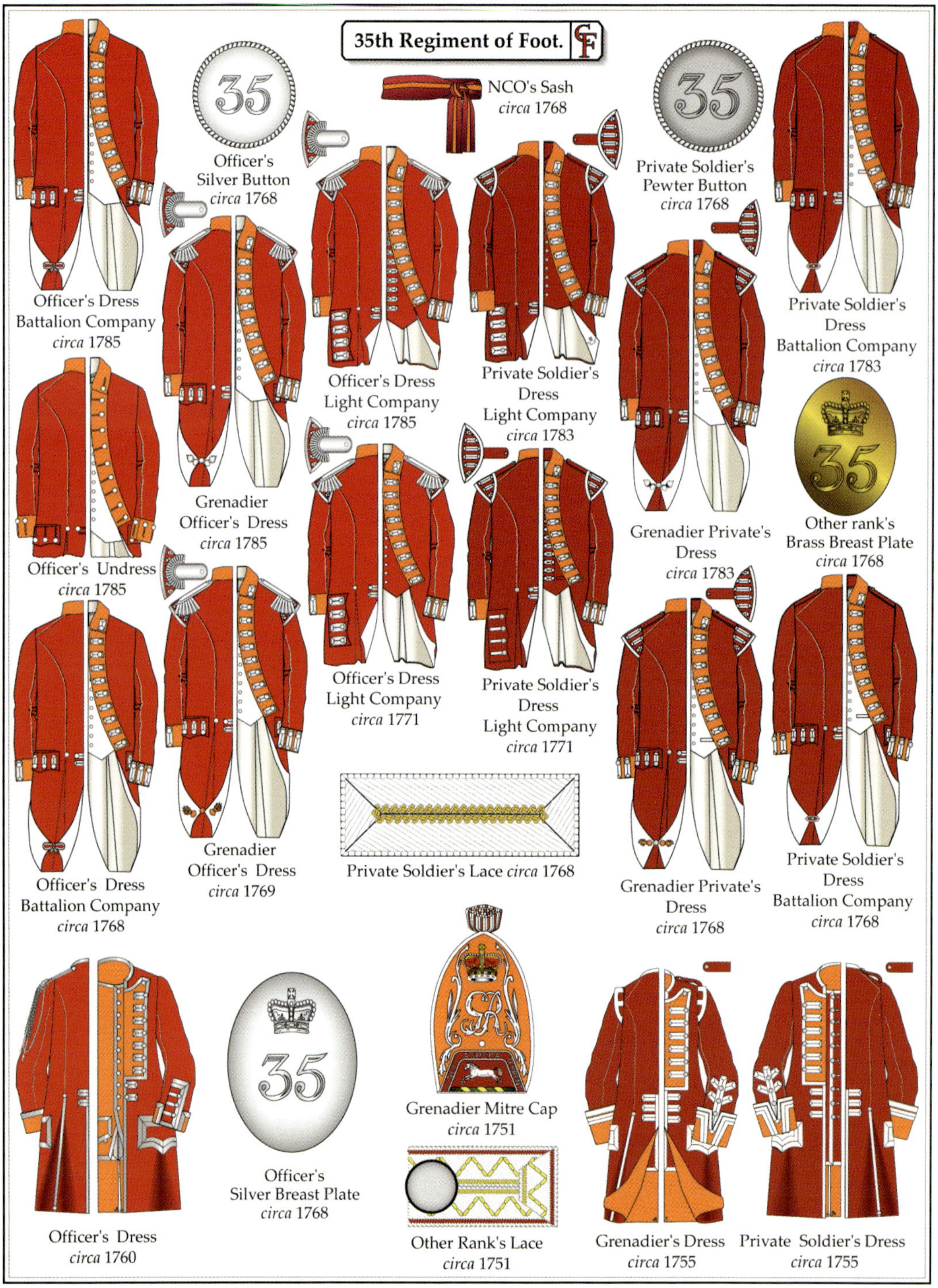
35th Regiment of Foot.
NCO's Sash *circa* 1768
Officer's Silver Button *circa* 1768
Private Soldier's Pewter Button *circa* 1768
Officer's Dress Battalion Company *circa* 1785
Officer's Dress Light Company *circa* 1785
Private Soldier's Dress Light Company *circa* 1783
Private Soldier's Dress Battalion Company *circa* 1783
Grenadier Officer's Dress *circa* 1785
Officer's Undress *circa* 1785
Grenadier Private's Dress *circa* 1783
Other rank's Brass Breast Plate *circa* 1768
Officer's Dress Light Company *circa* 1771
Private Soldier's Dress Light Company *circa* 1771
Officer's Dress Battalion Company *circa* 1768
Grenadier Officer's Dress *circa* 1769
Private Soldier's Lace *circa* 1768
Grenadier Private's Dress *circa* 1768
Private Soldier's Dress Battalion Company *circa* 1768
Grenadier Mitre Cap *circa* 1751
Officer's Dress *circa* 1760
Officer's Silver Breast Plate *circa* 1768
Other Rank's Lace *circa* 1751
Grenadier's Dress *circa* 1755
Private Soldier's Dress *circa* 1755

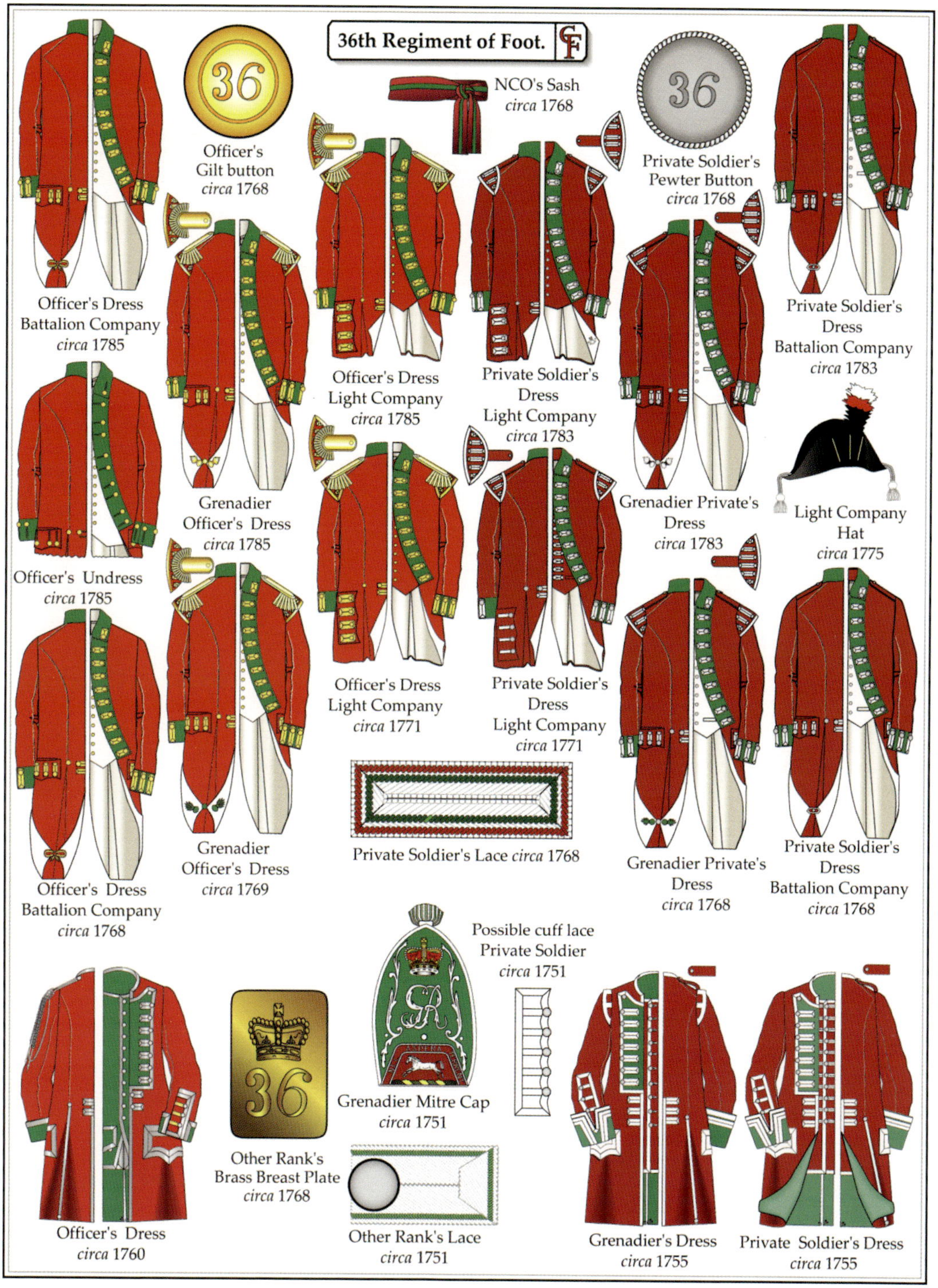
36th Regiment of Foot.
Officer's Dress
Battalion Company
circa 1785
36
Officer's
Gilt button
circa 1768
NCO's Sash
circa 1768
Officer's Dress
Light Company
circa 1785
Private Soldier's
Dress
Light Company
circa 1783
36
Private Soldier's
Pewter Button
circa 1768
Private Soldier's
Dress
Battalion Company
circa 1783
Grenadier
Officer's Dress
circa 1785
Grenadier Private's
Dress
circa 1783
Light Company
Hat
circa 1775
Officer's Undress
circa 1785
Officer's Dress
Light Company
circa 1771
Private Soldier's
Dress
Light Company
circa 1771
Officer's Dress
Battalion Company
circa 1768
Grenadier
Officer's Dress
circa 1769
Private Soldier's Lace circa 1768
Grenadier Private's
Dress
circa 1768
Private Soldier's
Dress
Battalion Company
circa 1768
Possible cuff lace
Private Soldier
circa 1751
Officer's Dress
circa 1760
36
Other Rank's
Brass Breast Plate
circa 1768
Grenadier Mitre Cap
circa 1751
Other Rank's Lace
circa 1751
Grenadier's Dress
circa 1755
Private Soldier's Dress
circa 1755

37th Regiment of Foot.
Officer's Dress
Battalion Company
circa 1785
Officer's
Silver Button
circa 1768
NCO's Sash
circa 1768
Private Soldier's
Pewter Button
circa 1768
Private Soldier's
Dress
Battalion Company
circa 1783
Officer's Dress
Light Company
circa 1785
Private Soldier's
Dress
Light Company
circa 1783
Grenadier
Officer's Dress
circa 1785
Officer's Undress
circa 1785
Grenadier Private's
Dress
circa 1783
Other rank's
Brass Breast Plate
circa 1768
Officer's Dress
Light Company
circa 1771
Private Soldier's
Dress
Light Company
circa 1771
Grenadier
Officer's Dress
circa 1769
Officer's Dress
Battalion Company
circa 1768
Other Rank's Lace circa 1768
Grenadier Private's
Dress
circa 1768
Private Soldier's
Dress
Battalion Company
circa 1768
Officer's Dress
circa 1760
Officer's
Silver Breast Plate
circa 1780
Grenadier Mitre Cap
circa 1751
Other Rank's Lace
circa 1751
Grenadier's Dress
circa 1755
Private Soldier's Dress
circa 1755

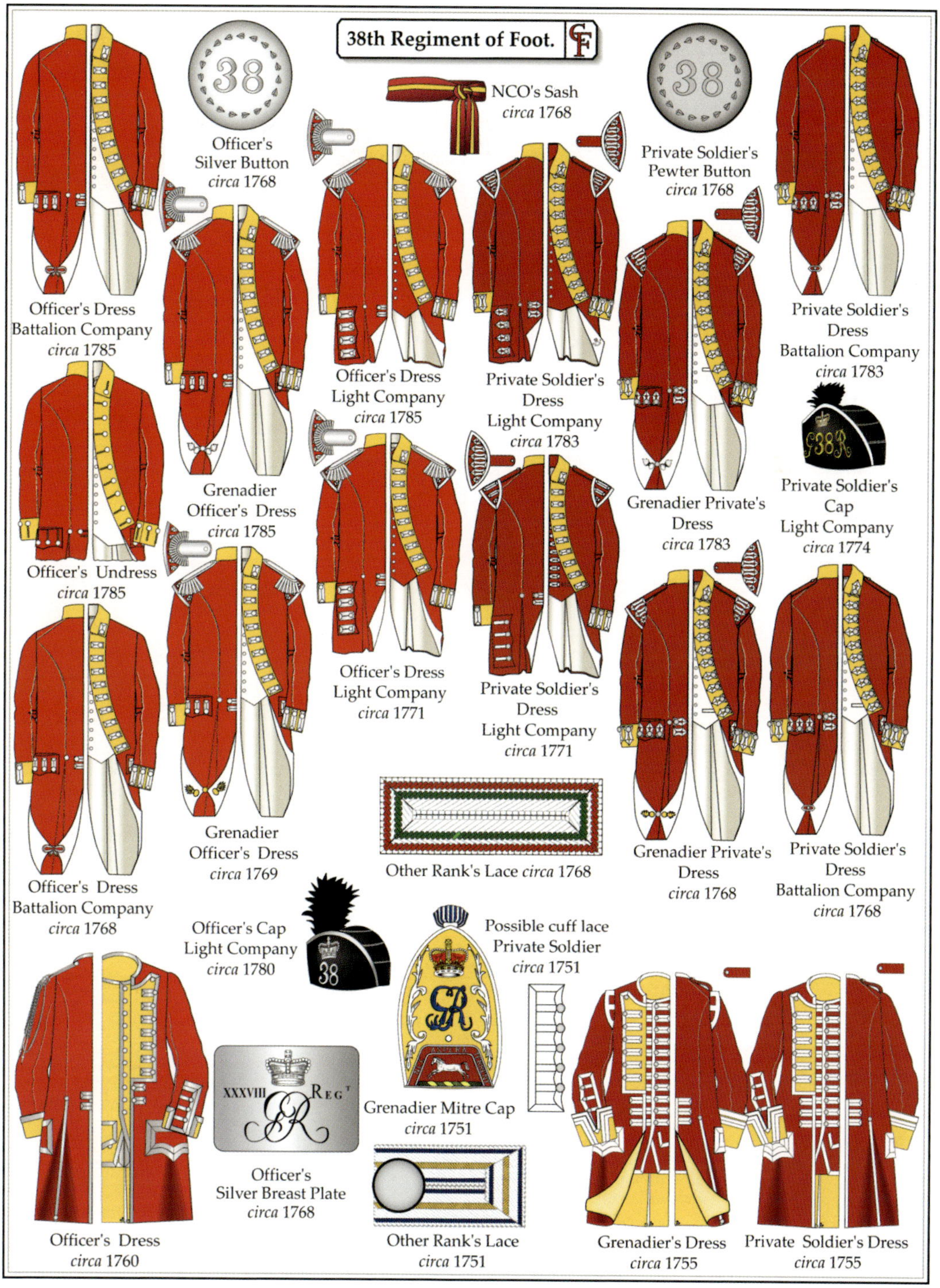
38th Regiment of Foot.
Officer's Dress Battalion Company circa 1785
Officer's Silver Button circa 1768
NCO's Sash circa 1768
Private Soldier's Pewter Button circa 1768
Private Soldier's Dress Battalion Company circa 1783
Grenadier Officer's Dress circa 1785
Officer's Dress Light Company circa 1785
Private Soldier's Dress Light Company circa 1783
Grenadier Private's Dress circa 1783
Private Soldier's Cap Light Company circa 1774
Officer's Undress circa 1785
Officer's Dress Battalion Company circa 1768
Grenadier Officer's Dress circa 1769
Officer's Dress Light Company circa 1771
Private Soldier's Dress Light Company circa 1771
Other Rank's Lace circa 1768
Grenadier Private's Dress circa 1768
Private Soldier's Dress Battalion Company circa 1768
Officer's Cap Light Company circa 1780
Possible cuff lace Private Soldier circa 1751
XXXVIII Reg^{T}
Officer's Silver Breast Plate circa 1768
Grenadier Mitre Cap circa 1751
Other Rank's Lace circa 1751
Officer's Dress circa 1760
Grenadier's Dress circa 1755
Private Soldier's Dress circa 1755

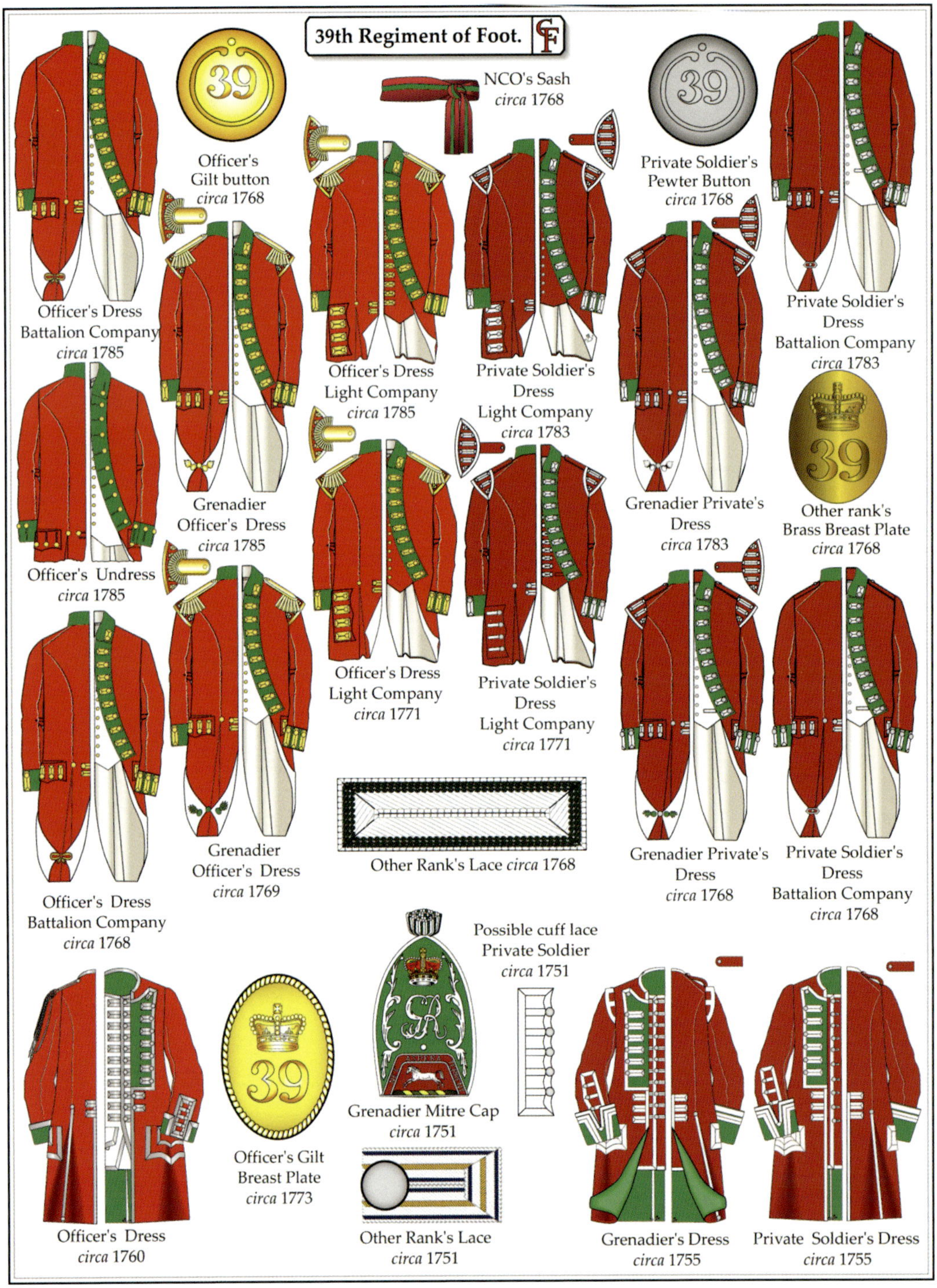
39th Regiment of Foot.
Officer's Dress
Battalion Company
circa 1785
Officer's
Gilt button
circa 1768
NCO's Sash
circa 1768
Private Soldier's
Pewter Button
circa 1768
Private Soldier's
Dress
Battalion Company
circa 1783
Grenadier
Officer's Dress
circa 1785
Officer's Dress
Light Company
circa 1785
Private Soldier's
Dress
Light Company
circa 1783
Grenadier Private's
Dress
circa 1783
Other rank's
Brass Breast Plate
circa 1768
Officer's Undress
circa 1785
Officer's Dress
Light Company
circa 1771
Private Soldier's
Dress
Light Company
circa 1771
Grenadier
Officer's Dress
circa 1769
Other Rank's Lace circa 1768
Grenadier Private's
Dress
circa 1768
Private Soldier's
Dress
Battalion Company
circa 1768
Officer's Dress
Battalion Company
circa 1768
Possible cuff lace
Private Soldier
circa 1751
Officer's Gilt
Breast Plate
circa 1773
Grenadier Mitre Cap
circa 1751
Officer's Dress
circa 1760
Other Rank's Lace
circa 1751
Grenadier's Dress
circa 1755
Private Soldier's Dress
circa 1755

40th Regiment of Foot.
CF
40
Officer's Gilt button circa 1768
NCO's Sash circa 1768
40
Private Soldier's Pewter Button circa 1768
Officer's Dress Battalion Company circa 1785
Officer's Dress Light Company circa 1785
Private Soldier's Dress Light Company circa 1783
Private Soldier's Dress Battalion Company circa 1783
Grenadier Officer's Dress circa 1785
Officer's Undress circa 1785
Grenadier Private's Dress circa 1783
40
Other rank's Brass Breast Plate circa 1768
Officer's Dress Light Company circa 1771
Private Soldier's Dress Light Company circa 1771
Officer's Dress Battalion Company circa 1768
Grenadier Officer's Dress circa 1769
Other Rank's Lace circa 1768
Grenadier Private's Dress circa 1768
Private Soldier's Dress Battalion Company circa 1768
Possible cuff lace Private Soldier circa 1751
Grenadier Mitre Cap circa 1751
40
Officer's Gilt Breast Plate circa 1779
Officer's Dress circa 1760
Other Rank's Lace circa 1751
Grenadier's Dress circa 1755
Private Soldier's Dress circa 1755

41st (Royal Invalids) Regiment of Foot.
CF
41
Officer's Gilt Button circa 1768
Grenadier Officer's Dress circa 1785
Officer's Grenadier Cap circa 1769
Private Soldier's Grenadier Cap circa 1769
Grenadier Private's Dress circa 1783
41
Private Soldier's Pewter Button circa 1768
Officer's Dress Battalion circa 1785
Officer's Badge on rear of Grenadier Cap circa 1768
Private Soldier's Badge on Rear of Grenadier Cap circa 1768
HONI SOIT QUI MAL Y PENSE
HONI SOIT QUI MAL Y PENSE
Private Soldier's Dress Battalion Company circa 1783
Officer's Dress Battalion circa 1785
Grenadier's Officer Dress circa 1768
NCO's Sash circa 1768
Private Soldier's Lace circa 1768
Grenadier Private's Dress circa 1768
Private Soldier's Dress Battalion Company circa 1768
Officer's Dress circa 1760
Drummer Cap circa 1751
Grenadier Mitre Cap circa 1751
Other Ranks wore no lace
Grenadier's Dress circa 1753
Private Soldier's Dress circa 1751

42nd (Royal Highland) Regiment of Foot.
Officer's Gilt button
circa 1768
Private Soldier's Pewter Button
circa 1768
Officer's Dress Battalion Company
circa 1785
Officer's Dress Light Company
circa 1785
Private Soldier's Dress Light Company
circa 1783
Private Soldier's Dress Battalion Company
circa 1783
Grenadier Officer's Dress
circa 1785
Grenadier Private's Dress
circa 1783
Officer's Undress
circa 1785
42nd Tartan
circa 1768
Officer's Dress Light Company
circa 1771
Private Soldier's Dress Light Company
circa 1771
Officer's Dress Battalion Company
circa 1768
Grenadier Officer's Dress
circa 1769
Other Rank's Lace
circa 1768
Grenadier Private's Dress
circa 1768
Private Soldier's Dress Battalion Company
circa 1768
Officer's Grenadier Fur Cap
circa 1751
Officer's Badge on rear of 1768 Grenadier Cap
42nd Grenadier Tartan
circa 1768
Private Soldier's Grenadier Fur Cap
circa 1751
Officer's Dress
circa 1760
Officer's Dress
circa 1759
Other Rank's Lace
circa 1751
Grenadier's Dress
circa 1759
Private Soldier's Dress
circa 1750

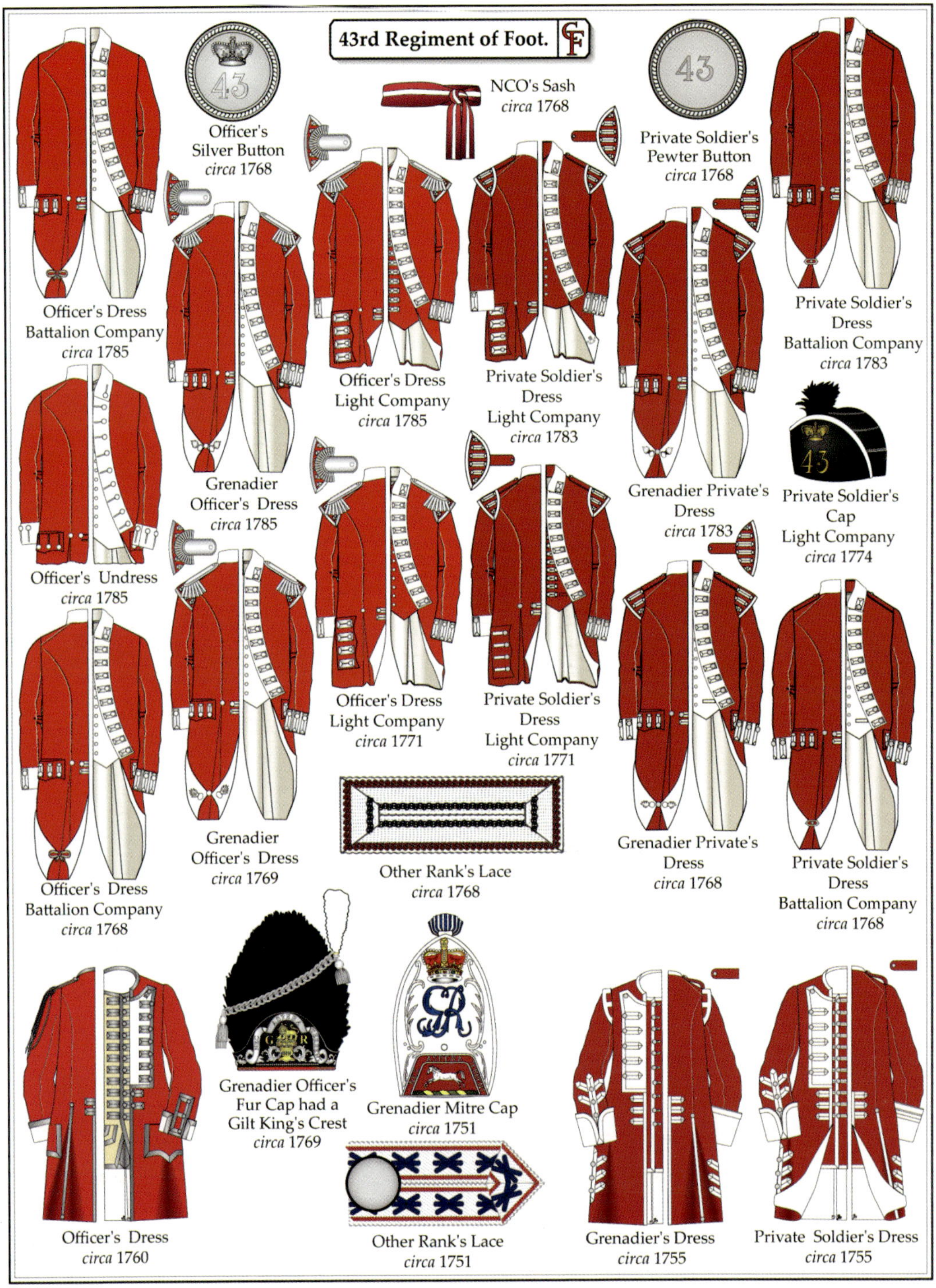
43rd Regiment of Foot.
CF
43
Officer's Silver Button circa 1768
NCO's Sash circa 1768
43
Private Soldier's Pewter Button circa 1768
Officer's Dress Battalion Company circa 1785
Officer's Dress Light Company circa 1785
Private Soldier's Dress Light Company circa 1783
Private Soldier's Dress Battalion Company circa 1783
Grenadier Officer's Dress circa 1785
Grenadier Private's Dress circa 1783
43
Private Soldier's Cap Light Company circa 1774
Officer's Undress circa 1785
Officer's Dress Light Company circa 1771
Private Soldier's Dress Light Company circa 1771
Officer's Dress Battalion Company circa 1768
Grenadier Officer's Dress circa 1769
Other Rank's Lace circa 1768
Grenadier Private's Dress circa 1768
Private Soldier's Dress Battalion Company circa 1768
G R
Grenadier Officer's Fur Cap had a Gilt King's Crest circa 1769
GR
Grenadier Mitre Cap circa 1751
Officer's Dress circa 1760
Other Rank's Lace circa 1751
Grenadier's Dress circa 1755
Private Soldier's Dress circa 1755

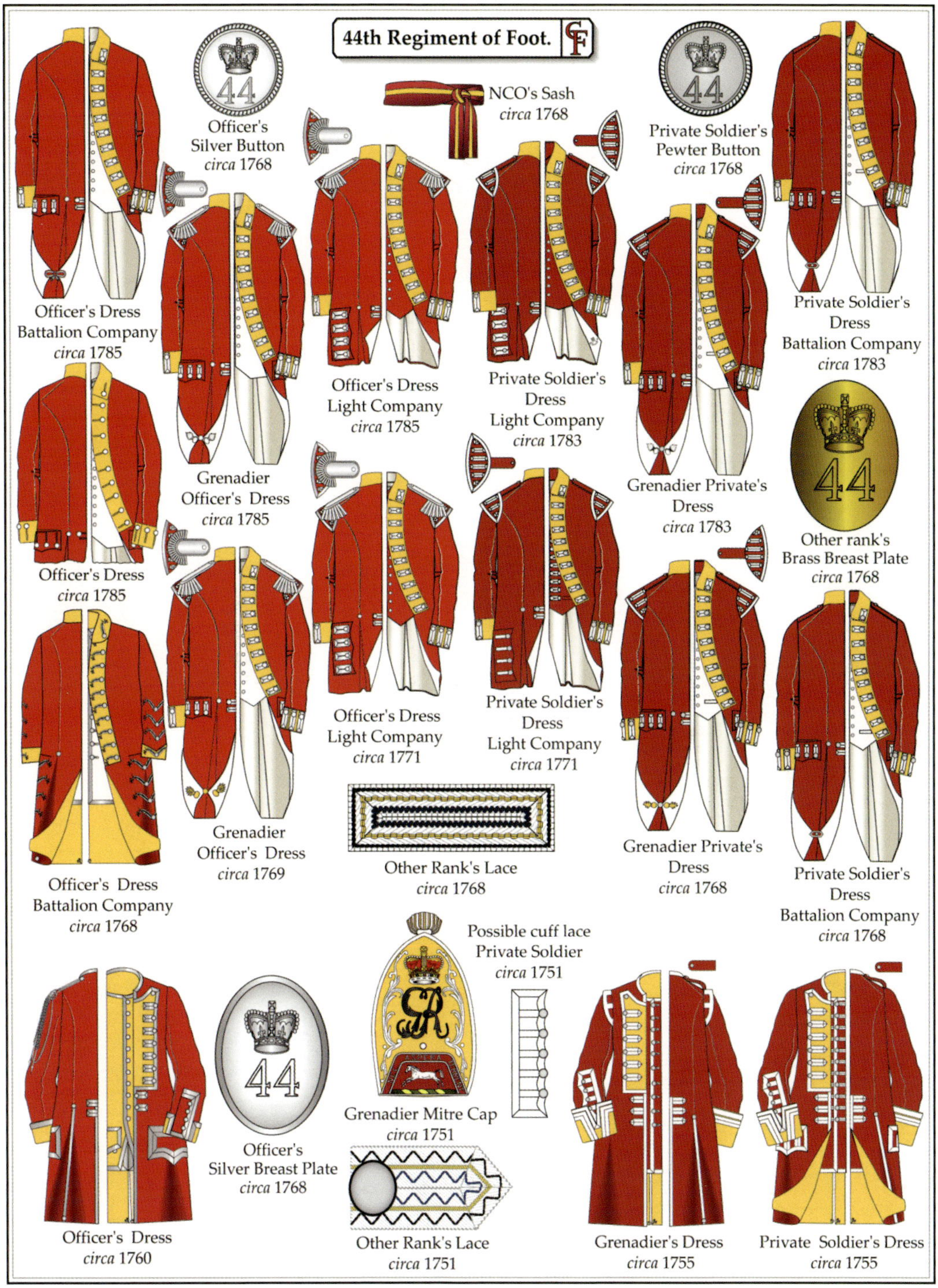
44th Regiment of Foot.
Officer's Silver Button circa 1768
NCO's Sash circa 1768
Private Soldier's Pewter Button circa 1768
Officer's Dress Battalion Company circa 1785
Officer's Dress Light Company circa 1785
Private Soldier's Dress Light Company circa 1783
Private Soldier's Dress Battalion Company circa 1783
Grenadier Officer's Dress circa 1785
Grenadier Private's Dress circa 1783
Officer's Dress circa 1785
Other rank's Brass Breast Plate circa 1768
Officer's Dress Light Company circa 1771
Private Soldier's Dress Light Company circa 1771
Grenadier Officer's Dress circa 1769
Other Rank's Lace circa 1768
Grenadier Private's Dress circa 1768
Officer's Dress Battalion Company circa 1768
Private Soldier's Dress Battalion Company circa 1768
Possible cuff lace Private Soldier circa 1751
Grenadier Mitre Cap circa 1751
Officer's Silver Breast Plate circa 1768
Officer's Dress circa 1760
Other Rank's Lace circa 1751
Grenadier's Dress circa 1755
Private Soldier's Dress circa 1755

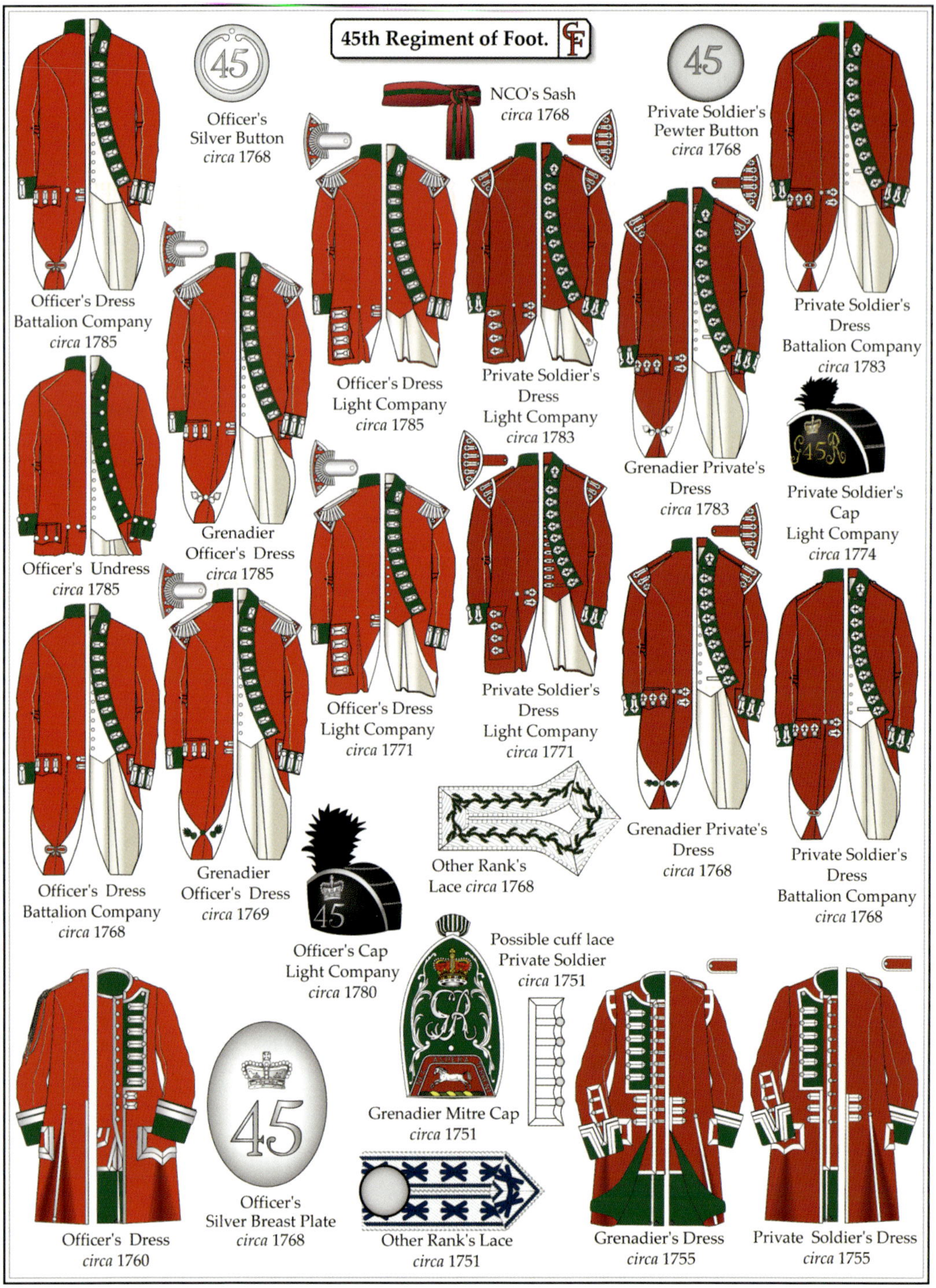
45th Regiment of Foot.
Officer's Dress Battalion Company circa 1785
Officer's Silver Button circa 1768
NCO's Sash circa 1768
Private Soldier's Pewter Button circa 1768
Private Soldier's Dress Battalion Company circa 1783
Officer's Dress Light Company circa 1785
Private Soldier's Dress Light Company circa 1783
Grenadier Private's Dress circa 1783
Officer's Undress circa 1785
Grenadier Officer's Dress circa 1785
Private Soldier's Cap Light Company circa 1774
Officer's Dress Light Company circa 1771
Private Soldier's Dress Light Company circa 1771
Officer's Dress Battalion Company circa 1768
Grenadier Officer's Dress circa 1769
Officer's Cap Light Company circa 1780
Other Rank's Lace circa 1768
Grenadier Private's Dress circa 1768
Private Soldier's Dress Battalion Company circa 1768
Possible cuff lace Private Soldier circa 1751
Grenadier Mitre Cap circa 1751
Officer's Dress circa 1760
Officer's Silver Breast Plate circa 1768
Other Rank's Lace circa 1751
Grenadier's Dress circa 1755
Private Soldier's Dress circa 1755

46th Regiment of Foot.
CF
Officer's Dress
Battalion Company
circa 1785
46
Officer's
Silver Button
circa 1768
NCO's Sash
circa 1768
46
Private Soldier's
Pewter Button
circa 1768
Private Soldier's
Dress
Battalion Company
circa 1783
Officer's Dress
Light Company
circa 1785
Private Soldier's
Dress
Light Company
circa 1783
Grenadier
Officer's Dress
circa 1785
Officer's Undress
circa 1785
Grenadier Private's
Dress
circa 1783
46
Other rank's
Brass Breast Plate
circa 1768
Officer's Dress
Light Company
circa 1771
Private Soldier's
Dress
Light Company
circa 1771
Officer's Dress
Battalion Company
circa 1768
Grenadier
Officer's Dress
circa 1769
Other Rank's Lace
circa 1768
Grenadier Private's
Dress
circa 1768
Private Soldier's
Dress
Battalion Company
circa 1768
46
Officer's
Silver Breast Plate
circa 1768
Grenadier Mitre Cap
circa 1751
Officer's Dress
circa 1760
Other Rank's Lace
circa 1751
Grenadier's Dress
circa 1755
Private Soldier's Dress
circa 1755

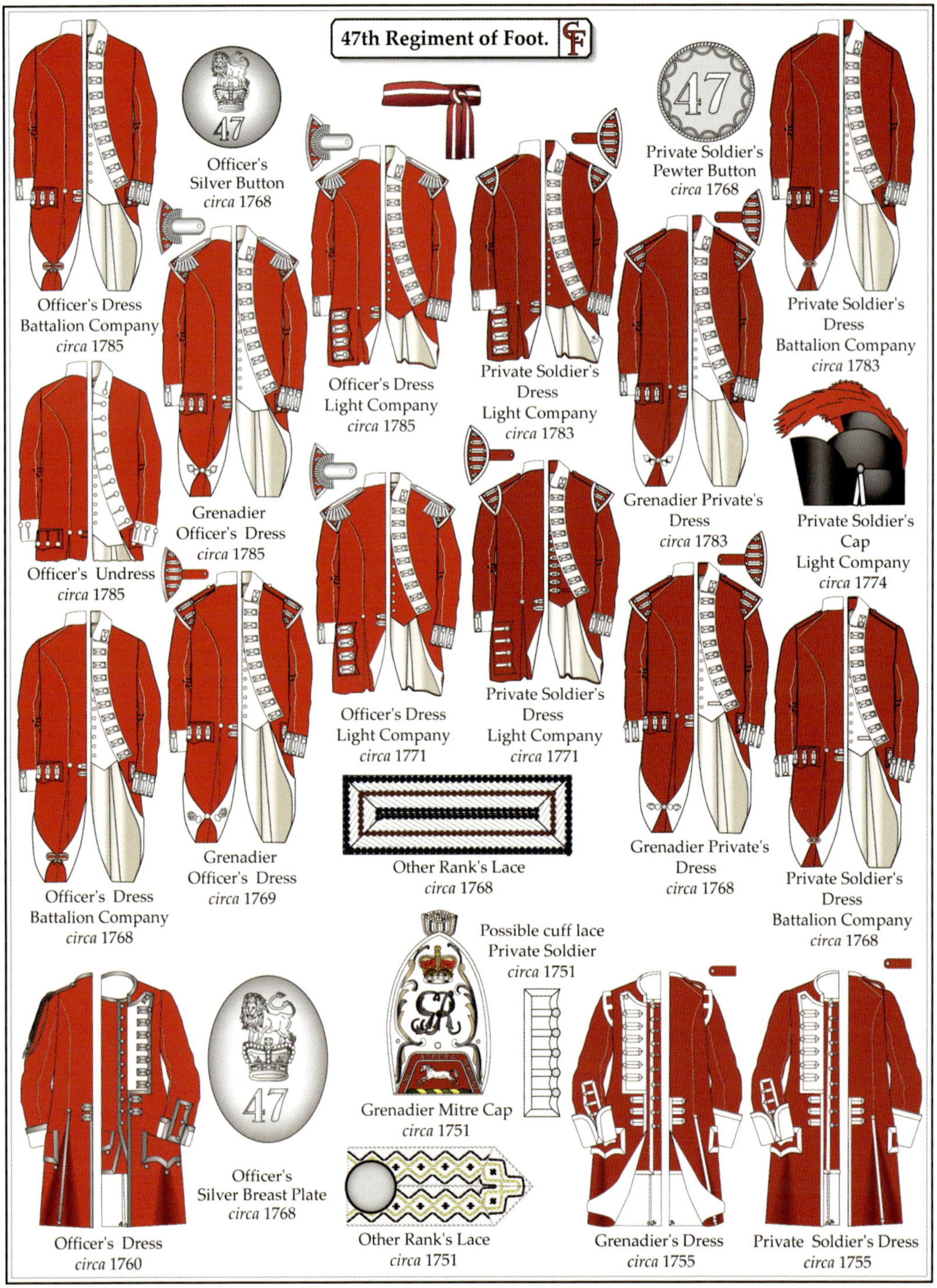

47th Regiment of Foot.
Officer's Silver Button circa 1768
Private Soldier's Pewter Button circa 1768
Officer's Dress Battalion Company circa 1785
Officer's Dress Light Company circa 1785
Private Soldier's Dress Light Company circa 1783
Private Soldier's Dress Battalion Company circa 1783
Grenadier Officer's Dress circa 1785
Grenadier Private's Dress circa 1783
Officer's Undress circa 1785
Private Soldier's Cap Light Company circa 1774
Officer's Dress Light Company circa 1771
Private Soldier's Dress Light Company circa 1771
Officer's Dress Battalion Company circa 1768
Grenadier Officer's Dress circa 1769
Other Rank's Lace circa 1768
Grenadier Private's Dress circa 1768
Private Soldier's Dress Battalion Company circa 1768
Possible cuff lace Private Soldier circa 1751
Grenadier Mitre Cap circa 1751
Officer's Dress circa 1760
Officer's Silver Breast Plate circa 1768
Other Rank's Lace circa 1751
Grenadier's Dress circa 1755
Private Soldier's Dress circa 1755

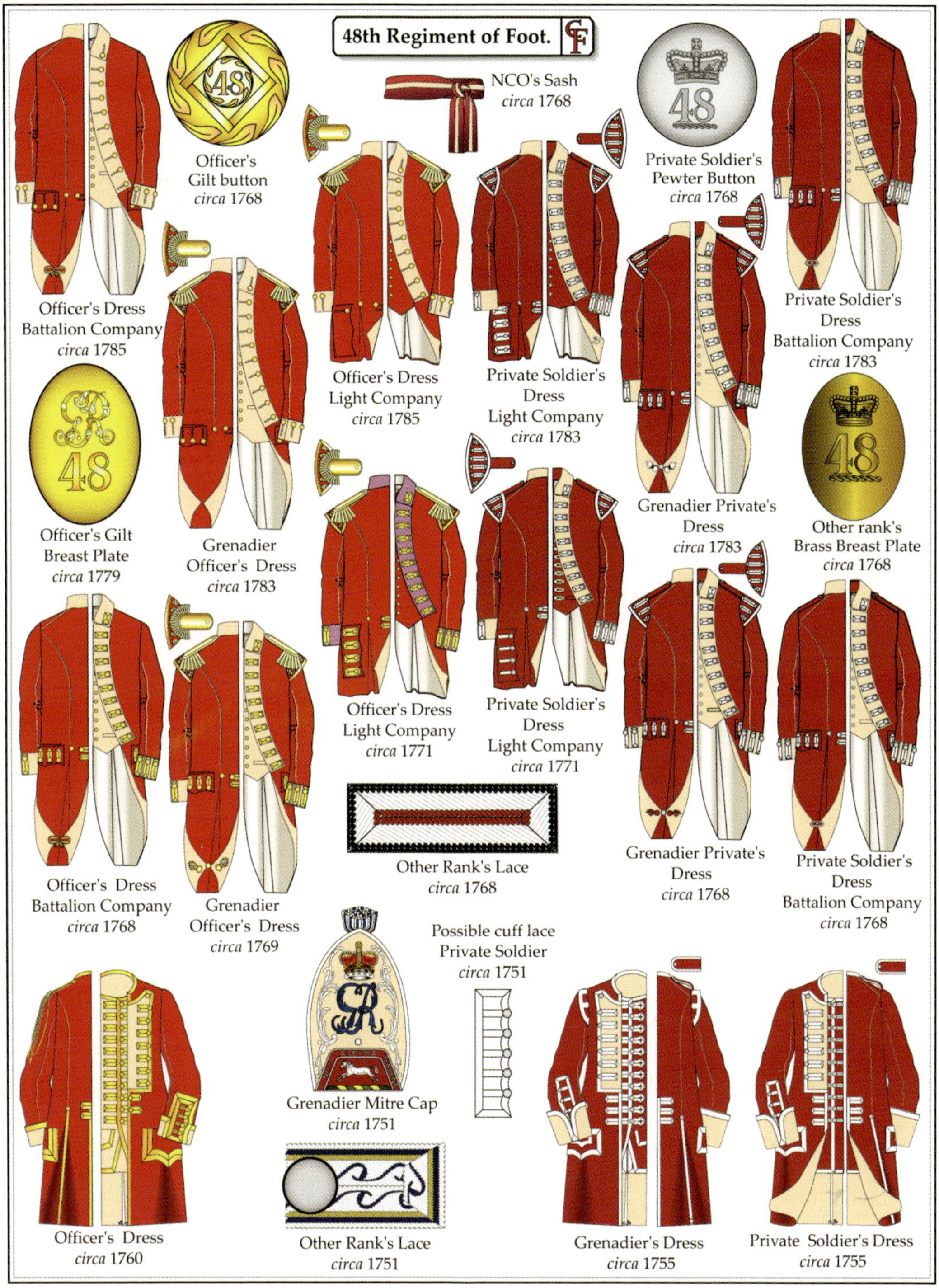
48th Regiment of Foot.
CF
Officer's Dress Battalion Company circa 1785
Officer's Gilt button circa 1768
NCO's Sash circa 1768
Private Soldier's Pewter Button circa 1768
Private Soldier's Dress Battalion Company circa 1783
Officer's Dress Light Company circa 1785
Private Soldier's Dress Light Company circa 1783
Officer's Gilt Breast Plate circa 1779
Grenadier Officer's Dress circa 1783
Grenadier Private's Dress circa 1783
Other rank's Brass Breast Plate circa 1768
Officer's Dress Light Company circa 1771
Private Soldier's Dress Light Company circa 1771
Officer's Dress Battalion Company circa 1768
Grenadier Officer's Dress circa 1769
Other Rank's Lace circa 1768
Grenadier Private's Dress circa 1768
Private Soldier's Dress Battalion Company circa 1768
Possible cuff lace Private Soldier circa 1751
Grenadier Mitre Cap circa 1751
Officer's Dress circa 1760
Other Rank's Lace circa 1751
Grenadier's Dress circa 1755
Private Soldier's Dress circa 1755

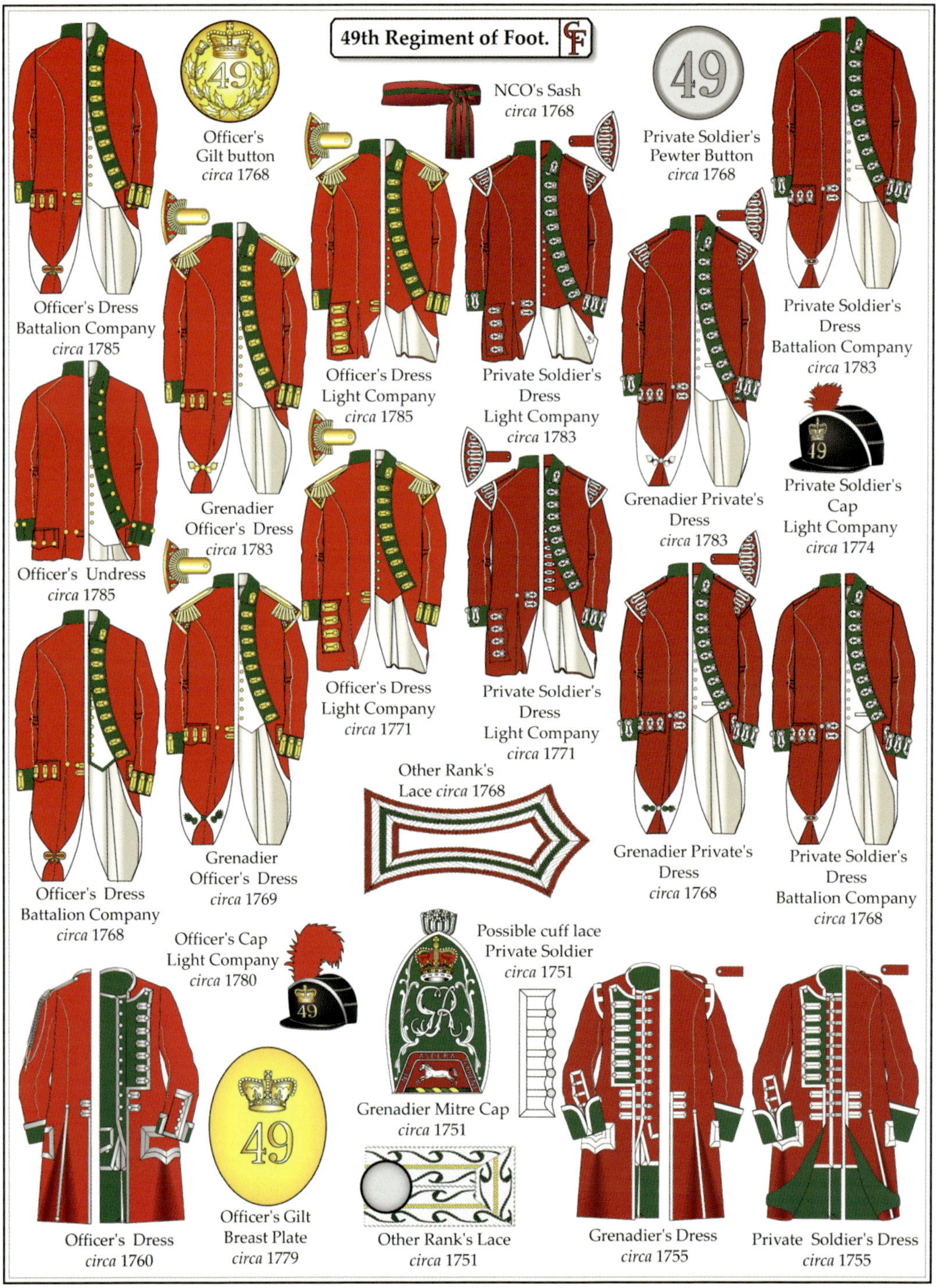
49th Regiment of Foot.
Officer's Dress Battalion Company circa 1785
Officer's Gilt button circa 1768
NCO's Sash circa 1768
Private Soldier's Pewter Button circa 1768
Private Soldier's Dress Battalion Company circa 1783
Officer's Dress Light Company circa 1785
Private Soldier's Dress Light Company circa 1783
Grenadier Officer's Dress circa 1783
Officer's Undress circa 1785
Grenadier Private's Dress circa 1783
Private Soldier's Cap Light Company circa 1774
Officer's Dress Light Company circa 1771
Private Soldier's Dress Light Company circa 1771
Other Rank's Lace circa 1768
Officer's Dress Battalion Company circa 1768
Grenadier Officer's Dress circa 1769
Grenadier Private's Dress circa 1768
Private Soldier's Dress Battalion Company circa 1768
Officer's Cap Light Company circa 1780
Possible cuff lace Private Soldier circa 1751
Grenadier Mitre Cap circa 1751
Officer's Dress circa 1760
Officer's Gilt Breast Plate circa 1779
Other Rank's Lace circa 1751
Grenadier's Dress circa 1755
Private Soldier's Dress circa 1755

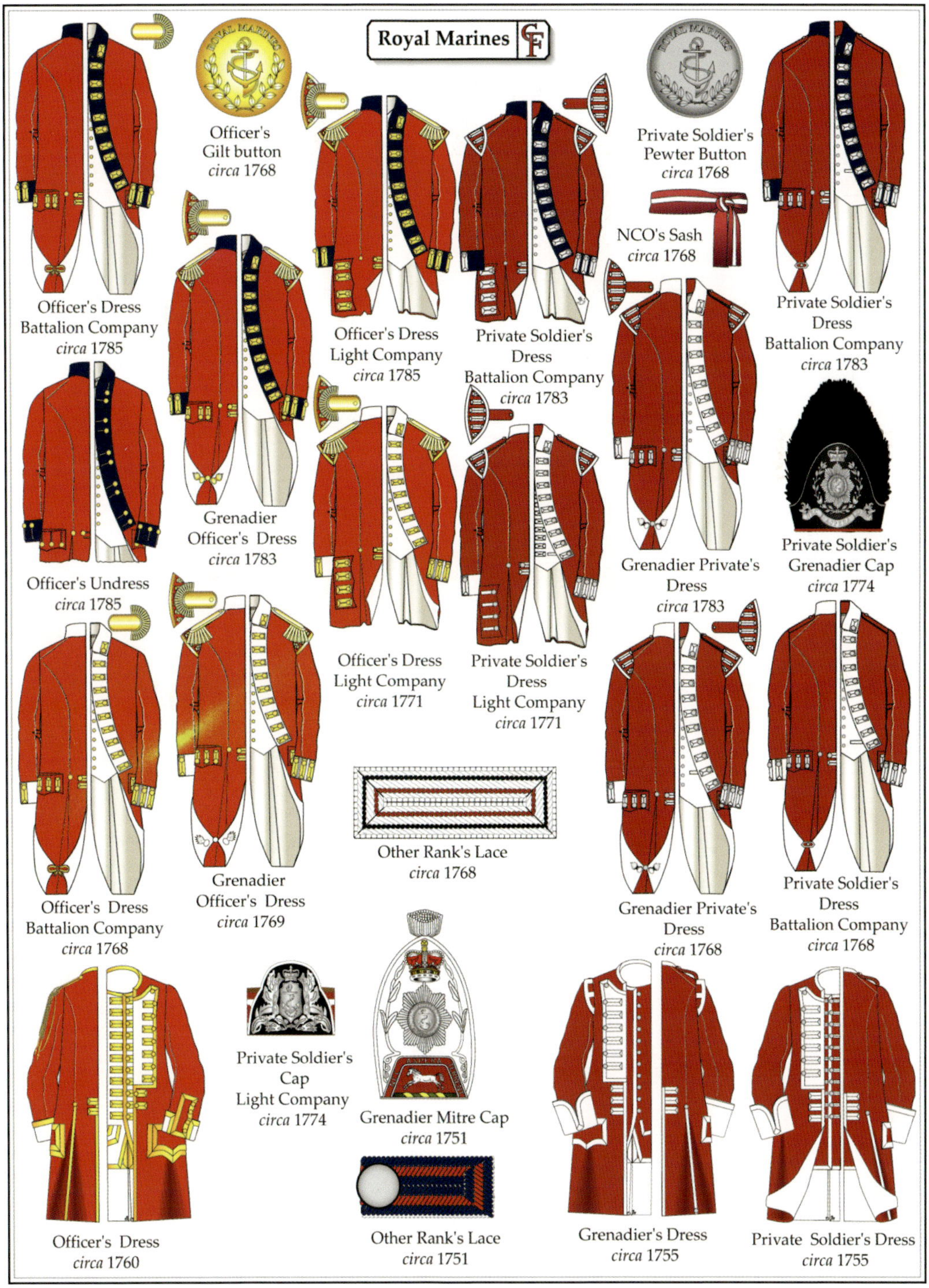
Royal Marines
Officer's Dress Battalion Company circa 1785
Officer's Undress circa 1785
Officer's Dress Battalion Company circa 1768
Officer's Dress circa 1760
Officer's Gilt button circa 1768
Grenadier Officer's Dress circa 1783
Grenadier Officer's Dress circa 1769
Private Soldier's Cap Light Company circa 1774
Officer's Dress Light Company circa 1785
Officer's Dress Light Company circa 1771
Private Soldier's Dress Battalion Company circa 1783
Private Soldier's Dress Light Company circa 1771
Other Rank's Lace circa 1768
Grenadier Mitre Cap circa 1751
Other Rank's Lace circa 1751
Private Soldier's Pewter Button circa 1768
NCO's Sash circa 1768
Grenadier Private's Dress circa 1783
Grenadier Private's Dress circa 1768
Grenadier's Dress circa 1755
Private Soldier's Dress Battalion Company circa 1783
Private Soldier's Grenadier Cap circa 1774
Private Soldier's Dress Battalion Company circa 1768
Private Soldier's Dress circa 1755

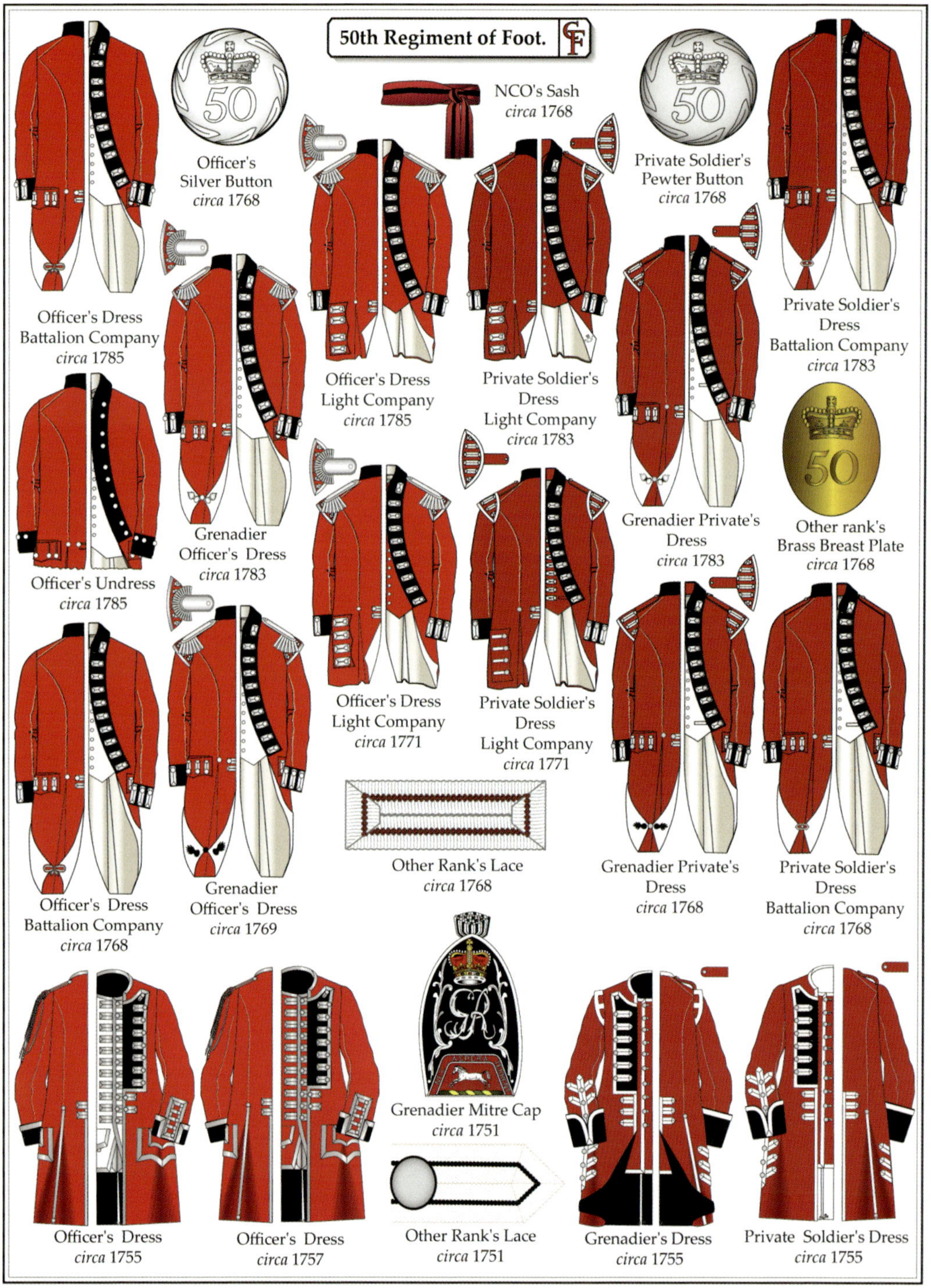

50th Regiment of Foot.
CF
Officer's Silver Button
circa 1768
NCO's Sash
circa 1768
Private Soldier's Pewter Button
circa 1768
Officer's Dress
Battalion Company
circa 1785
Officer's Dress
Light Company
circa 1785
Private Soldier's
Dress
Light Company
circa 1783
Private Soldier's
Dress
Battalion Company
circa 1783
Officer's Undress
circa 1785
Grenadier
Officer's Dress
circa 1783
Grenadier Private's
Dress
circa 1783
Other rank's
Brass Breast Plate
circa 1768
Officer's Dress
Light Company
circa 1771
Private Soldier's
Dress
Light Company
circa 1771
Officer's Dress
Battalion Company
circa 1768
Grenadier
Officer's Dress
circa 1769
Other Rank's Lace
circa 1768
Grenadier Private's
Dress
circa 1768
Private Soldier's
Dress
Battalion Company
circa 1768
Grenadier Mitre Cap
circa 1751
Officer's Dress
circa 1755
Officer's Dress
circa 1757
Other Rank's Lace
circa 1751
Grenadier's Dress
circa 1755
Private Soldier's Dress
circa 1755

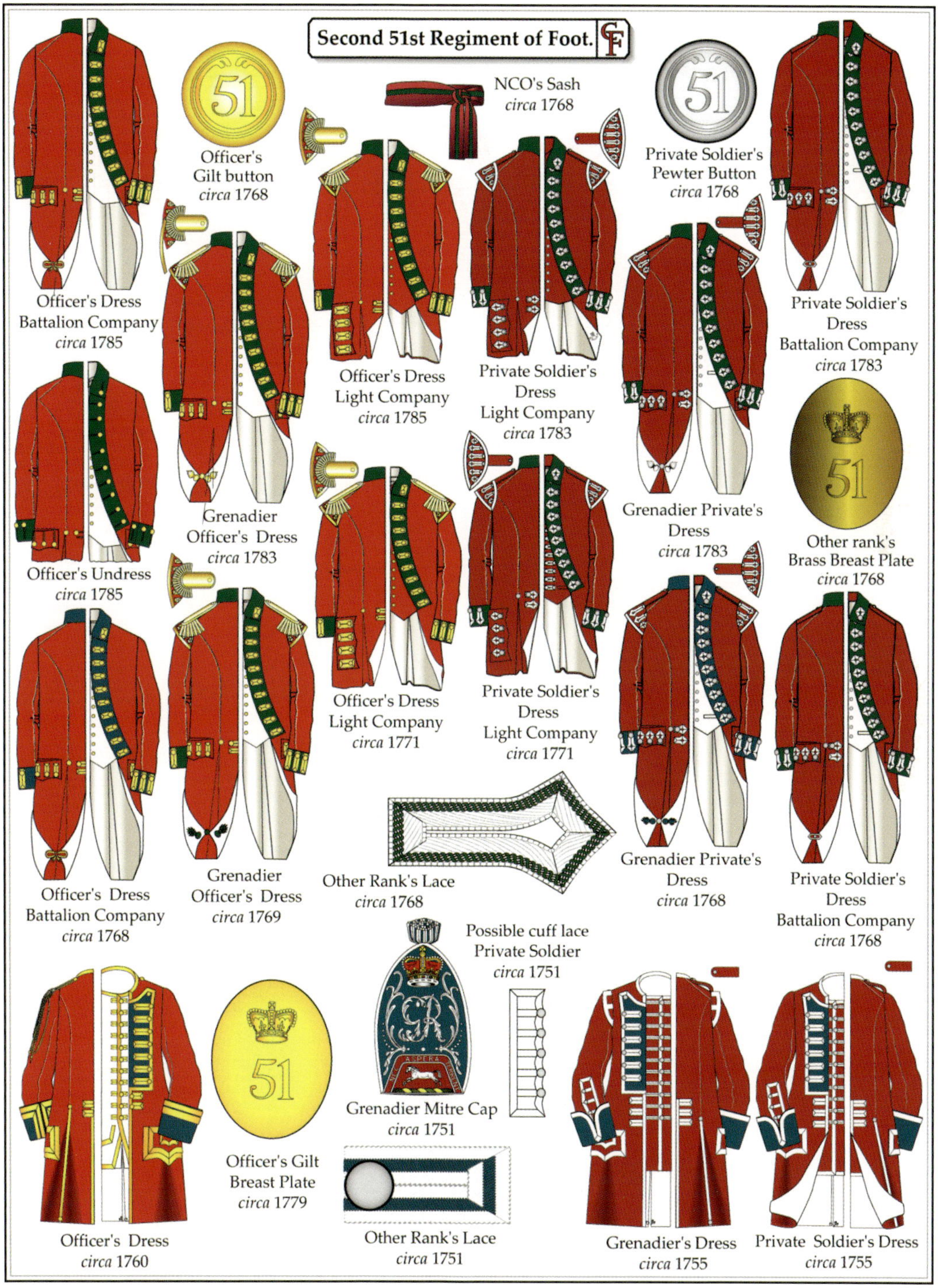
Second 51st Regiment of Foot.
Officer's Gilt button
circa 1768
NCO's Sash
circa 1768
Private Soldier's Pewter Button
circa 1768
Officer's Dress
Battalion Company
circa 1785
Officer's Dress
Light Company
circa 1785
Private Soldier's
Dress
Light Company
circa 1783
Private Soldier's
Dress
Battalion Company
circa 1783
Grenadier
Officer's Dress
circa 1783
Grenadier Private's
Dress
circa 1783
Officer's Undress
circa 1785
Other rank's
Brass Breast Plate
circa 1768
Officer's Dress
Light Company
circa 1771
Private Soldier's
Dress
Light Company
circa 1771
Officer's Dress
Battalion Company
circa 1768
Grenadier
Officer's Dress
circa 1769
Other Rank's Lace
circa 1768
Grenadier Private's
Dress
circa 1768
Private Soldier's
Dress
Battalion Company
circa 1768
Possible cuff lace
Private Soldier
circa 1751
Officer's Dress
circa 1760
Officer's Gilt
Breast Plate
circa 1779
Grenadier Mitre Cap
circa 1751
Other Rank's Lace
circa 1751
Grenadier's Dress
circa 1755
Private Soldier's Dress
circa 1755

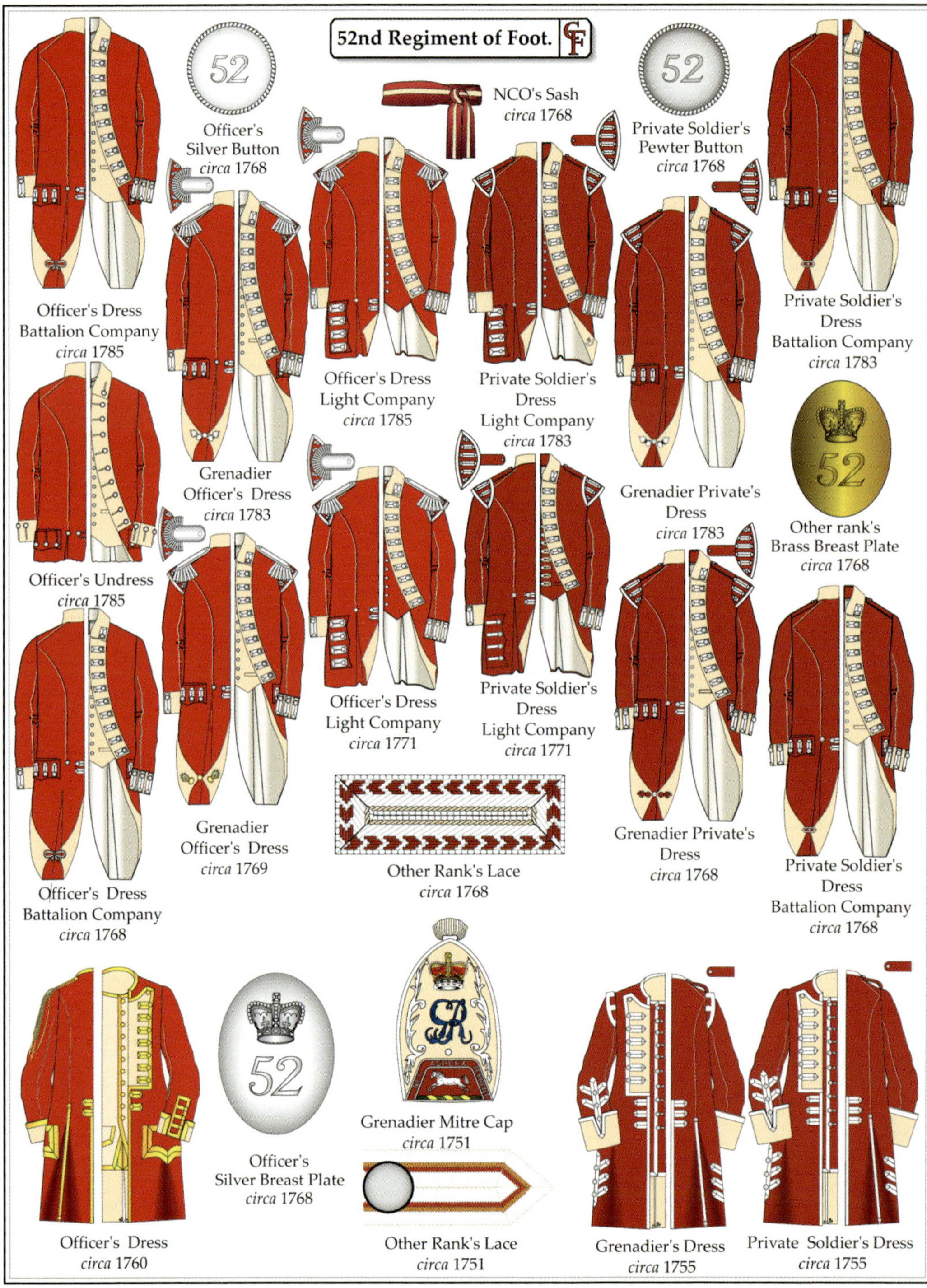
52nd Regiment of Foot.
CF
52
Officer's Silver Button circa 1768
NCO's Sash circa 1768
52
Private Soldier's Pewter Button circa 1768
Officer's Dress Battalion Company circa 1785
Officer's Dress Light Company circa 1785
Private Soldier's Dress Light Company circa 1783
Private Soldier's Dress Battalion Company circa 1783
Grenadier Officer's Dress circa 1783
Grenadier Private's Dress circa 1783
52
Other rank's Brass Breast Plate circa 1768
Officer's Undress circa 1785
Officer's Dress Light Company circa 1771
Private Soldier's Dress Light Company circa 1771
Grenadier Officer's Dress circa 1769
Other Rank's Lace circa 1768
Grenadier Private's Dress circa 1768
Officer's Dress Battalion Company circa 1768
Private Soldier's Dress Battalion Company circa 1768
52
Officer's Silver Breast Plate circa 1768
GR
Grenadier Mitre Cap circa 1751
Officer's Dress circa 1760
Other Rank's Lace circa 1751
Grenadier's Dress circa 1755
Private Soldier's Dress circa 1755

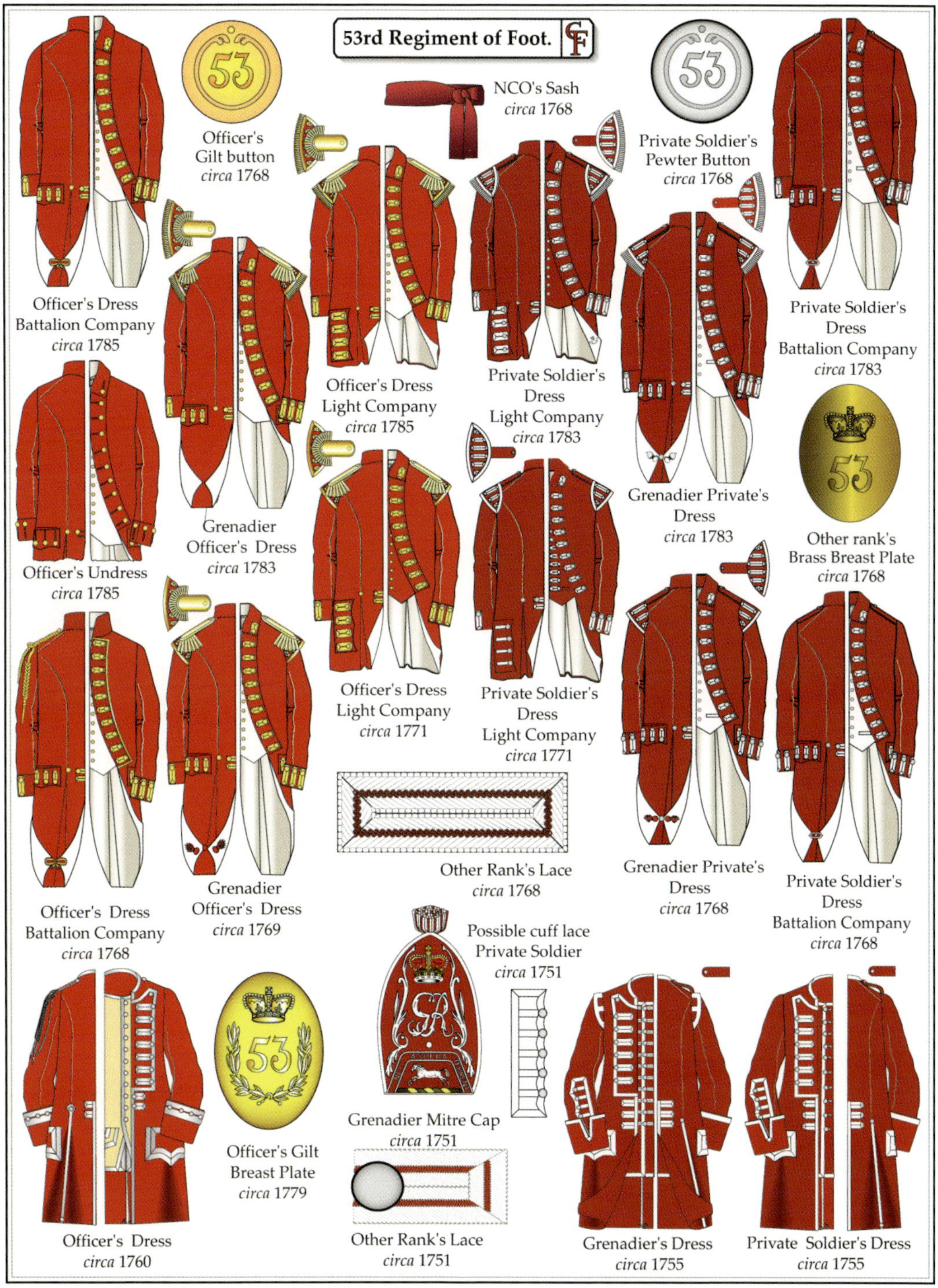
53rd Regiment of Foot.
NCO's Sash
circa 1768
Officer's
Gilt button
circa 1768
Private Soldier's
Pewter Button
circa 1768
Officer's Dress
Battalion Company
circa 1785
Officer's Dress
Light Company
circa 1785
Private Soldier's
Dress
Light Company
circa 1783
Private Soldier's
Dress
Battalion Company
circa 1783
Grenadier
Officer's Dress
circa 1783
Officer's Undress
circa 1785
Grenadier Private's
Dress
circa 1783
Other rank's
Brass Breast Plate
circa 1768
Officer's Dress
Light Company
circa 1771
Private Soldier's
Dress
Light Company
circa 1771
Other Rank's Lace
circa 1768
Grenadier Private's
Dress
circa 1768
Private Soldier's
Dress
Battalion Company
circa 1768
Officer's Dress
Battalion Company
circa 1768
Grenadier
Officer's Dress
circa 1769
Possible cuff lace
Private Soldier
circa 1751
Grenadier Mitre Cap
circa 1751
Officer's Gilt
Breast Plate
circa 1779
Other Rank's Lace
circa 1751
Officer's Dress
circa 1760
Grenadier's Dress
circa 1755
Private Soldier's Dress
circa 1755

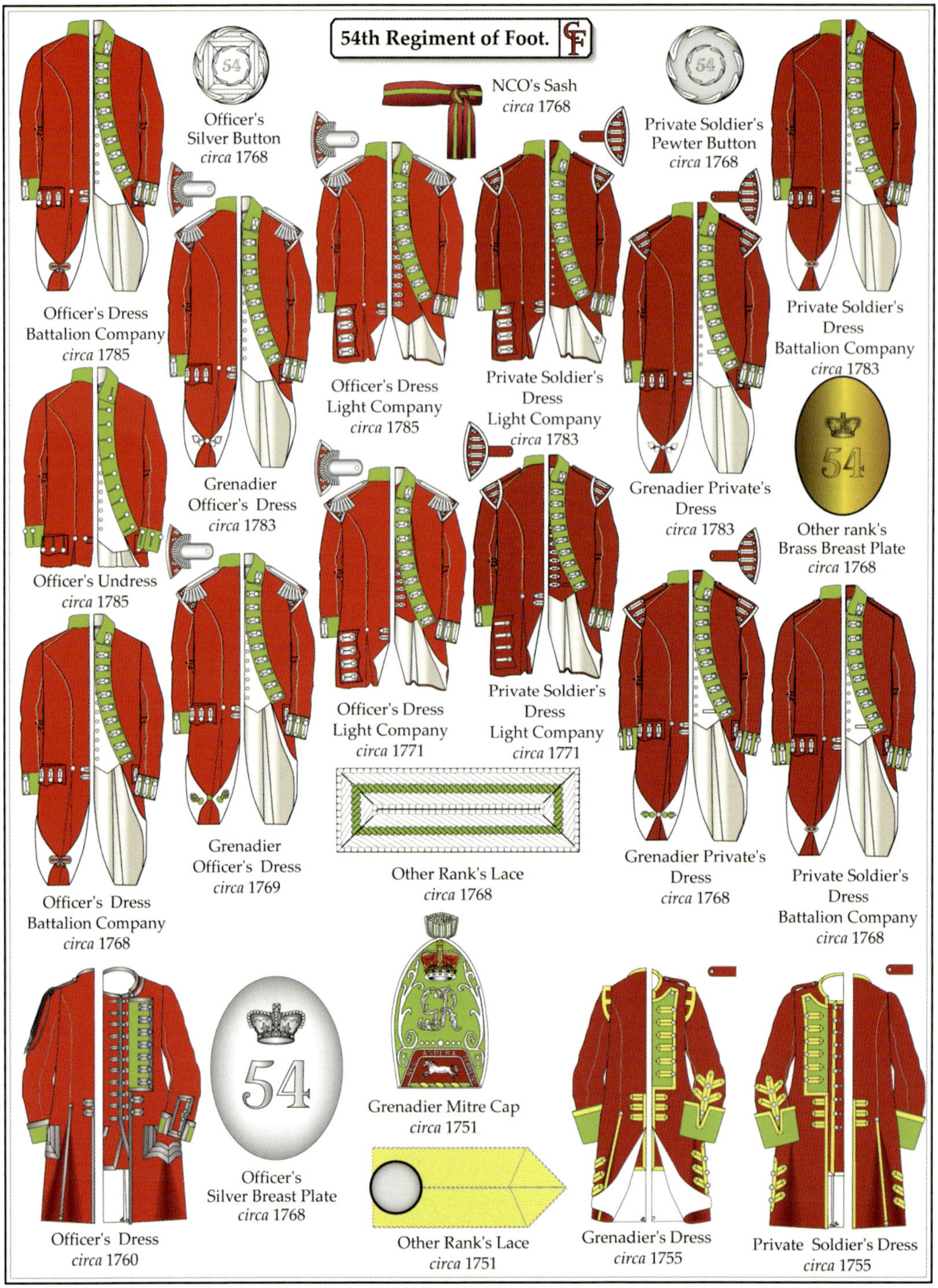
54th Regiment of Foot.
CF
Officer's Silver Button circa 1768
NCO's Sash circa 1768
Private Soldier's Pewter Button circa 1768
Officer's Dress Battalion Company circa 1785
Officer's Dress Light Company circa 1785
Private Soldier's Dress Light Company circa 1783
Private Soldier's Dress Battalion Company circa 1783
Grenadier Officer's Dress circa 1783
Grenadier Private's Dress circa 1783
Other rank's Brass Breast Plate circa 1768
Officer's Undress circa 1785
Officer's Dress Light Company circa 1771
Private Soldier's Dress Light Company circa 1771
Officer's Dress Battalion Company circa 1768
Grenadier Officer's Dress circa 1769
Other Rank's Lace circa 1768
Grenadier Private's Dress circa 1768
Private Soldier's Dress Battalion Company circa 1768
Officer's Dress circa 1760
Officer's Silver Breast Plate circa 1768
Grenadier Mitre Cap circa 1751
Other Rank's Lace circa 1751
Grenadier's Dress circa 1755
Private Soldier's Dress circa 1755

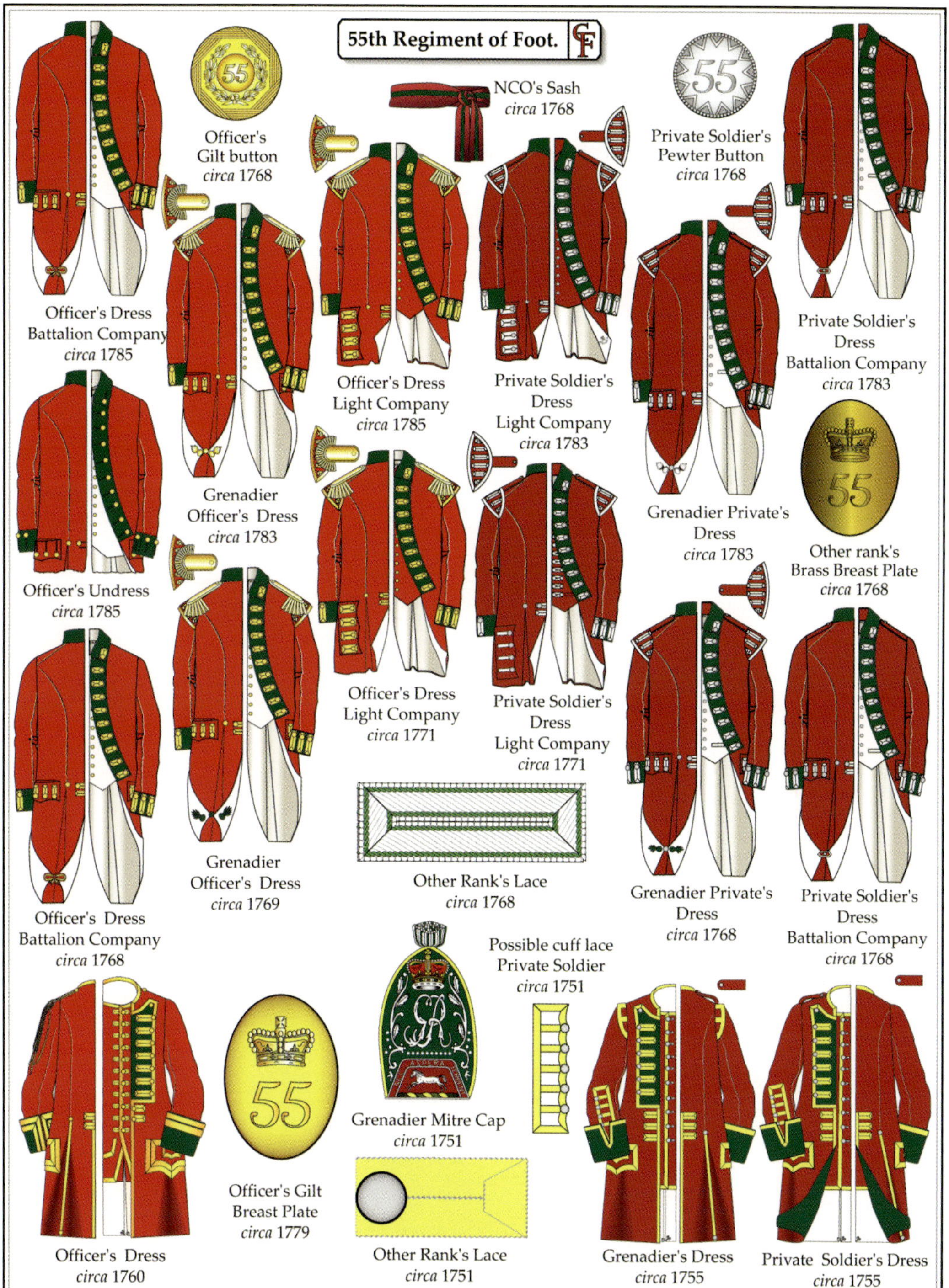
55th Regiment of Foot.
Officer's Dress Battalion Company circa 1785
Officer's Gilt button circa 1768
NCO's Sash circa 1768
Private Soldier's Pewter Button circa 1768
Private Soldier's Dress Battalion Company circa 1783
Officer's Dress Light Company circa 1785
Private Soldier's Dress Light Company circa 1783
Grenadier Officer's Dress circa 1783
Grenadier Private's Dress circa 1783
Other rank's Brass Breast Plate circa 1768
Officer's Undress circa 1785
Officer's Dress Light Company circa 1771
Private Soldier's Dress Light Company circa 1771
Officer's Dress Battalion Company circa 1768
Grenadier Officer's Dress circa 1769
Other Rank's Lace circa 1768
Grenadier Private's Dress circa 1768
Private Soldier's Dress Battalion Company circa 1768
Possible cuff lace Private Soldier circa 1751
Grenadier Mitre Cap circa 1751
Officer's Dress circa 1760
Officer's Gilt Breast Plate circa 1779
Other Rank's Lace circa 1751
Grenadier's Dress circa 1755
Private Soldier's Dress circa 1755

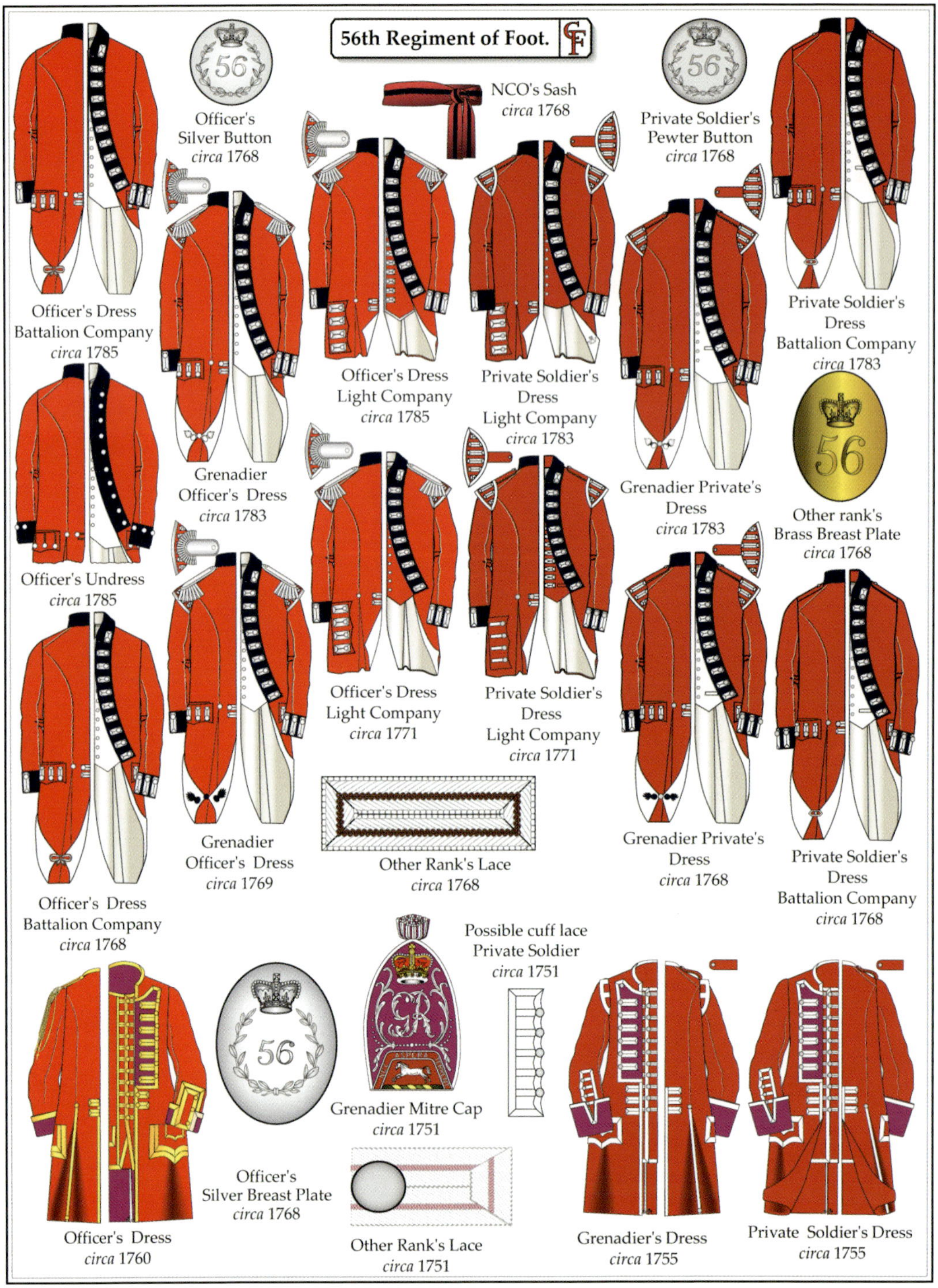
56th Regiment of Foot.
Officer's Silver Button circa 1768
NCO's Sash circa 1768
Private Soldier's Pewter Button circa 1768
Officer's Dress Battalion Company circa 1785
Private Soldier's Dress Battalion Company circa 1783
Officer's Dress Light Company circa 1785
Private Soldier's Dress Light Company circa 1783
Grenadier Officer's Dress circa 1783
Grenadier Private's Dress circa 1783
Officer's Undress circa 1785
Other rank's Brass Breast Plate circa 1768
Officer's Dress Light Company circa 1771
Private Soldier's Dress Light Company circa 1771
Grenadier Officer's Dress circa 1769
Other Rank's Lace circa 1768
Grenadier Private's Dress circa 1768
Private Soldier's Dress Battalion Company circa 1768
Officer's Dress Battalion Company circa 1768
Possible cuff lace Private Soldier circa 1751
Grenadier Mitre Cap circa 1751
Officer's Silver Breast Plate circa 1768
Officer's Dress circa 1760
Other Rank's Lace circa 1751
Grenadier's Dress circa 1755
Private Soldier's Dress circa 1755

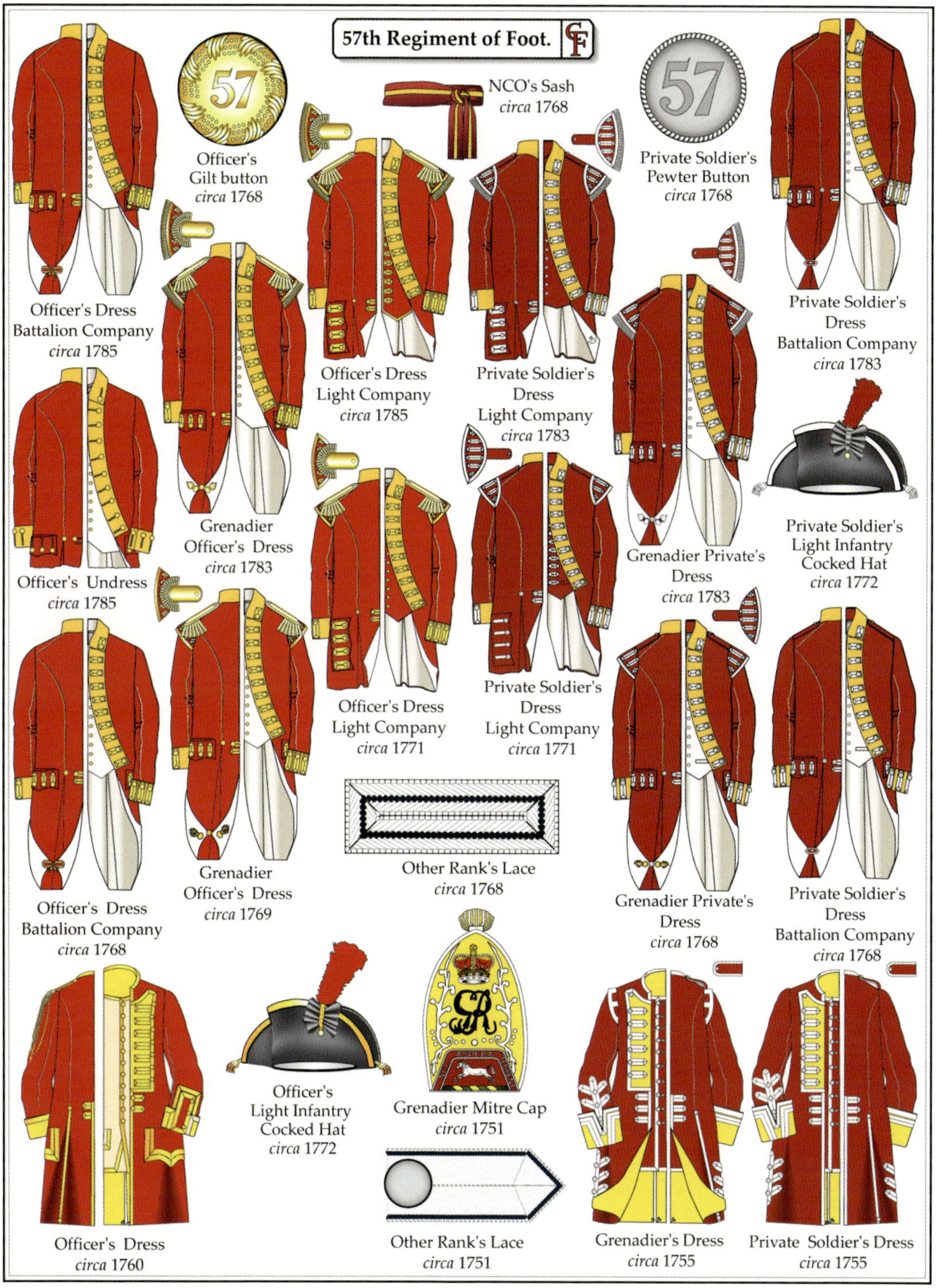
57th Regiment of Foot.
Officer's Gilt button circa 1768
NCO's Sash circa 1768
Private Soldier's Pewter Button circa 1768
Officer's Dress Battalion Company circa 1785
Officer's Dress Light Company circa 1785
Private Soldier's Dress Light Company circa 1783
Private Soldier's Dress Battalion Company circa 1783
Grenadier Officer's Dress circa 1783
Officer's Undress circa 1785
Grenadier Private's Dress circa 1783
Private Soldier's Light Infantry Cocked Hat circa 1772
Officer's Dress Light Company circa 1771
Private Soldier's Dress Light Company circa 1771
Officer's Dress Battalion Company circa 1768
Grenadier Officer's Dress circa 1769
Other Rank's Lace circa 1768
Grenadier Private's Dress circa 1768
Private Soldier's Dress Battalion Company circa 1768
Officer's Dress circa 1760
Officer's Light Infantry Cocked Hat circa 1772
Grenadier Mitre Cap circa 1751
Other Rank's Lace circa 1751
Grenadier's Dress circa 1755
Private Soldier's Dress circa 1755

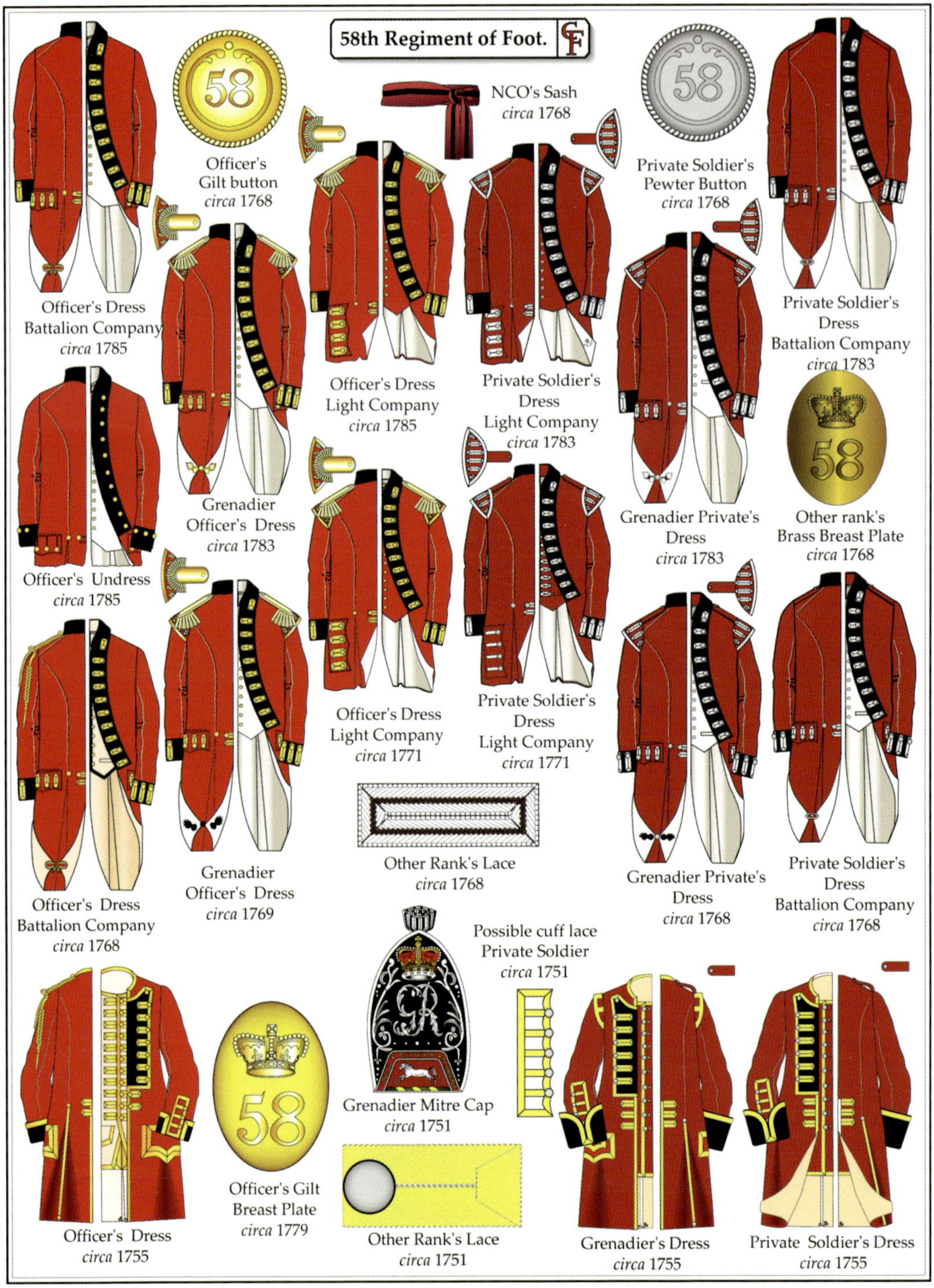
58th Regiment of Foot.
CF
Officer's Dress Battalion Company circa 1785
Officer's Gilt button circa 1768
58
NCO's Sash circa 1768
Private Soldier's Pewter Button circa 1768
58
Private Soldier's Dress Battalion Company circa 1783
Grenadier Officer's Dress circa 1783
Officer's Dress Light Company circa 1785
Private Soldier's Dress Light Company circa 1783
Grenadier Private's Dress circa 1783
Other rank's Brass Breast Plate circa 1768
58
Officer's Undress circa 1785
Officer's Dress Light Company circa 1771
Private Soldier's Dress Light Company circa 1771
Officer's Dress Battalion Company circa 1768
Grenadier Officer's Dress circa 1769
Other Rank's Lace circa 1768
Grenadier Private's Dress circa 1768
Private Soldier's Dress Battalion Company circa 1768
Possible cuff lace Private Soldier circa 1751
GR
Grenadier Mitre Cap circa 1751
58
Officer's Gilt Breast Plate circa 1779
Officer's Dress circa 1755
Other Rank's Lace circa 1751
Grenadier's Dress circa 1755
Private Soldier's Dress circa 1755

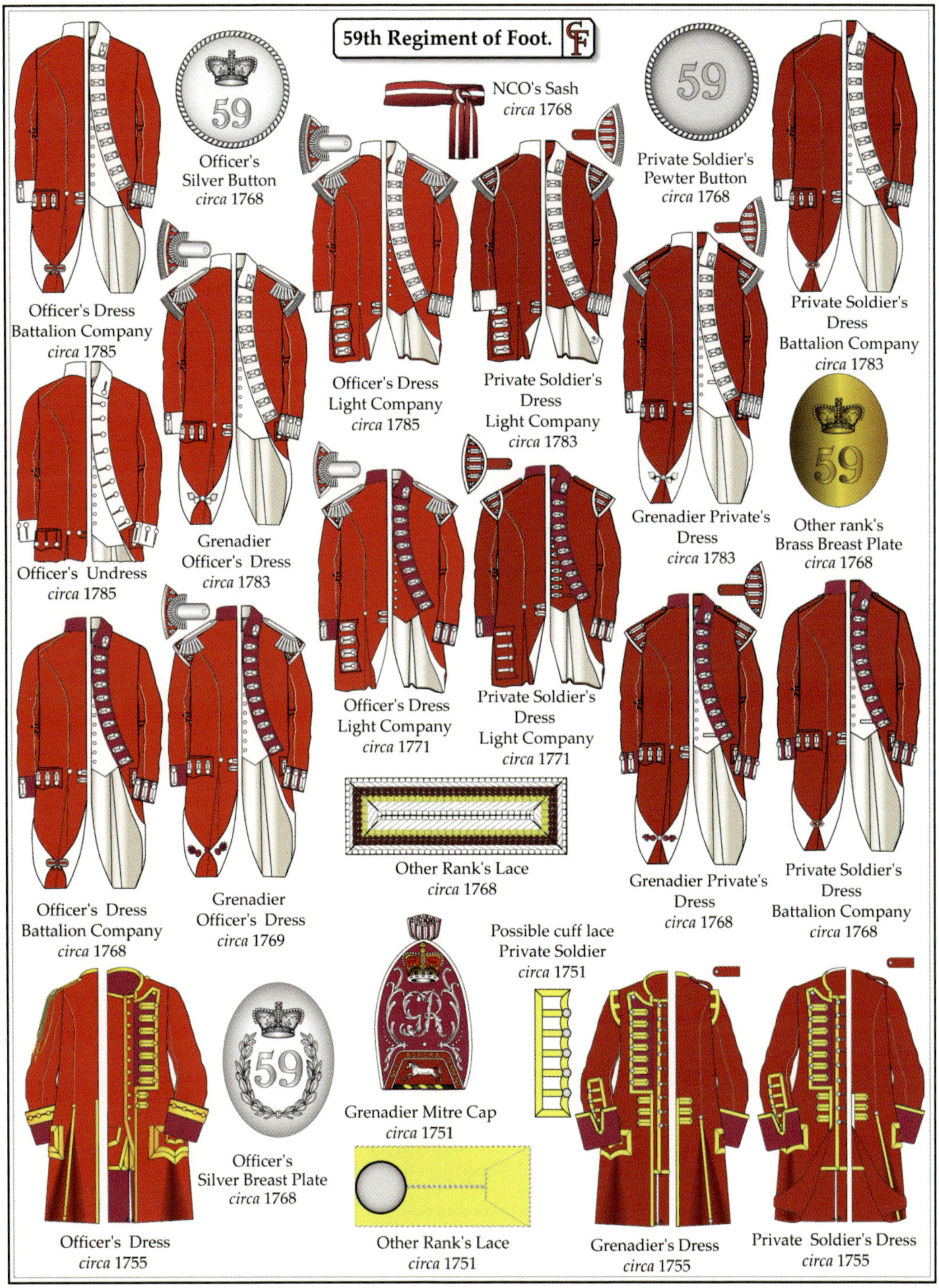
59th Regiment of Foot.
Officer's Silver Button circa 1768
NCO's Sash circa 1768
Private Soldier's Pewter Button circa 1768
Officer's Dress Battalion Company circa 1785
Officer's Dress Light Company circa 1785
Private Soldier's Dress Light Company circa 1783
Private Soldier's Dress Battalion Company circa 1783
Officer's Undress circa 1785
Grenadier Officer's Dress circa 1783
Grenadier Private's Dress circa 1783
Other rank's Brass Breast Plate circa 1768
Officer's Dress Light Company circa 1771
Private Soldier's Dress Light Company circa 1771
Officer's Dress Battalion Company circa 1768
Grenadier Officer's Dress circa 1769
Other Rank's Lace circa 1768
Grenadier Private's Dress circa 1768
Private Soldier's Dress Battalion Company circa 1768
Possible cuff lace Private Soldier circa 1751
Grenadier Mitre Cap circa 1751
Officer's Dress circa 1755
Officer's Silver Breast Plate circa 1768
Other Rank's Lace circa 1751
Grenadier's Dress circa 1755
Private Soldier's Dress circa 1755

60th (Royal American) Regiment of Foot.
Officer's Dress
Battalion Company
circa 1785
Officer's
Silver Button
circa 1768
NCO's Sash
circa 1768
Private Soldier's
Pewter Button
circa 1768
Private Soldier's
Dress
Battalion Company
circa 1783
Officer's Dress
Light Company
circa 1785
Private Soldier's
Dress
Light Company
circa 1783
Grenadier
Officer's Dress
circa 1783
Grenadier Private's
Dress
circa 1783
Officer's
Badge worn on rear
of the Grenadier Cap
circa 1768
Officer's Undress
circa 1785
Officer's Dress
Light Company
circa 1771
Private Soldier's
Dress
Light Company
circa 1771
Other Rank's Lace
circa 1768
Grenadier
Officer's Dress
circa 1769
Grenadier Private's
Dress
circa 1768
Officer's Dress
Battalion Company
circa 1768
Possible cuff lace
Private Soldier
circa 1751
Private Soldier's
Dress
Battalion Company
circa 1768
Grenadier Mitre Cap
circa 1751
Officer's Dress
circa 1755
Private Soldier's
With no lace
circa 1755
Other Rank's Lace
circa 1751
Grenadier's Dress
circa 1755
Private Soldier's Dress
circa 1755

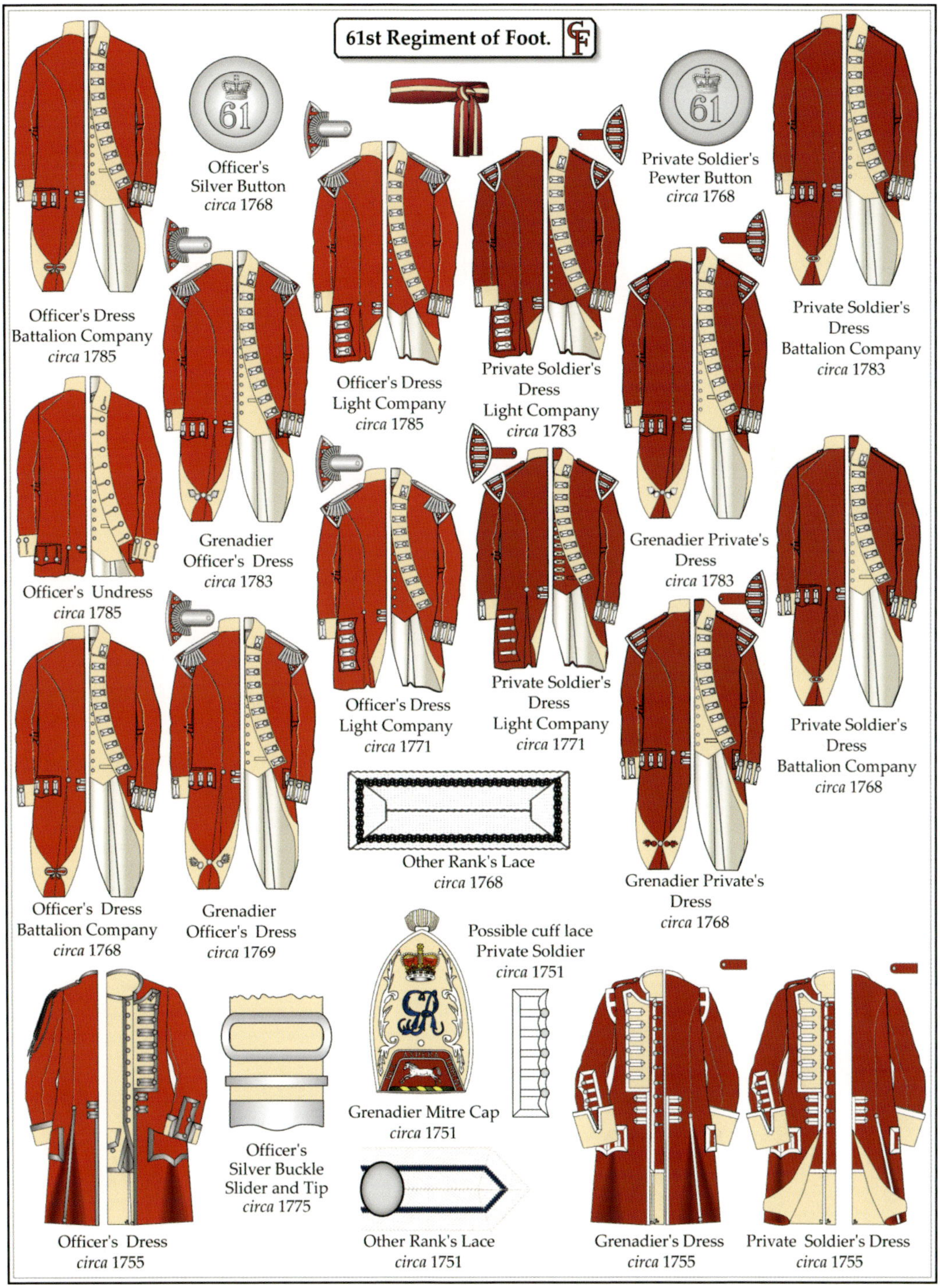
61st Regiment of Foot.
Officer's Dress
Battalion Company
circa 1785
Officer's
Silver Button
circa 1768
Officer's Dress
Light Company
circa 1785
Private Soldier's
Dress
Light Company
circa 1783
Private Soldier's
Pewter Button
circa 1768
Private Soldier's
Dress
Battalion Company
circa 1783
Officer's Undress
circa 1785
Grenadier
Officer's Dress
circa 1783
Officer's Dress
Light Company
circa 1771
Private Soldier's
Dress
Light Company
circa 1771
Grenadier Private's
Dress
circa 1783
Private Soldier's
Dress
Battalion Company
circa 1768
Officer's Dress
Battalion Company
circa 1768
Grenadier
Officer's Dress
circa 1769
Other Rank's Lace
circa 1768
Grenadier Private's
Dress
circa 1768
Possible cuff lace
Private Soldier
circa 1751
Officer's Dress
circa 1755
Officer's
Silver Buckle
Slider and Tip
circa 1775
Grenadier Mitre Cap
circa 1751
Other Rank's Lace
circa 1751
Grenadier's Dress
circa 1755
Private Soldier's Dress
circa 1755

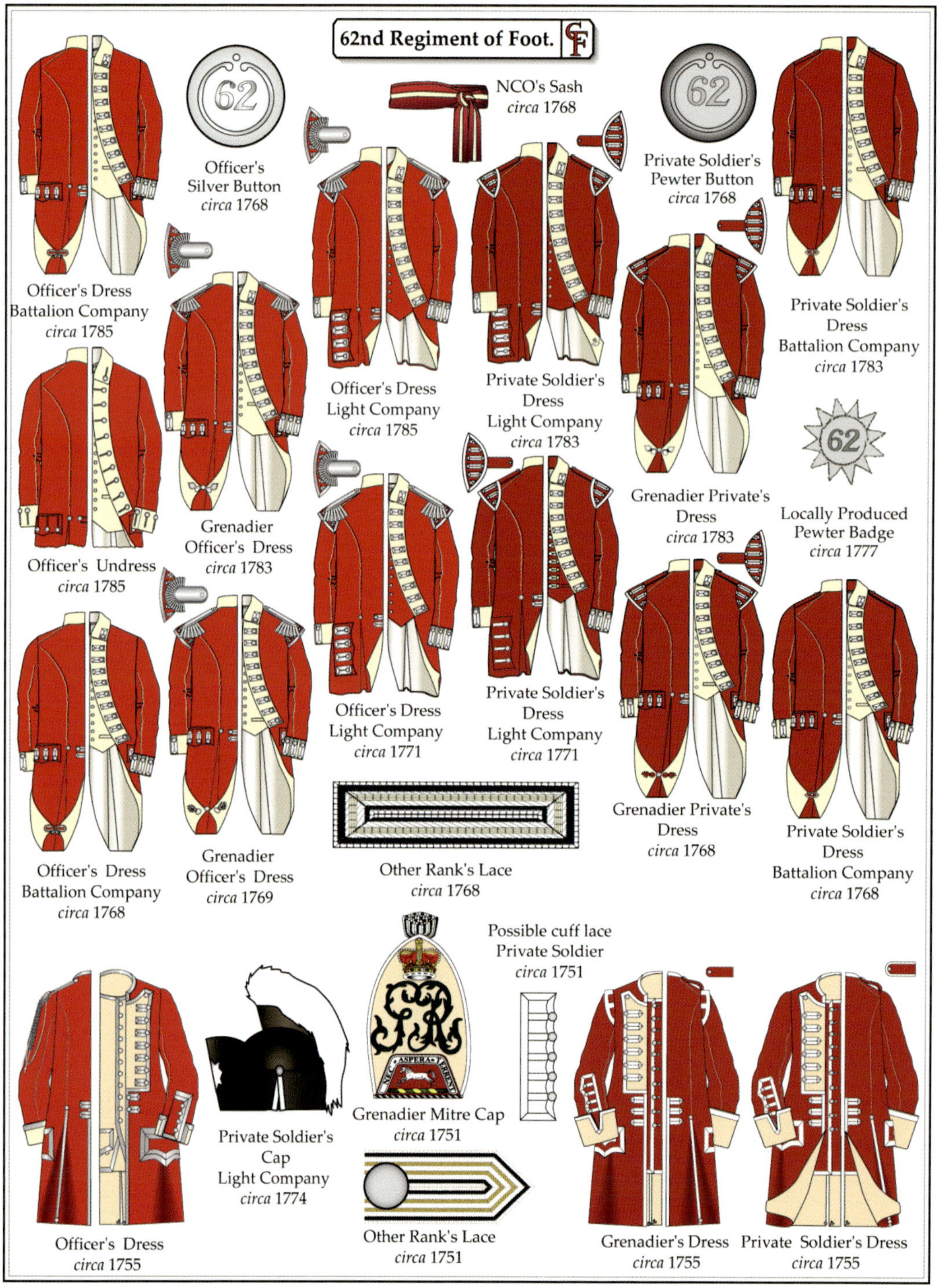
62nd Regiment of Foot.
Officer's Silver Button circa 1768
NCO's Sash circa 1768
Private Soldier's Pewter Button circa 1768
Officer's Dress Battalion Company circa 1785
Officer's Dress Light Company circa 1785
Private Soldier's Dress Light Company circa 1783
Private Soldier's Dress Battalion Company circa 1783
Officer's Undress circa 1785
Grenadier Officer's Dress circa 1783
Grenadier Private's Dress circa 1783
Locally Produced Pewter Badge circa 1777
Officer's Dress Light Company circa 1771
Private Soldier's Dress Light Company circa 1771
Officer's Dress Battalion Company circa 1768
Grenadier Officer's Dress circa 1769
Other Rank's Lace circa 1768
Grenadier Private's Dress circa 1768
Private Soldier's Dress Battalion Company circa 1768
Possible cuff lace Private Soldier circa 1751
NEC ASPERA TERRENT
Grenadier Mitre Cap circa 1751
Officer's Dress circa 1755
Private Soldier's Cap Light Company circa 1774
Other Rank's Lace circa 1751
Grenadier's Dress circa 1755
Private Soldier's Dress circa 1755

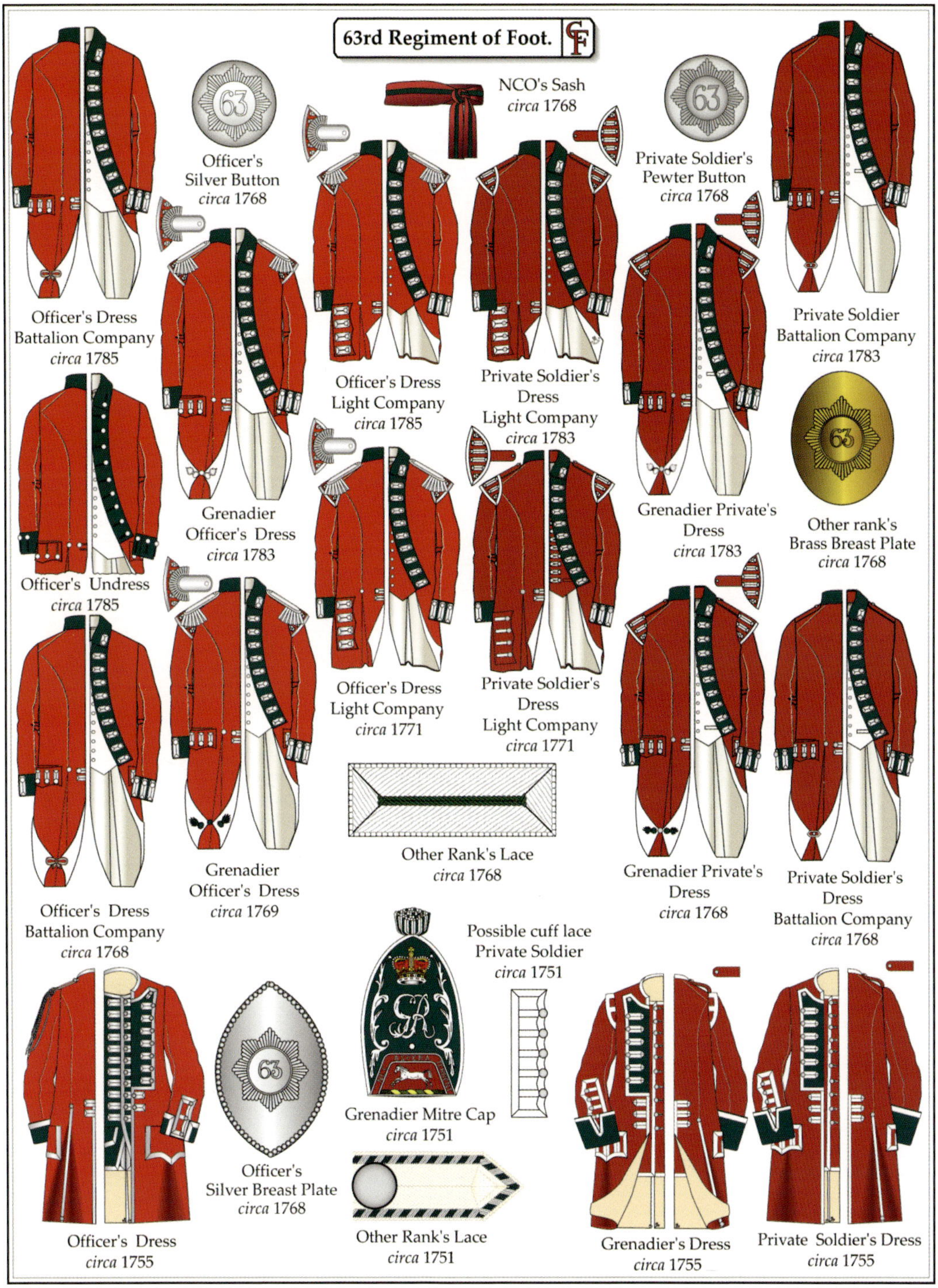
63rd Regiment of Foot.
Officer's Dress Battalion Company circa 1785
Officer's Silver Button circa 1768
NCO's Sash circa 1768
Private Soldier's Pewter Button circa 1768
Private Soldier Battalion Company circa 1783
Officer's Dress Light Company circa 1785
Private Soldier's Dress Light Company circa 1783
Grenadier Officer's Dress circa 1783
Officer's Undress circa 1785
Grenadier Private's Dress circa 1783
Other rank's Brass Breast Plate circa 1768
Officer's Dress Light Company circa 1771
Private Soldier's Dress Light Company circa 1771
Other Rank's Lace circa 1768
Officer's Dress Battalion Company circa 1768
Grenadier Officer's Dress circa 1769
Grenadier Private's Dress circa 1768
Private Soldier's Dress Battalion Company circa 1768
Possible cuff lace Private Soldier circa 1751
Grenadier Mitre Cap circa 1751
Officer's Silver Breast Plate circa 1768
Other Rank's Lace circa 1751
Officer's Dress circa 1755
Grenadier's Dress circa 1755
Private Soldier's Dress circa 1755

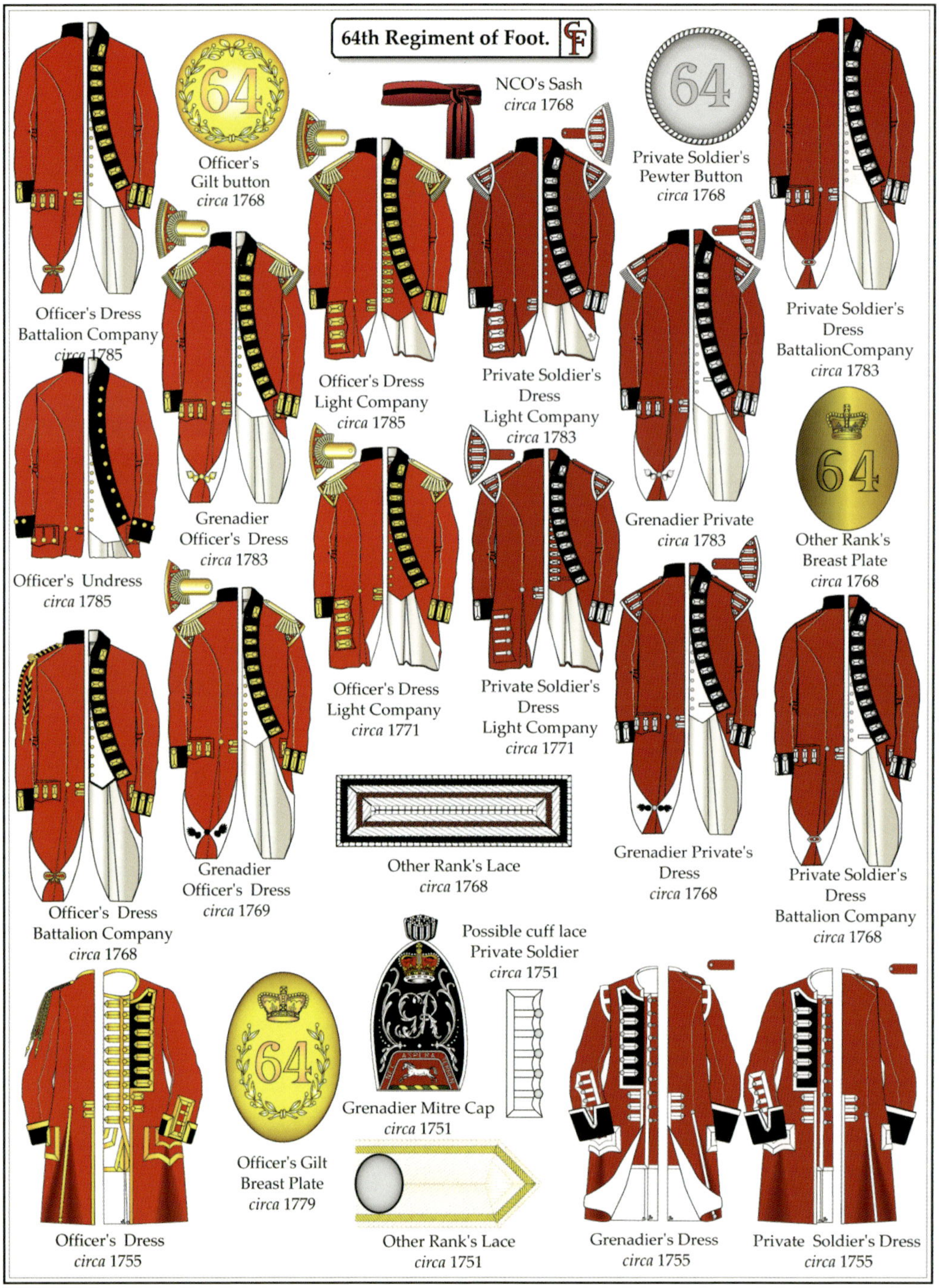
64th Regiment of Foot.
Officer's Gilt button circa 1768
NCO's Sash circa 1768
Private Soldier's Pewter Button circa 1768
Officer's Dress Battalion Company circa 1785
Officer's Dress Light Company circa 1785
Private Soldier's Dress Light Company circa 1783
Private Soldier's Dress BattalionCompany circa 1783
Officer's Undress circa 1785
Grenadier Officer's Dress circa 1783
Grenadier Private circa 1783
Other Rank's Breast Plate circa 1768
Officer's Dress Light Company circa 1771
Private Soldier's Dress Light Company circa 1771
Officer's Dress Battalion Company circa 1768
Grenadier Officer's Dress circa 1769
Other Rank's Lace circa 1768
Grenadier Private's Dress circa 1768
Private Soldier's Dress Battalion Company circa 1768
Possible cuff lace Private Soldier circa 1751
Grenadier Mitre Cap circa 1751
Officer's Dress circa 1755
Officer's Gilt Breast Plate circa 1779
Other Rank's Lace circa 1751
Grenadier's Dress circa 1755
Private Soldier's Dress circa 1755

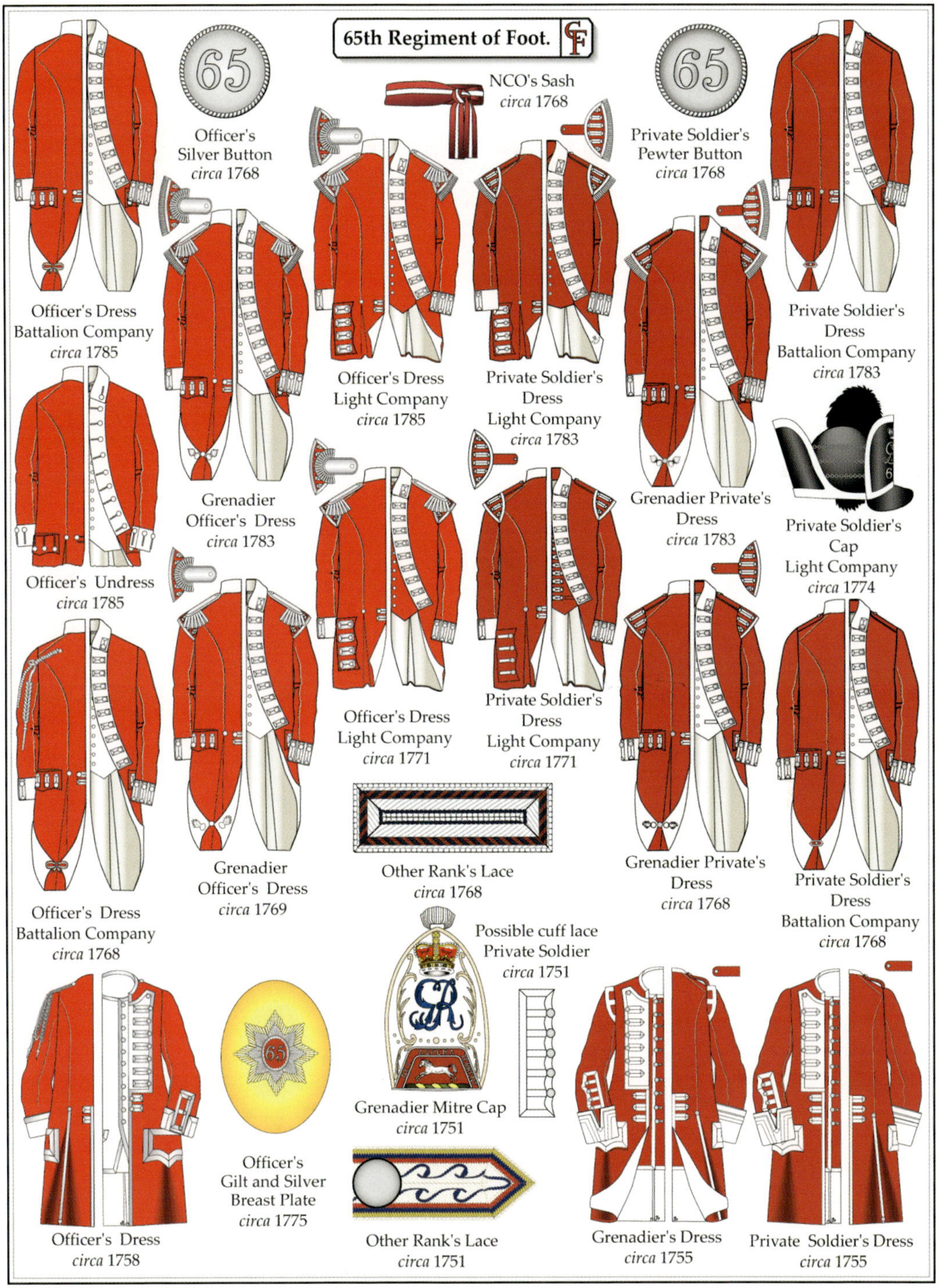
65th Regiment of Foot.
NCO's Sash
circa 1768
Officer's
Silver Button
circa 1768
Private Soldier's
Pewter Button
circa 1768
Officer's Dress
Battalion Company
circa 1785
Officer's Dress
Light Company
circa 1785
Private Soldier's
Dress
Light Company
circa 1783
Private Soldier's
Dress
Battalion Company
circa 1783
Grenadier
Officer's Dress
circa 1783
Grenadier Private's
Dress
circa 1783
Private Soldier's
Cap
Light Company
circa 1774
Officer's Undress
circa 1785
Officer's Dress
Light Company
circa 1771
Private Soldier's
Dress
Light Company
circa 1771
Other Rank's Lace
circa 1768
Grenadier Private's
Dress
circa 1768
Private Soldier's
Dress
Battalion Company
circa 1768
Grenadier
Officer's Dress
circa 1769
Officer's Dress
Battalion Company
circa 1768
Possible cuff lace
Private Soldier
circa 1751
Grenadier Mitre Cap
circa 1751
Officer's
Gilt and Silver
Breast Plate
circa 1775
Officer's Dress
circa 1758
Other Rank's Lace
circa 1751
Grenadier's Dress
circa 1755
Private Soldier's Dress
circa 1755

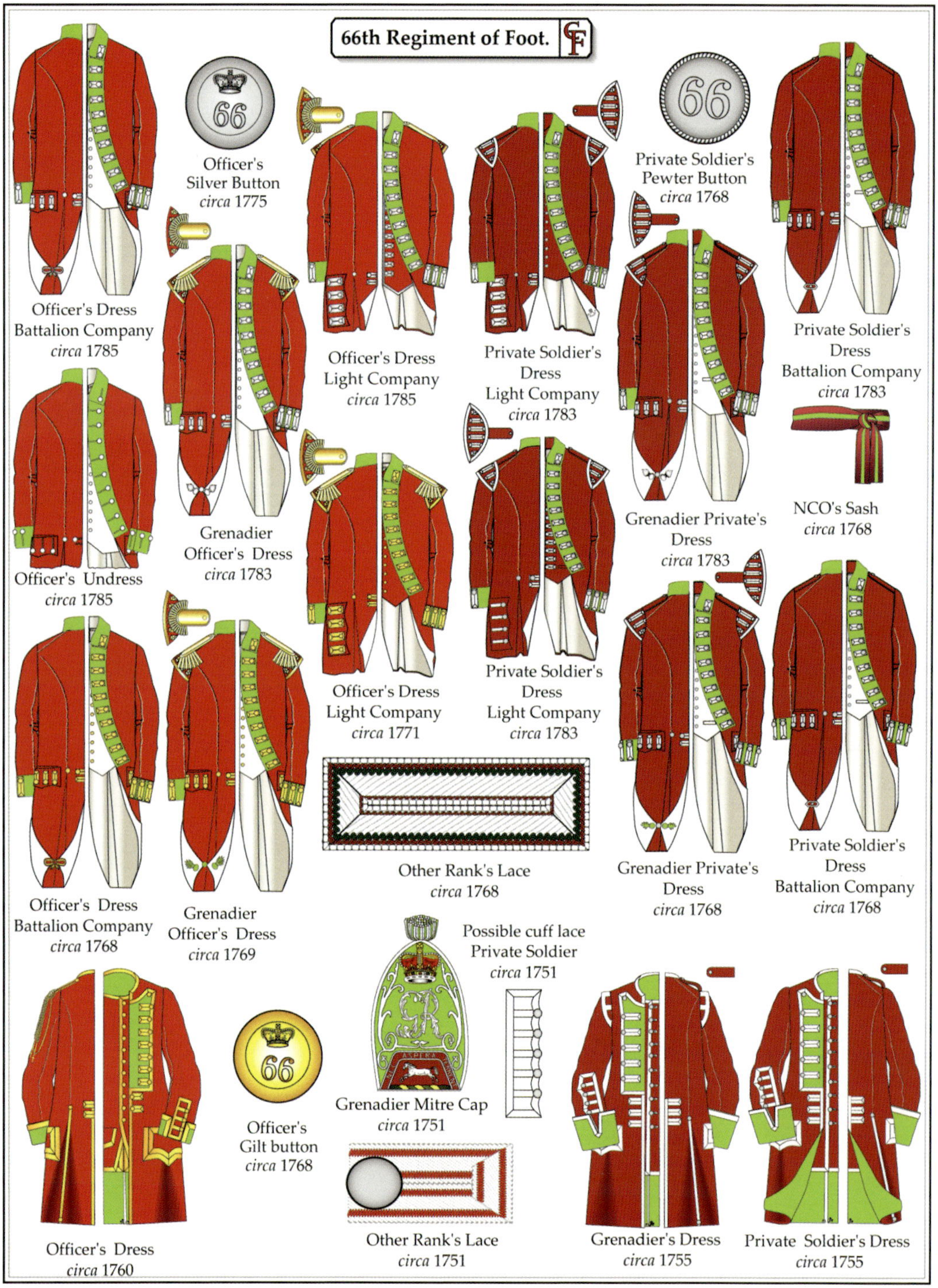
66th Regiment of Foot.
Officer's Silver Button circa 1775
Private Soldier's Pewter Button circa 1768
Officer's Dress Battalion Company circa 1785
Officer's Dress Light Company circa 1785
Private Soldier's Dress Light Company circa 1783
Private Soldier's Dress Battalion Company circa 1783
Officer's Undress circa 1785
Grenadier Officer's Dress circa 1783
Grenadier Private's Dress circa 1783
NCO's Sash circa 1768
Officer's Dress Light Company circa 1771
Private Soldier's Dress Light Company circa 1783
Officer's Dress Battalion Company circa 1768
Grenadier Officer's Dress circa 1769
Other Rank's Lace circa 1768
Grenadier Private's Dress circa 1768
Private Soldier's Dress Battalion Company circa 1768
Possible cuff lace Private Soldier circa 1751
Grenadier Mitre Cap circa 1751
Officer's Dress circa 1760
Officer's Gilt button circa 1768
Other Rank's Lace circa 1751
Grenadier's Dress circa 1755
Private Soldier's Dress circa 1755

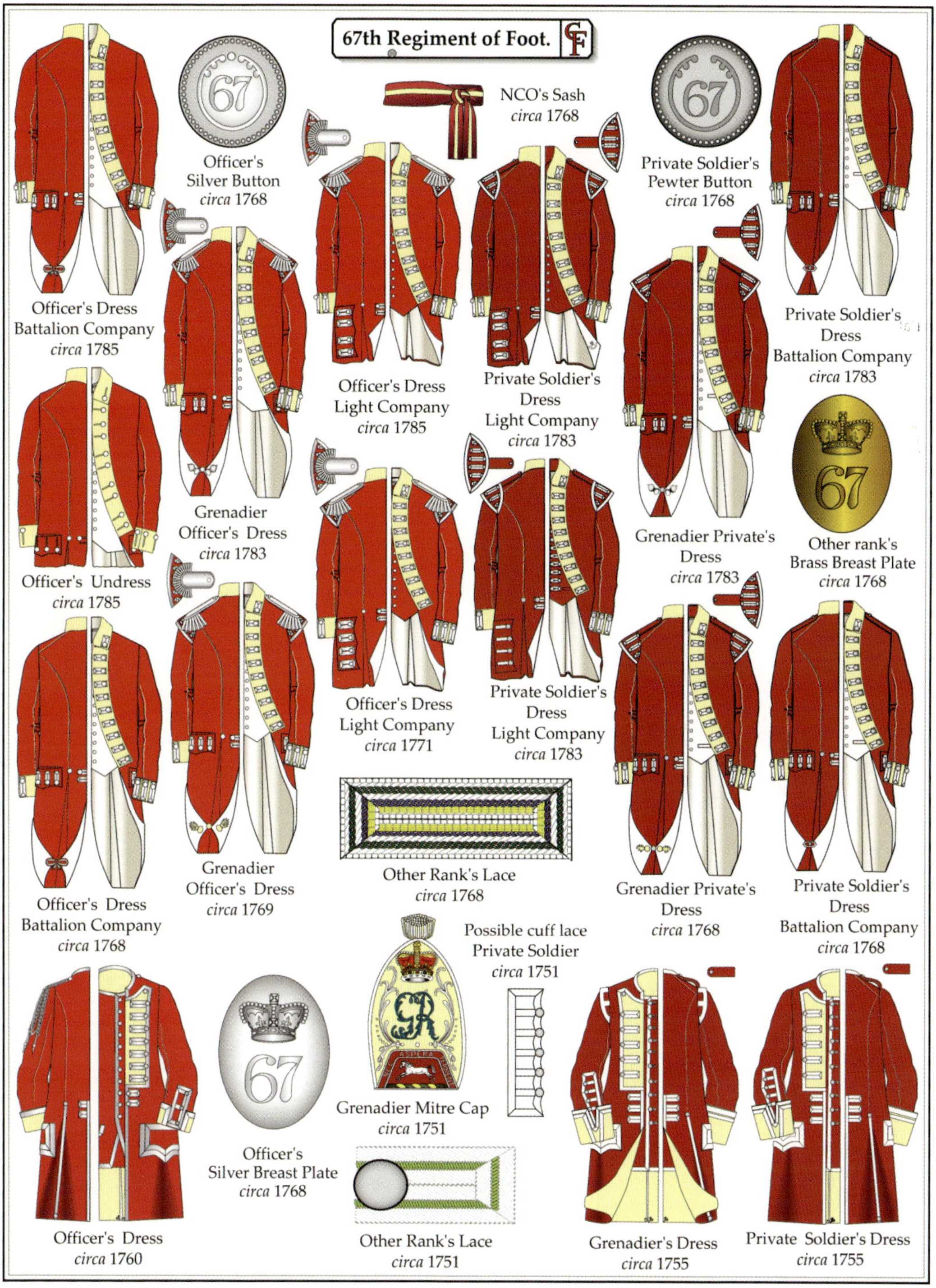
67th Regiment of Foot.
Officer's Dress Battalion Company circa 1785
Officer's Silver Button circa 1768
NCO's Sash circa 1768
Private Soldier's Pewter Button circa 1768
Private Soldier's Dress Battalion Company circa 1783
Officer's Dress Light Company circa 1785
Private Soldier's Dress Light Company circa 1783
Grenadier Officer's Dress circa 1783
Officer's Undress circa 1785
Grenadier Private's Dress circa 1783
Other rank's Brass Breast Plate circa 1768
Officer's Dress Light Company circa 1771
Private Soldier's Dress Light Company circa 1783
Officer's Dress Battalion Company circa 1768
Grenadier Officer's Dress circa 1769
Other Rank's Lace circa 1768
Grenadier Private's Dress circa 1768
Private Soldier's Dress Battalion Company circa 1768
Possible cuff lace Private Soldier circa 1751
Grenadier Mitre Cap circa 1751
Officer's Dress circa 1760
Officer's Silver Breast Plate circa 1768
Other Rank's Lace circa 1751
Grenadier's Dress circa 1755
Private Soldier's Dress circa 1755

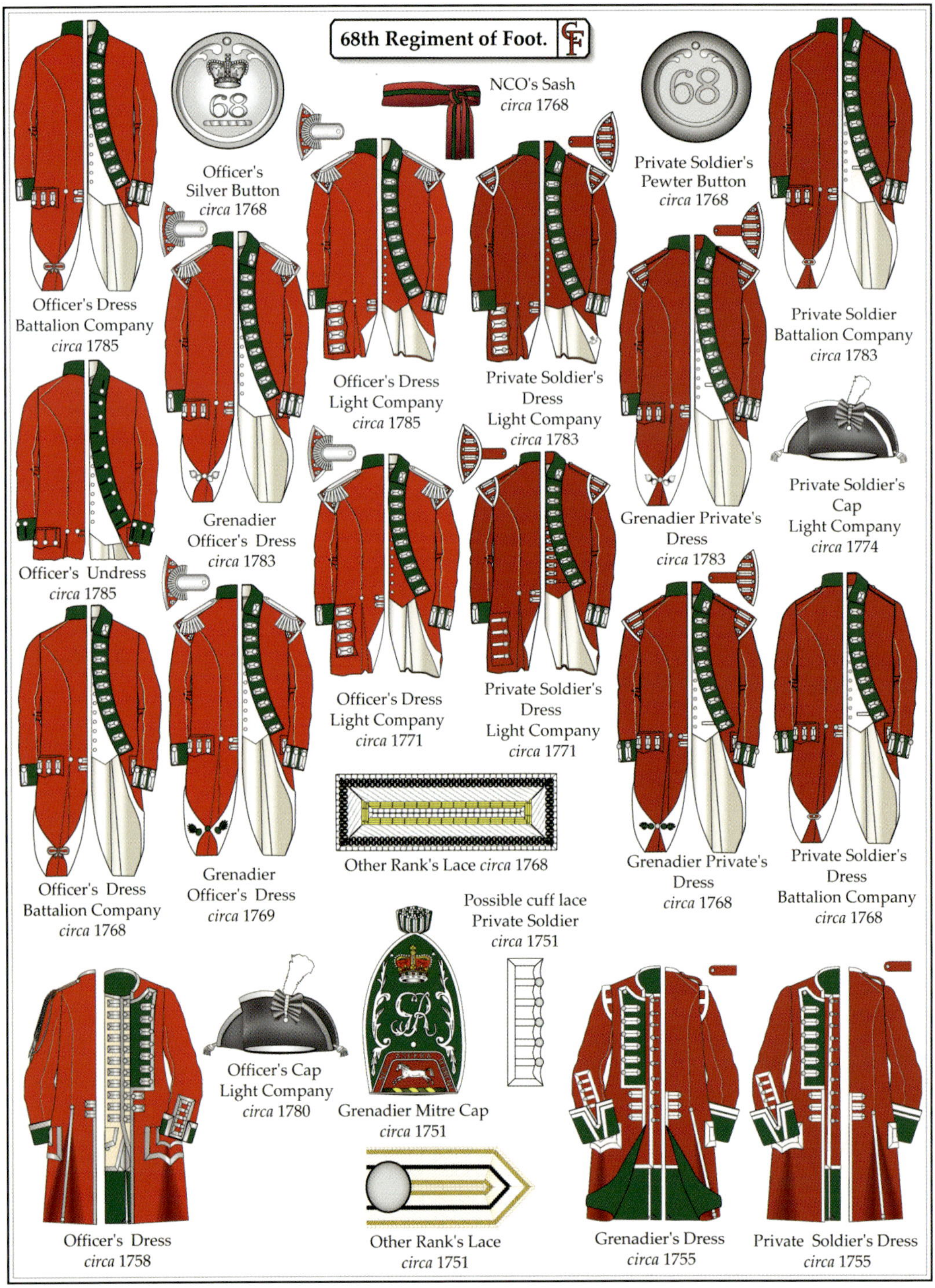
68th Regiment of Foot.
NCO's Sash
circa 1768
Officer's
Silver Button
circa 1768
Private Soldier's
Pewter Button
circa 1768
Officer's Dress
Battalion Company
circa 1785
Officer's Dress
Light Company
circa 1785
Private Soldier's
Dress
Light Company
circa 1783
Private Soldier
Battalion Company
circa 1783
Grenadier
Officer's Dress
circa 1783
Grenadier Private's
Dress
circa 1783
Private Soldier's
Cap
Light Company
circa 1774
Officer's Undress
circa 1785
Officer's Dress
Light Company
circa 1771
Private Soldier's
Dress
Light Company
circa 1771
Other Rank's Lace circa 1768
Officer's Dress
Battalion Company
circa 1768
Grenadier
Officer's Dress
circa 1769
Grenadier Private's
Dress
circa 1768
Private Soldier's
Dress
Battalion Company
circa 1768
Possible cuff lace
Private Soldier
circa 1751
Officer's Cap
Light Company
circa 1780
Grenadier Mitre Cap
circa 1751
Officer's Dress
circa 1758
Other Rank's Lace
circa 1751
Grenadier's Dress
circa 1755
Private Soldier's Dress
circa 1755

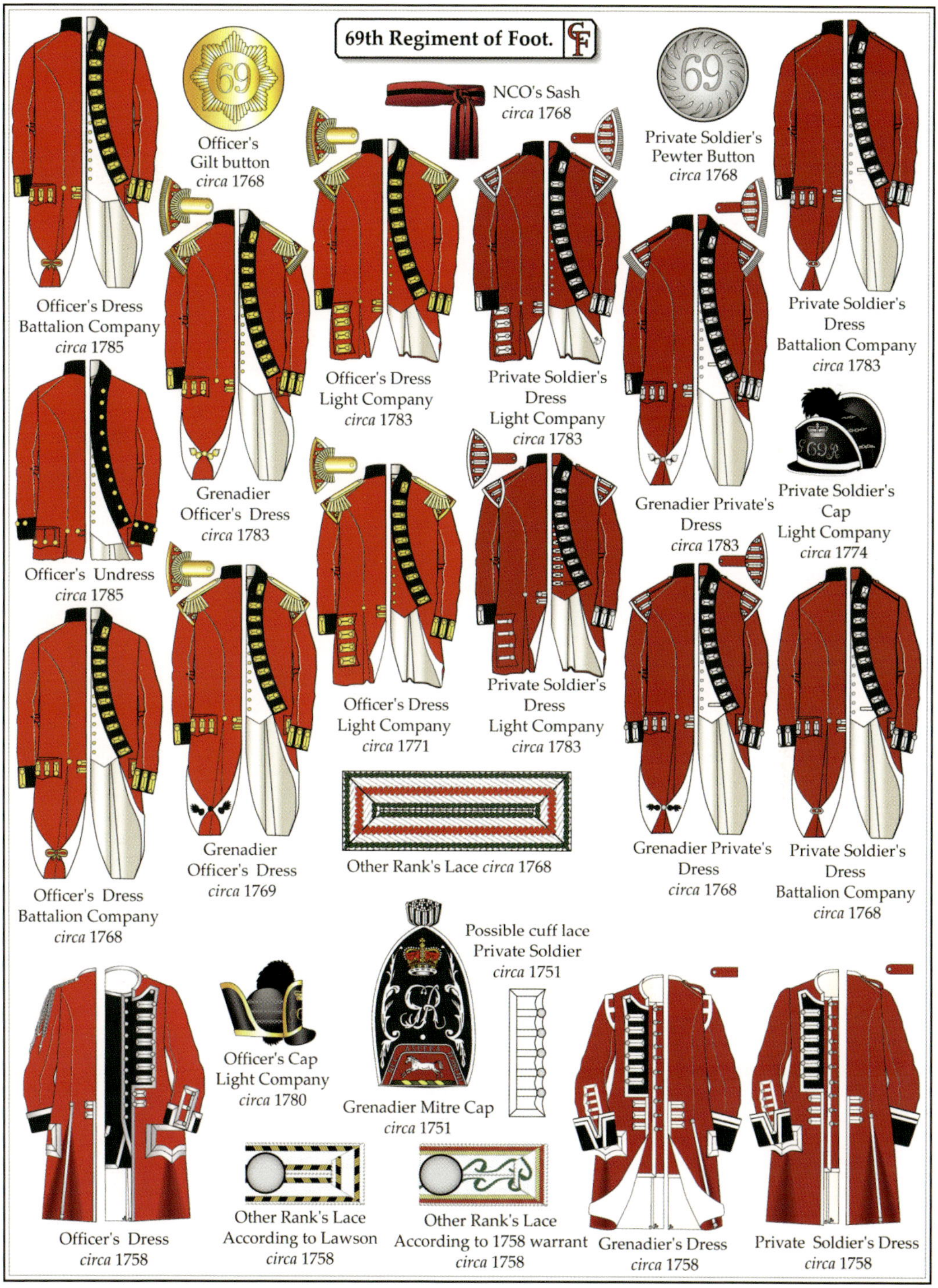

69th Regiment of Foot.
CF
69
Officer's Gilt button circa 1768
NCO's Sash circa 1768
69
Private Soldier's Pewter Button circa 1768
Officer's Dress Battalion Company circa 1785
Grenadier Officer's Dress circa 1783
Officer's Dress Light Company circa 1783
Private Soldier's Dress Light Company circa 1783
Grenadier Private's Dress circa 1783
Private Soldier's Dress Battalion Company circa 1783
Private Soldier's Cap Light Company circa 1774
Officer's Undress circa 1785
Officer's Dress Light Company circa 1771
Private Soldier's Dress Light Company circa 1783
Officer's Dress Battalion Company circa 1768
Grenadier Officer's Dress circa 1769
Other Rank's Lace circa 1768
Grenadier Private's Dress circa 1768
Private Soldier's Dress Battalion Company circa 1768
Possible cuff lace Private Soldier circa 1751
Officer's Cap Light Company circa 1780
Grenadier Mitre Cap circa 1751
Officer's Dress circa 1758
Other Rank's Lace According to Lawson circa 1758
Other Rank's Lace According to 1758 warrant circa 1758
Grenadier's Dress circa 1758
Private Soldier's Dress circa 1758

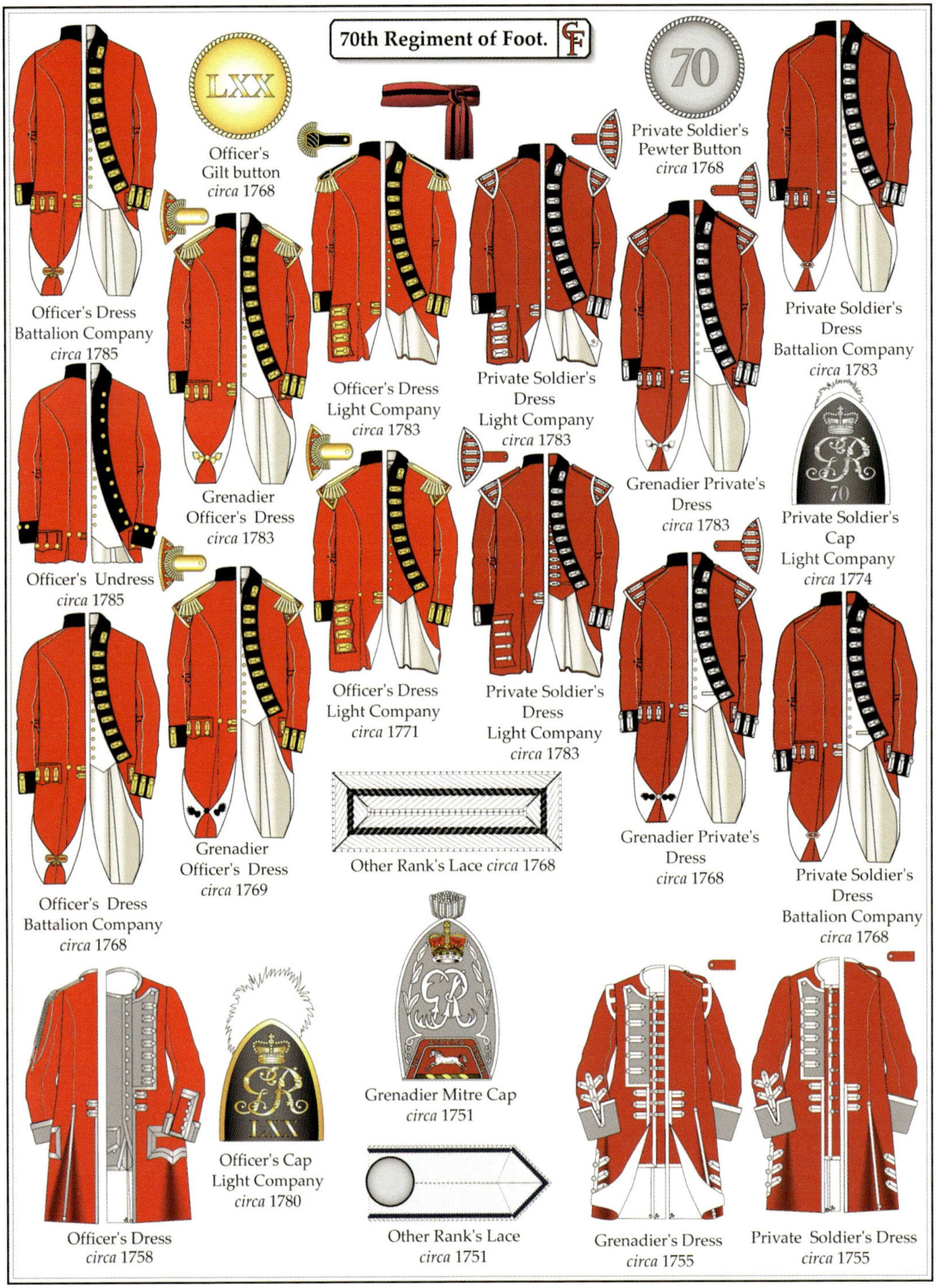
70th Regiment of Foot.
Officer's Gilt button circa 1768
Private Soldier's Pewter Button circa 1768
Officer's Dress Battalion Company circa 1785
Officer's Dress Light Company circa 1783
Private Soldier's Dress Light Company circa 1783
Private Soldier's Dress Battalion Company circa 1783
Grenadier Officer's Dress circa 1783
Grenadier Private's Dress circa 1783
Officer's Undress circa 1785
Private Soldier's Cap Light Company circa 1774
Officer's Dress Light Company circa 1771
Private Soldier's Dress Light Company circa 1783
Officer's Dress Battalion Company circa 1768
Grenadier Officer's Dress circa 1769
Other Rank's Lace circa 1768
Grenadier Private's Dress circa 1768
Private Soldier's Dress Battalion Company circa 1768
Grenadier Mitre Cap circa 1751
Officer's Dress circa 1758
Officer's Cap Light Company circa 1780
Other Rank's Lace circa 1751
Grenadier's Dress circa 1755
Private Soldier's Dress circa 1755

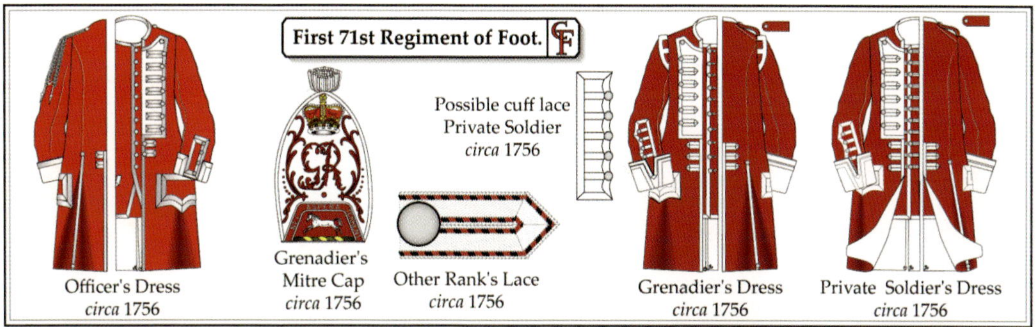
First 71st Regiment of Foot.
Officer's Dress circa 1756
Grenadier's Mitre Cap circa 1756
Possible cuff lace Private Soldier circa 1756
Other Rank's Lace circa 1756
Grenadier's Dress circa 1756
Private Soldier's Dress circa 1756

Second 71st (Invalids) Regiment of Foot.
Officer's Dress circa 1757
Drummer's Cap circa 1757
Grenadier's Mitre Cap circa 1757
Other Ranks wore no lace
Grenadier's Dress circa 1757
Private Soldier's Dress circa 1757

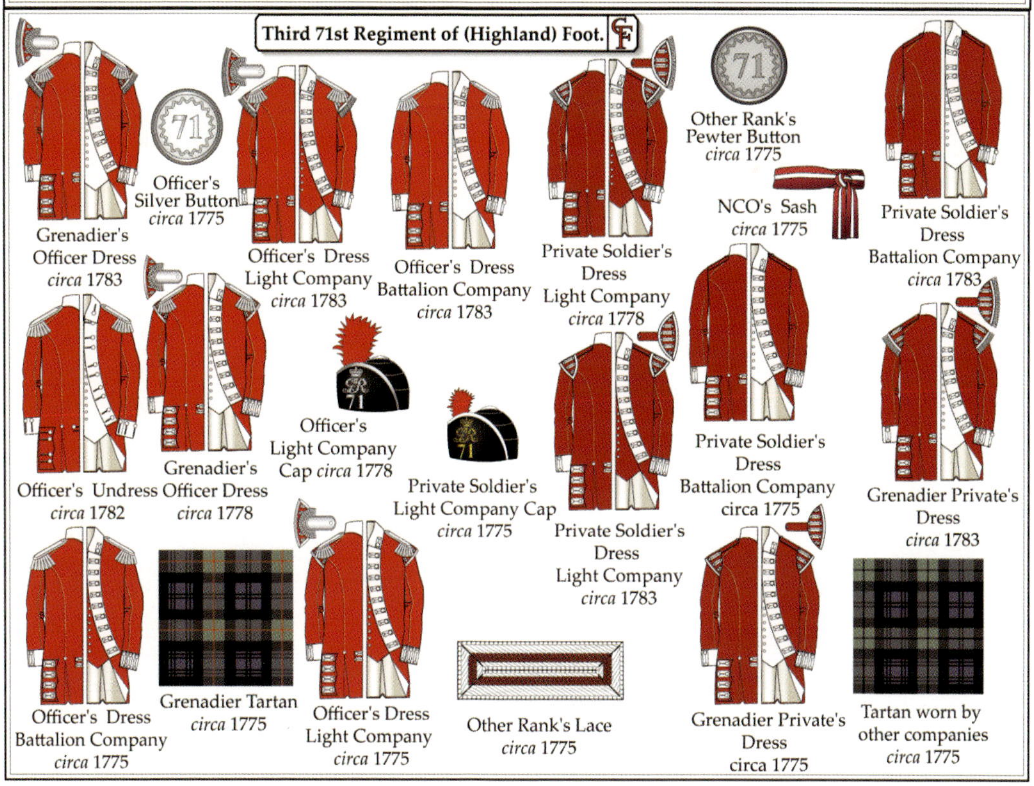
Third 71st Regiment of (Highland) Foot.
Grenadier's Officer Dress circa 1783
Officer's Silver Button circa 1775
Officer's Dress Light Company circa 1783
Officer's Dress Battalion Company circa 1783
Private Soldier's Dress Light Company circa 1778
Other Rank's Pewter Button circa 1775
NCO's Sash circa 1775
Private Soldier's Dress Battalion Company circa 1783
Officer's Undress circa 1782
Grenadier's Officer Dress circa 1778
Officer's Light Company Cap circa 1778
Private Soldier's Light Company Cap circa 1775
Private Soldier's Dress Light Company circa 1783
Private Soldier's Dress Battalion Company circa 1775
Grenadier Private's Dress circa 1783
Officer's Dress Battalion Company circa 1775
Grenadier Tartan circa 1775
Officer's Dress Light Company circa 1775
Other Rank's Lace circa 1775
Grenadier Private's Dress circa 1775
Tartan worn by other companies circa 1775

First 71st Regiment of Foot.
Officer's Dress
circa 1756
Grenadier's
Mitre Cap
circa 1756
Possible cuff lace
Private Soldier
circa 1756
Other Rank's Lace
circa 1756
Grenadier's Dress
circa 1756
Private Soldier's Dress
circa 1756
Second 71st (Invalids) Regiment of Foot.
Officer's Dress
circa 1757
Drummer's Cap
circa 1757
Grenadier's Mitre Cap
circa 1757
Other Ranks
wore no lace
Grenadier's Dress
circa 1757
Private Soldier's Dress
circa 1757
Third 71st Regiment of (Highland) Foot.
Grenadier's
Officer Dress
circa 1783
Officer's
Silver Button
circa 1775
Officer's Dress
Light Company
circa 1783
Officer's Dress
Battalion Company
circa 1783
Private Soldier's
Dress
Light Company
circa 1778
Other Rank's
Pewter Button
circa 1775
NCO's Sash
circa 1775
Private Soldier's
Dress
Battalion Company
circa 1783
Officer's
Light Company
Cap circa 1778
Private Soldier's
Light Company Cap
circa 1775
Officer's Undress
circa 1782
Grenadier's
Officer Dress
circa 1778
Private Soldier's
Dress
Light Company
circa 1783
Private Soldier's
Dress
Battalion Company
circa 1775
Grenadier Private's
Dress
circa 1783
Officer's Dress
Battalion Company
circa 1775
Grenadier Tartan
circa 1775
Officer's Dress
Light Company
circa 1775
Other Rank's Lace
circa 1775
Grenadier Private's
Dress
circa 1775
Tartan worn by
other companies
circa 1775

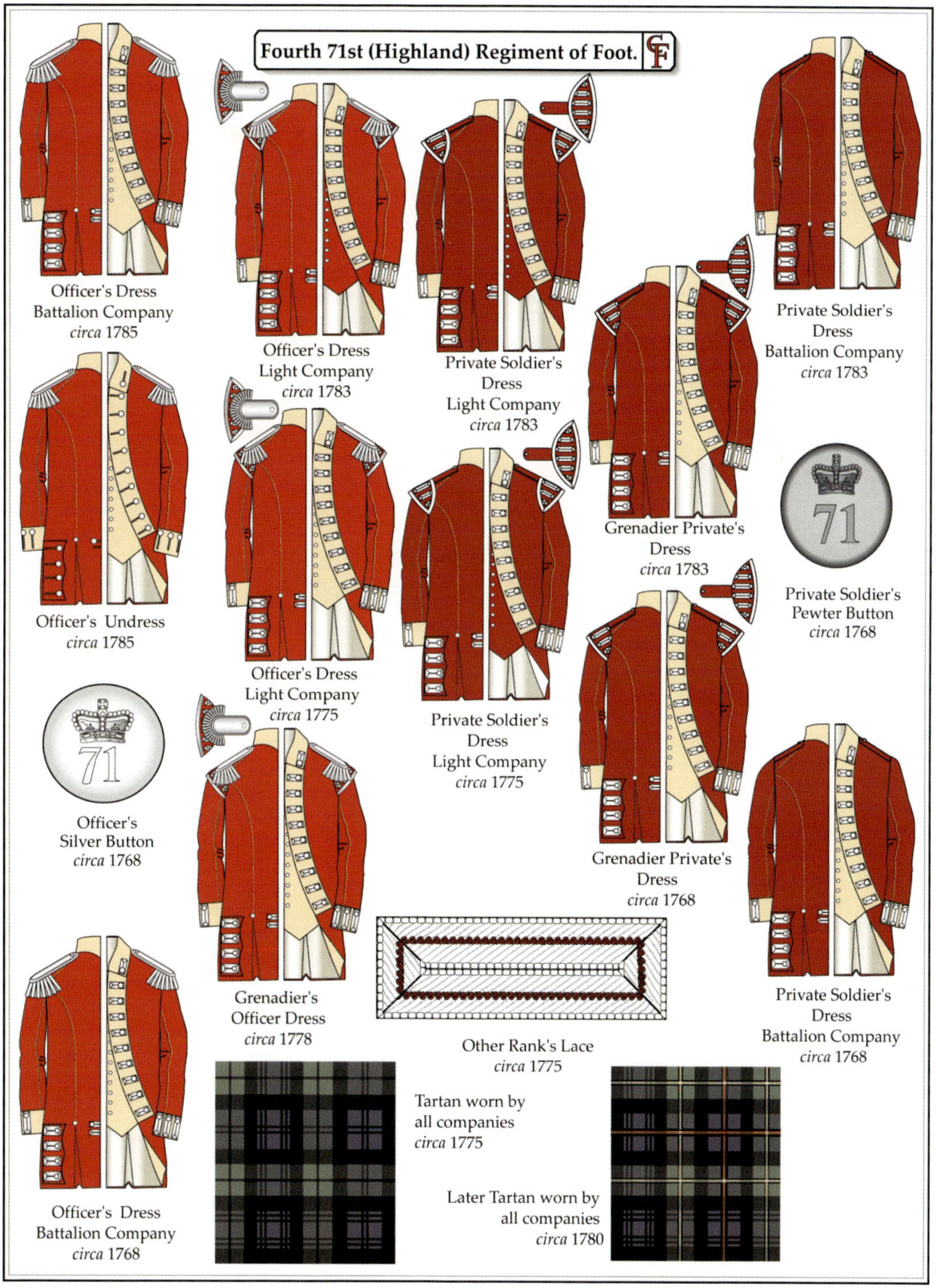
Fourth 71st (Highland) Regiment of Foot.
CF
Officer's Dress
Battalion Company
circa 1785
Officer's Dress
Light Company
circa 1783
Private Soldier's
Dress
Light Company
circa 1783
Private Soldier's
Dress
Battalion Company
circa 1783
Grenadier Private's
Dress
circa 1783
Officer's Undress
circa 1785
Officer's Dress
Light Company
circa 1775
Private Soldier's
Dress
Light Company
circa 1775
71
Private Soldier's
Pewter Button
circa 1768
71
Officer's
Silver Button
circa 1768
Grenadier Private's
Dress
circa 1768
Grenadier's
Officer Dress
circa 1778
Other Rank's Lace
circa 1775
Private Soldier's
Dress
Battalion Company
circa 1768
Tartan worn by
all companies
circa 1775
Later Tartan worn by
all companies
circa 1780
Officer's Dress
Battalion Company
circa 1768

First 72nd Regiment of Foot.

Officer's Dress
circa 1760

Grenadier
Mitre Cap
circa 1758

Possible cuff lace
Private Soldier
circa 1758

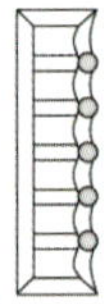

Other Ranks Lace
circa 1758

Grenadier's Dress
circa 1758

Private Soldier's Dress
circa 1758

Second 72nd (Invalids) Regiment of Foot.

Officer's Dress
circa 1757

Drummer Cap
circa 1757

Grenadier Mitre Cap
circa 1757

Other Ranks wore no lace

Grenadier's Dress
circa 1757

Private Soldier's Dress
circa 1757

Fourth 72nd (Royal Manchester Volunteers) Regiment of Foot.

Officer's Dress
Battalion Company
circa 1783

Grenadier
Officer's Dress
circa 1769

Officer's Dress
Light Company
circa 1783

Private Soldier's
Dress
Light Company
circa 1777

Grenadier Private's
Dress
circa 1783

Private Soldier's
Dress
Battalion Company
circa 1783

Officer's Dress
Battalion Company
circa 1777

Officer's
Gilt button
circa 1777

Officer's
Gilt Breast plate
circa 1777

Officer's Dress
Light Company
circa 1777

Private Soldier's
Pewter Button
circa 1768

Other Ranks lace not known

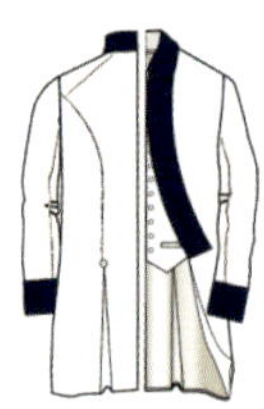

Private Soldier's
Dress
Battalion Company
circa 1768

Third 73rd (Invalids) Regiment of Foot.
Other Rank's wore no lace
Officer's Dress *circa* 1757
Drummer Cap *circa* 1757
Grenadier Mitre Cap *circa* 1757
Grenadier's Dress *circa* 1757
Private Soldier's Dress *circa* 1757

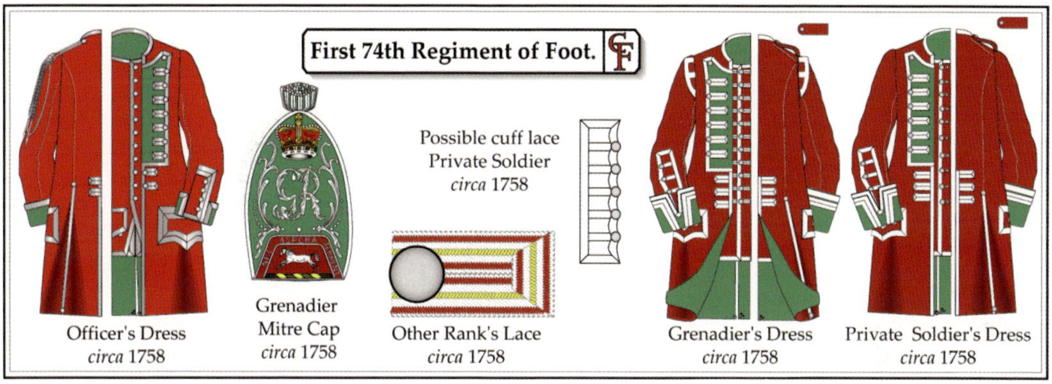
First 74th Regiment of Foot.
Possible cuff lace Private Soldier *circa* 1758
Officer's Dress *circa* 1758
Grenadier Mitre Cap *circa* 1758
Other Rank's Lace *circa* 1758
Grenadier's Dress *circa* 1758
Private Soldier's Dress *circa* 1758

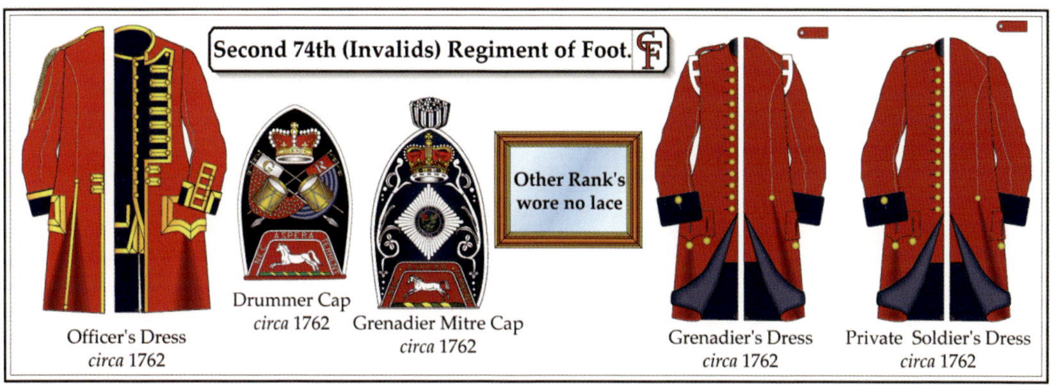
Second 74th (Invalids) Regiment of Foot.
Other Rank's wore no lace
Officer's Dress *circa* 1762
Drummer Cap *circa* 1762
Grenadier Mitre Cap *circa* 1762
Grenadier's Dress *circa* 1762
Private Soldier's Dress *circa* 1762

Third 74th (Highland) Regiment of Foot.
Grenadier Officer's Dress circa 1783
Officer's Dress Light Company circa 1783
Officer Dress Battalion Company circa 1783
Private Soldier's Dress Light Company circa 1783
Private Soldier's Dress Battalion Company circa 1783
Officer's Undress circa 1785
Grenadier Officer's Dress circa 1777
74
Officer's Silver Button circa 1777
Private Soldier's Dress Light Company circa 1777
Grenadier Private's Dress circa 1783
Officer's Dress Battalion Company circa 1777
Officer's Dress Light Company circa 1777
74
Private Soldier's Pewter Button circa 1777
NCO's Sash circa 1777
Grenadier Private's Dress circa 1777
Private Soldier's Dress Battalion Company circa 1777
Tartan worn by Battalion and Light Companies circa 1777
74
Officer's Silver Breast Plate circa 1768
Other Rank's Lace circa 1777
74
Private Soldier's Brass Breast Plate circa 1780
Tartan worn by Grenadier companies circa 1777

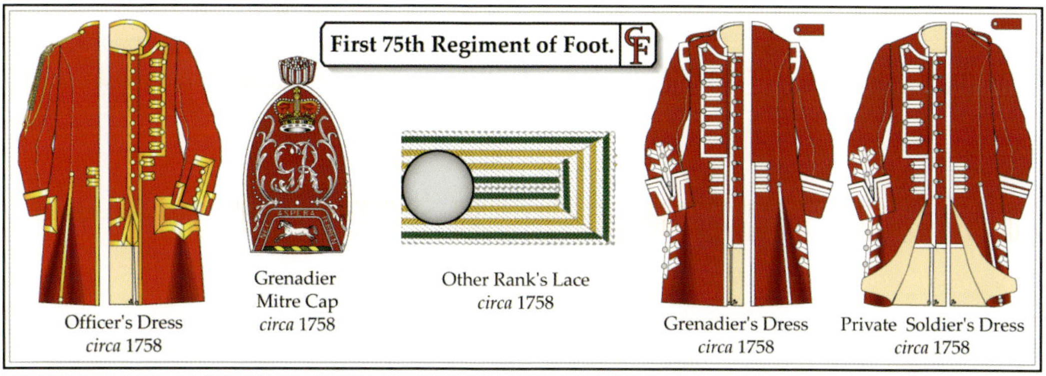
First 75th Regiment of Foot.
Officer's Dress
circa 1758
Grenadier
Mitre Cap
circa 1758
Other Rank's Lace
circa 1758
Grenadier's Dress
circa 1758
Private Soldier's Dress
circa 1758

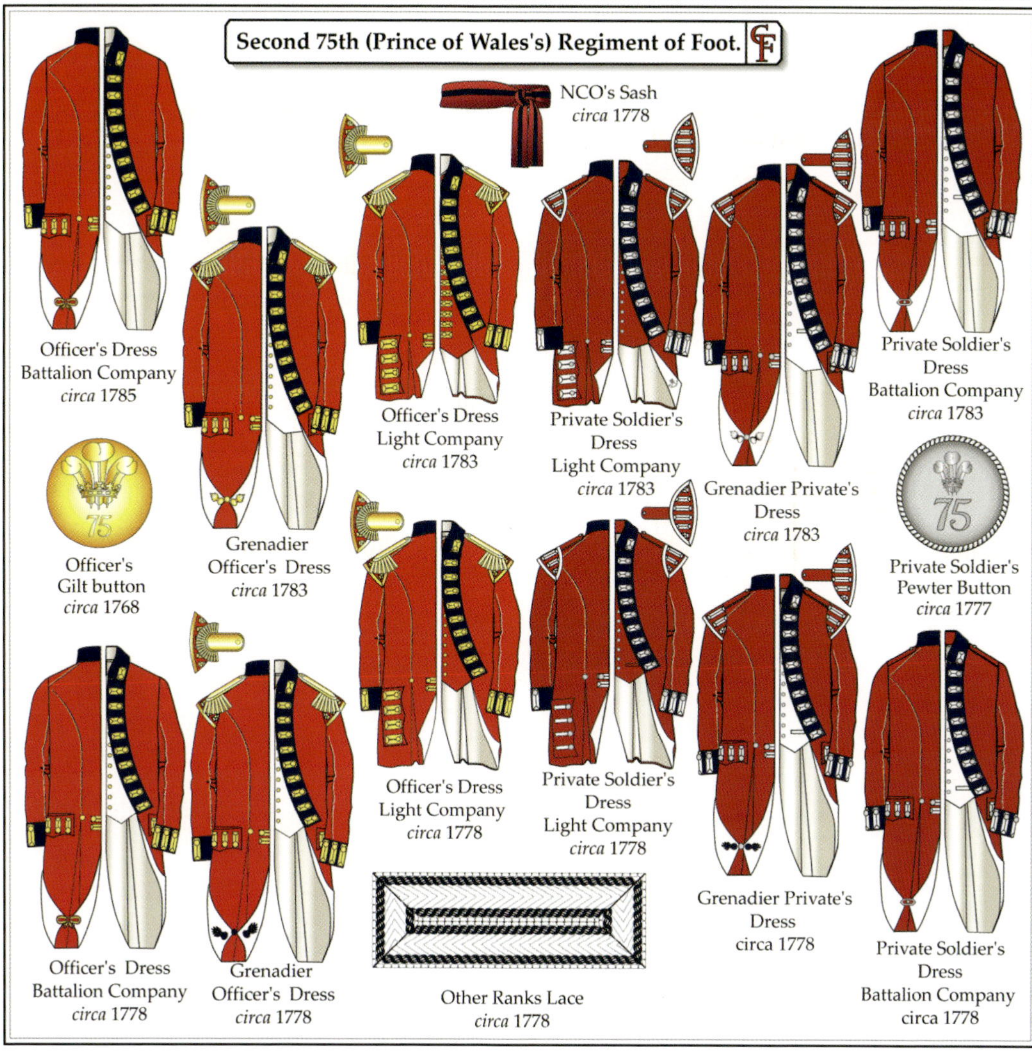
Second 75th (Prince of Wales's) Regiment of Foot.
Officer's Dress
Battalion Company
circa 1785
NCO's Sash
circa 1778
Officer's Dress
Light Company
circa 1783
Private Soldier's
Dress
Light Company
circa 1783
Grenadier Private's
Dress
circa 1783
Private Soldier's
Dress
Battalion Company
circa 1783
Officer's
Gilt button
circa 1768
Grenadier
Officer's Dress
circa 1783
Private Soldier's
Pewter Button
circa 1777
Officer's Dress
Light Company
circa 1778
Private Soldier's
Dress
Light Company
circa 1778
Grenadier Private's
Dress
circa 1778
Officer's Dress
Battalion Company
circa 1778
Grenadier
Officer's Dress
circa 1778
Other Ranks Lace
circa 1778
Private Soldier's
Dress
Battalion Company
circa 1778

1st 76th Regiment of Foot.
Officer's Dress *circa* 1756
Grenadier Mitre Cap *circa* 1756
Other Rank's Lace *circa* 1756
Grenadier's Dress *circa* 1756
Private soldier's Dress *circa* 1756

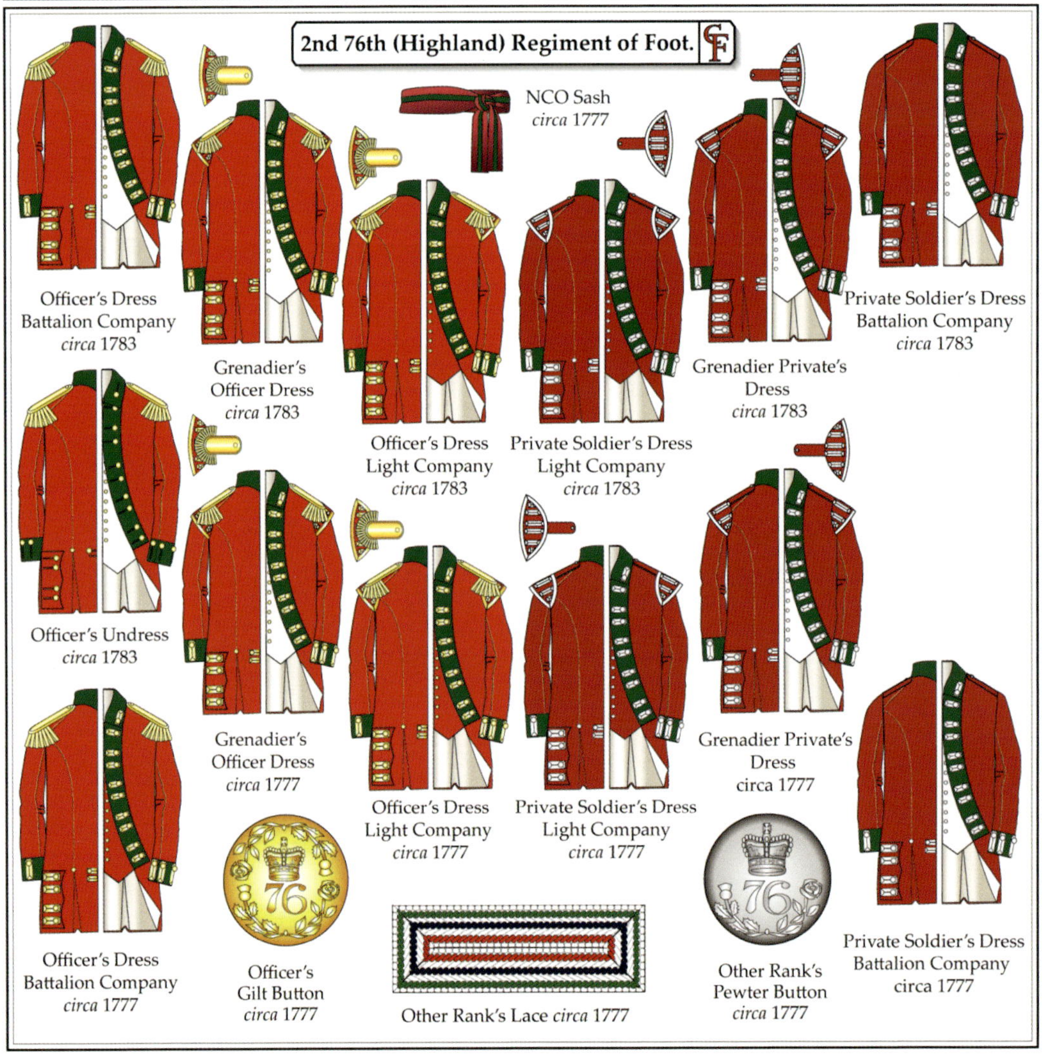
2nd 76th (Highland) Regiment of Foot.
NCO Sash *circa* 1777
Officer's Dress Battalion Company *circa* 1783
Grenadier's Officer Dress *circa* 1783
Officer's Dress Light Company *circa* 1783
Private Soldier's Dress Light Company *circa* 1783
Grenadier Private's Dress *circa* 1783
Private Soldier's Dress Battalion Company *circa* 1783
Officer's Undress *circa* 1783
Grenadier's Officer Dress *circa* 1777
Officer's Dress Light Company *circa* 1777
Private Soldier's Dress Light Company *circa* 1777
Grenadier Private's Dress circa 1777
Officer's Dress Battalion Company *circa* 1777
Officer's Gilt Button *circa* 1777
Other Rank's Lace *circa* 1777
Other Rank's Pewter Button *circa* 1777
Private Soldier's Dress Battalion Company circa 1777

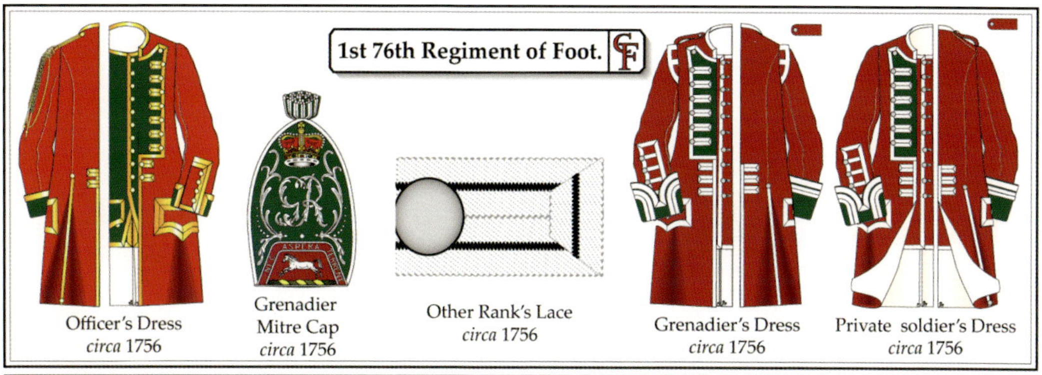
1st 76th Regiment of Foot.
Officer's Dress
circa 1756
Grenadier
Mitre Cap
circa 1756
Other Rank's Lace
circa 1756
Grenadier's Dress
circa 1756
Private soldier's Dress
circa 1756

2nd 76th (Highland) Regiment of Foot.
NCO Sash
circa 1777
Officer's Dress
Battalion Company
circa 1783
Grenadier's
Officer Dress
circa 1783
Officer's Dress
Light Company
circa 1783
Private Soldier's Dress
Light Company
circa 1783
Grenadier Private's
Dress
circa 1783
Private Soldier's Dress
Battalion Company
circa 1783
Officer's Undress
circa 1783
Grenadier's
Officer Dress
circa 1777
Officer's Dress
Light Company
circa 1777
Private Soldier's Dress
Light Company
circa 1777
Grenadier Private's
Dress
circa 1777
Officer's Dress
Battalion Company
circa 1777
Officer's
Gilt Button
circa 1777
Other Rank's Lace circa 1777
Other Rank's
Pewter Button
circa 1777
Private Soldier's Dress
Battalion Company
circa 1777

1st 78th (Highland) Regiment of Foot.
No details of Other Rank's Lace
Officer's Dress *circa* 1758
Tartan *circa* 1758
Grenadier Mitre Cap *circa* 1758
Grenadier's Dress *circa* 1758
Private Soldier's Dress *circa* 1758

2nd 78th (Highland) Regiment of Foot.
Officer's Dress Battalion Company *circa* 1783
Officer's Dress Light Company *circa* 1783
Officer's Silver Button *circa* 1777
Grenadier's Officer Dress *circa* 1783
Other Rank's Pewter Button *circa* 1777
Private Soldier's Dress Light Company *circa* 1783
Private Soldier's Dress Battalion Company *circa* 1783
NCO Sash *circa* 1780
Officer's Undress *circa* 1783
Grenadier's Officer Dress *circa* 1777
Other Rank's Lace *circa* 1777
Private Soldier's Dress Light Company *circa* 1777
Grenadier Private's Dress *circa* 1783
Officer's Dress Battalion Company *circa* 1777
Officer's Light Company Cap *circa* 1777
Officer's Dress Light Company *circa* 1777
Grenadier Private's Dress circa 1777
Other Rank's Light Company Cap *circa* 1777
Private Soldier's Dress Battalion Company circa 1777

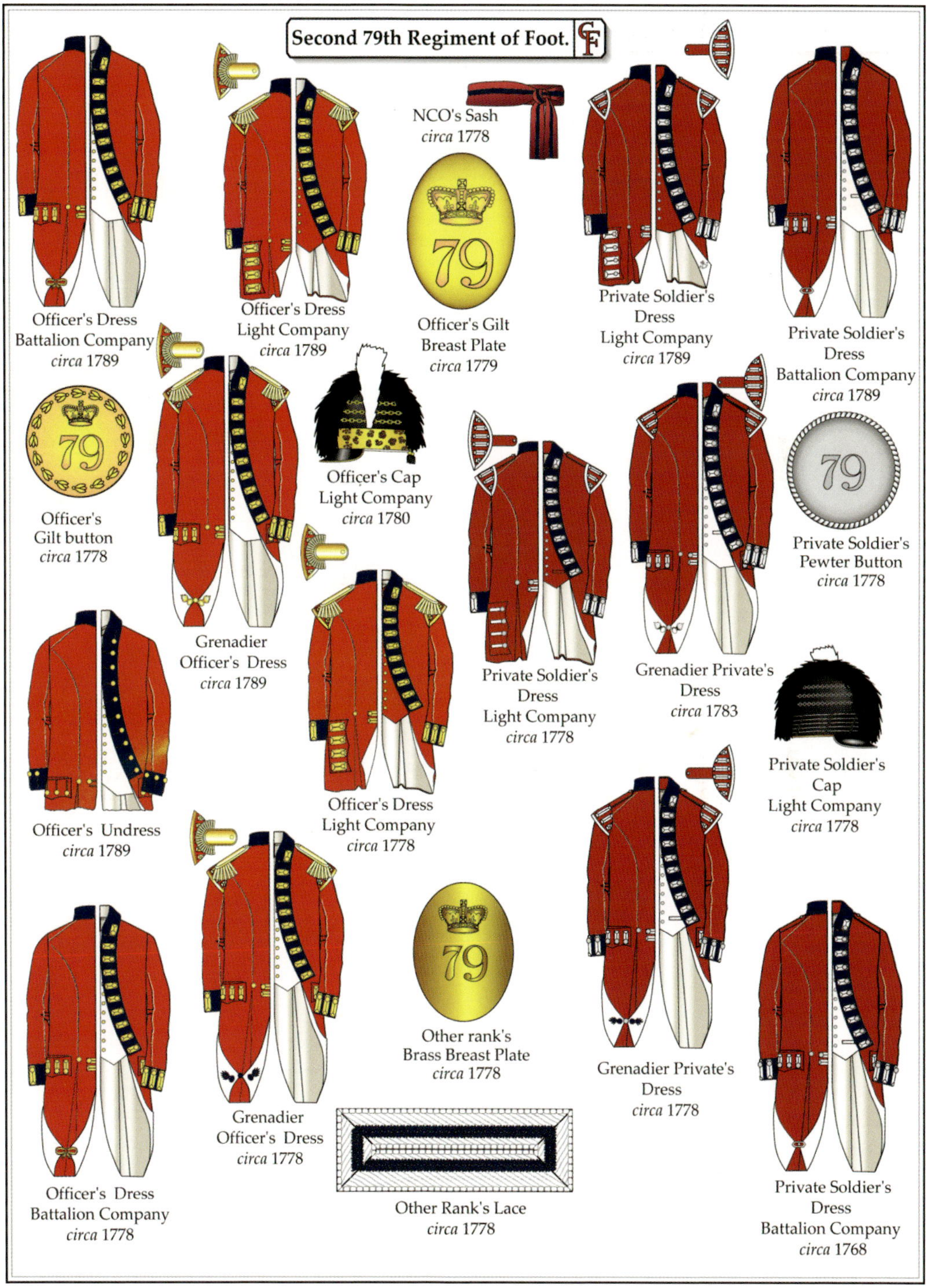
Second 79th Regiment of Foot.
CF
Officer's Dress
Battalion Company
circa 1789
Officer's Dress
Light Company
circa 1789
NCO's Sash
circa 1778
79
Officer's Gilt
Breast Plate
circa 1779
Private Soldier's
Dress
Light Company
circa 1789
Private Soldier's
Dress
Battalion Company
circa 1789
79
Officer's
Gilt button
circa 1778
Grenadier
Officer's Dress
circa 1789
Officer's Cap
Light Company
circa 1780
Private Soldier's
Dress
Light Company
circa 1778
Grenadier Private's
Dress
circa 1783
79
Private Soldier's
Pewter Button
circa 1778
Officer's Undress
circa 1789
Officer's Dress
Light Company
circa 1778
Private Soldier's
Cap
Light Company
circa 1778
79
Other rank's
Brass Breast Plate
circa 1778
Grenadier Private's
Dress
circa 1778
Officer's Dress
Battalion Company
circa 1778
Grenadier
Officer's Dress
circa 1778
Other Rank's Lace
circa 1778
Private Soldier's
Dress
Battalion Company
circa 1768

First 80th Regiment of Light-armed Foot.

Second 80th (Royal Edinburgh Volunteers) Regiment of Foot.

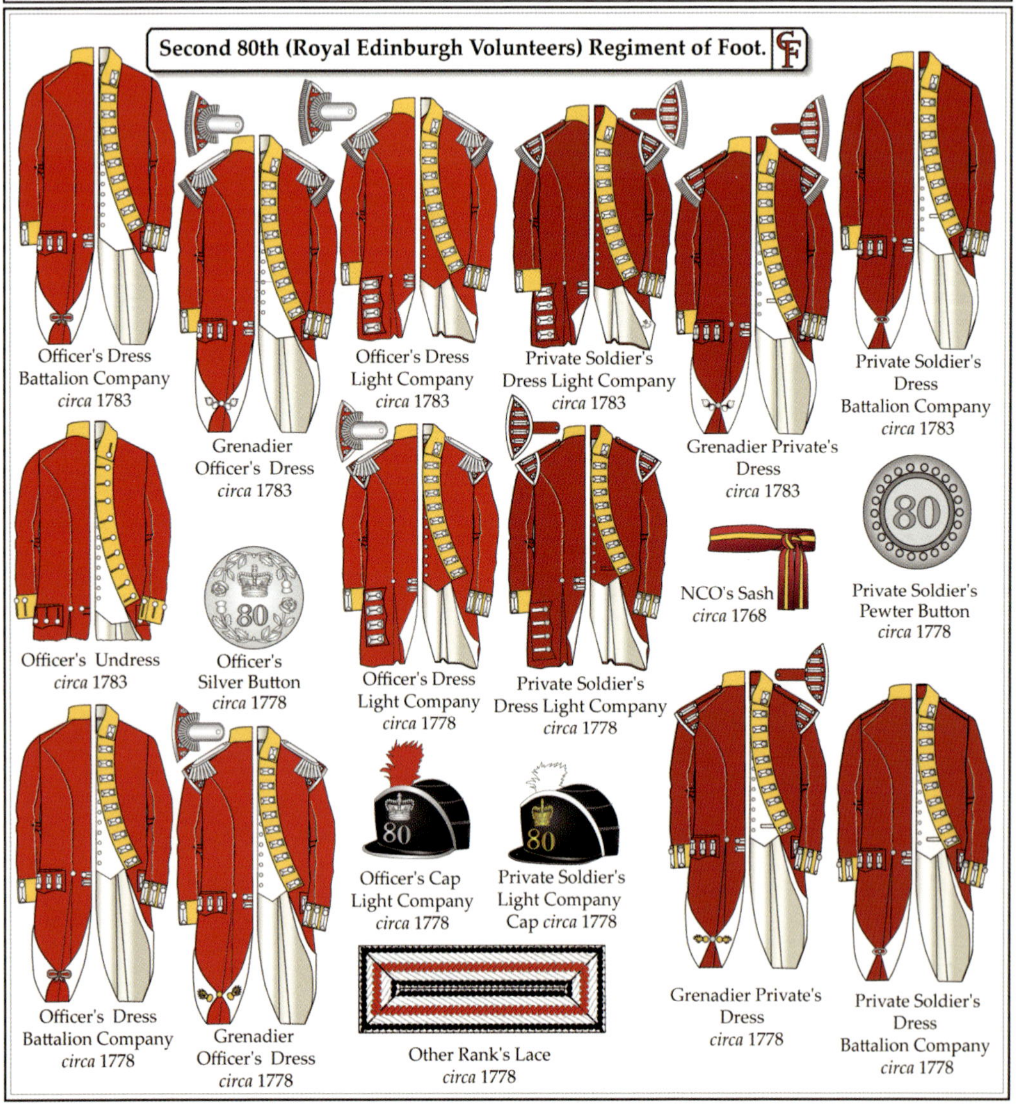

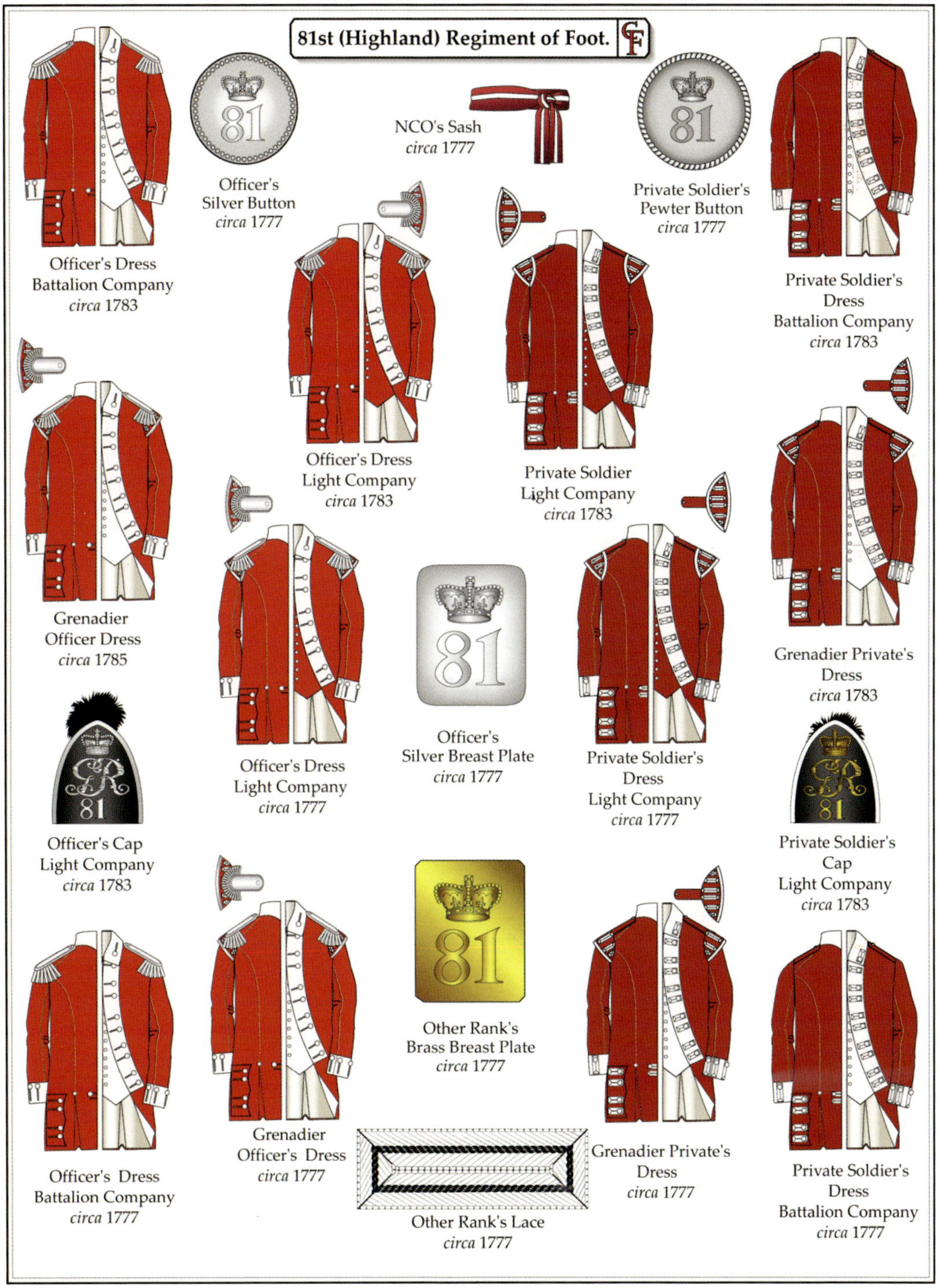
81st (Highland) Regiment of Foot.
CF
Officer's Dress
Battalion Company
circa 1783
81
Officer's
Silver Button
circa 1777
NCO's Sash
circa 1777
81
Private Soldier's
Pewter Button
circa 1777
Private Soldier's
Dress
Battalion Company
circa 1783
Officer's Dress
Light Company
circa 1783
Private Soldier
Light Company
circa 1783
Grenadier
Officer Dress
circa 1785
Grenadier Private's
Dress
circa 1783
Officer's Dress
Light Company
circa 1777
81
Officer's
Silver Breast Plate
circa 1777
Private Soldier's
Dress
Light Company
circa 1777
GR
81
Officer's Cap
Light Company
circa 1783
GR
81
Private Soldier's
Cap
Light Company
circa 1783
Officer's Dress
Battalion Company
circa 1777
Grenadier
Officer's Dress
circa 1777
81
Other Rank's
Brass Breast Plate
circa 1777
Grenadier Private's
Dress
circa 1777
Private Soldier's
Dress
Battalion Company
circa 1777
Other Rank's Lace
circa 1777

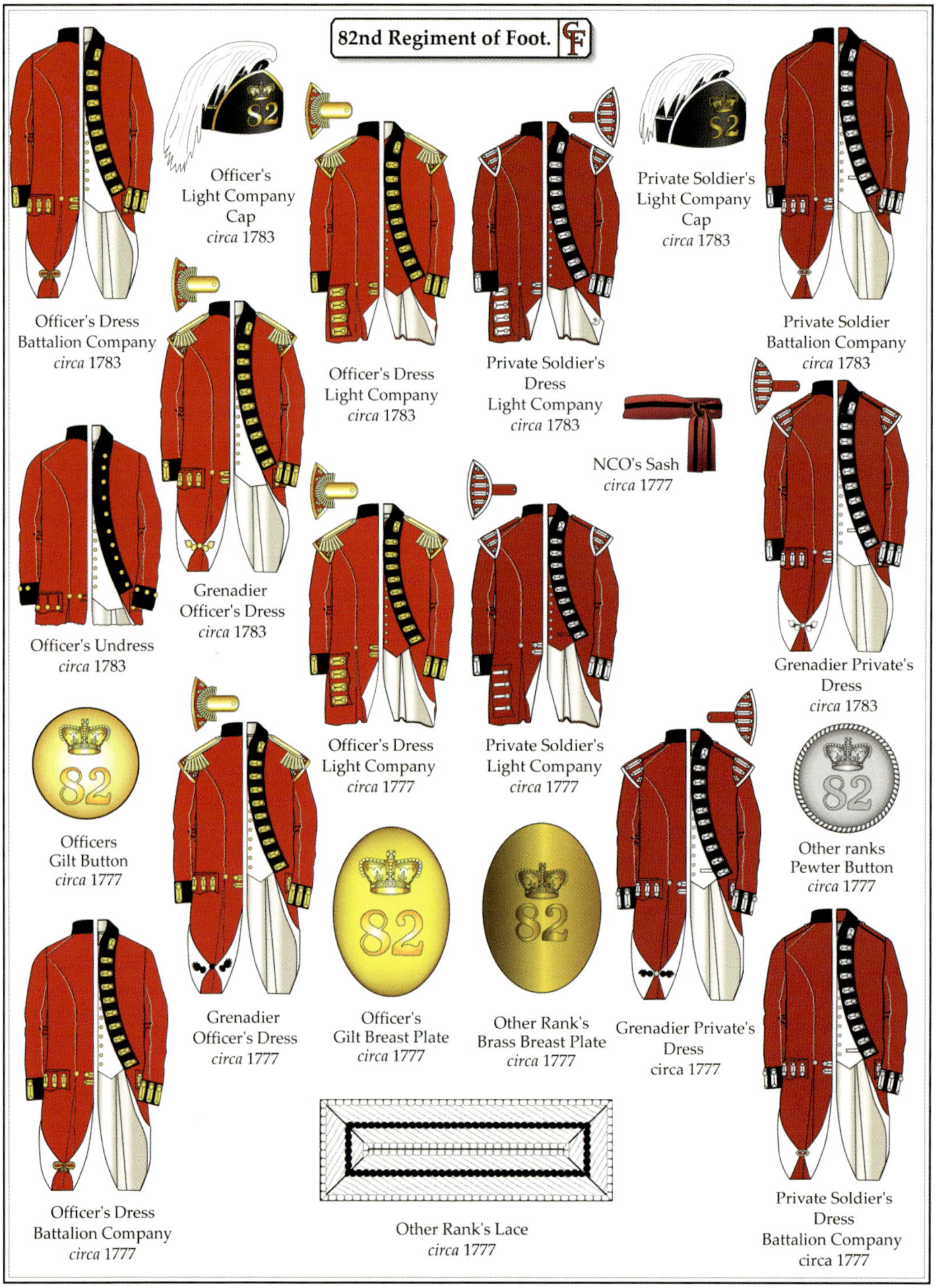
82nd Regiment of Foot.
Officer's Dress Battalion Company circa 1783
Officer's Light Company Cap circa 1783
Officer's Dress Light Company circa 1783
Private Soldier's Dress Light Company circa 1783
Private Soldier's Light Company Cap circa 1783
Private Soldier Battalion Company circa 1783
Grenadier Officer's Dress circa 1783
NCO's Sash circa 1777
Officer's Undress circa 1783
Officer's Dress Light Company circa 1777
Private Soldier's Light Company circa 1777
Grenadier Private's Dress circa 1783
Officers Gilt Button circa 1777
Other ranks Pewter Button circa 1777
Grenadier Officer's Dress circa 1777
Officer's Gilt Breast Plate circa 1777
Other Rank's Brass Breast Plate circa 1777
Grenadier Private's Dress circa 1777
Officer's Dress Battalion Company circa 1777
Other Rank's Lace circa 1777
Private Soldier's Dress Battalion Company circa 1777

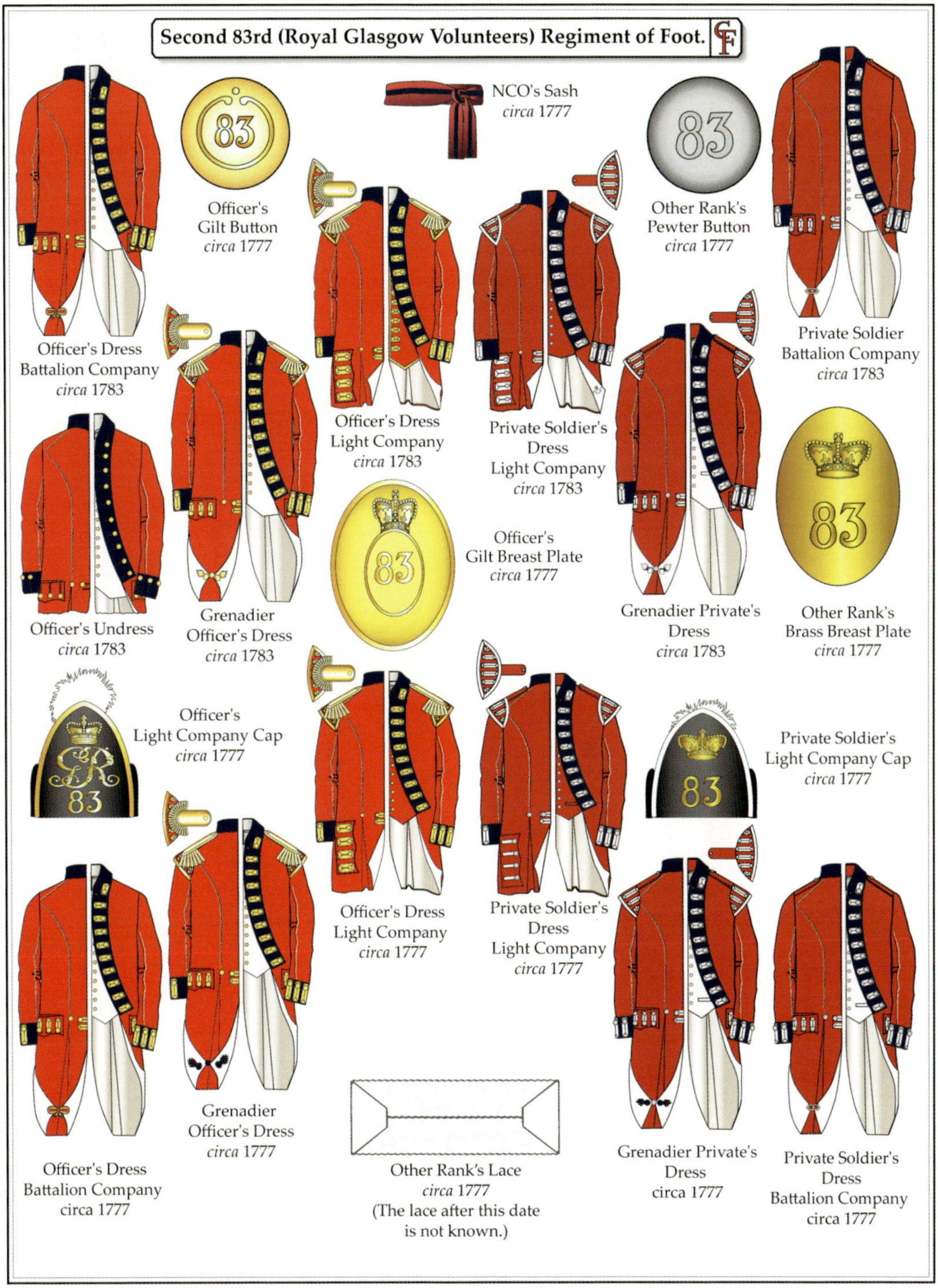
Second 83rd (Royal Glasgow Volunteers) Regiment of Foot.
CF
NCO's Sash circa 1777
Officer's Gilt Button circa 1777
83
Other Rank's Pewter Button circa 1777
83
Officer's Dress Battalion Company circa 1783
Officer's Dress Light Company circa 1783
Private Soldier's Dress Light Company circa 1783
Private Soldier Battalion Company circa 1783
Officer's Undress circa 1783
Grenadier Officer's Dress circa 1783
Officer's Gilt Breast Plate circa 1777
83
Grenadier Private's Dress circa 1783
Other Rank's Brass Breast Plate circa 1777
83
Officer's Light Company Cap circa 1777
GR
83
Private Soldier's Light Company Cap circa 1777
83
Officer's Dress Light Company circa 1777
Private Soldier's Dress Light Company circa 1777
Officer's Dress Battalion Company circa 1777
Grenadier Officer's Dress circa 1777
Other Rank's Lace circa 1777 (The lace after this date is not known.)
Grenadier Private's Dress circa 1777
Private Soldier's Dress Battalion Company circa 1777

Second 84th (Royal Highland Emigrants) Regiment of Foot.
CF
Grenadier Officer's Dress circa 1783
Officer's Dress Light Company circa 1783
Officer's Dress Battalion Company circa 1783
Private Soldier's Dress Light Company circa 1783
Private Soldier's Dress Battalion Company circa 1783
Officer's Undress circa 1782
Grenadier Officer's Dress circa 1779
Officer's Gilt Button circa 1779
Private Soldier's Dress Light Company circa 1779
Grenadier Private's Dress circa 1783
Other Rank's Pewter Button circa 1779
Officer's Dress Battalion Company circa 1779
Officer's Dress Light Company circa 1779
Officer's Light Company Cap circa 1779
Grenadier Private's Dress circa 17789
Private Soldier's Dress Battalion Company circa 1779
NCO's Sash circa 1779
Private Soldier's Light Company Cap circa 1779
Grenadier Tartan circa 1779
Officer's Gilt Breast Plate circa 1779
Other Rank's Lace circa 1779
Tartan worn by Companies circa 1779

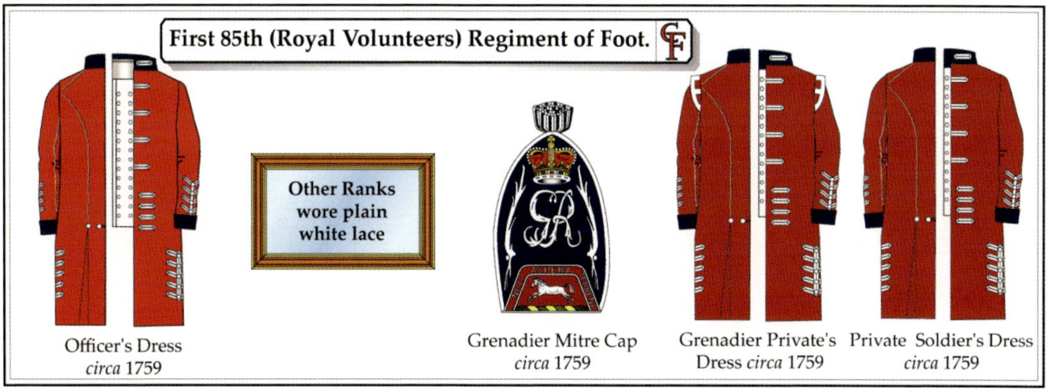
First 85th (Royal Volunteers) Regiment of Foot.
Other Ranks wore plain white lace
Officer's Dress *circa* 1759
Grenadier Mitre Cap *circa* 1759
Grenadier Private's Dress *circa* 1759
Private Soldier's Dress *circa* 1759

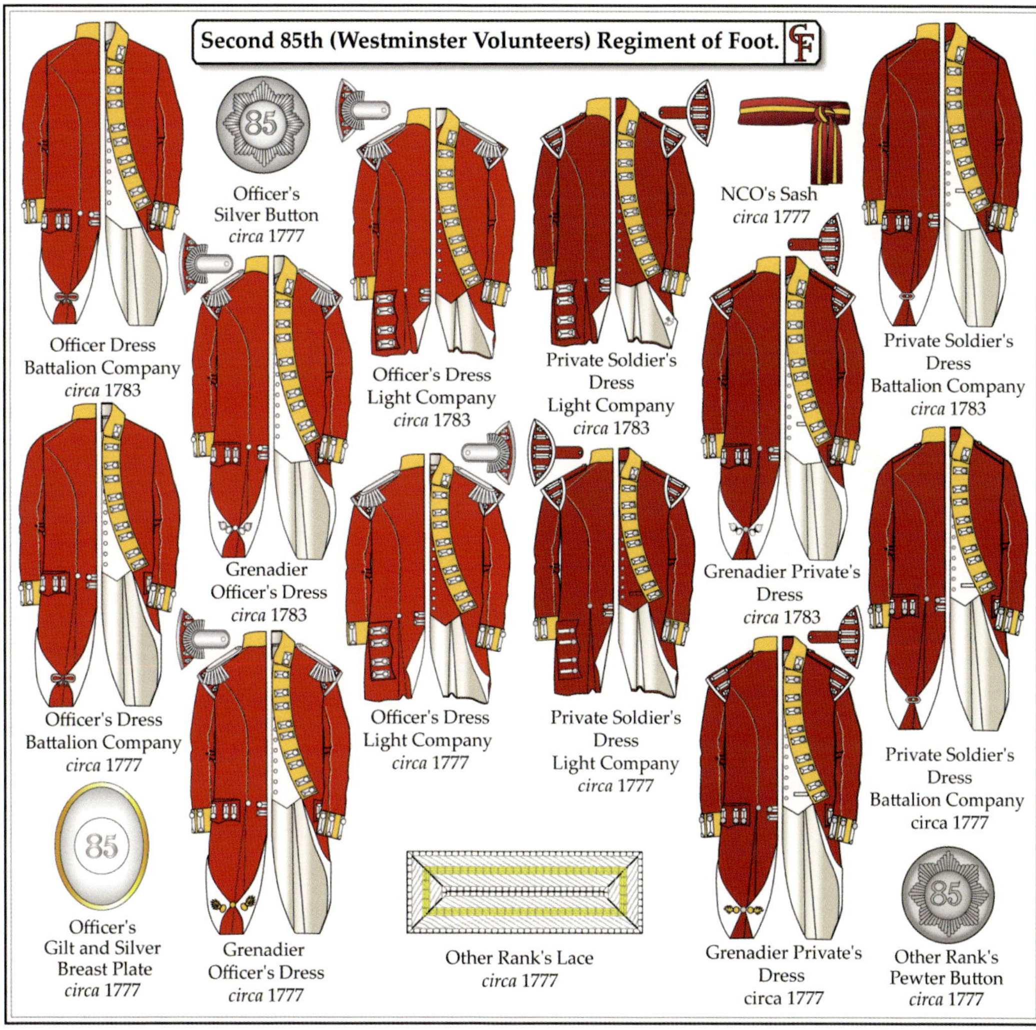
Second 85th (Westminster Volunteers) Regiment of Foot.
Officer's Silver Button *circa* 1777
NCO's Sash *circa* 1777
Officer Dress Battalion Company *circa* 1783
Officer's Dress Light Company *circa* 1783
Private Soldier's Dress Light Company *circa* 1783
Private Soldier's Dress Battalion Company *circa* 1783
Grenadier Officer's Dress *circa* 1783
Grenadier Private's Dress *circa* 1783
Officer's Dress Battalion Company *circa* 1777
Officer's Dress Light Company *circa* 1777
Private Soldier's Dress Light Company *circa* 1777
Private Soldier's Dress Battalion Company circa 1777
Officer's Gilt and Silver Breast Plate *circa* 1777
Grenadier Officer's Dress *circa* 1777
Other Rank's Lace *circa* 1777
Grenadier Private's Dress circa 1777
Other Rank's Pewter Button *circa* 1777

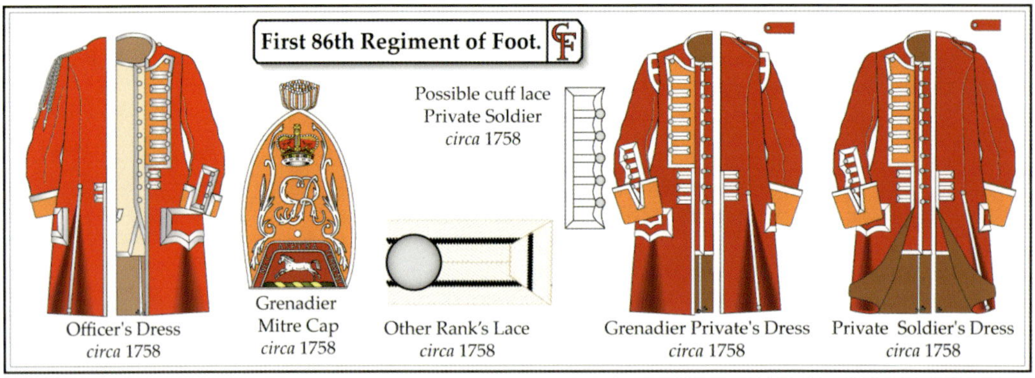

Officer's Dress *circa* 1758

Grenadier Mitre Cap *circa* 1758

Other Rank's Lace *circa* 1758

Grenadier Private's Dress *circa* 1758

Private Soldier's Dress *circa* 1758

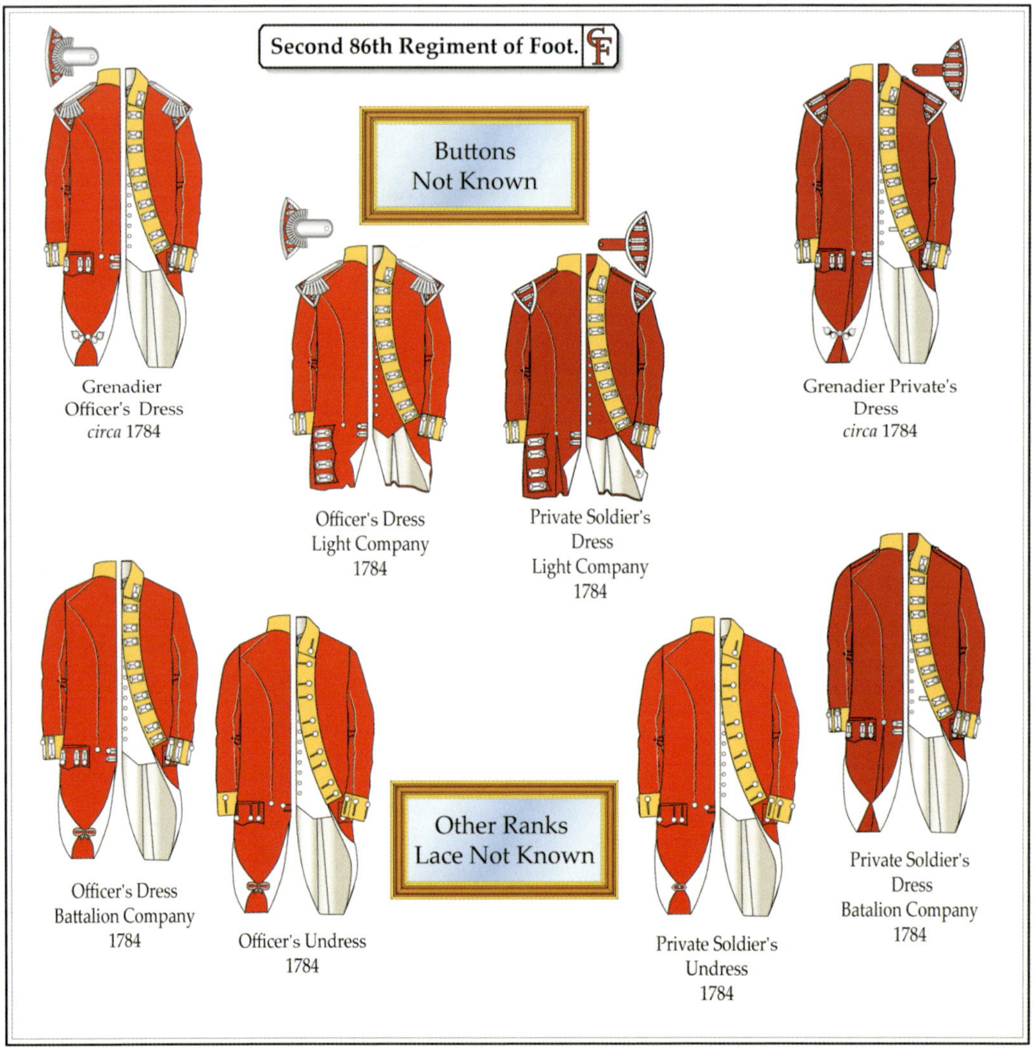

Grenadier Officer's Dress *circa* 1784

Officer's Dress Light Company 1784

Private Soldier's Dress Light Company 1784

Grenadier Private's Dress *circa* 1784

Officer's Dress Battalion Company 1784

Officer's Undress 1784

Private Soldier's Undress 1784

Private Soldier's Dress Batalion Company 1784

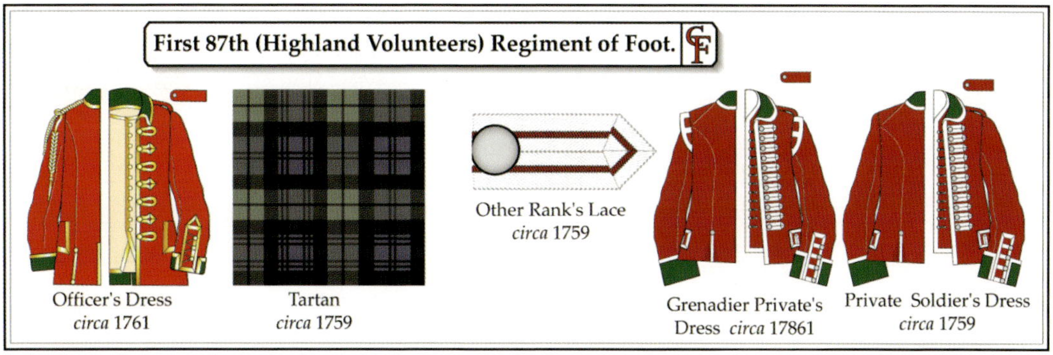
First 87th (Highland Volunteers) Regiment of Foot.
Officer's Dress
circa 1761
Tartan
circa 1759
Other Rank's Lace
circa 1759
Grenadier Private's
Dress circa 17861
Private Soldier's Dress
circa 1759

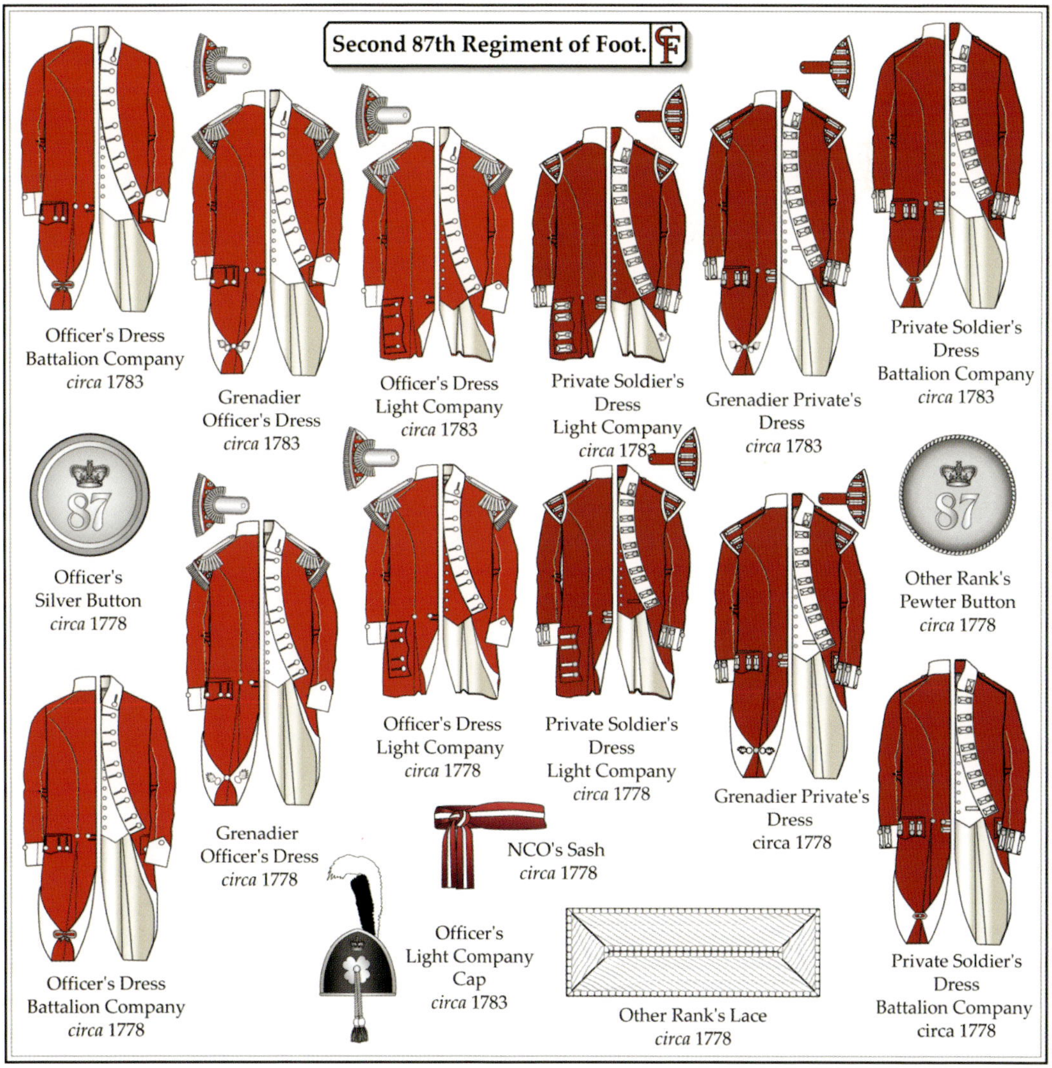
Second 87th Regiment of Foot.
Officer's Dress
Battalion Company
circa 1783
Grenadier
Officer's Dress
circa 1783
Officer's Dress
Light Company
circa 1783
Private Soldier's
Dress
Light Company
circa 1783
Grenadier Private's
Dress
circa 1783
Private Soldier's
Dress
Battalion Company
circa 1783
87
Officer's
Silver Button
circa 1778
87
Other Rank's
Pewter Button
circa 1778
Officer's Dress
Light Company
circa 1778
Private Soldier's
Dress
Light Company
circa 1778
Grenadier Private's
Dress
circa 1778
Officer's Dress
Battalion Company
circa 1778
Grenadier
Officer's Dress
circa 1778
NCO's Sash
circa 1778
Officer's
Light Company
Cap
circa 1783
Other Rank's Lace
circa 1778
Private Soldier's
Dress
Battalion Company
circa 1778

First 88th (Highland Volunteers) Regiment of Foot.
CF
Officer's Dress
circa 1760
Tartan
circa 1759
No details of Other Rank's Lace
Grenadier's Dress
circa 1755
Private Soldier's Dress
circa 1755

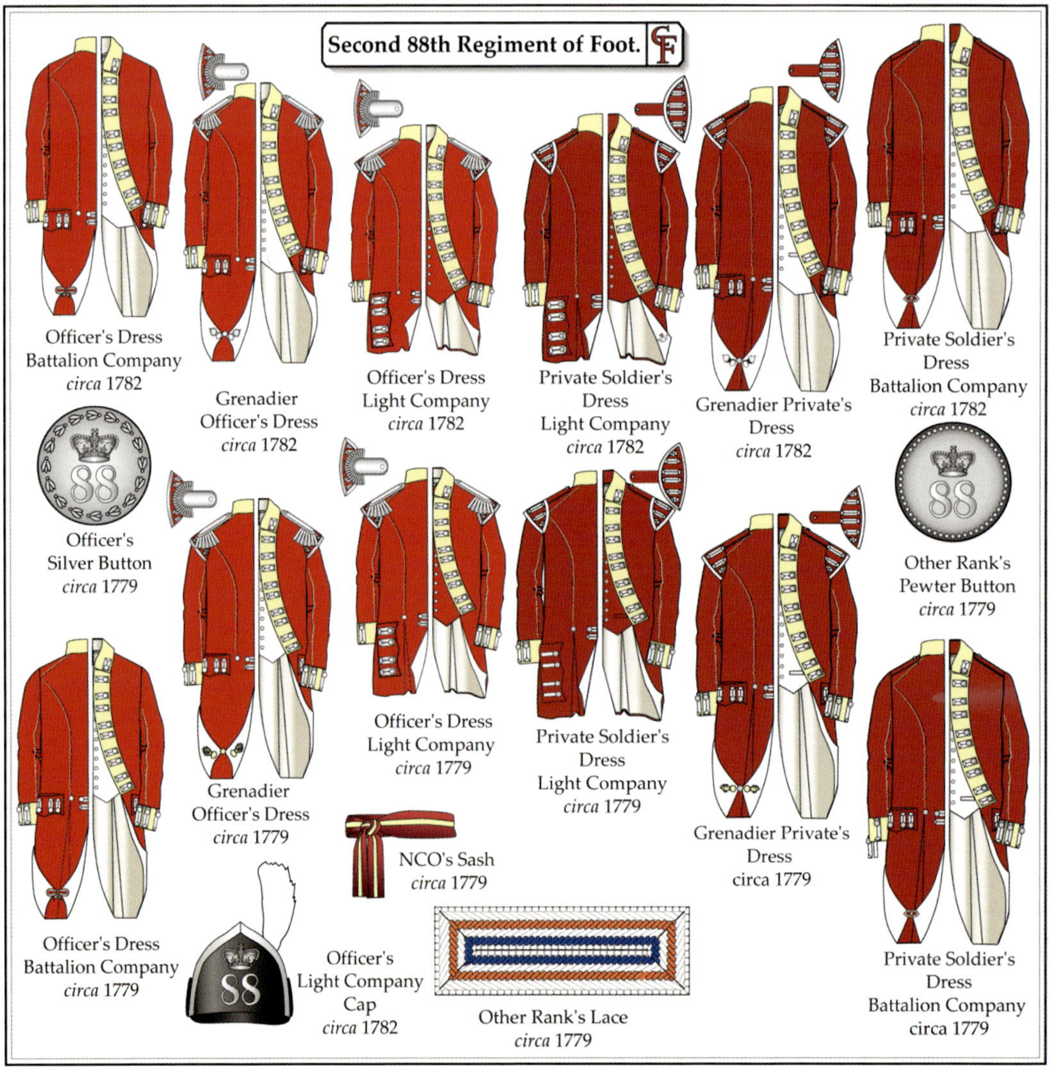
Second 88th Regiment of Foot.
CF
Officer's Dress Battalion Company
circa 1782
Grenadier Officer's Dress
circa 1782
Officer's Dress Light Company
circa 1782
Private Soldier's Dress Light Company
circa 1782
Grenadier Private's Dress
circa 1782
Private Soldier's Dress Battalion Company
circa 1782
88
Officer's Silver Button
circa 1779
88
Other Rank's Pewter Button
circa 1779
Grenadier Officer's Dress
circa 1779
Officer's Dress Light Company
circa 1779
Private Soldier's Dress Light Company
circa 1779
Grenadier Private's Dress
circa 1779
Officer's Dress Battalion Company
circa 1779
NCO's Sash
circa 1779
88
Officer's Light Company Cap
circa 1782
Other Rank's Lace
circa 1779
Private Soldier's Dress Battalion Company
circa 1779

First 89th (Highland) Regiment of Foot.

Officer's Dress
circa 1761

Tartan
circa 1759

No details of Other Rank's Lace

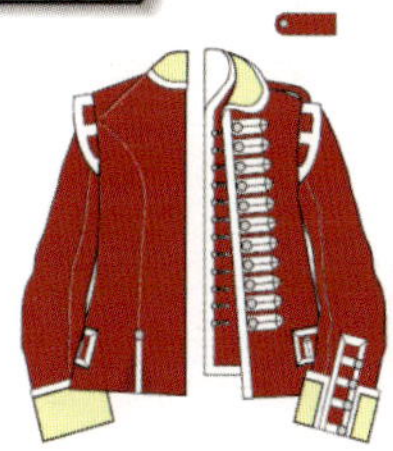

Grenadier's Dress
circa 1760

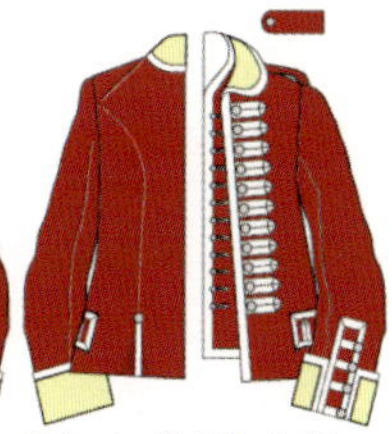

Private Soldier's Dress
circa 1759

Second 89th (Worcester Volunteers) Regiment of Foot.

Officer's Dress
Battalion Company
circa 1782

Grenadier
Officer's Dress
circa 1782

Officer's Dress
Light Company
circa 1782

Private Soldier's
Dress
Light Company
circa 1782

Grenadier Private's
Dress
circa 1782

Private Soldier's
Dress
Battalion Company
circa 1782

Officer's
Gilt button
circa 1779

Grenadier
Officer's Dress
circa 1779

Officer's Dress
Light Company
circa 1779

Private Soldier's
Dress
Light Company
circa 1779

Private Soldier's
Pewter Button
circa 1779

Grenadier Private's
Dress
circa 1779

Officer's Dress
Battalion Company
circa 1779

Private Soldier's
Dress
Battalion Company
circa 1779

Officer's Cap
Light Company
circa 1782

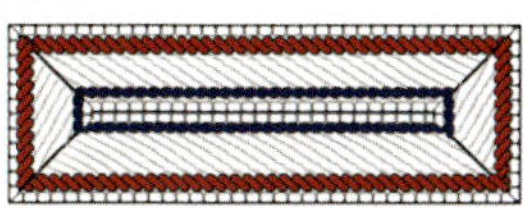

Other Rank's Lace
circa 1779

NCO's Sash
circa 1779

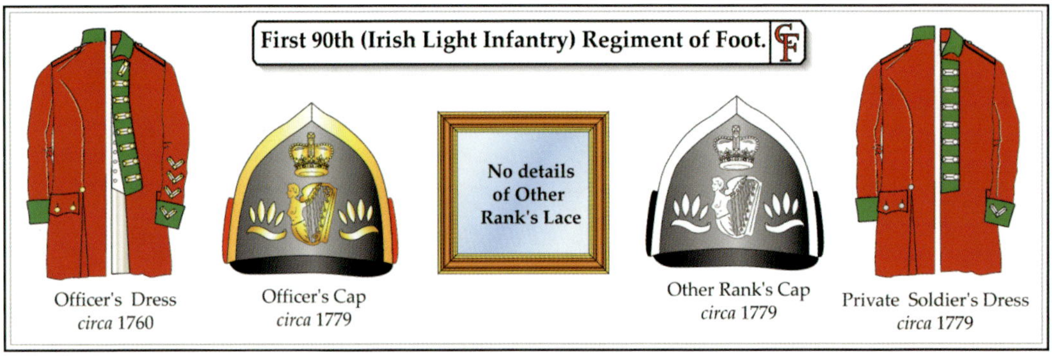
First 90th (Irish Light Infantry) Regiment of Foot.
CF
Officer's Dress
circa 1760
Officer's Cap
circa 1779
No details of Other Rank's Lace
Other Rank's Cap
circa 1779
Private Soldier's Dress
circa 1779

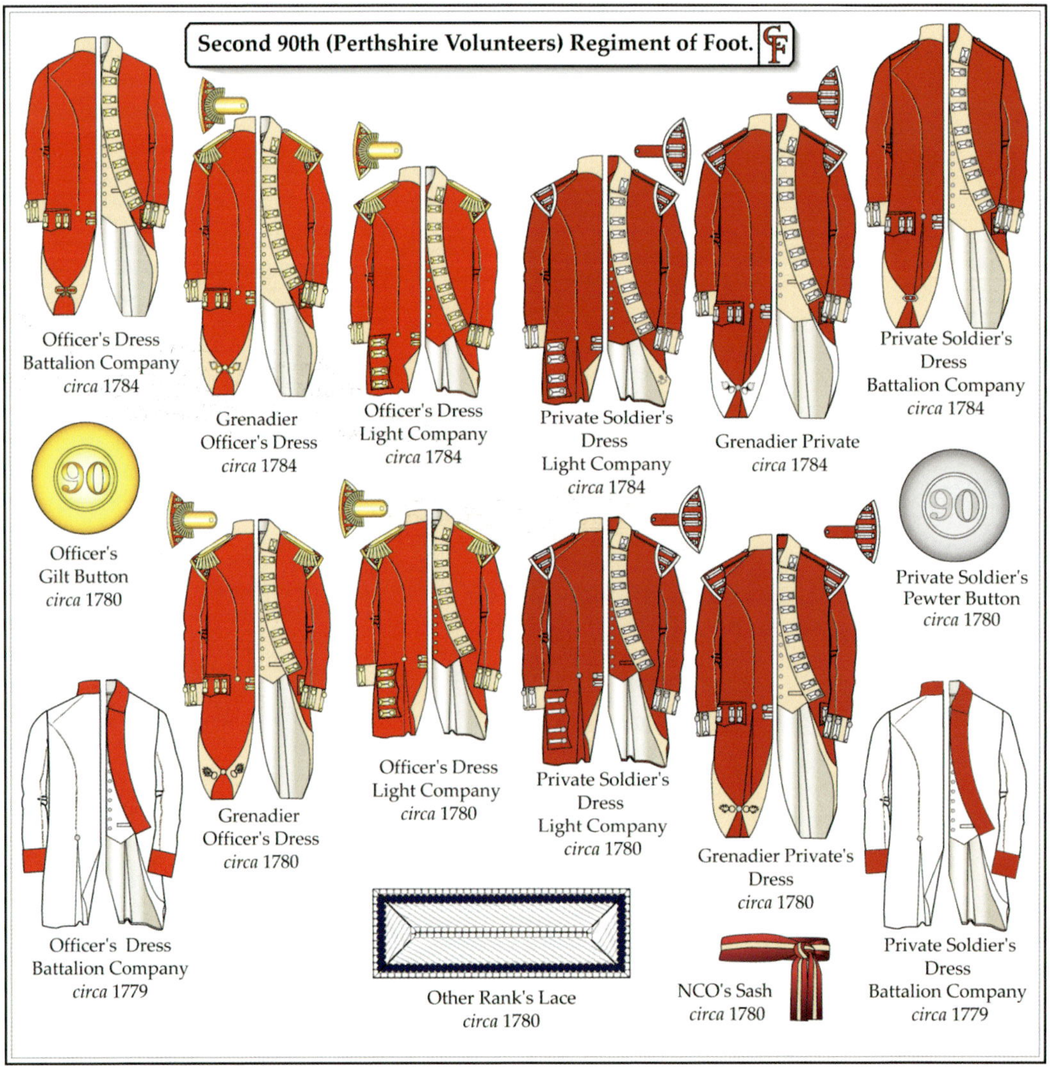
Second 90th (Perthshire Volunteers) Regiment of Foot.
CF
Officer's Dress Battalion Company
circa 1784
Grenadier Officer's Dress
circa 1784
Officer's Dress Light Company
circa 1784
Private Soldier's Dress Light Company
circa 1784
Grenadier Private
circa 1784
Private Soldier's Dress Battalion Company
circa 1784
90
Officer's Gilt Button
circa 1780
90
Private Soldier's Pewter Button
circa 1780
Grenadier Officer's Dress
circa 1780
Officer's Dress Light Company
circa 1780
Private Soldier's Dress Light Company
circa 1780
Grenadier Private's Dress
circa 1780
Officer's Dress Battalion Company
circa 1779
Other Rank's Lace
circa 1780
NCO's Sash
circa 1780
Private Soldier's Dress Battalion Company
circa 1779

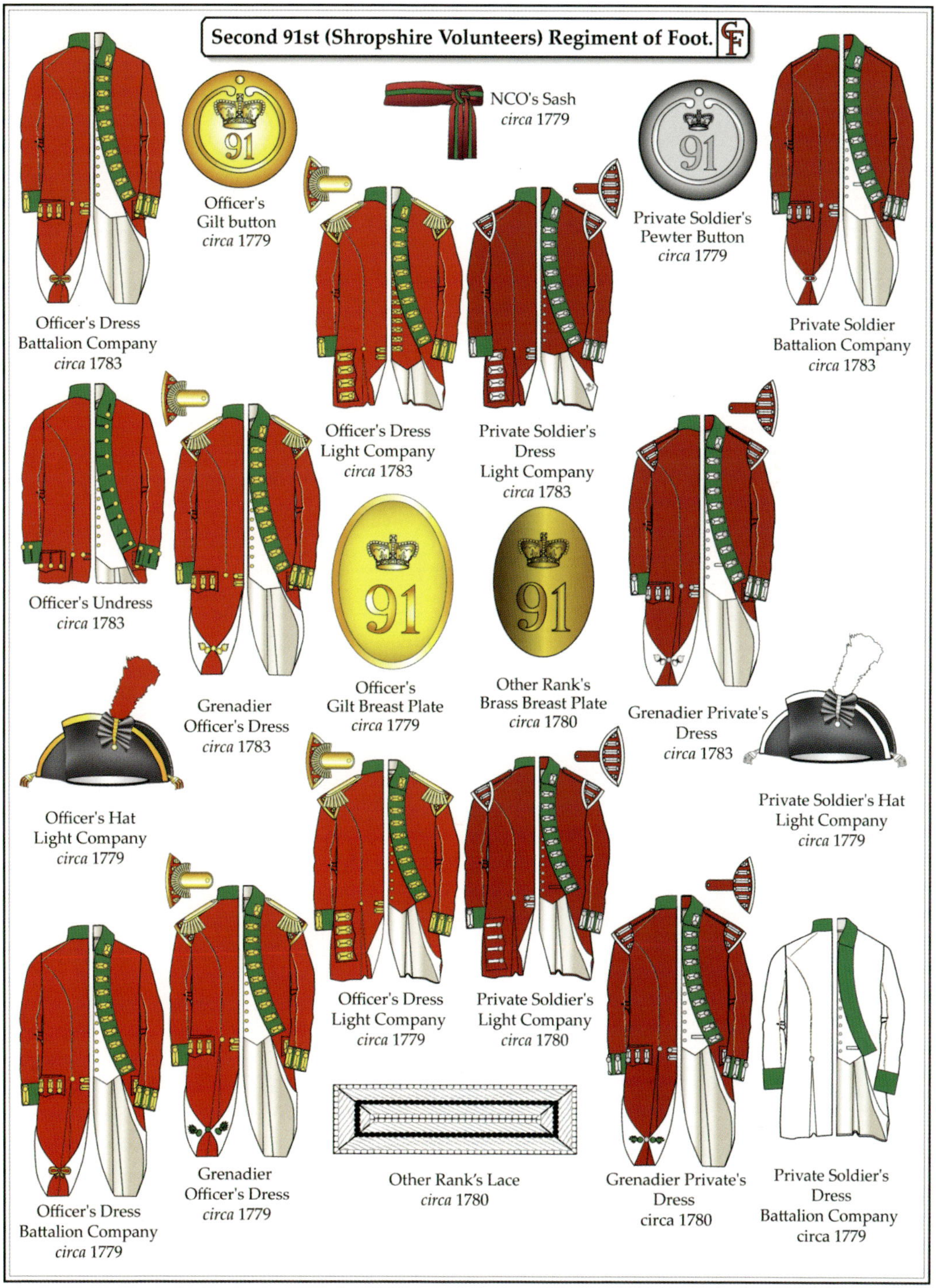
Second 91st (Shropshire Volunteers) Regiment of Foot.
Officer's Dress Battalion Company *circa* 1783
Officer's Gilt button *circa* 1779
NCO's Sash *circa* 1779
Private Soldier's Pewter Button *circa* 1779
Private Soldier Battalion Company *circa* 1783
Officer's Dress Light Company *circa* 1783
Private Soldier's Dress Light Company *circa* 1783
Officer's Undress *circa* 1783
Grenadier Officer's Dress *circa* 1783
Officer's Gilt Breast Plate *circa* 1779
Other Rank's Brass Breast Plate *circa* 1780
Grenadier Private's Dress *circa* 1783
Officer's Hat Light Company *circa* 1779
Private Soldier's Hat Light Company *circa* 1779
Officer's Dress Light Company *circa* 1779
Private Soldier's Light Company *circa* 1780
Officer's Dress Battalion Company *circa* 1779
Grenadier Officer's Dress *circa* 1779
Other Rank's Lace *circa* 1780
Grenadier Private's Dress circa 1780
Private Soldier's Dress Battalion Company circa 1779

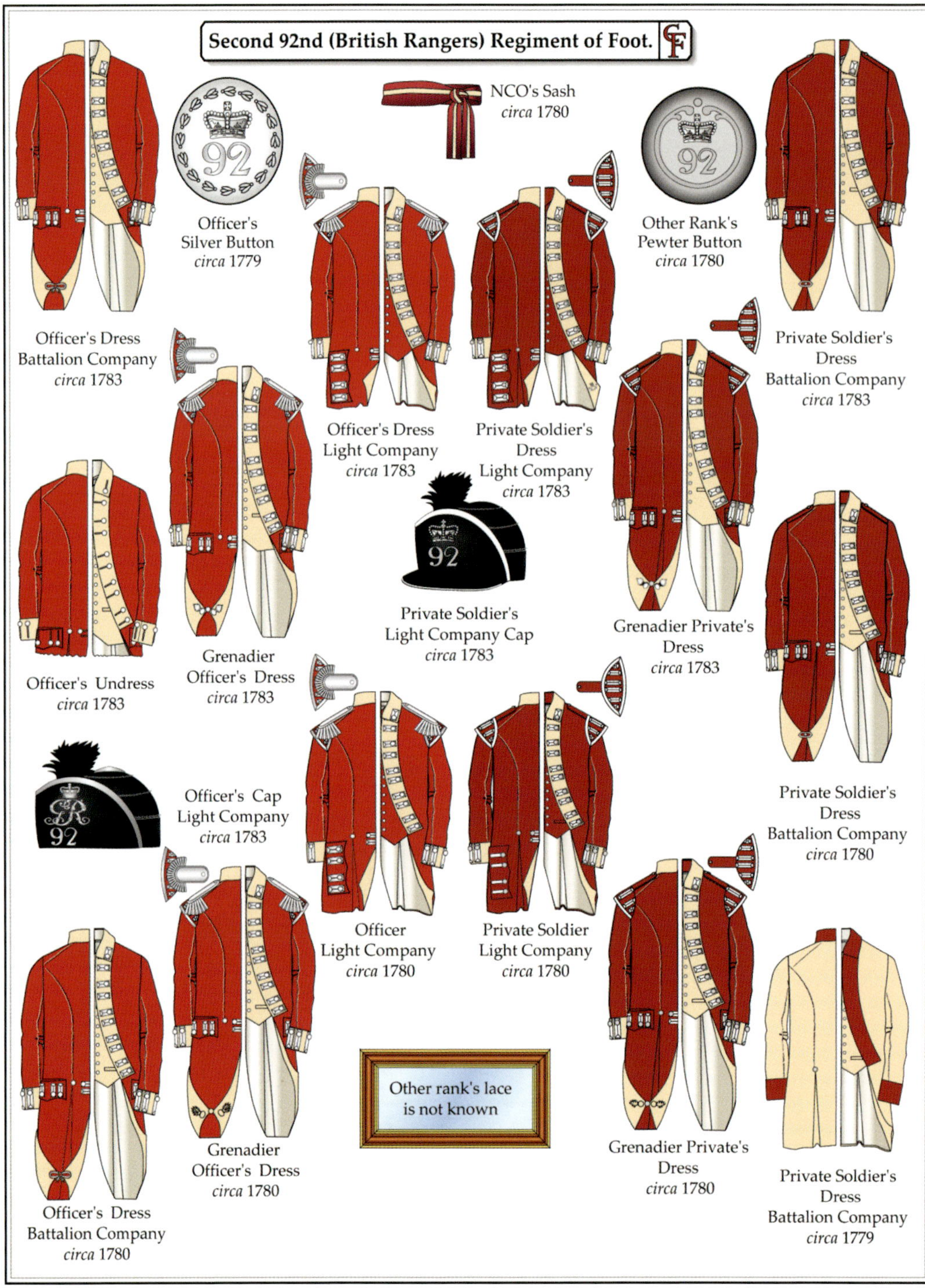
Second 92nd (British Rangers) Regiment of Foot.
CF
92
Officer's Silver Button circa 1779
NCO's Sash circa 1780
92
Other Rank's Pewter Button circa 1780
Officer's Dress Battalion Company circa 1783
Officer's Dress Light Company circa 1783
Private Soldier's Dress Light Company circa 1783
Private Soldier's Dress Battalion Company circa 1783
92
Private Soldier's Light Company Cap circa 1783
Grenadier Private's Dress circa 1783
Officer's Undress circa 1783
Grenadier Officer's Dress circa 1783
GR
92
Officer's Cap Light Company circa 1783
Private Soldier's Dress Battalion Company circa 1780
Officer Light Company circa 1780
Private Soldier Light Company circa 1780
Other rank's lace is not known
Grenadier Private's Dress circa 1780
Grenadier Officer's Dress circa 1780
Officer's Dress Battalion Company circa 1780
Private Soldier's Dress Battalion Company circa 1779

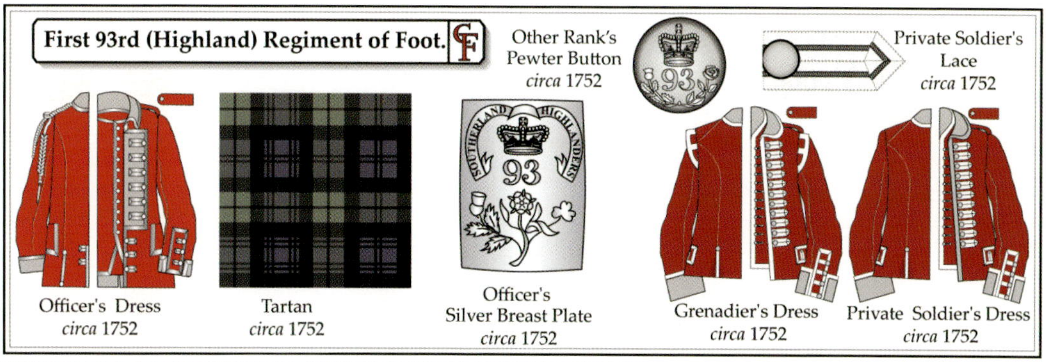
First 93rd (Highland) Regiment of Foot.
CF
Other Rank's Pewter Button *circa* 1752
Private Soldier's Lace *circa* 1752
Officer's Dress *circa* 1752
Tartan *circa* 1752
Officer's Silver Breast Plate *circa* 1752
SOUTHERLAND HIGHLANDERS 93
Grenadier's Dress *circa* 1752
Private Soldier's Dress *circa* 1752

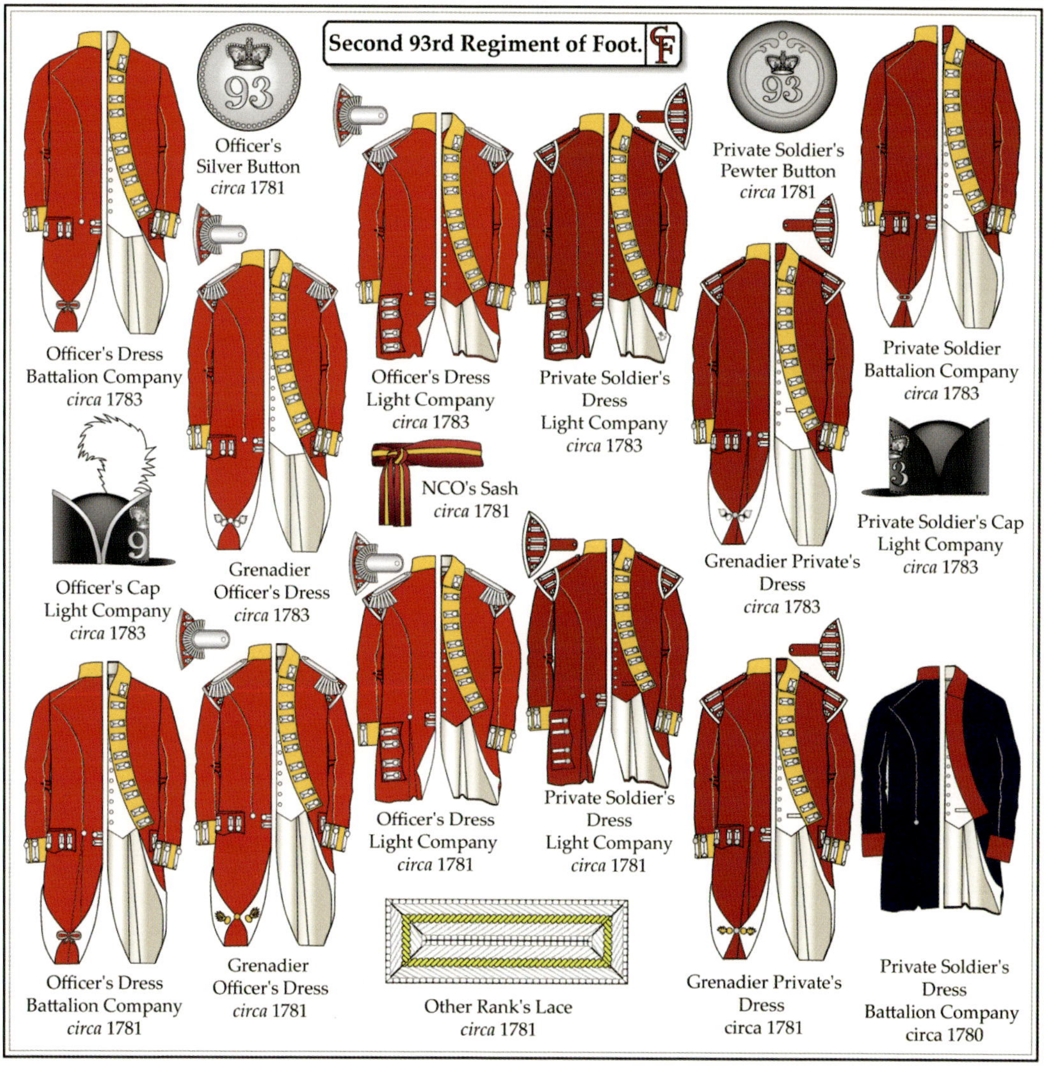
Second 93rd Regiment of Foot.
CF
Officer's Silver Button *circa* 1781
Private Soldier's Pewter Button *circa* 1781
Officer's Dress Battalion Company *circa* 1783
Officer's Dress Light Company *circa* 1783
Private Soldier's Dress Light Company *circa* 1783
Private Soldier Battalion Company *circa* 1783
Grenadier Officer's Dress *circa* 1783
NCO's Sash *circa* 1781
Grenadier Private's Dress *circa* 1783
Private Soldier's Cap Light Company *circa* 1783
Officer's Cap Light Company *circa* 1783
Officer's Dress Light Company *circa* 1781
Private Soldier's Dress Light Company *circa* 1781
Officer's Dress Battalion Company *circa* 1781
Grenadier Officer's Dress *circa* 1781
Other Rank's Lace *circa* 1781
Grenadier Private's Dress circa 1781
Private Soldier's Dress Battalion Company circa 1780

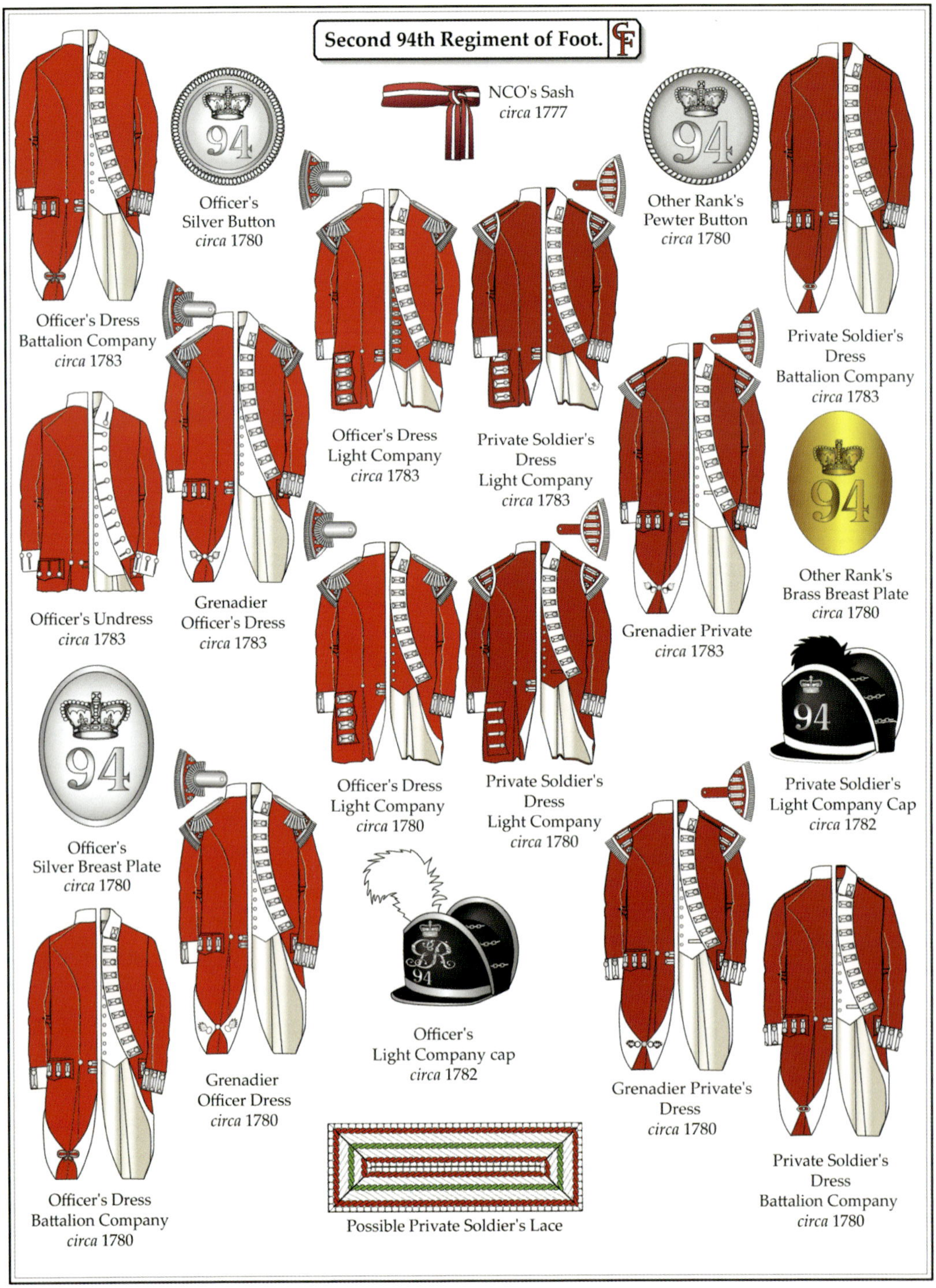
Second 94th Regiment of Foot.
CF
NCO's Sash
circa 1777
Officer's Silver Button
circa 1780
Other Rank's Pewter Button
circa 1780
94
Officer's Dress Battalion Company
circa 1783
Officer's Dress Light Company
circa 1783
Private Soldier's Dress Light Company
circa 1783
Private Soldier's Dress Battalion Company
circa 1783
Officer's Undress
circa 1783
Grenadier Officer's Dress
circa 1783
Grenadier Private
circa 1783
Other Rank's Brass Breast Plate
circa 1780
Officer's Dress Light Company
circa 1780
Private Soldier's Dress Light Company
circa 1780
Private Soldier's Light Company Cap
circa 1782
Officer's Silver Breast Plate
circa 1780
Officer's Light Company cap
circa 1782
GR
Grenadier Officer Dress
circa 1780
Grenadier Private's Dress
circa 1780
Officer's Dress Battalion Company
circa 1780
Possible Private Soldier's Lace
Private Soldier's Dress Battalion Company
circa 1780

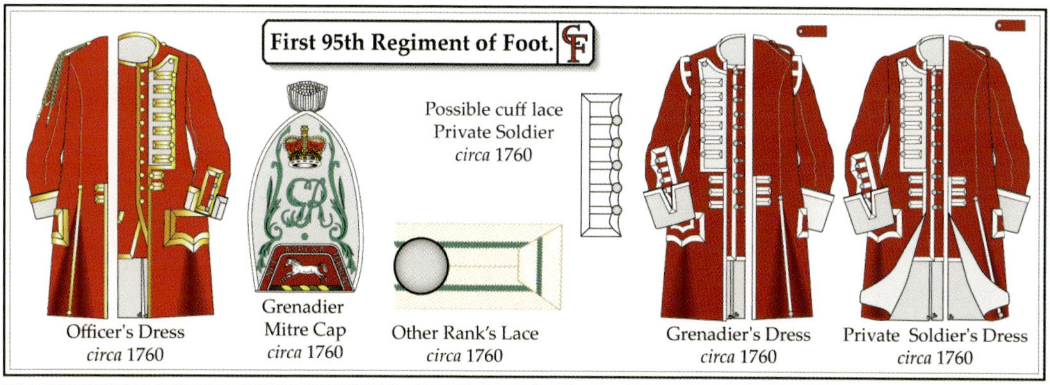
First 95th Regiment of Foot.
Officer's Dress
circa 1760
Grenadier
Mitre Cap
circa 1760
Possible cuff lace
Private Soldier
circa 1760
Other Rank's Lace
circa 1760
Grenadier's Dress
circa 1760
Private Soldier's Dress
circa 1760

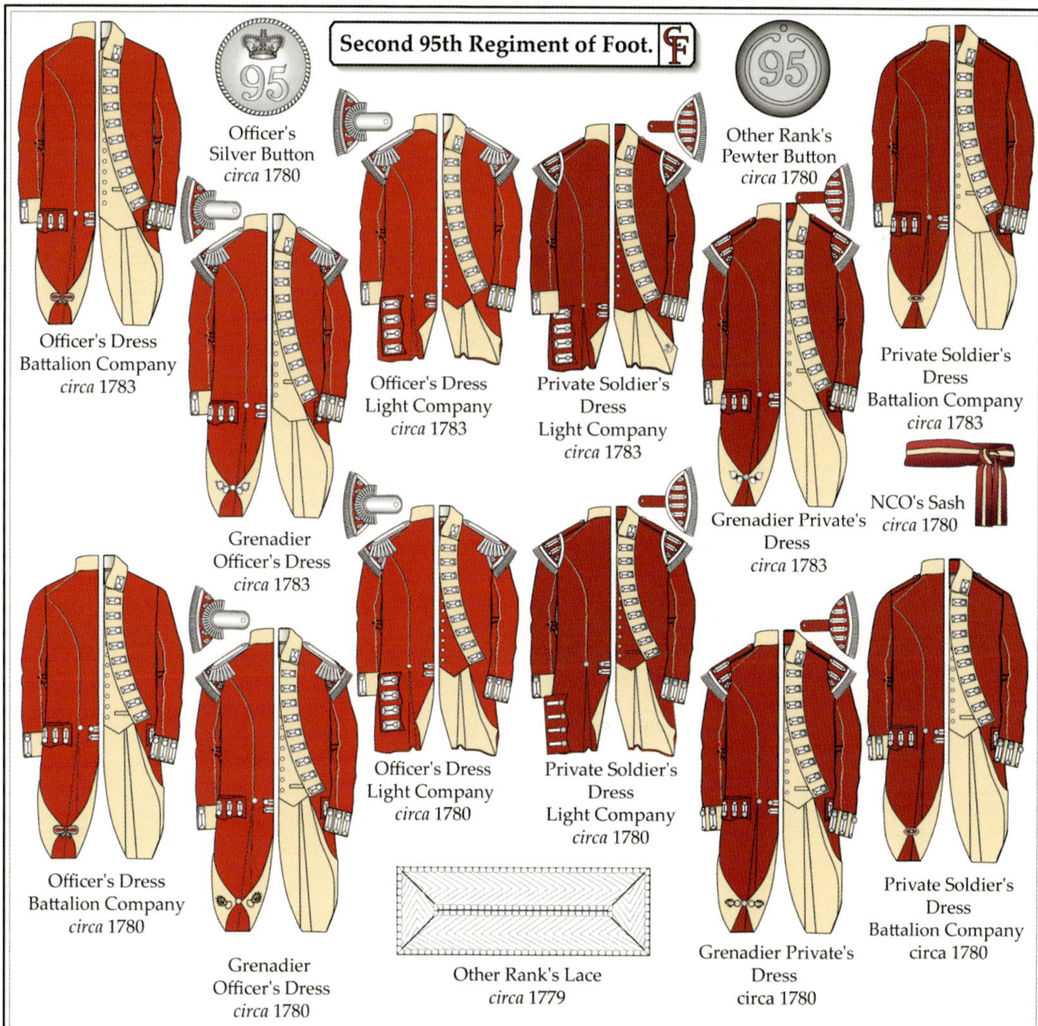
Second 95th Regiment of Foot.
Officer's Silver Button
circa 1780
Other Rank's Pewter Button
circa 1780
Officer's Dress
Battalion Company
circa 1783
Grenadier
Officer's Dress
circa 1783
Officer's Dress
Light Company
circa 1783
Private Soldier's
Dress
Light Company
circa 1783
Grenadier Private's
Dress
circa 1783
Private Soldier's
Dress
Battalion Company
circa 1783
NCO's Sash
circa 1780
Officer's Dress
Battalion Company
circa 1780
Grenadier
Officer's Dress
circa 1780
Officer's Dress
Light Company
circa 1780
Private Soldier's
Dress
Light Company
circa 1780
Other Rank's Lace
circa 1779
Grenadier Private's
Dress
circa 1780
Private Soldier's
Dress
Battalion Company
circa 1780

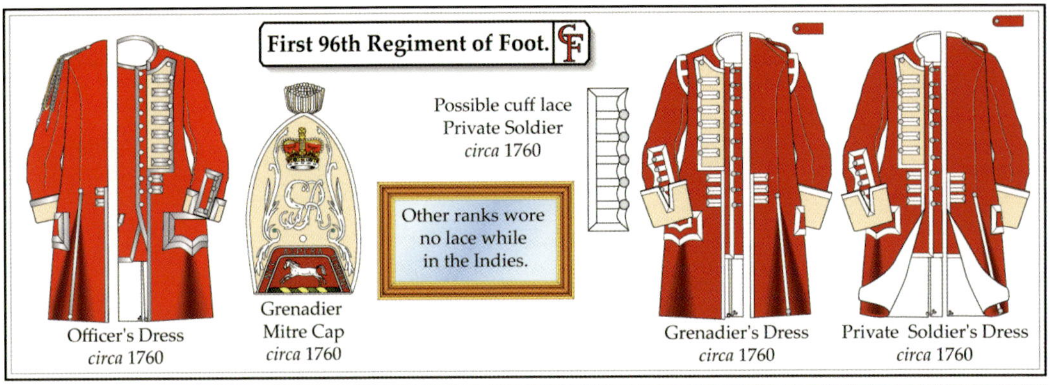
First 96th Regiment of Foot.
Officer's Dress
circa 1760
Grenadier
Mitre Cap
circa 1760
Possible cuff lace
Private Soldier
circa 1760
Other ranks wore
no lace while
in the Indies.
Grenadier's Dress
circa 1760
Private Soldier's Dress
circa 1760

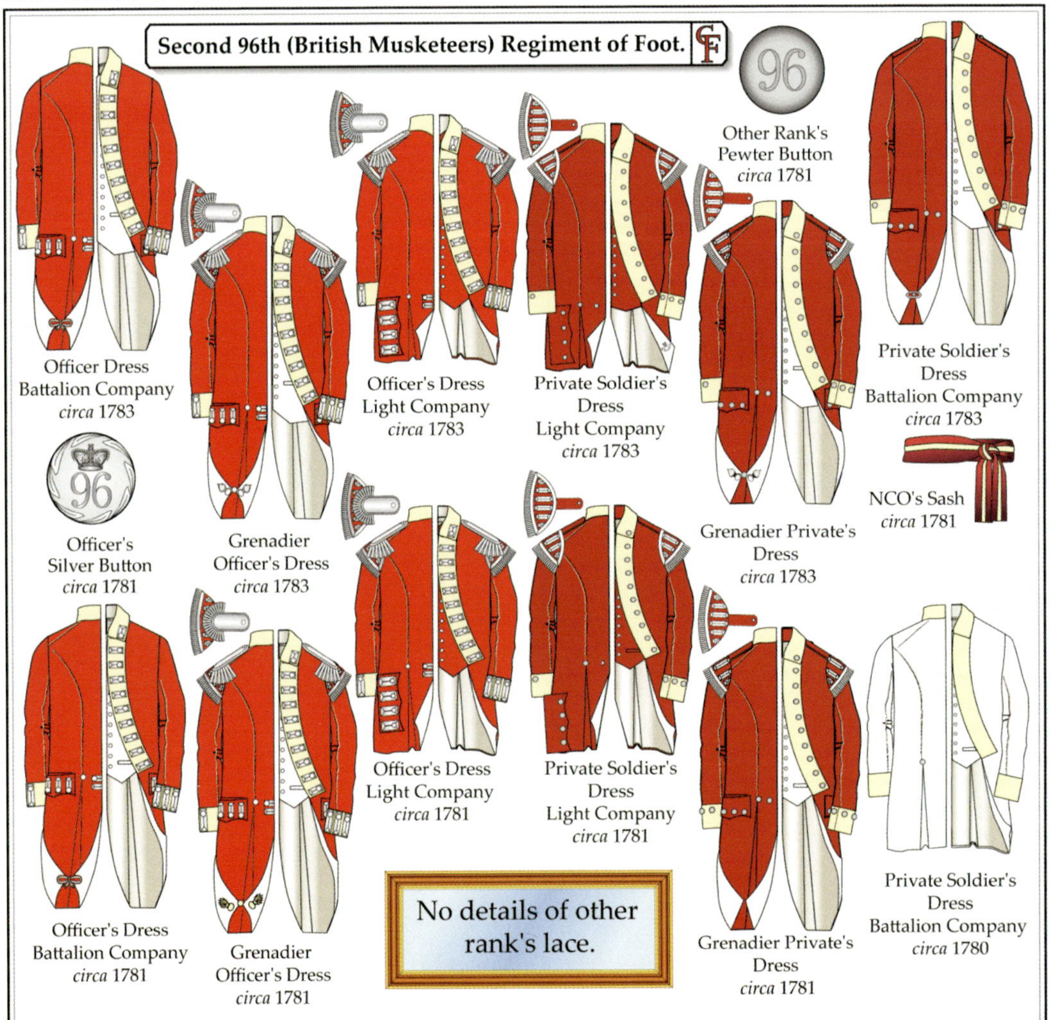
Second 96th (British Musketeers) Regiment of Foot.
Other Rank's
Pewter Button
circa 1781
Officer Dress
Battalion Company
circa 1783
Officer's Dress
Light Company
circa 1783
Private Soldier's
Dress
Light Company
circa 1783
Private Soldier's
Dress
Battalion Company
circa 1783
Officer's
Silver Button
circa 1781
Grenadier
Officer's Dress
circa 1783
Grenadier Private's
Dress
circa 1783
NCO's Sash
circa 1781
Officer's Dress
Light Company
circa 1781
Private Soldier's
Dress
Light Company
circa 1781
Officer's Dress
Battalion Company
circa 1781
Grenadier
Officer's Dress
circa 1781
No details of other
rank's lace.
Grenadier Private's
Dress
circa 1781
Private Soldier's
Dress
Battalion Company
circa 1780

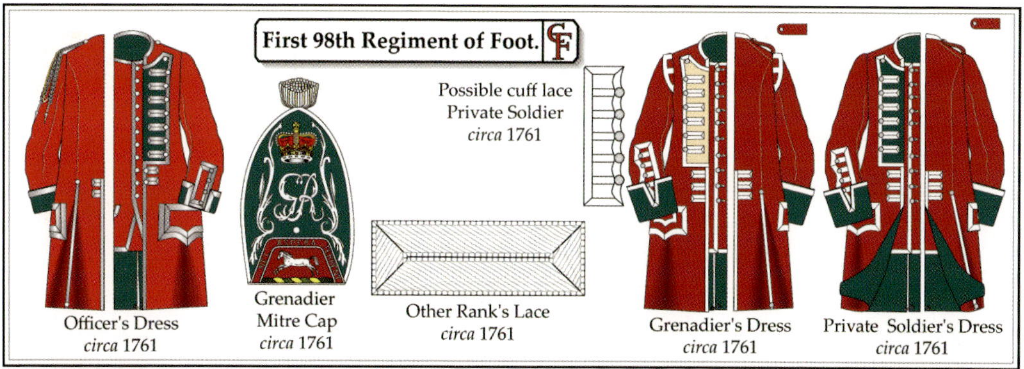
First 98th Regiment of Foot.
CF
Officer's Dress
circa 1761
Grenadier
Mitre Cap
circa 1761
Possible cuff lace
Private Soldier
circa 1761
Other Rank's Lace
circa 1761
Grenadier's Dress
circa 1761
Private Soldier's Dress
circa 1761

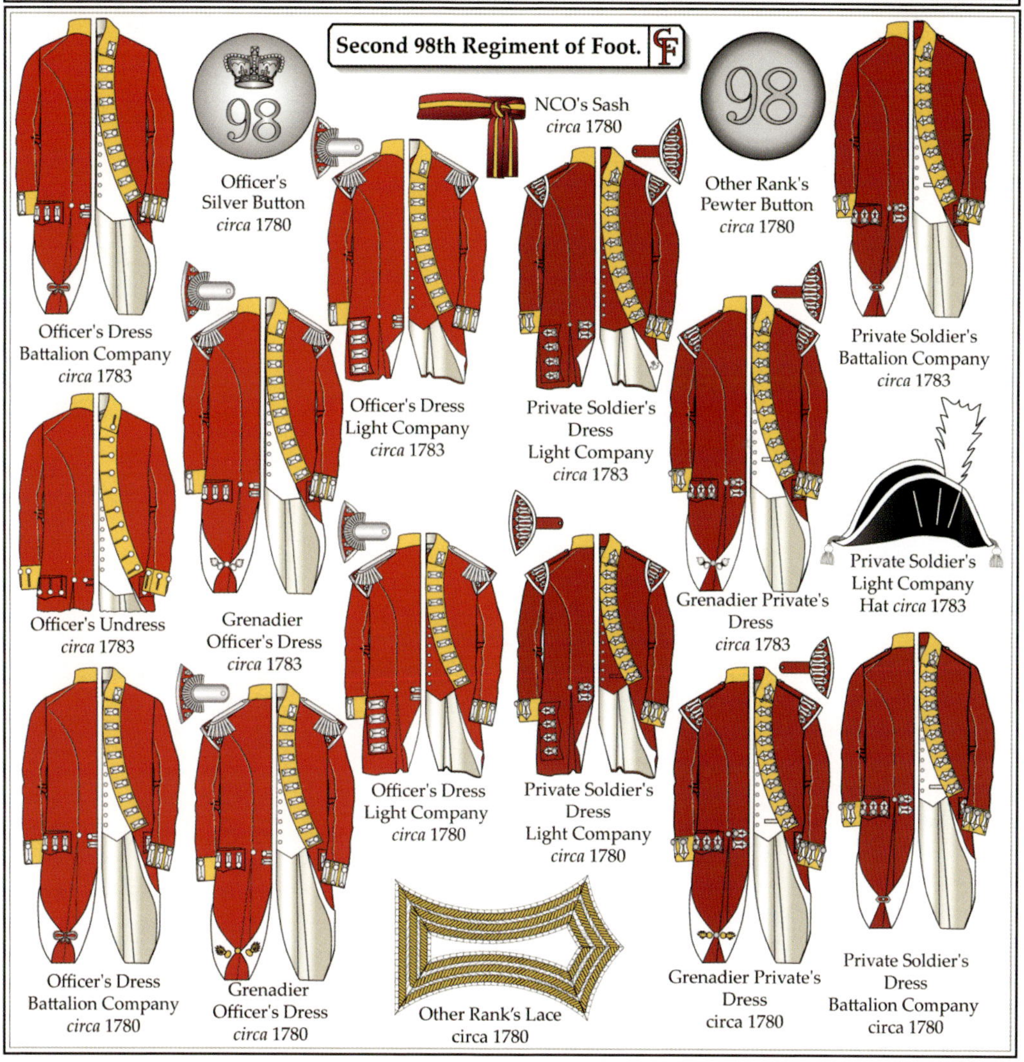
Second 98th Regiment of Foot.
CF
98
Officer's
Silver Button
circa 1780
NCO's Sash
circa 1780
98
Other Rank's
Pewter Button
circa 1780
Officer's Dress
Battalion Company
circa 1783
Officer's Dress
Light Company
circa 1783
Private Soldier's
Dress
Light Company
circa 1783
Private Soldier's
Battalion Company
circa 1783
Officer's Undress
circa 1783
Grenadier
Officer's Dress
circa 1783
Grenadier Private's
Dress
circa 1783
Private Soldier's
Light Company
Hat circa 1783
Officer's Dress
Light Company
circa 1780
Private Soldier's
Dress
Light Company
circa 1780
Officer's Dress
Battalion Company
circa 1780
Grenadier
Officer's Dress
circa 1780
Other Rank's Lace
circa 1780
Grenadier Private's
Dress
circa 1780
Private Soldier's
Dress
Battalion Company
circa 1780

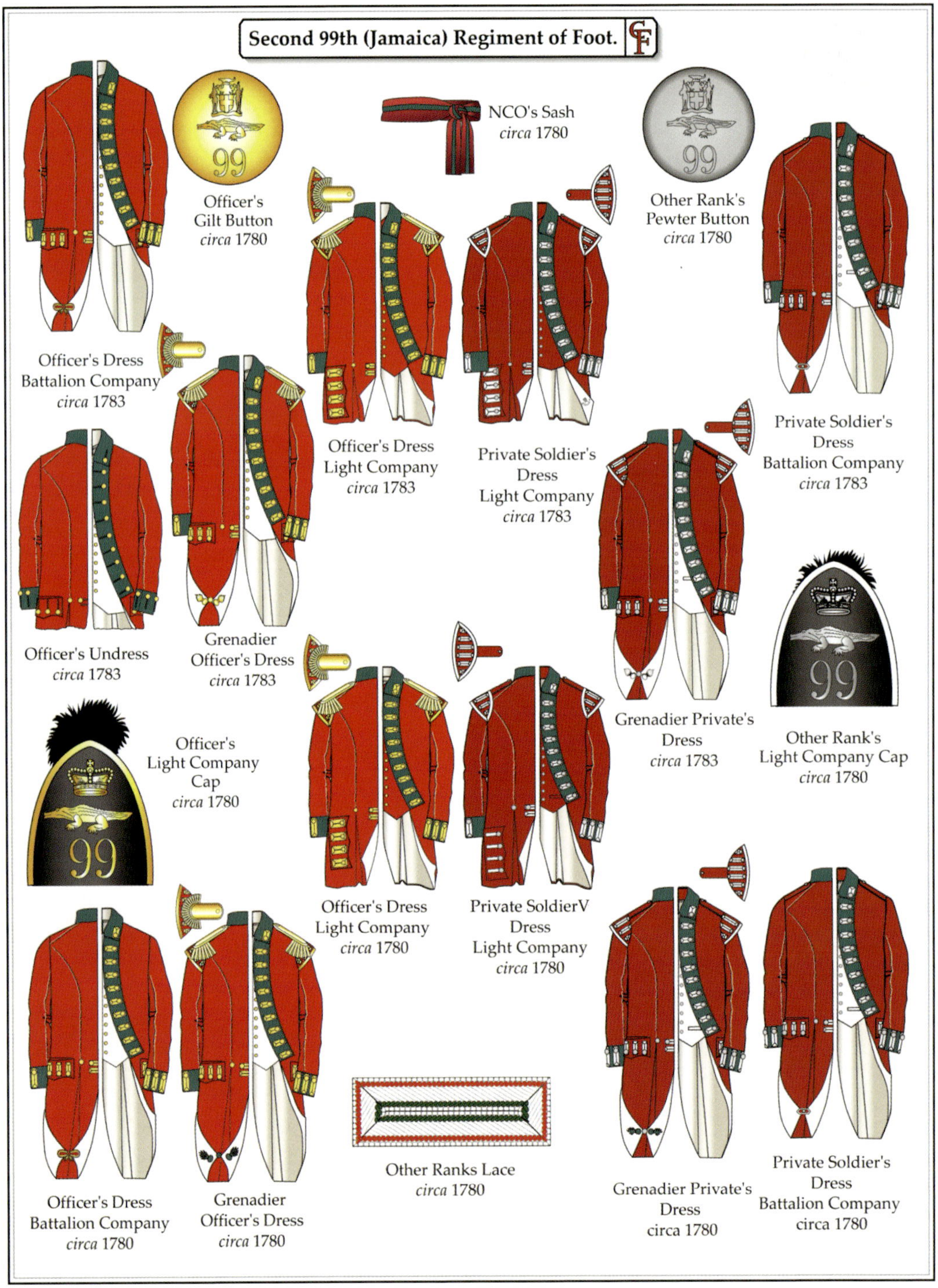
Second 99th (Jamaica) Regiment of Foot.
CF
Officer's Gilt Button circa 1780
NCO's Sash circa 1780
Other Rank's Pewter Button circa 1780
Officer's Dress Battalion Company circa 1783
Officer's Dress Light Company circa 1783
Private Soldier's Dress Light Company circa 1783
Private Soldier's Dress Battalion Company circa 1783
Officer's Undress circa 1783
Grenadier Officer's Dress circa 1783
Grenadier Private's Dress circa 1783
Other Rank's Light Company Cap circa 1780
Officer's Light Company Cap circa 1780
Officer's Dress Light Company circa 1780
Private SoldierV Dress Light Company circa 1780
Officer's Dress Battalion Company circa 1780
Grenadier Officer's Dress circa 1780
Other Ranks Lace circa 1780
Grenadier Private's Dress circa 1780
Private Soldier's Dress Battalion Company circa 1780

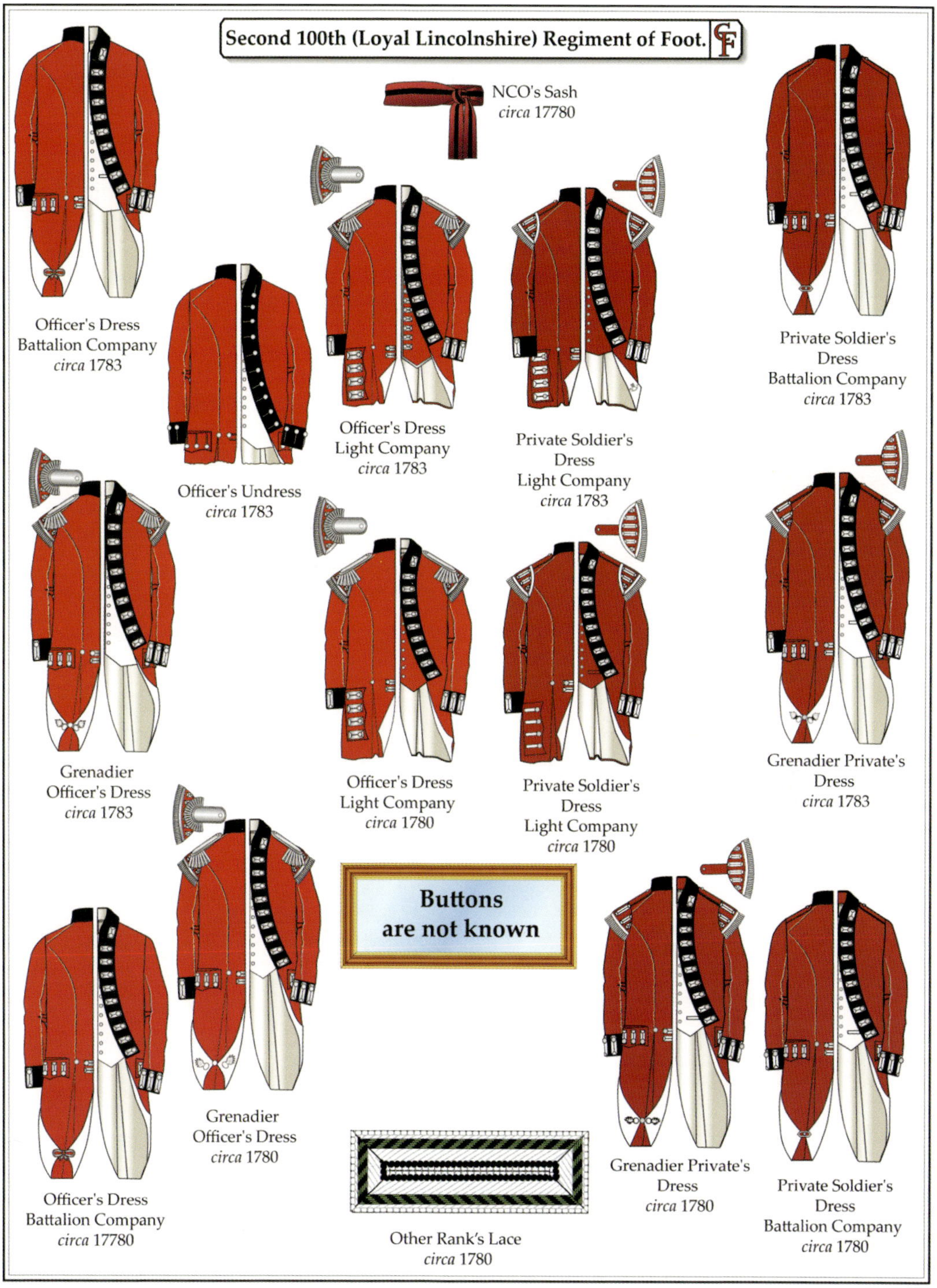
Second 100th (Loyal Lincolnshire) Regiment of Foot.
NCO's Sash
circa 17780
Officer's Dress
Battalion Company
circa 1783
Officer's Undress
circa 1783
Officer's Dress
Light Company
circa 1783
Private Soldier's
Dress
Light Company
circa 1783
Private Soldier's
Dress
Battalion Company
circa 1783
Grenadier
Officer's Dress
circa 1783
Officer's Dress
Light Company
circa 1780
Private Soldier's
Dress
Light Company
circa 1780
Grenadier Private's
Dress
circa 1783
Buttons
are not known
Officer's Dress
Battalion Company
circa 17780
Grenadier
Officer's Dress
circa 1780
Other Rank's Lace
circa 1780
Grenadier Private's
Dress
circa 1780
Private Soldier's
Dress
Battalion Company
circa 1780

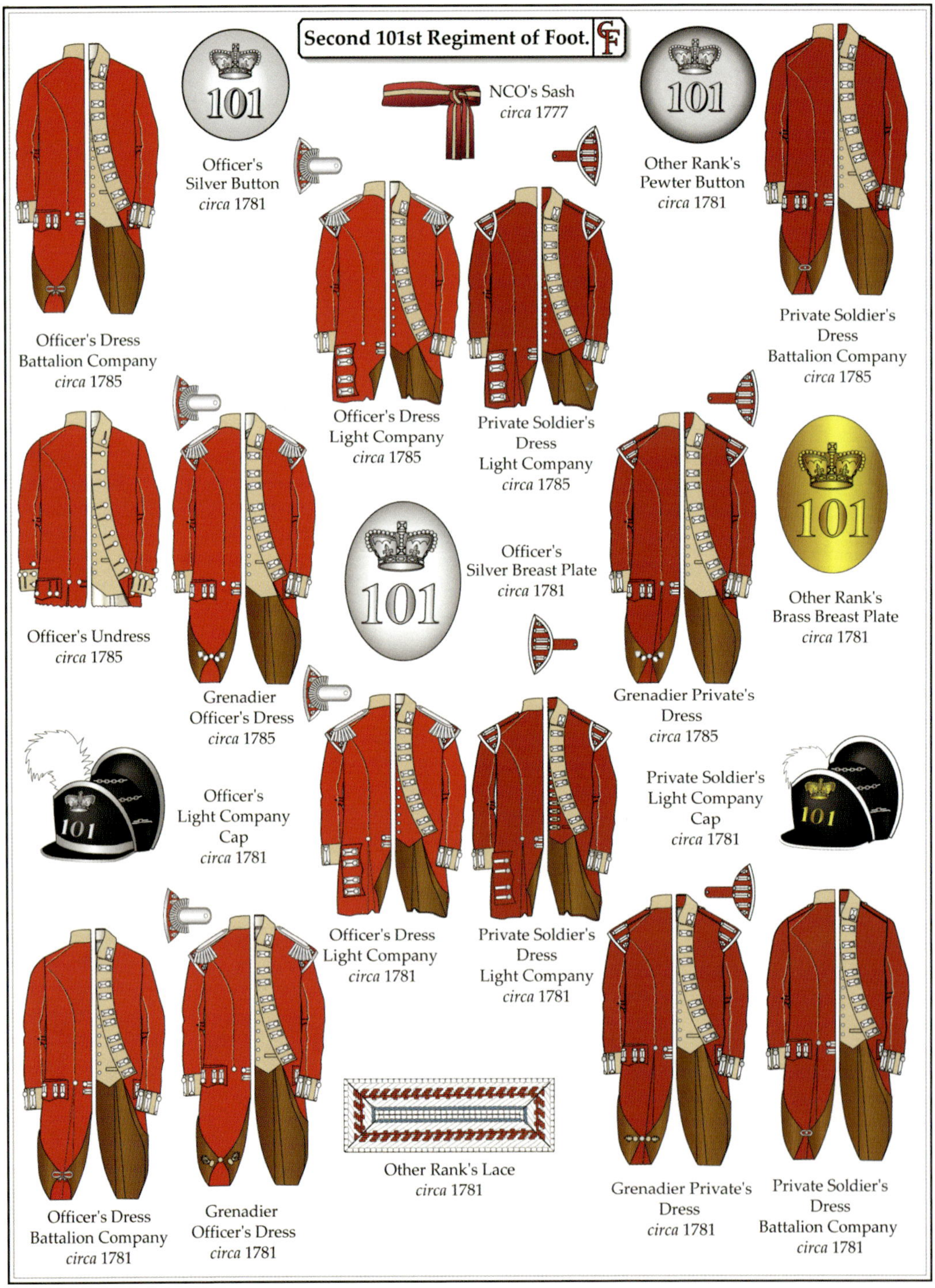
Second 101st Regiment of Foot.
CF
NCO's Sash
circa 1777
Officer's Silver Button
circa 1781
Other Rank's Pewter Button
circa 1781
Officer's Dress Battalion Company
circa 1785
Officer's Dress Light Company
circa 1785
Private Soldier's Dress Light Company
circa 1785
Private Soldier's Dress Battalion Company
circa 1785
Officer's Undress
circa 1785
Grenadier Officer's Dress
circa 1785
Officer's Silver Breast Plate
circa 1781
Grenadier Private's Dress
circa 1785
Other Rank's Brass Breast Plate
circa 1781
Officer's Light Company Cap
circa 1781
Private Soldier's Light Company Cap
circa 1781
Officer's Dress Light Company
circa 1781
Private Soldier's Dress Light Company
circa 1781
Other Rank's Lace
circa 1781
Officer's Dress Battalion Company
circa 1781
Grenadier Officer's Dress
circa 1781
Grenadier Private's Dress
circa 1781
Private Soldier's Dress Battalion Company
circa 1781

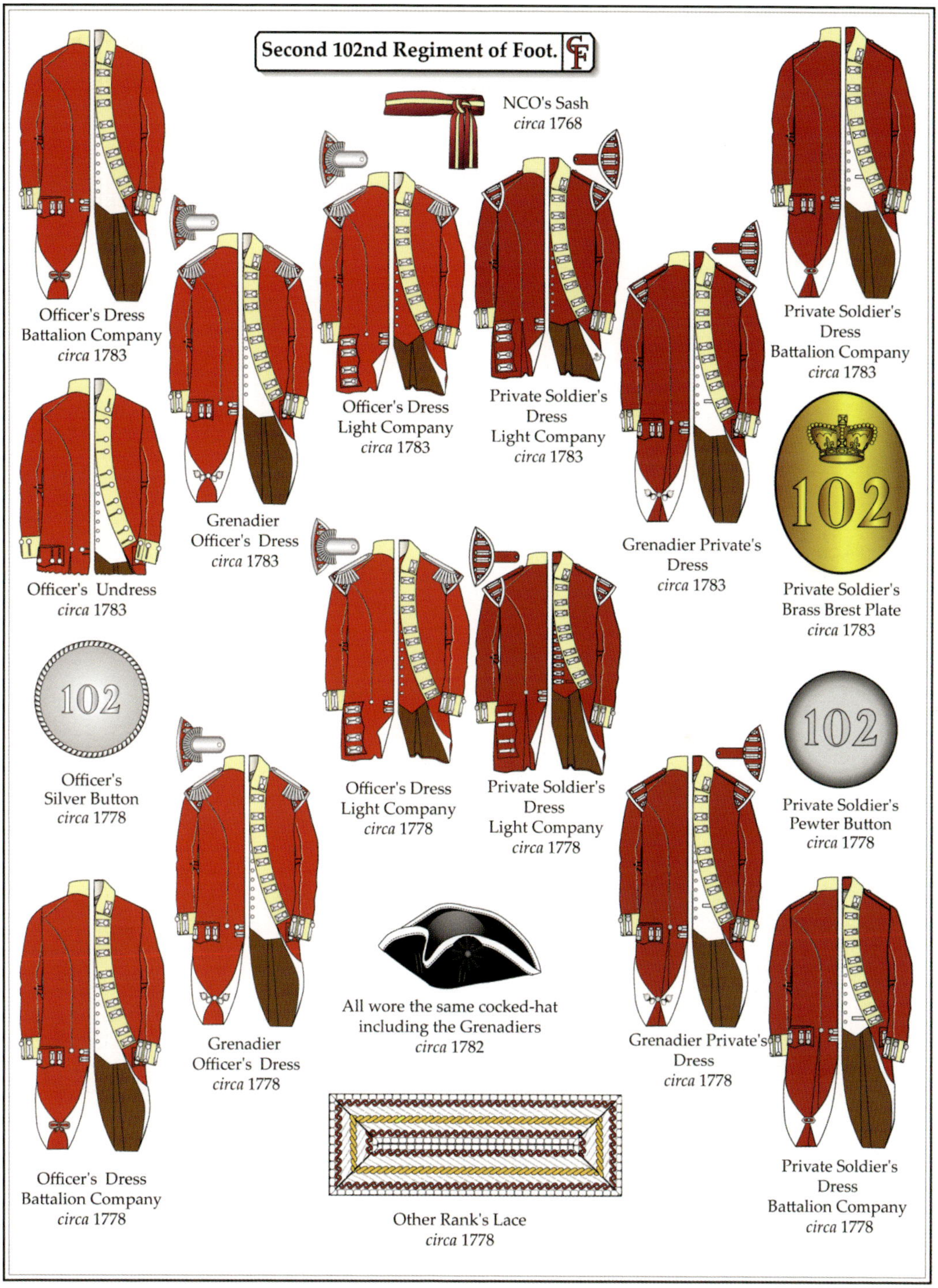
Second 102nd Regiment of Foot.
NCO's Sash
circa 1768
Officer's Dress
Battalion Company
circa 1783
Officer's Dress
Light Company
circa 1783
Private Soldier's
Dress
Light Company
circa 1783
Private Soldier's
Dress
Battalion Company
circa 1783
Grenadier
Officer's Dress
circa 1783
Officer's Undress
circa 1783
Grenadier Private's
Dress
circa 1783
102
Private Soldier's
Brass Brest Plate
circa 1783
102
Officer's
Silver Button
circa 1778
Officer's Dress
Light Company
circa 1778
Private Soldier's
Dress
Light Company
circa 1778
102
Private Soldier's
Pewter Button
circa 1778
All wore the same cocked-hat
including the Grenadiers
circa 1782
Grenadier
Officer's Dress
circa 1778
Grenadier Private's
Dress
circa 1778
Officer's Dress
Battalion Company
circa 1778
Other Rank's Lace
circa 1778
Private Soldier's
Dress
Battalion Company
circa 1778

Second 103rd (King's Irish) Regiment of Foot.

Officer's Dress
Battalion Company
circa 1784

NCO's Sash
circa 1782

Officer's Dress
Grenadier Company
circa 1784

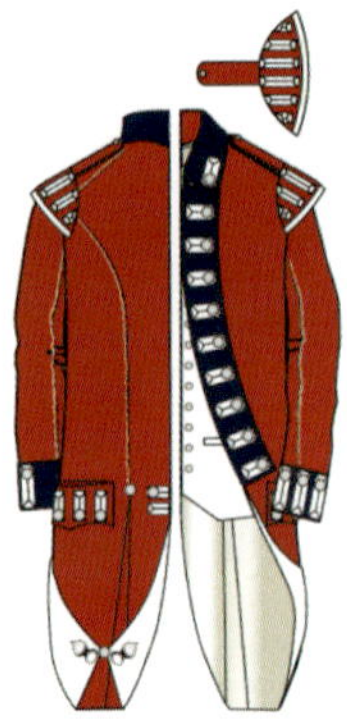

Private Soldier's
Dress
Grenadier Company
circa 1784

Private Soldier's
Dress
Battalion Company
circa 1784

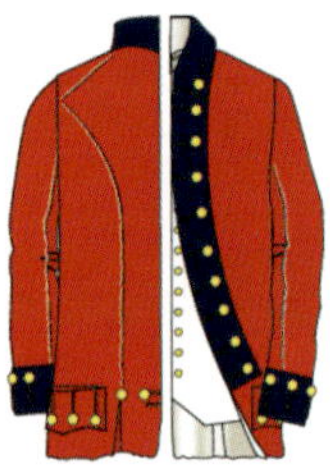

Officer's Undress
circa 1784

Other Rank's
Brass Breast Plate
circa 1781

Officer's
Silver Button
circa 1781

Other Rank's
Pewter Button
circa 17781

Officer's Dress
Light Company
circa 1781

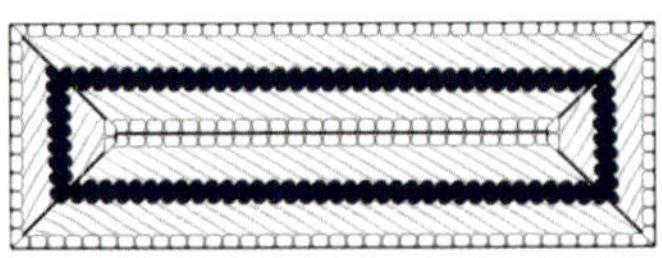

Other Rank's Lace
circa 1781

Private Soldier's
Dress
Light Company
circa 1781

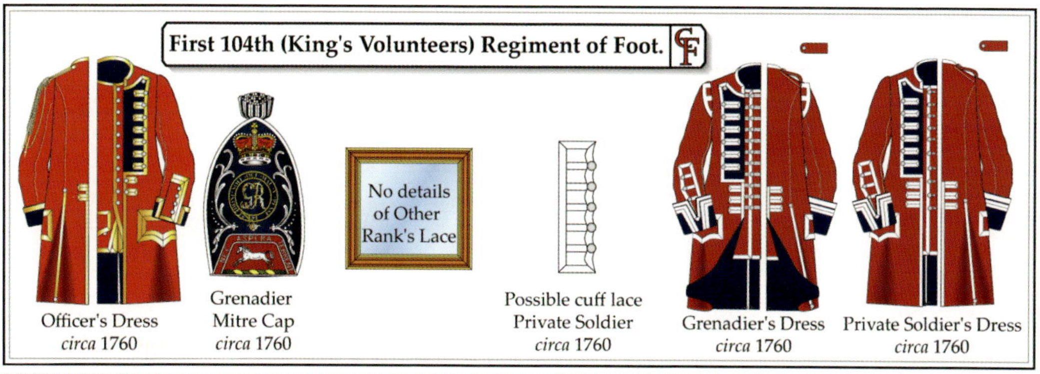
First 104th (King's Volunteers) Regiment of Foot.
Officer's Dress
circa 1760
Grenadier
Mitre Cap
circa 1760
No details
of Other
Rank's Lace
Possible cuff lace
Private Soldier
circa 1760
Grenadier's Dress
circa 1760
Private Soldier's Dress
circa 1760

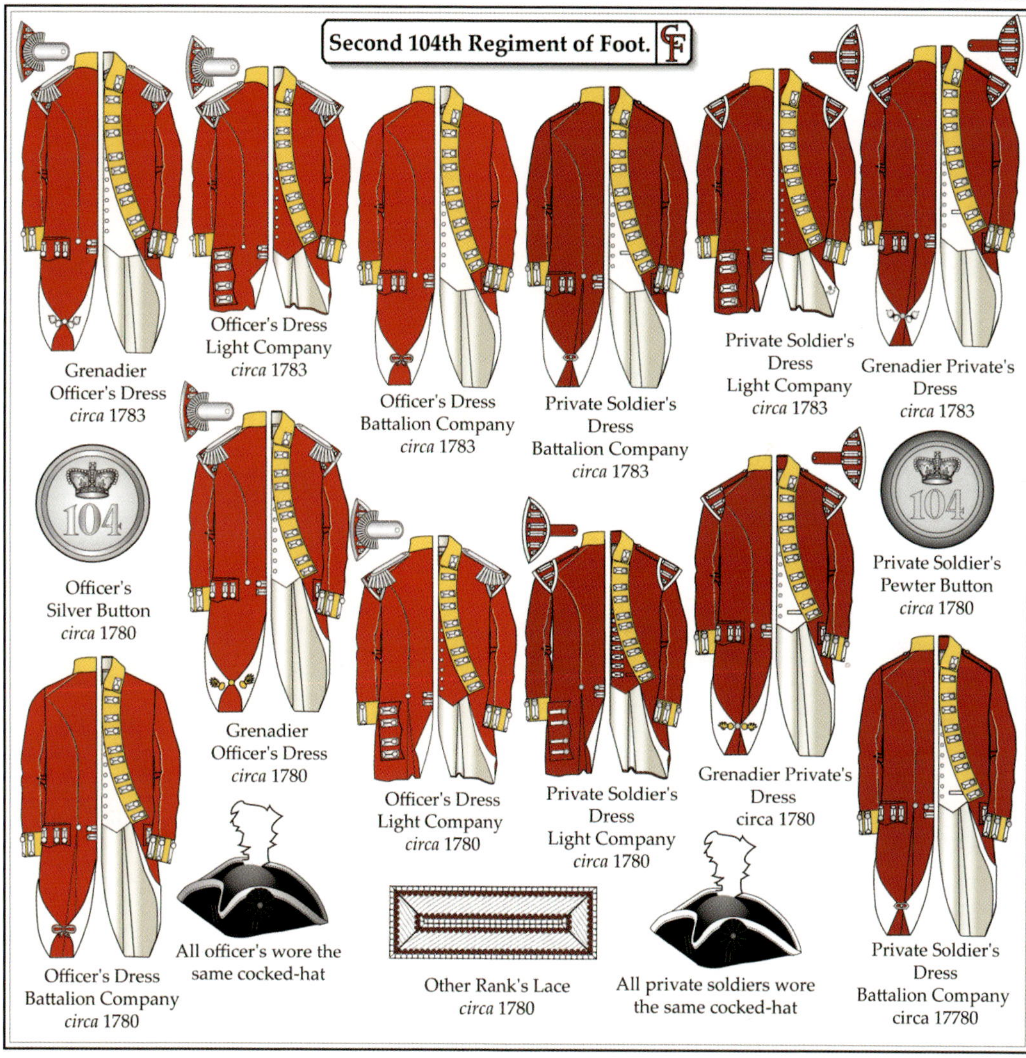
Second 104th Regiment of Foot.
Grenadier
Officer's Dress
circa 1783
Officer's Dress
Light Company
circa 1783
Officer's Dress
Battalion Company
circa 1783
Private Soldier's
Dress
Battalion Company
circa 1783
Private Soldier's
Dress
Light Company
circa 1783
Grenadier Private's
Dress
circa 1783
Officer's
Silver Button
circa 1780
Grenadier
Officer's Dress
circa 1780
Officer's Dress
Light Company
circa 1780
Private Soldier's
Dress
Light Company
circa 1780
Grenadier Private's
Dress
circa 1780
Private Soldier's
Pewter Button
circa 1780
Officer's Dress
Battalion Company
circa 1780
All officer's wore the
same cocked-hat
Other Rank's Lace
circa 1780
All private soldiers wore
the same cocked-hat
Private Soldier's
Dress
Battalion Company
circa 17780

First 105th (Queen's Own Royal Highland) Regiment of Foot.

Officer's Dress
circa 1761

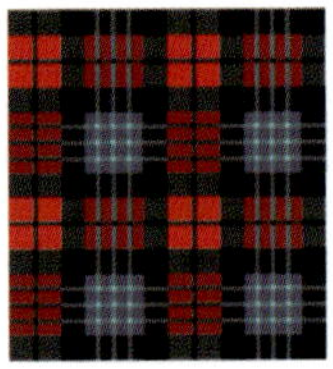

Tartan
circa 1760

No details of Other Rank's Lace

Grenadier's Dress
circa 1760

Private Soldier's Dress
circa 1760

Second 105th Regiment of Foot.

Officer's Dress
Battalion Company
circa 1782

Officer's Dress
Light Company
circa 1782

Private Soldier's Dress
Light Company
circa 1782

Private Soldier's Dress
Battalion Company
circa 1782

Grenadier Officer's Dress
circa 1782

NCO's Sash
circa 1782

Grenadier Private's Dress
circa 1782

Officer's Cap
(Conjectural)
circa 1782

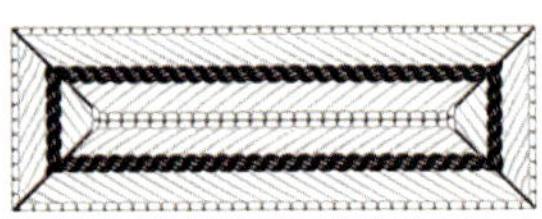

Other Rank's Lace
circa 1782

Other Rank's Cap
circa 1782

Royal Regiment of Artillery
CF
Officer's Dress
circa 1783
Officer's Undress
circa 1783
Officer's
Gilt Button
circa 1760
Private soldier's
Pewter Button
circa 1760
Private soldier's Undress
circa 1783
Private soldier's Dress
circa 1788
Officer's Undress
circa 1764
Officer's Dress
circa 1778
Officer's
Gilt Button
circa 1783
Trooper
Pewter Button
circa 1783
ROYAL
GR
ARTILLERY
Officer's
Gilt Breast Plate
circa 1783
Private soldier's Dress
circa 1778
Private Soldier's Cocked Hat
circa 1770
Officer's Dress
circa 1760
Officer's and Trooper's
Cocked Hat
1751
Officer's Cocked Hat
circa 1770
Officer's
Gold Lace
1751
Private Soldier's
YellowLace
1751
Private soldier's Dress
circa 1751

APPENDIX A

Rank distinctions of Officers and Enlisted Men

Officers and Enlisted Men

The commissioned officer ranks were divided into four groups: general officers; colonels, lieutenant colonels and majors; captains and subalterns - lieutenants, cornets, ensigns. Some authorities would describe captains as subaltern officers as well. The enlisted men consisted of non-commissioned officers (NCOs), who were the sergeant-majors and sergeants, the junior NCOs who were the corporals and 'chosen men' and lastly the private soldiers.

Officer Regimental and Brevet Ranks

There were three different forms of officer rank: the first was the regimental rank, which defined the role in which the officer was normally employed in his regimental duties; the second was his brevet rank, often awarded for particular achievement or performance (an officer with brevet wore his higher rank but was still required to undertake the duties associated with his regimental rank but, in the event he was detached to a different unit, or in the absence of a senior officer, he was permitted to act in his brevet rank). The last form of rank was local rank which was usually awarded to an officer to ensure that he could outrank any other officer assigned under his command.

Shoulder Knots

At the beginning of the period and certainly by 1751 the symbol of an officer and an NCO or corporal was the shoulder knot. This could take many different forms but was usually in the form of an aiguillette made from silver or gold cords, often pleated together with free ends; they were worn by officers but other ranks wore less expensive material.

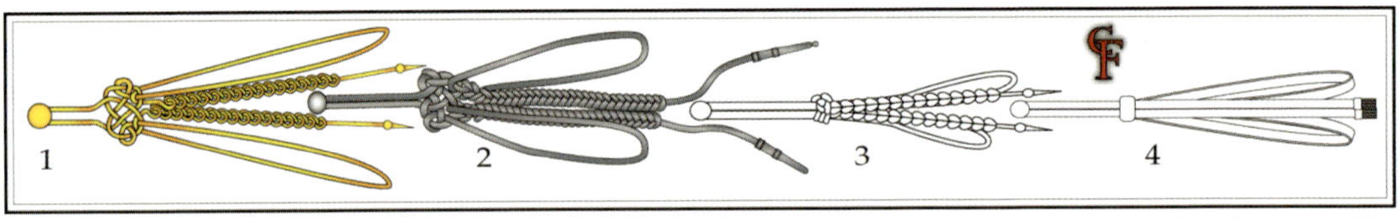

These are examples of shoulder knots: those of a gold-laced regiment (1), another example from a silver - laced regiment (2), those of the enlisted men were either silk or worsted (3) and others were of a much more simple construction (4).

Epaulettes

As the style of these shoulder knots became more elaborate they may well have led to the beginnings of the epaulette, but there is no specific date when shoulder knots began to be discontinued. However 1768 must be the date that regiments were required to wear epaulettes although many persisted in the shoulder knot. The inspection returns make it clear that, by 1770, all had followed this trend while other regiments adopted the use of the epaulette well before the 1768 warrant.

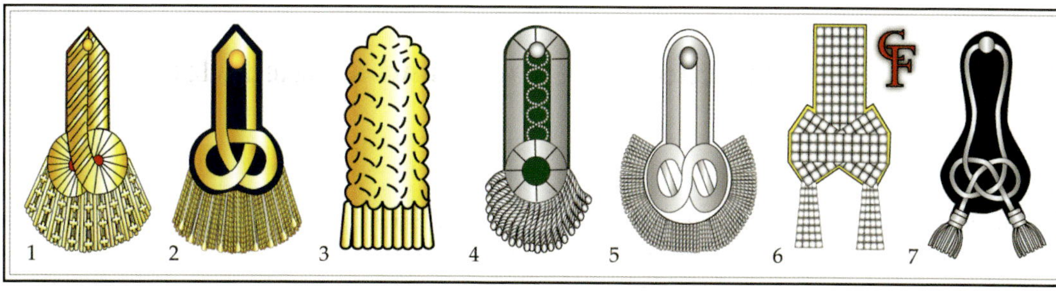

Epaulettes were of regimental design and there were many different styles and fashions: some had pointed ends while others were round. The first of the unregulated epaulettes was that of Lieutenant Colonel Murray Keith (1), 3rd Foot Guards of 1774 (2), 1st Royal Dragoons of 1767 (3), 4th Dragoons of 1770 (4), 7th Dragoons of 1770 (5), 8th Dragoons of 1764 (6) and 16th Light Dragoons of 1773 (7).

Officer Early Rank

After 1768 the cavalry and infantry were warranted to adopt the epaulette. Light Dragoons, field officers, grenadier officers, highland regiment and fusilier officers were required to wear an epaulette on each shoulder. Company officers wore one epaulette, on the right for infantry and on the left for dragoon guards. It was only in 1788 that cavalry were ordered to wear two epaulettes. Epaulettes were either gold or silver, according to the colour of the regimental metal. The nature of the epaulette changed over time and it could be embroidered or laced, on facing material or scarlet; in some cases it was a plain, flat, pleated cord but in most cases it had a two - or three-inch bullion or fringe. The officers of the Dragoon Guards and Dragoons wore an epaulette on the left shoulder only while Light Dragoons and Horse wore two epaulettes and the troopers wore shoulder straps. There were, of course, exceptions to this rule and other officers adopted the wearing of two epaulettes, particularly the 2nd Dragoons who considered that they were grenadiers. Epaulettes with crescents began to make their appearance towards the end of the period; this was a curved bar of material that served to connect the bullion to the end of the strap.

	Regiments of Foot and Foot Guards		Fusiliers
	Battalion Company	Grenadier Company	
Colonel	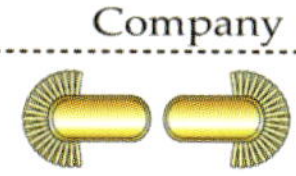		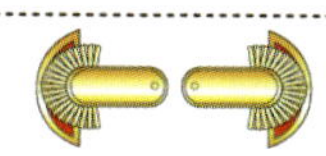
Lieutenant Colonel	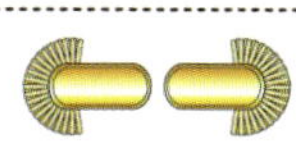		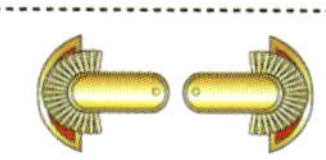
Major	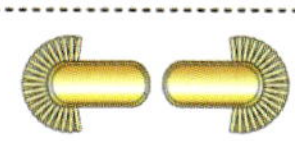		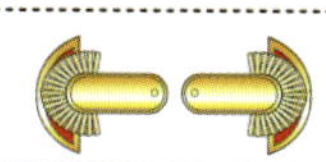
Captain	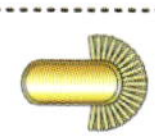	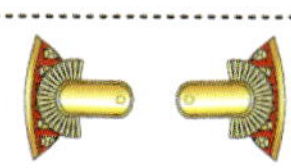	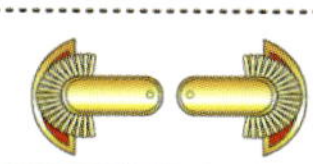
Lieutenant and Ensign	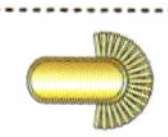	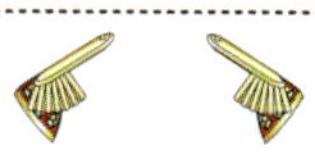	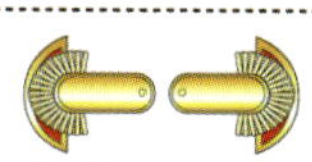

Rank Epaulettes. Senior officers wore two epaulettes, as did fusiliers (1), captains and lieutenants wore an epaulette on the right shoulder (2), while the grenadier and later light companies wore an epaulette on each shoulder (3) and fusiliers wore one on each shoulder.

Gorget

Infantry officers on duty were required to wear the gorget of gold or silver according to the regimental metal. This was stipulated in the Royal Warrant of 1684, but no evidence has been found to suggest that the cavalry ever wore them. The style and nature of the engraving had many variations, with a simple engraved crown and foliate designs, others with added parts in the appropriate metal. The infantry gorget was worn with two rosettes and suspended from a ribbon around the neck; the ribbons were half-an-inch wide and usually the same colour as the regimental facings, but not in all cases. Infantry gorgets carried the 'King's Arms' and the number of the regiment; special badges were worn when a regiment was so entitled. The Warrant of 1768 directed that the metal of the gorget should be that of the metal of the regiment but in 1796 it was ordered that all gorgets would be gilt. The gorget was eventually abolished in 1830.

The Different Gorgets and Breast Plates. Silver Gorget (1), 1st Regiment of Foot (2), 93rd (Highland) Regiment of Foot (3), 72nd Regiment of Foot (4), the rear of a breast plate (5), 24th Regiment of Foot (6) and a gold gorget of a regiment faced green.

Sashes

One of the other distinctions of rank was the sash. The original sash worn by officers was of crimson silk net, six inches wide by eighty-eight inches long with a ten-inch fringe, and was large enough to form a hammock stretcher. At the start of the period, officers wore the crimson net sash over the right shoulder while the highland regiments wore it over the left. In 1768 it was worn around the waist, over the waistcoat and tied on the left while highland regiments still wore the sash over the left shoulder. The officers of heavy cavalry often wore their sashes at the back or on the left to avoid interference with the sword arm. Light company officers were initially required to wear the crimson silk net sash, but soon adopted the whip pattern secured with cords and tassels.

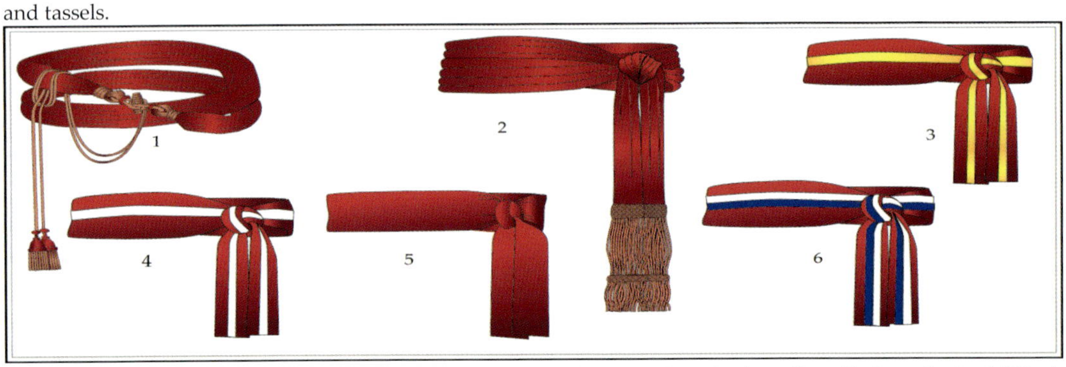

Sashes of officers and NCOs. The whip sash adopted by the light infantry (1), the sash of an officer (2), the sash of an NCO of a yellow-faced regiment (3), the sash of an NCO of the 1st Foot Guards or that of a line regiment with white facings (4), the sash of an NCO of the 2nd Foot Guards or an NCO of a regiment with purple or red facings (5) and the sash of the 3rd Foot Guards (6).

Sashes of the Enlisted Ranks

Sashes for sergeants were of crimson worsted with a central stripe of facing colour but, when the facing colour was red or purple, they wore a plain crimson sash. The sashes of NCOs of Foot Guards were different: the 1st Foot Guards wore a crimson sash with a white line, the 2nd (Coldstream) Foot Guards wore a plain crimson sash and the 3rd Foot Guards wore a sash of crimson, with white and blue, but later adopted a plain crimson. The NCOs of highland regiments wore their sashes over the left shoulder and tied at the right hip in the same manner as the officers.

Wings

The officers of grenadiers, after the change to the uniforms of the Foot Guards, soon adopted the wear of a fringed wing with an epaulette worn over it on each shoulder. Later the Grenadier officers wore a grenade on the broad part of the turn-back; earlier it was another form of distinction which according to Bennet was a grenade made of material. Light company officers later wore the bugle horn but rarely before the 1780s, although it is clear that the practice of using the scarlet waistcoat and wings with lace on both edges had started by 1771. It is also clear that there was a multitude of regimental variations in the styles and fashions.

Sword Knots

The other indication of an officer was the sword knot which was unregulated prior to 1768 but after that date gold sword knots with a crimson centre were specified. These were attached to the hilt of the sword or strapped to it in a manner and were used to wrap around the wrist in the event of the loss of the sword from the hand.

Sword Knots. The sword knot of 1751 (1), the sword knot of 1768 (2), the sword knot before regulation for a silver-metalled regiment (3) the gilt sword knot of a gold-metalled regiment (4) and the sword knot introduced in 1768 (5).

Rank Distinctions of the Foot Guards (the NCOs and private soldiers)

The Foot Guards used a system of ranking for sergeants and corporals, with gold lace for sergeants on the collar and cuffs and silver lace for corporals on the collar and cuffs. Sergeants wore epaulettes with a gold fringe. The distinction for corporals was an epaulette with silver fringe. The non-commissioned officers wore a similar uniform, but of a lesser scarlet cloth of 'superior' quality and cut. The rank distinctions used by the Foot Guards were different to those of the regiments of the line.

Rank Distinctions of the Infantry Enlisted Men (the NCOs and private soldiers)

In 1752 it was ordered that sergeants should wear white or yellow lace to reflect the officers who wore either silver or gilt. Sergeant Majors of infantry wore a silver or gold epaulette with a bullion fringe on each shoulder, and sergeants wore a silk epaulette with fringe on each shoulder; their jackets were laced with plain white lace - silk in the Foot Guards and the 42nd Regiment. Corporals wore a plain silk epaulette with fringe on the right shoulder, but the jacket was laced as the private soldier's with coloured stitches. After 1768 grenadier companies wore their epaulettes on both shoulders over the wings, as did the fusiliers. Silver or gilt lace on the uniform distinguished NCOs of cavalry and corporals wore similar lace, but only to the collar and cuffs. In the cavalry a corporal of horse was equivalent to a sergeant of infantry. It is also very clear that there was considerable variation from regiment to regiment and many appear to have adopted their own pattern and style.

The Foot Guards had their own method of denoting rank. Sergeant Majors and sergeants wore a gold-laced epaulette on each shoulder and gold hat lace; corporals wore silver lace to the cuff, cape and hat lace, grenadier corporals wore two silver laced epaulettes while, the grenadier rank and file wore two worsted epaulettes.

	Regiments of Foot		Regiments of Foot Guards		Fusiliers
	Battalion Company	Flank Company	Battalion Company	Flank Company	
Sergeant Major					
Sergeant					
Corporal	Silk	Silk			

Rank Distinctions of the Cavalry Enlisted Men (the NCOs and private soldiers)

The men of the Dragoon Guards wore an embroidered or laced epaulette with fringe on the left shoulder while those of the Light Dragoons wore one on each shoulder with the cloth of the epaulette that of the facing colour. Sergeants of the Dragoon Guards, Horse, Dragoons and Light Dragoons wore gold or silver lace to their coats and similar lace round the cape and epaulettes. The cloth was to be of facing colour with a gold or silver lace round the epaulettes and a similar fringe. Corporals wore a similar lace to the coat and cape and to the cuffs, and epaulettes of facing colour with yellow or white silk tape round the shoulder straps and a silk fringe. The troopers of the Horse wore red shoulder straps lined with facing colour, as did the Royal Horse Guards and the Horse Grenadier Guards. Troopers of the Life Guards wore lace to the cuff and round the shoulder strap. Dragoons wore a plain shoulder strap on the left shoulder in 1751.

	Regiments of Dragoons and Dragoon Guards	Regiments of Horse	Regiments of Light Dragoons
Sergeant	Worn on left shoulder	Worn on each shoulder	Worn on each shoulder
Corporal	Worn on left shoulder	Worn on each shoulder	Worn on each shoulder

Wings of Enlisted Ranks

Wings were worn by the private soldiers of the grenadiers and later, after 1770, by the light companies. The pattern of the wings changed over the period but generally the pattern worn by grenadier companies had the outer edge laced while those of the light company had lace all round the wing; in each case the lace on the wing echoed that on the lapels. When the clothing of the Foot Guards was addressed after the 1768 Warrant they adopted a variety of grenadier wings in blue. Those the private soldier of the regiments of foot of were a madder-red, but the officers of line regiments were scarlet.

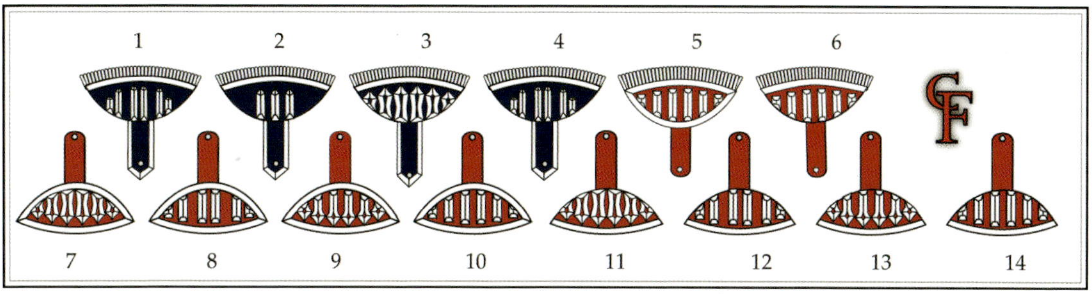

The wings. The grenadier wing introduced for the reclothed Foot Guards with fringe. The grenadier wing for the 3rd Foot Guards (1), the second wing of a grenadier of the 3rd Foot Guards with pointed loops (2). The 1st Foot Guards in 1770 (3) and the 2nd (Coldstream) Foot Guards (4). The resultant changes to the wing of the light company in 1771 (7 to 10) and the grenadier wing of 1768 (11 to14).

APPENDIX B

Regimental Facing Colours

(0C5M100Y0K) Lemon	(0C10M100Y0K) Bright yellow	(0C25M95Y0K) Yellow	(0C25M95Y5K) Philimot Yellow	(0C0M55Y0K) Pale yellow
(0C40M100Y0K) Deep yellow	(0C70M100Y0K) Orange	(0C15M35Y0K) Buff	(0C5M15Y0K) Pale buff	(0C3M30Y0K) Yellowish buff
(0C0M0Y0K) White	(0C0M0Y8K) Grayish white	(90C0M100Y40K) Full green	(100C0M90Y40K) Deep green	(90C0M100Y10K) Willow green
(90C0M100Y10K) Green	(70C0M100Y16K) Gosling green	(35C0M100Y10K) Popinjay green	(82C0M56Y40K) Pale or Grass green	(100C0M70Y55K) Very deep green
(40C0M100Y0K) Yellowish green	(100C0M50Y40K) Sea green	(100C14M70Y40K) Dark green	(10C100M30Y15K) Rose pompadore	(30C90M100Y30K) Brown
(100C100M0Y50K) Purple	(100C40M0Y80K) Light Cavalry Blue	(100C85M35Y30K) Royal blue	(76C50M20Y20K) Pale blue	(20C100M70Y15K) Crimson
(0C100M100Y0K) Scarlet	(7C100M100Y0K) NCO Crimson	(14C100M100Y0K) Madder red		

The colours are from a study of the facings in the "The Royal Collection © 2009, Her Majesty Queen Elizabeth II". Comparison has been made with the Pantone range of colours and the best colour chosen that most closely resembles the facing. The precise colours of scarlet and, madder-red are impossible to determine as the different dyes and mordant would have had a considerable effect and it is clear that the madder-red faded quickly. The colour of a facing material has a given texture and fades over the many years since 1768. While every effort has been made to assure the colour match there will be always be some discrepancy. If this is the case, I can only request the reader's understanding of a most difficult problem!

APPENDIX C

Lineage of the Cavalry and Infantry

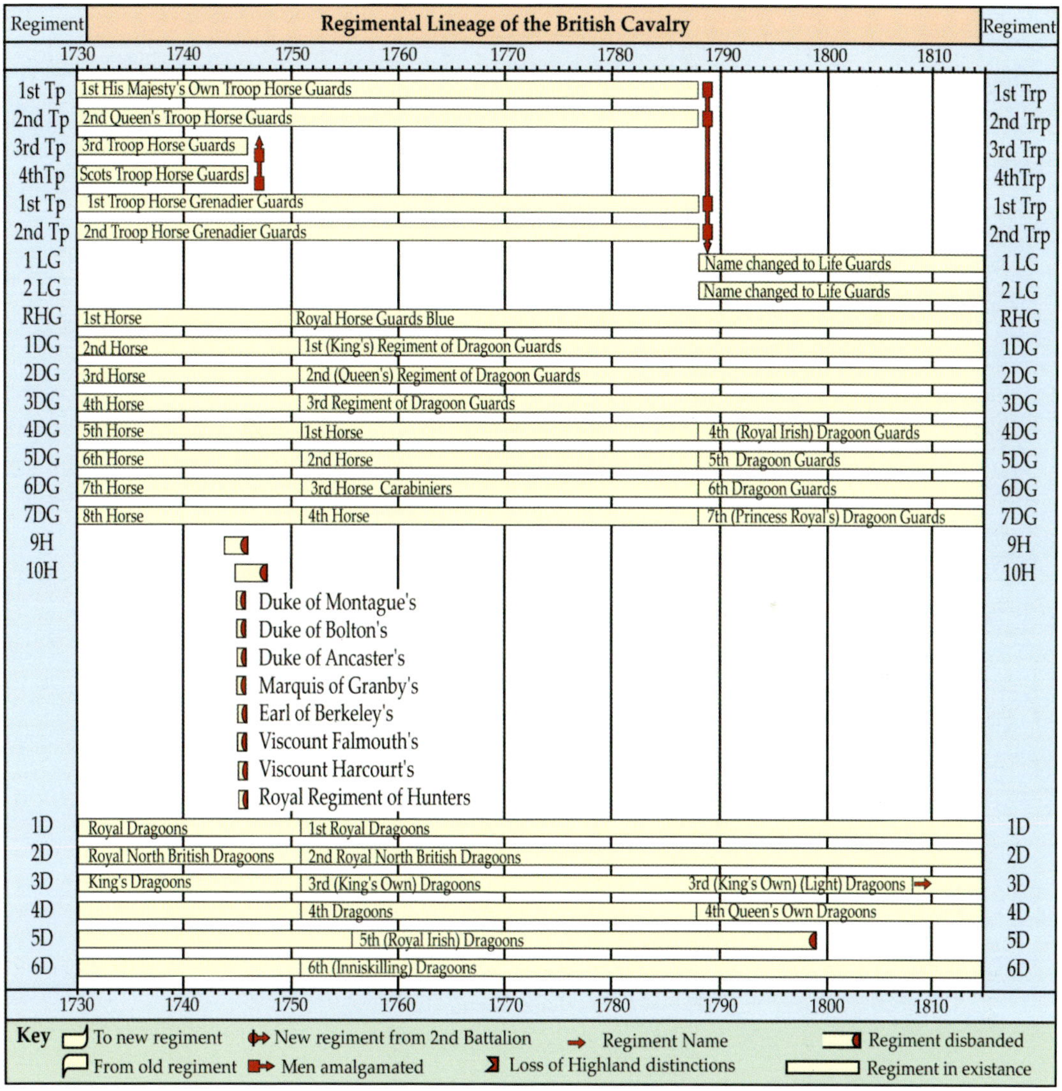

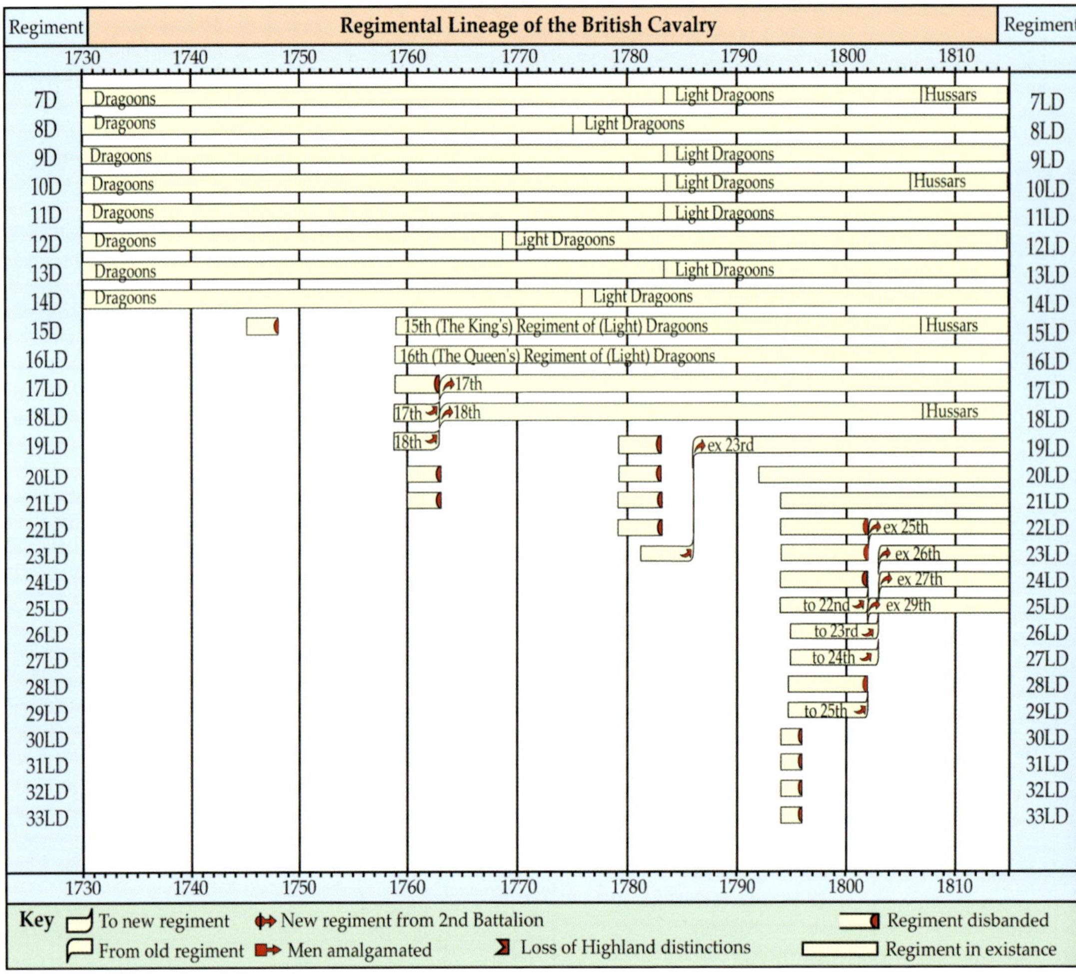
Regimental Lineage of the British Cavalry
Regiment
1730 1740 1750 1760 1770 1780 1790 1800 1810
7D Dragoons Light Dragoons Hussars 7LD
8D Dragoons Light Dragoons 8LD
9D Dragoons Light Dragoons 9LD
10D Dragoons Light Dragoons Hussars 10LD
11D Dragoons Light Dragoons 11LD
12D Dragoons Light Dragoons 12LD
13D Dragoons Light Dragoons 13LD
14D Dragoons Light Dragoons 14LD
15D 15th (The King's) Regiment of (Light) Dragoons Hussars 15LD
16LD 16th (The Queen's) Regiment of (Light) Dragoons 16LD
17LD 17th 17LD
18LD 17th 18th Hussars 18LD
19LD 18th ex 23rd 19LD
20LD
21LD
22LD ex 25th
23LD ex 26th
24LD ex 27th
25LD to 22nd ex 29th
26LD to 23rd
27LD to 24th
28LD
29LD to 25th
30LD
31LD
32LD
33LD
Key
To new regiment
From old regiment
New regiment from 2nd Battalion
Men amalgamated
Loss of Highland distinctions
Regiment disbanded
Regiment in existance

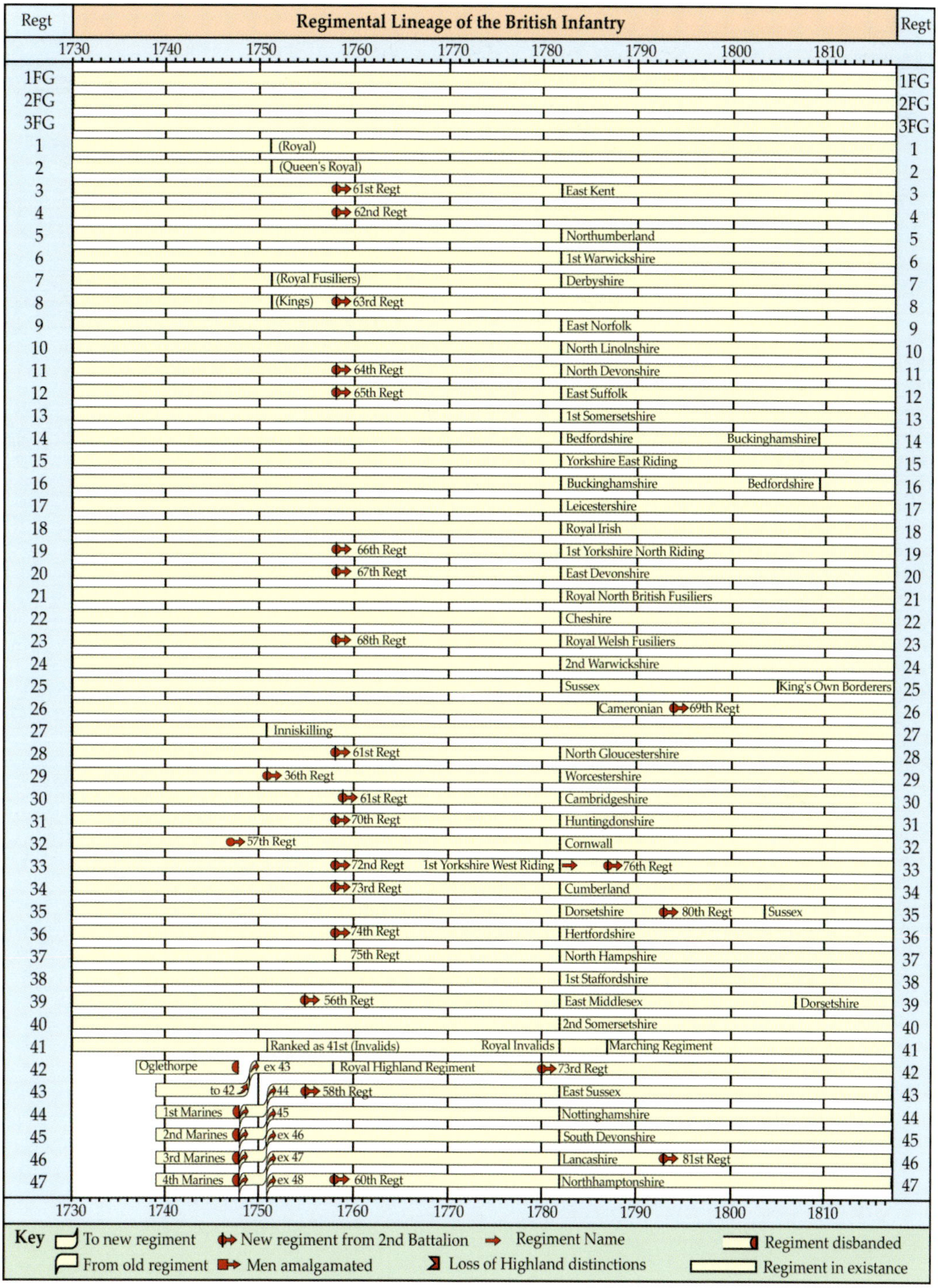
Regimental Lineage of the British Infantry
Regt
1730 1740 1750 1760 1770 1780 1790 1800 1810
1FG
2FG
3FG
1 (Royal)
2 (Queen's Royal)
3 61st Regt East Kent
4 62nd Regt
5 Northumberland
6 1st Warwickshire
7 (Royal Fusiliers) Derbyshire
8 (Kings) 63rd Regt
9 East Norfolk
10 North Linolnshire
11 64th Regt North Devonshire
12 65th Regt East Suffolk
13 1st Somersetshire
14 Bedfordshire Buckinghamshire
15 Yorkshire East Riding
16 Buckinghamshire Bedfordshire
17 Leicestershire
18 Royal Irish
19 66th Regt 1st Yorkshire North Riding
20 67th Regt East Devonshire
21 Royal North British Fusiliers
22 Cheshire
23 68th Regt Royal Welsh Fusiliers
24 2nd Warwickshire
25 Sussex King's Own Borderers
26 Cameronian 69th Regt
27 Inniskilling
28 61st Regt North Gloucestershire
29 36th Regt Worcestershire
30 61st Regt Cambridgeshire
31 70th Regt Huntingdonshire
32 57th Regt Cornwall
33 72nd Regt 1st Yorkshire West Riding 76th Regt
34 73rd Regt Cumberland
35 Dorsetshire 80th Regt Sussex
36 74th Regt Hertfordshire
37 75th Regt North Hampshire
38 1st Staffordshire
39 56th Regt East Middlesex Dorsetshire
40 2nd Somersetshire
41 Ranked as 41st (Invalids) Royal Invalids Marching Regiment
42 Oglethorpe ex 43 Royal Highland Regiment 73rd Regt
43 to 42 44 58th Regt East Sussex
44 1st Marines 45 Nottinghamshire
45 2nd Marines ex 46 South Devonshire
46 3rd Marines ex 47 Lancashire 81st Regt
47 4th Marines ex 48 60th Regt Northhamptonshire
Key
To new regiment
From old regiment
New regiment from 2nd Battalion
Men amalgamated
Regiment Name
Loss of Highland distinctions
Regiment disbanded
Regiment in existance

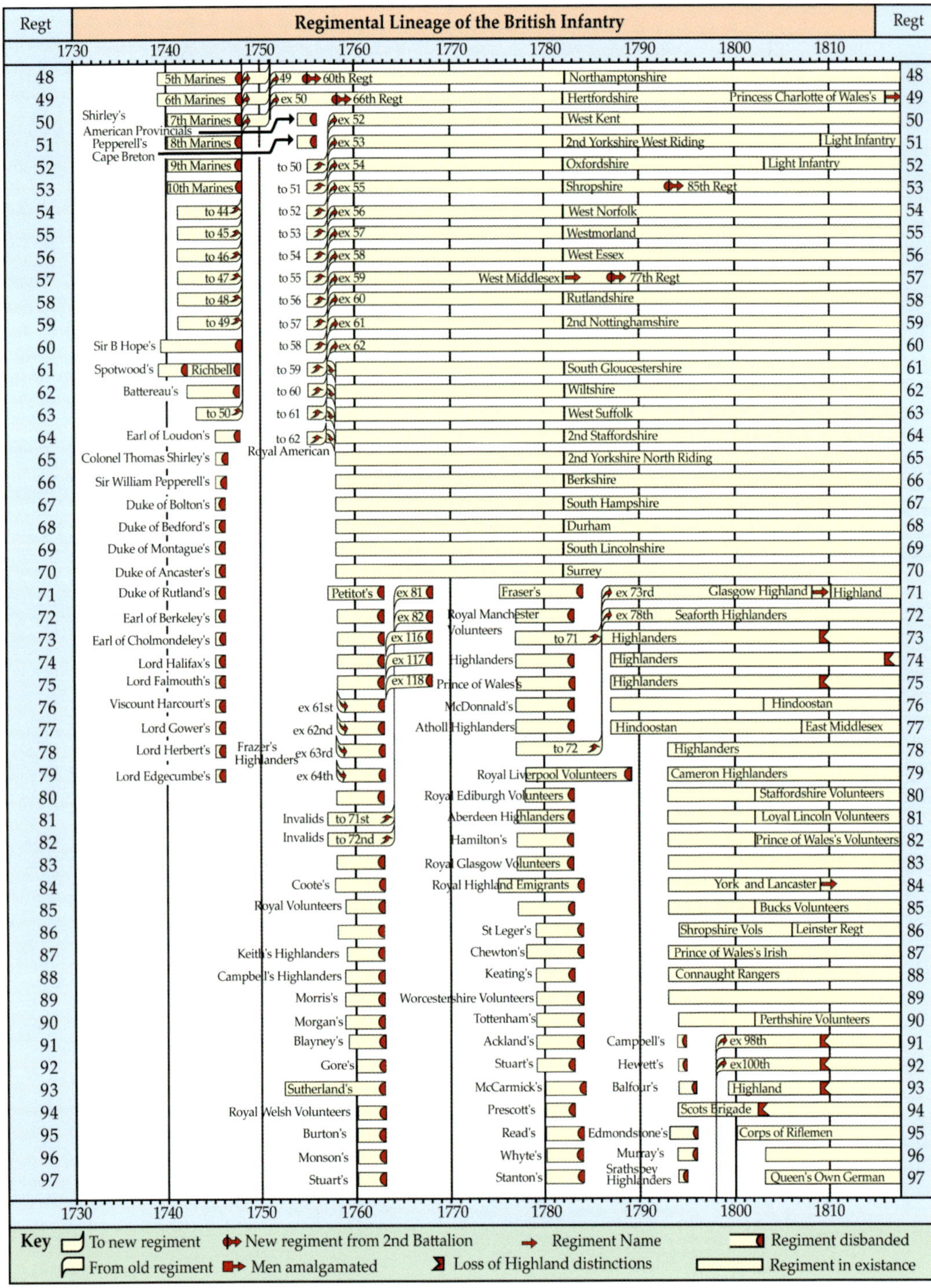
Regt
Regimental Lineage of the British Infantry
Regt
1730 1740 1750 1760 1770 1780 1790 1800 1810
48 5th Marines 49 60th Regt Northamptonshire 48
49 6th Marines ex 50 66th Regt Hertfordshire Princess Charlotte of Wales's 49
50 Shirley's American Provincials 7th Marines ex 52 West Kent 50
51 Pepperell's Cape Breton 8th Marines ex 53 2nd Yorkshire West Riding Light Infantry 51
52 9th Marines to 50 ex 54 Oxfordshire Light Infantry 52
53 10th Marines to 51 ex 55 Shropshire 85th Regt 53
54 to 44 to 52 ex 56 West Norfolk 54
55 to 45 to 53 ex 57 Westmorland 55
56 to 46 to 54 ex 58 West Essex 56
57 to 47 to 55 ex 59 West Middlesex 77th Regt 57
58 to 48 to 56 ex 60 Rutlandshire 58
59 to 49 to 57 ex 61 2nd Nottinghamshire 59
60 Sir B Hope's to 58 ex 62 60
61 Spotwood's Richbell to 59 South Gloucestershire 61
62 Battereau's to 60 Wiltshire 62
63 to 50 to 61 West Suffolk 63
64 Earl of Loudon's to 62 2nd Staffordshire 64
65 Colonel Thomas Shirley's Royal American 2nd Yorkshire North Riding 65
66 Sir William Pepperell's Berkshire 66
67 Duke of Bolton's South Hampshire 67
68 Duke of Bedford's Durham 68
69 Duke of Montague's South Lincolnshire 69
70 Duke of Ancaster's Surrey 70
71 Duke of Rutland's Petitot's ex 81 Fraser's ex 73rd Glasgow Highland Highland 71
72 Earl of Berkeley's ex 82 Royal Manchester Volunteers ex 78th Seaforth Highlanders 72
73 Earl of Cholmondeley's ex 116 to 71 Highlanders 73
74 Lord Halifax's ex 117 Highlanders Highlanders 74
75 Lord Falmouth's ex 118 Prince of Wales's Highlanders 75
76 Viscount Harcourt's ex 61st McDonnald's Hindoostan 76
77 Lord Gower's ex 62nd Atholl Highlanders Hindoostan East Middlesex 77
78 Lord Herbert's Frazer's Highlanders ex 63rd to 72 Highlanders 78
79 Lord Edgecumbe's ex 64th Royal Liverpool Volunteers Cameron Highlanders 79
80 Royal Ediburgh Volunteers Staffordshire Volunteers 80
81 Invalids to 71st Aberdeen Highlanders Loyal Lincoln Volunteers 81
82 Invalids to 72nd Hamilton's Prince of Wales's Volunteers 82
83 Royal Glasgow Volunteers 83
84 Coote's Royal Highland Emigrants York and Lancaster 84
85 Royal Volunteers Bucks Volunteers 85
86 St Leger's Shropshire Vols Leinster Regt 86
87 Keith's Highlanders Chewton's Prince of Wales's Irish 87
88 Campbell's Highlanders Keating's Connaught Rangers 88
89 Morris's Worcestershire Volunteers 89
90 Morgan's Tottenham's Perthshire Volunteers 90
91 Blayney's Ackland's Campbell's ex 98th 91
92 Gore's Stuart's Hewett's ex100th 92
93 Sutherland's McCarmick's Balfour's Highland 93
94 Royal Welsh Volunteers Prescott's Scots Brigade 94
95 Burton's Read's Edmondstone's Corps of Riflemen 95
96 Monson's Whyte's Murray's 96
97 Stuart's Stanton's Strathspey Highlanders Queen's Own German 97
1730 1740 1750 1760 1770 1780 1790 1800 1810
Key
To new regiment
From old regiment
New regiment from 2nd Battalion
Men amalgamated
Regiment Name
Loss of Highland distinctions
Regiment disbanded
Regiment in existance

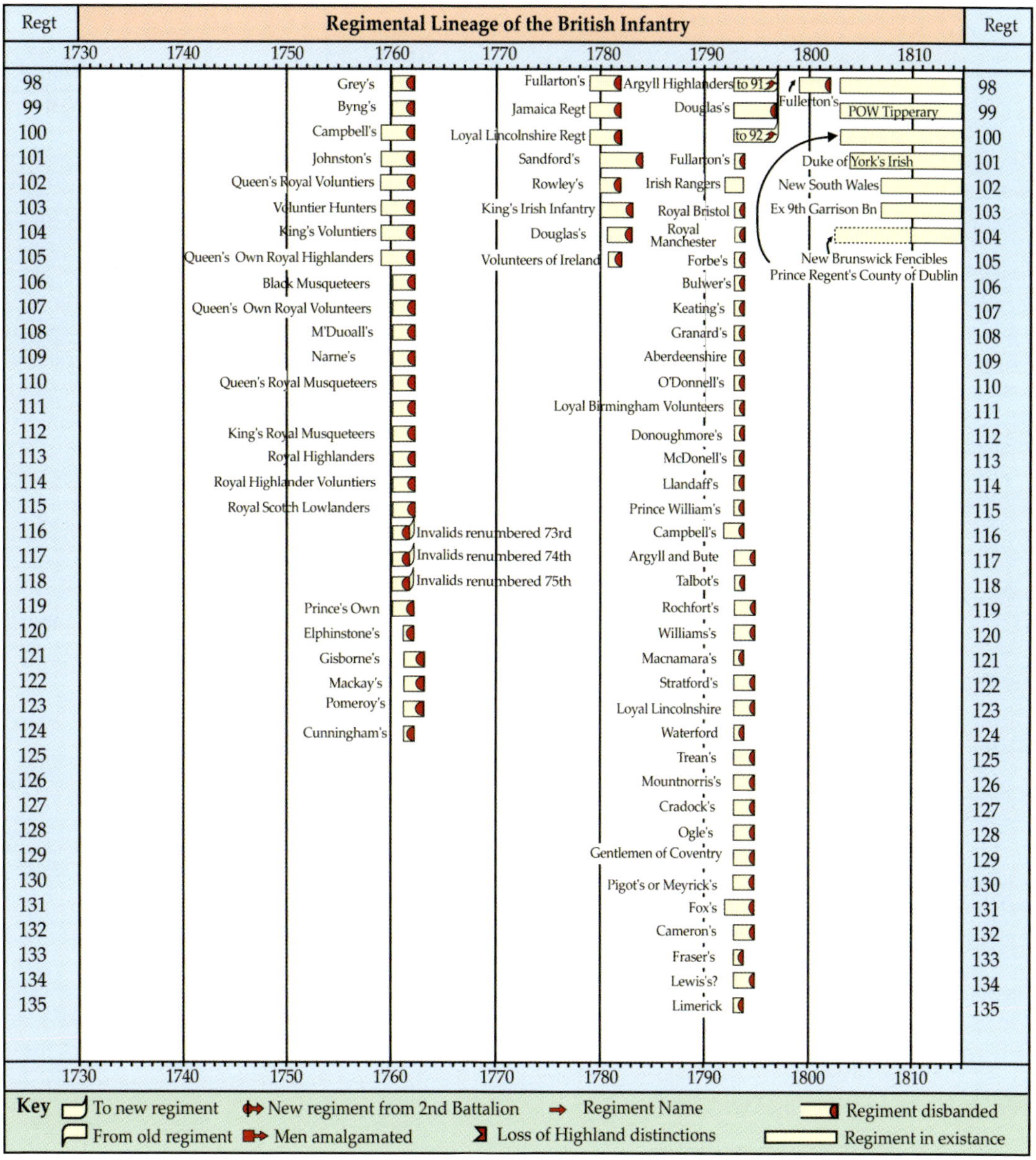
Regimental Lineage of the British Infantry
Regt
1730
1740
1750
1760
1770
1780
1790
1800
1810
98 Grey's
Fullarton's
Argyll Highlanders
to 91
Fullerton's
99 Byng's
Jamaica Regt
Douglas's
POW Tipperary
100 Campbell's
Loyal Lincolnshire Regt
to 92
101 Johnston's
Sandford's
Fullarton's
Duke of York's Irish
102 Queen's Royal Voluntiers
Rowley's
Irish Rangers
New South Wales
103 Voluntier Hunters
King's Irish Infantry
Royal Bristol
Ex 9th Garrison Bn
104 King's Voluntiers
Douglas's
Royal Manchester
105 Queen's Own Royal Highlanders
Volunteers of Ireland
Forbe's
New Brunswick Fencibles
Prince Regent's County of Dublin
106 Black Musqueteers
Bulwer's
107 Queen's Own Royal Volunteers
Keating's
108 M'Duoall's
Granard's
109 Narne's
Aberdeenshire
110 Queen's Royal Musqueteers
O'Donnell's
111 Loyal Birmingham Volunteers
112 King's Royal Musqueteers
Donoughmore's
113 Royal Highlanders
McDonell's
114 Royal Highlander Voluntiers
Llandaff's
115 Royal Scotch Lowlanders
Prince William's
116 Invalids renumbered 73rd
Campbell's
117 Invalids renumbered 74th
Argyll and Bute
118 Invalids renumbered 75th
Talbot's
119 Prince's Own
Rochfort's
120 Elphinstone's
Williams's
121 Gisborne's
Macnamara's
122 Mackay's
Stratford's
123 Pomeroy's
Loyal Lincolnshire
124 Cunningham's
Waterford
125 Trean's
126 Mountnorris's
127 Cradock's
128 Ogle's
129 Gentlemen of Coventry
130 Pigot's or Meyrick's
131 Fox's
132 Cameron's
133 Fraser's
134 Lewis's?
135 Limerick
Key
To new regiment
From old regiment
New regiment from 2nd Battalion
Men amalgamated
Regiment Name
Loss of Highland distinctions
Regiment disbanded
Regiment in existance

APPENDIX D

The Sources Used for this Study

The sources used to ascertain the regimental identification during the period are given below. They represent just a small sample of the information made available and to this must be added the assistance of many well-known authors and artists as well as regimental museums and other military institutions.

The 1751 paintings by Morier are used by the courtesy of "The Royal Collection © 2009, Her Majesty Queen Elizabeth II"; these show in detail the regimental uniforms of the infantry and cavalry. In addition, the series of lace samples in the Royal Collection at Windsor Castle provide a clear indication of the type of stitching and the shape of the loops and facings for each of the seventy Regiments of Foot that were listed in the 1768 Regulations.

The Prince Consort's Library at Aldershot has a copy of the 'Clothing Regulations Book' of 1768, which shows drawings of the grenadier for each regiment at that time. Many of the watercolours have faded and the colours changed over time, but the book provides a further insight into the lacing of the period. The library also has a copy of the Uniforms of Plates by Edward Dayes of the Foot Guards, the 1st to the 7th, and 15th Regiments of Foot.

Another source used was the Army Museums Ogilby Trust file boxes at the National Army Museum. These files contain collections of text, illustrations and photographs of many military portraits. These have been used to provide corroborating details of the uniforms. A further source of invaluable assistance are the Reynolds' manuscripts in the Victoria and Albert Museum.

The uniform items and accoutrements of the period that have survived the passage of time have been a critical source. Whenever possible these have been used to correlate and compare with the other sources to ensure – within their time frame – the material used to compile this book. In spite of this, it has been not possible to reconcile all of the differences between the sources, and it has proven impossible to say, particularly for the higher numbered regiments, which version may be correct. It could be that the distinctions for these regiments changed over time as they evolved or changed with their name or status but, in each case where a significant variation is noted, the different versions are illustrated and the reader must decide which is the most appropriate.

Possibly the most important of the sources are the records held by the National Archives at Kew. These contain the multiplicity of regulations published by Horse Guards and are contained in many volumes and books of correspondence. Generally they are prefixed WO: as an example the document relating to Royal Warrants is WO30/13B. Miscellany Book: Clothing Correspondence. 'His Majesty's Warrant for the Regulation of the Colours, Clothing, etc. of the Marching Regiments of Foot', 19 December 1768', and WO 30/13A.

The information on the tartans worn by the highland regiments was taken from the Wilson of Bannockburn's Pattern book. They were the major manufacturer of the kilts and plaids of the highland regiments and their detailed notes regarding the thread count, colours and sett size was used throughout this study.

Throughout this book there has been a constant reference to the The Society for Journal of Army Historical Research and particular and special thanks are due to David Rowlands and the multiplicity of Regimental Museums who contributed.

To this must be added the many other books and publications that have made significant contribution to this study:

Barnes, Major, R.M.
The Uniforms & History of the Scottish Regiments, Seeley Service & Co Ltd, London, 1959. *The History of the Uniforms & Regiments of the British Army*, Seeley Service & Co Ltd, London, 1957.

Barthorp, Michael,
British Cavalry Uniform Since 1660, Blandford Press, Poole, Dorset,1984.
British Infantry Uniform Since 1660, Blandford Press, Poole, Dorset, 1984.

Blackmore, D,
British Cavalry Uniforms in the Mid 18th Century, Partizan Press, Nottingham, 2008.

Campbell, D.A,
The Dress of the Royal Artillery, Arms & Armour Press, London, 1971.

Carman, W.Y.
British Military Uniforms, Henry VII to the present day, Leonard Hill Ltd, London, 1957.

Cuthbertson, B,
A System for the Complete Interior Management and Oeconomy of a Battalion of Infantry. 2nd Edition. London: J. Millan, 1779.

De Witt, Bailey,
Small Arms of the British Forces in America 1664-1815, Andrew Mobrey Inc Publishers, USA, 2009.

Gale, Ryan R,
A. Soldier Like Way. United States of America, Tack of the Wolf Inc, 2007.

Haswell Miller, A.E, & Dawney, N.P,
Military drawings and Paintings in the collection of Her Majesty the Queen, Phaidon, London, 1966.

Lawson, C.P,
A History of the Uniforms of the British Army, Norman Military Publications, Volumes 1 to 4, 1941.

May, R,
The British Army in North America, Osprey Publishing Ltd, Reading, 1974.

Mollo, J,
The Uniforms of the Seven Years War, Blandford Press, Dorset, 1977.*The Uniforms of the American Revolution*, Blandford Press, Dorset, 1975.

Rodgers, Colonel, H.C.B,
The Mounted Troops of the British Army, Seeley Service & Co Ltd, London, 1959.

Simkin, R. (Carman, W.Y,)
The Uniforms of the British Army - The Cavalry Regiments', Web & Bower, Exeter, 1982.

The Uniforms of the British Army - The Infantry Regiments', Web & Bower, Exeter, 1982.

Simes, Thomas,
The Military Guide of Young Officers. London, 1772

Stuart, R,
18th Century Highlanders, Osprey Publishing Ltd, London, 1993.

Strachan, Hew,
British Military Uniforms. 1768- 1796, The Dress of the British Army from Official Sources. London, Arms and Armour Press, 1975.

Troiani, Don,
Soldiers of the American Revolution, Mowbray Publishing, USA, 2007

Tylden Major, D,
Horses and Saddlery, JAA Allen & Company, London, 1980.

Glossary

Accoutrements – belts, pouches, straps packs or other equipment excluding the uniform and the weapons.
Aiguillette – pleated cord ending with needles, points or aglets, worn to distinguish certain ranks or indications of status. Often combined with a corded and unfringed epaulette.
Apron – worn to protect the uniform by those who were expected to perform particularly dirty tasks, a particular distinction of pioneers; they were also worn by drummers to protect the uniform from the friction of the swinging drum.
Arch – semicircular bridge connecting the two sideboards of a saddletree.
Artificer – title for army craftsman such as wheelers, carpenters and blacksmiths.
Austrian Knot – special knot worn on the uniforms of many troops; also known as crow's feet.

Backing – badges were frequently worn on coloured cloth to enhance their appearance and visibility. This applied particularly to the dubby, the grenades and bugle-horns of the flank companies or particular regiments.
Baldrick – correct term for a belt worn over the right shoulder to the left hip and normally holding a sword or a drum.
Battalion – basic formation of a battalion, notionally one hundred men. The introduction of grenadiers and later light companies were more usually known as flank companies and the battalion companies as centre companies.
Belted plaid – before the introduction of the 'little kilt' the tartan or sett of the highland regiments was a large piece of plaid, pleated and belted around the waist. The lower part formed the kilt and the upper protected the body or was folded back and fastened at the shoulder.
Billot – an extension of a buckled strap, designed to pass around an object and back through the buckle.
Bit – metal bar bearing upon the jaws of a horse and providing the means of control.
Black Line (in lace) – usually adopted to enhance the pattern of the lace. Often wrongly attributed to a sign of mourning for some famous person.
Boot – leather tube used to support the muzzle of the musket or carbine. Usually carried at the front offside of the saddle.
Boots – made from straight lasts until 1838. The boots were not made to fit left or right and were expected to be worn on alternate feet to give even wear.
Braid –used to describe the metallic braid of officers and the woven braid of the other ranks, usually called lace in documents of the period.
Breeches – various forms of nether-garment reaching to the knee and fastened with buttons or tapes. Initially the regular wear for all units, by the end of the period they had been relegated to dress and trousers worn for undress.
Bridoon – a bridle that uses a curb bit in conjunction with a snaffle bit.
Breastplate – Y-shaped harness passing around the neck of the horse, between the front legs and attached to the girth and the saddle to prevent it moving backwards.
Bridle – harness applied to the head of the horse to control the bits.
Broken bias – lace in which horizontal sections break a diagonal pattern.
Bucket – see boot
Buff – buffalo leather used to manufacture belts, sword and musket slings. Buff leather was usually whitened, but regiments with buff-coloured facings usually wore the belts plain.
Bullion – gold or silver wire drawn into a hollow spiral. Used on epaulettes and in other embellishments of army uniforms.
Burs – extension of the sideboards beyond the front arch to which attachments are made.

Cantle – rear edge of the saddle.

Cap – usually associated with a hat without a brim all round, it may have a peak at either the front or rear.
Cape – an alternative 1768 term for a collar.
Carbine – shortened firearm used by cavalrymen, later used to describe any rifled weapon where the projectile did not complete one full turn before leaving the barrel.
Clubbed – a style of hair worn in a tight form of bun during the early part of the period.
Coat – term used to describe a garment that extends below the waist. The term coatee did not come into official use until much later.
Collar – also known in 1768 as a cape.
Crupper – A strap running from the rear of the saddle and passing around the horse's tail or dock to prevent the saddle moving forwards.

Darts – decorative chevrons on the sleeves of drummers or trumpeters, they could point either up or down.
Dragoons – heavy cavalry
Dubby – decorative shape placed over the point where the two turnbacks of a coat or jacket came together.

Ensign – lowest commissioned rank in the infantry of the period; also the name for the flag or colour he carried.
Epaulette – decorative ornament and fringe worn at the shoulder, often as an indication of rank.

Facings – colour of the material used to differentiate one regiment from another. Usually applied to the collar and cuffs, it was also applied to the lapels when they were worn, and the turnbacks of certain regiments.
Fan – continuation of the sideboards of a saddletree to beyond the rear arch to carry equipment and harness.
Fatigue Dress – garments worn by military personnel when engaged in non-military duties.
Flank companies – armies had always placed the most reliable men on the right flank, the shield being carried on the left side. It was the position of the grenadier company of line regiments. After the light companies came into existence, they were positioned on the left flank.
Flap – the sidepieces of a saddle, also the overhanging part that protected a pocket from water.
Fleur-de-lys – an emblem representing the early royal coat of arms. Worn particularly by drummers and trumpeters of certain regiments.
Frog – an attachment to a belt to hold the bayonet or sword; also an attachment to go over a button or toggle.
Flounce – a fur, leather or canvas protector to prevent the reins abrading the cloak.
Full Dress – the uniform worn on ceremonial occasions. Levee dress included most full dress items but usually included different nether-wear and bicorne hats.
Furniture – that which is furnished, particularly applied to the shabraque, sheepskin and holster flounces of the cavalry.
Fusilier – term originally used to indicate a regiment had been equipped with a fusil, an old term for flintlock.

Gaiters – cloth leg protectors introduced to protect the hose. Usually buttoning on the outside and fitted to fit over the shoe.
Gaiter trousers – originally worn over breeches to protect them, tight fitting at the knee and leg, they were usually buttoned at the lower extremities; they became popular for troops serving in the tropics and also became known as mosquito trousers.
Gilt – thin covering of gold applied to military braid.
Girth – web or canvas strap securing the saddle to the horse.
Gorget – decorative item worn at the neck by infantry officers, a relic of the old armoured breastplate.
Grenadier – originally a person selected to throw grenades. By this period they were the selected men who protected the right flank and wore a badge in the form of a grenade as a distinction.

Hackle – bunch of short feathers worn as a distinction by highland regiments.

Hair powder – used to whiten the hair.
Half-gaiters – gaiters usually reached to the knees. When light infantry were formed, they preferred shorter gaiters that reached to the calf. When trousers were introduced, they were often worn with half gaiters.
Halter – see head collar
Head collar – head harness of leather or canvas for securing the horse in stalls or on the picquet line.
Helmet – metal or leather head protector.
Housings –part of horse furniture, usually made of cloth.

Jacket – short coat to the waist worn by cavalry, also used to describe the short coat used by infantry light companies after 1770.

Keeper – A band of leather on a belt that is stitched to the belt; a runner is similar but is free to move.
Kerseymere – old name for cassimere, a soft white cloth used for turn-backs, linings and breeches.
Kilt – short skirt-type garment worn from the waist to the knee by highland regiments.
Knapsack – sack used to carry a soldier's necessaries, developed into a canvas backpack.

Lace –Term used to describe the metallic and woven braid of military personnel.
Lapel – decorative turn-back to the front of a jacket or coat.
Levee dress – elaborate dress worn at royal levees.
Light company – men selected to protect the left flank of the regiment; also the most agile and distinguished by the right to wear a bugle-horn on the turn-back of the jacket.
Light dragoons – light cavalry.

Mess tin – a metal container for the consumption of food and drink.

Near-side – the left side of a horse facing forwards.
Needle – point of an aiguillette

Off-side – on the right side of a horse facing forwards.

Pantaloons – a nether garment of breeches and stockings in one piece, called after the Italian clown. Worn as close-fitting trousers to the ankles and often shown with short gaiters or short boots. Blue pantaloons made from stockinette were popular with Royal Artillery and light cavalrymen, while other regiments wore scarlet pantaloons laced at the front for dress.
Pickers – metal pins used to clean the touchholes of weapons.
Picquet line – rope line where the horses are secured.
Pleat – a fold of cloth made by doubling the material upon itself or at a seam; also spelt pleat.
Popinjay – light-green colour worn as a facing by the 54th Regiment.

Queue – a tail of hair, false or real, worn by all ranks until 1806.

Runner – loose band of leather on belt that is free to move and keep the free end in place. A keeper is similar but is not free to move.

Sash – a silk net crimson sash was the sign of a commissioned officer. Originally a long fringed sash that could be used to carry a wounded officer, the sash later became simplified. Senior non-commissioned officers wore a plain crimson worsted sash with a central stripe of facing colour.
Saddletree – framework that forms the basis of the saddle.

Sett – The pattern of a tartan and its size.
Sideboards – two parts of the saddletree that transmitted the weight of the rider to the horse's back.
Slide – band of leather or metal on belt that is free to move and keep the free end in place.
Snaffle –horse's bit, usually joined at its centre.
Stock – band passing around the soldier's neck to make him hold his head up, in this period usually of leather, but later changed to cloth.
Surcingle – leather or web straps that passed under the horse and over the saddle and saddlecloth or sheepskin to retain it.

Tommy – term used to describe the rear skirt of a jacket where there was an overlapped pleat, like the modern riding jacket.
Tricorne – hat with three corners or points.
Trousers – loose nether garments reaching to the ankles, originally used for fatigues.
Turn-backs – coat tails of a soldier's coat when folded back. Originally intended to provide ease of movement.

Undress – dress of a lower order than ceremonial or parade dress. Usually worn on informal occasions or on campaign.

Wing – A shoulder ornament worn particularly by grenadier companies, light companies, fusiliers and light infantry.

Index

Plain text is used to referto page numbers relating to the subject, bold test is used to refer to regimental plates and other illustrations.

Regimental Index